68000 Assembly Language Programming

68000 Assembly Language Programming

Gerry Kane
Doug Hawkins
Lance Leventhal

OSBORNE/McGraw-Hill
Berkeley, California

Published by
Osborne/McGraw-Hill
2600 Tenth Street
Berkeley, California 94710
U.S.A.

For information on translations and book distributors outside of the U. S. A., please write OSBORNE/McGraw-Hill at the above address.

68000 ASSEMBLY LANGUAGE PROGRAMMING

90 DODO 898765

ISBN 0-07-931062-1

Cover design by Timothy Sullivan.

Technical editor on this book was Joaquin Miller.

Acknowledgments

We gratefully acknowledge Motorola Microsystems, Mesa, Arizona and, in particular, Jeff Lavell, their former General Manager, for supplying equipment and information needed to write this book.

Special thanks go to Mr. Hans Kalldall for his excellent work in testing all of the example programs. Mr. Kalldall also suggested numerous corrections and improvements which greatly enhanced this book.

Doug Hawkins wishes to express his gratitude to his loving wife Peggy for the assistance, support, patience and understanding she provided throughout this project.

About the Authors

Gerry Kane, a member of Osborne/McGraw-Hill's technical staff, is co-author of several volumes of the well-known series, *An Introduction to Microcomputers.* Most recently, he authored the *CRT Controller Handbook* and the *68000 Microprocessor Handbook,* both part of the new Osborne Handbook Series. He received his B.S. degree from the United States Coast Guard Academy.

Doug Hawkins is Vice President of Engineering for Phoenix Digital Corporation, Phoenix, Arizona with responsibility for the design and implementation of microprocessor-based systems for distributive plant monitoring and process control. Previously, Mr. Hawkins worked for Motorola Microsystems, the primary source for the MC68000, as Manager of Language Systems. He received his BSEE degree from Michigan State University, and MSEE and MBA degrees from Arizona State University.

Lance Leventhal is a partner in Emulative Systems Company, Inc., a San Diego-based consulting firm specializing in microprocessors and microprogramming. He is a national lecturer on microprocessors for the IEEE, the author of ten books and over sixty articles on microprocessors, and a regular contributor to such publications as *Simulation* and *Microcomputing.* He also serves as technical editor for the Society for Computer Simulation and as contributing editor for *Digital Design* magazine.

Dr. Leventhal authored the original books in this series and has just begun work on a new series, Assembly Language Subroutines. He received a B.A. degree from Washington University in St. Louis, and M.S. and Ph.D. degrees from the University of California at San Diego. He is a member of SCS, ACM, IEEE, and the IEEE Computer Society.

Contents

Section I. Fundamental Concepts

Section II. Introductory Problems

Section III. Advanced Topics

Section V. 68000 Instruction Set

Section VI. Appendices

Index

Program Examples

I
Fundamental Concepts

This book describes assembly language programming. It assumes that you are familiar with *An Introduction to Microcomputers: Volume 1 — Basic Concepts* (Berkeley: Osborne/McGraw-Hill, 1980). Chapters 6 and 7 of that book are especially relevant. This book does not discuss the general features of computers, microcomputers, addressing methods, or instruction sets; you should refer to *An Introduction to Microcomputers: Volume 1* for that information.

The chapters in this section provide basic information on assembly language in general and the MC68000 in particular. Chapter 1 discusses the purpose of assembly language and compares it with higher level computer languages. Chapter 2 discusses assemblers and, briefly, loaders. Chapter 3 describes the architecture of the MC68000 microprocessor, compares it with similar processors, and discusses important features of Motorola's MC68000 assemblers.

HOW THIS BOOK HAS BEEN PRINTED

This book contains both boldface and lightface type. The material in lightface type only expands on information presented in the previous boldface type. Thus you can skip subject areas with which you are familiar by skipping the material in lightface type. When you reach an unfamiliar subject, read both the material in boldface type and the material in lightface type.

1

Introduction to Assembly Language Programming

A computer program is ultimately a series of numbers and therefore has very little meaning to a human being. In this chapter we will discuss the levels of human-like language in which a computer program may be expressed. We will also discuss the reasons for and uses of assembly language, which is the subject of this book.

THE MEANING OF INSTRUCTIONS

The instruction set of a microprocessor is the set of binary inputs that produce defined actions during an instruction cycle. An instruction set is to a microprocessor what a function table is to a logic device such as a gate, adder, or shift register. Of course, the actions that the microprocessor performs in response to its instruction inputs are far more complex than the actions that logic devices perform in response to their inputs.

Binary Instructions

An instruction is a binary digit pattern — it must be available at the data inputs to the microprocessor at the proper time in order to be interpreted as an instruction. For example, when the MC68000 microprocessor receives the 16-bit binary pattern 1101001100000000 as the input during an instruction fetch operation, the pattern means:

"Add the contents of Data Register D0 to Data Register D1."

Similarly, the pattern 00010000001110100000000011111111 means:

"Move 11111111 into Data Register D0."

The microprocessor (like any other computer) only recognizes binary patterns as instructions or data; it does not recognize characters or octal, decimal, or hexadecimal numbers.

A COMPUTER PROGRAM

A program is a series of instructions that causes a computer to perform a particular task.

Actually, a computer program includes more than instructions; it also contains the data and the memory addresses that the microprocessor needs to accomplish the tasks defined by the instructions. Clearly, if the microprocessor is to perform an addition, it must have two numbers to add and a place to put the result. The computer program must determine the sources of the data and the destination of the result as well as the operation to be performed.

All microprocessors execute instructions sequentially unless an instruction changes the order of execution or halts the processor. That is, the processor gets its next instruction from the next higher memory address unless the current instruction specifically directs it to do otherwise.

Ultimately, every program is a set of binary numbers. For example, this is a MC68000 program that adds the contents of memory locations 6000_{16} and 6002_{16} and places the result in memory location 6004_{16}:

```
0011000000111000
0110000000000000
1101000001111000
0110000000000010
0011000111000000
0110000000000100
```

This is a machine language, or object, program. If this program were entered into the memory of a MC68000-based microcomputer, the microcomputer would be able to execute it directly.

THE BINARY PROGRAMMING PROBLEM

There are many difficulties associated with creating programs as object, or binary machine language, programs. These are some of the problems:

- The programs are difficult to understand or debug. (Binary numbers all look the same, particularly after you have looked at them for a few hours.)
- The programs are slow to enter since you must set a front panel switch for each bit and load memory one word at a time.
- The programs do not describe the task which you want the computer to perform in anything resembling a human-readable format.
- The programs are long and tiresome to write.
- The programmer often makes careless errors that are very difficult to locate and correct.

For example, **the following version of the addition object program contains a single bit error. Try to find it:**

```
0011000000111000
0110000000000000
1100000001111000
0110000000000010
0011000111000000
0110000000000100
```

Although the computer handles binary numbers with ease, people do not. People find binary programs long, tiresome, confusing, and meaningless. Eventually, a programmer may start remembering some of the binary codes, but such effort should be spent more productively.

USING OCTAL OR HEXADECIMAL

We can improve the situation somewhat by writing instructions using octal or hexadecimal numbers, rather than binary. We will use hexadecimal numbers in this book because they are shorter, and because they are the standard for the microprocessor industry. Table 1-1 defines the hexadecimal digits and their binary equivalents. **The MC68000 program to add two numbers now becomes:**

```
3038
6000
D078
6002
31C0
6004
```

At the very least, the hexadecimal version is shorter to write and not quite so tiring to examine.

Table 1-1. Hexadecimal Conversion Table

Hexadecimal Digit	Binary Equivalent	Decimal Equivalent
0	0000	0
1	0001	1
2	0010	2
3	0011	3
4	0100	4
5	0101	5
6	0110	6
7	0111	7
8	1000	8
9	1001	9
A	1010	10
B	1011	11
C	1100	12
D	1101	13
E	1110	14
F	1111	15

Errors are somewhat easier to find in a sequence of hexadecimal digits. The erroneous version of the addition program, in hexadecimal form, becomes:

```
3038
6000
C078
6002
31C0
6004
```

The mistake is far more obvious.

What do we do with this hexadecimal program? The microprocessor understands only binary instruction codes. If your front panel has a hexadecimal keyboard instead of bit switches, you can key the hexadecimal program directly into memory — the keyboard logic translates the hexadecimal digits into binary numbers. But what if your front panel has only bit switches? You can convert the hexadecimal digits to binary by yourself, but this is a repetitive, tiresome task. People who attempt it make all sorts of petty mistakes, such as looking at the wrong line, dropping a bit, or transposing a bit or a digit. Besides, once we have converted our hexadecimal program we must still place the bits in memory through the switches on the front panel.

Hexadecimal Loader

These repetitive, grueling tasks are, however, perfect jobs for a computer. The computer never gets tired or bored and almost never makes mistakes. **The idea is to write a program that accepts hexadecimal numbers, converts them into binary numbers, and places them in memory. This is a standard program provided with many microcomputers; it is called a hexadecimal loader.**

The hexadecimal loader is a program like any other. It occupies memory space. In some systems, it resides in memory just long enough to load another program; in others, it occupies a reserved, read-only section of memory. Your microcomputer may not have bit switches on its front panel; it may not even have a front panel. This reflects the machine designer's decision that binary programming is not only impossibly tedious but also wholly unnecessary. The hexadecimal loader in your system may be part of a larger program called a monitor, which also provides a number of tools for program debugging and analysis.

A hexadecimal loader certainly does not solve every programming problem. The hexadecimal version of the program is still difficult to read or understand; for example, it does not distinguish operations from data or addresses, nor does the program listing provide any suggestion as to what the program does. What does 3038 or 31C0 mean? Memorizing a card full of codes is hardly an appetizing proposition. Furthermore, the codes will be entirely different for a different microprocessor and the program will require a large amount of documentation.

INSTRUCTION CODE MNEMONICS

An obvious programming improvement is to assign a name to each instruction code. The instruction code name is called a "mnemonic" or memory jogger. The instruction mnemonic should describe, in a minimum number of characters, what the instruction does.

Devising Mnemonics

In fact, all microprocessor manufacturers provide a set of mnemonics for the microprocessor instruction set (they cannot remember hexadecimal codes either). **You do not have to abide by the manufacturer's mnemonics;** there is nothing sacred about them. **However, they are standard for a given microprocessor, and therefore understood by all users.** These are the instruction codes that you will find in manuals, cards, books, articles, and programs. The problem with selecting instruction mnemonics is that not all instructions have "obvious" names. Some instructions do (for example, ADD, AND, OR), others have obvious contractions (such as SUB for subtraction, XOR for exclusive-OR), while still others have neither. The result is such mnemonics as WMP, PCHL, and even SOB. Most manufacturers come up with some reasonable names and some hopeless ones. However, users who devise their own mnemonics rarely do much better.

Standard Mnemonics

There is a proposed standard set of assembly language mnemonics.[1] The amount of use that it will receive is uncertain, but it should at least serve as a basis for comparing instruction sets and for selecting mnemonics for future processors.

Along with the instruction mnemonics, the manufacturer will usually assign names to the CPU registers. As with the instruction names, some register names are obvious (such as A for Accumulator) while others may have only historical significance. Again, we will use the manufacturer's suggestions simply to promote standardization.

An Assembly Language Program

If we use standard MC68000 instruction and register mnemonics, as defined by Motorola, our MC68000 addition program becomes:

```
MOVE    $6000,D0
ADD     $6002,D0
MOVE    D0,$6004
```

The program is still far from obvious, but at least some parts are comprehensible. ADD is a considerable improvement over D078. The MOVE mnemonics do suggest moving data into a register or memory location. We now see that some parts of the program are operations and others are addresses. **Such a program is an assembly language program.**

THE ASSEMBLER PROGRAM

How do we get the assembly language program into the computer? We have to translate it, either into hexadecimal or into binary numbers. **You can translate an assembly language program by hand,** instruction by instruction. This is called hand assembly.

The following table illustrates the hand assembly of the addition program:

Instruction Mnemonic	Register/Memory Location	Hexadecimal Equivalent
MOVE	$6000,D0	30386000
ADD	$6002,D0	D0786002
MOVE	D0,$6004	31C06004

As with hexadecimal-to-binary conversion, hand assembly is a rote task which is uninteresting, repetitive, and subject to numerous minor errors. Picking the wrong line, transposing digits, omitting instructions, and misreading the codes are only a few of the mistakes that you may make. Most microprocessors complicate the task even further by having instructions with different lengths. Some instructions are one word long while others may be two or three. Some instructions require data in the second and third words; others require memory addresses, register numbers, or who knows what?

Assembly is another rote task that we can assign to the microcomputer. The microcomputer never makes any mistakes when translating codes; it always knows how many words and what format each instruction requires. The program that does this job is an "assembler." The assembler program translates a user program, or "source" program written with mnemonics, into a machine language program, or "object" program, which the microcomputer can execute. The assembler's input is a source program and its output is an object program.

An assembler is a program, just as the hexadecimal loader is. However, assemblers are more difficult to write, occupy more memory, and require more peripherals and execution time than do hexadecimal loaders. While users may (and often do) write their own loaders, few care to write their own assemblers.

Assemblers have their own rules that you must learn. These include the use of certain markers (such as spaces, commas, semicolons, or colons) in appropriate places, correct spelling, the proper control of information, and perhaps even the correct placement of names and numbers. These rules are usually simple and can be learned quickly.

Additional Features of Assemblers

Early assemblers did little more than translate the mnemonic names of instructions and registers into their binary equivalents. However, most assemblers now provide such additional features as:

- Allowing the user to assign names to memory locations, input and output devices, and even sequences of instructions
- Converting data or addresses from various number systems (for example,

decimal or hexadecimal) to binary and converting characters into their ASCII or EBCDIC binary codes

- Performing some arithmetic as part of the assembly process
- Telling the loader program where in memory parts of the program or data should be placed
- Allowing the user to assign areas of memory as temporary data storage and to place fixed data in areas of program memory
- Providing the information required to include standard programs from program libraries, or programs written at some other time, in the current program
- Allowing the user to control the format of the program listing and the input and output devices employed

Choosing an Assembler

All of these features, of course, involve additional cost and memory. Microcomputers generally have much simpler assemblers than do larger computers, but the tendency is always for the size of assemblers to increase. You will often have a choice of assemblers. The important criterion is not how many off-beat features the assembler has, but rather how convenient it is to use in normal practice.

DISADVANTAGES OF ASSEMBLY LANGUAGE

The assembler, like the hexadecimal loader, does not solve all the problems of programming. One problem is the tremendous gap between the microcomputer instruction set and the tasks which the microcomputer is to perform. Computer instructions tend to do things like add the contents of two registers, shift the contents of the Accumulator one bit, or place a new value in the Program Counter. On the other hand, a user generally wants a microcomputer to do something like print a number, look for and react to a particular command from a teletypewriter, or activate a relay at the proper time. An assembly language programmer must translate such tasks into a sequence of simple computer instructions. The translation can be a difficult, time-consuming job.

Furthermore, **if you are programming in assembly language, you must have detailed knowledge of the particular microcomputer that you are using.** You must know what registers and instructions the microcomputers has, precisely how the instructions affect the various registers, what addressing methods the computer uses, and a mass of other information. None of this information is relevant to the task which the microcomputer must ultimately perform.

Lack of Portability

In addition, assembly language programs are not portable. Each microcomputer has its own assembly language which reflects its own architecture. An assembly language program written for the MC68000 will not run on a 6809, 8080, or Z8000 microprocessor. For example, the addition program written for the Z8000 would be:

```
LD      R0,%6000
ADD     R0,%6002
LD      %6004,R0
```

The lack of portability not only means that you will not be able to use your assembly language program on a different microcomputer, but also that you will not be able to use any programs that were not specifically written for the microcomputer you are using. This is a particular drawback for 16-bit microcomputers like the MC68000, since these devices are new and few assembly language programs exist for them. The result, too frequently, is that you are on your own. If you need a program to perform a particular task, you are not likely to find it in the small program libraries that most manufacturers provide. Nor are you likely to find it in an archive, journal article, or someone's old program file. You will probably have to write it yourself.

HIGH-LEVEL LANGUAGES

The solution to many of the difficulties associated with assembly language programs is to use, instead, "high-level" or "procedure-oriented" languages. Such languages allow you to describe tasks in forms that are problem-oriented rather than computer-oriented. Each statement in a high-level language performs a recognizable function; it will generally correspond to many assembly language instructions. A program called a compiler translates the high-level language source program into object code or machine language instructions.

FORTRAN — A HIGH-LEVEL LANGUAGE

Many different high-level languages exist for different types of tasks. **If, for example, you can express what you want the computer to do in algebraic notation, you can write your program in FORTRAN (Formula Translation Language), the oldest and most widely used of the high-level languages.** Now, if you want to add two numbers, you just tell the computer:

```
SUM = NUMB1 + NUM2
```

That is a lot simpler (and a lot shorter) than either the equivalent machine language program or the equivalent assembly language program. Other high-level languages include COBOL (for business applications), Pascal (a language designed for structured programming), PL/I (a combination of FORTRAN and COBOL), APL (designed for writing very compact programs), BASIC (popular for smaller microcomputers), and C (a systems-programming language developed at Bell Telephone Laboratories).

ADVANTAGES OF HIGH-LEVEL LANGUAGES

Clearly, high-level languages make programs easier and faster to write. A common estimate is that a programmer can write a program about ten times as fast in a high-level language as in assembly language.[2-4] That is just writing the program; it does not include problem definition, program design, debugging, testing, or documentation, all of which become simpler and faster. The high-level language program is, for instance, partly self-documenting. Even if you do not know FORTRAN, you probably could tell what the statement illustrated above does.

Machine Independence

High-level languages solve many other problems associated with assembly language programming. The high-level language has its own syntax (usually defined by a national or international standard). The language does not mention the instruction set, registers, or other features of a particular computer. The compiler takes care of all such details. Programmers can concentrate on their own tasks; they do not need a detailed understanding of the underlying CPU architecture — for that matter, they do not need to know anything about the computer they are programming.

Portability

Programs written in a high-level language are portable — at least, in theory. They will run on any computer that has a standard compiler for that language.

At the same time, all previous programs written in a high-level language for prior computers are available to you when programming a new computer. This can mean thousands of programs in the case of a common language like FORTRAN or BASIC.

DISADVANTAGES OF HIGH-LEVEL LANGUAGES

If all the good things we have said about high-level languages are true — if you can write programs faster and make them portable besides — why bother with assembly languages? Who wants to worry about registers, instruction codes, mnemonics, and all that garbage! As usual, there are disadvantages that balance the advantages.

Syntax

One obvious problem is that, as with assembly language, **you have to learn the "rules" or "syntax" of any high-level language** you want to use. A high-level language has a fairly complicated set of rules. You will find that it takes a lot of time just to get a program that is syntactically correct (and even then it probably will not do what you want). A high-level computer language is like a foreign language. If you have talent, you will get used to the rules and be able to turn out programs that the compiler will accept. Still, learning the rules and trying to get the program accepted by the compiler does not contribute directly to doing your job.

Here, for example, are a few rules for some FORTRAN compilers:

- Labels must be numbers placed in the first five card columns
- Statements must start in column 7
- Integer variables must start with the letters I, J, K, L, M, or N

Cost of Compilers

Another obvious problem is that you need a compiler to translate programs written in a high-level language into machine language. Compilers are expensive and use a large amount of memory. While most assemblers occupy 2K to 16K bytes of memory (1K = 1024), compilers occupy 4K to 64K bytes. So the amount of overhead involved in using the compiler is rather large.

Adapting Tasks to a Language

Furthermore, **only some compilers will make the implementation of your task simpler.** FORTRAN, for example, is well-suited to problems that can be expressed as algebraic formulas. If, however, your problem is controlling a display terminal, editing a string of characters, or monitoring an alarm system, your problem cannot be easily expressed in FORTRAN. In fact, formulating the solution in FORTRAN may be more awkward and more difficult than formulating it in assembly language. The answer is, of course, to use a more suitable high-level language. Languages specifically designed for tasks such as those mentioned above do exist — they are called system implementation languages. However, these languages are less widely used and standardized than FORTRAN.

Inefficiency

High-level languages do not produce very efficient machine language programs. The basic reason for this is that compilation is an automatic process which is riddled with compromises to allow for many ranges of possibilities. The compiler works much like a computerized language translator — sometimes the words are right but the sentence structures are awkward. A simple compiler cannot know when a variable is no longer being used and can be discarded, when a register should be used rather than a memory location, or when variables have simple relationships. The experienced programmer can take advantage of shortcuts to shorten execution time or reduce memory usage. A few compilers (known as optimizing compilers) can also do this, but such compilers are much larger than regular compilers.

SUMMARY OF ADVANTAGES AND DISADVANTAGES

Advantages of High-Level Languages:

- Easier to learn (and teach to others)
- More convenient descriptions of tasks
- Less time spent writing programs
- Easier documentation
- Standard syntax
- Independence of the structure of a particular computer
- Portability
- Availability of library and other programs

Disadvantages of High-Level Languages:

- Special rules
- Extensive hardware and software support required
- Orientation of common languages to mathematical or business problems
- Inefficient programs
- Difficulty of optimizing code to meet time and memory requirements
- Inability to use special features of a computer conveniently

HIGH-LEVEL LANGUAGES FOR MICROPROCESSORS

Microprocessor users will encounter several special difficulties when using high-level languages. Among these are:

- **Few high-level languages exist for microprocessors.** This is particularly true for processors that are new, relatively unpopular, or intended for simple control applications.
- **Few standard languages are widely available.**
- **Compilers usually require a large amount of memory or even a completely different computer.**
- **Many microprocessor applications are not well-suited to high-level languages.**
- **Many microprocessor languages produce no object program.** That is, they translate the program and run it line by line — this is referred to as interpreting rather than compiling — **or they produce an output that requires special systems software** (a run-time package) **to execute**. Either approach may result in programs that execute slowly and use a large amount of memory. BASIC and PASCAL, the most commonly available high-level languages, generally use one of these approaches.
- **Memory costs are often critical in microprocessor applications.**

The relatively small number of high-level languages for microcomputers is a result of the short history of microprocessors and their origin in the semiconductor industry, rather than in the computer industry. Among the high-level languages that are most often available are BASIC[5], Pascal[6, 7], FORTRAN, C[8], and the PL/I-type languages such as PL/M[9].

Many of the high-level languages that exist do not conform to recognized standards, so the microprocessor user cannot expect to gain much program portability, access to program libraries, or use of previous experience or programs. The main advantages remaining are the reduction in programming effort, easier documentation, and the smaller amount of detailed understanding of the computer architecture that is necessary.

Overhead for High-Level Languages

The overhead involved in using a high-level language with microprocessors is considerable. Until very recently, microprocessors have been better suited to control applications and slow interactive applications than to the character manipulation and language analysis involved in compilation. Therefore, compilers for some microprocessors will not run on a microprocessor-based system. Instead, they require a much larger computer; that is, they are cross-compilers rather than self-compilers. A user must not only bear the expense of the larger computer, but must also transfer the program from the larger computer to the micro.

Some self-compilers are available. These compilers run on the microcomputer for which they produce object code. Unfortunately, they usually require large amounts of memory, plus special supporting hardware and software.

Unsuitability of High-Level Languages

High-level languages also are not generally well-suited to certain microprocessor applications. Most of the common languages were devised either to help solve scientific problems or to handle large-scale business data processing. Many microprocessor applications do not fall in either of these areas. Instead they involve sending data and control information to output devices and receiving data and status information from input devices. Often the control and status information consists of a few binary digits with very precise hardware-related meanings. If you try to write a typical control program in a high-level language, you may feel like someone who is trying to eat soup with chopsticks. For tasks in such areas as test equipment, terminals, navigation systems, signal processing, and business equipment, the high-level languages work much better than they do in instrumentation, communications, peripherals, and automotive applications.

Application Areas for Language Levels

Applications better suited to high-level languages are those which require large memories. If, as in a valve controller, electronic game, appliance controller, or small instrument, the cost of a single memory chip is important, then the inefficient memory use of high-level languages is intolerable. If, on the other hand, as in a terminal or test equipment, the system has many thousands of bytes of memory anyway, this inefficiency is not as important. Clearly the size and volume of the product are important factors as well. A large program will greatly increase the advantages of high-level languages. On the other hand, a high-volume application will mean that fixed software development costs are not as important as memory costs that are part of each system.

WHICH LEVEL SHOULD YOU USE?

Which language level you use depends on your particular application. Let us briefly note some of the factors which may favor particular levels:

Applications for Machine Language:

- Virtually no one programs in machine language because it wastes human time and is difficult to document. An assembler costs very little and greatly reduces programming time.

Applications for Assembly Language:

- Short to moderate-sized programs
- Applications where memory cost is a factor
- Real-time control applications
- Limited data processing
- High-volume applications
- Applications involving more input/output or control than computation

Applications for High-Level Language:

- Long programs
- Low-volume applications
- Applications where the amount of memory required is already very large
- Applications invoing more computation than input/output or control
- Compatibility with similar applications using larger computers
- Availability of specific programs in a high-level language which can be used in the application
- Programs which are expected to undergo many changes

Other Considerations

Many other factors are also important, such as the availability of a large computer for use in development, experience with particular languages, and compatibility with other applications.

If hardware will ultimately be the largest cost in your application, or if speed is critical, you should favor assembly language. But be prepared to spend much extra time in software development in exchange for lower memory costs and higher execution speeds. If software will be the largest cost in your application, you should favor a high-level language.But be prepared to spend the extra money required for the supporting hardware and software.

Of course, no one except some theorists will object if you use both assembly and high-level languages. You can write the program originally in a high-level language and then patch some sections in assembly language.[10, 11] However, most users prefer not to do this because it can create havoc in debugging, testing, and documentation.

FUTURE TRENDS IN LANGUAGE LEVELS

We expect the future will favor high-level languages for the following reasons:

- Programs always add extra features and grow larger
- Hardware and memory are becoming less expensive
- Software and programmers are becoming more expensive
- Memory chips are becoming available in larger sizes, at lower "per bit" cost, so actual savings in chips are less likely
- More suitable and more efficient high-level languages are being developed

- More compilers are becoming available
- More standardization of high-level languages will occur

Assembly language programming of microprocessors will not be a dying art any more than it is for large computers. But longer programs, cheaper memory, and more expensive programmers will make software costs a larger part of most applications. The edge in many applications will therefore go to high-level languages.

WHY THIS BOOK?

If the future favors high-level languages, why have a book on assembly language programming? The reasons are:

1. Most industrial microcomputer users program in assembly language (almost two thirds, according to a recent survey).
2. Many microcomputer users will continue to program in assembly language since they need the detailed control that it provides.
3. No suitable high-level language has yet become widely available or standardized.
4. Many applications require the efficiency of assembly language.
5. An understanding of assembly language can help in evaluating high-level languages.
6. **Almost all microcomputer programmers ultimately find that they need some knowledge of assembly language,** most often to debug programs, write I/O routines, speed up or shorten critical sections of programs written in high-level languages, utilize or modify operating system functions, and understand other people's programs.

The rest of this book will deal exclusively with assemblers and assembly language programming. However, we do want readers to know that assembly language is not the only alternative. You should watch for new developments that may significantly reduce programming costs if such costs are a major factor in your application.

REFERENCES

1. W. P. Fischer, "Microprocessor Assembly Language Draft Standard," *Computer,* December 1979, pp. 96-109.

2. M. H. Halstead, *Elements of Software Science,* American Elsevier, New York, 1977.

3. L. H. Putnam and A. Fitzsimmons, "Estimating Software Costs," *Datamation,* September 1979, pp. 189-98.

4. M. Phister, Jr., *Data Processing Technology and Economics,* Santa Monica Publishing Co., Santa Monica, Calif., 1976. Also available from Digital Press, Educational Services, Digital Equipment Corp., Bedford, Mass.

5. Albrecht, Finkel, and Brown, *BASIC for Home Computers,* Wiley, New York, 1978.

6. G. M. Schneider et al., *An Introduction to Programming and Problem Solving with PASCAL,* Wiley, New York, 1978.

7. K. L. Bowles, *Microcomputer Problem Solving Using PASCAL,* Springer-Verlag, New York, 1977.

8. B. W. Kernighan and D.M. Ritchie, *The C Programming Language,* Prentice-Hall, Englewood Cliffs, N. J., 1978.

9. D. D. McCracken, *A Guide to PL/M Programming for Microcomputer Applications,* Addison-Wesley, Reading, Mass., 1978.

10. P. Caudill, "Using Assembly Coding to Optimize High-Level Language Programs," *Electronics,* February 1, 1979, pp. 121-24.

11. D. B. Wecker et al., "High Level Design Language Develops Low Level Microprocessor-Independent Software," *Computer Design,* June 1979, pp. 140-49.

2
Assemblers

This chapter discusses the functions performed by assemblers, beginning with features common to most assemblers and proceeding through more elaborate capabilities such as macros and conditional assembly. You may wish to skim this chapter for the present and return to it when you feel more comfortable with the material.

FEATURES OF ASSEMBLERS

As we mentioned previously, today's assemblers do much more than translate assembly language mnemonics into binary codes. But we will describe how an assembler handles the translation of mnemonics before describing additional assembler features. Finally we will explain how assemblers are used.

ASSEMBLY LANGUAGE FIELDS

Assembly language instructions (or "statements") are divided into a number of "fields," as shown in Table 2-1.

The operation code field is the only field which can never be empty; it always contains either an instruction mnemonic or a directive to the assembler, sometimes called a "pseudo-instruction," "pseudo-operation," or "pseudo-op."

The operand or address field may contain an address or data, or it may be blank.

Table 2-1. The Fields of an Assembly Language Instruction

Label Field	Operation Code or Mnemonic Field	Operand or Address Field	Comment Field
VALUE1:	DC.W	$201E	FIRST VALUE
VALUE2:	DC.W	$0774	SECOND VALUE
RESULT:	DS.W	1	16-BIT STORAGE FOR ADDITION RESULT
•			
•			
•			
START	MOVE	VALUE1,DO	GET FIRST VALUE
	ADD	VALUE2,DO	ADD SECOND VALUE TO FIRST VALUE
	MOVE	DO,RESULT	STORE RESULT OF ADDITION
NEXT:	?	?	NEXT INSTRUCTION

The comment and label fields are optional. A programmer will assign a label to a statement or add a comment as a personal convenience: namely, to make the program easier to read and use.

Of course, the assembler must have some way of telling where one field ends and another begins. Assemblers often require that each field start in a specific column. This is a "fixed format." However, fixed formats are inconvenient when the input medium is paper tape; fixed formats are also a nuisance to programmers. The alternative is a "free format" where the fields may appear anywhere on the line.

Delimiters

If the assembler cannot use the position on the line to tell the fields apart, it must use something else. **Most assemblers use a special symbol or "delimiter" at the beginning or end of each field.** The most common delimiter is the space character. Commas, periods, semicolons, colons, slashes, question marks, and other characters which would not otherwise be used in assembly language programs also may serve as delimiters. Table 2-2 lists standard MC68000 assembler delimiters.

You will have to exercise a little care with delimiters. Some assemblers are fussy about extra spaces or the appearance of delimiters in comments or labels. A well-written assembler will handle these minor problems, but many assemblers are not well-written. Our recommendation is simple: avoid potential problems if you can. The following rules will help:

- Do not use extra spaces, in particular, do not put spaces after commas that separate operands.
- Do not use delimiter characters in names or labels.
- Include standard delimiters even if your assembler does not require them. Then it will be more likely that your programs are in correct form for another assembler.

Table 2-2. Standard MC68000 Assembler Delimiters

'space'	Between label and operation code, between operation code and address, and before an entry in the comment field
comma	Between operands in the address field
asterisk	Before an entire line of comment

Labels

The label field is the first field in an assembly language instruction; it may be blank. If a label is present, the assembler defines the label as equivalent to the address into which the first byte of the object code generated for that instruction will be loaded. You may subsequently use the label as an address or as data in another instruction's address field. The assembler will replace the label with the assigned value when creating an object program.

Motorola's assembler uses two different delimiters to terminate label fields. If the label starts at the beginning of a line, as we discussed in the preceding paragraph, then a space will terminate the label field. However, this assembler also allows you to have the label start anywhere along a line, in which case you must use a colon (:) as the delimiter to terminate the label field.

Labels are most frequently used in Jump, Branch or TRAP instructions. These instructions place a new value in the program counter and so alter the normal sequential execution of instructions. JMP 150_{16} means "place the value 150_{16} in the program counter." The next instruction to be executed will be the one in memory location 150_{16}. The instruction JMP START means "place the value assigned to the label START in the program counter." The next instruction to be executed will be the on at the address corresponding to the label START. Table 2-3 contains an example.

Why use a label? Here are some reasons:

- A label makes a program location easier to find and remember.
- The label can easily be moved, if required, to change or correct a program. The assembler will automatically change all instructions that use the label when the program is reassembled.
- The assembler or loader can relocate the whole program by adding a constant (a "relocation constant") to each address in which a label was used. Thus we can move the program to allow for the insertion of other programs or simply to rearrange memory.
- The program is easier to use as a library program; that is, it is easier for someone else to take your program and add it to some totally different program.
- You do not have to figure out memory addresses. Figuring out memory addresses is particularly difficult with microprocessors which have instructions that vary in length.

You should assign a label to any instruction that you might want to refer to later.

The next question is how to choose a label. The assembler often places some

Table 2-3. Assigning and Using a Label

Assembly Language Program
START MOVE VALUE1,D0 . . . . (MAIN PROGRAM) . . . JMP START
When the machine language version of this program is executed, the instruction JMP START causes the address of the instruction labeled STRT to be placed in the program counter. That instruction will then be executed.

restrictions on the number of characters (usually 5 or 6), the leading character (often must be a letter), and the trailing characters (often must be letters, numbers, or one of a few special characters). Beyond these restrictions, the choice is up to you.

Our own preference is to **use labels that suggest their purpose,** i.e., mnemonic labels. Typical examples are ADDW in a routine that adds one word into a sum, SRCHETX in a routine that searches for the ASCII character ETX, or NKEYS for a location in data memory that contains the number of key entries. Meaningful labels are easier to remember and contribute to program documentation. Some programmers use a standard format for labels, such as starting with L0000. These labels are self-sequencing (you can skip a few numbers to permit insertions), but they do not help document the program.

Some label selection rules will keep you out of trouble. We recommend the following:

- Do not use labels that are the same as operation codes or other mnemonics. Most assemblers will not allow this usage; others will, but it is confusing.
- Do not use labels that are longer than the assembler recognizes. Assemblers have various rules, and often ignore some of the characters at the end of a long label.
- Avoid special characters (non-alphabetic and non-numeric) and lower-case letters. Some assemblers will not permit them; others allow only certain ones. The simplest practice is to stick to capital letters and numbers.
- Start each label with a letter. Such labels are always acceptable.
- Do not use labels that could be confused with each other. Avoid the letters I, O, and Z and the numbers 0, 1, and 2. Also avoid things like XXXX and XXXXX. There's no sense in tempting fate and Murphy's Law.
- When you are not sure if a label is legal, do not use it. You will not get any real benefit from discovering exactly what the assembler will accept.

These are recommendations, not rules. You do not have to follow them but don't blame us if you waste time on unnecessary problems.

ASSEMBLER OPERATION CODES (MNEMONICS)

One main task of the assembler is the translation of mnemonic operation codes into their binary equivalents. The assembler performs this task using a fixed table much as you would if you were doing the assembly by hand.

The assembler must, however, do more than just translate the operation codes. It **must also somehow determine how many operands the instruction requires and what type they are.** This may be rather complex — some instructions (like a Stop) have no operands, others (like a Jump instruction) have one, while still others (like a transfer between registers or a multiple-bit shift) require two. Some instructions may even allow alternatives; for example, some computers have instructions (like Shift or Clear) which can either apply to a register in the CPU or to a memory location. We will not discuss how the assembler makes these distinctions; we will just note that it must do so.

ASSEMBLER DIRECTIVES

Some assembly language instructions are not directly translated into machine language instructions. These instructions are directives to the assembler; they assign the program to certain areas in memory, define symbols, designate areas of memory for data storage, place tables or other fixed data in memory, allow references to other programs, and perform minor housekeeping functions.

To use these assembler directives or pseudo-operations a programmer places the directive's mnemonic in the operation code field, and, if the specified directive requires it, an address or data in the address field.

The most common directives are:

DATA
EQUATE or DEFINE
ORIGIN
RESERVE

Linking directives (used to connect separate programs) are:

ENTRY
EXTERNAL

Different assemblers use different names for those operations but their functions are the same. Housekeeping directives include:

END
LIST
NAME
PAGE
SPACE
TITLE
PUNCH

We will discuss these pseudo-operations briefly, although their functions are usually obvious.

The DATA Directive

The DATA or DEFINE CONSTANT directive allows the programmer to enter fixed data into program memory. This data may include:

- Lookup tables
- Code conversion tables
- Messages
- Synchronization patterns
- Thresholds
- Names
- Coefficients for equations
- Commands
- Conversion factors
- Weighting factors
- Characteristic times or frequencies
- Subroutine addresses
- Key identifications
- Test patterns
- Character generation patterns
- Identification patterns
- Tax tables
- Standard forms
- Masking patterns
- State transition tables

The DATA directive treats the data as a permanent part of the program.

The format of a DATA directive is usually quite simple. An instruction like:

```
DZCON    DATA    12
```

will place the number 12 in the next available memory location and assign that location the name DZCON. Every DATA directive usually has a label, unless it is one of a series. The data and label may take any form that the assembler permits.

Most assemblers allow more elaborate DATA directives that handle a large amount of data at one time, for example:

```
EMESS    DATA    'ERROR'
SQRS     DATA    1,4,9,16,25
```

A single directive may fill many bytes of program memory, limited perhaps by the length of a line or by the restrictions of a particular assembler. Of course, you can always overcome any restrictions by following one DATA directive with another:

```
MESSG    DATA    'NOW IS THE'
         DATA    'TIME FOR ALL'
         DATA    'GOOD MEN'
         DATA    'TO COME TO THE'
         DATA    'AID OF THEIR'
         DATA    'COUNTRY'
```

Microprocessor assemblers typically have some variations of standard DATA directives. DEFINE BYTE or FORM CONSTANT BYTE handles 8-bit numbers; DEFINE WORD or FORM CONSTANT WORD handles 16-bit numbers or addresses. Other special directives may handle character-coded data.

The EQUATE (or DEFINE) Directive

The EQUATE directive allows the programmer to equate names with addresses or data. This pseudo-operation is almost always given the mnemonic EQU or =. The names may refer to device addresses, numeric data, starting addresses, fixed addresses, etc.

The EQUATE directive assigns the numeric value in its operand field to the label in its label field. Here are two examples:

```
TTY     EQU     5
LAST    EQU     5000
```

Most assemblers will allow you to define one label in terms of another, for example:

```
LAST    EQU     FINAL
ST1     EQU     START+1
```

The label in the operand field must, of course, have been previously defined. Often, the operand field may contain more complex expressions, as we shall see later. Double name assignments (two names for the same data or address) may be useful in patching together programs that use different names for the same variable (or different spellings of what was supposed to be the same name).

Note that an EQU directive does not cause the assembler to place anything in memory. The assembler simply enters an additional name into a table (called a "symbol table") which the assembler maintains.

When do you use a name? The answer is: whenever you have a parameter that you might want to change or that has some meaning besides its ordinary numeric value. We typically assign names to time constants, device addresses, masking patterns, conversion factors, and the like. A name like DELAY, TTY, KBD, KROW, or OPEN not only makes the parameter easier to change, but it also adds to program documentation. We also assign names to memory locations that have special purposes; they may hold data, mark the start of the program, or be available for intermediate storage.

What name do you use? The best rules are much the same as in the case of labels, except that here meaningful names really count. Why not call the teletypewriter TTY instead of X15, a bit time delay BTIME or BTDLY rather than WW, the number of the "GO" key on a keyboard GOKEY rather than HORSE? This advice seems straightforward, but a surprising number of programmers do not follow it.

Where do you place the EQUATE directives? The best place is at the start of the program, under appropriate comment headings such as I/O ADDRESSES, TEMPORARY STORAGE, TIME CONSTANTS, or PROGRAM LOCATIONS. This makes the definitions easy to find if you want to change them. Furthermore, another user will be able to look up all the definitions in one centralized place. Clearly this practice improves documentation and makes the program easier to use.

Definitions used only in a specific subroutine should appear at the start of the subroutine.

The ORIGIN Directive

The ORIGIN directive (almost always abbreviated ORG) allows the programmer to specify the memory locations where programs, subroutines, or data will reside. Programs and data may be located in different areas of memory depending on the memory configuration. Startup routines, interrupt service routines, and other required programs may be scattered around memory at fixed or convenient addresses.

The assembler maintains a location counter (comparable to the computer's program counter) which contains the location in memory of the instruction or data item being processed. An ORG directive causes the assembler to place a new value in the location counter, much as a Jump instruction causes the CPU to place a new value in the program counter. The output from the assembler must not only contain instructions and data, but must also indicate to the loader program where in memory it should place the instructions and data.

Microprocessor programs often contain several ORIGIN statements for the following purposes:

- Reset (startup) address
- Interrupt service addresses
- Trap (software interrupt) addresses
- RAM storage
- Stack
- Main program
- Subroutines
- Memory addresses used for input/output devices or special functions

Still other ORIGIN statements may allow room for later insertions, place tables or data in memory, or assign vacant memory space for data buffers. Program and data memory in microcomputers may occupy widely separate addresses to simplify the hardware.

Typical ORIGIN statements are:

```
ORG     RESET
ORG     1000
ORG     INT3
```

Most assemblers assume an origin of zero if the programmer does not put an ORG statement at the start of the program. The convenience is slight; we recommend the inclusion of an ORG statement to avoid confusion.

The RESERVE Directive

The RESERVE or DEFINE STORAGE directive allows the programmer to allocate memory for various purposes such as data tables, temporary storage, indirect addresses, a Stack, etc.

Using the RESERVE directive, you assign a name to the memory area and declare the number of locations to be assigned. Here are some examples:

```
NOKEY   RESERVE   1
TEMP    RESERVE   50
VOLTG   RESERVE   80
BUFR    RESERVE   100
```

You can use the RESERVE directive to reserve memory locations in program memory or in data memory; however, the RESERVE directive will normally be used in data memory.

In reality, all the RESERVE directive does is increase the assembler's location counter by the amount declared in the operand field. The assembler does not actually produce any object code.

Note the following features of RESERVE:

1. **The label of the RESERVE directive is assigned the value of the first address reserved.** For example, the pseudo-operation:

   ```
   TEMP     RESERVE    20
   ```

   reserves 20 words of memory and assigns the name TEMP to the address of the first byte.
2. **You must specify the number of locations to be reserved. There is no default case.**
3. **No data is placed in the reserved locations.** Any data that, by chance, may be in these locations will be left there.

Some assemblers allow the programmer to specify initial values for the RESERVE area in memory. We strongly recommend that you do not use this feature; it assumes that the program (along with the initial values) will be loaded from an external device (e.g., paper tape or floppy disk) each time it is run. Microprocessor programs, on the other hand, often reside in non-volatile read-only-memory (ROM) and start when power comes on. The data memory (often referred to as random recess memory or 'RAM') in such situations does not retain its contents, nor is it reloaded. Therefore, always include instruction sequences to initialize RAM in your program; this will insure that initialization occurs every time the program is executed and not just during load time.

Linking Directives

We often want statements in one program or subroutine to use names that are defined in a different assembly. Such uses are called "external references"; a special linking program is necessary to actually fill in the values and determine if any names are undefined or doubly defined.

The directive EXTERNAL, usually abbreviated EXT or XREF, signifies that the name is defined elsewhere.

The directive ENTRY, usually abbreviated ENT or XDEF, signifies that the name is available for use elsewhere; that is, it is defined in this program.

The precise way in which **linking directives** are implemented varies greatly from assembler to assembler. We will not refer to these directives again, but they **are very important in actual applications.**

Output Control Directives

There are various assembler directives that affect the operation of the assem-

bler and its program listing rather than the object program itself. Common directives include:

- END, which marks the end of the assembly language source program.
- LIST, which tells the Assembler to print the source program. Some assemblers allow such variations as NO LIST or LIST SYMBOL TABLE.
- NAME or TITLE, which prints a name at the top of each page of the listing.
- PAGE or SPACE, which skips to the next page or next line, respectively, and improves the appearance of the listing, making it easier to read.
- PUNCH, which transfers subsequent object code to the paper tape punch. This pseudo-operation may in some cases be the default option and therefore unnecessary.

When to Use Labels

Users often wonder if or when they can assign a label to an assembler directive. These are our recommendations:

- **All EQUATE directives must have labels;** they are useless otherwise, since the purpose of an EQUATE is to define its label.
- **DATA and RESERVE directives usually have labels.** The label identifies the first memory location used or assigned.
- **Other directives should not have labels.** Some assemblers allow such labels, but we recommend against their use because there is no standard way to interpret them.

OPERANDS AND ADDRESSES

Most assemblers allow the programmer a lot of freedom in describing the contents of the operand or address field. But remember that the assembler has built-in names for registers and instructions and may have other built-in names. We will now describe some common options for the operand field.

Decimal Numbers

Most assemblers assume all numbers to be decimal unless they are marked otherwise. So:

```
ADD     100
```

means "add the contents of memory location 100_{10} to the contents of the Accumulator."

Other Number Systems

Most assemblers will also accept binary, octal, or hexadecimal entries. But **you must identify these number systems in some way:** for example, by preceding or following the number with an identifying character or letter. Here are some common identifiers:

- B or % for binary
- O,@, Q, or C for octal (the letter O should be avoided because of the confusion with zero)
- H or $ for hexadecimal (or standard BCD)
- D for decimal; or no identifiers if it is the default case.

Assemblers often require hexadecimal numbers to start with a digit (for example, 0A36 instead of A36) in order to distinguish between numbers and names or labels. It is good practice to enter numbers in the base in which their meaning is the clearest: that is, decimal constants in decimal; addresses and BCD numbers in hexadecimal; masking patterns or bit outputs in binary if they are short, and in hexadecimal if they are long.

Names

Names can appear in the operand field; they will be treated as the data that they represent. Remember, however, that **there is a difference between operands and addresses.** In a MC68000 assembly language program the sequence:

```
FIVE    EQU     5
        ADD     FIVE,D0
```

will add the contents of memory location 5 (not necessarily the number 5) to the contents of data register D0. A sequence which adds in the number 5 itself would be

```
FIVE    EQU     5
        ADDI    #FIVE,D0
```

The symbol # tells the assembler that the number represented by the name FIVE is the value of the operand FIVE, itself, instead of the contents of the memory location addressed by FIVE.

The Location Counter

You can use **the current value of the location counter**, which **is usually referred to as * or $**. This is useful mainly in Jump instructions; for example:

```
JMP     *+6
```

causes a Jump to the memory location 6 bytes beyond the byte that contains the first byte of the JMP instruction.

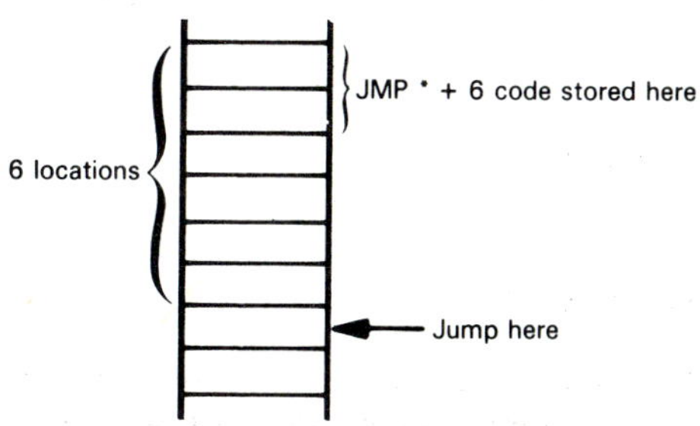

One reason to use this technique is to reduce the number of symbols in an assembly language program. This may be necessary if the assembler can handle only a limited number of symbols. Reducing the number of symbols may also decrease assembly time. Such benefits are almost negligible, however, unless your program is extremely large or your assembler rather primitive.

Most microprocessors have many two and three-byte instructions. Thus you will have difficulty determining exactly how far apart two assembly language statements are. Using offsets from the location counter therefore frequently results in errors that you can avoid if you use labels. Therefore. in almost every case, **you should not use the location counter symbol.**

Character Codes

Most assemblers allow text to be entered as ASCII strings. Such strings may be surrounded either with single or double quotation marks; some assemblers may also use a beginning or ending symbol such as A or C. **A few assemblers also permit EBCDIC strings as used by IBM machines.**

We recommend that you use character strings for all text. It improves the clarity and readability of the program.

Arithmetic and Logical Expressions

Assemblers permit combinations of the data forms described above, connected by arithmetic, logical, or special operators. These combinations are called expressions. Almost all assemblers allow simple arithmetic expressions such as START + 1. Some assemblers also permit multiplication, division, logical functions, shifts, etc. Note that the assembler evaluates expressions at assembly time; if a symbol appears in an expression, the address is used (i.e., the location counter or EQUATE value).

Assemblers vary in what expressions they accept and how they interpret them. Complex expressions make a program difficult to read and understand.

General Recommendations

We have made some recommendations during this section but will repeat them and add others here. **In general, the user should strive for clarity and simplicity.** There is no payoff for being an expert in the intricacies of an assembler or in having the most complex expression on the block. **We suggest the following approach:**

- Use the clearest number system or character code for data.
- Masks and BCD numbers in decimal, ASCII characters in octal, or ordinary numerical constants in hexadecimal serve no purpose and therefore should not be used.
- Remember to distinguish data from addresses.
- Don't use offsets from the location counter.
- Keep expressions simple and obvious. Don't rely on obscure features of the assembler.

CONDITIONAL ASSEMBLY

Some assemblers allow you to include or exclude parts of the source program, depending on conditions existing at assembly time. This is called conditional assembly; it gives the assembler some of the flexibility of a compiler. **Most microcomputer assemblers have limited capabilities for conditional assembly. A typical form is:**

```
IF      COND
.
.       (CONDITIONAL PROGRAM)
.
.
ENDIF
```

If the expression COND is true at assembly time, the instructions between IF and ENDIF (two pseudo-operations) are included in the program.

Typical uses of conditional assembly are:

- To include or exclude extra variables
- To place diagnostics or special conditions in test runs
- To allow data of various bit lengths

Unfortunately, conditional assembly tends to clutter programs and make them difficult to read. Use conditional assembly only if it is necessary.

Assembler Input	Assembler Output	
Source Program	**Object Code**	**Corresponding Mnemonics**
(Macro definition) MACRO ADDQ #1,D0 LSL.L #1,D1 BPL *-6 ENDM (End of macro definition)		
(Beginning of main program) LSL.B #1,D1 ADDX D0,D0 TST D1 BNE PARITY LOOP MAC1	E309 D140 4A41 66F8	LSL.B #1,D1 ADDX D0,D0 TST D1 BNE PARITY LOOP MAC1
	5240 E389 6AFA	ADDQ #1,D0 LSL.L #1,D1 BPL *-6 MAC1
BTST #0,D0 BNE NEXT CHAR MAC1	80000099 00000080	BTST #0,D0 BNE NEXT CHAR
	5240 E389 6AFA	ADDQ #1,D0 LSL.L #1,D1 BPL *-6
BSET #7,-(A0)	08E80007FFFF	BSET #7,-1(A0)

Figure 2-1. Expansion of a Macro by the Assembler

MACROS

You will often find that particular sequences of instructions occur many times in a source program. Repeated instruction sequences may reflect the needs of your program logic, or they may be compensating for deficiencies in your microprocessor's instruction set. You can avoid repeatedly writing out the same instruction sequence by using a "macro."[1]

Macros allow you to assign a name to an instruction sequence. You then use the macro name in your source program instead of the repeated instruction sequence. The assembler will replace the macro name with the appropriate sequence of instructions. The shaded parts of Figure 2-1 illustrate the assembler's treatment of a macro in an example program. Do not bother trying to figure out what the program or the instructions do; just observe that the assembler expands the macro MAC1 into the defined sequence.

A macro resembles a subroutine because it is a shorthand reference to a frequently used instruction sequence. However, macros are not the same as subroutines. The code for a subroutine occurs once in a program, and program execution branches to the subroutine. In contrast, the assembler replaces each occurrence of a macro name with the specified sequence of instructions; therefore program execution does not branch to a macro as it does to a subroutine. A macro name is a user-defined assembler directive; it directs assembly rather than program execution.

Advantages of Macros:

- Shorter source programs
- Better program documentation
- Use of debugged instruction sequences. Once the macro has been debugged, you are sure of an error-free instruction sequence every time you use the macro correctly.
- Easier changes. Change the macro definition and the assembler makes the change for you every time the macro is used.
- Inclusion of new operations in the basic instruction set. You can use macros to extend or clarify the instruction set.

Disadvantages of Macros:

- Since the macro is expanded every time it is used, memory space may be wasted by the repetition of instruction sequences.
- A single macro may create a lot of instructions.
- Lack of standardization makes programs difficult to read and understand.
- Possible effects on registers and flags may not be clearly described.

COMMENTS

All assemblers allow you to place comments in a source program. Comments have no effect on the object code, but they help you to read, understand, and document the program. Good commenting is an essential part of writing computer programs; programs without comments are very difficult to understand.

We will discuss commenting along with documentation in a later chapter, but here are some guidelines:

- Use comments to tell what application task the program is performing, not how the microcomputer executes the instructions.

  Comments should say things like "IS TEMPERATURE ABOVE LIMIT?," "LINE FEED TO TTY," or "EXAMINE LOAD SWITCH."

  Comments should not say things like "ADD 1 TO ACCUMULATOR," "JUMP TO START," or "LOOK AT CARRY." You should describe how the program is affecting the system; internal effects on the CPU should be obvious from the code.
- Keep comments brief and to the point. Details should be available elsewhere in the documentation.
- Comment all key points.
- Do not comment standard instructions or sequences that change counters or pointers; pay special attention to instructions that may not have an obvious meaning.
- Do not use obscure abbreviations.
- Make the comments neat and readable.
- Comment all definitions, describing their purposes. Also mark all tables and data storage areas.
- Comment sections of the program as well as individual instructions.
- Be consistent in your terminology. You can (should) be repetitive; you need not consult a thesaurus.
- Leave yourself notes at points that you find confusing: for example, "REMEMBER CARRY WAS SET BY LAST INSTRUCTION." If such points get cleared up later in program development, you may drop these comments in the final documentation.

A well-commented program is easy to use. You will recover the time spent in commenting many times over. We will try to show good commenting style in the programming examples, although we often over-comment for instructional purposes.

TYPES OF ASSEMBLERS

Although all assemblers perform the same tasks, their implementations vary greatly. We will not try to describe all the existing types of assemblers; we will merely define the terms and indicate some of the choices.

A cross-assembler is an assembler that runs on a computer other than the one for which it assembles object programs.

The computer on which the cross-assembler runs is typically a large computer with extensive software support and fast peripherals — such as an IBM 370, a Univac 1108, or a Burroughs 6700. The computer for which the cross-assembler assembles programs is typically a micro like the 6809 or MC68000. Many cross-assemblers are written in FORTRAN or another high-level language so that they are portable.

When a new microcomputer is introduced, a cross-assembler is often provided to run on existing development systems. For example, Motorola provides an MC68000 cross-assembler that will run on a 6809 development system.

A self-assembler or resident assembler is an assembler that runs on the computer for which it assembles programs. The self-assembler will require some memory and peripherals, and it may run quite slowly compared to a cross-assembler.

A macroassembler is an assembler that allows you to define sequences of instructions as macros.

A microassembler is an assembler used to write the microprograms which define the instruction set of a computer. Microprogramming has nothing specifically to do with programming microcomputers, but has to do with the internal operation of the computer.[2, 3]

A meta-assembler is an assembler that can handle many different instruction sets. The user must define the particular instruction set being used.

A one-pass assembler is an assembler that goes through the assembly language program only once. Such an assembler must have some way of resolving forward references, for example, Jump instructions which use labels that have not yet been defined.

A two-pass assembler is an assembler that goes through the assembly language source program twice. The first time the assembler simply collects and defines all the symbols; the second time it replaces the references with the actual definitions. A two-pass assembler has no problems with forward references but may be quite slow if no backup storage (like a floppy disk) is available; then the assembler must physically read the program twice from a slow input medium (like a teletypewriter paper tape reader). Most microprocessor-based assemblers require two passes.

ERRORS

Assemblers normally provide error messages, often consisting of a single coded letter. Some typical errors are:

- Undefined name (often a misspelling or an omitted definition)
- Illegal character (such as a 2 in a binary number)
- Illegal format (wrong delimiter or incorrect operands)
- Invalid expression (for example, two operators in a row)
- Illegal value (usually too large)
- Missing operand
- Double definition (two different values assigned to one name)
- Illegal label (such as a label on a pseudo-operation that cannot have one)
- Missing label
- Undefined operation code.

In interpreting assembler errors, you must remember that the assembler may get on the wrong track if it finds a stray letter, an extra space, or incorrect punctuation. Many assemblers will then proceed to misinterpret the succeeding instructions and produce meaningless error messages. Always look at the first error very carefully; subsequent ones may depend on it. Caution and consistent adherence to standard formats will eliminate many annoying mistakes.

LOADERS

The loader is the program which actually takes the output (object code) from the assembler and places it in memory. Loaders range from the very simple to the very complex. We will describe a few different types.

A "bootstrap loader" is a program that uses its own first few instructions to load the rest of itself or another loader program into memory. The bootstrap loader may be in ROM, or you may have to enter it into the computer memory using front panel switches. The assembler may place a bootstrap loader at the start of the object program that it produces.

A "relocating loader" can load programs anywhere in memory. It typically loads each program into the memory space immediately following that used by the previous program. The programs, however, must themselves be capable of being moved around in this way; that is, they must be relocatable. **An "absolute loader," in contrast, will always place the programs in the same area of memory.**

A "linking loader" loads programs and subroutines that have been assembled separately; it resolves cross-references — that is, instructions in one program that refer to a label in another program. Object programs loaded by a linking loader must be created by an assembler that allows external references. An alternative approach is to separate the linking and loading functions and have the linking performed by a program called a "link editor" and the loading done by a loader.

REFERENCES

1. A complete monograph on macros is M. Campbell-Kelly, *An Introduction to Macros,* American Elsevier, New York, 1973.

2. A. Osborne, *An Introduction to Microcomputers: Volume 1 — Basic Concepts,* Osborne/McGraw-Hill, Berkeley, Calif., 1980.

3. A. K. Agrawala and T. G. Rauscher, *Foundations of Microprogramming,* Academic Press, New York, 1976.

4. D. W. Barron, *Assemblers and Loaders,* American Elsevier, New York, 1972.

5. C. W. Gear, *Computer Organization and Programming,* McGraw-Hill, New York, 1974.

3
68000 Machine Structure and Assembly Language

This chapter outlines the MC68000 processor's architecture and describes the syntax rules of the Motorola assembler. The hardware aspects of the MC68000 microprocessor, including its output signals and interfaces, are described in *The 68000 Microprocessor Handbook.*[1] This book considers the MC68000 from the point of view of the assembly language programmer, to whom pins and signals are irrelevant and microcomputers and minicomputers essentially identical. Later chapters of this book describe the MC68000's stack and exception processing system in more detail.

Table 3-1 through 3-3 divide the MC68000 instruction set into instructions that are frequently used (Table 3-1), occasionally used (Table 3-2), and seldom used (Table 3-3). If you are an experienced assembly language programmer, you will probably not find this division important, and you may even disagree with it. However, if you are a novice, we recommend that you write your first program using only the frequently used instructions (Table 3-1). This restriction will help you overcome the obstacle of learning both the entire MC68000 instruction set and the basic methods of assembly language programming at the same time. Once you have mastered the concepts of assembly language programming, you should start using other instructions (Table 3-2 and 3-3).

Table 3-1. Frequently Used Instructions of the MC68000

Operation Mnemonic	Meaning	Operation Mnemonic	Meaning
ADD	Add	JMP	Jump
AND	AND	JSR	Jump to Subroutine
ASL	Arithmetic Shift Left	LSL	Logical Shift Left
ASR	Arithmetic Shift Right	LSR	Logical Shift Right
B_{CC}	Branch Conditionally	MOVE	Move
BRA	Branch Always	OR	OR
BSR	Branch to Subroutine	ROL	Rotate Left
CLR	Clear Operand	ROR	Rotate Right
CMP	Compare	RTS	Return from Subroutine
EOR	Exclusive OR	SUB	Subtract

Only word versions of instructions are listed. Byte and long word versions, where available, have the same use frequency.

Table 3-2. Occasionally Used Instructions of the MC68000

Operation Mnemonic	Meaning	Operation Mnemonic	Meaning
ABCD	Add Decimal with Extend	NEG	Negate
BTST	Bit Test	NOP	No Operation
DB_{CC}	Test Condition, Decrement and Branch	ROXL	Rotate Left wth Extend
		ROXR	Rotate Right with Extend
EXG	Exchange Registers	RTE	Return from Exception
MOVEM	Move Multiple Registers	RTR	Return and Restore
MOVEP	Move Peripheral Data	SBCD	Subtract Decimal with Extend
MULS	Multiply Signed	STOP	Stop
MULU	Multiply Unsigned	SWAP	Swap Data Register Halves
		TST	Test

Only word versions of instructions are listed. Byte and long word versions, where available, have the same use frequency.

Table 3-3. Seldom Used Instructions of the MC68000

Operation Mnemonic	Meaning	Operation Mnemonic	Meaning
BCHG	Bit Test and Change	LINK	Link Stack
BCLR	Bit Test and Clear	NBCD	Negate Decimal with Extend
BSET	Bit Test and Set	PEA	Push Effective Address
CHK	Check Register against Bounds	RESET	Reset
		S_{CC}	Set Conditional
DIVS	Divide Signed	TAS	Test and Set Operand
DIVU	Divide Unsigned	TRAP	Trap
EXT	Sign Extend	TRAPV	Trap on Overflow
LEA	Load Effective Address	UNLNK	Unlink Stack

Only word versions of instructions are listed. Byte and long word versions, when available, have the same use frequency.

MC68000 OPERATING MODES

The MC68000 can operate in either a supervisor (system) mode or in a user (normal) mode. A status flag setting determines the mode of operation.

Certain instructions can be executed only in supervisor mode, not in user mode. Also, two separate stack pointers are provided so that separate stacks are maintained in memory for supervisor and user modes.

If you are a novice assembly language programmer, keep the MC68000 in supervisor mode and ignore user mode; then you will be able to execute any MC68000 instruction. If you operate the MC68000 in user mode, you may encounter instructions that execute in supervisor mode only, and that will simply confuse you.

But there is a good reason for having separate supervisor and user modes. As any experienced assembly language programmer will tell you, assembly language programs can be divided into *system software* and *applications programs.* System software includes those programs that tie the components of a computer system together; system software may be written in system mode when required. Application programs cause the computer to perform a user's specific task, and should always be written in user mode.

MC68000 REGISTERS AND FLAGS

The MC68000 has eight 32-bit data registers, seven 32-bit address registers, two 32-bit stack pointer registers, a 32-bit program counter, and a 16-bit status register. Figure 3-1 illustrates the registers of the MC68000.

The MC68000 status register contains five status flags, three interrupt mask bits, one bit to set either supervisor or user mode, and one bit to set the trace mode. The five status flags are:

Carry (C)
Overflow (V)
Zero (Z)
Negative (N)
Extend (E)

The flags occupy the least significant five bits of the status register as shown in Figure 3-2.

MC6800 REGISTERS

The eight data registers can be used to handle 8-bit bytes, 16-bit words, or 32-bit long words. The following illustration shows how the various-sized operands are positioned within the data registers.

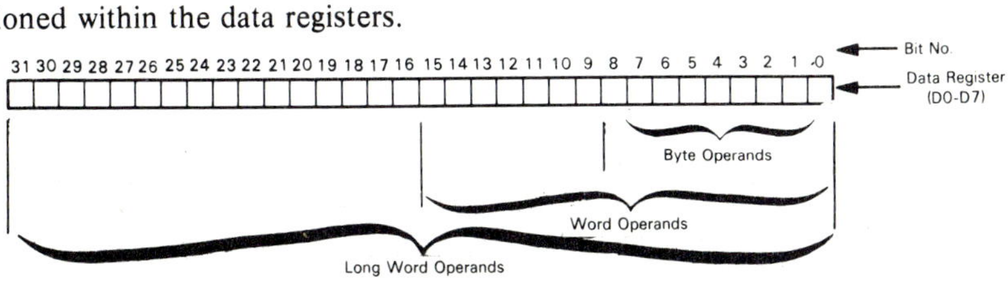

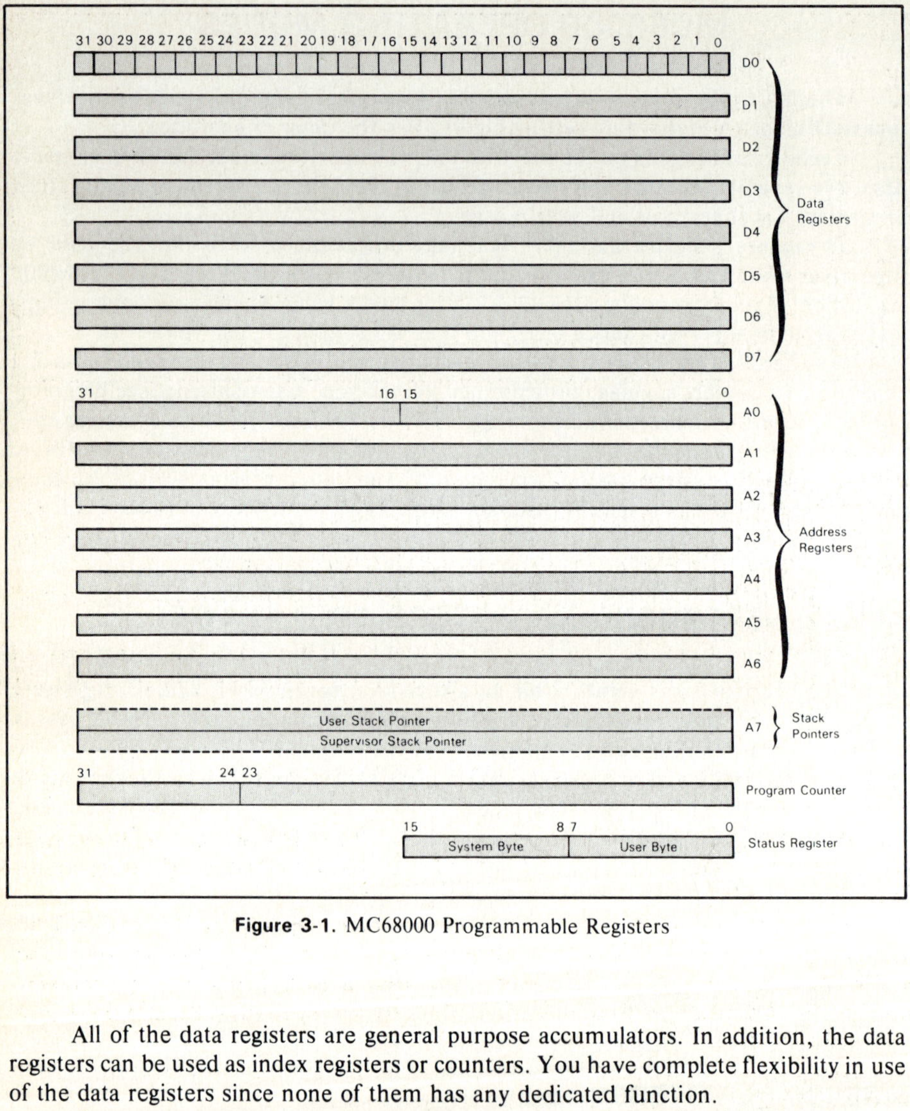

Figure 3-1. MC68000 Programmable Registers

All of the data registers are general purpose accumulators. In addition, the data registers can be used as index registers or counters. You have complete flexibility in use of the data registers since none of them has any dedicated function.

There are seven general purpose address registers (A0-A6). These registers can handle either 16-bit word operands or 32-bit long word operands. The address registers cannot be used for 8-bit bytes. As their name implies, the address registers will typically be used to hold addresses rather than data, and they can also be used as index registers for indexed memory addressing. When either the data registers or address registers are used as index registers, they function as typical microcomputer index registers as described in *An Introduction to Microcomputers: Volume 1.*

Address register A7 functions as the stack pointer in addition to serving as a general purpose address regiser or index register. Register A7 actually consists of two registers: different registers are used in supervisor mode and user mode. Therefore, if

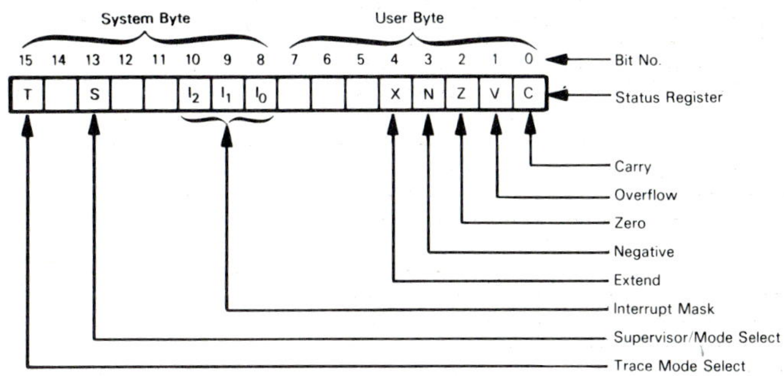

Figure 3-2. MC68000 Status Register Bit Assignments

you write into A7 in supervisor mode, then switch to user mode and read from A7, you will not read what you just wrote. These duplicate supervisor and user mode registers allow separate stacks to be maintained in supervisor and user modes.

The program counter is a typical program counter, as described in Volume 1 of *An Introduction to Microcomputers*.

Although the address registers and program counter contain 32 bits, only 24 bits are used to address memory. The high-order eight bits are ignored in making memory references.

STATUS REGISTER

The MC68000 has a 16-bit status register which is divided into two 8-bit bytes: the system byte and the user byte. The bit assignments for the status register are shown in Figure 3-2.

The Carry bit holds the carry from the most significant bit produced by arithmetic operations or shifts. Like most microprocessors, the MC68000 inverts the actual carry after subtraction so that **the Carry bit acts as a borrow bit after subtraction. In the MC68000, logical operations clear the Carry flag, as do moves, multiplies, and divides.**

The Zero bit is standard. It is set to 1 when an operation produces a zero result. It is set to 0 when an operation produces a non-zero result.

The Negative (sign) bit is standard. It takes on the value of the most significant bit of a result. Thus a negative bit value of 1 indicates a negative result and a negative bit value of 0 identifies a positive result if the standard two's complement signed number representation is being used. This bit will be set or reset on the assumption that you are using two's complement binary arithmetic. If you are using unsigned arithmetic you can ignore the negative bit or you can use it to identify the value of the most significant bit of the result.

The Overflow bit represents standard arithmetic overflow as described in Volume 1 of *An Introduction to Microcomputers;* that is, the bit is set when an arithmetic result is greater in magnitude than can be represented in the register. The processor implements this function by setting the Overflow flag when the carry out of the most significant bit is different from the carry out of the next most significant bit; that is, an overflow is the exclusive-OR of the carry into and out of the high-order bit. In the MC68000, logical operations clear the Overflow flag, as do moves, rotates, multiplies, and several other instructions.

The Extend bit will always be set to the same state as the Carry bit whenever it is affected by an instruction. This bit is provided for use in multiprecision arithmetic operations.

Many microprocessor instructions modify status bits, even when such modifications are not relevant to the operation performed. You should therefore consult the instruction summary table in Appendix A in order to determine how a particular status bit is affected by the execution of a specific instruction.

The system byte of the status register contains information that is system-related, unlike the instruction-related status bits of the user byte. Bits in the system byte of the status register can only be altered when the MC68000 is in the supervisor mode.

The three least significant bits of the status register's system byte provide the interrupt priority mask. The MC68000 has three encoded interrupt request inputs providing seven prioritized levels of interrupt. The interrupt mask in the status register determines which levels of interrupt requests will be recognized by the processor. For example, if you set the interrupt mask to 100, interrupt levels four and lower will be disabled and interrupt requests with those bit patterns (000, 001, 010, 011, 100) will be ignored.

The S bit in the status register is used to switch between supervisor and user modes. When this bit is 1, the processor operates in the supervisor mode, and when this bit is 0, the processor operates in the user mode. Recall that supervisor and user modes have their own stack pointers; also, certain privileged instructions can only be executed in supervisor mode.

The T bit in the status register is used to place the MC68000 in trace mode. This will be discussed in Chapter 19.

MC68000 MEMORY

The memory of the MC68000 is organized, just like the registers, into bytes, words, and long words. Each byte has an address which is a 24-bit number. Byte addresses may have any value. Word and double word addresses must be even numbers. In the illustrations in this book we will show the memory organized into words. Each word is made up of two bytes. The address of the word is shown to the right of the word. This is the address of the high-order byte of the word. The address of the low-order byte is one greater. In the illustration below the byte containing XX is at address 6020; the byte containing YY is at address 6021.

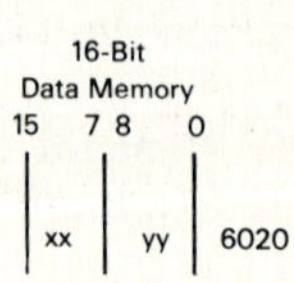

MC68000 ADDRESSING MODES

Assembly language instructions tell the processor what operation to perform and what addresses to use in performing the operation — that is, where to find the data to be operated upon. The part of the instruction that tells the processor what operation to perform is the *operation code.* Appendix C lists the MC68000 microprocessor's mnemonic operation codes and their numerical equivalents. The part of an instruction that tells the processor what addresses to use is the *operand* or *address field.* The processor may use this part of an instruction to determine where to obtain the operands or where to store the results.

GENERAL DESCRIPTION OF ADDRESSING MODES

There are many different ways to specify what addresses the processor is to use. These ways are called *addressing modes.* We will describe them generally before discussing how the MC68000 processor implements them. The following two modes do not involve memory at all:

1. **Inherent addressing** means that the operation code alone tells the processor what to do.
2. **Register addressing** means that the operand is contained in a register.

Common addressing modes that involve memory are as follows:

3. **Immediate addressing** means that operand is located immediately after the operation code in program memory.
4. **Direct addressing** means that the address to be used follows the operation code in program memory.
5. **Index addressing** means that the address to be used is the sum of a base address and an index or offset.
6. **Indirect addressing** means that the address to be used is either in a register or in memory. That is, the instruction tells the processor where the address is, not where the data is.
7. **Relative addressing** means that the operand is located a certain distance from the current position of the program.

Chapter 6 of *An Introduction to Microcomputers: Volume 1* describes all these addressing modes and their common combinations.

MC68000 Addressing Modes

The MC68000 has a powerful and versatile set of addressing modes. The available modes are the following, listed in the order in which we will describe them:

1. **Inherent operand** (instructions that require no addresses)
2. **Registers as operands** (instructions that use only register contents as operands)

The other modes specify memory addresses; they are:

3. **Immediate**
4. **Absolute or direct**
5. **Address register indirect**
6. **Address register indirect with displacement**
7. **Address register indirect with postincrement**
8. **Address register indirect with predecrement**
9. **Address register indirect with index and displacement**
10. **Program counter relative with displacement**
11. **Program counter relative with index and displacement**

EFFECTIVE ADDRESS

In describing how the processor executes these addressing modes and how the programmer uses them, we must often refer to the actual address that the processor ultimately uses to perform the specified operation. We call that address the *effective address;* it is the place from which the processor obtains an operand or in which the processor stores the result. In some modes (for example, immediate) the effective address is simply the location immediately following the operation code of the instruction. In other modes, determining the effective address may be complicated. The address may be part of the instruction, the contents of a base register, or the contents of memory locations. Determining the effective address may involve computations, such as adding an offset to a base register. Some of the addressing modes are difficult to understand, since they involve sequences of operations that finally culminate in an effective address. We will explain why these sequences are useful and describe typical cases from real applications. You should try to trace each sequence, since the various addressing modes are the keys to writing programs that are both general and powerful. Remember, the processor always determines the effective address correctly, no matter how complex the required operations are.

ADDRESSING MODES WHICH DO NOT SPECIFY MEMORY LOCATIONS

INHERENT ADDRESSING

In this mode, the processor knows from the operation code alone which addresses to use. For example, RTE (Return from Exception), RTS (Return from Subroutine), RTR (Return and Restore Condition Codes) all force the processor to use the stack pointer to move data to or from memory. Similarly, the TRAPV (Trap on Overflow) instruction forces the processor to use the supervisor stack pointer to store the program counter contents in memory, and also uses a predetermined memory address to obtain the appropriate vector for the trap operation. NOP (No Operation) and RESET require no operands. In all of these instructions, the operation codes are complete by themselves; no further addressing information is necessary.

Motorola literature includes the instructions we have just described, which use inherent addressing within a category of addressing which they describe as implicit. The instructions included in this implicit reference category by Motorola are all those instructions which make implicit reference to any of the MC68000 registers. This category includes Branch instructions which always affect the program counter, certain Move instructions which affect specific registers such as the status register or stack pointer, and Jump instruction, which always affect the program counter. These instructions are not, however, inherent addressing in the strict sense since they all allow or demand additional addressing information; the operation codes for these instructions are not complete by themselves.

REGISTER ADDRESSING

Many of the MC68000 instructions can be used to specify operands that reside only within the processor's registers and they thus require no memory addressing information. There are only a few MC68000 instructions which *must* use registers as operands. The EXG (Exchange Registers), EXT (Sign Extend), SWAP (Swap Register Values), and certain MOVE instructions operate only on operands contained in the registers and can never refer to operands located in memory.

The EXG instruction causes the contents of any two data or address registers to be exchanged with one another. The exchange is always a long word (32-bit) operation, thus completely exchanging the entire contents of the two registers involved. Two 3-bit fields within the instruction operation code designate the register numbers and a mode field specifies whether the registers are data registers, address registers, or a data register and an address register. The operation code for the EXG instruction can be illustrated as follows:

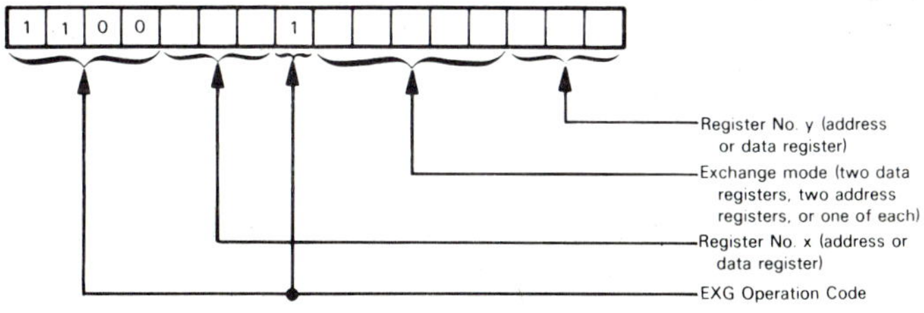

For details on how the register are coded, see the description of the EXG instruction in Chapter 22.

While only a few instructions *must* use register contents as operands, most of the MC68000 instructions *allow* you to specify that the operands reside within registers. **There are two modes of register direct addressing: data register direct and address register direct. The only difference between the two modes is the first, of course, uses a data register as the operand, while the second uses an address register.**

Some instructions that let you use the register direct addressing mode require that one of the registers involved be a data register while other instructions demand that one of the registers be an address register. For example, the ADD (Add Binary) instruction requires that one of the operands be contained in a data register. You can specify, however, that the other operand be from either a data register (data register direct addressing) or an address register (address register direct addressing). **Figure 3-3 illustrates data register direct addressing for an Add Binary (ADD) instruction.** Both of the operands used in this ADD operation are held in data registers; there is no need to reference operands held in memory.

Figure 3-4 illustrates the same ADD instruction but with address register direct addressing used. As we mentioned earlier, this instruction requires that one of the operands be held in a data register (in this case, D3). Since address register direct addressing is used, however, the other operand is taken from an address register (A6).

The MC68000 has a similar instruction (ADDA — Add Address) that requires that one of the operands be held in an address register. This instruction also requires that the destination of the add be that same address register. The second operand used in the ADDA instruction can be either an address register or a data register. (Both of these Add instructions also allow the second operand to be located in memory; however, since we are discussing register direct addressing, at this point we will defer a discussion of these options until later when we describe the other addressing modes.)

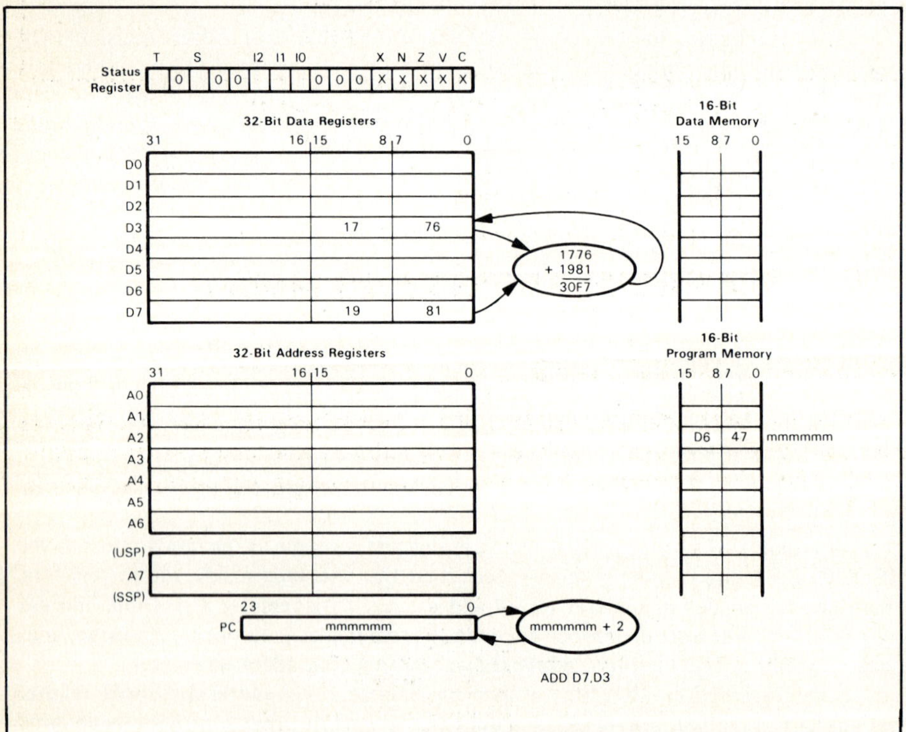

Figure 3-3. Data Register Direct Addressing

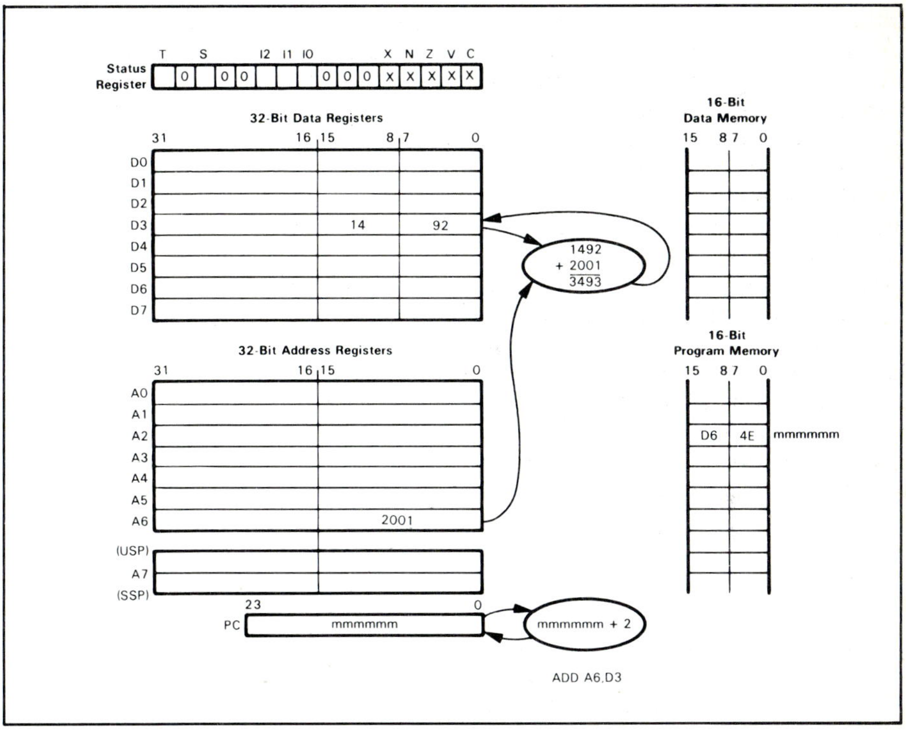

Figure 3-4. Address Register Direct Addressing

MEMORY ADDRESSING MODES

IMMEDIATE ADDRESSING

In immediate addressing, the data follows immediately after the operation code in memory. That is, the effective address is simply the contents of the program counter after the processor has fetched the operation code. We can illustrate this mode as follows:

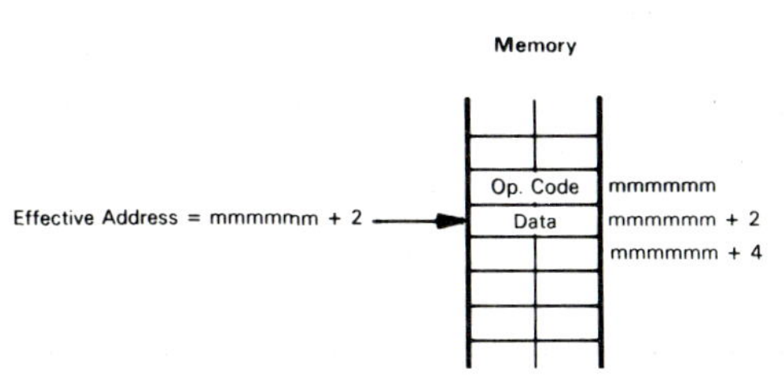

The MC68000 has byte, word and long word immediate instructions. Byte and word immediate instructions provide the immediate operand in the word immediately following the instruction's object code, as shown in the preceding illustration. For byte immediate instructions, the immediate data is in the low-order byte of the word immediately following the instruction's object code. The high-order byte of that word should consist of all zeros. This may be illustrated as follows:

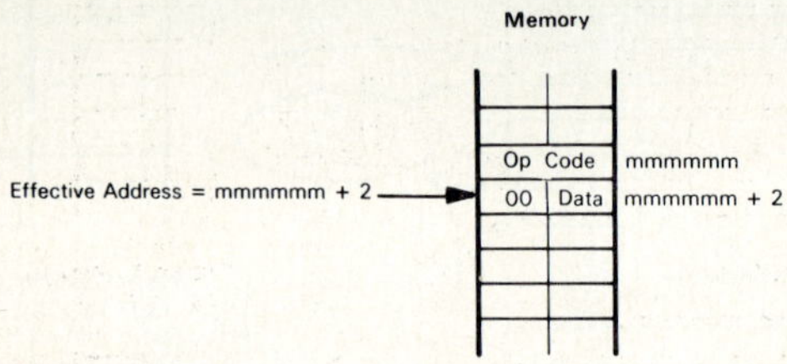

In standard MC68000 assembly language, we specify immediate addressing by preceding the operand with the # symbol. For example, the MC68000 assembler converts the statement

```
ADD #$1066,D3
    (# sign means "immediate addressing," and
    $ sign means "hexadecimal")
```

into an ADD instruction that adds the value 1066_{16} to data register D3. Figure 3-5 illustrates the execution of this instruction.

Register D3 contains 1848_{16} initially. After the processor executes ADD #$1066,D3 the contents of register D3 will be $1848_{16} + 1066_{16} = 28AE_{16}$. The processor increments its program counter four times, twice after fetching the operation code and twice after fetching the immediate data, 1066_{16} in this example.

In the example we have just given, the ADD instruction operates on a 16-bit word. This is the default data size that is assumed for nearly all instructions where data size is relevant. Most instructions can operate on more than one data size. If you want to specify a data size other than the default size of word, you must append a data size code to the instruction operation code. The standard MC68000 assembler allows three different data size codes to be appended to the operation codes: B indicates byte (8-bit data), W indicates word (16-bit data), and L indicates long word (32-bit data). You append these data size codes to the operation code using a period (.) followed by B, W or L. For example, the ADD instruction in our preceding illustration could have been written as ADD.W #$1066,D3. We did not need to specify a data size of word in that example, however, since the word size is the default.

The MC68000 also has a special immediate addressing mode for small operands. In this "quick" mode, the data is actually contained in the operation code word itself. ADDQ (Add Quick) and SUBQ (Subtract Quick) can be used to add or subtract numbers from one to eight. MOVEQ (Move Quick) can be used to move numbers in the range of −128 to +127 to a register or memory location.

ABSOLUTE SHORT (DIRECT) ADDRESSING

In this mode, the low-order half of the effective address follows the operation code in memory. The high-order half of the effective address is obtained by extending

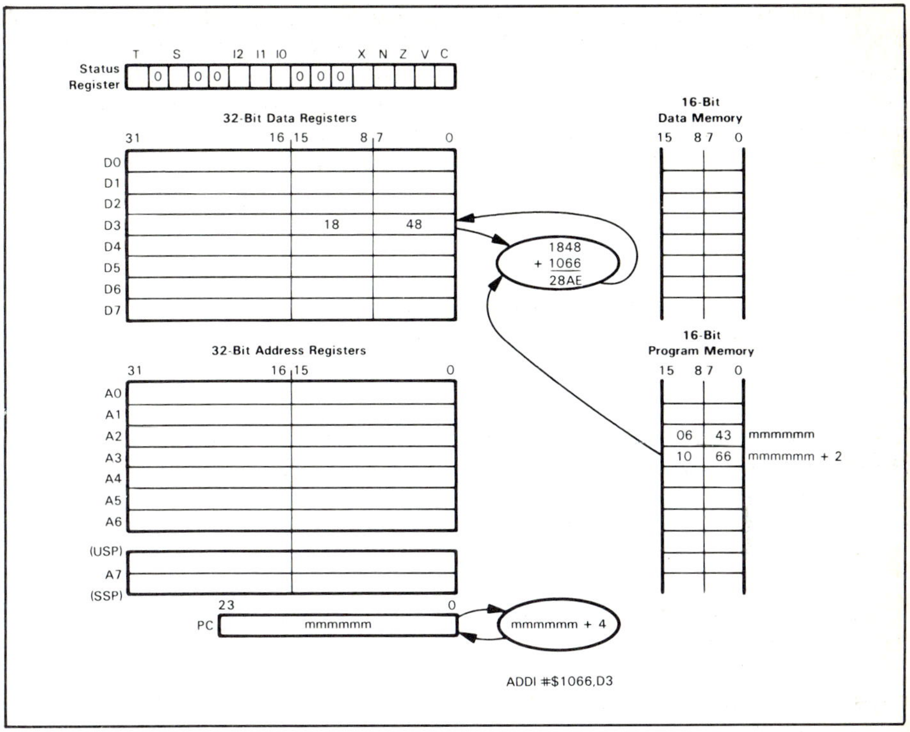

Figure 3-5. Immediate Addressing

the sign-bit (bit 15) of the low-order half of the address. Thus, 24-bit addresses can be generated for the address range 000000_{16} through $007FFF_{16}$ and $FF8000_{16}$ through $FFFFFF_{16}$. We can illustrate absolute short (direct) addressing as follows:

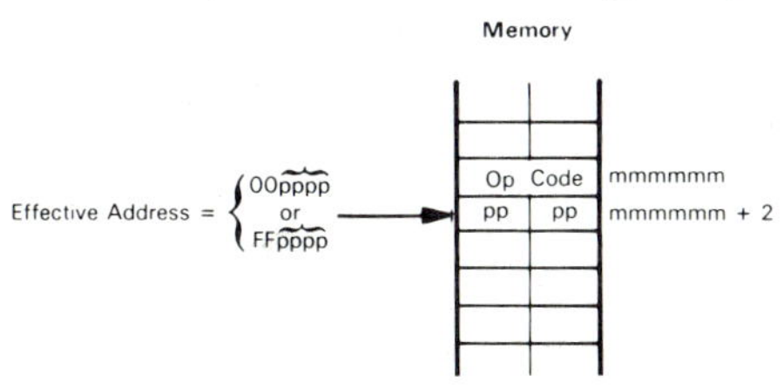

Absolute short addresses in the range 0000_{16} through $7FFF_{16}$ refer to the same locations in memory. However, **absolute short addresses in the range 8000_{16} to $FFFF_{16}$ refer to the highest possible memory addresses, because of sign extension.**

You should note that while MC68000 literature refers to this mode as *absolute short,* Volume 1 of *An Introduction to Microcomputers* describes this mode as *base page direct.* In this case, the base page for direct addressing consists of the bottom 32K bytes of memory and the top 32K bytes of memory. This mode provides a short, quick way to use programs or temporary storage on what is effectively the base page. It is short and quick because it saves a word of program memory and a read cycle.

The standard MC68000 assembler uses absolute short addressing whenever the mode is available, no other mode is specified, and the address is within the range that can be obtained.

Figure 3-6 illustrates absolute short addressing used with an ADD instruction. The instruction illustrated causes the contents of memory location 007100_{16} to be added to the contents of data register D3. After the processor executes the instruction, the sum in register D3 will be 1234_{16} + (007100_{16}) = 1234_{16} + 5678_{16}. The processor increments its program counter four times; twice after fetching the operation code and twice after fetching the direct address.

The absolute short address occupies only one word even if the instruction (such ADD.L) handles 32-bit operands. In that case, the processor would use the addresses 007100_{16} and 007102_{16} (in our example) to fetch the high-order and low-order words of data, respectively.

ABSOLUTE LONG (DIRECT) ADDRESSING

In this mode, the effective address occupies the two words of program memory immediately following the operation code. The high-order half of the address is in the

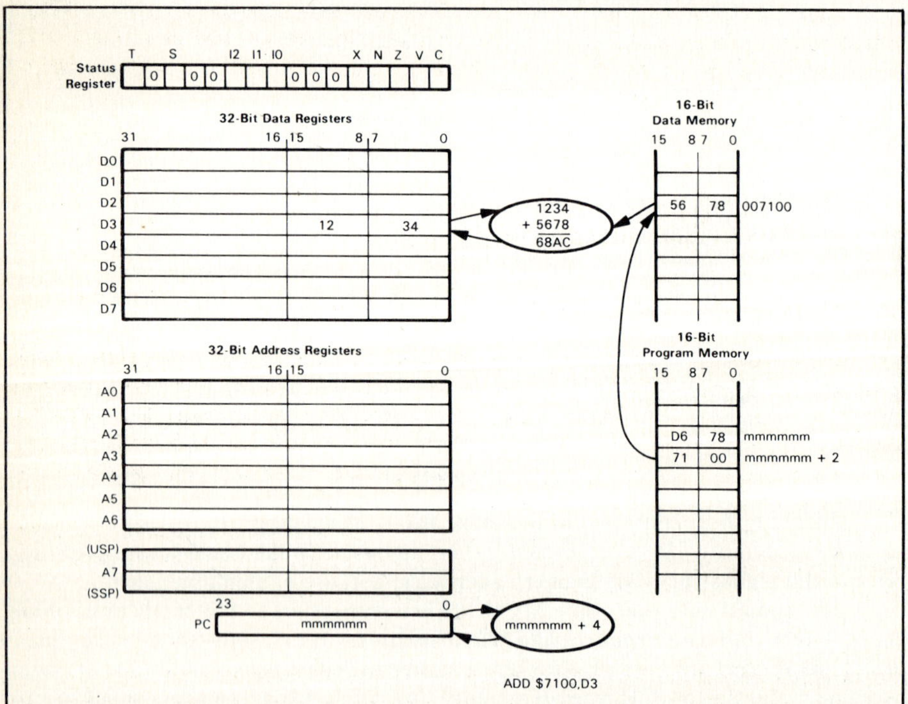

Figure 3-6. Absolute Short (Direct) Addressing

first word; this is the standard MC68000 format. We can illustrate absolute long direct addressing as follows:

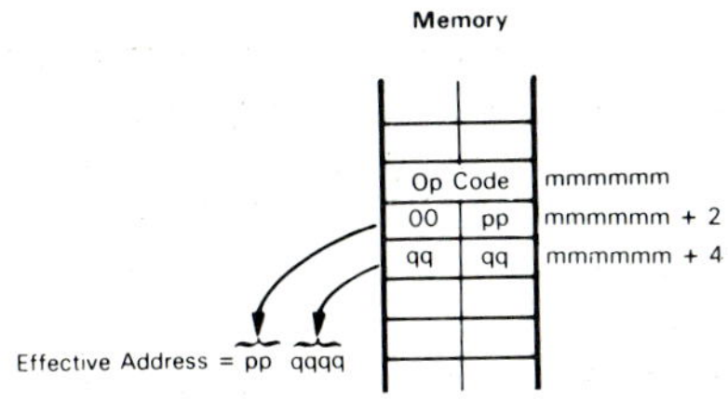

You should note that MC68000 literature refers to this mode as *absolute long,* whereas Volume 1 of *An Introduction to Microcomputers* refers to it as *direct* or *extended direct.*

This mode allows the processor to access any specific memory location. Of course, you need not use the absolute long addressing for memory locations that are within the lowest or highest 32K bytes of memory since the absolute short mode is shorter and faster. However, absolute long addressing is the usual approach for handling a fixed address that is not within the range of the absolute short addressing mode.

The standard MC68000 assembler uses absolute long addressing whenever the mode is available, no other mode is specified, and the address is not within the range of the absolute short addressing. Thus, absolute long addressing is a general default mode.

Figure 3-7 illustrates an ADD instruction used with absolute long addressing. This addressing mode and the execution of the instruction are the same as we illustrated for absolute short addressing except that 32 bits of address are held in program memory following the operation code.

ADDRESS REGISTER INDIRECT ADDRESSING

In this mode, the address of the operand to be used with the instruction is held in one of the address registers. You should note that this is not true *indirect* addressing; in standard indirect addressing, a memory location contains the effective address — not a register. In *An Introduction to Microcomputers: Volume 1,* register indirect addressing is described as "implied addressing." The MC68000 does not provide a memory indirect addressing mode.

In the standard MC68000 assembler format, you specify register indirect addressing by placing the address register specification within parentheses: for example, (A3). Thus, the assembler converts a statement

```
ADD (A3),D3
```

into an ADD instruction that adds the contents of the memory location pointed to by A3, to the contents of D3. Figure 3-8 illustrates address register indirect addressing for an ADD instruction. In this illustration, the ADD instruction uses the address ppqqqq which is held in register A3 to obtain the operand held in data memory.

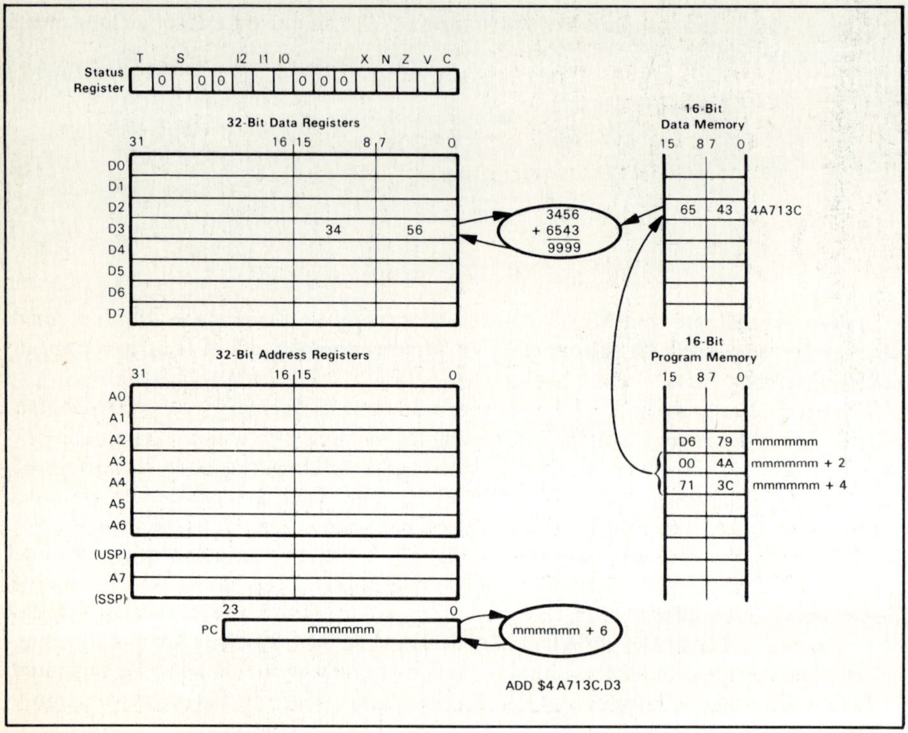

Figure 3-7. Absolute Long (Direct) Addressing

AUTOINCREMENT AND AUTODECREMENT

In processing arrays, strings, or lists, we frequently want to process one byte or word at a time and then proceed to the next byte or word located at the next higher address (if we are moving forward), or at the next lower address (if we are moving backwards). For example, if we are printing a string of characters, we must send the characters one by one to the printer. Similarly, if we are averaging a set of ten readings, we must add them together one by one (for instance, start with 0, add the first reading, add the second reading, etc.) and finally divide by ten.

Thus, to handle one byte and move forward, we may:

- Reach the byte using the address in an address register.
- Add one to the address register to make it point to the next byte.

The effect is like the action of a typewriter, which both prints the character for the key you press and moves the carriage along to the next position. Subtracting one from the address register would correspond to backspacing the typewriter carriage. Unlike the typewriter, the computer does not prefer forward over backward.

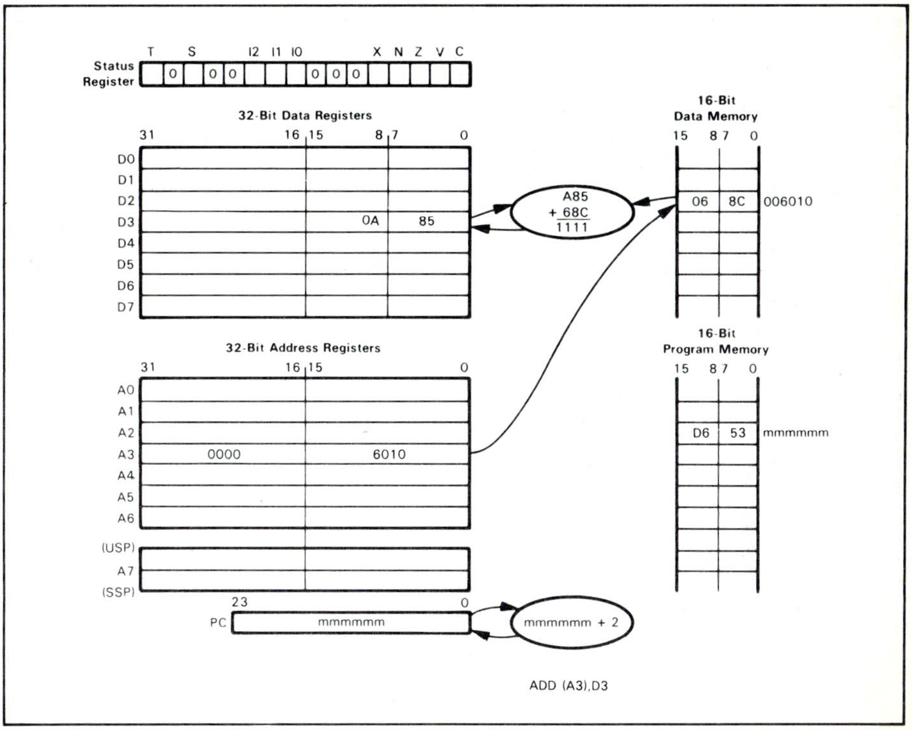

Figure 3-8. Address Register Indirect Addressing

Variations of Autoincrement and Autodecrement

The MC68000 offers different step sizes for autoincrementing and autodecrementing. The base address register may be:

- Incremented by one after it is used.
- Incremented by two after it is used.
- Incremented by four after it is used.
- Decremented by one before it is used.
- Decremented by two before it is used.
- Decremented by four before it is used.

The increment or decrement by two approach is used when the array consists of 16-bit data or addresses, and the increment or decrement by four approach would be used when the array consists of 32-bit data or addresses. The processor thus moves on to the next element automatically, even though that element is located two or four bytes away from the current element. Applying the increment after using the base but applying decrement before using the base maintains compatibility with the automatic use of stack pointers (in BSR, JSR, RTE, RTR, RTS, and TRAP instructions and in exception processing). Any access/change-pointer sequence could be implemented, but this is the most popular approach. All the user must remember is to load the base address register with the starting address of the array or string for autoincrementing, but with the ending address plus 1, 2, or 4 for autodecrementing (because the first autodecrement will reduce the base address register before using it).

Autoincrementing or autodecrementing is the simplest way to process arrays or strings since it provides automatic updating of the implied memory address as part of instruction execution. See Chapters 5 and 6 for further discussion of autoincrementing and autodecrementing.

MC68000 manufacturers' literature describes *autoincrement addressing* as *address register indirect with postincrement* and refers to *autodecrement addressing* as *address register indirect with predecrement.* As this implies, the autoincrement/ autodecrement modes can only be used with address register indirect addressing.

In the standard MC68000 assembler format, you specify address register indirect with postincrement addressing by placing the address register specification within parentheses and following it with a plus sign: for example (A3) +. Thus, the assembler converts the statement

```
ADD (A3)+,D3
```

into an ADD instruction that adds the contents of the memory location whose address is held in A3 to the contents of D3. After the ADD operation is performed, the contents of A3 are incremented by two. Note that since there was no size specification appended to the ADD instruction, a word size was assumed. Therefore, the contents of register A3 were incremented by two following the ADD operation. Had you specified a byte size, then A3 would have been incremented by one, and had you specified a long word size, A3 would have been incremented by four.

Figure 3-9 illustrates the execution of the ADD instruction using address register indirect with postincrement addressing.

In the standard MC68000 assembler format, you specify address register indirect addressing with predecrement by placing the address register number within parentheses and preceding the address specification with a minus sign: for example, −(A3). Thus, the assembler converts the statement

```
ADD -(A3), D3
```

into an ADD instruction that first decrements the contents of address register A3 by two, then adds the contents of the memory location whose address is held in A3 to the contents of D3.

Figure 3-10 illustrates the execution of the ADD instruction with address register indirect with predecrement addressing.

ADDRESS REGISTER INDIRECT WITH DISPLACEMENT

In this mode, the effective address is the sum of a fixed displacement or offset and the contents of an address register. The displacement follows the operation code in program memory and is a constant since program memory generally does not change during program execution. The contents of the address register may vary since the program can determine the values in the address register. This addressing mode allows us to refer to a particular element in an array or list. For example, we might have a set of ten temperature readings taken at different points in a tank; to change or display a particular one, we must know where the set of readings starts (the base address) and which reading we want (the displacement or offset). If, as is usual, we store the readings in successive memory locations, we can find one by using a constant displacement from the base address.

Similarly, we may store a record in memory consisting of a person's name, address, social security number, age, and job classification. If we want to send notices of change of wage rates to all people in a particular job classification, we can find the job classification by specifying how far it is from the start of the record (for example, 97 bytes further). This is much like telling all the students who are taking an examination to put their names on the top line, their class levels on the fifth line, and their dates of birth on the tenth line. Each student locates the required line relative to the top of her or his form. So, in our records, the name might occupy the first 24 bytes, the address the next 70, the social security number the next 9, and the age the next 3. We can locate a particular field in a particular record (for example, employee Sue's social security number) by specifying the base address (in this case, the address where employee Sue's record starts) and how far beyond that we must go for the desired field (in our example, 94 bytes to the social security number).

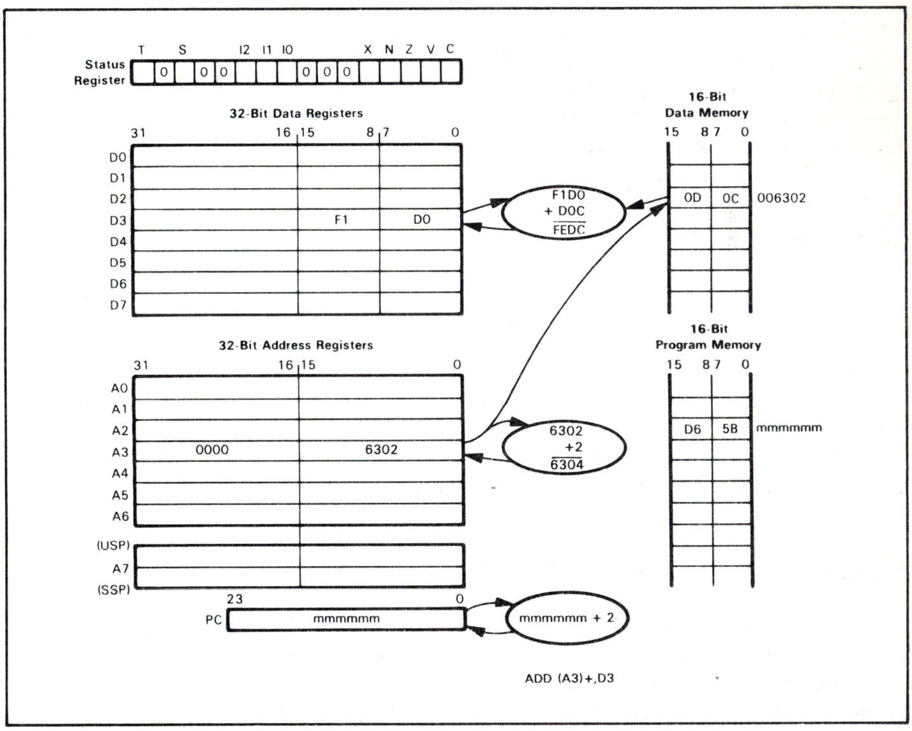

Figure 3-9. Address Register Indirect Addressing with Postincrement

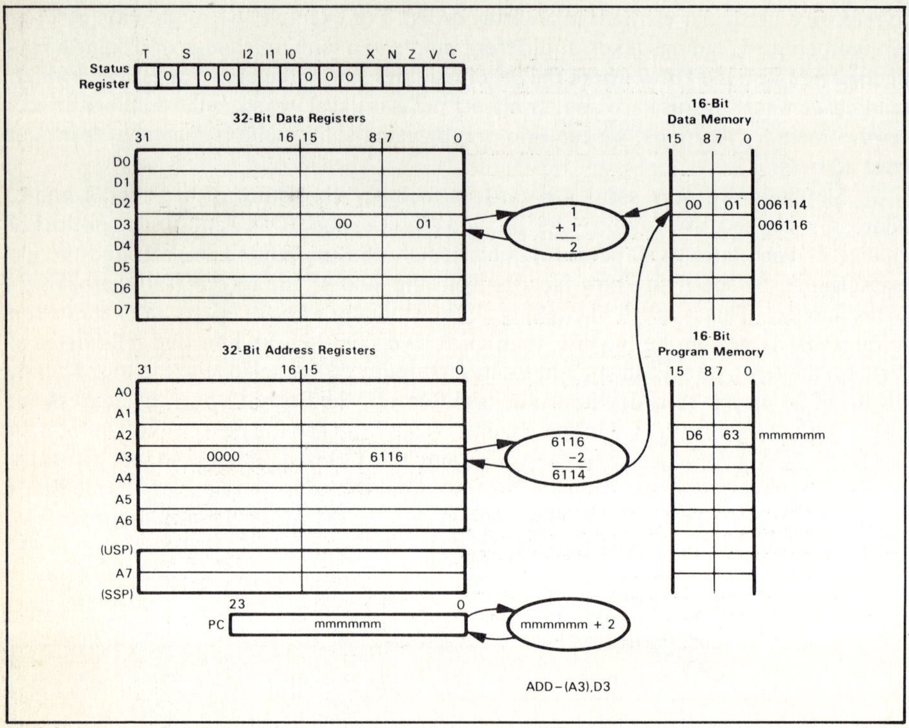

Figure 3-10. Address Register Indirect Addressing with Predecrement

The 16-bit displacement is contained in the lower half of the word following the operation code. Thus, the displacement from the base address contained in the address register can be as much as plus or minus 32K bytes. The displacement is considered to be a two's complement number, so if bit 15 is a one, it is considered to be a negative number.

In the standard MC68000 assembler format, you specify register indirect with displacement addressing by preceding the address register specification, which is enclosed in parentheses, with a label or immediate value representing the displacement. For example, the assembler converts the statement

```
ADD $56(A3),D3
```

into an ADD instruction that adds the contents of the address specified by register A3 plus 56_{16}, to the contents of register D3. If the displacement were 8000_{16} or greater, it would be treated as a two's complement negative number.

Figure 3-11 illustrates the execution of this instruction using register indirect with displacement addressing.

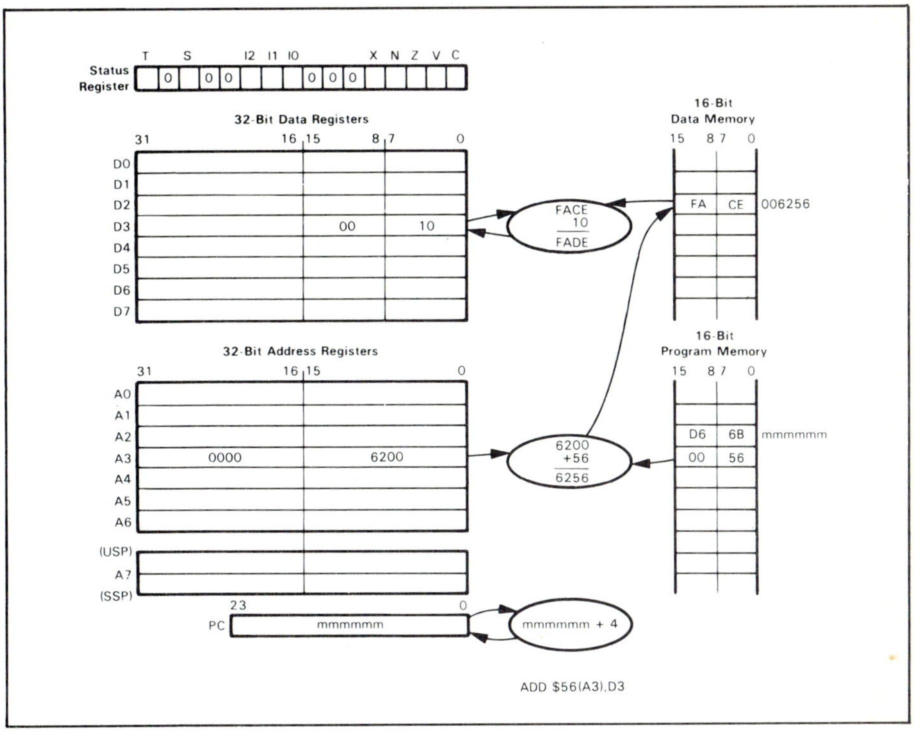

Figure 3-11. Address Register Indirect Addressing with Displacement

ADDRESS REGISTER INDIRECT WITH INDEX AND DISPLACEMENT

In this mode of addressing, the effective address is the sum of three addresses: the contents of an address register, the contents of an index register which can be any of the address or data registers, and a displacement provided as part of the instruction object code. A common use of this mode is to access structured data. For example, the address register would provide the origin for an array of records. The index register would be used to select a particular record; it would contain the distance of the particular record from the beginning of the array. Then the displacement would select a particular field of the record.

The standard MC68000 assembler format for this mode is quite similar to that used for register indirect with offset addressing. The register specification is preceded by the offset value. The address register and the register that is to be used as the index register are enclosed within parentheses; the address register is specified first, followed by a comma, then the index register specification. For example, the assembler converts the statement

```
ADD $20(A3,A6),D3
```

into an ADD instruction which adds the contents of an address obtained by adding the contents of registers A3 and A6 and the value 20_{16} to the contents of register D3. Register A3 is the base register in this example, A6 is used as the index register, and the displacement (20_{16}) is obtained from the low-order byte following the instruction object code in program memory.

Figure 3-12 illustrates the execution of the ADD instruction using address register indirect addressing with index and displacement.

The index register can be any of the address or data registers. You can specify that the index consist of the sign-extended low-order word from the index register as was illustrated in Figure 3-12, or that the entire 32-bit contents of the register be used as the index. The index size specification is contained in the high-order byte of the word following the instruction operation code in program memory. You specify to the assembler that the entire long-word contents of an index register are to be used by appending a period followed by the letter L to the index register specification. For example, if we wanted to use the entire contents of register A6 as an index in our ADD instruction, the standard MC68000 assembler format is

```
ADD $20(A3,A6.L),D3
```

In our original example of indexed addressing we did not specify an index size, and therefore the assembler assumes the default size of word (.W).

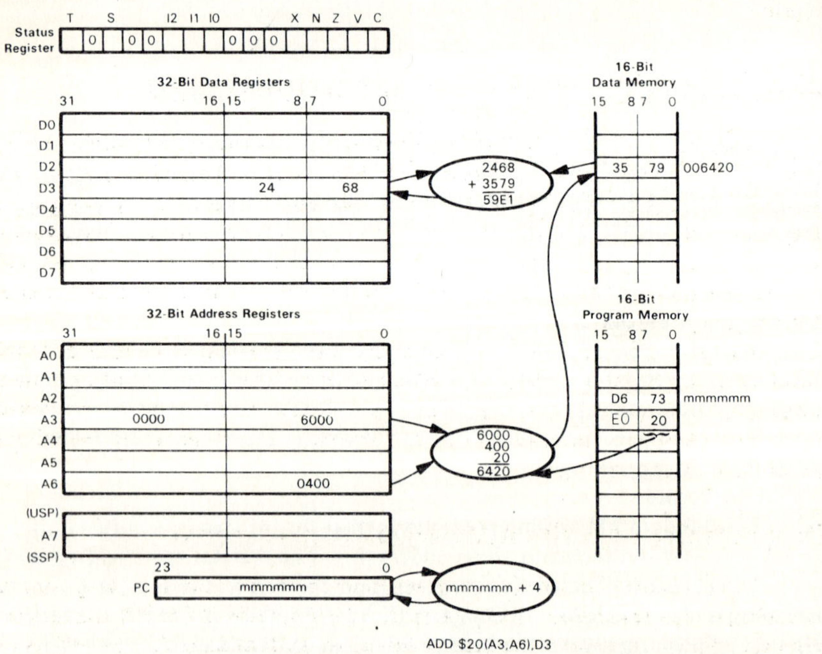

Figure 3-12. Address Register Indirect Addressing with Index and Displacement

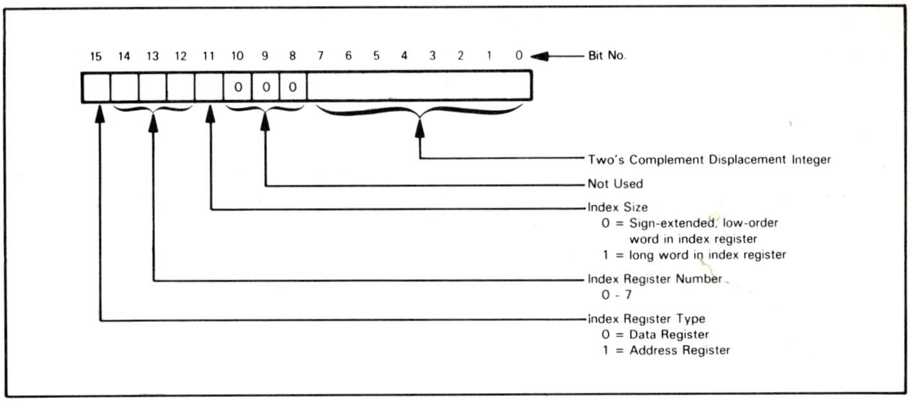

Figure 3-13. Bit Assignments in Extension Word for Address Register Indirect Addressing with Index and Displacement

The object code format in the extension word required for indexed register indirect addressing is shown in Figure 3-13. The low-order byte is the displacement integer. The displacement is considered to be a two's complement number and is sign-extended. Thus it can have the range +127 to −128. Bit 11 indicates the index size that is to be used. Bits 12-14 specify the register number that is to supply the index and bit 15 specifies whether it is a data register or address register that is to be used as the index register.

PROGRAM COUNTER RELATIVE ADDRESSING

Addressing modes that use offsets from the program counter help us write position-independent code, that is, programs that work regardless of where they are placed in memory. Such programs can be moved, without changes, to any available memory locations and can be used with any combination of other programs. The easiest way to make a program position-independent is for it to specify any addresses it uses relative to its own position. How does a program know its own position? By using the contents of the program counter.

We can move an entire program along with its own data if we refer to addresses relative to the program counter. The idea here is to refer to data as being "twenty locations from where we are," rather than at a particular address. If we then move everything, the relative positions of instructions and data remain the same, even though their absolute addresses change.

Program Counter Relative with Displacement

In this mode, a constant displacement or offset from the program counter is provided in the instruction's object code. The standard MC68000 assembler format for this addressing mode is basically the same as that used for the address register indirect with displacement mode. The assembler format is the same because **the program counter relative mode is simply a special case of the register indirect addressing**

mode; in this case, the register used must be the program counter instead of one of the address registers. The assembler converts the statement

```
ADD $6(PC),D3
```

into an instruction that adds the contents of the memory word six bytes beyond the location of the instruction to the contents of register D3.

Figure 3-14 illustrates the execution of this ADD instruction using program counter relative with displacement addressing. You will note in this illustration that the displacement is applied, not to the value that the program counter held (mmmmmm) when the instruction object code word was fetched, but to the program counter contents after it has been incremented to address the displacement word. The assembler will automatically make this correction if you use the location counter symbol (*). Typically, however, you would be using a label to specify the displacement and the assembler would then take care of generating the appropriate absolute value.

Program Counter Relative With Index and Displacement

This addressing mode operates identically to the address register indirect with index and displacement mode except the program counter is used as the base register

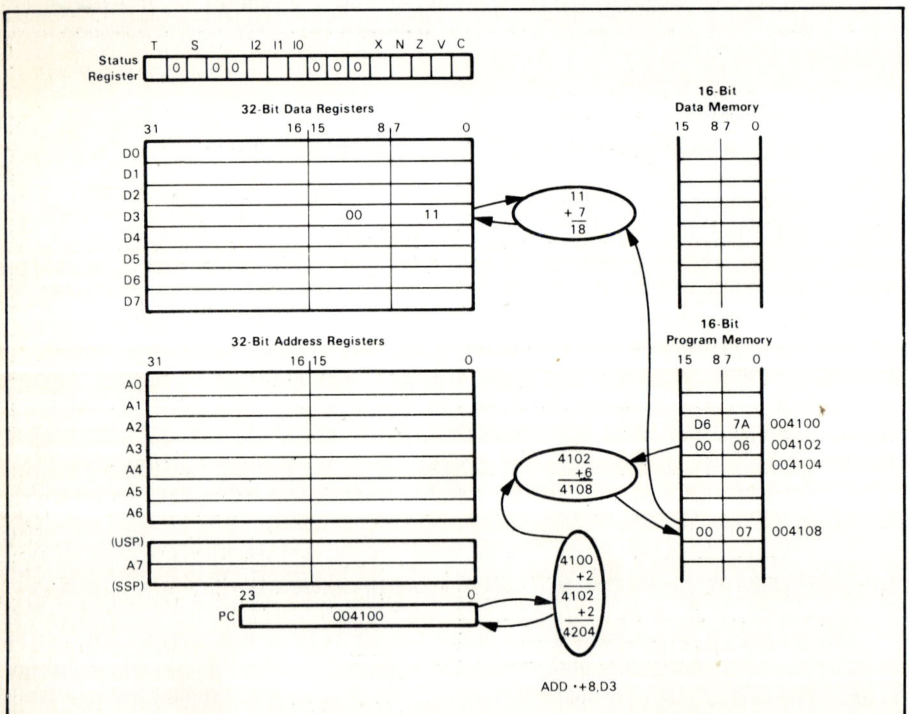

Figure 3-14. Program Counter Relative Addressing with Displacement

instead of an address register. The MC68000 standard assembler format for this addressing mode is essentially the same as for the indexed register indirect addressing. For example, the assembler converts the statement

```
ADD RSYMBOL(A3),D3
```

into an instruction that adds the contents of an address obtained by adding the contents of the program counter and register A3, and the displacement value of RSYMBOL to the contents of register D3. In this example, the program counter is the base register, A3 is the index register, and the displacement is the sign-extended value obtained from the low-order byte following the instruction code in program memory.

Note that the displacement value must be defined using a relative (rather than absolute) symbol since this form implicitly specifies the program counter as the base register. A more easily understood form of this addressing mode would be expressed as

```
ADD $4E(PC,A3),D3
```

and this form may be accepted by some assemblers. Always consult the documentation provided with your assembler to determine allowable forms.

Figure 3-15 illustrates the execution of the ADD instruction using program counter relative addressing with index and displacement.

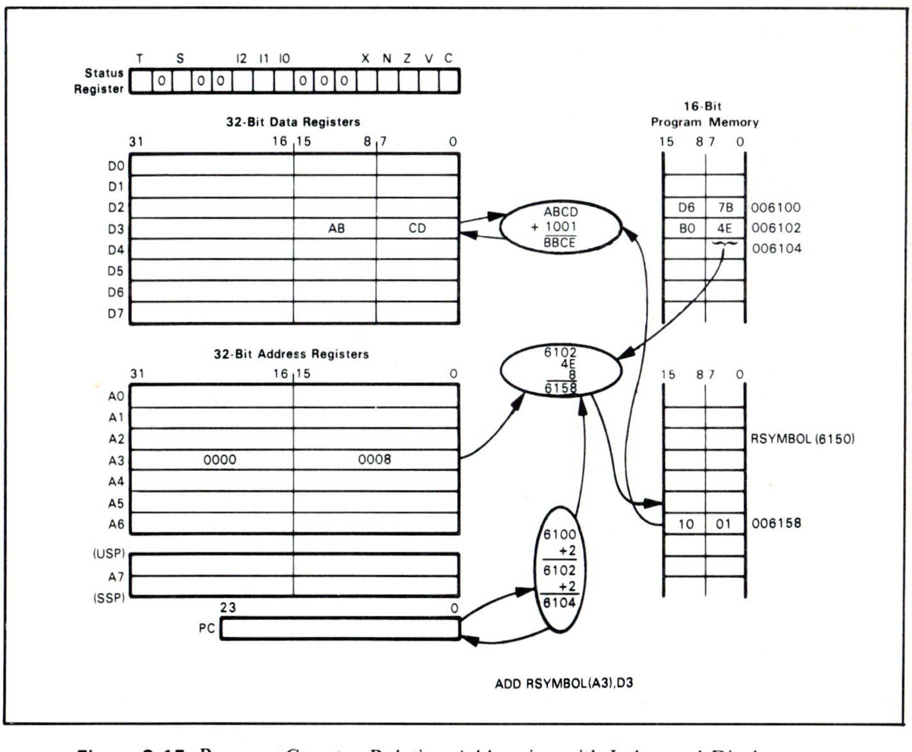

Figure 3-15. Program Counter Relative Addressing with Index and Displacement

The index register can be any of the address or data registers. You can specify that the index consist of the sign-extended low-order word from the index register as illustrated in Figure 3-15, or that the entire 32-bit contents of the register be used as the index. The index size specification is contained in the high-order byte of the word following the instruction operation code in program memory. The object code format for the extension word required for program counter relative addressing with index and displacement is identical to that used for address register indirect addressing with index and displacement (see Figure 3-13 earlier in this chapter).

ADDRESS MODE SPECIFICATION

For many instructions, you have no option in specifying the address mode: for example, the Exchange instructions always use operands that reside in registers. In other instructions, **for example RESET or NOP,** no address mode specification is relevant since there is no operand. **For those instructions where you do have options in specifying the addressing mode to be used, the six least significant bits of the instruction's operation code word are used to specify the addressing mode.** Bits 0, 1, and 2 specify a register number for some of the addressing modes and are used in conjunction with bits 3, 4, and 5 to further specify the addressing mode for other types.

Table 3-4 shows how these six bits determine which addressing mode is to be used. As you can see, in modes 000 through 110 the three least significant bits specify a register number. All of these modes use either a data register or an address register as part of the address formation operation. In the remaining address modes, the mode bits are all set to 1 and the three least significant bits of the operation code no longer specify a register number, but instead select one of the addressing modes that does not use an address register or data register as a primary or base register. Motorola literature categorizes these addressing modes as special address modes but the only thing that is "special" about them is that they do not use the three least significant bits to specify a register number.

Table 3-4. Addressing Mode Specification

Addressing Mode	Mode	Reg. No.
Bit No. →	5 4 3	2 1 0
Data register direct	0 0 0	r r r
Address register direct	0 0 1	r r r
Address register indirect	0 1 0	r r r
Address register indirect with postincrement	0 1 1	r r r
Address register indirect with predecrement	1 0 0	r r r
Address register indirect with displacement	1 0 1	r r r
Address register indirect with index and displacement	1 1 0	r r r
Absolute short	1 1 1	0 0 0
Absolute long	1 1 1	0 0 1
Program counter relative with displacement	1 1 1	0 1 0
Program counter relative with index and displacement	1 1 1	0 1 1
Immediate or status register	1 1 1	1 0 0

MOTOROLA MC68000 ASSEMBLER CONVENTIONS

The standard MC68000 assembler is available from Motorola and on many major time-sharing networks. It is also included in most development systems. Cross-assembler versions are also available for most large computers and minicomputers. The standard resident assembler differs in some ways from the various cross-assemblers. You should study your assembler manual.

ASSEMBLER FIELD DELIMITERS

The assembly language instructions have a standard field structure (see Table 2-1). The required delimiters are:

1. **A space or colon after a label.** A label that starts in column 1 must be followed by at least one space and a label that starts in a column other than column 1 must be terminated with a colon. All statements that are not labeled must start with at least one space.
2. **A space after the operation code.** Those instructions that can operate on more than one data size can have a data size code added to the operation code without a space. In this case, the data size code is appended to the operation code using a period (.) followed by B,W, or L (B = byte, W = word, L = long word). For example, ADD.L for "add long word" (32-bit operand) or ADD.B for "add byte" (8-bit operand). If no size specification is included, the default size of word is assumed by the assembler.
3. **A comma between operands in the address field** — for example between an immediate value and a register. ADD#5,D1 adds the value 5 to register D1.
4. **Parentheses — ( ) — around register designations when the register is to be used indirectly to form an address.**
5. **A plus sign after parentheses to indicate postincrement addressing; a minus sign before parentheses to indicate predecrement addressing.**
6. **A space before a comment that appears on the same line as an instruction, and an asterisk before an entire line of comments.**

LABELS

With the Motorola MC68000 assembler, only the first eight characters of a label are significant or meaningful. Additional characters are ignored by the assembler although it may print them when you put out a program listing. Thus, the assembler will not differentiate between LABELNUMBER1 and LABELNUMBER2 — they would be treated as the same label, LABELNUM. The first character must be an upper-case letter or the special character period (.). Each remaining character may be a letter, a digit (0-9), a dollar sign, a period, a hyphen, or an underscore. Although the standard MC68000 assembler allows the use of operation mnemonics as labels in some cases, this is usually not a good programming practice because of the obvious confusion that may result.

ASSEMBLER DIRECTIVES

The assembler has the following explicit pseudo-operations:

ORG — Set (location counter to) origin
SECTION — Establish program counter value for a relocatable program section
END — End of source program
EQU — Equate or define a permanent symbolic name
SET — Define a temporary symbolic name
REG — Define a register list
DC — Define constant data
DCB — Define constant block of data
DS — Define storage space in memory

DC and DCB — Data Directives

DC and DCB are the data directives used to place constant data in program memory — data such as tables, messages, and numerical factors — that is necessary for the execution of the program but does not consist of instructions. DC is used to define decimal, hexadecimal, or ASCII constants. The constants defined can be aligned on a byte boundary, word boundary, or long word boundary. You specify the size of the constant by appending B (byte), W (word), or L (long word) to the DC directive. A single DC directive can be used to define multiple constants, each of which is separated by a comma.

Examples:

```
DC.B 10,5,7
```

places the decimal numbers 10, 5, and 7 in three successive bytes of memory. Note that if you define an odd number of bytes, the odd byte will be zero-filled unless the next statement is another DC.B.

```
DC.B 'ERROR'
```

places the 7-bit ASCII character representation of E, R, R, O, and R (hexadecimal 45, 52, 52, 4F, and 52) in the next five bytes of program memory. Note that you must use the single quote (') character to enclose an ASCII string.

```
DC.L 10,5,7
```

Memory would have three contiguous long words defined. The value 10 would be contained in the first four bytes right justified with zero fill to the left (more significant) portion of the long word. The value 5 would be in the second long word, and the value 7 in the third long word.

DCB — Define Constant Block

DCB is the define constant block directive. It is used to initialize a block of

bytes, words, or long words (depending on the size code appended to the directive) to some initial value.

Example:

```
DCB.B 5.0
```

This directive loads a value of 0 into five contiguous bytes of memory. This directive will seldom be used within program logic and will usually be used simply to establish initial values (such as all zeros or all ones) in memory.

DS — Define Storage

DS is the define storage directive used to reserve locations in memory for specific purposes. The DS directive allocates a specified number of bytes (.B), words (.W), or long words (.L) depending on the size specification appended to the directive. The memory that is reserved is not initialized in any way.

EQU — Equate

EQU is the equate directive used to define names.

SET

The SET directive is used to define names and is thus similar to the EQU directive. The difference is that the SET directive **allows a symbol to be redefined later in the program using another SET directive.**

ORG

ORG is the standard origin directive. MC68000 assembly language programs usually have several origins, which are used for the following purposes:

1. To specify the starting address of the main program
2. To specify the starting address of subroutines
3. To define areas of memory for data storage
4. To define areas of memory for the user stacks
5. To specify addresses used for I/O ports and special functions

SECTION

The SECTION directive is similar to the origin directive in that it establishes starting points for programs and subroutines. It **is used to create relocatable program sections** and operates in conjunction with a linkage editor to subsequently create executable programs.

END

END simply marks the end of the assembly language program.

ADDRESSES

The Motorola MC68000 assembler allows entries in the address field in any of the following forms:

1. Decimal (the default case)
   Example: 12345
2. Hexadecimal (must start with $)
   Example: $CE00
3. Octal (must start with a @)
   Example: @1247
4. Binary (must start with %)
   Example: %00101
5. ASCII (must be enclosed by apostrophes)
   Example: 'ABCD'
6. As an offset from the current value of the location counter (asterisk)
   Example: *+10

Assembler, Arithmetic and Logical Expressions

The assembler also allows expressions in an address field. The expresssions consist of numbers and names separated by the arithmetic operators:

+	addition
—	subtraction
*	multiplication
/	division
>>	shift right
<<	shift left
&	logical AND
!	logical OR

The precedence of the various operators is as follows:

1. Expressions within parentheses are evaluated first.
2. Shift operations are performed next.
3. Logical AND and logical OR operations have the next priority.
4. Multiplication operators have precedence over addition and subtraction.
5. Operators with the same precedence are evaluated from left to right.

All results including intermediate results are truncated 32-bit integers.

We recommend that you avoid expressions within address fields whenever possible, since there are no standards for calculating such addresses. If you must compute an address, comment any unclear expressions and be sure that the evaluation of the expressions never produces a result which is too large for its ultimate use.

OTHER ASSEMBLER FEATURES

Most MC68000 assemblers have additional features, including both macro and conditional assembly capabilities. Others (such as SECTION) are closely related to the use of the linking editor and you should refer to the manufacturer's literature for a discussion of those capabilities. You should consult a particular assembler's manual for a description of how all of the assembler's features are implemented.

MC68000 INSTRUCTION SET

Table 3-5 lists the MC68000 instruction mnemonics. For a detailed description of the MC68000 instruction set, see the last sections of this book. In Chapter 22, we discuss each instruction's operation; refer to that chapter when you need to understand how a particular instruction works. Appendix A summarizes the available MC68000 instructions, grouping them by function. This provides a survey of the MC68000's capabilities, and will also be useful when you need a certain kind of operation but are either unsure of the specific mnemonics or not yet familiar with what instructions are available. The rest of the appendices serve as reference tables for

Table 3-5. Instruction Mnemonics

Mnemonic	Description	Mnemonic	Description
ABCD	Add Decimal with Extend	MOVE	Move
ADD	Add	MOVEM	Move Multiple Registers
AND	Logical AND	MOVEP	Move Peripheral Data
ASL	Arithmetic Shift Left	MULS	Signed Multiply
ASR	Arithmetic Shift Right	MULU	Signed Multiply
B_{CC}	Branch Conditionally	NBCD	Negate Decimal with Extend
BCHG	Bit Test and Change	NEG	Negate
BCLR	Bit Test and Clear	NOP	No Operation
BRA	Branch Always	NOT	One's Complement
BSET	Bit Test and Set	OR	Logical OR
BSR	Branch to Subroutine	PEA	Push Effective Address
BTST	Bit Test	RESET	Reset External Devices
CHK	Check Register Against Bounds	ROL	Rotate Left without Extend
CLR	Clear Operand	ROR	Rotate Right without Extend
CMP	Compare	ROXL	Rotate Left with Extend
DB_{CC}	Tst Cond, Decrement and Branch	ROXR	Rotate Right with Extend
		RTE	Return from Exception
DIVS	Signed Divide	RTR	Return and Restore
DIVU	Unsigned Divide	RTS	Return from Subroutine
EOR	Exclusive OR	SBCD	Subtract Decimal with Extend
EXG	Exchange Registers	S_{CC}	Set Conditional
EXT	Sign Extend	STOP	Stop
JMP	Jump	SUB	Subtract
JSR	Jump to Subroutine	SWAP	Swap Data Register Halves
LEA	Load Effective Address	TAS	Test and Set Operand
LINK	Link Stack	TRAP	Trap
LSL	Logical Shift Left	TRAPV	Trap on Overflow
LSR	Logical Shift Right	TST	Test
		UNLK	Unlink

Table 3-6. Variations of Instruction Types

Instruction Type	*Variation*	*Description*
ADD	*ADD*	Add
	ADDA	AddAddress
	ADDQ	Add Quick
	ADDI	Add Immediate
	ADDX	Add with Extend
AND	*AND*	Logical And
CMP	*CMP*	Compare
	CMPA	Compare Address
	CMPM	Compare Memory
	CPI	Compare Immediate
EOR	*EOR*	Exclusive Or
	EORI	Exclusive Or Immediate
MOVE	*MOVE*	Move
	MOVEA	Move Address
	MOVEQ	Move Quick
	MOVE from SR	Move from Status Register
	MOVE to SR	Move from Status Register
	MOVE to CCR	Move to Condition Codes
	MOVE USP	Move User Stack Pointer
NEG	*Neg*	Negate
	NEGX	Negate with Extend
OR	*OR*	Logical Or
	ORI	Or Immediate
SUB	*SUB*	Subtract
	SUBA	Subtract Address
	SUBI	Subtract Immediate
	SUBQ	Subtract Quick
	SUBX	Subtract with Extend

calculating program execution time and memory requirements, and for hand assembly and disassembly.

Instructions often frighten microcomputer users who are new to programming. Yet taken in isolation, the operations involved in the execution of a single instruction are usually easy to follow. The purpose of the last section of this book is to isolate and explain those operations. Furthermore, you need not attempt to understand all the instructions at once. As you study each of the programs in this book you will learn about the specific instructions involved.

Why are a microprocessor's instructions referred to as an instruction *set?* Because the microprocessor designer selects the instruction complement with great care; it must be easy to execute complex operations as a sequence of simple events, each of which is represented by one instruction from a well-designed instruction set.

REFERENCES

1. G. Kane, *68000 Microprocessor Handbook*, Osborne/McGraw-Hill, Berkeley, California, 1981.

II
Introductory Problems

The only way to learn assembly language programming is through experience. The next six chapters of this book contain examples of simple programs that perform actual microprocessor tasks. You should read each example carefully and try to execute the program on a MC68000-based microcomputer. Then work the problems at the end of each chapter and run the resulting programs to ensure that you understand the material.

You should use the examples as guidelines for solving the problems at the end of each chapter. Don't forget to run your solutions on a MC68000-based microcomputer to ensure that they are correct.

GENERAL FORMAT OF EXAMPLES

Each program example contains the following parts:

- **A title** that describes the general problem
- **A statement of purpose** that describes the task the program performs and the memory locations used
- **A sample problem** with data and results
- **A flowchart if the program logic is complex**
- **The source program** or assembly language listing
- **The object program** or hexadecimal machine language listing
- **Explanatory notes** that discuss the instructions and methods used in the program

Each example is written and assembled as a stand-alone program. Each program is assigned a name which identifies the chapter within which the program occurs, and the sequential position of the program within the chapter. This may be illustrated generally as follows:

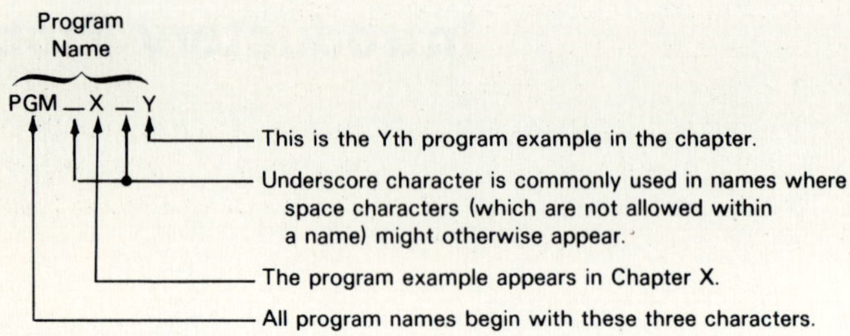

X and Y represent any decimal numbers. Thus the declaration:

PGM 6 3

names the third program example in Chapter 6.

Program Listing Format

The program listings in this book will show the object code program alongside the source program — this is a common assembler output format. For example, here is a portion of program 4-1:

```
       00006000    DATA      EQU      $6000
       00004000    PROGRAM   EQU      $4000

       00006000              ORG      DATA
006000 00000002    VALUE     DS.W     1            VALUE TO TRANSFER
006002 00000002    RESULT    DS.W     1            STORAGE FOR TRANSFERRED DATA

       00004000              ORG      PROGRAM

004000 30386000    PGM_4_1   MOVE.W   VALUE,D0     GET DATA TO BE MOVED
004004 31C06002              MOVE.W   D0,RESULT    SAVE DATA

004008 4E75                  RTS

                             END      PGM_4_1
```

The six-digit number starting in the far left column of each line is the hexadecimal address of the first byte of object code shown on that line. In the first line above, 004000 is the address of the first object code byte of the four-byte MOVE.W VALUE,DO instruction; the hexadecimal object code for this instruction is 3038 6000, and the first byte, 30, is in location 4000. Location 4001 contains the byte 38 — we infer this from the fact that 38 follows the byte in address 4000 — and locations 4002 and 4003 hold the bytes 60 and 00, respectively. The words to the right of the object code are the assembly language fields which were described in Chapter 2. These fields comprise the source program.

If you wish to assemble these examples on your microcomputer, key in the source statements only; do not enter the addresses or object codes, since the assembler program will generate them. You will also need to enter some assembler directives (for example, to tell the assembler where to start program addresses). We show some of these directives, but the ones you use will be determined by your assembler and the requirements of your microcomputer's operating system.

If you wish to execute the program examples without assembling source code, you can key the object code into the specified addresses. Before you do this, however, make sure that you will not be trying to load areas of memory reserved for the monitor or operating system. To avoid such problems, you may need to change addresses before you load the programs. As we will discuss in guideline 7 below, you may also need to change the instruction at the end of the program.

Guidelines for Examples

We have used the following guidelines in constructing the examples:

1. Standard Motorola MC68000 assembler notation is used, as summarized in Chapter 3.
2. The forms in which data and addresses appear are selected for clarity rather than for consistency. We use hexadecimal numbers for memory addresses, instruction codes, and BCD data; decimal for numeric constants; binary for logical masks; and ASCII for characters.
3. Frequently used instructions and programming techniques are emphasized.
4. Examples illustrate tasks that microprocessors perform in communications, instrumentation, computers, business equipment, industrial, and military applications.
5. Detailed comments are included.
6. Simple and clear structures are emphasized, but programs are written as efficiently as possible within this guideline. Notes accompanying programs often describe more efficient procedures.
7. Programs use consistent memory allocation. Each program starts in memory location 4000_{16} and ends with the RTS (Return from Subroutine) instruction. Each program is written as an independent procedure or subroutine although no assumptions are made concerning the state of the microprocessor on procedure entry. You may prefer to modify the way a program ends. This could be done by replacing the RTS instruction with a STOP instruction or by an endless loop instruction such as:

   HERE: JMP HERE

8. Programs use standard Motorola assembler directives. We introduced assembler directives conceptually in Chapter 2. When first examining programming examples, you can ignore assembler directives if you do not understand them. Assembler directives do not contribute to program logic, which is what you will be trying to understand initially; but they are a necessary part of every assembly language program, so you will have to learn how to use them before you write any executable programs. Including assembler directives in all program examples will help you become familiar with the functions they perform.

Trying the Examples

To test an example program on your microcomputer system, first place the object program in memory. Your assembler program may do this automatically, or it may create an object code file which a separate loader program must then place in memory.

In most of the program examples, the locations to be used for test data have been specified using the Define Storage (DS) directive. This directive simply establishes memory locations that are to be reserved for references by the program. Unlike the Define Constant (DC) directive, the Define Storage directive does not establish any initial values in the specified memory locations. We also use the DS directive to reserve memory locations which will hold variable addresses — such as the address of an array or table to be accessed. Therefore, **once the program is in memory, you must put the test data (and/or addresses) in the appropriate locations. Then run the program. After the program terminates, examine the result locations.** To test different sets of data, simply change the appropriate data locations before running the program again. (If your system does not allow you to enter data directly into memory, you must use Define Constant directives to enter the data.)

Note that this use of memory locations to provide variable information for use by a program is known as parameter passing. The data to be operated on, and some of the addresses to be used, are the parameters. This is a common technique used in conjunction with subroutines. We will discuss this subject in detail in Chapters 10 and 11. All you need to concern yourself with, at this point, is that you load the required test data and address information into the defined memory areas when you are trying the examples.

PROGRAM INITIALIZATION

All of the programming examples presented in Chapter 4, and in subsequent chapters, pay particular attention to the correct initialization of constants and operands. Often this requires additional instructions that may appear superfluous, in that they do not contribute directly to the solution of the stated problem. Nevertheless, correct initialization is important in order to ensure the proper execution of the program every time.

We want to stress correct initialization; that is why we are going to emphasize this aspect of problems.

SPECIAL CONDITIONS

For the same reasons that we emphasize correct initialization, we also pay particular attention to special conditions that can cause a program to fail. Empty lists and zero indexes are two of the most common circumstances overlooked in sample problems. **It is critically important** when using microprocessors in general, and powerful 16-bit microprocessors in particular, **that you learn with your very first program to anticipate unusual circumstances; they frequently cause your program to fail. You must build in the necessary programming steps to account for these potential problems.**

PROGRAMMING GUIDELINES FOR SOLVING PROBLEMS

Use the following guidelines in solving the problems at the end of each chapter:

1. Comment each program so that others can understand it. The comments can be brief and ungrammatical. They should explain the purpose of a section or instruction in the program, but should not describe the operation of instructions; that description is available in manuals. You do not have to comment each statement or explain the obvious. You may follow the format of the examples but provide less detail.
2. Emphasize clarity, simplicity, and good structure in programs. While programs should be reasonably efficient, do not worry about saving a single byte of program memory or a few microseconds.
3. Make programs reasonably general. Do not confuse parameters (such as the number of elements in any array) with fixed constants (such as π or ASCII C).
4. Never assume fixed initial values for parameters.
5. Use assembler notation as shown in the examples and defined in Chapter 3.
6. Use symbolic notation for address and data references. Symbolic notation should also be used even for constants (such as DATA SELECT instead of %00000100). Also use the clearest possible form for data (such as 'C' instead of $43).
7. If your system allows it, start all programs in memory location 4000_{16} and use memory locations starting with 6000_{16} for data and temporary storage. Use location 7000_{16} as the base of the stack. Otherwise, establish equivalent addresses for your microcomputer and use them consistently. Again, consult the user's manual.
8. Use meaningful names for labels and variables; e.g., SUM or CHECK rather than X or Z.
9. Execute each program on your microcomputer. There is no other way of ensuring that your program is correct. We have provided sample data with each problem. Be sure that the program works for special cases. Chapters 19 and 20 provide some useful guidelines you can follow when testing your programs.

4
Beginning Programs

This chapter contains some very elementary programs. They will introduce some fundamental features of the MC68000. In addition, these programs demonstrate some primitive tasks that are common to assembly language programs for many different applications.

PROGRAM EXAMPLES

4-1. 16-BIT DATA TRANSFER

Purpose: Move the contents of one 16-bit variable VALUE at location 6000 to another 16-bit variable RESULT at location 6002.

Sample Problem:

Input: VALUE-(6000)=2E56
Output: RESULT-(6002)=2E56

Program 4-1:

```
              00006000     DATA      EQU      $6000
              00004000     PROGRAM   EQU      $4000

              00006000               ORG      DATA
006000 00000002     VALUE     DS.W     1                 VALUE TO TRANSFER
006002 00000002     RESULT    DS.W     1                 STORAGE FOR TRANSFERRED DATA

              00004000               ORG      PROGRAM

004000 30386000     PGM_4_1   MOVE.W   VALUE,D0          GET DATA TO BE MOVED
004004 31C06002               MOVE.W   D0,RESULT         SAVE DATA

004008 4E75                   RTS

                              END      PGM_4_1
```

This program solves the problem in two simple steps. The first instruction loads data register D0 with the 16-bit value in location VALUE. The next instruction saves the 16-bit contents of data register D0 in location RESULT.

Remember — if you want to try this program with some sample data, *you* must first load the data that is to be transferred into the variable VALUE at memory location 6000. If your system does not allow this, use the Define Constant directive.

During the execution of this program, only the least significant 16 bits of the 32-bit data register D0 are affected. The most significant 16 bits are not modified, since both instructions specified an operation size of word (16 bits) by using the '.W' instruction suffix. If a data transfer of one byte (8 bits) or one long word (32 bits) is desired, a size suffix of '.B' or '.L', respectively, should be used.

The MC68000 combines three classes of instruction provided by most microprocessors — load register, store register, and transfer between registers — into a single class of instructions — MOVE. Using a register as the source operand (first operand) with a MOVE instruction is similar to a typical microprocessor's store register operation. Using a register specified as a destination operand with the MOVE instruction is similar to a typical microprocessor's load register operation. Using internal registers to provide both the source and destination operands with a MOVE instruction accomplishes the same function as a typical microprocessor's register transfer instruction.

When you use the MOVE instruction to accomplish the LOAD, STORE, or TRANSFER function, it generally affects the status flags in the status register. The execution of most MOVE instructions sets or clears the Negative (N) and Zero (Z) flags depending on the value moved, while clearing the Overflow (V) and Carry (C) flags. The Extend (X) flag is not affected.

In addition to moving data between registers, and between registers and memory, the MOVE instruction can also be used to move data between two memory locations. As a result, the two MOVE instructions in PGM 4-1 can be replaced by the single instruction:

```
MOVE.W VALUE, RESULT
```

This version of the MOVE instruction moves the 16-bit word contained in memory location VALUE to memory location RESULT without utilizing any of the data or address registers. The status register is still affected.

If you examine the instruction set of the MC68000 you will see that a number of other instructions are capable of operating on memory in this same manner.

4-2. ONE'S COMPLEMENT

Purpose: Form the bitwise complement of the contents of the 16-bit variable VALUE at location 6000.

Sample Problem:

Input: VALUE-(6000)=7F3E
Output: VALUE-(6000)=80C1

Program 4-2:

```
       00006000    DATA      EQU     $6000
       00004000    PROGRAM   EQU     $4000

       00006000              ORG     DATA
006000 00000002    VALUE     DS.W    1               VALUE TO BE COMPLEMENTED

       00004000              ORG     PROGRAM

004000 30386000    PGM_4_2   MOVE.W  VALUE,D0        FETCH VALUE
004004 4640                  NOT.W   D0              LOGICAL COMPLEMENT OF VALUE
004006 31C06000              MOVE.W  D0,VALUE        STORE COMPLEMENTED RESULT

00400A 4E75                  RTS

                             END     PGM_4_2
```

This program solves the problem in three steps. The first instruction moves the contents of location VALUE into data register D0. The next instruction takes the logical complement of data register D0. Finally, in the third instruction the result of the logical complement is stored in VALUE.

Note that any data register may be referenced in any instruction that uses data registers. (The same is true of address registers although you must pay special attention to register A7 which the processor uses as the stack pointer.) Thus, in the MOVE instruction we've just illustrated, any of the eight data registers could have been used.

The two MOVE instructions in this program, like those in Program 4-1, demonstrate two of the MC68000's addressing modes. The data reference to VALUE as either a source or destination operand is an example of absolute addressing. In absolute addressing the address for the data being referenced is contained in the extension word(s) following the operation word of the instruction. As shown in the assembly listing, the address (6000) corresponding to VALUE is found in the extension word for the MOVE instructions.

Since the address of VALUE requires only one extension word, the MC68000 refers to this form of absolute addressing as short absolute. Addresses in the ranges from 00000000 to 00007FFF and FFFF8000 to FFFFFFFF may be referenced using short absolute addressing. This range may appear somewhat different than expected, but it is consistent with the MC68000's treatment of 16-bit addresses and address displacements which are always sign-extended to 32 bits. This technique of addressing memory allows the system designer to organize his or her memory map so as to permit the usage of efficient short absolute addressing for both memory and peripheral device references. One way of achieving this would be to organize random access memory (RAM) starting at address 0 and peripheral devices in the upper 64K memory bytes.

Another form of absolute addressing is long absolute. This form is similar to short absolute except that two extension words are required to reference the data. Therefore to reduce your program size, you should strive to keep your frequently referenced variables in the short absolute addressing range.

Most programs in this book use short absolute addressing. Try modifying the value of DATA to a value outside the short absolute addressing range such as 9000_{16}. What happens to the generated object code? To ensure that the assembler generates the short absolute form whenever possible, you should try to define all data references prior to their use. Try moving the two assembler psuedo-instructions ORG DATA and VALUE DS.W 1 to the end of the program. Note the resulting object code.

The other addressing mode used in all instructions in Program 4-2 is data register direct. In this mode, the contents of the data register are directly affected. The contents are either loaded, modified, or stored as specified by the instruction.

The MOVE instruction allows any of the processor's 14 different addressing modes to be used to specify the source operand. However, the destination operand must be specified using addressing modes which reference memory locations that are "alterable." Thus you cannot use program counter relative or immediate addressing modes since such memory locations may be located in nonalterable, read-only memory.

If you want to perform a MOVE-type instruction with an address register as the destination, the MOVEA instruction must be used. The MOVEA instruction performs the same function as the MOVE instruction, but it does not affect the status register. Motorola's MC68000 assemblers allow you to specify an address register as the destination operand in a MOVE instruction. However, in this case the assembler actually generates the machine code for a MOVEA instruction; thus the status flags are unchanged.

Program 4-2 is another example where a single instruction may replace two or more instructions. The three instructions in this program may be replaced by the single instruction:

```
NOT.W VALUE
```

With this instruction, the contents of the variable VALUE are complemented without using the data or address registers. The operation is performed directly on the designated memory location VALUE.

4-3. 16-BIT ADDITION

Purpose: Add the contents of the 16-bit variable VALUE1 at location 6000 to the contents of the 16-bit variable VALUE2 at location 6002 and place the result in the 16-bit variable RESULT at location 6004.

Sample Problem:

```
 Input: VALUE1-(6000)=10F5
        VALUE2-(6002)=2621
Output: RESULT-(6004)=3716
```

Program 4-3a:

```
       00006000      DATA      EQU     $6000
       00004000      PROGRAM   EQU     $4000

       00006000                ORG     DATA
006000 00000002      VALUE1    DS.W    1              FIRST VALUE
006002 00000002      VALUE2    DS.W    1              SECOND VALUE
006004 00000002      RESULT    DS.W    1              16 BIT STORAGE FOR ADDITION RESULT
```

```
       00004000               ORG     PROGRAM

004000 30386000     PGM_4_3A  MOVE.W  VALUE1,D0      GET FIRST VALUE
004004 D0786002               ADD.W   VALUE2,D0      ADD SECOND VALUE TO FIRST VALUE
004008 31C06004               MOVE.W  D0,RESULT      STORE RESULT OF ADDITION

00400C 4E75                   RTS

                              END     PGM_4_3A
```

The ADD instruction in this program is another example of a two-operand instruction. However, unlike the MOVE instruction, this instruction's second operand not only represents the instruction's destination but also is operated upon to calculate the result. The format

SOURCE Operation DESTINATION → DESTINATION

is common to many of the MC68000's instructions.

We should note at this point that the MC68000 processor provides an external 16-bit data bus for data accesses to memory. Internally, however, the processor also supports 8- and 32-bit data operations. Therefore, the ADD instruction, just like the MOVE and most other MC68000 instructions, permits data operations on all three data sizes. By simply changing the .W suffix to .B or .L anywhere in the programs we have shown, the programs would be converted to 8-bit or 32-bit addition programs.

As we noted in Program 4-1, the MC68000 allows many instructions to have both operands in memory. You should note, however, that this capability is not available with all instructions; for example, the ADD instruction only allows the source or destination operand to reference memory. Thus you could not add the contents of one memory location directly to the contents of another memory location.

As with any microprocessor, there are many instruction sequences you can execute with the MC68000 which will solve the same problem. Program 4-3*b*, for example, is a modification of Program 4-3*a* and uses address register indirect addressing instead of absolute short addressing. If you use address register indirect addressing, the address of the actual operand may not (need not) be known until execution time.

Program 4-3b:

```
       00006000       DATA      EQU     $6000
       00004000       PROGRAM   EQU     $4000


       00006000                 ORG     DATA
006000 00000002       VALUE1    DS.W    1              FIRST VALUE
006002 00000002       VALUE2    DS.W    1              SECOND VALUE
006004 00000002       RESULT    DS.W    1              16 BIT STORAGE FOR ADDITION RESULT

       00004000                 ORG     PROGRAM

004000 207C00006000   PGM_4_3B  MOVEA.L #VALUE1,A0     INITIALIZE A0 WITH ADDRESS OF VALUE
004006 3010                     MOVE.W  (A0),D0        GET FIRST VALUE IN D0
004008 D1FC00000002             ADDA.L  #2,A0          INCREMENT ADDRESS REGISTER A0 BY 2
00400E D050                     ADD.W   (A0),D0        ADD SECOND VALUE TO FIRST VALUE
004010 D1FC00000002             ADDA.L  #2,A0          INCREMENT A0 BY 2 AGAIN
004016 3080                     MOVE.W  D0,(A0)        STORE RESULT OF ADDITION

004018 4E75                     RTS

                                END     PGM_4_3B
```

The MOVEA instruction introduces two addressing modes — immediate and address register direct, which we have not used previously. Immediate addressing lets you define a data constant and include that constant in the instruction's associated object code. Motorola assembler format identifies immediate addressing with a pound sign (#) preceding the data constant. The size of the data constant varies depending on the instruction. Immediate addressing is extremely useful when small data constants must be referenced.

The second addressing mode — address register direct — is similar to data register direct except the address register is affected instead of the data register. Only word or long word references are permitted with address direct. When word size operands are used to modify an address register, the 16-bit operand is always sign-extended to 32 bits.

Program 4-3*b* also demonstrates the use of address register indirect addressing. In this mode the address of the operand is contained in the specified 32-bit address register. Since an extension word is not required, the address register indirect mode of addressing is more memory-efficient than absolute addressing. Because of the need to set up the address register, several references must be made to a particular data item before this mode really becomes more memory-efficient.

Another advantage of this addressing mode is its faster execution time as compared to absolute addressing. This improvement occurs because the address extension word(s) does not have to be fetched from memory prior to the actual data references.

A final advantage is the flexibility provided by having the reference address in an address register instead of fixed as part of the instruction. This flexibility allows the same code to be used for more than one address. Thus if you wanted to add the values contained in consecutive variables VALUE3 and VALUE4, you could simply change the contents of A0.

4-4. SHIFT LEFT ONE BIT

Purpose: Shift the contents of the 16-bit variable VALUE at location 6000 to the left one bit. Store the result back in VALUE.

Sample Problem:

Input: VALUE-(6000)=57B6 0101 0111 1011 0110_2
Output: VALUE-(6000)=AF6C 1010 1111 0110 1100_2

Program 4-4:

```
        00006000        DATA       EQU     $6000
        00004000        PROGRAM    EQU     $4000

        00006000                   ORG     DATA
006000  00000002        VALUE      DS.W    1               VALUE TO BE SHIFTED LEFT

        00004000                   ORG     PROGRAM

004000  30386000        PGM_4_4    MOVE.W  VALUE,D0        GET VALUE TO BE SHIFTED
004004  E348                       LSL.W   #1,D0           SHIFT LEFT LOGICALLY ONE BIT
004006  31C06000                   MOVE.W  D0,VALUE        STORE SHIFTED RESULT

00400A  4E75                       RTS

                                   END     PGM_4_4
```

The LSL instruction is used to perform a logical shift left. Using the operand format of the LSL instruction shown in Program 4-4, a data register can be shifted from 1 to 8 bits on either a byte, word or long word basis. Another form of the LSL instruction allows a shift count (modulo 64) to be specified in another data register. A final form of the LSL instruction, which uses only one operand, allows the contents of a memory location to be shifted one bit to the left without the use of a data register.

Except for different status register results, the following sequences all could replace the instruction LSL #1, D0, and produce the same results in D0:

```
MOVE    #1,D1
LSL     D1,D0

LSL     VALUE
MOVE    VALUE,D0

ROL     #1,D0
BCLR    #0,D0

ADD     D0,D0
```

How many others can you find? Which of those presented will execute the fastest?

4-5. BYTE DISASSEMBLY

Purpose: Divide the least significant byte of the 8-bit variable VALUE at location 6000 into two 4-bit nibbles and store one nibble in each byte of 16-bit variable RESULT at location 6002. The low-order four bits of the byte will be stored in the low-order four bits of the least significant byte of RESULT. The high-order four bits of the byte will be stored in the low-order four bits of the most significant byte of RESULT.

Sample Problem:

Input: VALUE-(6000)=5F
Output: RESULT-(6002)=050F

Program 4-5a:

```
       00006000   DATA       EQU      $6000
       00004000   PROGRAM    EQU      $4000

       00006000              ORG      DATA
       0000000F   MASK       EQU      $000F             MASK FOR LOWER NIBBLE
006000 00000001   VALUE      DS.B     1                 BYTE TO BE DISASSEMBLED
006001 00000001              DS.B     1                 ALIGN RESULT ON WORD BOUNDARY
006002 00000002   RESULT     DS.W     1                 STORAGE FOR DISASSEMBLED BYTE

       00004000              ORG      PROGRAM

004000 10386000   PGM_4_5A   MOVE.B   VALUE,D0          GET BYTE TO BE DISASSEMBLED
004004 0200000F              AND.B    #MASK,D0          ISOLATE LOWER NIBBLE OF BYTE
004008 11C06003              MOVE.B   D0,RESULT+1       SAVE LOWER ORDER NIBBLE
00400C 10386000              MOVE.B   VALUE,D0          GET BYTE TO BE DISASSEMBLED
004010 E808                  LSR.B    #4,D0             ISOLATE HIGH NIBBLE
004012 11C06002              MOVE.B   D0,RESULT         SAVE HIGH ORDER NIBBLE

004016 4E75                  RTS

                             END      PGM_4_5
```

This is an example of byte manipulation. The MC68000 allows most instructions which operate on words also to operate on bytes. Thus, by using the .B suffix, all the instructions in Program 4-5*a* perform byte operations.

Remember that the MOVE instruction, in addition to performing register-to-memory and memory-to-register transfers also performs register-to-register transfers. This use of the MOVE instruction is quite frequent.

Generally, it is more efficient in terms of program memory usage and execution time to minimize references to memory. Program 4-5*b* is a modification of the above problem which demonstrates this.

Program 4-5b:

```
         00006000       DATA      EQU     $6000
         00004000       PROGRAM   EQU     $4000

         00006000                 ORG     DATA
006000   00000001       VALUE     DS.B    1              BYTE TO BE DISASSEMBLED
006001   00000001                 DS.B    1              ALIGN RESULT ON WORD BOUNDARY
006002   00000002       RESULT    DS.W    1              STORAGE FOR DISASSEMBLED BYTE

         00004000                 ORG     PROGRAM

004000   4240           PGM_4_5B  CLR.W   D0             CLEAR DATA REGISTER D0(0:15)
004002   10386000                 MOVE.B  VALUE,D0       BYTE TO BE DISASSEMBLED IN D0(0:7)
004006   E958                     ROL.W   #4,D0          MOVE BYTE TO D0(4:11)
004008   E808                     LSR.B   #4,D0          SHIFT D0(4:7) TO D0(0:3)
00400A   31C06002                 MOVE.W  D0,RESULT      STORE DISASSEMBLED BYTE

00400E   4E75                     RTS

                                  END     PGM_4_5B
```

The CLR.W instruction is required to clear the least significant 16 bits of data register D0. Only the least significant byte of D0 is affected by the byte transfer from VALUE. The ROL instruction rotates the least significant word of D0 such that the high-order nibble of VALUE is in the second byte of D0. Could the ROXL instruction be used in place of the ROL instruction?

Although the MC68000 allows manipulation of various data sizes, you must take care when you define a program's data. All of the processor's instructions, when making memory references to 16-bit or 32-bit data, assume the least significant bit of the memory address to be zero — that is, an even address. For this reason, an additional byte of memory storage is required to align the variable RESULT on an even address (6002_{16}) instead of at the next available memory location which would be 6001_{16}. Would the results of Program 4-5*a* have been the same if the memory addresses associated with RESULT had been 6001_{16}? What about Program 4-5*b*?

4-6. FIND THE LARGER OF TWO NUMBERS

Purpose: Find the larger of two 32-bit variables VALUE1 (at location 6000) and VALUE2 (at location 6004). Place the results in the variable RESULT at location 6008. Assume the values are unsigned.

Sample Problems:

```
a.    Input:  VALUE1 - (6000) = 12345678
              VALUE2 - (6004) = 87654321
     Output:  RESULT - (6008) = 87654321

b.    Input:  VALUE1 - (6000) = 12345678
              VALUE2 - (6004) = 0ABCDEF1
     Output:  RESULT - (6008) = 12345678
```

Program 4-6:

```
        00006000      DATA     EQU      $6000
        00004000      PROGRAM  EQU      $4000


        00006000               ORG      DATA
006000 00000004       VALUE1   DS.L     1                FIRST VALUE
006004 00000004       VALUE2   DS.L     1                SECOND VALUE
006008 00000004       RESULT   DS.L     1                RESERVE LONG WORD STORAGE

        00004000               ORG      PROGRAM

004000 4CF800036000 PGM_4_6  MOVEM.L  VALUE1,D0/D1     LOAD VALUES TO BE COMPARED
004006 B280                  CMP.L    D0,D1            COMPARE 32 BIT VALUES
004008 62000004              BHI      STORE            IF VALUE2 >= VALUE1 THEN GOTO STORE
00400C 2200                  MOVE.L   D0,D1            ...ELSE D1 = VALUE1
00400E 21C16008     STORE    MOVE.L   D1,RESULT        STORE LARGER VALUE

004012 4E75                  RTS

                             END      PGM_4_6
```

The MOVE Multiple instruction, MOVEM, used in Program 4-6, lets us transfer the contents of selected address/data registers to or from a block of consecutive memory locations. In Program 4-6, D0 and D1 are loaded via the MOVEM instruction with the contents of the variables VALUE1 and VALUE2, respectively.

While you can specify which registers are to be selected with the MOVEM instruction, the order in which the register contents are transferred is not subject to your control. The transfer order is always data register D0 (or the lowest data register number you have specified) through data register D7 (or the highest data register you have specified) and then address registers A0 through A7 (once again, with the same limitations). The only exception to this sequence occurs when you use the predecrement addressing mode; in this case, the order is just the reverse of that which we have described. For details on the register specification and sequence, refer to the description of the MOVEM instruction in Chapter 22.

The Compare instruction, CMP, in Program 4-6 sets the status register flags as if the source, D0, were subtracted from the destination, D1. The order of the operands is the same as the operands in the subtract instruction, SUB.

The conditional transfer instruction BHI transfers control to the statement labeled FINI if the unsigned contents of D1 are greater than or equal to the contents of D0. Otherwise, the next instruction, (MOVE.L D0,D1) is executed. At STORE, register D1 will always contain the larger of the two values.

The BHI instruction is one of fourteen conditional branch instructions. To change the program to operate on signed numbers, simply change the BHI to BGE:

```
-
-
CMP.L   D0,D1
BGE     STORE
-
-
```

You can use the following table to determine which conditionals to use when performing signed and unsigned comparisons:

Compare Condition	Signed	Unsigned
greater than or equal	BGE	BCC
greater than	BGT	BHI
equal	BEQ	BEQ
not equal	BNE	BNE
less than or equal	BLE	BLS
less than	BLT	BCS

Note that the same instructions are used for signed and unsigned addition, subtraction, or comparison; however, the comparison operations are different.

The branch conditionally instructions are an example of program counter relative addressing. In other words, if the branch condition is satisfied, control will be transferred to an address relative to the current value of the program counter. The MC68000 permits two sizes of relative displacement, either 8-bit or 16-bit. Since the displacement is a two's complement byte displacement, and the displacement is from the program counter after it has been incremented, the branch instructions permit a maximum backward reference of either 126 or 32766 bytes, or a maximum forward reference of either 128 or 32768 bytes.

Dealing with compares and branches is an important part of programming the MC68000. Don't confuse the sense of the CMP instruction. **After a compare, the relation tested is:**

DESTINATION condition **SOURCE.**

For example, if the condition is "less than," then you test for destination less than source. Become familiar with all of the conditions and their meanings. Unsigned compares are very useful when comparing two addresses.

4-7. 64-BIT ADDITION

Purpose: Add the contents of two 64-bit variables VALUE1 (at location 6000) and VALUE2 (at location 6008). Store the result in RESULT (at location 6010).

Sample Problem:

```
Input:  VALUE1 - (6000) = 12A2
                 (6002) = E640   12A2E640F210123
                 (6004) = F210
                 (6006) = 0123
        VALUE2 - (6008) = 0010
                 (600A) = 19BF   001019BF40023F51
                 (600C) = 4002
                 (600E) = 3F51
Output: RESULT - (6010) = 12B3
                 (6012) = 0000   12B3000032124074
                 (6014) = 3212
                 (6016) = 4074
```

Program 4-7:

```
       00006000        DATA      EQU       $6000
       00004000        PROGRAM   EQU       $4000

       00006000                  ORG       DATA
006000 00000008        VALUE1    DS.L      2               FIRST VALUE
006008 00000008        VALUE2    DS.L      2               SECOND VALUE
006010 00000008        RESULT    DS.L      2               RESERVE 64 BITS FOR RESULT

       00004000                  ORG       PROGRAM

004000 4CF8000F6000 PGM_4_7      MOVEM.L   VALUE1,D0-D3    D0-D1 := VALUE1 AND D2-D3 := VALUE2
004006 D283                      ADD.L     D3,D1           ADD LEAST SIGNIFICANT LONG WORD
004008 D182                      ADDX.L    D2,D0           ADD MOST SIG. LONG WORD WITH EXTEND
00400A 48F800036010              MOVEM.L   D0-D1,RESULT    STORE 64 BIT ADDITION RESULT

004010 4E75                      RTS

                                 END       PGM_4_7
```

The usefulness of the Move Multiple (MOVEM) instruction is again demonstrated in this 128-bit transfer to data registers D0 through D3. The status register flags are not affected by the transfer. Both the Carry and Extend flags are affected by the ADD instruction. The condition of the Extend flag is used in the ADDX (Add with Extend) instruction to include in the addition the carry from the previous 32-bit addition operation.

4-8. TABLE OF FACTORIALS

Purpose: Calculate the factorial of the 8-bit variable VALUE at location 6010 from a table of factorials FTABLE which occupies memory locations 6000 through 600F. Store result in the 16-bit variable RESULT at location 6012. Assume VALUE has a value between 0 and 7.

Sample Problem:

```
Input:  FTABLE-   (6000) = 0000 0! = 1
                  (6002) = 0001 1! = 1
                  (6004) = 0002 2! = 2
                  (6006) = 0006 3! = 6
                  (6008) = 0018 4! = 24
                  (600A) = 0078 5! = 120
                  (600C) = 02D0 6! = 720
                  (600E) = 13B0 7! = 5040
        VALUE -   (6010) = 05
Output: RESULT -  (6012) = 0078 5! = 120
```

(All factorial values above are decimal, subscript 10.)

Program 4-8a:

```
       00006000  DATA      EQU      $6000
       00004000  PROGRAM   EQU      $4000

       00006000            ORG      DATA

                 * TABLE OF FACTORIALS

006000 0001      FTABLE    DC       1                  0! := 1
006002 0001                DC       1                  1! := 1
006004 0002                DC       2                  2! := 2
006006 0006                DC       6                  3! := 6
006008 0018                DC       24                 4! := 24
00600A 0078                DC       120                5! := 120
00600C 02D0                DC       720                6! := 720
00600E 13B0                DC       5040               7! := 5040

006010 00000001  VALUE     DS.B     1                  DETERMINE FACTORIAL FOR THIS VALUE
006011 00000001            DS.B     1                  ALIGNMENT STORAGE
006012 00000002  RESULT    DS.W     1                  RESULT OF FACTORIAL

       00004000            ORG      PROGRAM

004000 4240      PGM_4_8A  CLR.W    D0                 D0(0:15) := 0
004002 10386010            MOVE.B   VALUE,D0           GET VALUE
004006 D000                ADD.B    D0,D0              D0(0:7) := 2 * VALUE
004008 307C6000            MOVEA.W  #FTABLE,A0         INITIALIZE POINTER TO FACTORIAL TABLE
00400C 31F000006012        MOVE.W   0(A0,D0),RESULT    STORE FACTORIAL RESULT

004012 4E75                RTS

                           END      PGM_4_8A
```

The approach to this table lookup problem, as implemented in Program 4-8*a*, demonstrates the use of the address register indirect addressing mode with index. The first two instructions, CLR and MOVE, load the index register D0 with the contents of

VALUE. The CLR instruction is required since the data size of VALUE is byte and the index register size used in this addressing mode is either word or long word. The MC68000 allows either a data register or an address register to be used as the index register.

The Move Address (MOVEA) instruction initializes address register A0 with the address of the factorial table. All 32 bits of the address register are affected by the move regardless of the instruction's data size. When the data size is word, as in Program 4-8*a*, the source operand is sign-extended to 32 bits.

The actual calculation of the entry in the table is determined by the first operand of the MOVE.W instruction. The long word contents of address register A0 are added to the sign-extended word contents of data register D0 to form the effective address used to address the table entry. When D0 is used in this manner, it is referred to as an index register. As in most MC68000 addressing modes, the usage of an address or data register in determining the effective address does not alter the contents of the register. The direct, postincrement, and predecrement addressing modes are exceptions to this rule.

The address register indirect with index mode permits either the 16-bit or 32-bit contents of the index register to be used in the calculation of the effective address. The size of the index register to be used is specified by the size suffix of the index register operand specification. As in the specification of the instruction size, the default suffix is '.W' or word. Why can't the suffix .L be used for index register D0 in Program 4-8*a*?

In addition to allowing the effective address to be determined by the contents of the address and index registers, the address register indirect with index mode also permits a small displacement. The displacement field allows for an 8-bit value. However, like the 16-bit index, this displacement is sign-extended. Thus, displacements of from −126 bytes to +129 bytes are possible.

Program 4-8b:

```
       00006000         DATA      EQU      $6000
       00004000         PROGRAM   EQU      $4000

       00006000                   ORG      DATA

                        *  TABLE OF FACTORIALS

006000 0001             FTABLE    DC       1                    0! := 1
006002 0001                       DC       1                    1! := 1
006004 0002                       DC       2                    2! := 2
006006 0006                       DC       6                    3! := 6
006008 0018                       DC       24                   4! := 24
00600A 0078                       DC       120                  5! := 120
00600C 02D0                       DC       720                  6! := 720
00600E 13B0                       DC       5040                 7! := 5040

006010 00000001         VALUE     DS.B     1                    DETERMINE FACTORIAL FOR THIS VALUE
006011 00000001                   DS.B     1                    ALIGNMENT STORAGE
006012 00000002         RESULT    DS.W     1                    RESULT OF FACTORIAL

       00004000                   ORG      PROGRAM

004000 4240             PGM_4_8B  CLR.W    D0                   D0(0:15) := 0
004002 10386010                   MOVE.B   VALUE,D0             GET VALUE
004006 D000                       ADD.B    D0,D0                D0(0:7) := 2 * VALUE
004008 3040                       MOVEA.W  D0,A0                MOVE TABLE OFFSET TO ADDRESS REG
00400A 31E860006012               MOVE.W   FTABLE(A0),RESULT    STORE FACTORIAL RESULT

004010 4E75                       RTS

                                  END      PGM_4_8B
```

Program 4-8*b* performs the same function as Program 4-8*a* except it demonstrates the use of another addressing mode – it uses address register indirect with displacement addressing. In this addressing mode, the effective address of the operand is the sum of the address register and the sign-extended 16-bit displacement. The displacement is stored in the extension word following the instruction in program memory.

In Program 4-8*b*, the "displacement" is actually the base of the table, while the address register is the offset into the table. It is very important to remember that the 16-bit displacement is sign-extended when used. Therefore, if FTABLE had been located at any address of 8000_{16} or higher, the sign extension of bit 15 (=1) would cause an address of $FF8000_{16}$ through $FFFFFF_{16}$ to be loaded as the table base address. Thus, for example, Program 4-8*b* would not work if FTABLE were located at address 015000_{16}. This method of using the "displacement" as a base address is only useful in the address range of 0-$7FFF_{16}$ or $FF8000_{16}$ through $FFFFFF_{16}$.

Program 4-8*b* usage of address register indirect with displacement addressing is not a typical example of this addressing mode. Generally, the address register will contain the address of a table or data structure while the displacement will represent a fixed offset from the base of the table or structure.

PROBLEMS

4-1. 64-BIT DATA TRANSFER

Purpose: Move the contents of memory locations 6000 through 6006 to locations 6800 through 6806.

Sample Problem:

```
 Input:  (6000) = 3E2A
         (6002) = 42A1
         (6004) = 21F2
         (6006) = 60A0
Output:  (6800) = 3E2A
         (6802) = 42A1
         (6804) = 21F2
         (6806) = 60A0
```

4-2. 16-BIT SUBTRACTION

Purpose: Subtract the contents of the 16-bit variable VALUE1 at location 6000 from the contents of the 16-bit variable VALUE2 at location 6002 and store the result back in VALUE1.

Sample Problem:

```
 Input:  VALUE1 -  (6000) = 3977
         VALUE2 -  (6002) = 2182
Output:  VALUE1 -  (6000) = 17F5
```

4-3. SHIFT RIGHT THREE BITS

Purpose: Shift the contents of the 16-bit variable VALUE1 at location 6000 right three bits. Clear the three most significant bit positions.

Sample Problem:

a. Input: VALUE1 - (6000) = 415D
Output: VALUE1 - (6000) = 082B

b. Input: VALUE1 - (6000) = C15D
Output: VALUE1 - (6000) = 182B

4-4. WORD ASSEMBLY

Purpose: Combine the low four bits of each of the four consecutive bytes beginning at location 6000 into one 16-bit word. The value at 6000 goes into the most significant nibble of the result; the value at 6003 becomes the least significant nibble. Store the result in location 6004.

Sample Problems:

Input: (6000) = 0C
(6001) = 02
(6002) = 06
(6003) = 09
Output: (6004) = C269

4-5. FIND SMALLEST OF THREE NUMBERS

Purpose: Locations 6000, 6002, and 6004 each contain an unsigned number. Store the smallest of these numbers in location 6006.

Sample Problem:

Input: (6000) = 9125
(6002) = 102C
(6004) = 7040
Output: (6006) = 102C

4-6. SUM OF SQUARES

Purpose: Calculate the squares of the contents of word VALUE1 at location 6000 and word VALUE2 at 6002 and add them together. Place the result into the long word RESULT at location 6004. Use signed arithmetic.

Sample Problem:

Input: VALUE1 - (6000) = 0007
VALUE2 - (6002) = 0032
Output: RESULT - (6004) = 000009F5

That is, $7^2 + 50^2 = 49 + 2500 = 2549$ (decimal)
$7^2 + 32^2 = 31 + 9C4 = 9F5$ (hexadecimal)

Sample Answer:

```
MOVE.W   VALUE1,D0
MULS.W   VALUE1,D0
MOVE.W   VALUE2,D1
MULS.W   VALUE2,D1
ADD.L    D0,D1
MOVE.L   D1,RESULT
```

4-7. SHIFT LEFT VARIABLE NUMBER OF BITS

Purpose: Shift the contents of the word VALUE at memory location 6000 left. The number of positions to shift is contained in the word COUNT at memory location 6002. Assume that the shift count is less than 32. The low-order bits should be cleared.

Sample Problems:

a.	Input:	(6000) = 182B	
		(6002) = 0003	shift left 3 positions
	Output:	(6000) = C158	
b.	Input:	(6000) = 182B	
		(6002) = 0010	shift left 16 positions
	Output:	(6000) = 0000	

Sample Answer:

```
MOVEM.W   VALUE,D0/D1
LSL.W     D1,D0
MOVE.W    D0,VALUE
```

5

Simple Program Loops

The program loop is the basic structure that forces the CPU to repeat a sequence of instructions. Loops have four sections:

1. **The initialization section,** which establishes the starting values of counters, pointers, and other variables.
2. **The processing section,** where the actual data manipulation occurs. This is the section that does the work.
3. **The loop control section,** which updates counters and pointers for the next iteration.
4. **The concluding section,** that may be needed to analyze and store the results.

The computer performs Sections 1 and 4 only once, while it may perform Sections 2 and 3 many times. Therefore, the execution time of the loop depends mainly on the execution time of Sections 2 and 3. Those sections should execute as quickly as possible, while the execution times of Sections 1 and 4 have less effect on overall program speed.

Figure 5-1 and 5-2 contain two alternative flowcharts for a typical program loop. Following the flowchart in Figure 5-1 results in the computer always executing the processing section at least once. On the other hand, the computer may not execute the processing section in Figure 5-2 at all. The order of operations in Figure 5-1 is more natural, but the order in Figure 5-2 is often more efficient and eliminates the problem of the computer going through the processing sequence once even where there is no data for it to handle.

The computer can use the loop structure to process large sets of data (usually called "arrays"). The simplest way to use one sequence of instructions to handle an array of data is to have the program increment a register (usually an index register or

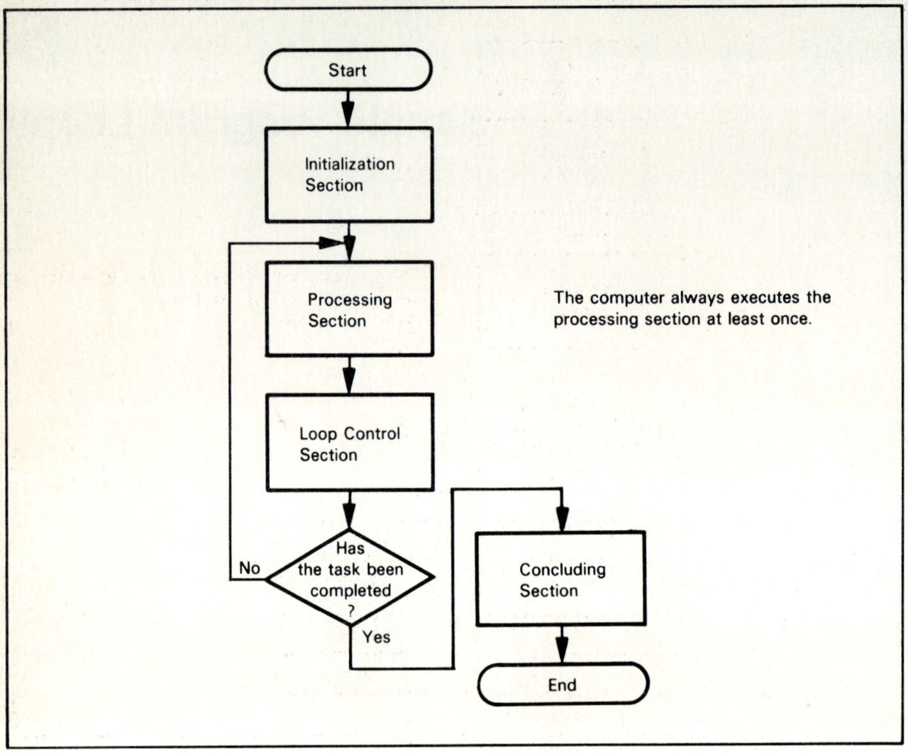

Figure 5-1. Flowchart of a Program Loop

stack pointer) after each iteration. Then the register will contain the address of the next element in the array when the computer repeats the sequence of instructions. The computer can then handle arrays of any length with a single program.

Register indirect addressing is the key to processing arrays with the MC68000 microprocessor, since that mode allows you to vary the actual address of the data (the "effective address") by changing the contents of a register. In the absolute addressing modes, the instruction completely determines the effective address; that address is therefore fixed if program memory is read-only.

The MC68000's autoincrementing mode is particularly convenient for processing arrays since it automatically updates the address register for the next iteration. No additional instruction is necessary. You can even have an automatic increment by 2 or 4 if the array contains 16-bit or 32-bit data or addresses.

Although our examples show the processing of arrays with autoincrementing (adding 1, 2, or 4 after each iteration), **the procedure is equally valid with autodecrementing** (subtracting 1, 2, or 4 before each iteration). Many programmers find moving backward through an array somewhat awkward and difficult to follow, but it is more efficient in many situations. The computer obviously does not know backward from forward. **The programmer, however, must remember that the MC68000 increments an address register after using it but decrements an address register before using it.** This

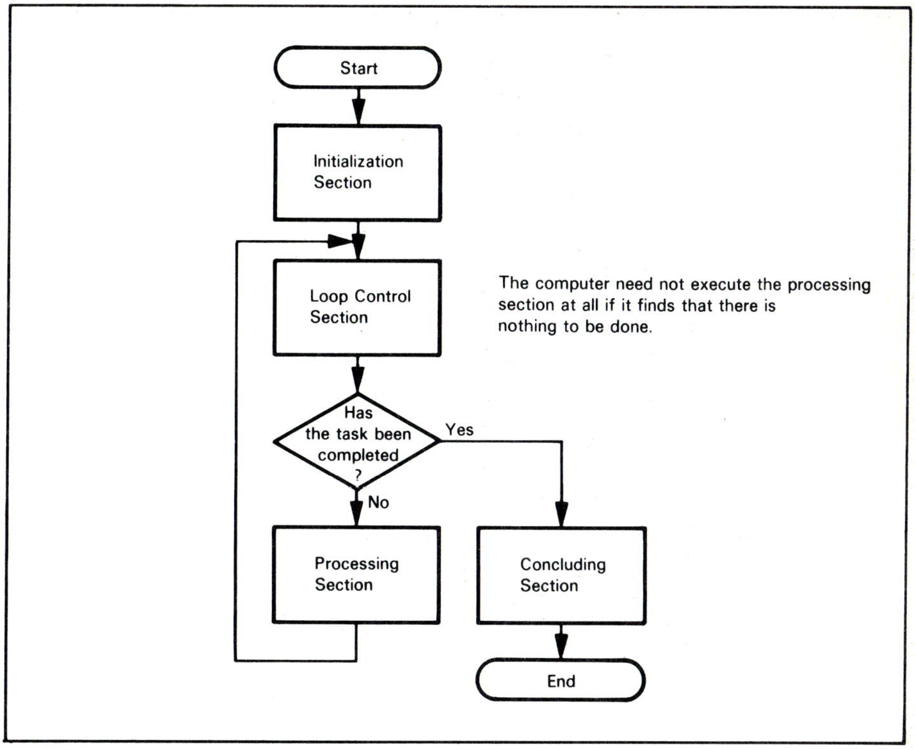

Figure 5-2. An Alternative for a Program Loop

difference affects initialization as follows:

1. When moving forward through an array (autoincrementing), start the address register at the lowest address occupied by the array.
2. When moving backward through an array (autodecrementing), start the address register one step (1, 2, or 4) beyond the highest address occupied by the array.

PROGRAM EXAMPLES

5-1. 16-BIT SUM OF DATA

Purpose: Calculate the sum of a series of numbers. The length of the series (in words) is defined by the variable LENGTH at location 6000. The starting address of the series is contained in the long-word variable START at location 6002. Store the sum in the variable TOTAL at location 6006. Assume that the sum is a 16-bit number so that you can ignore carries.

Sample Problem:

```
Input:  LENGTH  -  (6000)  =  0003
        START   -  (6002)  =  00005000
                   (5000)  =  2040
                   (5002)  =  1C22
                   (5004)  =  0242
Output: TOTAL   -  (6006)  =  (5000) + (5002) + (5004)
                           =  2040 + 1C22 + 0242
                           =  3EA4
```

Flowchart 5-1:

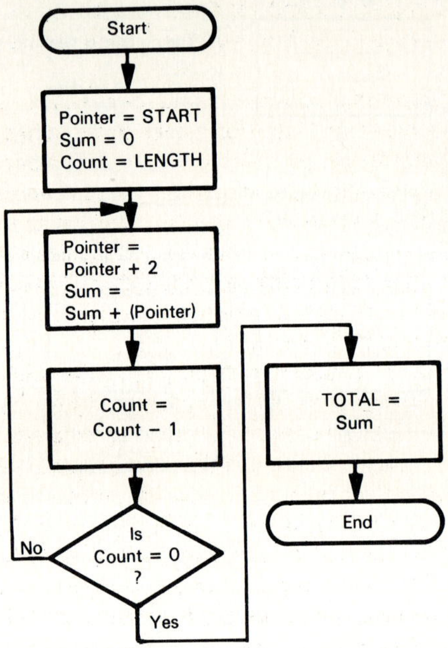

Program 5-1a:

```
       00006000   DATA      EQU      $6000
       00004000   PROGRAM   EQU      $4000

       00006000             ORG      DATA
006000 00000002   LENGTH    DS.W     1           NUMBER OF DATA ELEMENTS
006002 00000004   START     DS.L     1           ADDRESS OF DATA ELEMENTS
006006 00000002   TOTAL     DS.W     1           SUM OF DATA ELEMENTS

       00004000             ORG      PROGRAM

004000 20786002   PGM_5_1A  MOVEA.L  START,A0    INITIALIZE POINTER REGISTER
004004 7000                 MOVEQ    #0,D0       INITIALIZE SUM TO ZERO
004006 32386000             MOVE.W   LENGTH,D1   INITIALIZE ELEMENT COUNT

00400A D058       LOOP      ADD.W    (A0)+,D0    SUM NEXT ELEMENT
00400C 5341                 SUBQ.W   #1,D1       UPDATE ELEMENT COUNT
00400E 66FA                 BNE      LOOP        IF COUNT NOT ZERO THEN GOTO LOOP

004010 31C06006             MOVE.W   D0,TOTAL    STORE SUMMATION

004014 4E75                 RTS

                            END      PGM_5_1A
```

The initialization section of the program consists of the first three instructions, which set the data pointer, sum, and counter to the appropriate initial values. In this program we encounter the first example of parameter passing where the parameters include an address (the contents of START) along with such parameters as size or count (LENGTH) which we have encountered in previous programs. The first MOVE instruction in the program loads the beginning address (from location START) of the data elements into address register A0. Once again we will defer a detailed discussion of parameter passing until Chapters 10 and 11; at this point, you must simply ensure that the required starting address is in the long word at location 6002 prior to attempting to execute this program.

Frequently in programming, you must initialize a data register with a small data value as we have done in Program 5-1*a*. For values in the range −128 to +127, you should use the MOVEQ instruction. The MOVEQ instruction encodes the value within the instruction word, thus eliminating an additional operand word that would otherwise be needed to define the initial value. You should note that the MOVEQ instruction, unlike most other MC68000 instructions, only has a data size of long word. We could have used the CLR instruction to initialize the sum to zero; both the MOVEQ and CLR instructions require the same number of bytes and microprocessor cycles. In what cases is the use of the CLR instruction preferred?

The processing section of Program 5-1*a* consists of the single instruction ADD.W (A0)+,D0 which adds the contents of the memory location addressed by address register A0 to the contents of data register D0. This instruction does all the real work of the program and is the first example of the address register indirect with postincrement mode of addressing. You probably noticed that the program contained no explicit instruction to update the address register to the next word in the series. Instead, the address register is implicitly updated by execution of the ADD instruction. Thus, this instruction is also part of the loop control section. In the postincrement addressing mode, the processor increments the contents of the address register after the address register has been used to determine the effective address of the data references. The contents of the address register are incremented by either 1, 2, or 4 depending on the size of the data being referenced. An increment of 1 is used for byte references, 2 for word references and 4 for long word references. Thus, the instruction ADD.W (A0)+,D0 results in the contents of address register A0 being incremented by 2. This addressing mode is extremely useful when you are performing operations on data tables.

The loop control section of the program consists of the single instruction SUBQ.W, since the instruction ADD.W (A0)+,D0 updates the pointer automatically. The SUBQ instruction decrements the counter that keeps track of the number of iterations the processor has left to perform. The Subtract Quick (SUBQ) instruction is another instruction which you'll find useful in reducing the size of your programs. Like the MOVEQ instruction, SUBQ allows the encoding of small data values within a single instruction word. Unlike the MOVEQ instruction, SUBQ only allows data values in the range from 1 to 8. However, you can use the SUBQ instruction to operate on byte, word or long word data and SUBQ can be used to operate on memory directly, or on any address register as well as a data register.

The instruction BNE causes a branch if the Zero (Z) flag is reset (that is, if the result of decrementing D1 *was not* zero). The offset part of the BNE instruction is a two's complement number, determined by the distance between the destination and the instruction. In this case, the distance is from memory location 4010 (the address of the BNE instruction+2) to memory location 400A (the destination). So the offset (using two's complement arithmetic) is:

```
      400A              400A
  -(400E+2)    =      +BFF0
                      -----
                       FFFA
```

The offset of $FA corresponds to a negative six (−6) bytes which is the number of bytes to the label LOOP from the location of the branch instruction plus two. This single byte sign-extended form of the branch instruction allows offsets in the range −63 words to +64 words from the location of the branch instruction. The address range is described in words rather than bytes since all MC68000 instructions must start on a word boundary and have sizes which are word multiples. Another form of the branch instruction allows a 16-bit sign-extended offset, thus providing a branching range of −16383 words to +16384 words. When you use this form, an additional operand word is required.

If the Zero flag is 1 (that is, if the result of decrementing D1 *was* zero), the processor continues its normal sequence. Thus the result of executing BNE is:

```
         LOOP if the result of decrementing D1 is zero
PC =
         (PC) + 2 if the result of decrementing D1 is zero
```

The extra 2, as usual, comes from the two bytes occupied by the BNE instruction itself. This is true for either form of the branch instruction since the PC is incremented by two in either case, before adding the offset. With the 16-bit offset, the PC is incremented by another two if the branch is not taken. The result is the same for both the 8-bit and the 16-bit offset; the instruction following the conditional branch will be executed if the test fails.

Most programmers make computer loops count down rather than up so that they can use the setting of the Zero flag as an exit condition. Remember that the Zero flag is 1 if the most recent result was zero and 0 if that result was not zero. Try rewriting the program so that it loads register D1 with zero initially and increments it after each iteration. Which approach is more efficient?

Program 5-1*a* executes correctly for all initial values unless the number of elements is zero. This problem is solved by modifying Program 5-1*a* to include a specific check for this condition prior to the loop processing as shown in Program 5-1*b*.

Program 5-1b:

```
       00006000   DATA     EQU      $6000
       00004000   PROGRAM  EQU      $4000

       00006000            ORG      DATA
006000 00000002   LENGTH   DS.W     1              NUMBER OF DATA ELEMENTS
006002 00000004   START    DS.L     1              ADDRESS OF DATA ELEMENTS
006006 00000002   TOTAL    DS.W     1              SUM OF DATA ELEMENTS

       00004000            ORG      PROGRAM

004000 20786002   PGM_5_1B MOVEA.L  START,A0       INITIALIZE POINTER REGISTER
004004 7000                MOVEQ    #0,D0          INITIALIZE SUM TO ZERO
004006 32386000            MOVE.W   LENGTH,D1      INITIALIZE ELEMENT COUNT

00400A 6706                BEQ.S    DONE           IF LENGTH = 0 THEN DONE
```

```
00400C D058          LOOP      ADD.W     (A0)+,D0          SUM NEXT ELEMENT
00400E 5341                    SUBQ.W    #1,D1             UPDATE ELEMENT COUNT
004010 66FA                    BNE       LOOP              IF COUNT NOT ZERO THEN GOTO LOOP

004012 31C06006      DONE      MOVE.W    D0,TOTAL          STORE SUMMATION

004016 4E75                    RTS

                               END       PGM_5_1B
```

In this program, the single instruction BEQ is used to check for number of elements equal to zero, and it will cause the program's flow of control to be transferred to DONE if there are no numbers in the series. You may have noticed that the BEQ branch instruction had a suffix of ".S". This suffix is used by the assembler to determine which offset form of the branch instruction should be used. This suffix is only necessary when the label in the operand field is a forward reference and the assembler default is the long offset form.

The order in which the processor executes instructions is often very important. In Program 5-1*b*, BEQ must come immediately after the MOVE.W LENGTH,D1 instruction; otherwise, an intervening instruction might change the Zero flag. Similarly, the SUBQ instruction must be followed immediately by the BNE instruction.

5-2. 32-BIT SUM OF DATA

Purpose: Calculate the sum of a series of unsigned 16-bit numbers. The length of the series (in words) is defined by the variable LENGTH at location 6000. The starting address of the series is contained in the long-word variable START at location 6002. Store the sum in the long word (32-bit) variable TOTAL at location 6006. Take carries into account.

Sample Problem:

```
Input:   LENGTH  - (6000) = 0003
         START   - (6002) = 00005000
                   (5000) = 2040
                   (5002) = 1C22
                   (5004) = E242
Output:  TOTAL   - (6006) = (5000)+(5002)+(5004)
                          = 2040 + 1C22 + E242
                          = 00011EA4
```

Program 5-2a:

```
       00006000      DATA      EQU       $6000
       00004000      PROGRAM   EQU       $4000


       00006000                ORG       DATA
006000 00000002      LENGTH    DS.W      1                 NUMBER OF DATA ELEMENTS
006002 00000004      START     DS.L      1                 ADDRESS OF DATA ELEMENTS
006006 00000004      TOTAL     DS.L      1                 SUM OF DATA ELEMENTS
       00010000      CARRYBIT  EQU       $10000            CARRY BIT VALUE

       00004000                ORG       PROGRAM

004000 20786002      PGM_5_2A  MOVEA.L   START,A0          INITIALIZE POINTER REGISTER
004004 7000                    MOVEQ     #0,D0             INITIALIZE SUM TO ZERO
004006 32386000                MOVE.W    LENGTH,D1         INITIALIZE ELEMENT COUNT

00400A 670E                    BEQ.S     DONE              IF LENGTH = 0 THEN DONE
```

```
00400C D058          LOOP     ADD.W    (A0)+,D0          SUM NEXT ELEMENT
00400E 6406                   BCC.S    LOOPTEST          IF CARRY = 0 THEN GOTO LOOPTEST

004010 068000010000           ADDI.L   #CARRYBIT,D0      ...ELSE ADD 16-BIT CARRY

004016 5341          LOOPTEST SUBQ.W   #1,D1             UPDATE ELEMENT COUNT
004018 66F2                   BNE      LOOP              IF COUNT NOT ZERO THEN GOTO LOOP

00401A 21C06006      DONE     MOVE.L   D0,TOTAL          STORE SUMMATION

00401E 4E75                   RTS

                              END      PGM_5_2A
```

Flowchart 5-2:

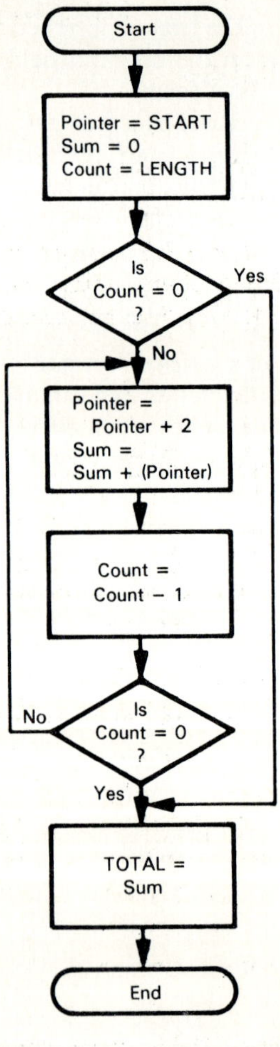

This program differs only slightly from the 16-bit addition program. Since a 32-bit sum is to be generated, we must now handle the carry generated by the ADD instruction. The two new instructions (BCC and ADDI) test for the carry during addition and add the carry bit back into the sum when a carry occurs.

The instruction BCC causes a jump to memory location LOOPTEST if the Carry (C) flag = 0. Thus, if there is no carry from the 16-bit addition, the program jumps around the statement that increments the most significant 16 bits of the sum. The relative offset for BCC LOOPTEST is:

```
  4016              4016
-(400E +2)   =    -4010
                  -----
                     06
```

The relative offset for BNE LOOP is:

```
  400C              400C
-(4018 +2)   =    -401A
                  -----
                  - 0E  =  FFF2
```

The relative offset for BEQ.S DONE is:

```
  401A              401A
-(400A+2)    =    -400C
                  -----
                     0E
```

The long word form of the ADD instruction might simplify this program. However, since the series consists of 16-bit values we must do some extra work to make these values into long words. Program 5-2*b* accomplishes this.

Program 5-2b:

```
       00006000     DATA     EQU      $6000
       00004000     PROGRAM  EQU      $4000

       00006000              ORG      DATA
006000 00000002     LENGTH   DS.W     1             NUMBER OF DATA ELEMENTS
006002 00000004     START    DS.L     1             ADDRESS OF DATA ELEMENTS
006006 00000004     TOTAL    DS.L     1             SUM OF DATA ELEMENTS

       00004000              ORG      PROGRAM

004000 20786002     PGM_5_2B MOVEA.L  START,A0      INITIALIZE POINTER REGISTER
004004 7000                  MOVEQ    #0,D0         INITIALIZE SUM TO ZERO
004006 2400                  MOVE.L   D0,D2         CLEAR TEMPORARY REGISTER
004008 32386000              MOVE.W   LENGTH,D1     INITIALIZE ELEMENT COUNT

00400C 6708                  BEQ.S    DONE          IF LENGTH = 0 THEN DONE

00400E 3418         LOOP     MOVE.W   (A0)+,D2      D2[15-0] := DATA ELEMENT
004010 D082                  ADD.L    D2,D0         ADD DATA ELEMENT TO SUM
004012 5341                  SUBQ.W   #1,D1         UPDATE ELEMENT COUNT
004014 66F8                  BNE      LOOP          IF COUNT NOT ZERO THEN GOTO LOOP

004016 21C06006     DONE     MOVE.L   D0,TOTAL      STORE SUMMATION

00401A 4E75                  RTS

                             END      PGM_5_2B
```

We clear the most significant 16-bits of register D2 during the initialization section; since these bits will never change, we don't need to clear them each time through the loop. The 16-bit values from memory are then loaded into the low-order 16 bits of D2 and then a long add (ADD.L) is used to add the 32-bit contents of D2 to register D0.

Because the purpose said the values were unsigned numbers, the high-order 16 bits will always be zero.

Note that we need not check for carry in the loop processing section since, with a 32-bit operation, any carry from the low-order 16 bits will automatically be propagated into the high-order portion of D0. The changes in the loop processing section reduced the number of instructions in the loop and perhaps make the program easier to understand. The number of bytes in the loop is also reduced. However, does this make the loop execute faster? The processing section in Program 5-2*a* takes 18 or 36 cycles:

```
ADD       8 cycles
BCC       10 cycles (12 if branch not taken)
ADDI.L    (16) cycles (not always executed)
          ------------
          18 (36) cycles (if BCC.S used - 18 (32) cycles)
```

The second version takes 16 cycles:

```
MOVE      8 cycles
ADD.L     (8) cycles
          ---------
          16 cycles
```

The second version is both smaller and faster. However, you may not always find this to be the case. A single more powerful instruction may take longer to execute than two or more simpler instructions that perform the same task. Can you find an example of this?

5-3. NUMBER OF NEGATIVE ELEMENTS

Purpose: Determine the number of negative elements in a series of signed 16-bit numbers. Negative elements are identified by a 1 in the most significant bit position (bit 15). The length of the series is defined by the variable LENGTH at location 6000. The starting address of the series is defined by the long word variable START at location 6002. Store the number of negative elements in the variable TOTAL at location 6006.

Sample Problem:

```
Input:  LENGTH  -  (6000)  =  0003
        START   -  (6002)  =  00005000
                   (5000)  =  F1DC
                   (5002)  =  7E0A
                   (5004)  =  824B
Output: TOTAL   -  (6006)  =  0002, since memory locations 5000 and
                              5004 contain negative numbers
```

Program 5-3:

```
       00006000    DATA     EQU      $6000
       00004000    PROGRAM  EQU      $4000

       00006000             ORG      DATA
006000 00000002    LENGTH   DS.W     1                NUMBER OF DATA ELEMENTS
006002 00000004    START    DS.L     1                ADDRESS OF DATA ELEMENTS
006006 00000002    TOTAL    DS.W     1                SUM OF DATA ELEMENTS

       00004000             ORG      PROGRAM

004000 20786002    PGM_5_3  MOVEA.L  START,A0         INITIALIZE POINTER REGISTER
004004 7000                 MOVEQ    #0,D0            NNEG := 0
004006 32386000             MOVE.W   LENGTH,D1        INITIALIZE ELEMENT COUNT
```

```
00400A 670A                BEQ.S    DONE          IF LENGTH = 0 THEN DONE

00400C 4A58      LOOP      TST.W    (A0)+         TEST DATA ELEMENT
00400E 6A02                BPL.S    LOOPTEST      IF  > 0 THEN GOTO LOOPTEST

004010 5240                ADDQ.W   #1,D0           ...ELSE NNEG := NNEG + 1

004012 5341      LOOPTEST  SUBQ.W   #1,D1           UPDATE ELEMENT COUNT
004014 66F6                BNE      LOOP          IF COUNT NOT ZERO THEN GOTO LOOP

004016 31C06006  DONE      MOVE.W   D0,TOTAL      STORE NUMBER OF NEGATIVE ELEMENTS

00401A 4E75                RTS

                           END      PGM_5_3
```

Flowchart 5-3:

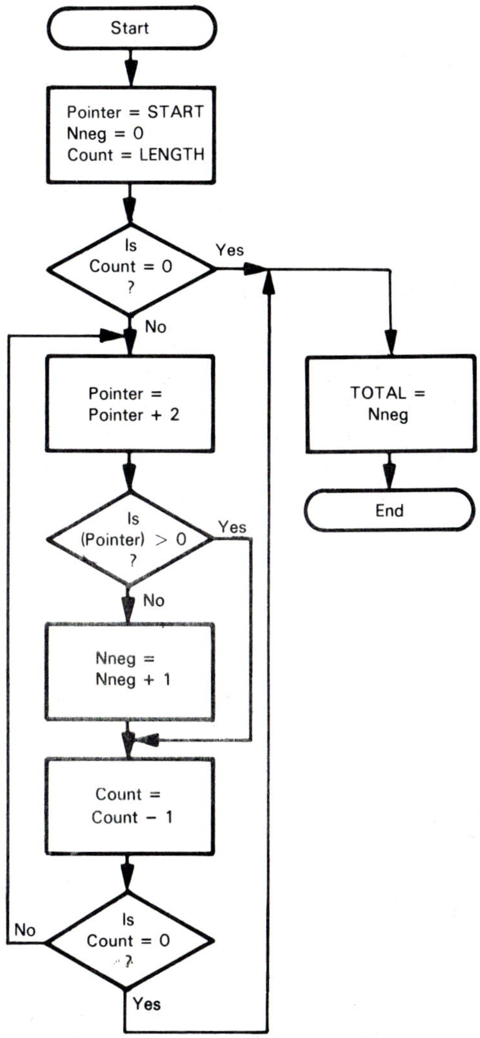

The TST instruction is used to determine if the next element in the series is a negative number. TST compares the operand with zero and sets the status flags accordingly. Thus, the operation of the TST instruction is essentially equivalent to:

```
SUBQ #0,(A0)+
```

Why should you use TST instead of SUBQ in cases like this? Because it provides clearer documentation.

While testing the operand, TST sets the Negative (N) and Zero (Z) flags according to the results of the comparison. The Carry (C) and Overflow (V) flags are always reset to zero.

The Negative (N) flag simply reflects the value of bit 15 of the most recent result. If you are using signed numbers, bit 15 is, in fact, the sign (0 for positive, 1 for negative); the mnemonics for Branch if Plus (BPL) and Branch if Minus (BMI) assume that you are using signed numbers. However, you can use equally well bit 15 for other purposes, such as the status of peripherals or other 1-bit data. In these cases you can still test bit 15 with BMI (bit 15 = 1) or BPL (bit 15 = 0); although the mnemonics no longer make sense, the operations work. The computer performs its operations without considering whether the user thinks they are sensible or meaningful. The interpretation of the results is the programmer's problem, not the computer's.

Negative signed numbers all have a most significant bit of 1 and thus are actually larger, when considered as unsigned numbers, than positive numbers.

In Program 5-3, the BPL (Branch if Plus) instruction causes a branch if the Negative flag is 0. Which other branch instructions could you use in place of BPL?

We could also replace:

```
TST (A0)+
BPL LOOPTEST
```

with

```
MOVE (A0)+,D3
BTST #15,D3
BEQ LOOPTEST
```

The BTST instruction tests a specific bit in the destination. If the bit is zero, the Zero (Z) flag is set; if the bit is one, the Zero (Z) flag is reset to zero. This instruction is most useful in testing bits other than the sign bit; for example, when you need to test the status of a peripheral device. Although the BTST instruction allows you to directly test the contents of memory, only bits within a single byte can be tested in this mode. How could you rewrite Program 5-3 so that BTST tests the most significant byte of a 16-bit element in memory?

5-4. FIND MAXIMUM VALUE

Purpose: Find the largest element in a series of 16-bit unsigned binary numbers. The length of the series is defined by the variable LENGTH at location 6000 and the starting address of the series is defined by the long word variable START at location 6002. Store the maximum (largest unsigned element) in the value MAXNUM at location 6006.

Sample Problem:

Input:	LENGTH	- (6000)	=	0004
	START	- (6002)	=	00005000
		(5000)	=	A48E
		(5002)	=	71AC
		(5004)	=	34F1
		(5006)	=	E57A
Output:	MAXNUM	- (6006)	=	E57A, since this is the largest of the four unsigned numbers.

Flowchart: 5-4a:

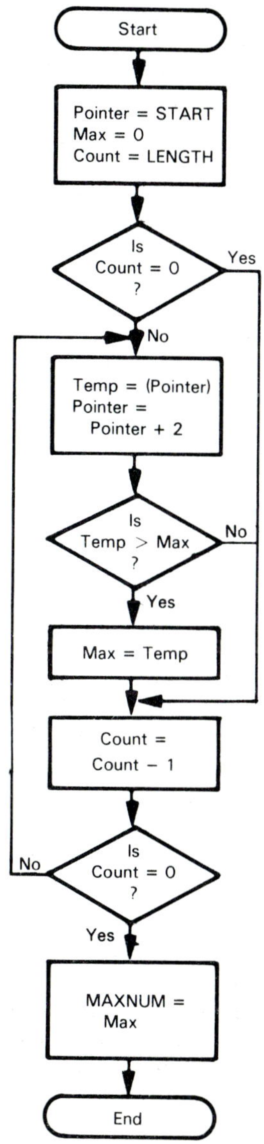

Program 5-4a:

```
         00006000    DATA      EQU      $6000
         00004000    PROGRAM   EQU      $4000

         00006000              ORG      DATA
006000   00000002    LENGTH    DS.W     1              NUMBER OF DATA ELEMENTS
006002   00000004    START     DS.L     1              ADDRESS OF DATA ELEMENTS
006006   00000002    MAXNUM    DS.W     1              MAXIMUM NUMBER IN SERIES

         00004000              ORG      PROGRAM

004000 20786002      PGM_5_4A MOVEA.L  START,A0       INITIALIZE POINTER REGISTER
004004 7000                   MOVEQ    #0,D0          MAX := 0
004006 32386000               MOVE.W   LENGTH,D1      INITIALIZE ELEMENT COUNT

00400A 670C                   BEQ.S    DONE           IF LENGTH = 0 THEN DONE

00400C 3418          LOOP     MOVE.W   (A0)+,D2       TEMP := NEXT DATA ELEMENT
00400E B042                   CMP.W    D2,D0          COMPARE TEMP WITH MAX, "MAX-TEMP" !
004010 6402                   BCC.S    LOOPTEST       IF MAX > OR = TEMP GOTO LOOPTEST

004012 3002                   MOVE.W   D2,D0          ...ELSE NEW MAX, MAX := TEMP

004014 5341          LOOPTEST SUBQ.W   #1,D1            UPDATE ELEMENT COUNT
004016 66F4                   BNE      LOOP           IF COUNT NOT ZERO THEN GOTO LOOP

004018 31C06006      DONE     MOVE.W   D0,MAXNUM      STORE MAXIMUM NUMBER IN SERIES

00401C 4E75                   RTS

                              END      PGM_5_4A
```

The first three instructions of this program form the initialization section.

In this program we take advantage of the fact that zero is the smallest unsigned binary number. If you make zero the initial estimate of the maximum, then the program will set the maximum to a larger value unless all elements in the array are zeros. The maximum will also be set to zero if the series contains no elements.

The two instruction sequence MOVE.W (A0)+,D2 and CMP.W D2,D0 compares the next element in the series with the current maximum value. The CMP instruction affects the Carry and Zero flags as follows (TEMP is the value of the current element and MAX is the current maximum value):

Carry = 0 if MAX > TEMP (Higher or Same)
Carry = 1 if MAX < TEMP (Lower)
Zero = 0 if MAX = TEMP (Not Equal)
Zero = 1 if MAX = TEMP (Equal)

The program uses the branch BCC (Carry Clear) instruction which tests both the Carry and Zero flags. If either flag is set, the program replaces the maximum with the current element using the instruction MOVE.W D2,D0. The branch instruction BHI could have been used instead of BCC and would have been easier to understand. Why is BCC a better choice of branch instructions?

The program does not work properly if the numbers are signed, because negative numbers all appear to be larger than positive numbers. You must use the Sign (Negative) flag instead of the Carry in the comparison. However, you must also consider the fact that two's complement overflow can affect the sign; that is, the magnitude of a signed result could overflow into the sign bit. The MC68000 has special instructions — BGT, BGE, BLE and BLT — which perform signed comparison branches and automatically handle two's complement overflow.

As we have seen before, the MC68000 allows for some operations to be performed directly on memory without requiring the use of an additional data register. Program 5-4*b* uses this feature to eliminate the MOVE.W (A0)+,D2 instruction in Program 5-4*a*.

Program 5-4b:

```
         00006000   DATA      EQU      $6000
         00004000   PROGRAM   EQU      $4000

         00006000             ORG      DATA
006000 00000002     LENGTH    DS.W     1            NUMBER OF DATA ELEMENTS
006002 00000004     START     DS.L     1            ADDRESS OF DATA ELEMENTS
006006 00000002     MAXNUM    DS.W     1            MAXIMUM NUMBER IN SERIES

         00004000             ORG      PROGRAM

004000 20786002     PGM_5_4B  MOVEA.L  START,A0     INITIALIZE POINTER REGISTER
004004 7000                   MOVEQ    #0,D0        MAX := 0
004006 32386000               MOVE.W   LENGTH,D1    INITIALIZE ELEMENT COUNT

00400A 670C                   BEQ.S    DONE         IF LENGTH = 0 THEN DONE

00400C B058         LOOP      CMP.W    (A0)+,D0     COMPARE DATA ELEMENT WITH MAX
00400E 6404                   BCC.S    LOOPTEST     IF MAX > OR = ELEMENT GOTO LOOPTEST

004010 3028FFFE               MOVE.W   -2(A0),D0    ...ELSE NEW MAX, MAX := ELEMENT

004014 5341         LOOPTEST  SUBQ.W   #1,D1        UPDATE ELEMENT COUNT
004016 66F4                   BNE      LOOP         IF COUNT NOT ZERO THEN GOTO LOOP

004018 31C06006     DONE      MOVE.W   D0,MAXNUM    STORE MAXIMUM NUMBER IN SERIES

00401C 4E75                   RTS

                              END      PGM_5_4B
```

Although the CMP.W (A0)+,D0 instruction appears to simplify this program, it does cause one slight problem — it increments register A0 while performing the compare. Now, when updating the maximum value, the new maximum is no longer in any data register or pointed to by any address register. The address register indirect with displacement addressing mode can be used to overcome this problem. By using a displacement of −2, we essentially back the pointer up to the element we just compared. The effective address for the instruction MOVE −2(A0),D0 is calculated as follows:

Effective Address of −2(A0) = (A0) −2

The contents of register A0 are not changed by this calculation.

At first glance CMP.W (A0)+,D0 may appear not to optimize the loop processing since the loop processing of Program 5-4*b* requires the same number of words as Program 5-4*a*. However, the execution cycles for program 5-4*a* are 17 or 20 cycles:

MOVE	8	cycles
CMP	4	cycles
BCC	5	cycles (4 if branch not taken)
MOVE	(4)	cycles (not always executed)
	17	(20) cycles

compared to 13 or 24 cycles for Program 5-4*b:*

CMP	8	cycles
BCC	5	cycles (4 if branch not taken)
MOVE	(12)	cycles (not always executed)
	13	(24) cycles

Although both programs require the same number of loop cycles to update the maximum, the second program is slightly more efficient when no update is required.

5-5. NORMALIZE A BINARY NUMBER

Purpose: Shift a 32-bit binary number until the most significant bit of the number is 1. The address of the number is defined by the long word variable NUMBER at location 6000. Store the normalized number (shifted number) in the variable NORMNUM at location 6004. Store the number of left shifts required in the byte variable SHIFTNUM at location 6008. If the number is zero, clear both variables NORMNUM and SHIFTNUM.

The processing is just like converting a number to a scientific notation; for example:

$$0.0057 \quad 5.7 \times 10^{-3}$$

Sample Problems:

```
a.   Input:  NUMBER   - (6000) = 00005000
                        (5000) = 30001000
    Output:  NORMNUM  - (6004) = C0004000
             SHIFTNUM - (6008) = 02
b.   Input:  NUMBER   - (6000) = 00005000
                        (5000) = 00000001
    Output:  NORMNUM  - (6004) = 80000000
             SHIFTNUM - (6008) = 1F
c.   Input:  NUMBER   - (6000) = 00005000
                        (5000) = 00000000
    Output:  NORMNUM  - (6004) = 00000000
             SHIFTNUM - (6008) = 00
d.   Input:  NUMBER   - (6000) = 00005000
                        (5000) = C1234567
    Output:  NORMNUM  - (6004) = C1234567
             SHIFTNUM - (6008) = 00
```

Program 5-5:

```
       00006000    DATA      EQU      $6000
       00004000    PROGRAM   EQU      $4000

       00006000              ORG      DATA
006000 00000004    NUMBER    DS.L     1              ADDRESS OF NUMBER TO BE NORMALIZED
006004 00000004    NORMNUM   DS.L     1              NORMALIZED NUMBER
006008 00000001    SHIFTNUM  DS.B     1              NUMBER OF SHIFT REQUIRED TO NORMALIZE

       00004000              ORG      PROGRAM

004000 7000        PGM_5_5   MOVEQ    #0,D0          INITIALIZE SHIFT COUNT
004002 20786000              MOVEA.L  NUMBER,A0      GET ADDRESS OF NUMBER TO NORMALIZE
004006 2210                  MOVE.L   (A0),D1        GET NUMBER TO BE NORMALIZED
004008 6F06                  BLE.S    DONE           IF ZERO OR NORMALIZED THEN DONE

00400A 5240        JUSTIFY   ADDQ.W   #1,D0          INCREMENT SHIFT COUNT
00400C E389                  LSL.L    #1,D1          SHIFT NUMBER 1 BIT TO THE LEFT
00400E 6AFA                  BPL      JUSTIFY        AGAIN IF MSB = 0

004010 11C06008    DONE      MOVE.B   D0,SHIFTNUM    STORE SHIFT COUNT
004014 21C16004              MOVE.L   D1,NORM        STORE NORMALIZED NUMBER

004018 4E75                  RTS

                             END      PGM_5_5
```

Flowchart 5-5:

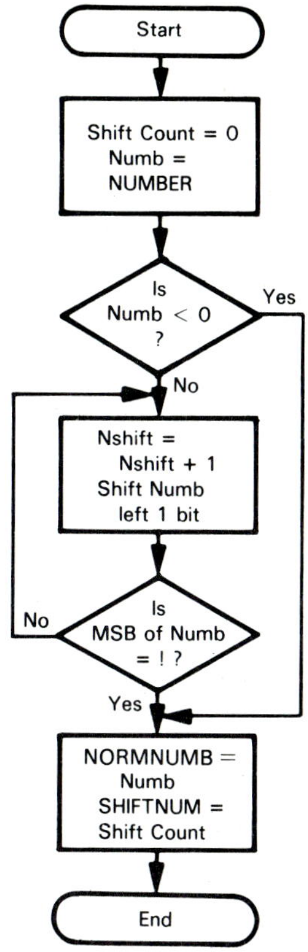

The BLE instruction performs both the test for number being zero and being already justified. The status conditions for the branch are set during the MOVE instruction which loads the number into data register D0. BLE causes a branch to DONE if the Zero flag is 1. If the number is already normalized, the most significant bit will be 1 and the Negative flag will be set by the MOVE. In this case, BLE causes a branch to DONE if the Negative flag is 1. Why can BLE be used to perform this last test, since the state of the Overflow (V) flag must also be taken into consideration when you use the BLE instruction?

LSL.L #1,D0 (Logical Shift Left Long) shifts the contents of the specified data register D0 left one bit and clears the least significant bit. The most significant bit ends up in the Carry flag and the old Carry value is lost. This use of LSL is equivalent to adding D0 to itself; the result is, of course, twice the original number.

BPL causes a branch to JUSTIFY if the Negative flag is 0. This condition may mean that the result was a positive number, or it may just mean that the most significant bit of the result was 0; the microprocessor simply performs the operation; only the programmer can provide the interpretation. Since the LSL instruction affects the state of the Carry flag, how could you modify this program to use BCC (Branch if Carry Clear) instead of BPL?

PROBLEMS

5-1. CHECKSUM OF DATA

Purpose: Calculate the checksum of a series of 8-bit numbers. The length of the series is defined by the variable LENGTH at location 6000. The starting address of the series is contained in the long-word variable START at location 6002. Store the checksum in the variable CHECKSUM at location 6006. The checksum is formed by Exclusive-ORing all the numbers in the list.

Note: Checksums are often used by paper tape and cassette systems to ensure that data has been correctly read. A checksum calculated when reading the data is compared to a checksum that is stored with the data on the tape. If the two checksums do not agree, the system will usually indicate an error, or automatically read the data again.

Sample Problem:

```
Input:  LENGTH   - (6000) = 0003
        START    - (6002) = 00005000
                   (5000) = 28
                   (5001) = 55
                   (5002) = 26
Output: CHECKSUM - (6006) = (5000)⊕(5001)⊕(5002)
                          = 28⊕55⊕26
                          =  01101000
                          = ⊕01010101
                            --------
                             01111101
                            ⊕00100110
                            --------
                             01011011
                          = 5B
```

5-2. NUMBER OF ZERO, POSITIVE, AND NEGATIVE NUMBERS

Purpose: Determine the number of zero, positive (most significant bit zero, but entire number not zero), and negative (most significant bit 1) elements in a series of signed 16-bit numbers. The length of the series is defined by the variable LENGTH at location 6000 and the starting address is defined by the contents of the long word variable START at location 6002. Place the number of negative elements in variable NUMNEG at location 6006, the number of zero elements in variable NUMZERO at location 6008, and the number of positive elements in variable NUMPOS at location 600A.

Sample Problem:

```
Input:  LENGTH - (6000) = 0006
        START  - (6002) = 00005000
                 (5000) = 7602
                 (5002) = 8D48
                 (5004) = 2120
                 (5006) = 0000
                 (5008) = E605
                 (500A) = 0004
```

Output: 2 negative, 1 zero, 3 positive, so

NUMNEG	-	(6006)	=	0002
NUMZERO	-	(6008)	=	0001
NUMPOS	-	(600A)	=	0003

5-3. FIND MINIMUM

Purpose: Find the smallest element in a series of unsigned byte data. The length of the series is defined by the variable LENGTH at location 6000 and the starting address of the series is contained in the long-word variable START at location 6002. Store the minimum byte value in the variable NUMMIN at location 6006.

Sample Problem:

Input:	LENGTH	-	(6000)	=	0005
	START	-	(6002)	=	00005000
			(5000)	=	65
			(5001)	=	79
			(5002)	=	15
			(5003)	=	E3
			(5004)	=	72
Output:	NUMMIN	-	(6006)	=	15, since this is the smallest of five unsigned numbers.

5-4. COUNT 1 BITS

Purpose: Determine the number of bits which are one in the 16-bit variable NUM at location 6000, and store the result in the variable NUMBITS at location 6002.

Sample Problem:

Input: NUM −(6000) = B794 = 1011011110010100
Output: NUMBITS − (6002) = 09

5-5. FIND ELEMENT WITH MOST 1 BITS

Purpose: Determine which element in a series of 16-bit numbers has the largest number of bits that are one. The length of the series is defined by the variable LENGTH at location 6000 and the starting address of the series is contained in the long-word variable START at location 6002. Store the value with the most 1 bits in the variable NUM at location 6006. If two or more elements have the same number of 1 bits, use the value of the earliest element in the series.

Sample Problem:

Input:	LENGTH	-	(6000)	=	0005
	START	-	(6002)	=	00005000
			(5000)	=	6779 = 0110011101111001
			(5002)	=	15E3 = 0001010111100011
			(5004)	=	68F2 = 0110100011110010
			(5006)	=	8700 = 1000011100000000
			(5008)	=	592A = 0101100100101010
Output:	NUM	-	(6006)	=	6779, since this element is the first element in the series to have ten bits = 1

6

Character-Coded Data

Microprocessors often handle data which represents printed characters rather than numeric quantities. Not only do keyboards, teletypewriters, communications devices, displays, and computer terminals expect or provide character-coded data, but many instruments, test systems, and controllers also require data in this form. ASCII (American Standard Code for Information Interchange) is the most commonly used code; others include Baudot (telegraph) and EBCDIC (Extended Binary-Coded-Decimal Interchange Code).

Throughout this book, we will assume all of our character-coded data to be seven-bit ASCII, as shown in Table 6-1; the character code occupies the low-order seven bits of the byte, and the most significant bit of the byte holds a 0 or a parity bit.

HANDLING DATA IN ASCII

Here are some principles to remember in handling ASCII-coded data:

1. **The codes for the numbers and letters form ordered sequences.** Since the ASCII codes for the numbers 0 through 9 are 30_{16} through 39_{16}, you can convert a decimal digit to the equivalent ASCII characters (and ASCII to decimal) by means of a simple additive factor: 30_{16} = ASCII 0. Since the codes for the upper-case letters (41_{16} through $5A_{16}$) are ordered alphabetically, you can alphabetize strings by sorting them according to their numerical values.
2. **The computer does not distinguish between printing and non-printing characters.** Only the I/O devices make that distinction.
3. **An ASCII I/O device handles data only in ASCII.** For example, if you want an ASCII printer to print the digit 7, you must send it 37_{16} as the data; 07_{16} is the bell character. Similarly, if an operator presses the 9 key on an ASCII keyboard, the input data will be 39_{16}; 09_{16} is the horizontal tab character.

Table 6-1. Hexadecimal ASCII Character Codes

LSBs \ MSBs	0	1	2	3	4	5	6	7	Control Characters			
0	NUL	DLE	SP	0	@	P	`	p	NUL	Null	DC1	Device control 1
1	SOH	DC1	!	1	A	Q	a	q	SOH	Start of heading	DC2	Device control 2
2	STX	DC2	"	2	B	R	b	r	STX	Start of text	DC3	Device control 3
3	ETX	DC3	#	3	C	S	c	s	ETX	End of text	DC4	Device control 4
4	EOT	DC4	$	4	D	T	d	t	EOT	End of transmission	NAK	Negative acknowledge
5	ENQ	NAK	%	5	E	U	e	u	ENQ	Enquiry	SYN	Synchronous idle
6	ACK	SYN	&	6	F	V	f	v	ACK	Acknowledge	ETB	End of transmission block
7	BEL	ETB	'	7	G	W	g	w	BEL	Bell, or alarm	CAN	Cancel
8	BS	CAN	(	8	H	X	h	x	BS	Backspace	EM	End of medium
9	HT	EM	)	9	I	Y	i	y	HT	Horizontal tabulation	SUB	Substitute
A	LF	SUB	*	:	J	Z	j	z	LF	Line feed	ESC	Escape
B	VT	ESC	+	;	K	[	k	{	VT	Vertical tabulation	FS	File separator
C	FF	FS	,	<	L	\	l	|	FF	Form feed	GS	Group separator
D	CR	GS	–	=	M	]	m	}	CR	Carriage return	RS	Record separator
E	SO	RS	.	>	N	^	n	~	SO	Shift out	US	Unit separator
F	SI	US	/	?	O	_	o	DEL	SI	Shift in	SP	Space
									DLE	Data link escape	DEL	Delete

4. **Many ASCII devices do not use the entire character set.** For example, devices may ignore many control characters and may not print lower-case letters.
5. **ASCII control characters often have widely varying interpretations.** Each ASCII device typically uses control characters in a special way to provide features such as cursor control on a CRT, and to allow software control of characteristics such as rate of data transmission, print width, and line length.
6. **Some widely used ASCII control characters are:**

   $0A_{16}$ line feed (LF)
   $0D_{16}$ carriage return (CR)
   08_{16} backspace
   $7F_{16}$ rubout or delete character (DEL)

7. **Each ASCII character occupies eight bits.** This allows a large character set but is wasteful when only a few characters are actually being used. If, for example, the data consists entirely of decimal numbers, the ASCII format (allowing one digit per byte) requires twice as much storage, communications capacity, and processing time as does the BCD format (allowing two digits per byte).

Most assembly languages have features that make character-coded data easy to handle. In Motorola's assembly language, quotation marks around a character indicate the character's ASCII value. For example,

```
MOVE.B # 'A',D0
```

is the same as

```
MOVE.B # $41,D0
```

The first form is preferable for several reasons. It increases the readability of the instruction; it also avoids errors that may result from looking up a value in a table. The program does not depend on ASCII as the character set, since the assembler handles the conversion using whatever code has been designed into it.

PROGRAM EXAMPLES

6-1. LENGTH OF A STRING OF CHARACTERS

Purpose: Determine the length of a string of characters. The starting address is contained in the 32-bit variable START at location 6000. The end of the string is marked by an ASCII carriage return character ($0D_{16}$). Place the length of the string (excluding the carriage return) in the variable LENGTH at location 6004.

Sample Problems:

```
a.   Input:   START   —  (6000) = 00005000
                         (5000) = 0D
    Output:   LENGTH  —  (6004) = 0000
b.   Input:   START   —  (6000) = 00005000
                         (5000) = 4D  'M'
                         (5001) = 43  'C'
                         (5002) = 36  '6'
                         (5003) = 38  '8'
                         (5004) = 30  '0'
                         (5005) = 30  '0'
                         (5006) = 30  '0'
                         (5007) = 0D  CR
    Output:   LENGTH  —  (6004) = 07
```

Flowchart 6-1a:

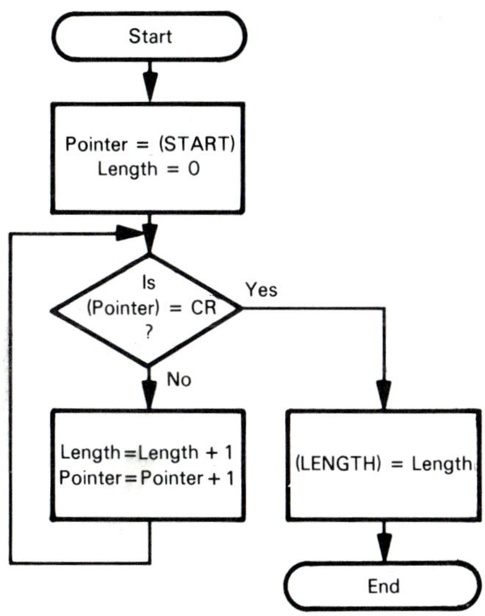

Program 6-1a:

```
       00006000         DATA      EQU      $6000
       00004000         PROGRAM   EQU      $4000

       00006000                   ORG      DATA
006000 00000004         START     DS.L     1            ADDRESS OF STRING
006004 00000002         LENGTH    DS.W     1            NUMBER OF CHARACTERS IN STRING
```

```
        0000000D        CR        EQU      $0D              ASCII VALUE FOR CARRIAGE RETURN

        00004000                  ORG      PROGRAM

004000 20786000        PGM_6_1A  MOVEA.L  START,A0         POINTER TO START OF STRING
004004 7000                      MOVEQ    #0,D0            INITIALIZE LENGTH COUNTER

004006 0C18000D        LOOP      CMPI.B   #CR,(A0)+        IS CURRENT CHAR A CARRIAGE RETURN?
00400A 6704                      BEQ.S    DONE             IF YES THEN DONE

00400C 5240                      ADDQ.W   #1,D0            ...ELSE INCREMENT LENGTH COUNTER
00400E 60F6                      BRA      LOOP             CONTINUE SCAN

004010 31C06004        DONE      MOVE.W   D0,LENGTH        SAVE STRING LENGTH

004014 4E75                      RTS

                                 END      PGM_6_1A
```

As far as the processor is concerned, the carriage return (CR) is just another ASCII code ($0D_{16}$). The fact that the carriage return can cause an output device to perform a control function rather than print a symbol does not affect the processor. The processor simply treats $0D_{16}$ as a value that is to be searched for.

The search is performed using the compare instruction CMPI. This instruction sets the flags as if the immediate operand, the carriage return ($0D_{16}$) character, had been subtracted from the destination operand. The destination operand (the next character in the string) is not affected. In this program the CMPI instruction affects the Zero (Z) flag as follows:

$Z = 1$ if the character in the string is a carriage return.

$Z = 0$ if it is not a carriage return.

In addition to performing the compare, the CMPI instruction also uses the postincrementing address mode to update the string character pointer. Thus, a portion of the loop control processing shown in Flowchart 6-1*a* has been completed. Normally, combining several instructions like this makes a program more efficient. However, how would the results of the flowchart and program differ if you also needed to save the pointer to the carriage return?

The postincrementing address mode is another variation of the MC68000 address register indirect modes. Like the address register indirect mode, the contents of the specified address registers are used to determine the address of operand. However after the data reference, the processor updates the contents of the register by incrementing it by the size associated with the data reference. Incrementing is by one, two, or four bytes depending on whether the data reference size is byte, word, or long word, respectively. The only exception to this occurs when address register A7 (the stack pointer) is used and the data size is byte. In this case the stack pointer is incremented by two bytes to ensure that the pointer is properly aligned on a word boundary.

The instruction ADDQ adds 1 to the string length counter in data register D0. This counter was initialized to zero before the loop began by the MOVEQ #0,D0 instruction. You must remember to initalize variables before using them in a loop; failure to do so is a common programming error.

By rearranging the logic and changing the initial conditions, you can shorten the program and decrease the execution time. If we rearrange the flowchart so that the program increments the string length before it checks for the carriage return, only one branch instruction is needed instead of two.

Program 6-1b:

```
         00006000     DATA      EQU      $6000
         00004000     PROGRAM   EQU      $4000

         00006000               ORG      DATA
006000 00000004       START     DS.L     1                 ADDRESS OF STRING
006004 00000002       LENGTH    DS.W     1                 NUMBER OF CHARACTERS IN STRING

         0000000D     CR        EQU      $0D               ASCII VALUE FOR CARRIAGE RETURN

         00004000               ORG      PROGRAM

004000 20786000       PGM_6_1B MOVEA.L START,A0           POINTER TO START OF STRING
004004 70FF                     MOVEQ    #-1,D0            INITIALIZE LENGTH COUNT
004006 720D                     MOVEQ    #CR,D1            INITIALIZE WITH ASCII VALUE OF CR

004008 5240           LOOP      ADDQ.W   #1,D0             INCREMENT LENGTH COUNT
00400A B218                     CMP.B    (A0)+,D1          IS CURRENT CHAR A CARRIAGE RETURN?
00400C 66FA                     BNE      LOOP              IF NO THEN CONTINUE SCAN

00400E 31C06004                 MOVE.W   D0,LENGTH         ...ELSE DONE, SAVE LENGTH COUNT

004012 4E75                     RTS

                                END      PGM_6_1B
```

Flowchart 6-1b:

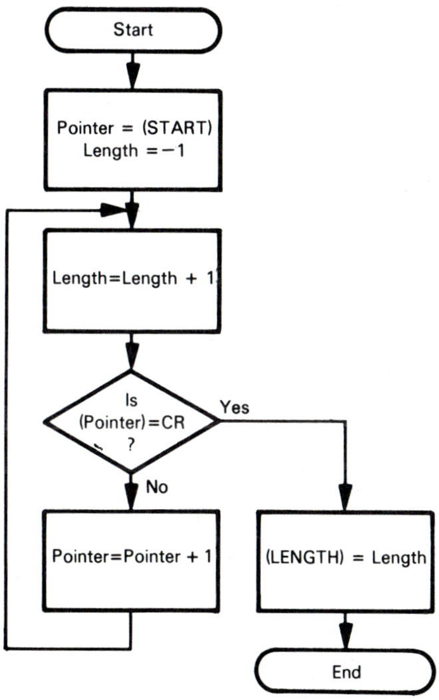

As you can see in Program 6-1*b*, incrementing the string length at the beginning of the loop rather than at the end allows elimination of one of the branch instructions. We have made another less obvious change in the loop of Program 6-1*b* that further decreases execution time of the loop: we have used data register direct addressing for the source operand of the Compare instruction instead of using immediate data as we did in Program 6-1*a*. This change reduces the object code for the Compare instruction by two bytes and saves the microprocessor from loading the ASCII value for carriage return each time through the loop. In general, eliminating the use of the immediate operands within loops can improve the loop efficiency. The family of "quick" instructions such as MOVEQ and ADDQ is an exception to this general rule. You should also note that the use of immediate operands does provide for better program documentation.

Neither of the preceding programs has loops which terminate by decrementing a counter to zero or by incrementing a counter to reach a maximum value. In fact, the processor will simply continue examining characters until it finds a carriage return. Obviously, this will create a problem if the string, because of an error or an omission, does not contain a carriage return. It is good programming practice to place a maximum count in a loop like this even though it does not appear to be necessary. What would happen if the example programs were used on a string which does not contain a carriage return? Program 6-1*c* corrects this problem.

Flowchart 6-1c

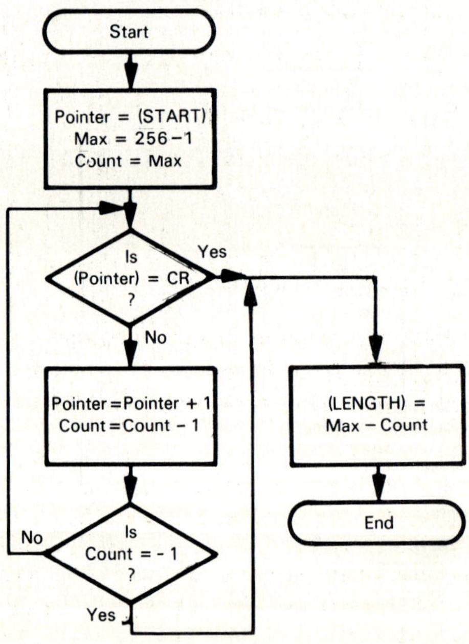

Program 6-1c:

```
       00006000   DATA      EQU      $6000
       00004000   PROGRAM   EQU      $4000

       00006000             ORG      DATA
006000 00000004   START     DS.L     1              ADDRESS OF STRING
006004 00000002   LENGTH    DS.W     1              NUMBER OF CHARACTERS IN STRING

       0000000D   CR        EQU      $0D            ASCII VALUE FOR CARRIAGE RETURN

       00004000             ORG      PROGRAM

004000 20786000   PGM_6_1C  MOVEA.L  START,A0       POINTER TO START OF STRING
```

```
004004 74FF                  MOVEQ    #256-1,D2        INITIALIZE MAX STRING LENGTH = 256
004006 3002                  MOVE.W   D2,D0            LENGTH COUNT := MAX STRING LENGTH
004008 720D                  MOVEQ    #CR,D1           INITIALIZE WITH ASCII VALUE OF CR

                  *  SCAN STRING FOR CARRIAGE RETURN. STOP SCAN WHEN
                  *  CARRIAGE RETURN FOUND OR 256 CHARACTERS SCANNED.

00400A B218       LOOP       CMP.B    (A0)+,D1         IS CURRENT CHAR A CARRIAGE RETURN?
00400C 57C8FFFC              DBEQ     D0,LOOP          IF NO AND NOT END OF STRING - CONT.

004010 9440                  SUB.W    D0,D2                DETERMINE STRING LENGTH
004012 31C26004              MOVE.W   D2,LENGTH            SAVE STRING LENGTH

004016 4E75                  RTS

                             END      PGM_6_1C
```

This program makes use of one of the Test Condition, Decrement and Branch instructions, DBcc. This set of instructions can be very useful in loop or array processing. The DBcc instructions have the form

DBcc Dn, < label >

and perform the following steps:

1. If the condition being tested is satisfied, control passes to the instruction following the DBcc.
2. If the condition is not satisfied then
   a. The *lower 16-bits* of the specified data register are decremented by one.
   b. If the result is a −1, control passes to the instruction following the DBcc.
   c. If the result is not −1, control is transferred to the specified branch location. The location must be within a sign-extended 16-bit displacement from the current PC value.

The conditional tests allowed by the DBcc instructions are identical to the tests allowed by the Bcc instructions except that DBcc also permits the conditions "never true" or "false" (F) and "always true" (T). The Motorola MC68000 assembler allows DBRA as well as DBF.

With the DBEQ instruction, the two instruction sequences CMP and DBEQ will scan a string with a maximum length of 256 bytes for a carriage return character. The scan will terminate either when a carriage return is found or when the entire 256 character string has been searched. You will note that in either termination, the instruction immediately following the DBEQ will always be executed. In this program the same calculation will be performed regardless of the cause of termination. However, in some programs you may want to perform different operations based on which condition caused the termination. When this is necessary, you can follow the DBcc instruction with an appropriate Bcc branch instruction to transfer control to the program associated with the conditional test that caused termination.

When using the DBcc instructions, you must be careful to properly initialize data counters. In Program 6-1*c,* the counter was initialized to 256−1 (255), since **the loop terminates when the counter reaches −1, not zero.** The operand form 256−1 instead of 255 was used in order to more clearly document this initialization condition.

After the loop terminates, the counter does not contain the length of the string: we must calculate the string length by subtracting the counter contents from the maximum string length minus 1. (Remember the termination condition!)

6-2. FIND FIRST NON-BLANK CHARACTER

Purpose: Search a string of ASCII characters for a non-blank character. The starting address of the string is contained in the 32-bit variable START at location 6000. Store the address of the first non-blank character in the 32-bit variable POINTER at location 6004. A blank character is the same as a space and the ASCII code for this character is 20_{16}.

Sample Problems:

```
a.   Input:   START    —  (6000) = 00005000
                          (5000) = 37  '7'
     Output:  POINTER  —  (6004) = 00005000
b.   Input:   START    —  (6000) = 5000
                          (5000) = 20  blank
                          (5001) = 20  blank
                          (5002) = 20  blank
                          (5003) = 46  'F'
                          (5004) = 20  blank
     Output:  POINTER  —  (6004) = 00005003, since the previous
                          memory locations all contained blanks.
```

Flowchart 6-2:

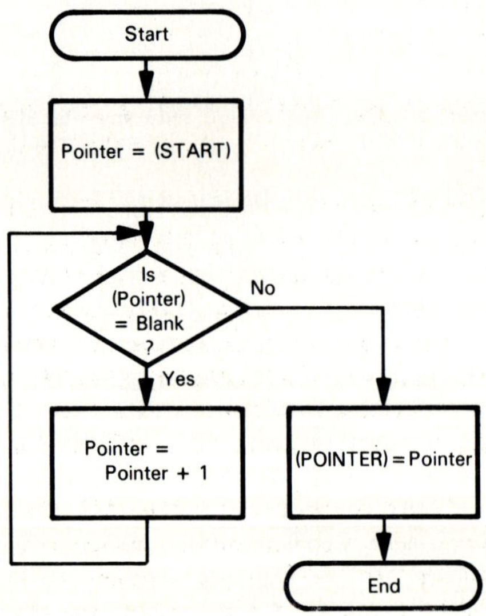

Program 6-2:

```
       00006000    DATA     EQU      $6000
       00004000    PROGRAM  EQU      $4000

       00006000             ORG      DATA
006000 00000004    START    DS.L     1              ADDRESS OF STRING
006004 00000004    POINTER  DS.L     1              ADDRESS OF FIRST NON-BLANK

       00000020    BLANK    EQU.B    ' '            ACSII VALUE FOR BLANK/SPACE

       00004000             ORG      PROGRAM

004000 20786000    PGM_6_2  MOVEA.L  START,A0       POINTER TO START OF STRING
004004 7220                 MOVEQ    #BLANK,D1      INITIALIZE WITH ASCII VALUE FOR ' '

004006 B218        LOOP     CMP.B    (A0)+,D1       IS CURRENT CHAR A BLANK?
```

```
004008 67FC                  BEQ      LOOP            IF YES THEN CONTINUE SCAN

00400A 5388                  SUBQ.L   #1,A0           ..ELSE ADJUST POINTER TO CURRENT CHAR
00400C 21C86004              MOVEA.L  A0,POINTER      SAVE ADDRESS OF FIRST NON-BLANK

004010 4E75                  RTS

                             END      PGM_6_2
```

Note the use of the apostrophes (') or single quotation marks before and after the ASCII character. You can place a single ASCII character in an MC68000 assembly language program by preceding it and following it with an apostrophe (') as in the EQU statements. The EQU is not a MC68000 instruction but rather an assembly language directive which assigns the expression in the operand field to the label in the label field. The .B suffix is required to put the ASCII code in the low-order byte; otherwise the assembler puts the ASCII value in the high-order byte of a 16-bit value and fills out the 16-bit value with zero bits.

You can place a string of ASCII characters in memory by using the DC (Define Constant) directive of the MC68000 assembler. Like the EQU directive, the string is placed within apostrophes in the DC's operand field. If an apostrophe is contained within the string, the apostrophe must be preceded by another apostrophe. Examples of some string definitions are:

```
DC  'ABCD'  Defines string ABCD
DC  'IT''S'  Defines string IT'S
```

Each ASCII character requires eight bits of storage, as compared to four bits for a BCD digit. Therefore, ASCII is a relatively inefficient format in which to store or transmit numerical data.

Looking for spaces in strings is a common task in microprocessor applications. Programs often reduce storage requirements by removing spaces that serve to increase readability or fit data in particular formats. Storing and transmitting extra space characters obviously can waste memory, communications capacity, and processor time. However, operators find it easier to enter data and programs when the computer accepts extra spaces; the entry is then said to be in free format rather than fixed format. One use for microcomputers is to convert data and commands between the forms that are easy for people to handle and the forms that are most efficient for computers and communication systems.

The autoincrement addressing mode used in the CMP (A0)+,D1 instruction provides us with a fast and simple way to step to the next character. However, once we have found the first non-blank character, we must remember that the pointer has already been incremented past the address we want to save. We must therefore explicitly subtract the increment of 1 with the instruction SUBQ #1,A0. This instruction would not be necessary if we were working backwards instead of forward, since the MC68000 autodecrements *before* using the address. However, as we noted earlier, if you use autodecrementing you must use a starting address that is one beyond the end of the string.

6-3. REPLACE LEADING ZEROS WITH BLANKS

Purpose: Edit a string of ASCII decimal characters by replacing all leading zeros with blanks. The starting address of the string is contained in the long-word variable START at location 6000. The first two bytes of the string represent the length of the string in bytes. The actual string of characters starts in the third byte.

a. Input: START — (6000) = 00005000
(5000) = 0002 Length of the string in bytes
(5002) = 36 '6'
(5003) = 39 '9'

The program leaves the string unchanged, since the leading digit is not zero.

b. Input: START — (6000) = 00005000
(5000) = 0008
(5002) = 30 '0'
(5003) = 30 '0'
(5004) = 38 '8'

(5002) = 20 Space
(5003) = 20 Space
(5004) = 38 '8'

The program replaces the two leading zeros with ASCII spaces. The printed result would be ' 8...' instead of '008...'.

Flowchart 6-3:

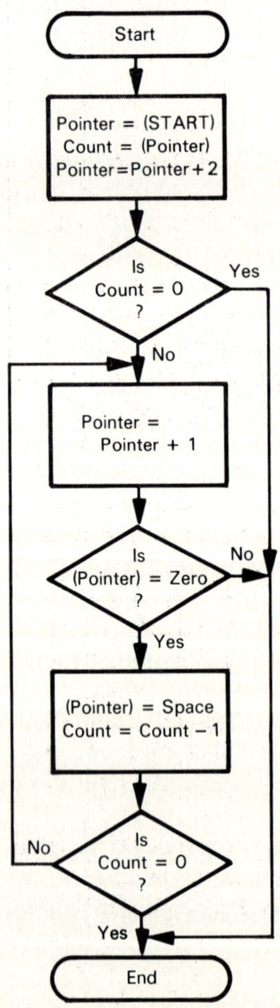

Program 6-3:

```
       00006000     DATA      EQU      $6000
       00004000.    PROGRAM   EQU      $4000

       00006000               ORG      DATA
006000 00000004     START     DS.L     1              ADDRESS OF STRING

       00000030     CHAR_0    EQU.B    '0'            ASCII VALUE FOR ZERO
       00000020     BLANK     EQU.B    ' '            ASCII VALUE FOR BLANK/SPACE

       00004000               ORG      PROGRAM

004000 20786000     PGM_6_3   MOVEA.L  START,A0       POINTER TO START OF STRING
004004 7030                   MOVEQ    #CHAR_0,D0     INITIALIZE  WITH ASCII ZERO
004006 7220                   MOVEQ    #BLANK,D1      INITIALIZE WITH ASCII BLANK
004008 3418                   MOVE.W   (A0)+,D2       STRING LENGTH TO D2
00400A 670E                   BEQ.S    DONE           IF LENGTH = 0 THEN DONE
00400C 5342                   SUBQ.W   #1,D2          ADJUST STRING COUNTER FOR DBRA

00400E B018         LOOP      CMP.B    (A0)+,D0       IS CURRENT CHAR A ZERO?
004010 6608                   BNE.S    DONE           IF NO THEN DONE

004012 1141FFFF               MOVE.B   D1,-1(A0)      REPLACE ZERO BY BLANK IN CURR CHAR
004016 51CAFFF6               DBRA     D2,LOOP        STOP SCAN IF ALL CHAR = '0'

       0000401A     DONE      EQU      *              DONE

00401A 4E75                   RTS

                              END      PGM_6_3
```

The string storage format with the length of the string immediately preceding the actual string is quite frequently used in microprocessor applications. With this format the length is known; thus you don't have to scan for a carriage return and can easily move strings in memory.

Editing strings of decimal digits to improve their appearance is a common task in microprocessor programs. Typical procedures include the removal of leading zeros, justification, the addition of signs (+ or −), delimiters or symbols for units (such as $, %, or #), and rounding. **Programs should print numbers in the form that the user wants and expects;** results like "0006", "$27.34382", or "135000000" are annoying and difficult to interpret.

This loop has two exits — one if the processor finds a non-zero digit and the other if it scans the entire string. In an actual application, you would have to be careful to leave one zero if all the digits in the string are zero. How would you modify the program to do this?

We have assumed that all the digits in the string are in ASCII; that is, the digits used are 30_{16} through 39_{16} rather than the binary representation of the numbers 0 to 9. Converting a digit from BCD to ASCII is simply a matter of adding 30_{16} (ASCII zero), while converting from ASCII to decimal involves subtracting the same number.

The instruction MOVE.B D1,−1(A0) places an ASCII space (20_{16}) in a memory location that previously contained an ASCII zero. Address register indirect addressing with a displacement of −1 is used to make up for the +1 that was added to register A0 by the CMP.B (A0)+,D0 instruction.

The DBRA instruction ensures that the program does not continue beyond the end of the string. DBRA is a form of the DBcc instruction for which the conditional test is never true. DBRA, or its equivalent form DBF, is functionally equal to the instruction sequence:

```
SUBI.W #1,D2
BNE LOOP
```

The DBRA instruction thus always causes a branch back to LOOP unless the entire string has been processed (D2 = −1).

6-4. ADD EVEN PARITY TO ASCII CHARACTERS

Purpose: Add even parity to a string of 7-bit ASCII characters. The starting address of the string is contained in the long word START at location 6000. The first word of the string represents the string length in bytes. The actual string of characters starts in the third byte. The parity bit is the most significant bit of a byte; for even parity the bit is set to 1 if that makes the total number of 1 bits in the byte an even number; otherwise it is set to 0. In either case the final number of 1 bits is even.

Sample Problem:

```
Input:  START  –  (6000) = 00005000
                  (5000) = 0006          string length
                  (5002) = 31            0011  0001
                  (5003) = 32            0011  0010
                  (5004) = 33            0011  0011
                  (5005) = 34            0011  0100
                  (5006) = 35            0011  0101
                  (5007) = 36            0011  0110
Output:           (5002) = B1            1011  0001
                  (5003) = B2            1011  0010
                  (5004) = 33            0011  0011
                  (5005) = B4            1011  0100
                  (5006) = 35            0011  0101
                  (5007) = 36            0011  0110
```

Program 6-4:

```
       00006000     DATA       EQU      $6000
       00004000     PROGRAM    EQU      $4000

       00006000                ORG      DATA
006000 00000004     START      DS.L     1                ADDRESS OF STRING

       00004000                ORG      PROGRAM

004000 20786000     PGM_6_4    MOVEA.L  START,A0         POINTER TO START OF STRING
004004 3418                    MOVE.W   (A0)+,D2         STRING LENGTH TO D2
004006 6720                    BEQ.S    DONE             IF LENGTH = 0 THEN DONE
004008 5342                    SUBQ.W   #1,D2            ADJUST STRING COUNTER FOR DBRA
00400A 7600                    MOVEQ    #0,D3            CONSTANT ZERO FOR ADDX INSTRUCTION

       0000400C     MAIN_LOOP  EQU      *
00400C 1218                    MOVE.B   (A0)+,D1         GET CURRENT CHARACTER
00400E 7000                    MOVEQ    #0,D0            CLEAR BIT COUNTER

       00004010     PARITY_LOOP EQU     *
004010 E309                    LSL.B    #1,D1            SHIFT MSB OF CHAR INTO C & X-BITS
004012 D103                    ADDX.B   D3,D0            ADD X-BIT TO BIT COUNT
004014 4A01                    TST.B    D1               TEST IF ALL BITS = 1 COUNTED
004016 66F8                    BNE      PARITY_LOOP      IF NO THEN CONTINUE COUNTING

004018 08000000                BTST.B   #0,D0            ...ELSE CHECK FOR ODD PARITY
00401C 6706                    BEQ.S    NEXT_CHAR        IF EVEN THEN PROCESS NEXT CHAR

00401E 08E80007FFFF            BSET.B   #7,-1(A0)        ...ELSE SET PARITY BIT

       00004024     NEXT_CHAR  EQU      *
004024 51CAFFE6                DBRA     D2,MAIN_LOOP     CONTINUE IF CHAR LEFT IN STRING

       00004028     DONE       EQU      *                STRING NOW HAS EVEN PARITY

004028 4E75                    RTS

                               END      PGM_6_4
```

Flowchart 6-4:

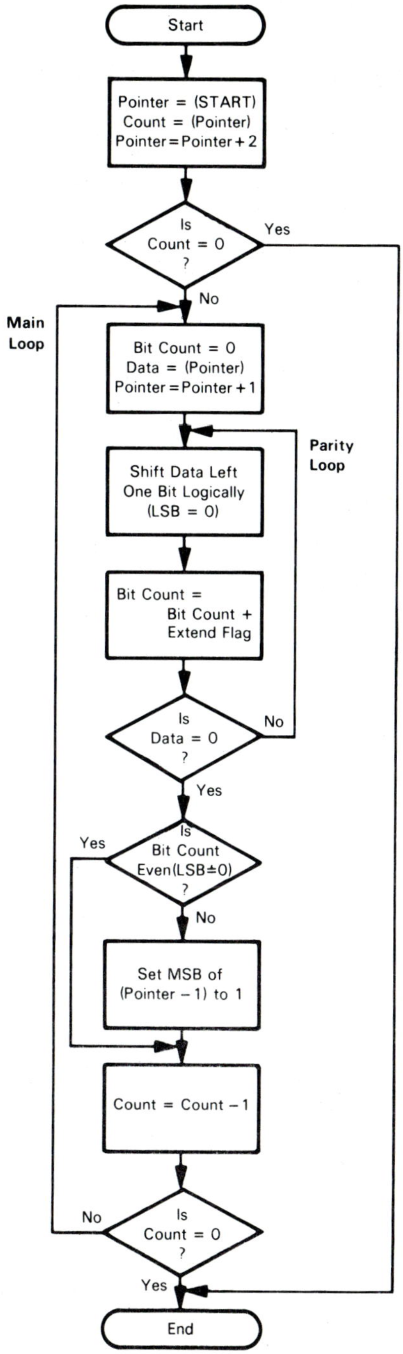

Parity provides a simple means of checking for errors on noisy communications lines. If the transmitter sends parity along with the actual data, the receiver can then check for correct parity of the data that it receives. If the parity is not correct, the receiver can request retransmission of the data. If there is a single bit in error, the parity will be incorrect, since the number of 1 bits in the data will clearly change from even to odd or odd to even. However, two bit errors will just as obviously result in the same parity as the original data. Thus we say that **parity detects single but not double bit errors.** Of course, single bit errors are usually more common than are double bit errors, so the test is still useful.

A more serious problem with **parity** is that it **provides no way to correct errors.** An error in any bit position will produce the same change in parity, so the receiver cannot determine which bit is wrong. **More advanced coding techniques provide for error correction as well as error detection. Parity, however, is easy to calculate and adequate in situations in which retransmission of data is tolerable.**

The procedure for calculating parity is to count the number of 1 bits in each byte of data. If that number is odd and even parity is desired, the program sets the most significant bit (MSB) of the data byte to 1 to make the parity even. One of the advantages of the 7-bit ASCII code is that it leaves the most significant bit available for parity; the 8-bit EBCDIC code does not.

The LSL instruction clears the least significant bit of the data register or memory location that it is shifting. Therefore, **a series of LSL instructions will eventually result in a zero value, regardless of the original data.** (Try it!) The bit counting procedure in the example program does not use a counter for termination since it stops as soon as all the remaining data bits are zero. This procedure is simple and reduces execution time in most cases.

Note that Program 6-4 assumes that the most significant bit (the parity bit) of each 8-bit data byte being processed is set to 0 at the outset; if this bit were initially set to 1, then Program 6-4 would generate odd parity instead of even.

In addition to clearing the least significant bit of the data byte, the LSL instruction affects the Carry (C) and Extend (X) flags as follows:

C=X=1 if MSB of data = 1 prior to shift
C=X=0 if MSB of data = 0 prior to shift

The state of the Extend flag is used in the ADDX.B D3,D0 instruction which has the same affect as:

D0=D0+D3+X=D0+0+X=D0+X

Thus the number of 1 bits in the byte is counted in register D0.

Like the other Add instructions, ADDX affects the status flags, so the TST instruction is used to determine if the LSL instruction cleared the data register. TST.B D1 compares the contents of the low-order byte of register D1 with zero and sets the status flags accordingly without modifying the data register contents. The TST instruction is thus an optimized form of the Compare Immediate instruction CMPI #0, D1.

Bit Manipulation Instructions

The MC68000 allows operations on individual bits within a *single byte or long word.* The Bit Clear (BCLR) instruction is used to clear a single bit. Bit Change (BCHG) is used to change the state of a specified bit. The Bit Set (BSET) instruction is used to set a specific bit to 1. Finally, you may use the Bit Test (BTST) instruction to test the state of a single bit without altering its state. All of these bit operation instructions perform an implicit Bit Test (BTST) instruction prior to operating on the specified bit.

6-5. PATTERN MATCH

Purpose: Compare two strings of ASCII characters to see if they are the same. The starting addresses of the strings are contained in the long word variables START1 at location 6000 and START2 at location 6004. The first byte of each string contains the string length (in bytes) and is followed by the string. If the two strings match, clear the variable MATCH at location 6008; otherwise set its value to -1 (all ones = $FFFF_{16}$).

Sample Problems:

```
a.   Input:  START1   —  (6000) = 00005000
             START2   —  (6004) = 00005400
                         (5000) = 03
                         (5001) = 43   'C'
                         (5002) = 41   'A'
                         (5003) = 54   'T'
                         (5400) = 03
                         (5401) = 43   'C'
                         (5402) = 41   'A'
                         (5403) = 54   'T'
    Output:  MATCH    —  (6008) = 0000   0, since the strings
                         match
b.   Input:  START1   —  (6000) = 00005000
             START2   —  (6008) = 00005400
                         (5000) = 03
                         (5001) = 43   'C'
                         (5002) = 41   'A'
                         (5003) = 54   'T'
                         (5400) = 03
                         (5401) = 52   'R'
                         (5402) = 41   'A'
                         (5403) = 54   'T'
    Output:  MATCH    —  (6008) = FFFF -1,   since the first
                         characters differ
c.   Input:  START1   —  (6000) = 00005000
             START2   —  (6004) = 00005400
                         (5000) = 03
                         (5400) = 04
    Output:  MATCH    —  (6008) = FFFF -1, since the strings are
                         not the same length
```

Note: the matching process ends as soon as we find a difference. The rest of the string is not examined.

Flowchart 6-5a:

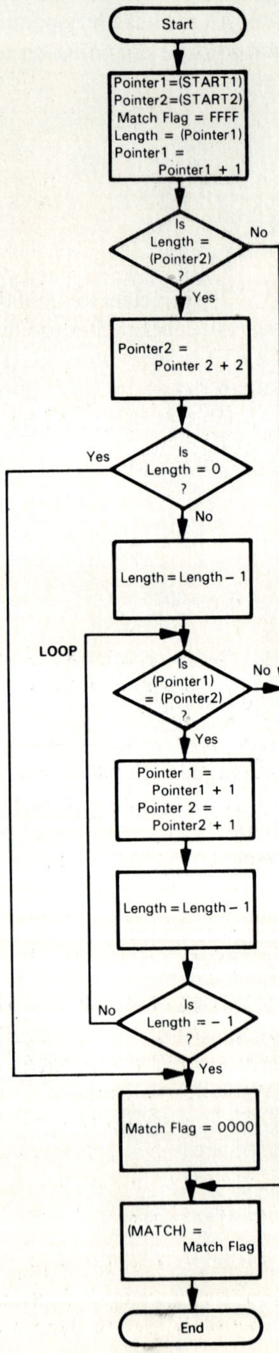

Program 6-5a:

```
        00006000        DATA     EQU      $6000
        00004000        PROGRAM  EQU      $4000


        00006000                 ORG      DATA
006000  00000004        START1   DS.L     1              ADDRESS OF FIRST STRING
006004  00000004        START2   DS.L     1              ADDRESS OF SECOND STRING
006008  00000002        MATCH    DS.W     1              MATCH FLAG

        00004000                 ORG      PROGRAM

004000  20786000        PGM_6_5A MOVEA.L  START1,A0      POINTER TO FIRST STRING
004004  22786004                 MOVEA.L  START2,A1      POINTER TO SECOND STRING
004008  72FF                     MOVEQ    #-1,D1         ASSUME NO MATCH
00400A  7000                     MOVEQ    #0,D0          LENGTH COUNTER := 0
00400C  1018                     MOVE.B   (A0)+,D0       INITIALIZE LENGTH COUNTER
00400E  B019                     CMP.B    (A1)+,D0       STRING LENGTHS EQUAL?
004010  6610                     BNE.S    DONE           IF NOT = THEN NO MATCH

004012  4A00                     TST.B    D0             STRING LENGTHS = 0?
004014  670A                     BEQ.S    SAME           IF = 0 THEN STRINGS MATCH

004016  5340                     SUBQ.W   #1,D0          ADJUST COUNTER FOR DBNE

004018  B308            LOOP     CMPM.B   (A0)+,(A1)+    COMPARE CURRENT STRING ELEMENTS
00401A  56C8FFFC                 DBNE     D0,LOOP        IF MATCH AND NOT END OF STRING-CONT

00401E  6602                     BNE.S    DONE           IF NO MATCH AND END THEN DONE

004020  4641            SAME     NOT.W    D1             STRING MATCH

004022  31C16008        DONE     MOVE.W   D1,MATCH       SAVE MATCH STATE

004026  4E75                     RTS

                                 END      PGM_6_5A
```

Matching strings of ASCII characters is an essential part of recognizing names or commands, identifying variables or operation codes in assemblers and compilers, accessing named files, and many other tasks.

The MOVEQ #−1,D1 instruction has the effect of assuming there will be no match. If a match is found, the match flag is cleared by using the NOT.W D1 instruction which complements the state of each bit in the destination operand; thus a zero bit becomes 1 and a one bit becomes 0. Had we not initialized the match flag in this way, the end of the program would have been more complicated:

```
         BNE      DONE
SAME:    MOVE     #-1,  MATCH
         BRA      DONE
FINI:    MOVE     #0,   MATCH
DONE:    RTS
```

Assuming a result is true until proven false, or false until proven true, is a common technique that simplifies many programs.

The Compare Memory instruction CMPM allows data in memory to be compared directly without first moving one of the data elements into a data register. The CMPM instruction is extremely useful and efficient in performing string comparisons. Note that only the postincrementing address mode can be used with this instruction to specify the operands. Of course, this is exactly the mode that is most useful for comparing strings since the addresses are automatically incremented to point to the next elements to be compared.

When control is passed to the instruction following the DBNE instruction, we know that either a match did not occur on a given pair of string elements, or that the two strings are identical. The BNE instruction is used to determine which condition caused the exit from DBNE. The correct execution of the BNE instruction depends on the fact that the DBNE instruction does not affect the status flags.

Why must the instruction MOVEQ #0,D0 be used prior to loading the lower byte of D0 with the string length?

This program is much more complicated than it need be. We can treat the length bytes of the strings as if they were part of the string. If the lengths are unequal, the strings are unequal.

Flowchart 6-5b:

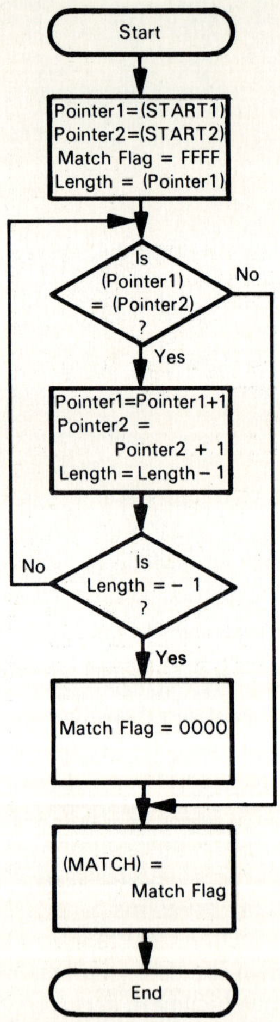

Program 6-5b:

```
       00006000     DATA      EQU     $6000
       00004000     PROGRAM   EQU     $4000


       00006000               ORG     DATA
006000 00000004     START1    DS.L    1                       ADDRESS OF FIRST STRING
006004 00000004     START2    DS.L    1                       ADDRESS OF SECOND STRING
```

```
006008 00000002    MATCH     DS.W     1              MATCH FLAG

       00004000              ORG      PROGRAM

004000 20786000    PGM_6_5B  MOVEA.L  START1,A0      POINTER TO FIRST STRING
004004 22786004              MOVEA.L  START2,A1      POINTER TO SECOND STRING
004008 72FF                  MOVEQ    #-1,D1         ASSUME NO MATCH
00400A 7000                  MOVEQ    #0,D0          LENGTH COUNTER := 0
00400C 1010                  MOVE.B   (A0),D0        INITIALIZE LENGTH COUNTER

00400E B308        LOOP      CMPM.B   (A0)+,(A1)+    COMPARE CURRENT STRING ELEMENTS
004010 56C8FFFC              DBNE     D0,LOOP        IF MATCH AND NOT END OF STRING-CONT

004014 6602                  BNE.S    DONE           IF NO MATCH AND END THEN DONE

004016 4641        SAME      NOT.W    D1             STRING MATCH

004018 31C16008    DONE      MOVE.W   D1,MATCH       SAVE MATCH STATE

00401C 4E75                  RTS

                             END      PGM_6_5B
```

If the string lengths are unequal, the program will terminate after the first iteration. Why can we use the string length as a loop counter without first decrementing it by 1?

PROBLEMS

6-1. LENGTH OF A TELETYPEWRITER MESSAGE

Purpose: Determine the length of an ASCII message. All characters are 7-bit ASCII with MSB=0. The string of characters in which the message is embedded has a starting address which is contained in the variable START at location 6000. The message itself starts with an ASCII STX character (02_{16}) and ends with ETX (03_{16}). Save the length of the message (the number of characters between the STX and the ETX but including neither) in the variable LENGTH at location 6004.

Sample Problem:

Input:	START	—	(6000)	=	00005000
			(5000)	=	02 STX
			(5001)	=	47 'G'
			(5002)	=	4F 'O'
			(5003)	=	03 ETX
Output:	LENGTH	—	(6004)	=	02, since there are two characters between the STX in location 5000 and ETX in location 5003.

6-2. FIND LAST NON-BLANK CHARACTER

Purpose: Search a string of ASCII characters for the last non-blank character. Starting address of the string is contained in the variable START at location 6000 and the string ends with a carriage return character ($0D_{16}$). Place the address of the last non-blank character in the variable ADDRESS at location 6004.

Sample Problems:

```
a.     Input:   START     —   (6000) = 00005000
                              (5000) = 37   '7'
                              (5001) = 0D   CR
       Output:  ADDRESS   —   (6004) = 5000
```

Since the last (and only) non-blank character is in memory location 5000.

```
b.     Input:   START     —   (6000) = 5000
                              (5000) = 41   'A'
                              (5001) = 20   SP
                              (5002) = 48   'H'
                              (5003) = 41   'A'
                              (5004) = 54   'T'
                              (5005) = 20   SP
                              (5006) = 20   SP
                              (5007) = 0D   CR
       Output:  ADDRESS   —   (6004) = 5004
```

6-3. TRUNCATE DECIMAL STRING TO INTEGER FORM

Purpose: Edit a string of ASCII decimal characters by replacing all digits to the right of the decimal point with ASCII blanks (20_{16}). The starting address of the string is contained in the variable START at location 6000 and the string is assumed to consist entirely of ASCII-coded decimal digits and a possible decimal point ($2E_{16}$). The length of the string is stored in the variable LENGTH at location 6004. If no decimal point appears in the string, assume that the decimal point is at the far right.

Sample Problems:

```
a.     Input:   START     —   (6000) = 00005000
                LENGTH    —   (6004) = 0004   Length of string
                              (5000) = 37   '7'
                              (5001) = 2E   '.'
                              (5002) = 38   '8'
                              (5003) = 31   '1'
       Output:                (5000) = 37   '7'
                              (5001) = 2E   '.'
                              (5002) = 20   SP
                              (5003) = 20   SP
b.     Input:   START     —   (6000) = 00005000
                LENGTH    —   (6004) = 0003   Length of string
                              (5000) = 36   '6'
                              (5001) = 37   '7'
                              (5002) = 31   '1'
```

Output: Unchanged, as number is assumed to be 671.

6-4. CHECK EVEN PARITY AND ASCII CHARACTERS

Purpose: Check for even parity in a string of ASCII characters. A string's starting address is contained in the variable START at location 6000. The first byte of the string is its length which is followed by the string itself. If the parity of all the characters in the string is correct, clear the variable PARITY at location 6004; otherwise, place all ones ($FFFF_{16}$) into PARITY.

Sample Problems:

a.	Input:	START	—	(6000) = 00005000
				(5000) = 03 Length of string
				(5001) = B1 = 1011 0001
				(5002) = B2 = 1011 0010
				(5003) = 33 = 0011 0011
	Output:	PARITY	—	(6004) = 0000, since all the characters have even parity.
b.	Input:	START	—	(6000) = 5000
				(5000) = 03 Length of string
				(5001) = B1 1011 0001
				(5002) = B6 1011 0110
				(5003) = 33 0011 0011
	Output:	PARITY	—	(6004) = FFFF, since the character in memory location 5002 does not have even parity.

6-5. STRING COMPARISON

Purpose: Compare two strings of ASCII characters to see which is larger (that is, which follows the other in alphabetical ordering). Both strings have the same length as defined by the variable LENGTH at location 6000. The strings' starting addresses are defined by the variables START1 at location 6002 and START at location 6006. If the string defined by START1 is greater than or equal to the other string, clear the variable GREATER at location 600A; otherwise, set GREATER to all ones ($FFFF_{16}$).

Sample Problems:

a.	Input:	LENGTH	—	(6000) = 0003 Length at each string
		START1	—	(6002) = 00005000
		START	—	(6006) = 00005400
				(5000) = 43 'C'
				(5001) = 41 'A'
				(5002) = 54 'T'
				(5400) = 42 'B'
				(5401) = 41 'A'
				(5402) = 54 'T'
	Output:	GREATER	—	(600A) = 0000, since CAT is "larger" than BAT.
b.	Input:	LENGTH	—	(6000) = 0003 Length at each string
		START1	—	(6002) = 00005000
		START	—	(6006) = 00005400
				(5000) = 43 'C'
				(5001) = 41 'A'
				(5002) = 54 'T'
				(5400) = 43 'C'
				(5401) = 41 'A'
				(5402) = 54 'T'
	Output:	GREATER	—	(600A) = 0000, since CAT is not "larger" than CAT.

```
c.   Input:   LENGTH   —  (6000) = 0003   Length of each string
              START1   —  (6002) = 00005000
              START    —  (6006) = 00005400
                          (5000) = 43   'C'
                          (5001) = 41   'A'
                          (5002) = 54   'T'
                          (5400) = 43   'C'
                          (5401) = 55   'U'
                          (5402) = 54   'T'
     Output:  GREATER  —  (600A) = FFFF, since CUT is
                          'larger' than CAT
```

7
Code Conversion

Code conversion is a continual problem in microcomputer applications. Peripherals provide data in ASCII, BCD, or various special codes. The microcomputer must convert the data into some standard form for processing. Output devices may require data in ASCII, BCD, seven-segment, or other codes. Therefore, the microcomputer must convert the results to the proper form after it completes the processing.

There are several ways to approach code conversion:

1. **Some conversions can easily be handled by algorithms involving arithmetic or logical functions.** The program may, however, have to handle special cases separately.
2. **More complex conversions can be handled with lookup tables.** The lookup table method requires little programming and is easy to apply. However, the table may occupy a large amount of memory if the range of input values is large.
3. **Hardware is readily available for some conversion tasks.** Typical examples are decoders for BCD to seven-segment conversion and Universal Asynchronous Receiver/Transmitters (UARTs) for conversion between parallel (ASCII) and serial (teletypewriter) formats.

In most applications, the program should do as much as possible of the code conversion work. This approach reduces parts counts and power dissipation, saves board space, and increases reliability. Furthermore, most code conversions are easy to program and require little execution time.

PROGRAM EXAMPLES

7-1. HEXADECIMAL TO ASCII

Purpose: Convert the contents of the variable DIGIT at location 6000 to an ASCII character representing the hexadecimal value of the variable. DIGIT contains a single hexadecimal digit (the four most significant bits are zero). Store the ASCII character in the variable CHAR at location 6001.

Sample Problems:

a. Input: DIGIT - (6000) = 0C
   Output: CHAR - (6001) = 43 'C'

b. Input: DIGIT - (6000) = 06
   Output: CHAR - (6001) = 36 '6'

Flowchart 7-1:

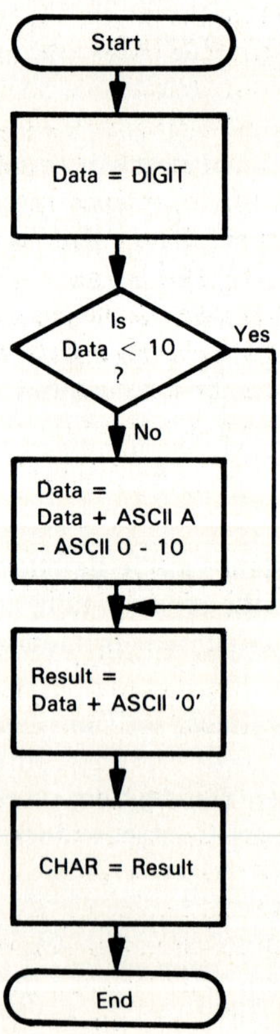

Program 7-1:

```
        00006000        DATA     EQU      $6000
        00004000        PROGRAM  EQU      $4000


        00006000        DIGIT    EQU      $6000             ADDRESS OF DIGIT
        00006001        CHAR     EQU      $6001             ADDRESS OF CHAR

        00004000                 ORG      PROGRAM

004000  10386000        PGM_7_1  MOVE.B   DIGIT,D0          GET HEX-DIGIT
004004  0C00000A                 CMP.B    #10,D0            IS DIGIT < 10?
004008  6D02                     BLT.S    ADD_0             IF YES THEN ADD '0' ONLY

00400A  5E00                     ADD.B    #'A'-'0'-10,D0    ...ELSE ADD OFFSET FOR 'A'-'F' ALSO

00400C  06000030        ADD_0    ADD.B    #'0',D0           CONVERT TO ASCII
004010  11C06001                 MOVE.B   D0,CHAR           STORE ASCII DIGIT

004014  4E75                     RTS

                                 END      PGM_7_1
```

The basic idea of this program is to add ASCII 0 (30_{16}) to all the hexadecimal digits. This addition converts the digits 0 through 9 to ASCII correctly. However, the letters A through F do not follow immediately after the digit 9 in the ASCII code; instead, there is a break between the ASCII code for 9 (39_{16}) and the ASCII code for A (41_{16}), so that **the conversion must add a further constant to the values greater than 9** (A, B, C, D, E, and F) to account for the break. The first ADD instruction does this by adding 'A' – '0' – 10 to data register D0. Can you explain why the extra factor for letter digits has the value 'A' – '0' – 10? Note that this value is small enough to fit into the 3-bit data field of an ADDQ instruction. The assembler discovers this and automatically generates the ADDQ object code (even though the instruction mnemonic does not indicate this). How can you force the assembler to create the object code for ADDI?

We have used the ASCII forms for the addition factors in the source program; a single quotation mark (apostrophe) before and after a character indicates the ASCII equivalent. We have also left the offset for the letters as an arithmetic expression to make its meaning as clear as possible. The extra assembly time is a small price to pay for the great increase in clarity. A routine like this is necessary in many applications; for example, monitor programs must convert hexadecimal digits to their ASCII equivalents in order to display the contents of memory locations in hexadecimal on an ASCII printer or CRT display.

7-2. DECIMAL TO SEVEN-SEGMENT

Purpose: Convert the contents of the variable DIGIT at location 6000 to a seven-segment code and store in the variable CODE at location 6001. If DIGIT does not contain a single decimal digit, clear CODE.

Figure 7-1 illustrates the seven-segment display and our representation of it as a binary code. The segments are usually assigned the letters a through g as shown in Figure 7-1. We have organized the seven-segment code as shown: segment g is in bit position 6, segment f in bit position 5, and so on. Bit position 7 is always zero. The segment names are standard, but the assignment of segments to bit positions is arbitrary; in actual applications, this assignment is a hardware function.

The table in Figure 7-1 is a typical example of those used to convert decimal numbers to seven-segment code; it assumes positive logic, that is, 1 = on and 0 = off. Note that the table uses 7D for 6 rather than the alternative 7C (top bar off) to avoid confusion with lower-case b, and 6F for 9 rather than 67 (bottom bar off) for symmetry with the 6.

Sample Problems:

a. Input: DIGIT - (6000) = 03
   Output: CODE - (6001) = 4F

b. Input: DIGIT - (6000) = 28
   Output: CODE - (6001) = 00

c. Input: DIGIT - (6000) = 0A
   Output: :CODE - (6001) = 00

Flowchart 7-2:

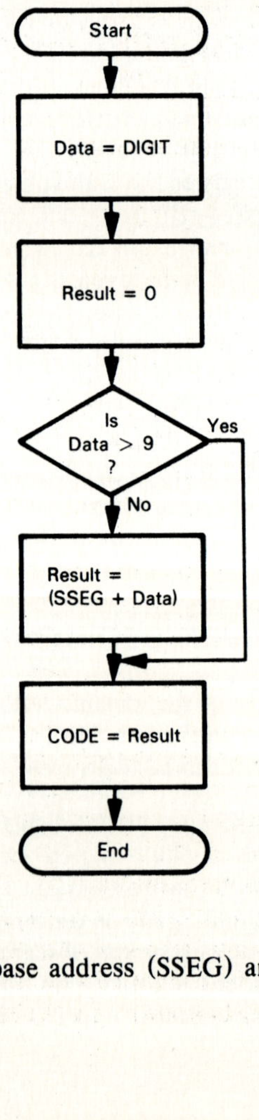

Note that the addition of base address (SSEG) and index (Data) produces the address that contains the answer.

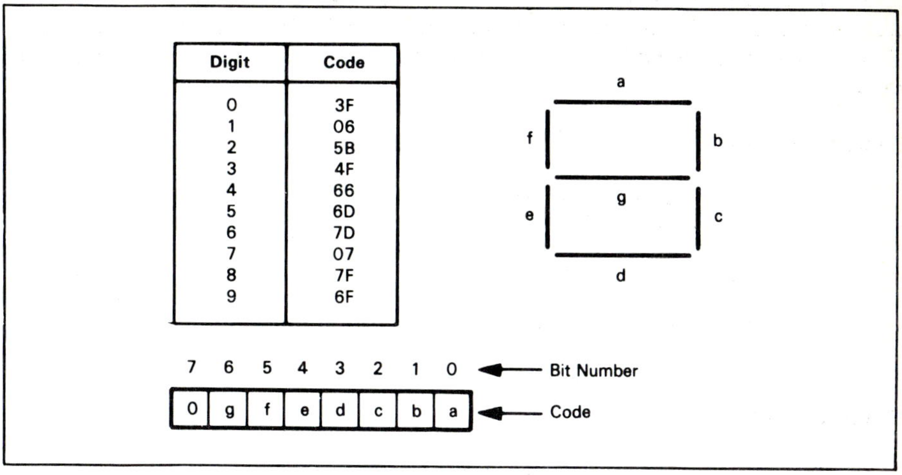

Digit	Code
0	3F
1	06
2	5B
3	4F
4	66
5	6D
6	7D
7	07
8	7F
9	6F

Figure 7-1. Seven-Segment Arrangement

Program 7-2:

```
       00006000     DATA      EQU      $6000
       00004000     PROGRAM   EQU      $4000

       00006000               ORG      DATA

006000 00000001     DIGIT     DS.B     1                           DIGIT
006001 00000001     CODE      DS.B     1                           BCD CODE
006002 3F           SSEG      DC.B     $3F,$06,$5B,$4F,$66,$6D,$7D,$07,$7F,$6F CONVERSION TABLE

       00004000               ORG      PROGRAM

004000 207C00006002 PGM_7_2   MOVEA.L  #SSEG,A0                    POINTER TO CONVERSION TABLE
004006 4201                   CLR.B    D1
004008 10386000               MOVE.B   DIGIT,D0                    GET DIGIT
00400C 0C000009               CMP.B    #9,D0                       VALID DIGIT?
004010 6206                   BHI.S    DONE                        IF NOT VALID THEN CLEAR RESULT

004012 4880                   EXT.W    D0                          MAKE INDEX BYTE LOOK LIKE A WORD
004014 12300000               MOVE.B   0(A0,D0),D1                 GET SEVEN-SEGMENT CODE FROM TABLE

004018 11C16001     DONE      MOVE.B   D1,CODE                     SAVE BCD CODE

00401C 4E75                   RTS

                              END      PGM_7_2
```

The Clear instruction (CLR), like the MOVEQ + instruction, can be used to clear all 32 bits of a data register and requires only one instruction word. However, CLR, unlike MOVEQ +, can also be used to clear just the lower byte or word of a data register. (In this program, we use CLR.B D1 to clear the least significant 8 bits of D1). In addition, we can clear a memory location directly with CLR. Why does the MC68000 have several means of clearing memory or registers?

The program calculates the memory address of the seven-segment code by adding an index — the digit to be converted — to the base address of the seven-segment code table. This procedure is known as a "table lookup." The addition does not require any explicit instructions, since the processor performs it automatically as part of the calculation of the effective address in the indexed addressing mode. Since all 32 bits of the address register are used in this indexing addition, we can place the table anywhere in memory.

When indexed addressing is used, all 32 bits of the primary address register are involved in the address calculation, but only the least significant word of the specified index register (or offset register) is used. In the program, the offset into the table is a byte value and loading this byte offset into a data register affects only the least significant 8 bits of the register. The other 24 bits of the register are not affected. Bits 8-15 of the data register must be cleared in order for the register to be used as an index register. This is accomplished by using the EXT instruction which extends the most significant bit (MSB) of the byte or word data in the data register to a word or long word. If the MSB is 0, all bits to the left of the data are cleared; if the bit is 1, all bits are set to one.

Using the Define Constant (DC) Directive

The assembler directive DC (Define Constant) places constant byte-length data in program memory. Such data may include tables, headings, error messages, prompting messages, format characters, threshold values, and mathematical constants. The optional label attached to a DC pseudo-operation is assigned the value of the address in which the assembler places the first byte of data.

The assembler assigns the data from the DC directive to consecutive memory addresses, with no changes other than numerical conversions. One DC directive can fill many bytes of memory; all the programmer must do is separate the entries with commas.

Tables are a simple, fast, and convenient approach to code conversion problems that are more complex than our hexadecimal-to-ASCII example. The required lookup tables simply contain all the possible results organized by input value; that is, the first entry is the code for input value zero and so on.

Seven-segment displays provide recognizable forms of the decimal digits and a few letters and other characters. They are relatively inexpensive and easy to handle with microprocessors. However, many people find seven-segment coded digits somewhat difficult to read. Their widespread use in calculators and watches has made them more familiar.

7-3. ASCII TO DECIMAL

Purpose: Convert the contents of the variable CHAR at location 6000 from an ASCII character to a decimal digit and store the result in the variable DIGIT at location 6001. If the contents of CHAR are not the ASCII representation of a decimal digit, set the contents of DIGIT to FF_{16}.

Sample Problems:

a. Input: CHAR - (6000) = 37 '7'
   Output: DIGIT - (6001) = 07

b. Input: CHAR - (6000) = 55 'U' (an invalid code, since it is not an ASCII decimal digit)
   Output: DIGIT - (6001) = FF

Flowchart 7-3:

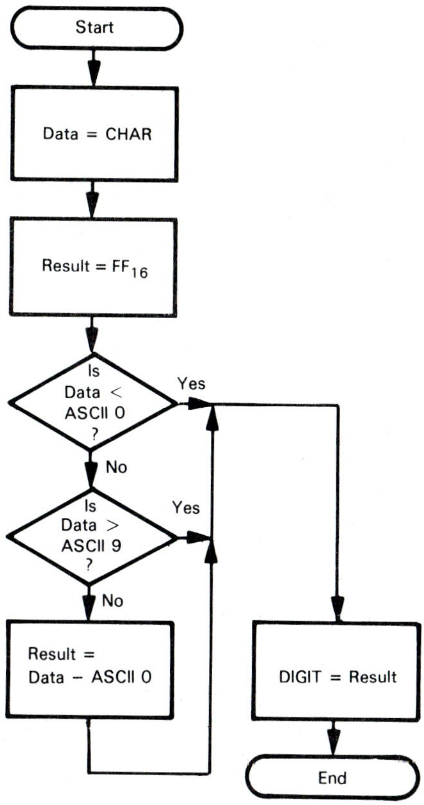

Program 7-3:

```
         00006000    DATA      EQU     $6000
         00004000    PROGRAM   EQU     $4000

         00006001    DIGIT     EQU     $6001          ADDRESS OF DIGIT
         00006000    CHAR      EQU     $6000          ADDRESS OF CHAR

         00004000              ORG     PROGRAM

004000 72FF          PGM_7_3   MOVEQ   #-1,D1         SET ERROR FLAG
004002 10386000                MOVE.B  CHAR,D0        GET CHARACTER
004006 04000030                SUB.B   #'0',D0        IS CHARACTER BELOW ASCII ZERO?
00400A 6508                    BCS.S   DONE           IF YES THEN NOT A DIGIT

00400C 0C000009                CMP.B   #9,D0          IS CHARACTER ABOVE ASCII NINE?
004010 6202                    BHI.S   DONE           IF YES THEN NOT A DIGIT

004012 C141                    EXG     D0,D1          GET NUMBER VALUE OF CHARACTER

004014 11C16001      DONE      MOVE.B  D1,DIGIT       SAVE DIGIT OR ERROR FLAG

004018 4E75                    RTS

                               END     PGM_7_3
```

This program handles ASCII-coded characters just like ordinary numbers. Since ASCII assigns an ordered sequence of codes to the decimal digits, **we can identify an ASCII character as a digit by determining if it falls within the proper range of numerical values.** We could use the order of ASCII codes similarly to determine if a character is in a particular group of letters or symbols, such as A through F. **This approach assumes detailed knowledge of a particular code and would not necessarily be valid for other codes.**

Subtracting ASCII 0 (30_{16}) from any ASCII decimal digit gives the decimal value of that digit. An ASCII character is a decimal digit if its value lies between 30_{16} and 39_{16} (including the endpoints). How would you determine if an ASCII character is a valid hexadecimal digit? ASCII-to-decimal conversion is necessary in applications in which decimal data is entered from an ASCII device such as a teletypewriter or terminal.

The program performs one comparison — to the lower limit — with an actual subtraction (SUB '0',D0) since the subtraction is necessary for the ASCII-to-decimal conversion. It performs the other comparison with an implied subtraction (CMP.B#9,D0) to avoid destroying the possible decimal digit in data register D0. **Implied subtractions (CMP) are far more common than actual subtractions (SUB) in programs, since the numerical value of the result of the comparison is often not of interest.**

The instruction EXG can exchange the contents of any 32-bit register with the contents of any other 32-bit register. Long word exchanges can be made between any two data registers, any two address registers, or between a data register and an address register.

7-4. BINARY-CODED DECIMAL TO BINARY

Purpose: Convert four BCD digits in the variable STRING at location 6000 to a binary number in the variable NUMBER at location 6004. The most significant BCD digit is in memory location 6000. There is one BCD digit in each byte of STRING.

Sample Problems:

a. Input: STRING - (6000) = 02
(6001) = 09
(6002) = 07
(6003) = 01
Output: NUMBER - (6004) = $0B9B_{16} = 2971_{10}$

b. Input: STRING - (6000) = 09
(6001) = 07
(6002) = 00
(6003) = 02
Output: NUMBER - (6004) = $25E6_{16} = 9702_{10}$

Program 7-4a:

```
00006000        DATA      EQU     $6000
00004000        PROGRAM   EQU     $4000

00006000        STRING    EQU     $6000              ADDRESS OF FOUR DIGIT BCD STRING
00006004        RESULT    EQU     $6004              ADDRESS OF RESULT

00004000                  ORG     PROGRAM
```

```
004000 307C6000     PGM_7_4A MOVEA.W #STRING,A0      POINTER TO FIRST BCD DIGIT
004004 7003                  MOVEQ   #4-1,D0         NUMBER OF DIGITS(-1) TO PROCESS
004006 4281                  CLR.L   D1              CLEAR FINAL RESULT - D1
004008 4282                  CLR.L   D2              CLEAR DIGIT REGISTER
00400A 6008                  BRA.S   NOMULT          SKIP MULTIPLY FIRST TIME

00400C D241         LOOP     ADD.W   D1,D1           2X
00400E 3601                  MOVE.W  D1,D3
004010 E54B                  LSL.W   #2,D3           8X = 2X * 4
004012 D243                  ADD.W   D3,D1           10X = 8X + 2X

004014 1418         NOMULT   MOVE.B  (A0)+,D2        NEXT BCD DIGIT,(D2[15-8] UNCHANGED)
004016 D242                  ADD.W   D2,D1           ADD NEXT DIGIT
004018 51C8FFF2              DBRA    D0,LOOP         CONTINUE PROCESSING IF STILL DIGITS

00401C 31C16004              MOVE.W  D1,RESULT       STORE RESULT

004020 4E75                  RTS

                             END     PGM_7_4A
```

Flowchart 7-4a:

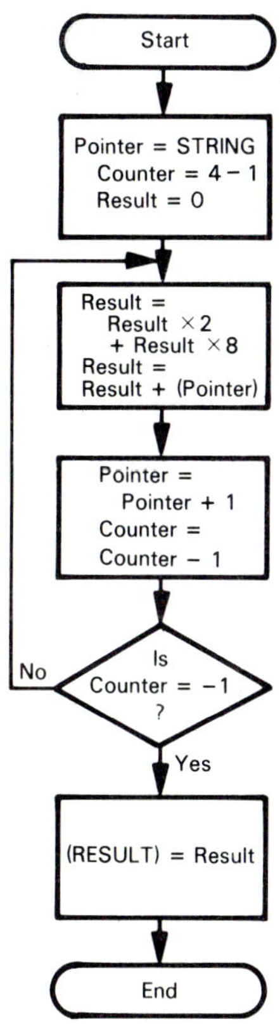

Program 7-4a multiplies each intermediate result by 10 using the formula $10x = 8x + 2x$. Multiplying by 2 requires one logical shift left (LSL), and multiplying by 8 requires three such shifts.

BCD entries are converted to binary in order to take advantage of the inherent binary operators provided by the processor. In addition, a binary representation requires less storage than the equivalent BCD form. However, in some cases, the program time and spacc rcquired for conversion may affect some of the advantages of binary storage and arithmetic.

Program 7-4a uses a word length ADD to add the BCD digit to the accumulated result in register D1. Had we used ADD.B D2,D1, the program would not have worked for all values. Consider the value 0257. Before adding the lowest digit, D1 would contain 0250_{10} or $00FA_{16}$. Adding 7 to the low byte of D1 yields FA + 07 = 01, and the high byte is still 0. Since we cannot directly add a byte value to a word value, we chose to load the value into a data register prior to the addition. Why don't we have to perform an extend operation prior to the addition?

This program skips the first multiply, since we know the initial value of D2 is 0. However, if we eliminated the branch instructions, we'd still get the same result.

There are often several ways to perform a function using assembly language instructions. In this program, we used the ADD instruction to shift a value left one place since this is the fastest means of performing this operation in the MC68000. Two ADD instructions would also be faster than the LSL instruction but would require two additional bytes of storage.

We could also use one of the MC68000 multiply instructions. The multiply instructions perform a multiplication operation on two 16-bit operands to produce a 32-bit result in one of the data registers. At least one of the 16-bit operands must be in a data register. The MC68000 allows for both signed and unsigned multiplication. If signed multiplication (MULS) is used, operands are treated as signed values and the result is signed. For unsigned multiplication (MULU), all values are unsigned. In program 7-4b, we have modified program 7-4a to use the MULU instruction instead of the ADD and shift (LSL) instructions:

Program 7-4b:

```
            00006000     DATA     EQU      $6000
            00004000     PROGRAM  EQU      $4000

            00006000     STRING   EQU      $6000         ADDRESS OF FOUR DIGIT BDC STRING
            00006004     CODE     EQU      $6004         ADDRESS OF RESULT

            00004000              ORG      PROGRAM


004000 307C6000          PGM_7_4B MOVEA.W  #STRING,A0    POINTER TO FIRST BCD DIGIT
004004 7003                       MOVEQ    #4-1,D0       NUMBER OF DIGITS(-1) TO PROCESS
004006 4281                       CLR.L    D1            CLEAR FINAL RESULT - D1
004008 4282                       CLR.L    D2            CLEAR DIGIT REGISTER
00400A 6004                       BRA.S    NOMULT        SKIP MULTIPLY FIRST TIME

00400C C2FC000A          LOOP     MULU.W   #10,D1        D1 = D1 * 10

004010 1418              NOMULT   MOVE.B   (A0)+,D2      NEXT BCD DIGIT(D2[15-8] UNCHANGED)
004012 D242                       ADD.W    D2,D1         ADD NEXT DIGIT
004014 51C8FFF6                   DBRA     D0,LOOP       CONTINUE PROCESSING IF STILL DIGITS

004018 31C16004                   MOVE.W   D1,CODE       STORE RESULT

00401C 4E75                       RTS

                                  END      PGM_7_4B
```

7-5. BINARY NUMBER TO ASCII STRING

Purpose: Convert the 16-bit binary number in the variable NUMBER at memory location 6000 into 16 ASCII characters (either ASCII 0 or ASCII 1). Store the ASCII characters in the 16-character string variable STRING located at memory location 6002.

Sample Problem:

```
 Input:  NUMBER -  (6000) = 31D2 = 0011 0001 1101 0010
Output:  STRING -  (6002) = 30  '0'
                   (6003) = 30  '0'
                   (6004) = 31  '1'
                   (6005) = 31  '1'
                   (6006) = 30  '0'
                   (6007) = 30  '0'
                   (6008) = 30  '0'
                   (6009) = 31  '1'
                   (600A) = 31  '1'
                   (600B) = 31  '1'
                   (600C) = 30  '0'
                   (600D) = 31  '1'
                   (600E) = 30  '0'
                   (600F) = 30  '0'
                   (6010) = 31  '1'
                   (6011) = 30  '0'
```

Program 7-5:

```
       00006000      DATA     EQU      $6000
       00004000      PROGRAM  EQU      $4000

       00006000      NUMBER   EQU      $6000            ADDRESS OF 16 BIT NUMBER
       00006002      STRING   EQU      $6002            ADDRESS OF EQUIVALENT ASCII STRING

       00004000               ORG      PROGRAM

004000 207C00006012  PGM_7_5  MOVEA.L  #STRING+16,A0    POINTER TO END OF STRING(+1)
004006 700F                   MOVEQ    #15,D0           LOOP COUNT(-1)
004008 123C0030               MOVE.B   #'0',D1
00400C 34386000               MOVE.W   NUMBER,D2        GET NUMERIC DATA

004010 1101          LOOP     MOVE.B   D1,-(A0)         ASSUME CURRENT LSB IS ZERO
004012 E25A                   ROR.W    #1,D2            TEST CURRENT LSB
004014 6404                   BCC.S    LOOPEND          IF ZERO THEN TRY NEXT BIT

004016 06100001               ADDI.B   #1,(A0)          CHANGE ASCII '0' TO ASCII '1'

00401A 51C8FFF4      LOOPEND  DBRA     D0,LOOP          PROCESS ALL BITS

00401E 4E75                   RTS

                              END      PGM_7_5
```

The ASCII digits form a sequence so ASCII 1 = ASCII 0 + 1. The ADD instruction can be used to directly increment the contents of a memory location. As a result, no explicit instructions are required to load the data from memory into a register or to store the result back into memory. Nor are any registers disturbed.

Note that the string pointer, A0, starts at the end of the string +1 ($6002+16_{10}$) and is decremented at the beginning of each step. When accessing data in this manner, note that the end-of-the-string address is actually the address of the first byte not in the string. For example, the byte at $6002 + 16_{10}$ is not in the string of ASCII digits. Finally, note that $6002 + 16_{10}$ is more easily identified with a 16-byte string than $6002 + 15_{10}$.

Binary-to-ASCII conversion is necessary if numbers are to be printed in binary on an ASCII device. Binary outputs are helpful in debugging and testing when each bit has a separate meaning; typical examples are inputs from a set of panel switches or outputs to a set of LEDs. If the programmer can only obtain the value in some other number system (such as octal or hexadecimal), he or she must perform an error-prone hand conversion to check the bits.

Flowchart 7-5:

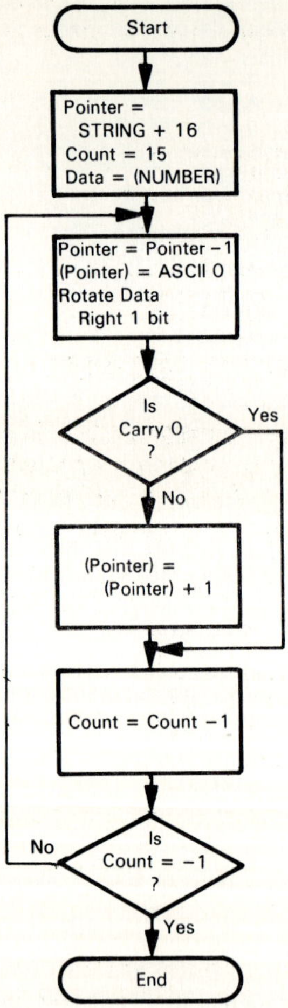

PROBLEMS

7-1. ASCII TO HEXADECIMAL

Purpose: Convert the contents of the variable A DIGIT at memory location 6000 from an ASCII character to a hexadecimal digit and store the result in the variable H DIGIT at memory location 6001. Assume that A DIGIT contains the ASCII representation of a hexadecimal digit (7 bits with MSB=0).

Sample Problems:

```
a.    Input:  A DIGIT - (6000) = 43  'C'
     Output:  H DIGIT - (6001) = 0C

b.    Input:  A DIGIT - (6000) = 36  '6'
     Output:  H DIGIT - (6001) = 06
```

7-2. SEVEN-SEGMENT TO DECIMAL

Purpose: Convert the contents of the variable CODE at memory location 6000 from a seven-segment code to a decimal number and store the result in the variable NUMBER at location 6001. If CODE does not contain a valid seven-segment code, set NUMBER to FF_{16}. Use the seven-segment table given in Figure 7-1 and try to match codes.

Sample Problems:

```
a.    Input:    CODE - (6000) = 4F
     Output:  NUMBER - (6001) = 03

b.    Input:    CODE - (6000) = 28
     Output:  NUMBER - (6001) = FF
```

7-3. DECIMAL TO ASCII

Purpose: Convert the contents of the variable DIGIT at memory location 6000 from a decimal digit to an ASCII character and store the result in the variable CHAR at memory location 6001. If the number in DIGIT is not a decimal digit, set the contents of CHAR to an ASCII space (20_{16}).

Sample Problems:

```
a.    Input:  DIGIT - (6000) = 07
     Output:  CHAR - (6001) = 37  '7'

b.    Input:  DIGIT - (6000) = 55
     Output:  CHAR - (6001) = 20  space
```

7-4. BINARY TO BCD

Purpose: Convert the contents of the variable NUMBER at memory location 6000 to four BCD digits in the variable STRING at location 6002 (most significant digit in 6002). The 16-bit number in NUMBER is unsigned and less than 10,000.

Sample Problem:

Input:	NUMBER -	(6000) = 1C52	(7250 decimal)
Output:	STRING -	(6002) = 07	
		(6003) = 02	
		(6004) = 05	
		(6005) = 00	

7-5. ASCII STRING TO BINARY NUMBER

Purpose: Convert the eight ASCII characters in the variable STRING starting at location 6000 to an 8-bit binary number in the variable NUMBER at location 6008 (the most significant bit-character is in location 6000). Clear the byte variable ERROR at location 6009 if all the ASCII characters are either ASCII 1 or ASCII 0; otherwise set ERROR to all ones (FF_{16}).

Sample Problems:

a.	Input:	STRING -	(6000) = 31	'1'
			(6001) = 31	'1'
			(6002) = 30	'0'
			(6003) = 31	'1'
			(6004) = 30	'0'
			(6005) = 30	'0'
			(6006) = 31	'1'
			(6007) = 30	'0'
	Output:	NUMBER -	(6008) = D2	
			(6009) = 0	
b.	Input:	Same as (a) above except		
			(6005) = 37	'7'
	Output:	ERROR -	(6009) = FF	

REFERENCES

Other BCD-to-binary conversion methods are discussed in M.L. Roginsky and J.A. Tabb, "Microprocessor Algorithms Make BCD-Binary Conversions Super-fast," *EDN,* January 5, 1977, pp. 46-50, and in J.B. Peatman, *Microcomputer-based Design.* New York: McGraw-Hill, 1977, pp. 400-06.

8
Arithmetic Problems

MULTIPLE-WORD AND DECIMAL ARITHMETIC

Much of the arithmetic in some microprocessor applications consists of multiple-word binary or decimal manipulations. A decimal correction (decimal adjust) or some other means for performing decimal arithmetic is frequently the only arithmetic instruction provided besides basic addition and subtraction. When this is the case, you must implement other arithmetic operations with sequences of instruction. The MC68000, however, provides both signed and unsigned multiply and divide instructions for 16-bit binary arithmetic, as well as decimal addition and subtraction instructions.

The MC68000 provides for both signed and unsigned binary arithmetic. Signed numbers are represented in two's complement form. This means that the operations of addition and subtraction are the same whether the numbers are signed or unsigned. Different instructions are needed for signed and unsigned multiplication and division, but not for addition and subtraction. Try some examples to convince yourself this is true.

Multiple-precision binary arithmetic requires simple repetitions of the basic instructions. The Extend bit transfers information between words. It is set when an addition results in a carry or a subtraction results in a borrow. Add with Extend and Subtract with Extend use this information from the previous arithmetic operation. You must be careful to clear the Extend bit before operating on the first words. (Obviously there is no carry into or borrow from the least significant bits.)

Decimal arithmetic is a common enough task for microprocessors that most have special instructions for this purpose. These instructions may either perform decimal operations directly or correct the results of binary operations to the proper decimal form. Decimal arithmetic is essential in such applications as point-of-sale terminals, check processors, order entry systems, and banking terminals. The MC68000 provides instructions for decimal addition and subtraction. Since the MC68000 performs decimal arithmetic directly, there is no need for a decimal adjust instruction such as is found in many other microprocessors.

You can implement decimal multiplication and division as series of additions and subtractions, respectively. Extra storage must be reserved for results, since a multiplication produces a result twice as long as the operands. A division contracts the length of the result. Multiplications and divisions are time-consuming when done in software because of the repeated operations that are necessary.

PROGRAM EXAMPLES

8-1. 64-BIT BINARY ADDITION

Purpose: Add two four-word (64-bit) binary numbers. The first number is the 64-bit variable NUM1 and occupies memory locations 6000 through 6007, the second is the 64-bit variable NUM2 and occupies locations 6200 through 6207. Place the sum in NUM1 at locations 6000 through 6007.

Sample Problem:

Input:	NUM1	—	(6000) = 6A4D	
			(6002) = ED05	$6A4DED05A9376414_{16}$ is the
			(6004) = A937	first number
			(6006) = 6414	
	NUM2	—	(6200) = 56C8	
			(6202) = 46E6	$56C846E676C84AEA_{16}$ is the
			(6204) = 76C8	second number
			(6206) = 4AEA	
Output:	NUM1	—	(6000) = C116	
			(6002) = 33EC	$C11633EC1FFFAEFE_{16}$ is sum
			(6004) = 1FFF	
			(6006) = AEFE	

Program 8-1a:

```
00006000        DATA       EQU     $6000
00004000        PROGRAM    EQU     $4000

00006000        NUM1       EQU     $6000                   ADDR. OF 1:ST 64-BIT BINARY NUMBER
00006200        NUM2       EQU     $6200                   ADDR. OF 2:ND 64 BIT BINARY NUMBER
00000008        BYTECOUNT  EQU     $8                      NUMBER OF BYTES TO ADD

00004000                   ORG     PROGRAM

004000 207C00006008 PGM_8_1A MOVEA.L #NUM1+BYTECOUNT,A0 ADDRESS BEYOND END OF FIRST NUMBER
004006 227C00006208          MOVEA.L #NUM2+BYTECOUNT,A1 ADDRESS BEYOND END OF SECOND NUMBER
00400C 44FC0000              MOVE    #0,CCR             CLEAR EXTEND FLAG(AND OTHER FLAGS)
004010 7407                  MOVEQ   #BYTECOUNT-1,D2    LOOPCOUNTER, ADJUSTED FOR DBRA
```

```
004012 1020        LOOP    MOVE.B   -(A0),D0
004014 1221                MOVE.B   -(A1),D1
004016 D101                ADDX.B   D1,D0          D0[0-7]:= D0[0-7] + D1[0-7] + (EXT)
004018 1080                MOVE.B   D0,(A0)        STORE RESULT
00401A 51CAFFF6            DBRA     D2,LOOP        CONTINUE

00401E 4E75                RTS

                           END      PGM_8_1A
```

Flowchart 8-1:

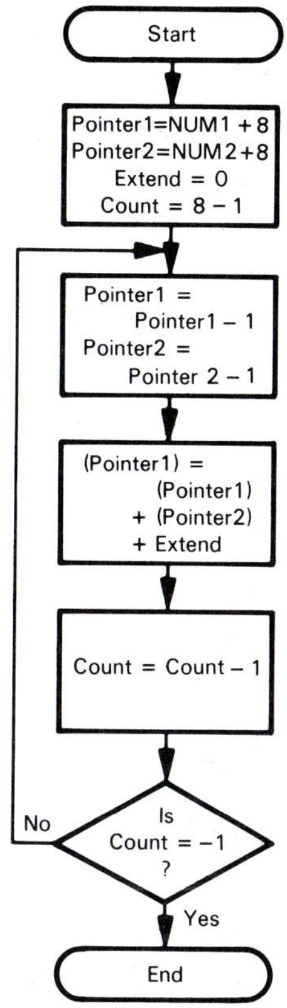

Clearing and Setting Flags

The instruction MOVE TO CCR sets *all the condition codes* in the processor's status register according to the contents of the source operand. Although the source operand is always a 16-bit word, only the least significant byte is used to set the condition codes. Therefore MOVE #0,CCR clears all the conditions (Negative, Zero, Overflow, Carry and Extend). This instruction is used to clear the Extend flag in preparation for the first ADDX instruction.

MOVE TO CCR is not the only instruction which can explicitly modify the contents of condition codes. The immediate instructions ANDI, EORI, and ORI can also be used to selectively clear, complement, and set individual condition codes. For example, by using the instruction ANDI #$EF,CCR we could clear only the Extend flag without modifying the other condition codes. The format for the immediate operand when modifying condition codes is:

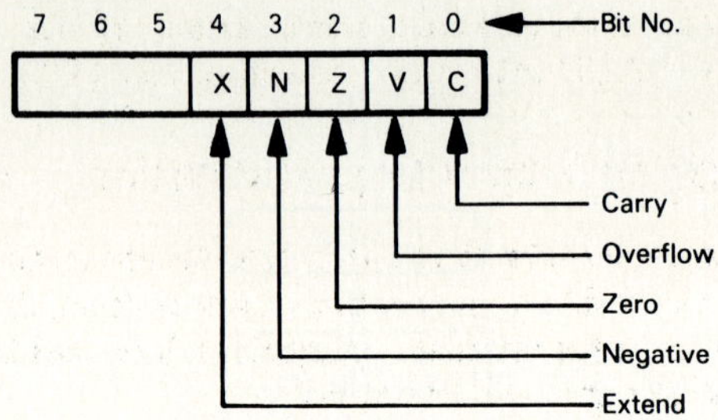

Add with Extend

The ADDX instruction, Add with Extend, adds the contents of the two registers. If the Extend flag is set, then 1 is added to the sum. Besides performing the addition, ADDX sets the Extend flag appropriately for future operations. Note that no other instruction in this program's loop affects the state of the Extend flag.

The Extend flag is similar to the Carry flag found in most other microprocessors. The MC68000 has both a Carry and Extend flag. As a general rule, the Carry flag is set if a carry occurs out of the most significant bit of the result for addition or if a borrow occurs during subtraction; otherwise it is cleared. The Extend flag is generally set to the same state as the Carry flag, except during data movement, when the state of the Extend flag is not affected.

Adding Memory Operands

A quicker and more elegant version of this addition program is shown in Program 8-1*b*. This program uses the second form of the Add with Extend instruction, the powerful MC68000 memory-to-memory form. This format requires the use of two address registers which point to the two operands in memory. The address registers are *decremented* according to the operand size *prior* to being used to fetch the operands. Note that the ADD with Extend instruction may be used to operate on 8-, 16-, or 32-bit data.

Program 8-1b:

```
       00006000      DATA      EQU       $6000
       00004000      PROGRAM   EQU       $4000

       00006000      NUM1      EQU       $6000          ADDR. OF 1:ST 64-BIT BINARY NUMBER
       00006200      NUM2      EQU       $6200          ADDR. OF 2:ND 64-BIT BINARY NUMBER

       00004000                ORG       PROGRAM

004000 207C00006008 PGM_8_1B   MOVEA.L   #NUM1+8,A0     ADDRESS BEYOND END OF 64-BIT NUMBER
004006 227C00006208            MOVEA.L   #NUM2+8,A1     ADDRESS BEYOND END OF SECOND NUMBER
00400C 44FC0000                MOVE      #0,CCR         CLEAR EXTEND FLAG(AND OTHER FLAGS)

004010 D189                    ADDX.L    -(A1),-(A0)    ADD LOWER LONG WORDS,RESULT IN NUM1
004012 D189                    ADDX.L    -(A1),-(A0)    ADD HIGHER LONG WORDS, RES IN NUM1

004014 4E75                    RTS

                               END       PGM_8_1B
```

In addition to the Add with Extend (ADDX) instruction, the MC68000 also supports binary addition with the ADD instruction. ADD is similar to ADDX except that the state of the Extend flag is not used in the addition operation. The ADD instruction also requires at least one of its operands to be in a data register. How could we modify Program 8-1*a* to use the ADD instruction instead of ADDX?

Decimal Precision in Binary Representation

Storing data in a binary format as opposed to decimal requires less memory. For example, **ten bits correspond to approximately three decimal digits** since $2^{10} = 1024$. **So you can calculate the approximate number of bits required to give a certain accuracy in decimal digits from the formula:**

Number of bits (10/3) $\times$ Number of decimal digits

Thus, twelve decimal digit accuracy requires:

$$12 \times 10/3 = 40 \text{ bits}$$

8-2. DECIMAL ADDITION

Purpose: Add two multiple-byte packed BCD numbers. The length of the numbers (in bytes) is defined by the variable LENGTH at location 6000. The first number (most significant bits first) is contained in the variable BCDNUM1 at location 6001. The second number is contained in the variable BCDNUM2 at location 6101. The sum replaces the number at BCDNUM1. Each byte of the BCD numbers contains two decimal digits.

Sample Problem:

Input:	LENGTH	—	(6000) = 04	Number of bytes in each number
	BCDNUM1	—	(6001) = 36	
			(6002) = 70	36701985 is first number
			(6003) = 19	
			(6004) = 85	
	BCDNUM2	—	(6101) = 12	
			(6102) = 66	12663459 is second number
			(6103) = 34	
			(6104) = 59	
Output:	BCDNUM1	—	(6001) = 49	
			(6002) = 36	49365444 is decimal sum
			(6003) = 54	
			(6004) = 44	

```
That is,  36701985
        + 12663459
        ----------
          49365444
```

Program 8-2a:

```
00006000    DATA       EQU    $6000
00004000    PROGRAM    EQU    $4000

00006000    LENGTH     EQU    $6000      LENGTH OF BCD NUMBER IN BYTES
00006001    BCDNUM1    EQU    $6001      ADDRESS OF FIRST BCD NUMBER
00006101    BCDNUM2    EQU    $6101      ADDRESS OF SECOND BCD NUMBER
```

```
              00004000             ORG       PROGRAM
004000 4242             PGM_8_2A   CLR.W     D2
004002 14386000                    MOVE.B    LENGTH,D2
004006 3442                        MOVE.W    D2,A2               A2[0-31] = BYTES IN BCD NUMBER
004008 41EA6001                    LEA       BCDNUM1(A2),A0      POINTS BEYOND END OF BCDNUM1
00400C 43EA6101                    LEA       BCDNUM2(A2),A1      POINTS BEYOND END OF BCDNUM2

004010 5342                        SUBQ      #1,D2               ADJUST LENGTH FOR LOOP TERMINATION
004012 44FC0000                    MOVE      #0,CCR              CLEAR EXTEND FLAG FOR ABCD

004016 C109             LOOP       ABCD.B    -(A1),-(A0)         BCD ADDITION WITH EXTEND
004018 51CAFFFC                    DBRA      D2,LOOP             CONTINUE

00401C 4E75                        RTS

                                   END       PGM_8_2A
```

Flowchart 8-2:

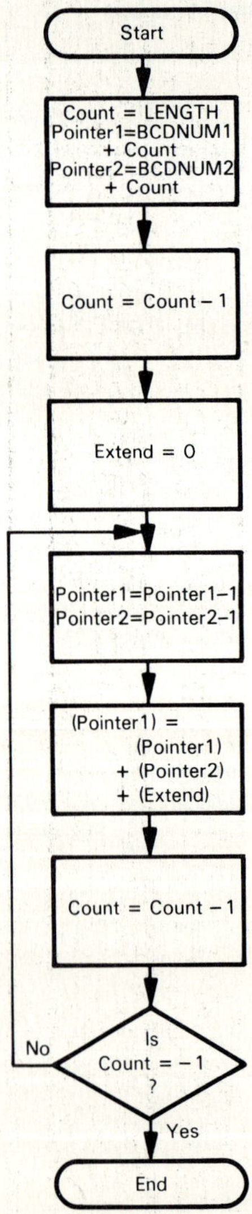

The MC68000, unlike most microprocessors, implements decimal addition in a single instruction ABCD, Add Decimal with Extend. Like the ADDX instruction, ABCD performs addition using the state of the Extend flag. However, the addition is performed using binary-coded decimal arithmetic. This eliminates the need for the typical decimal adjust instruction such as the DAA instruction on Motorola's 6809 microprocessor. The MC68000 also provides a decimal subtraction instruction, SBCD.

Program 8-2 uses the Load Effective Address, LEA, instruction to calculate the address of the decimal number's last byte plus one. This instruction calculates an effective address in the normal way, but then simply places that address in the specified address register rather than using it to transfer data. The effective address is available for later use and need not be recalculated.

We should note that use of the register indirect with displacement mode of addressing with the LEA instruction results in some restrictions being placed on Program 8-2*a:* since the displacement (BCDNUM1) that is part of the operand can only be 16-bits in length, the full addressing space of the processor cannot be utilized. We can make Program 8-1*b* more general purpose so that it can utilize the full addressing space, although this will require several additional instructions. Program 8-2*b* provides this more general solution.

Program 8-2b:

```
       00006000         DATA      EQU      $6000
       00004000         PROGRAM   EQU      $4000

       00006000         LENGTH    EQU      $6000          LENGTH OF BCD NUMBER IN BYTES
       00006001         BCDNUM1   EQU      $6001          ADDRESS OF FIRST BCD NUMBER
       00006101         BCDNUM2   EQU      $6101          ADDRESS OF SECOND BCD NUMBER

       00004000                   ORG      PROGRAM

004000 4242             PGM_8_2B  CLR      D2
004002 14386000                   MOVE.B   LENGTH,D2
004006 207C00006001               MOVEA.L  #BCDNUM1,A0    POINTER TO START OF BCDNUM1
00400C 227C00006101               MOVEA.L  #BCDNUM2,A1    POINTER TO START OF BCDNUM2
004012 41F02000                   LEA      0(A0,D2.W),A0  ADJUST TO POINT BEYOND END OF VALUE
004016 43F12000                   LEA      0(A1,D2.W),A1  ADJUST TO POINT BEYOND END OF VALUE

00401A 5342                       SUBQ.W   #1,D2          ADJUST LENGTH FOR LOOP TERMINATION
00401C 44FC0000                   MOVE     #0,CCR         CLEAR EXTEND FLAG FOR ABCD

004020 C109             LOOP      ABCD.B   -(A1),-(A0)    BCD ADDITION WITH EXTEND
004022 51CAFFFC                   DBRA     D2,LOOP        CONTINUE

004026 4E75                       RTS

                                  END      PGM_8_2B
```

The procedure used in both of these programs can add decimal (BCD) numbers of any length (up to 131,072 digits!). Since each decimal digit requires four bits, twelve digit precision requires

$$12 \times 4 = 48 \text{ bits}$$

as compared to 40 bits using binary addition. This is six bytes instead of five, a 20% increase.

Note that if we replaced the ABCD instruction in Program 8-2*a* or 8-2*b* with an ADDX instruction, these programs would provide a more general solution to the binary addition problem presented in Program 8-1.

8-3. 16-BIT BINARY MULTIPLICATION

Purpose: Multiply the 16-bit unsigned number in the variable NUM1 at location 6000 by the 16-bit unsigned binary number in the variable NUM2 at location 6002. Place the 32-bit result in the long word variable RESULT at location 6004 with the 16 most significant bits of the result in location 6004 and the 16 least significant bits in location 6006.

Sample Problems:

```
a.   Input:    NUM1     —   (6000) = 0003
                NUM2     —   (6002) = 0005
     Output:   RESULT   —   (6004) = 0000
                             (6006) = 000F
                             or in decimal, 3 × 5 = 15
b.   Input:    NUM1     —   (6000) = 706F
                NUM2     —   (6002) = 0161
     Output:   RESULT   —   (6004) = 009B
                             (6006) = 090F
                             or in decimal, 28783 × 353 = 10160399
```

Program 8-3a:

```
       00006000     DATA      EQU      $6000
       00004000     PROGRAM   EQU      $4000

       00006000               ORG      DATA
006000 00000002     NUM1      DS.W     1                16-BIT MULTIPLICAND
006002 00000002     NUM2      DS.W     1                16-BIT MULTIPLIER
006004 00000004     RESULT    DS.L     1                32-BIT  MULTIPLICATION RESULT

       00004000               ORG      PROGRAM

004000 30386000     PGM_8_3A  MOVE.W   NUM1,D0          MULTIPLICAND
004004 C0F86002               MULU     NUM2,D0          UNSIGNED MULTIPLICATION
004008 21C06004               MOVE.L   D0,RESULT        STORE 32-BIT MULTIPLICATION RESULTS

00400C 4E75                   RTS

                              END      PGM_8_3A
```

The MC68000 supports signed, as well as unsigned, binary multiplication or division. To multiply two signed 16-bit binary numbers, you simply replace MULU with MULS, the Signed Multiply instruction.

Besides its obvious uses in, for example, point-of-sale terminals, multiplication is also a key part of many mathematical algorithms. The speed at which a processor can perform multiplication determines its usefulness in process control, adaptive control, signal detection, and signal analysis.

Multidimensional Arrays

Another common use of multiplication is in locating elements in multidimensional arrays. For example, if we have an array of sensor readings organized by remote station number and sensor number, we can refer to the reading from the seventh sensor at station number 5 as R(5,7), where R is the name of the entire array. The usual method of storing such an array is to start at address RBASE with R(0,0) and continue with R(0,1), etc. If there are three stations (0,1, and 2) and four sensors at each station (0, 1, 2, and 3), we keep the readings in the following memory locations:

Memory Location	Reading
RBASE	R(0,0)
RBASE + 1	R(0,1)
RBASE + 2	R(0,2)
RBASE + 3	R(0,3)
RBASE + 4	R(1,0)
RBASE + 5	R(1,1)
RBASE + 6	R(1,2)
RBASE + 7	R(1,3)
RBASE + 8	R(2,0)
RBASE + 9	R(2,1)
RBASE + 10	R(2,2)
RBASE + 11	R(2,3)

In general, if we know the station number I and the sensor number J, the reading R(I,J) is located at address

$$\text{RBASE} + (\text{N} \times \text{I}) + \text{J}$$

where N is the number of sensors at each station. Thus, locating a particular reading in order to update it, display it, or perform some mathemetical operations on it requires a multiplication. For example, the operator might want an instrument to print the current reading of sensor 03 at station 02. To find that reading, the processor must calculate the address

$$\text{RBASE} + (4 \times 2) + 3 = \text{RBASE} + 11$$

Even more multiplications are necessary if the array has more dimensions. For example, we might organize the sensors by station number, position in the X direction, and position in the Y direction. (Each station thus has sensors at regular positions on a two-dimensional surface.) Now we can describe a reading R(2,3,1), which refers to the reading of the sensor at station 02, X position 03, and Y position 01. We can add even more dimensions, such as vertical position, type of sensor, or time of reading. Each added dimension means that the processor must perform more multiplications to locate elements in the essentially one-dimensional memory.

A Binary Multiplication Algorithm

It is interesting to look at a binary multiplication routine for two reasons: first, we can compare the execution time of the routine with the MULU or MULS instruction; and second, some other microprocessors don't have multiply instructions and understanding multiplication is important.

You can perform multiplication on a computer in the same way that you do long multiplication by hand. Since the numbers are binary, you will only multiply by 0 or 1; multiplying by zero obviously give zero as a result, while multiplying by one produces the same number you started with (the multiplicand). So each step in binary multiplication can be reduced to the following operation: if the current bit in the multiplier is 1, add the multiplicand to the partial product.

The only remaining problem is to ensure that you line everything up correctly each time. The following operations perform this task.

1. Shift the multiplier left one bit so that the bit to be examined is placed in the Carry.
2. Shift the product left one bit so that the next addition is lined up correctly.

To keep things simple, we will multiply two 8-bit values to produce a 16-bit result.

Step 1 - Initialization

Product = 0
Counter = 8

Step 2 - Shift Product so as to line up properly

Product = 2 × Product (LSB = 0)

Step 3 - Shift Multiplier so bit goes to Carry

Multiplier = 2 × Multiplier

Step 4 - Add Multiplicand to Product if Carry is 1

If Carry = 1, Product = Product + Multiplicand

Step 5 - Decrement Counter and check for zero

Counter = Counter − 1
If Counter > 0 go to Step 2

Assuming the multiplier is 61_{16} and the multiplicand is $6F_{16}$, the algorithm works as follows.

Initialization:

Product	0000	=	0000000000000000_2
Multiplier	61	=	01100001_2
Multiplicand	6F	=	01101111_2
Counter	08		

After first iteration of steps 2-5:

Product	0000	=	0000000000000000_2
Multiplier	C2	=	11000010_2
Multiplicand	6F	=	01101111_2
Counter	07		
Carry from Multiplier	0		

After second iteration:

Product	006F	=	0000000001101111_2
Multiplier	84	=	10000100_2
Multiplicand	6F	=	01101111_2
Counter	06		
Carry from Multiplier	1		

After third iteration:

Product	014D	=	0000000101001101_2
Multiplier	08	=	00001000_2
Multiplicand	6F	=	01101111_2
Counter	05		
Carry from Multiplier	1		

After fourth iteration:

Product	029A	=	0000001010011010_2
Multiplier	10	=	00010000_2
Multiplicand	6F	=	01101111_2
Counter	04		
Carry from Multiplier	0		

After fifth iteration:

Product	0534	=	0000010100110100_2
Multiplier	20	=	00100000_2
Multiplicand	6F	=	01101111_2
Counter	03		
Carry from Multiplier	0		

After sixth iteration:

Product	0A68	=	0000101001101000_2
Multiplier	40	=	01000000_2
Multiplicand	6F	=	01101111_2
Counter	02		
Carry from Multiplier	0		

After seventh iteration:

Product	14D0	=	0001010011010000_2
Multiplier	80	=	10000000_2
Multiplicand	6F	=	01101111_2
Counter	01		
Carry from Multiplier	0		

After eighth iteration:

Product	2A0F	=	0010101000001111_2
Multiplier	00	=	00000000_2
Multiplicand	6F	=	01101111_2
Counter	00		
Carry from Multiplier	1		

Program 8-3b:

```
       00006000     DATA      EQU      $6000
       00004000     PROGRAM   EQU      $4000

       00006000               ORG      DATA
006000 00000002     NUM1      DS       1             16-BIT MULTIPLICAND
006002 00000002     NUM2      DS       1             16-BIT MULTIPLIER
006004 00000004     RESULT    DS.L     1             32-BIT  MULTIPLICATION RESULT

       00004000               ORG      PROGRAM

004000 4280         PGM_8_3B  CLR.L    D0            CLEAR 32-BIT PRODUCT
004002 2200                   MOVE.L   D0,D1         UPPER WORD MUST BE CLEAR FOR ADD.L
004004 32386000               MOVE.W   NUM1,D1       16-BIT MULTIPLICAND
004008 34386002               MOVE.W   NUM2,D2       16-BIT MULTIPLIER
00400C 760F                   MOVEQ    #16-1,D3      LOOP COUNT := 16 (-1 FOR DBRA)

00400E D080         LOOP      ADD.L    D0,D0         SHIFT PRODUCT LEFT 1 BIT
004010 D442                   ADD.W    D2,D2         SHIFT MULTIPLIER LEFT 1 BIT
004012 6402                   BCC.S    STEP          IF MULTIPLIER[15] WAS 1

004014 D081                   ADD.L    D1,D0         ...THEN ADD MULTIPLICAND
```

```
004016 51CBFFF6      STEP     DBRA     D3,LOOP              ...ELSE CONTINUE
00401A 21C06004               MOVE.L   D0,RESULT            STORE RESULT

00401E 4E75                   RTS

                              END      PGM_8_3B
```

Flowchart 8-3b:

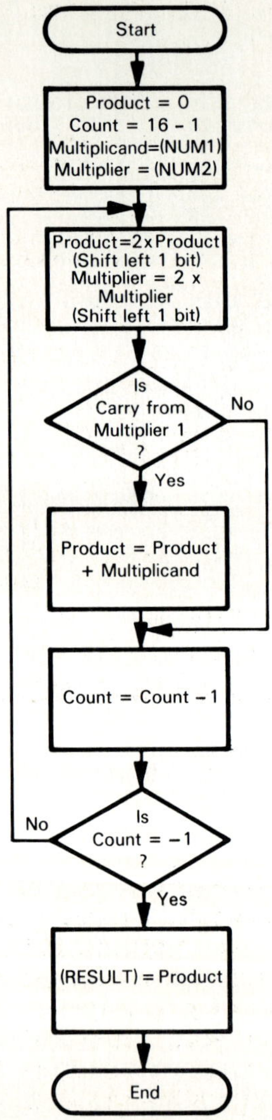

This program performs the same 16-bit multiplication operation as Program 8-3*a*. If you count clock cycles for the two versions, you will find the expected results: the MULU version takes less than 109 cycles while the long version (Program 8-3*b*) takes 58 cycles outside the loop, and 516 + 6n (n = number of 1 bits in multiplier) cycles inside the loop.

8-4. 32-BIT BINARY DIVIDE

Purpose: Divide the 32-bit unsigned number in variable NUM1 at location 6000 by the 16-bit unsigned binary number in variable NUM2 at location 6004. Place the 16-bit remainder in the variable REMAINDER at location 6006 and the 16-bit quotient in the variable QUOTIENT at location 6008.

Sample Problem:

Input:	NUM1	—	(6000) = 0074
			(6002) = CBB1 32-bit dividend
	NUM2	—	(6004) = 0141 16-bit divisor
Output:	REMAINDER	—	(6006) = 004C
	QUOTIENT	—	(6008) = 5D25
			or in decimal, 7654321 321 = 23845 with remainder of 76

Program 8-4:

```
         00006000    DATA      EQU     $6000
         00004000    PROGRAM   EQU     $4000

         00006000              ORG     DATA
006000 00000004    NUM1      DS.L    1              32-BIT DIVIDEND
006004 00000002    NUM2      DS.W    1              16-BIT DIVISOR
006006 00000002    REMAIND   DS.W    1              16-BIT REMAINDER
006008 00000002    QUOTIENT  DS.W    1              16-BIT QUOTIENT

         00004000              ORG     PROGRAM

004000 20386000    PGM_8_4   MOVE.L  NUM1,D0        32 BIT DIVIDEND
004004 80F86004              DIVU    NUM2,D0        UNSIGNED DIVIDE - NUM1/NUM2
004008 21C06006              MOVE.L  D0,REMAIND     STORE RESULTS-REMAINDER & QUOTIENT

00400C 4E75                  RTS

                             END     PGM_8_4
```

The MC68000 provides two instructions (DIVU and DIVS) which perform a divide operation using a 32-bit binary dividend and a 16-bit binary divisor. The operation results in a 16-bit binary quotient as well as a 16-bit binary remainder. The DIVU instruction should be used for unsigned arithmetic, while the DIVS instruction is used with signed numbers. When performing a signed divide, the sign of the remainder will be the same as the sign of the dividend. The sign of the quotient is positive if both operands have the same sign and negative if they have different signs. Both instructions place the remainder in the 16 most significant bits of the destination data register while the quotient is placed in the 16 least significant bits of the destination data register.

Two special conditions can occur when executing either of the Divide instruction. First, if the divisor equals zero, the processor will cause a zero divide trap. (A description of traps and of trap processing will be delayed until Chapter 15.) Secondly, the microprocessor may detect an overflow condition. In this case, the Overflow (V) bit in the status register will be set and the operands will be unaffected.

PROBLEMS

8-1. MULTIPLE PRECISION BINARY SUBTRACTION

Purpose: Subtract one multiple-word number from another. The length in words of both numbers is in the variable LENGTH at location 6000. The numbers themselves are stored (most significant bits first) in the variables NUM1 and NUM2 at locations 6002 and 6102, respectively. Subtract the number in NUM2 from the one in NUM1. Store the difference in NUM1.

Sample Problem:

Input:	LENGTH	—	(6000) = 0003
	NUM1	—	(6002) = 2F5B
			(6004) = 47C3
			(6006) = 306C
	NUM2	—	(6102) = 14DF
			(6104) = 85B8
			(6106) = 03BC
Output:	NUM1	—	(6002) = 1A7B
			(6004) = C20B
			(6006) = 2CBO

```
That is:   2F5B47C3306C
         - 14DF85B803BC
         --------------
           1A7BC20B2CBO
```

8-2. DECIMAL SUBTRACTION

Purpose: Subtract one multiple-byte packed decimal (BCD) number from another. The length in bytes of both numbers is in the byte variable LENGTH at location 6000. The numbers themselves (most significant digits first) are in the variables NUM1 and NUM2 at locations 6001 and 6101, respectively. Subtract the number contained in NUM2 from the one starting in NUM1. Store the difference in NUM1.

Sample Problem:

Input:	LENGTH	—	(6000) = 04
	NUM1	—	(6001) = 36
			(6002) = 70
			(6003) = 19
			(6004) = 85
	NUM2	—	(6101) = 12
			(6102) = 66
			(6103) = 34
			(6104) = 59
Output:	NUM1	—	(6001) = 24
			(6002) = 03
			(6003) = 85
			(6004) = 26

```
That is:   36701985
         - 12663459
         ----------
           24038526
```

8-3. 32-BIT BY 32-BIT MULTIPLY

Purpose: Multiply the 32-bit value in the variable NUM1 which begins in memory location 6000 (high-order) by the 32-bit value in variable NUM2 at location 6004. Do the multiply twice: first use the MULU instruction and place the results in the 64-bit variable PROD1 starting at location 6008; then use a shift and add method as illustrated in Program 8-3*b* and place the result in the 64-bit variable PROD2 starting at location 6010.

Sample Problem:

Input:	NUM1	—	(6000) = 0024
			(6002) = 68AC
	NUM2	—	(6004) = 0328
			(6006) = 1088
Output:	PROD1	—	(6008) = 0000
			(600A) = 72EC
			(600C) = BBC2
			(600E) = 5B60
	PROD2	—	(6010) = 0000
			(6012) = 72EC
			(6014) = B8C2
			(6016) = 5B60

REFERENCES

Other methods for implementing multiplication, division, and other arithmetic tasks are discussed in:

Ali, Z. "Know the LSI Hardware Tradeoffs of Digital Signal Processors," *Electronic Design,* June 21, 1979, pp. 66-71.

Geist, D. J. "MOS Processor Picks up Speed with Bipolar Multipliers," *Electronics,* July 7, 1977, pp. 113-15.

Kolodzinski, A. and D. Wainland. "Multiplying with a Microcomputer," *Electronic Design,* January 18, 1978, pp. 78-83.

Mor, S. "An 8 x 8 Multiplier and 8-Bit Microprocessor Perform 16 x 16-Bit Multiplication,"*EDN,* November 5, 1979, pp. 147-52.

Tao, T. F. et al. "Applications of Microprocessors in Control Problems," Proceedings of the 1977 Joint Automatic Control Conference, San Francisco, Ca., June 22-24, 1977.

Waser, S. "State-of-the-Art in High-Speed Arithmetic Integrated Circuits," *Computer Design,* July 1978, pp. 67-75.

Waser, S. and A. Peterson. "Medium-Speed Multipliers Trim Cost, Shrink Bandwidth in Speech Transmission," *Electronic Design,* February 1, 1979, pp. 58-65.

Weissberger, A. J. and T. Toal. "Tough Mathematical Tasks are Child's Play for Number Cruncher," *Electronics,* February 17, 1977, pp. 102-07.

9
Tables and Lists

Tables and lists are two of the basic data structures used with all computers. We have already seen tables used to perform code conversions and arithmetic. Tables may also be used to identify or respond to commands and instructions, provide access to files or records, define the meaning of keys or switches, and choose among alternate programs. Lists are usually less structured than tables. Lists may record tasks that the processor must perform, messages or data that the processor must record, or conditions that have changed or should be monitored. Tables are a simple way of making decisions or solving problems, since no computations or logical functions are necessary. The task, then, is reduced to organizing the table so that the proper entry is easy to find. Lists allow the execution of sequences of tasks, the preparation of sets of results, and the construction of interrelated data (or data bases). Problems include how to add elements to a list and remove elements from it.

PROGRAM EXAMPLES

9-1. ADD ENTRY TO LIST

Purpose: Add the contents of the word variable ITEM at memory location 6000 to a list if it is not already present in the list. The list is comprised of word elements and the starting address of the list is in the long-word variable LIST at memory location 6002. The first word of the list contains the list's length in words.

Sample Problems:

a.

Input:	ITEM —	(6000)	=	16B2	
	LIST —	(6002)	=	00005000	List's address
		(5000)	=	0004	Length of list
		(5002)	=	5376	
		(5004)	=	7618	
		(5006)	=	138A	
		(5008)	=	21DC	
Output:		(5000)	=	0005	Length of list
		.			
		.			
		.			
		(500A)	=	16B2	

b.

Input:	ITEM —	(6000)	=	16B2
	LIST —	(6002)	=	00005000
		(5000)	=	0003
		(5002)	=	5376
		(5004)	=	16B2
		(5006)	=	7431

Output: No change to list, since the item is already in the list at location 5004.

Flowchart 9-1a:

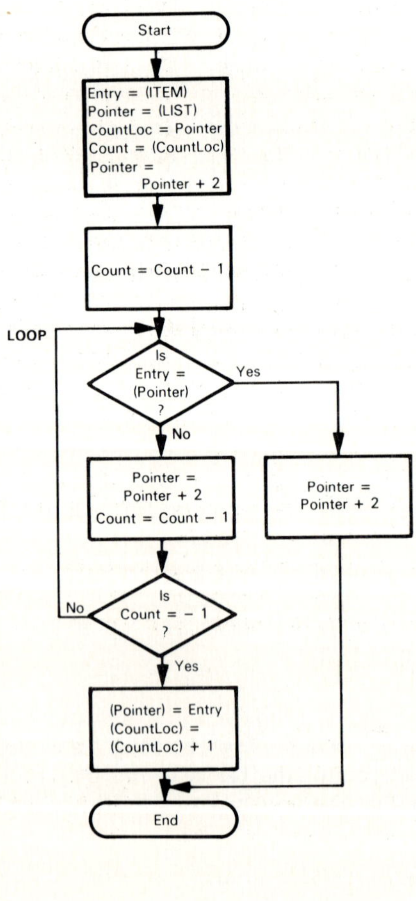

Program 9-1a:

```
         00006000        DATA      EQU      $6000
         00004000        PROGRAM   EQU      $4000

         00006000        ITEM      EQU      $6000        SEARCH ITEM
         00006002        LIST      EQU      $6002        POINTER TO START OF LIST

         00004000                  ORG      PROGRAM

004000 30386000          PGM_9_1A MOVE.W   ITEM,D0      GET SEARCH ITEM
004004 20786002                    MOVEA.L  LIST,A0      A0 - POINTER TO LIST
004008 2248                        MOVEA.L  A0,A1        SAVE POINTER TO LIST COUNT
00400A 3218                        MOVE.W   (A0)+,D1     D1.W - NUMBER OF ELEMENTS IN LIST
00400C 5341                        SUBQ.W   #1,D1        ADJUST FOR DBEQ

00400E B058              LOOP      CMP.W    (A0)+,D0     TEST NEXT ELEMENT FOR MATCH
004010 57C9FFFC                    DBEQ     D1,LOOP      CONTINUE UNTIL MATCH OR LIST END
004014 6704                        BEQ.S    DONE         IF MATCH THEN DONE

004016 3080                        MOVE.W   D0,(A0)      ...ELSE ADD ELEMENT TO LIST
004018 5251                        ADDQ.W   #1,(A1)      INCREMENT LIST COUNT

00401A 4E75              DONE      RTS

                                   END      PGM_9_1A
```

In this program, we use the autoincrement mode of addressing to access the list indirectly via register A0. When we move the length of the list to register D1, the pointer in A0 was also autoincremented so that it points to the first item in the list when LOOP is begun. When we exit from the loop due to no match being found, the pointer will have already been incremented to point to the location beyond the last item currently in the list; thus we don't have to adjust the pointer in order to add the new entry to the end of the list. You should compare this program to Program 5-4*b* to clarify those situations that require pointers to be adjusted and those that do not.

Clearly, the method of adding elements used in this program is very inefficient if the list is long. We could improve the procedure by limiting the search to part of the list or by ordering the list. We could limit the search by using the entry to get a starting point in the list. This method is called *hashing,* and is much like selecting a starting page in a dictionary or directory on the basis of the first letter in an entry.[1] We could order the list by numerical value. The search could end when the list values went beyond the entry (larger or smaller, depending on the ordering technique used). A new entry would have to be inserted properly, and all the other entries would have to be moved down in the list.

The program could be restructured to use two tables. One table could provide a starting point in the other table; for example, the search point could be based on the most or least significant 4-bit digit in the entry.

The program does not work if the length of the list is zero. (What happens?) We could avoid this problem by checking the length initially. The initialization procedure and other program changes required are shown in Program 9-1*b*.

Program 9-1b:

```
         00006000        DATA      EQU      $6000
         00004000        PROGRAM   EQU      $4000

         00006000        ITEM      EQU      $6000        SEARCH ITEM
         00006002        LIST      EQU      $6002        POINTER TO START OF LIST

         00004000                  ORG      PROGRAM
```

```
004000 30386000        PGM_9_1B MOVE.W   ITEM,D0        GET SEARCH OBJECT
004004 20786002                 MOVEA.L  LIST,A0        A0 - POINTER TO LIST
004008 2248                     MOVEA.L  A0,A1          SAVE POINTER TO LIST COUNT
00400A 3218                     MOVE.W   (A0)+,D1       D1.W - NUMBER OF ELEMENTS IN LIST
00400C 670A                     BEQ.S    INSERT         IF LENGTH = 0 THEN INSERT ITEM

00400E 5341                     SUBQ.W   #1,D1          ADJUST FOR DBEQ

004010 B058            LOOP     CMP.W    (A0)+,D0       TEST NEXT ELEMENT FOR MATCH
004012 57C9FFFC                 DBEQ     D1,LOOP        CONTINUE UNTIL MATCH OR LIST END
004016 6704                     BEQ.S    DONE           IF MATCH THEN DONE

004018 3080            INSERT   MOVE.W   D0,(A0)        ELSE ADD ELEMENT TO LIST
00401A 5251                     ADDQ.W   #1,(A1)        INCREMENT LIST COUNT

00401C 4E75            DONE     RTS

                                END      PGM_9_1B
```

If the length of the list is zero, it means that there are currently no elements in the list. Therefore, the element in ITEM cannot be in the list and must be inserted (as the first element of the list).

9-2. CHECK AN ORDERED LIST

Purpose: Check the contents of the word variable ITEM at memory location 6000 to see if it is in an ordered list. The list consists of 16-bit unsigned binary numbers in increasing order. The address of the first element in the list is in the variable LIST at location 6004. The first entry in the list is the list's length in words. If the contents of ITEM are in the list, place the index of its entry in the variable INDEX at 6002; otherwise, set INDEX to $FFFF_{16}$.

Sample Problems:

```
a.    Input:   ITEM —   (6000)  =  5376
               LIST —   (6004)  =  00005000
                        (5000)  =  0004          List's length
                        (5002)  =  138A
                        (5004)  =  21DC
                        (5006)  =  5376
                        (5008)  =  8613
      Output:  INDEX —  (6002)  =  0004, since the search item is at
                                         location 5006 = (5002+0004).

b.    Input:   ITEM —   (6000)  =  46B2
               LIST —   (6004)  =  00005000
                        (5000)  =  0002
                        (5002)  =  138A
                        (5004)  =  71DC
      Output:  INDEX —  (6002)  =  FFFF,  since the search item is
                                          not in the list.
```

Flowchart 9-2a:

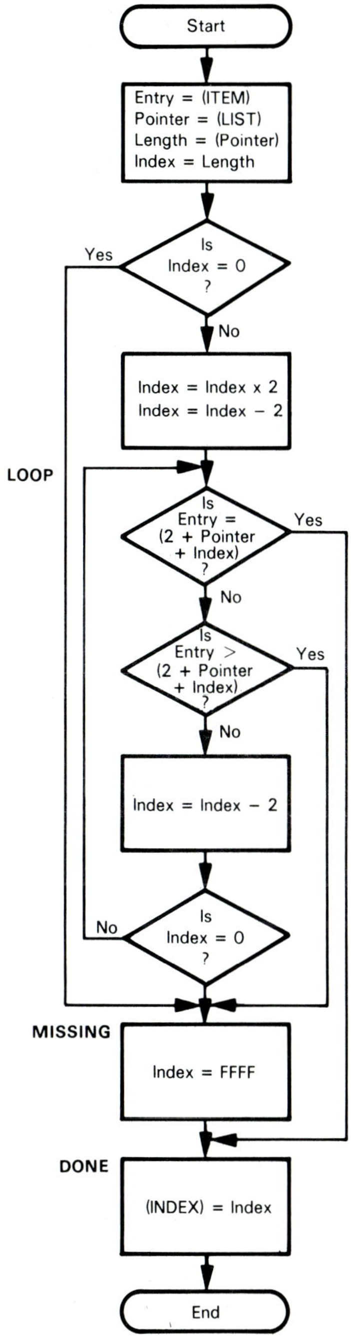

Program 9-2a:

```
         00006000       DATA      EQU      $6000
         00004000       PROGRAM   EQU      $4000

         00006000       ITEM      EQU      $6000
         00006002       INDEX     EQU      $6002
         00006004       LIST      EQU      $6004

         00004000                 ORG      PROGRAM

004000 30386000         PGM_9_2A  MOVE.W   ITEM,D0          GET SEARCH OBJECT
004004 20786004                   MOVEA.L  LIST,A0          GET START ADDRESS OF LIST
004008 7200                       MOVEQ    #0,D1            CLEAR THE ELEMENT COUNT
00400A 3210                       MOVE.W   (A0),D1          GET THE ELEMENT COUNT
00400C 6710                       BEQ.S    MISSING          IF LENGTH = 0,OBJECT IS NOT IN LIST

00400E D241                       ADD.W    D1,D1            EACH ELEMENT CONSISTS OF TWO BYTES
004010 5541                       SUBQ.W   #2,D1            INDEX RANGE = 0 - (LENGTH*2 - 2) !

004012 B0701002         LOOP      CMP.W    2(A0,D1.W),D0    SEARCH FROM END OF LIST TO START
004016 6708                       BEQ.S    DONE             OBJECT IS IN LIST, D1 HOLDS INDEX
004018 6204                       BHI.S    MISSING          LIST ELEM. SMALLER, OBJ NOT IN LIST
00401A 5541                       SUBQ.W   #2,D1            INDEX FOR NEXT SMALLER ELEMENT
00401C 64F4                       BCC      LOOP             INDEX >= 0   - CONTINUE

00401E 72FF             MISSING   MOVEQ    #$FF,D1          "NOT FOUND"-INDEX

004020 31C16002         DONE      MOVE.W   D1,INDEX         SAVE INDEX

004024 4E75                       RTS

                                  END      PGM_9_2A
```

The searching process of this program takes advantage of the fact that the elements are ordered. We begin the search with the last element in this list which will also be the largest. Once we find an element smaller than the entry, the search is over, since subsequent elements will be even smaller. You may want to try an example to convince yourself that the procedure works.

As in the previous problem, any method of choosing a good starting point will speed up the search. One such method starts in the middle of the list, determines which half of the list the entry is in, then divides the half into halves, and so on. This method is called a binary search since it divides the remaining part of the list into halves each time.[2,3]

Program 9-2*a* works if the length is zero since we test for zero length when forming the word index. Note the addressing mode used with the CMP.W instruction in the loop. This is a good example of how to use the indexed addressing with displacement mode. Address register A0 points to the "base" of a data structure, which in this case is an ordered list with the list's length being the first element in the list. The displacement is used to address a substructure, in this case the first number in the list. Register D1 is used as an index register to dynamically access the objects within the list. This addressing method can be illustrated as follows:

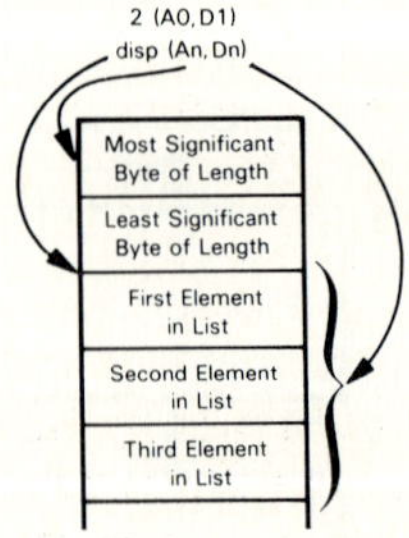

Remember that the displacement is interpreted as a two's complement number: it is possible to have a negative displacement. The size of the displacement is eight bits, and since the displacement is sign-extended, this allows for displacements in the range −128 bytes to +127 bytes.

The effective address is calculated by adding the sign-extended displacement to the *32-bit* contents of the address register and the index register. The value in the index register is treated as a signed number. If you define the index register size to be word, as we have done in this program with D1, the value in the index register is sign-extended to 32 bits for the effective address calculation. The actual contents of the index register are not, however, affected by the address calculation.

Because the index register may contain a negative number, the final effective address may be before or after the base address in the address register.

Note that an unsigned comparison, BHI, is used in this program. In the sample problems, a comparison using GT will not work correctly since the last entry in the list, 8613, has its sign bit set. Unsigned compares are particularly useful when dealing with addresses, which are always unsigned.

The two branch instructions (BEQ.S and BHI.S) in this program can be replaced by a single branch instruction which will speed up execution of the loop. Program 9-2*b* is the resultant program:

Program 9-2b:

```
       00006000    DATA      EQU      $6000
       00004000    PROGRAM   EQU      $4000

       00006000    ITEM      EQU      $6000
       00006002    INDEX     EQU      $6002
       00006004    LIST      EQU      $6004

       00004000              ORG      PROGRAM

004000 30386000    PGM_9_2B  MOVE.W   ITEM,D0            GET SEARCH OBJECT
004004 20786004              MOVEA.L  LIST,A0            GET START ADDRESS OF LIST
004008 7200                  MOVEQ    #0,D1              CLEAR THE ELEMENT COUNT
00400A 3210                  MOVE.W   (A0),D1            GET THE ELEMENT COUNT
00400C 6710                  BEQ.S    MISSING            IF LENGTH = 0,OBJECT IS NOT IN LIST

00400E D241                  ADD.W    D1,D1              EACH ELEMENT CONSISTS OF TWO BYTES
004010 5541                  SUBQ.W   #2,D1              INDEX RANGE = 0 - (LENGTH*2 - 2) !

004012 B0701002    LOOP      CMP.W    2(A0,D1.W),D0      SEARCH FROM END OF LIST TO START
004016 6404                  BCC.S    LPEXIT             DONE IF FOUND OR ITEM > LIST ELEM.
004018 5541                  SUBQ.W   #2,D1              INDEX FOR NEXT SMALLER ELEMENT
00401A 64F6                  BCC      LOOP               INDEX >= 0  - CONTINUE

00401C 6702        LPEXIT    BEQ.S    DONE               OBJECT IS IN LIST, D1 HOLDS INDEX

00401E 72FF        MISSING   MOVEQ    #$FF,D1            "NOT FOUND"-INDEX

004020 31C16002    DONE      MOVE.W   D1,INDEX           SAVE INDEX

004024 4E75                  RTS

                             END      PGM_9_2B
```

In this program, the first branch instruction in the loop transfers control to LPEXIT if the entry is equal to or greater than the list element being compared. There is one dangerous aspect that has been introduced in this program, however. Take a look at the

BEQ instruction at LPEXIT. There are two different ways in which the program can arrive at this instruction:

1. the BCC.S LPEXIT instruction in the loop can cause a branch to LPEXIT and in this case the status flags are set according to the result of the CMP.W instruction in the loop.
2. if all elements in the list have been tested without finding the entry item, then the loop is exhausted and the instruction immediately following BCC LOOP is executed. In this case, the status flags are set according to the results of the SUBQ instruction in the loop.

Thus, the BEQ instruction at LPEXIT tests the status flags that have been set by one of two possible instructions. You must be very careful to ensure that there are not conflicting conditions which will give you unexpected results and errors that are very difficult to find. The surest way to avoid errors is to make up a table to see what happens for all possible situations. Such a table for Program 9-2*b* would look like this:

		N	Z	V	C	
After CMP.W	item < (list)	?	0	?	1	These should cause exit from the loop. Use BCC to exit.
	item = (list)	0	1	0	0	
	item > (list)	?	0	?	0	
After SUBQ	D1 ≥ 0	?	?	?	0	This should cause loop to terminate. Use BCC to loop.
	D1 = −2	1	0	0	1	

As you can see from this table, the Z flag will always be 0 when the loop is exhausted. Thus, when the BEQ instruction at LPEXIT is executed following the BCC LOOP instruction, the branch to DONE will not be taken.

It is possible to speed up this program a bit more. Since the fastest loop in this case is the one that makes use of a CMP instruction with predecrement and the DBcc instruction, it may be worth the effort to write a program based on this construction. The changes required are shown in Program 9-2*c*.

Program 9-2c:

```
        00006000    DATA      EQU      $6000
        00004000    PROGRAM   EQU      $4000

        00006000    ITEM      EQU      $6000
        00006002    INDEX     EQU      $6002
        00006004    LIST      EQU      $6004

        00004000              ORG      PROGRAM

004000 20786004    PGM_9_2C  MOVEA.L  LIST,A0          GET START ADDRESS OF LIST
004004 3210                  MOVE.W   (A0),D1          GET THE ELEMENT COUNT
004006 6718                  BEQ.S    MISSING          IF LENGTH = 0,OBJECT IS NOT IN LIST

004008 5341                  SUBQ.W   #1,D1            ADJUST FOR DBCC AND INDEX RANGE
00400A 3401                  MOVE.W   D1,D2            D2 IS THE LOOP COUNTER

00400C D241                  ADD.W    D1,D1            EACH ELEMENT CONSISTS OF TWO BYTES
00400E 5441                  ADDQ.W   #2,D1            ADJUST FOR 1:ST PREDECREMENT IN LOP
004010 41F01002              LEA      2(A0,D1.W),A0    POINTER BEYOND END OF LIST

004014 30386000              MOVE.W   ITEM,D0          GET SEARCH OBJECT

004018 B060        LOOP      CMP.W    -(A0),D0         SEARCH FROM END OF LIST
00401A 54CAFFFC              DBCC     D2,LOOP          TEST NEXT IF ELEM>OBJ AND ELEM LEFT
00401E 6704                  BEQ.S    MATCHING         OBJECT IS IN LIST, D2 HAS INDEX
```

```
004020 74FF          MISSING   MOVEQ    #$FF,D2        "NOT FOUND"-INDEX
004022 6002                    BRA.S    DONE

004024 D442          MATCHING  ADD.W    D2,D2          ADJUST INDEX TO WORD SIZE
004026 31C26002      DONE      MOVE.W   D2,INDEX       SAVE IT

00402A 4E75                    RTS

                               END      PGM_9_2C
```

Flowchart 9-2c:

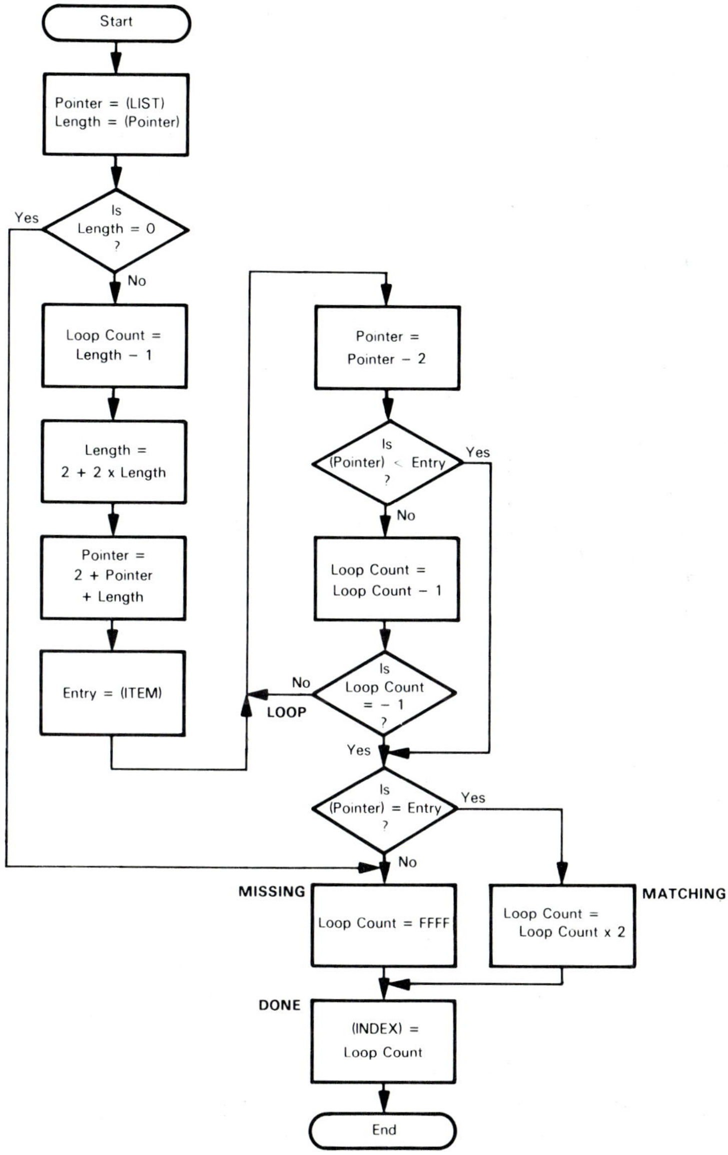

Besides changing the loop in the program, we have made some subtle changes to the initialization portion. First of all, note that we do not get the search object (entry) until we have first checked for length equal zero. There is no need to get the entry until we are sure that we have to perform a search.

The LEA instruction is used in this program to construct the address of the first element in the data structure in the same way as in Programs 9-2*a* and 9-2*b*, but in this case we form the starting address before we enter the loop.

Also note that Program 9-2*c* avoids the problem with the status flag that we discussed following Program 9-2*b*. Since the DBcc instruction does not affect the Condition codes, they are still set according to the result of the CMP.W instruction when the loop is exhausted and we can feel free to test in any way we want.

If you compare the clock cycles required to execute the loop in Program 9-2*c* you will see that it is more than twice as fast as the one in Program 9-2*a*. If it is possible that a loop may be executed many times, it is often worth the extra effort to reduce the execution time of the loop.

The average execution time of this simple search technique, regardless of which of the three programs you use, increases linearly with the length of the list. In comparison, the average execution time for a binary search increases logarithmically. For example, if the length of the list is doubled, the simple technique takes twice as long on the average while the binary search method only requires one extra iteration.

9-3. REMOVE AN ELEMENT FROM A QUEUE

Purpose: The variable QUEUE at memory location 6000 contains the address for the head of a queue. Save the address of the first element (head) of the queue in the variable POINTER at memory location 6002. Update the queue to remove the element. Each element in the queue is one word long and contains the address of the next element in the queue. The last element in the queue contains zero to indicate that there is no next element.

Queues are used to store data in the order in which it will be used, or tasks in the order in which they will be executed. The queue is a first-in, first-out (FIFO) data structure; that is, elements are removed from the queue in the same order in which they were entered. Operating systems place tasks in queues so that they will be executed in the proper order. I/O drivers transfer data to or from queues to ensure that the data will be transmitted or handled in the proper order. Buffers may be queued so that it becomes easy to find the next available buffer in a storage pool. Queues may also be used to link requests for storage, timing, or I/O to ensure that requests are satisfied in the correct order.

In real applications, each element in the queue would typically contain a large amount of information and/or storage space in addition to providing the address which links each element to the next one.

Linked Lists

One way to implement a queue is to make use of a linked list. Note that there is a difference between a data structure and the implementation of that data structure. For example, a queue is a data structure, and there are many different ways that you can implement a queue. However, the basic function of the queue (first-in, first-out) is always the same regardless of the way in which you implement this data structure.

The basic principle of a linked list is that each entry in the list contains the address to the next entry in the list, in addition to any data that may be found in a particular element. This can be illustrated as follows:

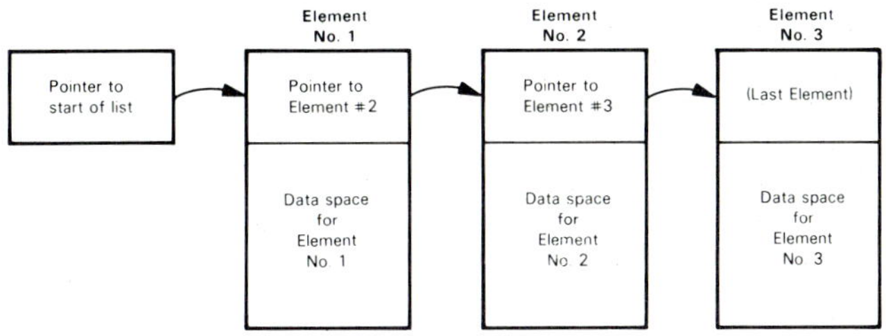

One advantage of this technique is that the elements in the list do not have to be stored sequentially in memory, since each entry contains the address pointing to the next entry. To change the order of two elements in a linked list, all you have to do is move the pointers — the data associated with each element need not be moved. Thus, to remove the first element in a queue we simply move a couple of pointers and the task is done; we don't have to move a single bit of data, just addresses. Linked lists require extra storage as compared to sequential lists, but elements are far easier to add, delete, or insert.

Sample Problems:

a.

Input:	QUEUE —	(6000)	=	00006020	Address of first element in queue
		(6020)	=	00006060	First element in queue
		(6060)	=	000060A0	
		(60A0)	=	00000000	Last element in queue
Output:	QUEUE —	(6000)	=	00006060	Address of new first element in queue
	POINTER —	(6004)	=	00006020	Address of element removed from queue

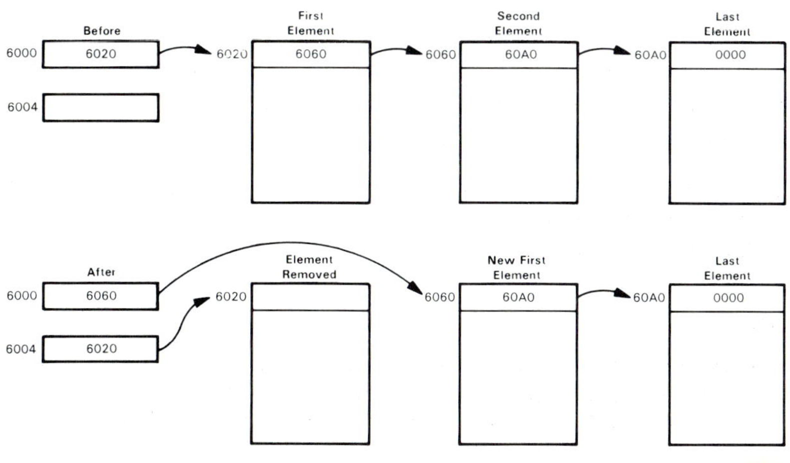

b.	Input:	QUEUE —	(6000)	=	00000000	Empty queue
	Output:	QUEUE —	(6000)	=	0000	
		POINTER —	(6004)	=	0000	No element available from queue

Flowchart 9-3:

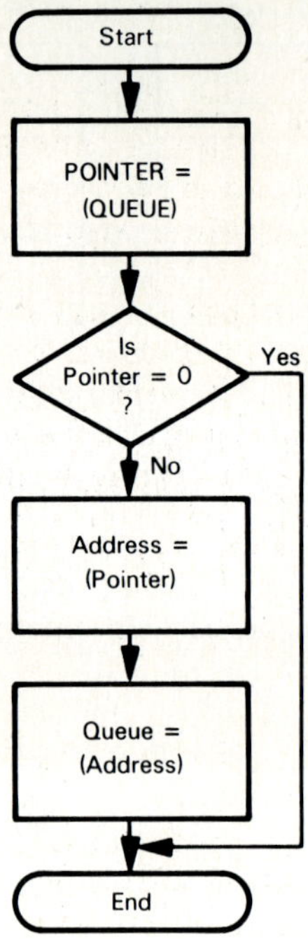

Program 9-3:

```
        00006000     DATA      EQU      $6000
        00004000     PROGRAM   EQU      $4000

        00006000     QUEUE     EQU      $6000              ADDRESS OF QUEUE HEAD
        00006004     POINTER   EQU      $6004              ADDRESS OF FORMER QUEUE HEAD

        00004000               ORG      PROGRAM

004000 21F860006004  PGM_9_3   MOVE.L   QUEUE,POINTER      SAVE OLD HEAD OF QUEUE
004006 6708                    BEQ.S    DONE               IF QUEUE EMPTY THEN DONE

004008 20786004                MOVE.L   POINTER,A0         ...ELSE REMOVE FIRST ELEMENT
00400C 21D06000                MOVE.L   (A0),QUEUE         AND REPLACE WITH SECOND
004010 4E75          DONE      RTS

                               END      PGM_9_3
```

Doubly Linked Lists

Sometimes you may want to maintain links in both directions. Then each element in the queue must contain the addresses of both the preceding and the following elements.[4,5] Such doubly linked lists allow you to retrace your steps easily (e.g., repeating the previous task if an error occurs in the current one) or access elements from either end (e.g., allowing you to remove or change the last two elements without having to go through the entire queue). **The data structure may then be used in either a first-in, first-out manner or in a last-in, first-out manner, depending on whether new elements are added to the head or to the tail.**

Empty Queue

If there are no elements in the queue, the program clears POINTER at location 6004. A program that requests an element from the queue must check this memory location to see if its request has been satisfied (i.e., if there was anything in the queue). Can you suggest other ways to indicate to the requesting program whether the queue is empty?

Another way of implementing a queue is as a list in sequential memory positions. The MC68000 architecture is well suited to manipulation of such queues. You can use any pair of address registers (A0 − A6) and the postincrement or predecrement mode of addressing to implement the queue. If the queue is to go from low to high memory, then the postincrement addressing mode is used, and if the queue goes from high to low memory, the predecrement mode would be used. For example, a queue going from low memory to high memory could be implemented using address registers A0 and A1 as shown in the following illustration:

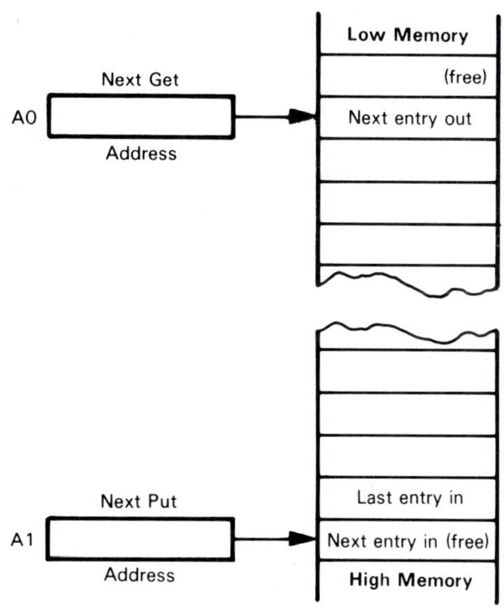

A0 points to the first or oldest entry in the queue while A1 points to the location where the next or newest entry in the queue will be made. If you use the postdecrement mode of addressing when accessing this queue, then A0 will always hold the next "get" address and register A1 will always hold the next "put" address for the queue.

Stack Operations

Another form of data structure similar to the queue is the stack: a stack is a last-in first-out (LIF0) list. Most microprocessors provide special push and pull instructions to manipulate stacks. In the MC68000, however, you can simply use the powerful MOVE instructions with predecrement or postincrement addressing to manipulate stacks.

You can implement a stack using a single address register in the predecrement or postincrement addressing mode. In fact, the processor itself uses address register A7 to maintain special system and user stacks. We will discuss the processor's use of these stacks further in Chapter 10.

Using Data Structures

The various indexed and indirect addressing modes allow us to use data structures in a very flexible way. If, for example, an address register contains the starting address of a block of information, we can refer to elements in the block with constant offsets.

How would we use such data structures? For example, we might want a piece of test equipment to execute a series of tests as specified by the operator. Using entries from a control panel, we will make up a queue of blocks of information, one for each test that the operator will eventually want to run. Each block of information contains:

1. The starting address of the next block (or 0 if there is no next block).
2. The starting address of the test program.
3. The address of the input device (e.g., keyboard, card reader, or communications line) from which data will be read during the test.
4. The address of the output device (e.g., printer, CRT terminal, or communications line) to which the results will be sent as the test is run.
5. The number of times the test will be repeated.
6. The starting address of the data area to be used for storing temporary data.
7. A flag that indicates whether failing a test should preclude continuing to the next test.

Clearly the block could contain even more information if there were more options for the operator to specify while setting up the test sequence. Note that some elements in the block contain data, others contain addresses, while still others may be 1-bit flags.

Consider what we mean by flexibility in this example. Some of the procedures that the operator can easily implement are:

1. Run the same test with different sets of I/O devices. A trial run might use data from a local keyboard and send the results to the CRT, while a production run might use data from a remote communications line and produce a permanent record on a printer.
2. Execute tests in any order, just by changing the order in the queue.
3. Place temporary data in an area where it can easily be displayed or retrieved by a debugging program.
4. Make alternative decisions as to whether tests should be continued, errors reported, or procedures repeated. Here again, trial or debugging runs may use one option, while production runs use another.

5. Delete or insert tests merely by changing the links which connect a test to its successor. The operator can thus correct errors or make changes without reentering the entire list of tests.

For example, assume that the operator enters the sequence TEST 1, TEST 2, TEST 4, and TEST 5, accidentally omitting TEST 3. The blocks are linked as follows:

Block 1 (for TEST 1) contains the starting address for block 2 (for TEST 2).

Block 2 (for TEST 2) contains the starting address for block 3 (for TEST 4).

Block 3 (for TEST 4) contains the starting address for block 4 (for TEST 5).

Block 4 (for TEST 5) contains a link address of zero to indicate that it is the last block.

To insert TEST 3 between TEST 2 and TEST 4 merely involves the following changes:

Block 2 (for TEST 2) must now contain the starting address for block 5 (for TEST 3).

Block 5 (for TEST 3) must contain the starting address for block 3 (for TEST 4).

No other changes are necessary and no blocks have to be moved. Note how much simpler it is to insert or delete using linked lists than to use lists that are stored in consecutive memory locations. There is no problem of moving elements up or down to remove or create empty spaces.

9-4. 8-BIT SORT

Purpose: Sort a list of unsigned binary 8-bit numbers into descending order. The address of the start of the list is in the variable LIST at memory location 6000. The first entry in the list is the number of remaining elements in the list — that is, the length of the list beyond this first entry. Thus, the list has 255 or fewer elements.

Sample Problem:

Input:	LIST —	(6000)	=	00005000	Address of beginning of list
		(5000)	=	06	Number of elements in list
		(5001)	=	2A	First element in list
		(5002)	=	B5	
		(5003)	=	60	
		(5004)	=	3F	
		(5005)	=	D1	
		(5006)	=	19	
Output:	LIST —	(6000)	=	00005000	
		(5000)	=	06	
		(5001)	=	D1	Largest element in list
		(5002)	=	B5	
		(5003)	=	60	
		(5004)	=	3F	
		(5005)	=	2A	
		(5006)	=	19	Smallest element in list

Simple Sorting Algorithm

A simple sorting technique works as follows:

Step 1. Clear a flag named EXCHANGE.

Step 2. Examine each consecutive pair of numbers in the list. If any are out of order, exchange them and set EXCHANGE.

Step 3. If EXCHANGE is set after the entire list has been examined, return to Step 1.

EXCHANGE will be set if any consecutive pair of numbers is found out of order. Therefore, if EXCHANGE is clear at the end of a pass through the entire list, the list is in proper order.

This sorting method is referred to as a "bubble sort." It is an easy algorithm to implement. However, it is slow; other sorting techniques should be considered when sorting long lists where speed is important.[6-8]

The technique operates as follows in a simple case. Let us assume that we want to sort a list into descending order; the list has four elements — 12, 03, 15, 08.

1st Iteration:

Step 1. EXCHANGE = 0

Step 2. Final order of the array is:

12
15
08
03

since the second pair (03, 15) is exchanged and so is the third pair (03, 08).

EXCHANGE = 1

2nd Iteration:

Step 1. EXCHANGE = 0

Step 2. Final order of the array is:

15
12
08
03

since the first pair (12, 15) is exchanged.

EXCHANGE = 1

3rd Iteration:

Step 1. EXCHANGE = 0

Step 2. The elements are already in order, so no exchanges are necessary and EXCHANGE remains 0.

This approach always requires one extra iteration to ensure that the elements are in the proper order. No exchanges are performed in the last iteration, so it does not really accomplish anything. **Tracing through the examples shows that many of the comparisons are wasted and even repetitive. Thus the method could be improved**

greatly, particularly if the number of elements is in the thousands or millions, as it commonly is in large data processing applications. New sorting techniques are an important area of current research.[9]

Flowchart 9-4:

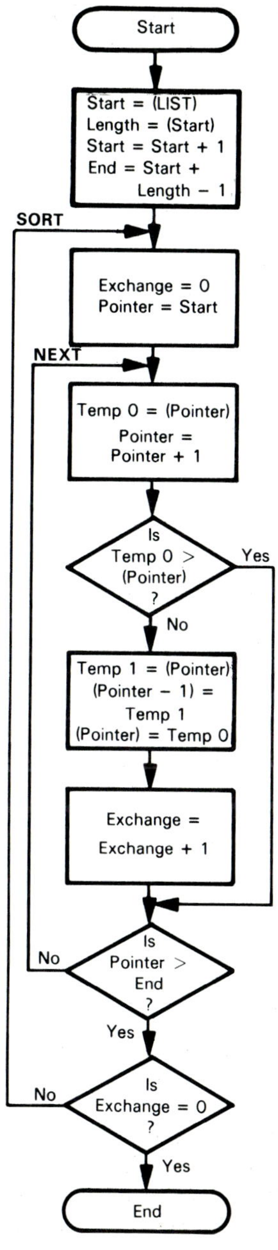

Program 9-4a:

```
        00006000        DATA      EQU       $6000
        00004000        PROGRAM   EQU       $4000

        00006000        LIST      EQU       $6000          ADDRESS TO START OF LIST

        00004000                  ORG       PROGRAM

004000 20786000         PGM_9_4A  MOVEA.L   LIST,A0        POINTER TO START OF LIST
004004 4240                       CLR.W     D0
004006 1018                       MOVE.B    (A0)+,D0       LENGTH OF LIST
004008 43F000FF                   LEA       -1(A0,D0.W),A1 POINTER TO LAST LIST ELEMENT

00400C 4241             SORT      CLR.W     D1             COUNTER FOR EXCHANGES
00400E 2448                       MOVEA.L   A0,A2          POINTER TO START OF LIST

004010 101A             NEXT      MOVE.B    (A2)+,D0       GET NEXT ELEMENT
004012 B012                       CMP.B     (A2),D0        COMPARE IT WITH FOLLOWING ELEMENT
004014 640A                       BCC.S     NSWITCH        IF PREVIOUS ELEMENT >= THEN DO NEXT

004016 1212                       MOVE.B    (A2),D1        ...ELSE EXCHANGE ELEMENTS
004018 1541FFFF                   MOVE.B    D1,-1(A2)
00401C 1480                       MOVE.B    D0,(A2)
00401E 5241                       ADDQ.W    #1,D1          INCREMENT EXCHANGE COUNT

004020 B3CA             NSWITCH   CMPA.L    A2,A1          END OF LIST
004022 62EC                       BHI       NEXT           IF NOT THEN LOOK AT NEXT ELEMENT
004024 4A41                       TST.W     D1             EXCHANGE OCCURRED?
004026 66E4                       BNE       SORT           YES, CONTINUE SORT
004028 4E75                       RTS

                                  END       PGM_9_4A
```

The program must reduce the end pointer A1 by 1 because the last element has no successor. The final comparison is between the next to last element and the last element. Before starting each sorting pass, we must be careful to reinitialize the pointer and the Exchange flag.

Previous examples in this chapter used counters to control loops. In this example we compare addresses. This avoids decrementing a counter on each step. It is interesting to note what happens if there are fewer than two elements in the list. Although the results are not as tragic as they would be if we used counters, the results are incorrect nevertheless. Actually, checking for this case is quite simple. We simply insert BRA.S NSWITCH before the statement labeled NEXT.

Two equal elements in the array must not be exchanged; if they are, the exchange will occur on every pass and the program will never end.

There are many ways to code this bubble sort program using the MC68000 instruction set. The memory-to-memory compare instruction can be used to reduce the program's size and improve loop processing. This variation, as well as others, are shown in Program 9-4*b*. What are the advantages and disadvantages of using the bit operate instructions to set the program's exchange flag? What happens if you don't test for zero elements in the list? Remember that DBRA tests for counter value = −1.

Program 9-4b:

```
        00006000        DATA      EQU       $6000
        00004000        PROGRAM   EQU       $4000

        00006000        LIST      EQU       $6000          START OF LIST

        00004000                  ORG       PROGRAM

004000 20786000         PGM_9_4B  MOVEA.L   LIST,A0        POINTER TO LIST LENGTH
004004 4280                       CLR.L     D0             CLEAR ALL 32 BITS OF D0
```

```
004006 1018                 MOVE.B  (A0)+,D0       LENGTH OF LIST
004008 6724                 BEQ.S   DONE           IF LENGTH = 0 THEN DONE
00400A 43E80001             LEA.L   1(A0),A1       POINTER TO SECOND ELEMENT
00400E 08810000             BCLR.B  #0,D1          EXCHANGE FLAG := 0
004012 5340                 SUBQ.W  #1,D0          ADJUST COUNTER FOR DBCC INSTRUCTION
004014 600E                 BRA.S   NSWITCH        CHECK FOR ONLY 1 ENTRY

004016 B308        NEXT     CMPM.B  (A0)+,(A1)+    COMPARE ADJACENT ENTRIES
004018 630A                 BLS.S   NSWITCH        IF FIRST <= SECOND THEN NO SWITCH
00401A 1420                 MOVE.B  -(A0),D2       EXCHANGE
00401C 10E1                 MOVE.B  -(A1),(A0)+    ... ENTRIES
00401E 12C2                 MOVE.B  D2,(A1)+
004020 08C10000             BSET.B  #0,D1          SET EXCHANGE FLAG

004024 51C8FFF0    NSWITCH  DBRA    D0,NEXT        COMPARE ALL ENTRIES
004028 08010000             BTST.B  #0,D1          EXCHANGE FLAG SET?
00402C 66D2                 BNE     PGM_9_4B       IF YES THEN REPEAT TESTING

00402E 4E75        DONE     RTS

                            END     PGM_9_4B
```

There have been entire books written on sorting and searching, so a discussion of sorting methods would be beyond our scope. However, there is one variation that should be considered. At the end of every step, we know that the smallest element is at the end of the list. Therefore the number of pairs we need to compare decreases by one each step. (Try a few examples to convince yourself this is true. Do you see how the method gets its name?) What changes to the program would take advantage of this?

9-5. USING AN ORDERED JUMP TABLE

Purpose: Use the contents of the variable INDEX at location 6000 as an index to a jump table starting at TABLE (location 6002). Each entry in the jump table contains a 16-bit address. The program should transfer control to the address with the appropriate index; that is, if the index is 6, the program jumps to address entry number 6 in the table. (Note that we start counting with entry number 0, the zeroth element in the table.)

Sample Problem:

INDEX —	(6000)	=	0002	
TABLE —	(6002)	=	4740	Zeroth element in jump table
	(6004)	=	47A6	
	(6006)	=	47D0	
	(6008)	=	4620	
	(600A)	=	4854	Fourth element in jump table

Result: (PC) = 0047D0 since that is entry number 2 (starting from zero) in the jump table. The next instruction to be executed will be the one located at that address.

Flowchart 9-5:

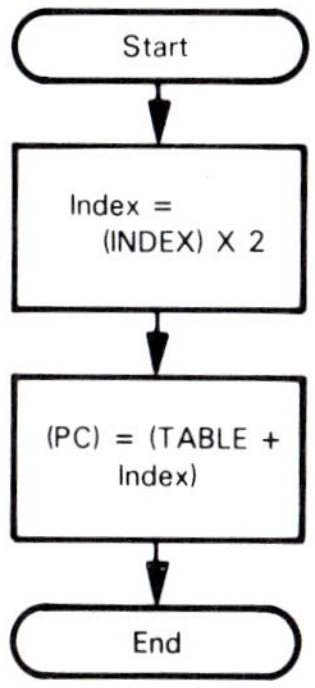

The last box in the flowchart results in a transfer of control to the address obtained from the table. No ending block is necessary. Such transfers do not bother the processor at all, but you may want to add special notes to your flowchart and program documentation so that the sequence does not appear to be a "dead-end street" to the reader.

Program 9-5a:

```
         00006000    DATA      EQU      $6000
         00004000    PROGRAM   EQU      $4000

         00006000    INDEX     EQU      $6000              INDEX INTO TABLE
         00006002    TABLE     EQU      $6002              START OF TABLE

         00004000              ORG      PROGRAM

004000 30786000      PGM_9_5A MOVEA.W  INDEX,A0            GET TABLE INDEX
004004 D0C8                   ADDA.W   A0,A0               ADJUST INDEX FOR WORD OFFSET
004006 32686002               MOVEA.W  TABLE(A0),A1        GET ADDRESS FROM TABLE
00400A 4ED1                   JMP      (A1)                TRANSFER TO ADDRESS

                              END      PGM_9_5A
```

When you run this program, be sure to place some executable code (such as a TRAP instruction) at each address to which control could be transferred. Otherwise the processor will be executing random code and you will have no way to tell which branch was taken.

Jump Tables

Jump tables are very useful in situations where the processor must select one of several routines for execution. Such situations arise in decoding commands (entered, for example, from a control keyboard), selecting test programs, choosing alternative methods or units, or selecting an I/O configuration. For example, a four-position switch on the front of an instrument or test system may select among the remote, self-test, automatic, or manual modes of operation. The processor reads the switch and selects the appropriate routine from a jump table. References 10 and 11 contain additional examples of the use of jump tables.

The jump table thus replaces a whole series of compare and jump operations. The program is compact, efficient and easily changed or extended.

The index into the jump table must be multiplied by 2 to give the correct word offset since each entry in the table is a 16-bit address occupying two bytes of memory. This assumes that the addresses in the table are short absolute references. What else does the program assume in regard to the length of the jump table?

If addresses in the table could reference anywhere in the processor's 16-megabyte address space, then each entry would require at least three bytes. By using entries of five bytes, this case could be handled by simply inserting an additional ADDA instruction and modifying the MOVE.W TABLE(A0),A1 to a MOVE.L instruction. However, you will encounter difficulties if you try to place the jump table in 9-5*a* at addresses greater than 7FFF. Why?

Program 9-5*b* illustrates another method of implementing the jump table using indexed addressing.

Program 9-5b:

```
         00006000      DATA      EQU       $6000
         00004000      PROGRAM   EQU       $4000

         00006000      INDEX     EQU       $6000                   INDEX INTO JUMP TABLE
         00006002      TABLE     EQU       $6002                   START OF JUMP TABLE

         00004000                ORG       PROGRAM

004000  207C00006002  PGM_9_5B   MOVEA.L   #TABLE,A0               GET TABLE ADDRESS
004006  30386000                 MOVE.W    INDEX,D0                GET TABLE INDEX
00400A  E540                     ASL.W     #2,D0                   ADJUST FOR 4 BYTE ENTRY
00400C  22700000                 MOVEA.L   0(A0,D0.W),A1           GET ADDRESS FROM JUMP TABLE
004010  4ED1                     JMP       (A1)

                                 END       PGM_9_5B
```

In both of these programs, the instruction JMP (A1) is an indirect jump which transfers the contents of register A1 to the program counter. This instruction sometimes causes confusion because of the "level of indirection." To clarify this, compare the action of JMP (A1) with MOVEA (A1),A0. In the case of JMP (A1), the program counter receives the value held in A1. In the MOVEA (A1),A0 instruction, A0 receives the value pointed to by A1.

This is an apparent inconsistency in the assembly language syntax. It can be resolved by reading the instruction JMP (A1) as:

"Jump to the location pointed to by A1."

What would happen if we had replaced the last two instructions in Program 9-5*a* with JMP TABLE(A0)?

How could you modify Program 9-5*b* to accept the address of the table in the variable TABLE, instead of the beginning of the table itself?

PROBLEMS

9-1. REMOVE ENTRY FROM LIST

Purpose: Remove the value in the variable ITEM at memory location 6000 from a list if the value is present. The address of the list is in the variable LIST at location 6002. The first entry in the list is the number (in words) of elements remaining in the list. Move entries below the one removed up one position and reduce the length of the list by 1.

Sample Problems:

a.	Input:	ITEM —	(6000)	=	D010	Entry to be removed
		LIST —	(6002)	=	00005000	Address of list
			(5000)	=	0004	Length of list
			(5002)	=	C121	First element in list
			(5004)	=	A346	
			(5006)	=	3A64	
			(5008)	=	6C20	
	Result:	No change to list since the entry is not in the list.				

b.	Input:	ITEM —	(6000)	=	D010	Entry to be removed
		LIST —	(6002)	=	00005000	Address of list
			(5000)	=	0004	Length of list
			(5002)	=	C121	First element in list
			(5004)	=	D010	
			(5006)	=	3A64	
			(5008)	=	6C20	
	Result:		(5000)	=	0003	Length of list reduced by 1
			(5002)	=	C121	
			(5004)	=	3A64	Other elements in list
			(5006)	=	6C20	moved up one position

9-2. ADD ENTRY TO ORDERED LIST

Purpose: Insert the value in the variable ITEM at location 6000 into an ordered list if it is not already there. The address of the list is in the variable LIST at location 6002. The first entry in the list is the list's length in words. The list itself consists of unsigned binary numbers in increasing order. Place the new entry in the correct position in the list, adjust the elements below it down, and increase the length of the list by 1.

Sample Problems:

a.	Input:	ITEM —	(6000)	=	7010	Entry to be added to list
		LIST—	(6002)	=	00005000	Address of list
			(5000)	=	0004	Length of list
			(5002)	=	0037	First element in list
			(5004)	=	5322	
			(5006)	=	A101	
			(5008)	=	C203	
	Result:		(5000)	=	005	Length of list increased
			(5002)	=	0037	by 1
			(5004)	=	5322	
			(5006)	=	7010	New entry
			(5008)	=	A101	Other elements moved
			(500A)	=	C203	down one position
b.	Input:	ITEM —	(6000)	=	7010	Entry to be added to list
		LIST —	(6002)	=	00005000	Address of list
			(5000)	=	0004	Length of list
			(5002)	=	0037	First element in list
			(5004)	=	5322	
			(5006)	=	7010	
			(5008)	=	C203	
	Result:	No change in the list since entry is already in the list.				

9-3. ADD ELEMENT TO QUEUE

Purpose: Add the value in the variable ITEM at memory location 6000 to a queue. The address of the first element in the queue is in the variable QUEUE at location 6002. Each element in the queue contains either the address of the next element in the queue or zero if there is no next element. The new element is placed at the end (tail) of the queue; the new element's address will be in the element that *was* at the end of the queue. The new element will contain zero to indicate that it is now the end of the queue.

Sample Problem:

Input:	ITEM —	(6000)	=	000060A0	
	QUEUE —	(6002)	=	00006020	Pointer to head of queue
		(6020)	=	00006030	
		(6030)	=	0000	Last element in queue
Result:	QUEUE —	(6002)	=	00006020	
		(6020)	=	00006030	
		(6030)	=	000060A0	Old last element points to new last element
		(60A0)	=	0000	New last element

How would you add an element to the queue if memory location 6006 contained the address of the tail of the queue (the last element)? Remember to update this end-of-queue pointer.

9-4. 4-BYTE SORT

Purpose: Sort a list of 4-byte entries into descending order. The first three bytes in each entry are an unsigned key with the first byte being the most significant. The fourth byte is additional information and should not be used to determine the sort order, but should be moved along with its key. The number of entries in the list is defined by the word variable LENGTH at location 6000. The list itself begins at location 6002 (LIST).

Sample Problem:

Input:	LENGTH —	(6000)	=	0004	4 entries in list
	LIST —	(6002)	=	41	Beginning of first entry key
		(6003)	=	42	
		(6004)	=	43	End of first entry key
		(6005)	=	07	First entry additional information
		(6006)	=	4A	Beginning of second entry
		(6007)	=	4B	
		(6008)	=	4C	
		(6009)	=	13	
		(600A)	=	4A	Beginning of third entry
		(600B)	=	4B	
		(600C)	=	41	
		(600D)	=	37	
		(600E)	=	44	Beginning of fourth entry
		(600F)	=	4B	
		(6010)	=	41	
		(6011)	=	3F	
Result:	LIST —	(6002)	=	4A	
		(6003)	=	4B	
		(6004)	=	4C	
		(6005)	=	13	End of first entry
		(6006)	=	4A	
		(6007)	=	4B	
		(6008)	=	41	
		(6009)	=	37	End of second entry
		(600A)	=	44	
		(600B)	=	4B	
		(600C)	=	41	
		(600D)	=	3F	End of third entry
		(600E)	=	41	
		(600F)	=	42	
		(6010)	=	43	
		(6011)	=	07	End of last entry

The data in the unsorted entries are 'ABC',\$07; 'JKL',\$13; 'JKA',\$37; 'DKA',\$3F.

9-5. USING A JUMP TABLE WITH A KEY

Purpose: Use the value in the variable INDEX at memory location 6000 as a key to a jump table (TABLE) starting at location 6002. Each entry in the jump table contains a 16-bit identifier followed by a 32-bit address to which the program should transfer control if the key is equal to that identifier.

Sample Problem:

Input:	INDEX –	(6000)	=	4142	
	TABLE –	(6002)	=	4348	First key
		(6004)	=	00004900	First transfer address
		(6008)	=	4142	Second entry
		(600A)	=	00004940	
		(600E)	=	4558	Third entry
		(6010)	=	00004A20	

Result: (PC) — 004940 since that address corresponds to key value 4142.

REFERENCES

1. J. Hemenway and E. Teja. "EDN Software Tutorial: Hash Coding," *EDN,* September 20, 1979, pp. 108-10.
2. D. Knuth. *The Art of Computer Programming, Volume III: Searching and Sorting.* Reading, Mass.: Addison-Wesley, 1978.
3. D. Knuth. "Algorithms," *Scientific American,* April 1977, pp. 63-80.
4. K. J. Thurber and P. C. Patton. *Data Structures and Computer Architecture.* Lexington Mass.: Lexington Books, 1977.
5. J. Hemenway and E. Teja. "Data Structures — Part 1," *EDN,* March 5, 1979, pp. 89-92; "Data Structures — Part 2," *EDN,* May 5, 1979, pp. 113-16.
6. See Reference 2.
7. B. W. Kernighan and P. J. Plauger. *The Elements of Programming Style.* New York: McGraw-Hill, 1978.
8. K. A. Schember and J. R. Rumsey. "Minimal Storage Sorting and Searching Techniques for RAM Applications," *Computer,* June 1977, pp. 92-100.
9. "Sorting 30 Times Faster with DPS," *Datamation,* February 1978, pp. 200-03.
10. L. A. Leventhal. "Cut Your Processor's Computation Time," *Electronic Design,* August 16, 1977, pp. 82-89.
11. J. B. Peatman. *Microcomputer-Based Design.* New York: McGraw-Hill, 1977, Chapter 7.

III
Advanced Topics

The following chapters will discuss more advanced areas of assembly language programming. Chapters 10 and 11 deal with subroutines, an important aspect of all levels of programming. Chapter 10 discusses MC68000 implementations of important parameter passing techniques while Chapter 11 defines and gives examples of subroutines. The following three chapters cover input and output, a microprocessor's contact with the outside world. In Chapter 12 we discuss time delays and different types of peripherals. Chapter 13 deals with the 6821 Peripheral Interface Adapter — a popular parallel I/O device for Motorola processors — and gives examples of basic program tasks for that device. Chapter 14 illustrates basic routines for a serial interface device, the 6850 Asynchronous Communications Interface Adapter. Chapter 15 treats the important and often confusing topic of interrupts and other types of MC68000 exception processing.

10
Parameter Passing Techniques

None of the examples that we have shown thus far is a typical program that would stand by itself. Most real programs perform a series of tasks, many of which may be used a number of times or be common to other programs.

SUBROUTINES

The standard method of producing programs which can be used in this manner is to write subroutines that perform particular tasks. The resulting sequences of instructions can be written once, tested once, and then used repeatedly.

In order to be really useful, a subroutine must be general. For example, a subroutine that can perform only a specialized task, such as looking for a particular letter in an input string of fixed length, will not be very useful. If, on the other hand, the subroutine can look for any letter, in strings of any length, it will be far more helpful.

In order to provide subroutines with this flexibility, it is necessary to provide them with the ability to receive various kinds of information. We call data or addresses that we provide the subroutine *parameters.* An important part of writing subroutines is providing for transferring the parameters to the subroutine. This process is called Parameter Passing.

GENERAL PARAMETER PASSING TECHNIQUES

There are three general approaches to passing parameters:

1. Place the parameters in registers.
2. Place the parameters immediately after the subroutine call in program memory.
3. Transfer the parameters and results on the hardware stack.

The registers often provide a fast, convenient way of passing parameters and returning results. The limitations of this method are that it cannot be expanded beyond the number of available registers; it often results in unforeseen side effects; and it lacks generality.

The trade-off here is between fast execution time and a more general approach. Such a trade-off is common in computer applications at all levels. General approaches are easy to learn and consistent; they can be automated through the use of macros. On the other hand, approaches that take advantage of the specific features of a particular task require less time and memory. The choice of one approach over the other depends on your application, but you should take the general approach (saving programming time and simplifying documentation and maintenance) unless time or memory constraints force you to do otherwise.

Passing Parameters In Registers

The first and simplest method of passing parameters to a subroutine is via the registers. After calling a subroutine, the calling program can load memory addresses, counters, and other data into registers. For example, suppose a subroutine operates on two data buffers of equal length. The subroutine might specify that the length of the two data buffers be in the register D0 while the two data buffer beginning addresses are in the registers A0 and A1. The calling program would then call the subroutine as follows:

```
MOVE.W   #BUFL,D0          LENGTH OF BUFFER IN D0
MOVEA.L  BUFA,A0           BUFFER A BEGINNING ADDRESS IN A0
MOVEA.L  BUFB,A1           BUFFER B BEGINNING ADDRESS IN A1
JSR      SUBR              CALL SUBROUTINE
```

Using this method of parameter passing, the subroutine can simply assume that the parameters are there. Results can also be returned in registers, or the addresses of locations for results can be passed as parameters via the registers. Of course, this technique is limited by the number of registers available. Such MC68000 features as register indirect addressing, indexed addressing, the ability to use any address register as a stack pointer, and the LEA instruction provide far more powerful and more general ways of passing parameters.

Passing Parameters In Program Memory

Parameters that are to be passed to a subroutine can also be placed directly after the subroutine call. The subroutine must then modify the return address at the top of the stack in addition to fetching the parameters. Using this technique, our example would be modified as follows:

```
        JSR       SUBR
        DC.W      BUFL                   BUFFER LENGTH
        DC.L      BUFA                   BUFFER A STARTING ADDRESS
        DC.L      BUFB                   BUFFER B STARTING ADDRESS
```

The subroutine saves prior contents of CPU registers, then loads parameters and adjusts the return address as follows:

```
SUBR    MOVEM.L  D0/A0-A2,-(A7)         SUBROUTINE USES D0,A0,A1,A2
        MOVEA.L  16(A7),A2              RETURN ADDRESS POINTS TO BUFL
        MOVE.W   (A2)+,D0               BUFL TO D0
        MOVEA.L  (A2)+,A0               BUFA TO A0
        MOVEA.L  (A2)+,A1               BUFB TO A1
        MOVEA.L  A2,16(A7)              ADJUST RETURN ADDRESS
```

The constant 16 is to adjust for the change in A7 when the four registers D0, A0, A1, and A2 are saved on the stack.

This parameter passing technique has the advantage of being easy to read. It has, however, the disadvantage of requiring parameters to be fixed when the program is written. A modification which allows parameters to vary uses an address pointer following the subroutine call. The pointer addresses an area of data memory where the parameters are actually found. This may be illustrated as follows:

```
        JSR      SUBR
        DC.L     PLIST                  BEGINNING ADDRESS OF PARAMETERS

PLIST   DC.W     BUFL
        DC.L     BUFA
        DC.L     BUFB


SUBR    MOVEM.L  D0/A0-A2,-(A7)         SUBROUTINE USES D0,A0,A1,A2
        MOVEA.L  16(A7),A1              RETURN ADDRESS POINTS TO PLIST
        MOVEA.L  (A1)+,A2               GET ADDRESS OF PARAMETER LIST
        MOVEA.L  A1,16(A7)              ... AND UPDATE RETURN ADDRESS
        MOVE.L   (A2)+,D0               BUFL IN D0
        MOVEA.L  (A2)+,A0               BUFA IN A0
        MOVEA.L  (A2)+,A1               BUFB IN A1
```

Parameters held in a separate area of memory are frequently referred to as a "parameter block." In the illustration above, we stored the beginning address for a three word parameter block after the JSR. The address of the parameter block could also be passed to the subroutine as follows:

```
        MOVE.L   #PLIST,-(A7)           PUSH ADDRESS OF PARAMETER BLOCK
        JSR      SUBR
```

The subroutine would fetch parameters as follows:

```
SUBR    MOVEM.L  D0/A0-A2,-(A7)         SUBROUTINE USES D0,A0,A1,A2
        MOVEA.L  20(A7),A2              GET PARAMETER ADDRESS
        MOVE.W   (A2)+,D0               BUFL IN D0
        MOVEA.L  (A2)+,A0               BUFA IN A0
        MOVEA.L  (A2)+,A1               BUFB IN A1
```

No adjustment of the stack pointer is required when this method is used.

Results can be returned by storing them in the same parameter block, or addresses for storing results can also be passed as parameters.

Passing Parameters On The Stack

Another common method of passing parameters to a subroutine is to push the parameters onto the stack. Using this parameter passing technique, the subroutine call illustrated above would occur as follows:

```
        MOVE.W   #BUFL,-(A7)          PUSH BUFFER LENGTH
        MOVEA.L  BUFA,-(A7)           PUSH TWO BUFFER STARTING ADDRESSES
        MOVEA.L  BUFB,-(A7)           ... ONTO STACK
        JSR      SUBR
```

The subroutine must begin by loading parameters into CPU registers as follows:

```
SUBR    MOVEM.L  D0/A0/A1,-(A7)       SAVE PRIOR REGISTER CONTENTS
        MOVEA.L  12(A7),A1            BUFFER B STARTING ADDRESS IN A1
        MOVEA.L  16(A7),A0            BUFFER A STARTING ADDRESS IN A0
        MOVE.W   20(A7),D0            BUFFER LENGTH IN D0
```

In this approach, all parameters are passed and results are returned on the stack.

The MC68000 stack grows downward (toward lower addresses). This occurs because elements are pushed onto the stack using the predecrement address mode. The use of the predecrement mode causes the stack pointer to always contain the address of the last occupied location, rather than the next empty one as on some other microprocessors, such as the 6800. This implies that you must initialize the stack pointer to a value higher than the largest address in the stack area.

When passing parameters on the stack, the programmer must implement this approach as follows:

1. Decrement the system stack pointer to make room for parameters on the system stack, and store them using offsets from the stack pointer; or simply push the parameters on the stack.
2. Access the parameters by means of offsets from the system stack pointer, remembering that JSR places the return address at the top of the stack.
3. Store the results on the stack by means of offsets from the systems stack pointer.
4. Clean up the stack before or after returning from the subroutine, so that the parameters are removed and the results are handled appropriately.

TYPES OF PARAMETERS

Regardless of our approach to passing parameters, we can specify the parameters in a variety of ways. For example, we can:

1. Place the actual values in the parameter list. This method is sometimes referred to as call-by-value, since only the values of the parameters are of concern.
2. Place the addresses of the parameters in the parameter list. This method is sometimes referred to as call-by-name, since we are concerned with the locations of the parameters as well as their values.

11
Subroutines

Most microprocessors have special instructions for transferring control to subroutines and restoring control to the main program. We often refer to the special instruction that transfers control to a subroutine as Call, Jump-to-Subroutine, Jump-and-Mark Place, or Jump-and-Link. The special instruction that restores control to the main program is usually called Return.

On the MC68000 microprocessor, the Jump-to-Subroutine (JSR) or Branch-to-Subroutine (BSR) instructions save the old value of the program counter on the stack before placing the starting address of the subroutine in the program counter; the Return-from-Subroutine (RTS) instruction gets the old value from the stack and puts it back in the program counter. The effect is to transfer program control, first to the subroutine and then back to the main program. Clearly, the subroutine may itself transfer control to a subroutine, and so on.

TYPES OF SUBROUTINES

Sometimes a subroutine must have special characteristics. **A subroutine is relocatable if it can be placed anywhere in memory.** You can use such a subroutine easily, regardless of other programs or the arrangement of the memory. **A relocating loader is necessary to place the program in memory properly; the loader will start the program after other programs and will add the starting address or relocation constant to all addresses in the program. Position independent code does not require a relocating loader — all program addresses are expressed relative to the program counter's current value. Data addresses are held in registers at all times.** We will discuss the writing of position independent code later in this chapter.

A subroutine is reentrant if it can be interrupted and called by the interrupting program and still give the correct results for both the interrupting and interrupted

programs. Reentrancy is important for standard subroutines in an interrupt-based system. Otherwise the interrupt service routines cannot use the standard subroutines without causing errors. Microprocessor subroutines are easy to make reentrant since the Call instruction uses the stack and use of the stack is automatically reentrant. The only remaining requirement is that the subroutine use only the registers and the stack rather than fixed memory locations for temporary storage.

A subroutine is recursive if it calls itself. Such a subroutine clearly must also be reentrant.

SUBROUTINE DOCUMENTATION

Most programs consist of a main program and several subroutines. This is advantageous because you can use proven routines when available and you can debug and test the other subroutines properly and remember their exact effects on registers and memory locations.

Subroutine listings must provide enough information that users need not examine the subroutine's internal structure. Among necessary specifications are:

- A description of the purpose of the subroutine
- A list of input and output parameters
- Registers and memory locations used
- A sample case, perhaps including a sample calling sequence

The subroutine will be easy to use if you follow these guidelines.

PROGRAM EXAMPLES

Examples in this chapter assume that the stack and stack pointer have already been initialized. Instructions that load an address into the stack pointer or clear the stack prior to use are not shown. If you wish to establish your own stack area, remember to save any prior stack pointer and to restore it in order to produce a proper return at the end of your program. Since the MC68000 allows any address register to be used as a stack pointer, it is better to use a stack for your needs and not change the system stack pointer (A7).

The MC68000 has no special instructions to load or save the current stack value. Instead you use the MOVEA instruction to alter the stack register as shown in the following program.

```
              00006000   DATA      EQU      $6000
              00004000   PROGRAM   EQU      $4000

              00006000   PSTACK    EQU      DATA
              00008000   STACK     EQU      $8000

              00004600   MAIN      EQU      $4600


              00004000             ORG      PROGRAM

       004000 21CF6000             MOVEA.L  A7,PSTACK         SAVE PRIOR STACK
```

```
004004 2E7C00008000        MOVEA.L #STACK,A7          SET UP OUR STACK
00400A 4EB84600            JSR     MAIN
00400E 2E786000            MOVEA.L PSTACK,A7          RESTORE PRIOR STACK

004012 4E75                RTS

                           END
```

The program illustrated above saves the prior stack pointer, sets up the main program's stack pointer, and then calls the main program. The stack base for the main program is then 8000. When the main program has completed execution, it can execute an RTS to transfer control to the setup routine, which restores the prior stack pointer and then returns control to the prior program.

11-1. CONVERTING HEXADECIMAL TO ASCII

Purpose: Convert the contents of data register D0 from a hexadecimal digit to an ASCII character. Assume that the original contents of data register D0 are less than 16.

Sample Problems:

a.	Input:	D0	=	0C	
	Result:	D0	=	43	'C'
b.	Input:	D0	=	06	
	Result:	D0	=	36	'6'

The JSR instruction saves the program counter (the address of the instruction following the JSR) on the system stack and then places the subroutine starting address in the program counter. The procedure is:

Step 1. Decrement the stack pointer by 4.

Step 2. Save the program counter in the top word of the stack.

Step 3. Place the subroutine start address in the program counter.

For program 11-1, the following occurs as a result of executing the JSR instruction:

```
Before JSR
  PC = 004604
  A7 = 7FFC
After executing the JSR
  PC     = 00460E
  A7     = 7FF8
  (7FF8) = 00004608
```

The stack pointer is always adjusted by four since all addresses are stored on the stack as 32-bit values, even if the return addresses can be referenced with short absolute addressing. Since the processor has fetched the entire JSR instruction, the program counter has been incremented to address the instruction following the JSR. This is the address that is saved as a 32-bit value on the stack.

The JSR instruction is similar to the JMP instruction except that JSR "remembers" where it came from. In this regard, the JSR instruction can call any-

where in memory. Like the JMP and its related instruction BRA, JSR has a relationship with the BSR instruction. BSR, like JSR, is used to call a subroutine and place the return address on the stack. However, the addressing modes of BSR are similar to the BRA instruction in that only instructions within an 8-bit or 16-bit displacement may be referenced by BSR.

The RTS instruction reverses the process:

Step 1. Place the value on the top of the stack in the program counter.
Step 2. Increment the stack pointer by 4.

For 11-1 the RTS instruction then causes the following to occur:

```
Before RTS
                  PC    =  00461A
                  A7    =  7FF8
                (7FF8)  =  00004608
```

Flowchart 11-1:

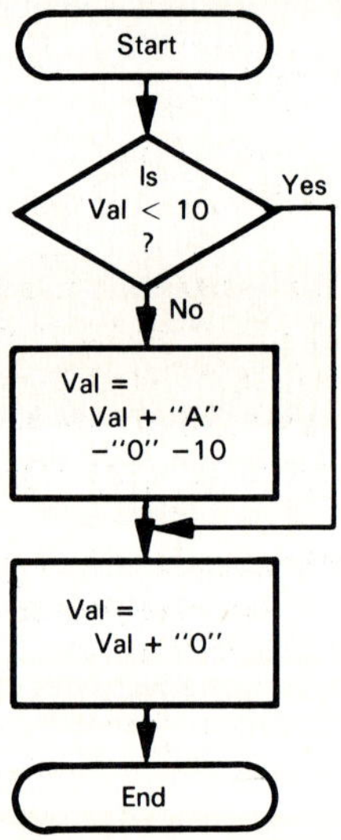

The calling program gets the data from the variable HDIGIT at memory location 6000, calls the conversion subroutine, and stores the result in the variable ACHAR at memory location 6001.

Program 11-1:

```
       00006000     DATA      EQU    $6000
       00004600     PROGRAM   EQU    $4600

       00006000               ORG    DATA

006000 00000001     HDIGIT    DS.B   1                HEX DIGIT TO BE CONVERTED
006001 00000001     ACHAR     DS.B   1                CONVERTED ASCII CHARACTER


       00004600               ORG    PROGRAM
```

```
004600 10386000      MAIN      MOVE.B  HDIGIT,D0           GET DATA: RANGE IS 00 - 0F
004604 4EB8460E                JSR     HEXDIGIT            CONVERT TO ASCII CHARACTER
004608 11C06001                MOVE.B  D0,ACHAR
00460C 4E75                    RTS

                     :: SUBROUTINE HEXDIGIT
                     ::
                     :: PURPOSE: HEXDIGIT CONVERTS A HEXADECIMAL DIGIT TO AN ASCII CHARACTER
                     ::
                     :: INITIAL CONDITIONS:  D0.B CONTAINS VALUE IN RANGE 00 - 0F
                     ::
                     :: FINAL CONDITIONS:    D0.B CONTAINS AN ASCII CHARACTER IN THE
                     ::                      RANGE '0'-'9' OR 'A' - 'F'
                     ::
                     :: REGISTERS CHANGED:   D0 ONLY
                     ::
                     :: SAMPLE CASE:         INITIAL CONDITIONS: D0.B = 6
                     ::                      FINAL CONDITIONS:   D0.B = 36 ('6')
                     ::

00460E 0C00000A      HEXDIGIT CMP.B   #$0A,D0             DECIMAL DIGIT OR HEX LETTER?
004612 6D02                   BLT.S   ADDZ                IF DIGIT GOTO ADDZ

004614 5E00                   ADD.B   #'A'-'0'-$0A,D0     OFFSET FOR LETTERS
004616 06000030      ADDZ     ADD.B   #'0',D0             CONVERT TO ASCII

00461A 4E75                   RTS

                              END     HEXDIGIT
```

After executing RTS
PC = 004608
A7 = 7FFC

The MC68000 always increments the stack pointer after pulling data from the stack, so the procedure is the same as in the postincrement addressing mode. RTS balances the JSR or BSR. The action of the RTS instruction, however, is simply to take the top four bytes in the stack and place them in the program counter. The programmer must be certain that these four bytes contain a legitimate return address — the processor does not examine them.

This subroutine has a single parameter and produces a single result. A data register is the obvious place to put both the parameter and the result.

The calling program consists of three steps:

- Placing the data into the data register.
- Calling the subroutine.
- Storing the result.

The overall initialization program must also load the stack pointer with the appropriate address.

This program is reentrant since it uses no data memory, and it is relocatable since the address ADDZ is referenced relative to the program counter. Using BSR (Branch to Subroutine) instead of JSR (Jump to Subroutine) would make the calling program relocatable as well.

The JSR instruction results in the execution of four or five instructions, taking either 44 or 48 clock cycles. A subroutine call may take a long time even though it appears to be only a single instruction in the program. Calling a routine always involves some overhead, since both the JSR and the BSR instructions take time. In fact, a JSR takes 10 clock cycles longer than the corresponding JMP (with the same addressing mode) because JSR must save the current program counter in the stack. RTS takes 16 clock cycles.

11-2. HEX WORD TO ASCII STRING

Purpose: Convert the value in the variable NUMBER at memory location 6000 to four ASCII hex digits in the four-byte array STRING starting at memory location 6002. Perform the task using a subroutine with the hex value and the string address as parameters.

Sample Problem:

Input:	NUMBER	(6000) = 4CD0	
Results:	STRING	(6002) = 34	'4'
		(6003) = 43	'C'
		(6004) = 44	'D'
		(6005) = 30	'0'

Program 11-2:

```
        00006000     DATA     EQU      $6000
        00004600     PROGRAM  EQU      $4600

        00006000              ORG      DATA

006000  00000002     NUMBER   DS.W     1                 NUMBER TO BE CONVERTED TO ASCII HEX
006002  00000004     STRING   DS.B     4                 CHARACTER STRING FOR ASCII HEX DIGI

        00004600              ORG      PROGRAM

004600  2F3C00006002 MAIN     MOVE.L   #STRING,-(A7)     PUSH ADDRESS OF STRING ON STACK
004606  3F386000              MOVE.W   NUMBER,-(A7)      PUSH 16 BIT NUMBER TO BE CONVERTED
00460A  4EB84610              JSR      BINHEX            BINARY TO ASCII/HEX

00460E  4E75                  RTS

                     * SUBROUTINE BINHEX
                     *
                     * PURPOSE: CONVERT A 16 BIT VALUE TO 4 ASCII HEX DIGITS
                     *
                     * INITIAL CONDITIONS: THE FIRST PARAMETER ON THE STACK IS THE
                     *                     VALUE; THE SECOND PARAMETER IS THE
                     *                     ADDRESS OF THE STRING TO BE BUILT
                     *
                     * FINAL CONDITIONS:   THE HEX STRING OCCUPIES 4 SUCCESSIVE
                     *                     BYTES BEGINNING WITH THE ADDRESS PASSED
                     *                     AS THE SECOND PARAMETER
                     *
                     * REGISTER USAGE:     NO REGISTERS ARE AFFECTED
                     *
                     * SAMPLE CASE:        INITIAL CONDITIONS: 4CD0 AT TOP OF STACK,
                     *                                         THEN 00006002
                     *                     FINAL CONDITIONS:   THE STRING '4CD0' IN ASCII
                     *                                         OCCUPIES MEMORY 6002-5
                     *

004610  48E7E080     BINHEX   MOVEM.L  D0-D2/A0,-(A7)    SAVE REGISTERS USED IN BINHEX
004614  7203                  MOVEQ    #3,D1             LOOP COUNTER:= 4-1
004616  342F0014              MOVE.W   16+4(A7),D2       GET VALUE
00461A  206F0016              MOVEA.L  16+6(A7),A0       GET STRING ADDRESS
00461E  D1FC00000004          ADDA.L   #4,A0             ADJUST POINTER PAST END OF STRING

004624  1002         LOOP     MOVE.B   D2,D0
004626  0200000F              ANDI.B   #$0F,D0           GET LOW NIBBLE
00462A  4EB84646              JSR      HEXDIGIT          CONVERT TO ASCII CHARCTER
00462E  1100                  MOVE.B   D0,-(A0)          SAVE ASCII DIGIT
004630  E84A                  LSR.W    #4,D2             SHIFT D2 TO GET NEXT NIBBLE
004632  51C9FFF0              DBRA     D1,LOOP           REPEAT FOR ALL 4 DIGITS

004636  4CDF0107              MOVEM.L  (A7)+,D0-D2/A0    RESTORE INITIAL REGISTER VALUES
00463A  2F570006              MOVE.L   (A7),6(A7)        MOVE RETURN ADDRESS DOWN
00463E  DFFC00000006          ADDA.L   #6,A7             ADJUST STACK POINTER TO RETURN ADDR
```

```
004644 4E75                 RTS


004646 0C00000A   HEXDIGIT CMP.B    #$0A,D0             DECIMAL DIGIT OR HEX LETTER ?
00464A 6D02                 BLT.S    ADDZ                IF DIGIT GOTO ADDZ
00464C 5E00                 ADD.B    #'A'-'0'-$0A,D0     OFFSET FOR LETTERS
00464E 06000030   ADDZ      ADD.B    #'0',D0             CONVERT TO ASCII

004652 4E75                 RTS

                            END      BINHEX
```

This program demonstrates another method of passing parameters. Instead of passing the two parameters in registers, the parameters are passed on the stack. Therefore, upon entry to the subroutine, the stack would look like this:

Address Parameter	(32 bits)	
Hex Digit Parameter	(16 bits)	
Return Address	(32 bits)	System Stack Pointer (A7)

The system stack pointer (A7) usually operates like any other register. However, since all word and long word references must be aligned on a word boundary, the MC68000 takes special precautions to ensure proper alignment. Thus, ***all* data pushed or pulled from the system stack is word-aligned — even byte data.** In the case of byte data, the data is stored in the high-order (most significant) byte of the word, the lower order (least significant) byte is left unchanged.

Unlike our first subroutine example, BINHEX modifies the contents of data and address registers other than those which are used to pass subroutine results. In some cases, the unexpected modification of registers by a subroutine may cause unpredictable results in the calling program. **It is good programming practice to define which registers are being affected by the execution of the subroutine.** This has been done for subroutine BINHEX in its introductory description block.

A common practice used to prevent any inadvertent effects due to modification of the registers is to save all registers used in a subroutine and to restore them upon subroutine exit. **The Move Multiple (MOVEM) instruction provides an efficient means of saving or restoring registers. Whenever two or more index registers (address or data register) are to be saved or restored, it is always more memory-efficient to use MOVEM. In terms of execution performance, it is *generally* better to use MOVEM when saving two or more index registers and when restoring three or more.** The order in which index registers are transferred via MOVEM is dependent upon the effective address mode. If the effective address is the postincrement mode, the registers are stored starting with data register 0 through data register 7, then address register 0 to address register 7. If the effective address is the predecrement mode, the registers are loaded in the reverse order starting with address register 7. Therefore, after the execution of the first MOVEM instruction in BINHEX, the system stack will be as follows:

Address Parameter	(32 bits)
Hex Digit Parameter	(16 bits)
Return Address	(32 bits)
A0	(32 bits)
D2	(32 bits)
D1	(32 bits)
D0(32 bits)	System Stack Pointer (A7)

The parameters are not passed in registers; they must be retrieved from the system stack. We must take care in retrieving the parameters from the stack, because other elements have been pushed onto the stack. The MOVEM instruction pushed 16 bytes onto the stack while JSR pushed the 4-byte return address (0000460E in our example). The MOVE.W 16+4(A7),A0 is used to load A0 with the 32-bit string address. The order of these two instructions makes no difference since the system stack register is not affected.

Both these MOVE instructions are examples of address register indirect with displacement addressing. This addressing mode is similar to the program counter with displacement mode used by the branch instruction, but it has two main differences. First, an address register is used instead of the program counter. And second, only a 16-bit displacement is allowed although it is still sign-extended. In program 11-2 the system stack pointer contains $7FFC upon MAIN entry. Thus the address referenced in the first MOVE is:

```
(A7) + 16 + 4
= $7FE2 + 16 + 4
= $7FF6 (the address of the digit value)
```

Prior to returning control back to program MAIN, the system stack must be restored. First, the saved registers are pulled by MOVEM (A7)+,D0-D2/A0. At this point we could return to MAIN by using an RTS instruction since the return address is on top of the system stack. However, this would leave the parameters still on the stack and the calling program would have to adjust the stack. This adjustment would have to be performed after each subroutine call to BINHEX. Instead, the system stack is adjusted in BINHEX by the instruction sequence:

```
MOVE.L (A7),6(A7)
ADDA O6,A7
```

Using the memory-to-memory move capability, the return address is stored at the system stack entry previously occupied by the address parameter. The system stack is then modified to point to this new return address entry. The same results could be obtained faster by substituting the instruction LEA 6(A7),A7 for the ADDA instruction. A picture of the stack before and after the MOVE and ADDA instructions is:

```
Before:
  (A7) → 7FF2 — 0000460E (return address)
         7FF6 — 4CD0 (value parameter)
         7FF8 — 00006002 (address parameter)

After:
         7FF2 — 0000460E
         7FF6 — 4CD0
  (A7) → 7FF8 — 0000460E (return address)
```

If results were to be returned on the stack, a different adjustment would be made.

This subroutine is both reentrant and position-independent since it uses no fixed memory addresses and only relative branches.

The BSR and JSR instructions allow the nesting of subroutines, since subsequent subroutine calls will place their return addresses further down the stack. No addresses are ever lost and the RTS instruction always returns control to the instruction just after the most recent BSR and JSR.

11-3. 64 BIT ADDITION

Purpose: Add two 64-bit (4-word) values and return the results in data registers D0 and D1. D0 shall contain the most significant word of the result.

Sample Problem:

Input:	Value 1	—	\$0420147AEB529CB8
	Value 2	—	\$3020EB8520473118
Result:	D0	—	34410000
	D1	—	0B99CDD0

Program 11-3a:

```
         00006000       DATA     EQU      $6000
         00004600       PROGRAM  EQU      $4600

         00006000                ORG      DATA


         00004600                ORG      PROGRAM

004600 4EB84616         MAIN     JSR      ADD64                 64 BIT ADDITION
004604 00000001                  DC.L     $1,$12345678          FIRST PARAMETER
00460C 00000001                  DC.L     $1,$12345             SECOND PARAMETER
004614 4E75                      RTS

                        * SUBROUTINE ADD64
                        *
                        * PURPOSE                     ADD TWO 64 BIT VALUES
                        *
                        * INITIAL CONDITIONS:         THE TWO PARAMETER VALUES ARE PASSED
                        *                             IMMEDIATELY FOLLOWING THE SUBROUTINE CALL
                        *
                        * FINAL CONDITIONS:           THE SUM OF THE TWO 64 BIT PARAMETERS
                        *                             IS RETURNED IN D0.L AND D1.L. THE EXTEND
                        *                             CONDITION CODE = 1 IF OVERFLOW, ELSE = 0
                        *
                        * REGISTER USAGE              NO REGISTERS ARE AFFECTED EXCEPT D0 AND D1
                        *
                        * SAMPLE CASE                 INITIAL CONDITIONS: 1ST PARAMETER = $112345678
                        *                                                 2ND PARAMETER = $100012345
                        *                             FINAL CONDITIONS    D0.L = $00000002
                        *                                                 D1.L = $123579BD
                        *                                                 CC.X = 0
                        *
                        *

004616 48E73080         ADD64    MOVEM.L D2-D3/A0,-(A7)   SAVE D2,D3 AND A0
00461A 206F000C                  MOVEA.L 12(A7),A0        A0 - ADDRESS OF FIRST PARAMETER
00461E 4CD8000F                  MOVEM.L (A0)+,D0-D3      D0-D1 = FIRST VALUE, D2-D3 = SECOND

004622 D283                      ADD.L    D3,D1           ADD LEAST SIGNIFICANT WORD
004624 D182                      ADDX.L   D2,D0           ADD MOST SIGNIFICANT 16 BIT WITH EX

004626 4CDF010C                  MOVEM.L (A7)+,D2-D3/A0   RESTORE D2,D3 AND A0
00462A 40E7                      MOVE.W   SR,-(A7)        SAVE EXTEND FLAG
00462C 06AF00000010
            0002                 ADDI.L   #16,2(A7)       ADJUST RETURN ADDRESS
004634 4E77                      RTR      .               RETURN AND RESTORE EXTEND FLAG

                                 END      ADD64
```

In Program 11-3*a* the parameters for the subroutine ADD64 are passed immediately following the subroutine call. Upon entry to ADD64, the address of this parameter block may be found on top of the system stack, since it is the return address for the JSR instruction. The MOVEA.L instruction loads address register A0 with this parameter block address. The displacement of 12 in this instruction is necessary because of the three 32-bit registers pushed onto the system stack.

The actual addition process is quite simple and was demonstrated in Chapter 8. Prior to returning to the calling program, MAIN, the return address must be adjusted since it points to the address following the JSR. An adjustment of 16 bytes is necessary to jump around the two 8-byte parameters. This adjustment is performed via the ADDI instruction on the return address without first having to move it into a register. The system stack (before and after the ADDI instruction) is pictured as follows:

```
Before:
  (A7) (7FF6) = Status Register (16 bits)
       (7FF8) = 4604

After:
  (A7) (7FF6) = Status Register
       (7FF8) = 4614
```

After the addition to adjust the stack pointer, the status register is pushed onto the stack in order to preserve the condition codes. This allows the calling program to test for overflow or carry as a result of the 64-bit addition. Such a test would normally be performed by a "branch conditional" instruction following the JSR or the JSR parameter list. In this instance the condition codes had to be saved since their state could have been changed by the ADDI. To accomplish this the MC68000 provides a special return instruction: RTR (return and restore condition codes). RTR pulls *both* the condition codes and the return address from the stack. The supervisor portion of the status register is not affected by this instruction. The RTR instruction can be extremely useful when error conditions from subroutines are indicated by the condition codes.

Generally you may assume that a subroutine call changes the condition codes unless it is specifically stated otherwise. If the main program needed the old condition codes (for checking later), it could have saved them on the system stack using MOVE SR,−(A7) before calling the subroutine. It would then be able to restore them afterwards using MOVE (A7)+,CCR.

This program lacks some generality since the values associated with the parameters are passed following the call. For example, if the program were placed in read-only memory the parameters could not be modified. To overcome this problem, the addresses of the parameters could have been passed instead of their values.

Program 11-3*b* shows how we might modify the program to pass addresses instead of values.

Program 11-3b:

```
       00006000    DATA     EQU    $6000
       00004600    PROGRAM  EQU    $4600

       00006000             ORG    DATA

006000 00000008    VALUE1   DS.L   2              FIRST 64-BIT VALUE
006008 00000008    VALUE2   DS.L   2              SECOND 64-BIT VALUE

       00004600             ORG    PROGRAM

004600 4EB8460E    MAIN     JSR    ADD64          64 BIT ADDITION
004604 00006000             DC.L   VALUE1         ADDRESS OF FIRST PARAMETER
004608 00006008             DC.L   VALUE2         ADDRESS OF SECOND PARAMETER
00460C 4E75                 RTS
```

```
                  :: SUBROUTINE ADD64
                  ::
                  :: PURPOSE:                ADD TWO 64 BIT VALUES
                  ::
                  :: INITIAL CONDITIONS      THE TWO PARAMETERVALUES ARE PASSED
                  ::                         IMMEDIATELY FOLLOWING THE SUBROUTINE CALL
                  ::
                  :: FINAL CONDITIONS        THE SUM OF THE TWO 64 BIT PARAMETERS
                  ::                         IS RETURNED IN D0.L AND D1.L. THE EXTEND
                  ::                         CONDITION CODE = 1 IF OVERFLOW, ELSE = 0
                  ::
                  :: REGISTER USAGE:         NO REGISTERS ARE AFFECTED EXCEPT D0 AND D1
                  ::
                  :: SAMPLE CASE:            INITIAL CONDITIONS: 1ST PARAMETER = $00006000
                  ::                                             2ND PARAMETER = $00006004
                  ::                                            ($6000) = $0420147AEB529CB8
                  ::                                            ($6004) = $3020EB8520473118
                  ::
                  ::                         FINAL CONDITIONS:   D0.L = $34410000
                  ::                                             D1.L = $0B99CDD0
                  ::                                             CC.X = 0
                  ::
                  ::

00460E 48E730C0 ADD64   MOVEM.L D2-D3/A0-A1,-(A7)  SAVE D2,D3,A0 AND A1
004612 206F0010         MOVEA.L 16(A7),A0          A0 - ADDRESS OF PARAMETER BLOCK

004616 2258             MOVEA.L (A0)+,A1           A1 - FIRST PARAMETER ADDRESS
004618 20290000         MOVE.L  0(A1),D0           MOST SIGNIFICANT WORD OF FIRST VALUE
00461C 22290004         MOVE.L  4(A1),D1           .. AND LEAST SIGNIFICANT

004620 2258             MOVEA.L (A0)+,A1           A1 - SECOND PARAMETER ADDRESS
004622 24290000         MOVE.L  0(A1),D2           MOST SIGNIFICANT WORD OF SECOND VALUE
004626 26290004         MOVE.L  4(A1),D3           ... AND LEAST SIGNIFICANT

00462A 2F480010         MOVEA.L A0,16(A7)          UPDATE RETURN ADDRESS
00462E D283             ADD.L   D3,D1              ADD LEAST SIGNIFICANT WORD
004630 D182             ADDX.L  D2,D0              ADD MOST SIGNIFICANT WORD

004632 4CDF030C         MOVEM.L (A7)+,D2-D3/A0-A1  RESTORE USED REGISTERS

004636 4E75             RTS

                        END     ADD64
```

The initial instructions in 11-3*b* are essentially the same as those found in 11-3*a*. However, once the address of the parameter block is determined (MOVE.L 16(A7),A0)), another instruction must be performed to obtain the parameter values:

```
MOVEA.L   (A0)+,A1    Get address of parameter
MOVE.L    0(A1),D0    Get value
MOVE.L    4(A1),D1    ...of parameter
```

The use of the predecrement mode in fetching the parameter addresses also aids in updating the return address. After the two MOVE.L (A0)+,A1 instructions, A0 contains the correct return address which is used to modify the return address on the system stack: (MOVEA.L A0,16(A7)). This means of updating the return address eliminates the ADDI instruction and therefore the need to push the condition codes onto the system stack.

11-4. FACTORIAL OF A NUMBER

Purpose: Determine the factorial of the number in the variable NUMB at memory location 6000. Store the result in the variable FNUMB at memory location 6002. Assume the number is less than nine but greater than zero.

Sample Problems:

a.	Input:	NUMB−(6000)	=	0002
	Result:	FNUMB−(6002)	=	0002
b.	Input:	NUMB−(6000)	=	0005
	Result:	FNUMB−(6002)	=	0078(120_{10})

Flowchart:

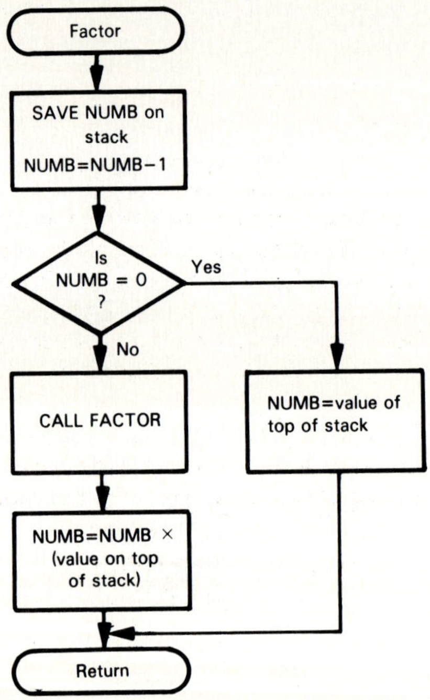

Program 11-4a:

```
         00006000       DATA     EQU      $6000
         00004600       PROGRAM  EQU      $4600

         00006000                ORG      DATA

006000 00000002         NUMB     DS.W     1              NUMBER
006002 00000002         F_NUMB   DS.W     1              FACTORIAL OF NUMBER

         00004600                ORG      PROGRAM

004600 30386000         MAIN     MOVE.W   NUMB,D0        GET NUMBER
004604 6106                      BSR.S    FACTOR         FIND FACTORIAL
004606 31C06002                  MOVE.W   D0,F_NUMB      STORE FACTORIAL

00460A 4E75                      RTS
```

```
                    * SUBROUTINE FACTOR
                    * PURPOSE:              DETERMINE THE FACTORIAL OF A GIVEN NUMBER
                    *
                    * INITIAL CONDITIONS: D0.W = NUMBER WHOSE FACTORIAL IS TO BE
                    *                      DETERMINED. D0.W > 0 AND < 9
                    *
                    * FINAL CONDITIONS:    D0.W = FACTORIAL OF INPUT NUMBER
                    *
                    * REGISTER USAGE:      NO REGISTERS EXCEPT D0 AFFECTED
                    *
                    * SAMPLE CASE:         INITIAL CONDITIONS: D0.W = 5
                    *                      FINAL CONDITIONS  : D0.W = 120
                    *

00460C 3F00         FACTOR  MOVE.W  D0,-(A7)          PUSH CURRENT NUMBER TO STACK
00460E 5340                 SUBQ.W  #1,D0             DECREMENT NUMBER
004610 6604                 BNE.S   F_CONT            NOT END OF FACTORIAL PROCESS

004612 301F                 MOVE.W  (A7)+,D0          FACTORIAL:= 1
004614 6004                 BRA.S   RETURN

004616 61F4         F_CONT  BSR     FACTOR
004618 C0DF                 MULU    (A7)+,D0          FACTORIAL: = N * (N-1)

00461A 4E75         RETURN  RTS

                            END     FACTOR
```

This subroutine is reentrant since it does not use any fixed data storage area. Instead, all temporary data is allocated space on the stack. In addition, this subroutine is recursive because it invokes itself via the BSR FACTOR instruction.

Recursive subroutines are a special case of subroutine nesting. Like any other subroutine call using a BSR or JSR instruction, the return address is placed on top of the stack. In this case, the processor does not care if identical return addresses appear at the top of the stack.

Subroutine FACTOR is a simple example of a recursive routine because it is easy to see that FACTOR calls itself. However, a subroutine can still be recursive if a routine it calls eventually invokes the calling subroutine. For example, FACTOR would still be recursive if:

```
F CONT:     BSR FACTOR
            MULU (A7)+,D0
```

were replaced with:

```
F CONT:     BSR MULTIPLY
```

where MULTIPLY was a subroutine like:

```
MULTIPLY:   BSR FACTOR
            MULU (A7)+,D0
            RTS
```

Like any subroutine which uses the stack for temporary storage, FACTOR *must* ensure that no data is left on the stack prior to the execution of return. Both the MOVE.W (A7)+,D0 and MULU (A7)+,D0 instructions ensure that the stack is properly restored.

In many instances, you may not be sure of the exact state of the stack prior to return. This could be especially true if you practice good programming techniques and use only one exit or return statement per program (as in subroutine FACTOR). More important, the execution of a subroutine frequently will not save temporary data on

the stack in an orderly manner. For these reasons, the MC68000 has implemented the LINK and UNLK instructions.

Subroutine FACTOR has been rewritten in Program 11-4*b* using LINK and UNLK. With the aid of the LINK instruction, we are able to dynamically reserve up to 32,768 bytes of storage on the stack, as well as set up a pointer to the top of the reserved area. In addition, the LINK instruction saves the current value of the pointer.

Program 11-4b:

```
       00006000     DATA     EQU      $6000
       00004600     PROGRAM  EQU      $4600

       00006000              ORG      DATA

006000 00000002     NUMB     DS.W     1                     NUMBER
006002 00000002     F_NUMB   DS.W     1                     FACTORIAL OF NUMBER

       00004600              ORG      PROGRAM

004600 30386000     MAIN     MOVE.W   NUMB,D0               GET NUMBER
004604 6106                  BSR.S    FACTOR                FIND FACTORIAL
004606 31C06002              MOVE.W   D0,F_NUMB             STORE FACTORIAL

00460A 4E75                  RTS

                    * SUBROUTINE FACTOR
                    * PURPOSE:             DETERMINE THE FACTORIAL OF A GIVEN NUMBER
                    *
                    * INITIAL CONDITIONS: D0.W = NUMBER WHOSE FACTORIAL IS TO BE
                    *                     DETERMINED. D0.W > 0 AND < 9
                    *
                    * FINAL CONDITIONS:   D0.W = FACTORIAL OF INPUT NUMBER
                    *
                    * REGISTER USAGE:     NO REGISTERS EXCEPT D0 AFFECTED
                    *
                    * SAMPLE CASE:        INITIAL CONDITIONS: D0.W = 5
                    *                     FINAL CONDITIONS  : D0.W = 120
                    *

00460C 4E50FFFE     FACTOR   LINK     A0,#-2          ALLOCATE TEMPORARY STACK STORAGE
004610 3140FFFE              MOVE.W   D0,-2(A0)       SAVE NUMBER
004614 5340                  SUBQ.W   #1,D0           DECREMENT NUMBER
004616 6604                  BNE.S    F_CONT          NOT END OF FACTORIAL PROCESS

004618 7001                  MOVEQ    #1,D0           FACTORIAL := 1
00461A 6006                  BRA.S    RETURN          RETURN TO CALLING ROUTINE

00461C 61EE         F_CONT   BSR      FACTOR          CONTINUE FACTORIAL PROCESS
00461E C0E8FFFE              MULU     -2(A0),D0       FACTORIAL:= N * (N-1)

004622 4E58         RETURN   UNLK     A0              FREE TEMPORARY STORAGE

004624 4E75                  RTS

                             END      FACTOR
```

In Program 11-4*b*, the instruction LINK A0,-2 has the following effect:

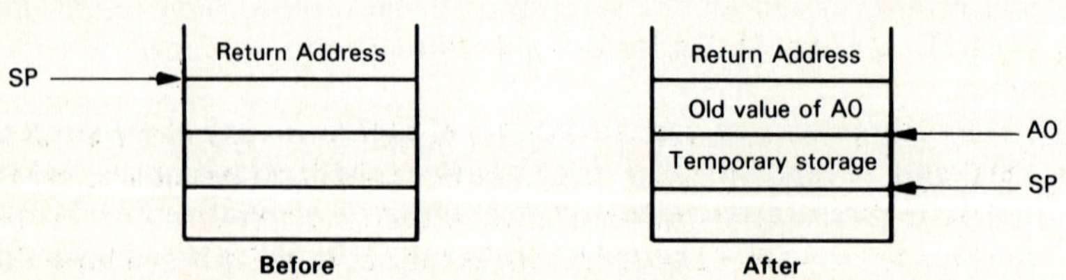

The UNLK instruction reverses the results of the LINK instruction, thus restoring the stack and address registers.

When using these two instructions, remember that the displacement for data storage is a negative displacement, since the stack expands toward low address memory. Offsets to the pointer register should also be negative, since the address register points to the top of the temporary data area.

PROBLEMS

Write both a calling program for the sample problem and at least one properly documented subroutine for each problem.

11-1. ASCII Hex to Binary

Purpose: Convert the least significant eight bits in data register D0 from the ASCII representation of a hexadecimal digit to the 4-bit binary representation of the digit. Place the result back into D0.

Sample Problems:

a.	Input:	DO	=	43	'C'
	Result:	DO	=	OC	
b.	Input:	DO	=	36	'6'
	Result:	DO	=	06	

11-2. ASCII Hex String to Binary Word

Purpose: Convert the four ASCII characters in the variable STRING starting in memory location 6002 into a 16-bit binary value. Store the value in the variable VALUE at memory location 6000. Write a subroutine that takes the string address from the stack and returns the value on the stack.

Sample Problem:

Input:	STRING – (6002)	=	42	'B'
	(6003)	=	32	'1'
	(6004)	=	46	'F'
	(6005)	=	30	'0'
Result:	VALUE – (6000)	=	B1FO	

11-3. Test for Alphabetic Character

Purpose: If the ASCII character in the variable CHAR at memory location 6000 is an alphabetic (upper- or lower-case), set the variable FLAG at memory location 6001 to FF_{16}; otherwise set FLAG to 0. Write a subroutine that finds its parameter in a register and returns its result using the condition code flags.

Sample Problems:

a.	Input:	CHAR – (6000)	=	47 'G'
	Results:			
		FLAG – (6001)	=	FF
b.	Input:	CHAR – (6000)	=	36 '6'
	Results:	FLAG – (6001)	=	00
c.	Input:	CHAR – (6000)	=	6A 'j'
	Results:			
		FLAG – (6001)	=	FF

11-4. Scan to Next Nonalphabetic

Purpose: The variable STRING at memory location 6000 contains the address of an ASCII string. Place the address of the first nonalphabetic character in this string in the variable ADDRESS at memory location 6002. Write a subroutine that takes the string address from a register and returns the result in the same register.

Sample Problems:

a.	Input:	STRING – (6000)	=	6100
		(6100)	=	43 'C'
		(6101)	=	61 'a'
		(6102)	=	74 't'
		(6103)	=	0D CR
	Result:	ADDRESS – (6002)	=	6103
b.	Input:	STRING – (6000)	=	6100
		(6100)	=	32 '2'
		(6101)	=	50 'P'
		(6102)	=	49 'I'
		(6103)	=	0D CR
	Result:	ADDRESS – (6002)	=	6100

11-5. Check Even Parity

Purpose: The variable LENGTH at memory location 6001 contains the length in bytes of a string variable STRING that begins at location 6002. If each byte in the string has even parity, set the variable FLAG at location 6000 to 0; if one or more bytes have odd parity, set FLAG to FF_{16}. Write a subroutine that obtains length and location from the stack and returns its result on the stack.

Sample Problems:

a.	Input:	LENGTH – (6001)	=	3
		STRING – (6002)	=	47
		(6003)	=	AF
		(6004)	=	18
	Result:	FLAG – (6000)	=	00
b.	Input:	LENGTH – (6001)	=	3
		STRING – (6002)	=	47
		(6003)	=	AF
		(6004)	=	19
	Result:	FLAG – (6000)	=	FF, since 19 = 00011001 has odd parity

11-6. Compare Two Strings

Purpose: Write a subroutine, and a main program that tests it, to compare two ASCII strings. The first byte in each string is its length. Return the information in the condition codes; i.e., the S flag will be set if the first string is lexically less than (prior to) the second, the Z flag will be set if the strings are equal, no flags are set if the second is prior to the first. Note that ABCD is lexically greater than ABC.

12
Input/Output

There are two problems in the design of input/output routines: one is how to interface peripherals to the computer and transfer data, status, and control signals; the other is how to address I/O devices so that the CPU can select a particular one for data transfer. Clearly, the first problem is both more complex and more interesting. **We will** therefore **discuss the interfacing of peripherals** here and leave addressing to a more hardware-oriented book.

I/O AND MEMORY

In theory, **the transfer of data to or from an I/O device is similar to the transfer of data to or from memory.** In fact, **we can consider the memory as just another I/O device. The memory is,** however, **special for the following reasons:**

1. It operates at almost the same speed as the processor.
2. It uses the same type of signals as the CPU. The only circuits usually needed to interface the memory to the CPU are drivers, receivers, and sometimes level translators.
3. It requires no special formats or any control signals besides a Read/Write pulse.
4. It automatically latches data sent to it.
5. Its word length is the same as the computer's.

Most I/O devices do not have such convenient features. They may operate at speeds much slower than the processor; for example, a teletypewriter can transfer only 30 characters per second, while a slow processor can transfer 10,000 characters per second. **The range of speeds is also very wide** — sensors may provide one reading per minute, while video displays or floppy disks may transfer 250,000 bits per second. Furthermore, **I/O devices may require continuous signals** (motors or thermometers), **currents rather than voltages** (older teletypewriters), **or voltages at far different levels than the signals used by the processor** (gas-discharge displays). I/O devices may also require special formats, protocols, or control signals. Their word lengths may be much shorter or much longer than the word length of the computer. **These variations make the design of I/O routines difficult, and mean that each peripheral presents its own special interfacing problem.**

I/O DEVICE CATEGORIES

We may, however, provide a general description of devices and interfacing methods. We may roughly separate devices into three categories, based on their data rates:

1. **Slow devices that change state no more than once per second.** Changing their states typically requires milliseconds or longer. Such devices include lighted displays, switches, relays, and many mechanical sensors and actuators.
2. **Medium-speed devices that transfer data at rates of 1 to 10,000 bits per second.** Such devices include keyboards, printers, card readers, paper tape readers and punches, cassettes, ordinary communications lines, and many analog data acquisition systems.
3. **High-speed devices that transfer data at rates of over 10,000 bits per second.** Such devices include magnetic tapes, magnetic disks, high-speed line printers, high-speed communications lines, and video displays.

INTERFACING SLOW DEVICES

The interfacing of slow devices is simple. Few control signals are necessary unless the devices are multiplexed, that is, several are handled from one port, as shown in Figures 12-1 to 12-4. Input data from slow devices need not be latched, since it remains stable for a long time. Output data must, of course, be latched. The only problems with input are transitions that occur while the computer is reading the data. One-shots, cross-coupled latches, or software delay routines can smooth the transitions.

A single port can handle several slow devices. Figure 12-1 shows a demultiplexer that automatically directs the next output data to the next device by counting output operations. Figure 12-2 shows a control port that provides select inputs to a demultiplexer. The data outputs here can come in any order, but an additional output instruction is necessary to change the state of the control port. Output demultiplexers are commonly used to drive several displays from the same output port. Figures 12-3 and 12-4 show the same alternatives for an input multiplexer.

Note the differences between input and output with slow devices.

1. **Input data need not be latched** since the input device holds the data for an enormous length of time by computer standards. Output data must be latched

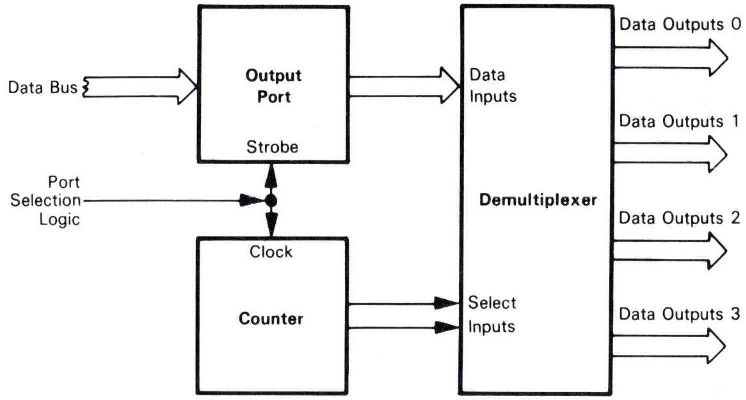

The Counter controls where the Demultiplexer sends the data.

Figure 12-1. An Output Demultiplexer Controlled by a Counter

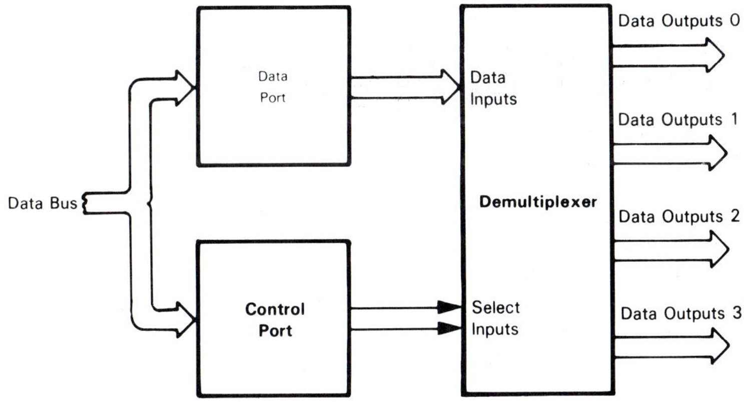

The CPU sends control information to the Control Port; that port then determines where the Demultiplexer sends the data.

Figure 12-2. An Output Demultiplexer Controlled by a Port

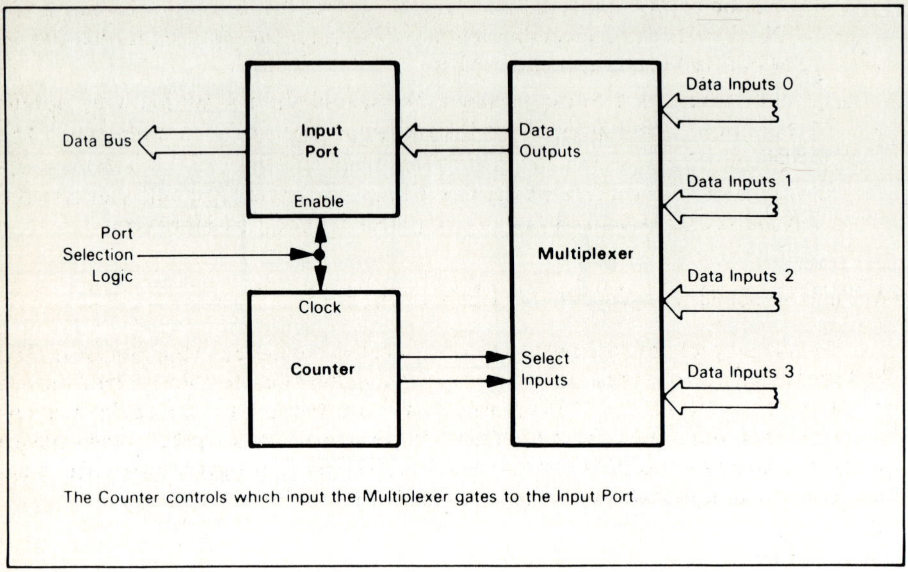

Figure 12-3. An Input Multiplexer Controlled by a Counter

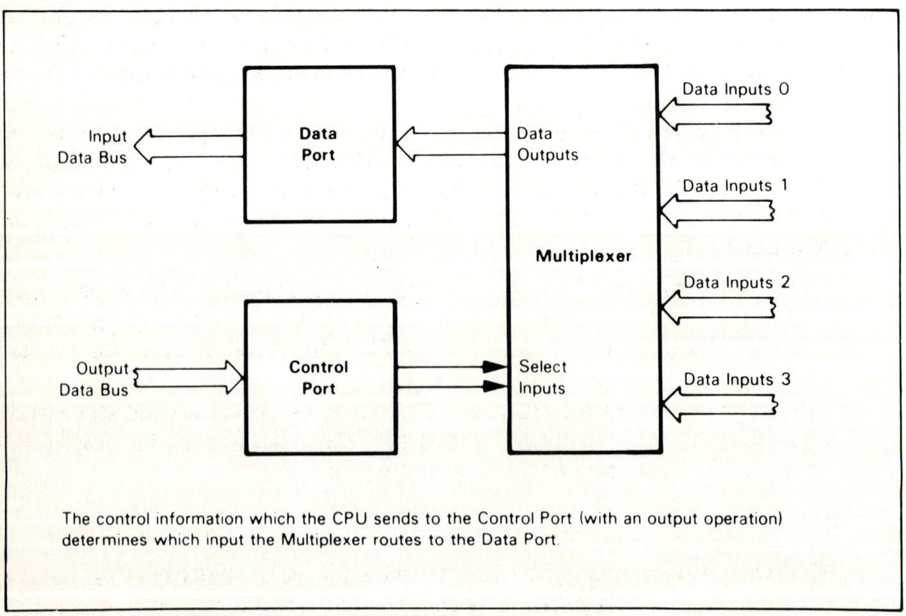

Figure 12-4. An Input Multiplexer Controlled by a Port

since the output device will not respond to data that is present for only a few CPU clock cycles. Remember that the CPU is constantly using its data bus to perform ordinary memory transfers.

2. **Input transitions cause problems because of their duration; brief output transitions cause no problems** because the output devices (or the observers) react slowly.
3. **The major constraints on input are reaction time and responsiveness; the major constraints on output are response time and observability.**

INTERFACING MEDIUM-SPEED DEVICES

Medium-speed devices must be synchronized in some way to the processor. The CPU cannot simply treat these devices as if they held their data forever or could receive data at any time. Instead, the CPU must be able to determine when a device has new input data or is ready to receive output data. It must also have a way of telling a device that new output data is available or that the previous input data has been accepted. Note that **the peripheral may be or contain another processor.**

Handshake

The standard unclocked synchronization procedure is the handshake. Here the sender indicates the availability of data to the receiver and transfers the data; the receiver completes the handshake by acknowledging the receipt of the data. The receiver may control the situation by initially requesting the data or by indicating its readiness to accept data; the sender then sends the data and completes the handshake by indicating that data is available. In either case, the sender knows that the transfer has been completed successfully and the receiver knows when new data is available. The handshake procedure can operate at any speed, since the sender and receiver (not a clock) control the sequence of events.

Figures 12-5 and 12-6 show typical input and output operations using the handshake method. The procedure whereby the CPU checks the readiness of the peripheral before transferring data is called "polling." Clearly, polling can occupy a large amount of processor time if there are many I/O device. **There are several ways of providing the handshake signals. Among these are:**

- **Separate dedicated I/O lines.** The processor may handle these as additional I/O ports or through special lines or interrupts. The MC68000 microprocessor does not have special I/O lines, but the 6821 Peripheral Interface Adapter (or programmable parallel interface chip) does.
- **Special patterns on the I/O lines.** These may be single start and stop bits or entire characters or groups of characters. The patterns must be easy to distinguish from background noise or inactive states.

Strobe

We often call a separate I/O line that indicates the availability of data or the occurrence of a transfer a "strobe." A strobe may, for example, clock data into a latch or fetch data from a buffer.

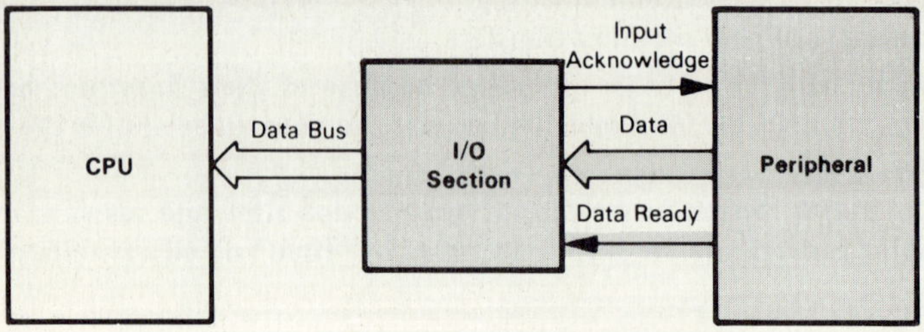

a. Peripheral provides data and Data Ready signal to computer I/O section.

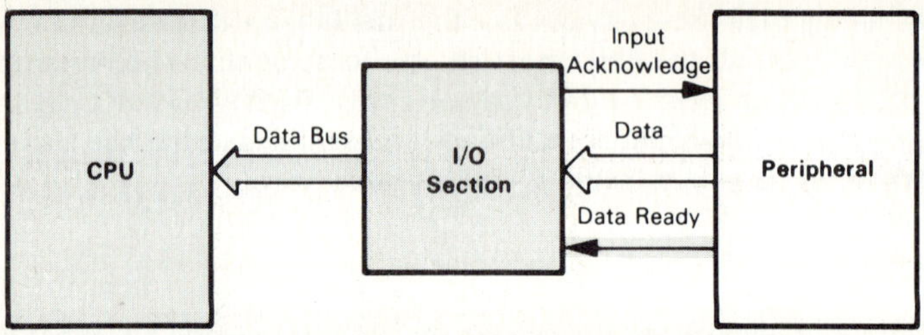

b. CPU reads Data Ready signal from I/O section (this may be a hardware, interrupt connection).

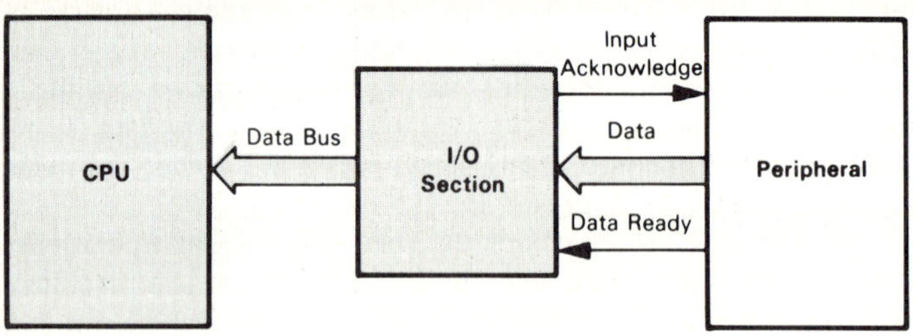

c. CPU reads data from I/O section.

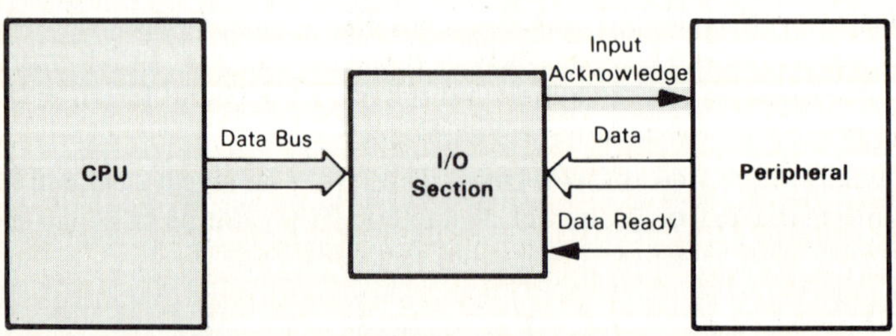

d. CPU sends Input Acknowledge signal to I/O section which then provides Input Acknowledge signal to Peripheral (this may be a hardware connection).

Figure 12-5. An Input Handshake

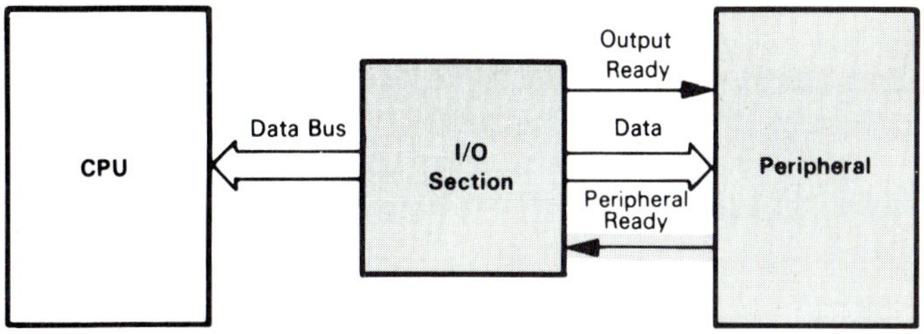

a. Peripheral provides Peripheral Ready signal to computer I/O section.

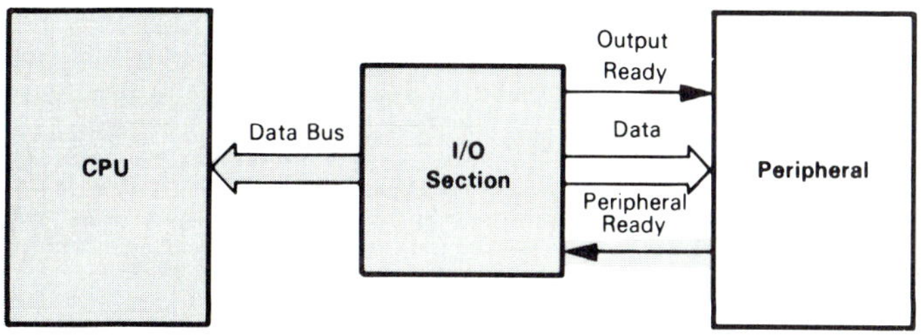

b. CPU reads Peripheral Ready signal from I/O section (this may be a hardware, e.g., interrupt connection).

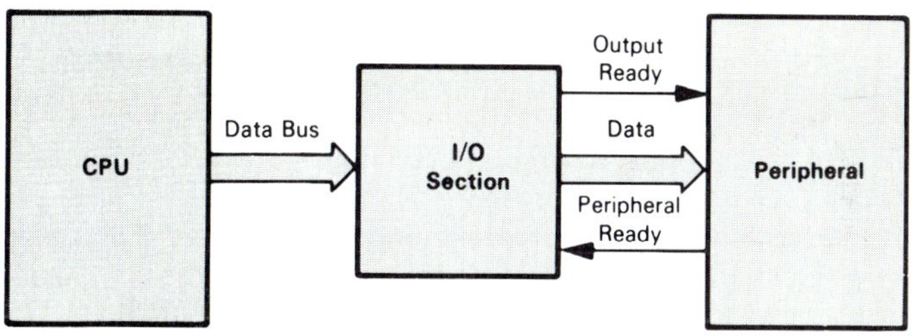

c. CPU sends data to Peripheral.

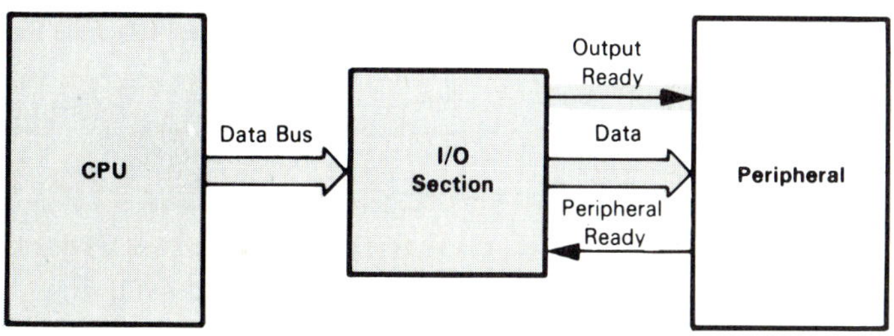

d. CPU sends Output Ready signal to Peripheral (this may be a hardware connection).

Figure 12-6. An Output Handshake

CLOCK

Many peripherals transfer data at regular intervals: i.e., synchronously. Here the only problem is starting the process by lining up to the first input or marking the first output. In some cases, the peripheral provides a clock output from which the processor can obtain timing information. **In synchronous I/O, the clock controls the speed of the transfers, rather than the sender and receiver.**

Reducing Transmission Errors

Transmission errors are a problem with medium-speed devices. Several methods can lessen the likelihood of such errors; they include:

- **Sampling input data at the center of the transmission interval** in order to avoid edge effects; that is, you should keep away from the edges where the data is changing.
- **Sampling each input several times and using majority logic.** For example, one could read each bit five times and choose the value that occurred most often.[1]
- **Generating and checking parity;** an extra bit is used that makes the number of 1 bits in the correct data even or odd.
- **Using other error detecting and correcting codes** such as checksums, LRC (longitudinal redundancy check), and CRC (cyclic redundancy check).[2]

INTERFACING HIGH-SPEED DEVICES

High-speed devices that transfer more than 10,000 bits per second require special methods. The usual technique is to construct a special purpose controller that transfers data directly between the memory and the I/O device. This process is called direct memory access (DMA). The DMA controller must force the CPU off the busses, provide addresses and control signals to the memory, and transfer the data. Such a controller will be fairly complex, typically consisting of 50 to 100 chips, although LSI devices such as the MC68450 DMA controller[3] for the MC68000 will be introduced throughout 1981. The CPU must initially load the address and data counters in the controller so the controller will know where to start and how much data to transfer.

TIME INTERVALS

A common problem in I/O programming is how to provide time intervals of various lengths between operations. Such intervals are necessary to debounce mechanical switches (i.e., to smooth their irregular transitions), to provide pulses with specified lengths and frequencies for displays, and to time I/O operations for devices that transfer data regularly (e.g., a teletypewriter that sends or receives one bit every 9.1 ms).

METHODS FOR PRODUCING TIME INTERVALS

We can produce time intervals in several ways:

1. **In hardware** with one-shots or monostable multivibrators. These devices produce a single pulse of fixed duration in response to a pulse input. However, one-shots create reliability problems and should be avoided whenever possible.
2. **In a combination of hardware and software** with a flexible device such as the 6840 Programmable Timer for MC68000-based microcomputers.[4] The 6840 device can provide time intervals of various lengths with a variety of starting and ending conditions.
3. **In software with delay routines.** A delay routine has no purpose other than to count time. We can easily specify how much time the computer is to count, since we know the clock speed of our particular microcomputer (this is system-dependent) and the number of clock cycles required to execute instructions (Appendix B). The problem with pure delay routines is that the processor cannot do other tasks while it is counting time; however, delay routines require no hardware and may use processor time that would be wasted anyway.

The choice among these three methods depends on your application. The software method is inexpensive but may overburden the processor. The programmable timers are relatively expensive but are easy to interface and may be able to handle many complex timing tasks.

DELAY ROUTINES

A simple delay routine works as follows:

1. **Load a register with a specified value.**
2. **Decrement the register.**
3. **If the result is not zero, repeat 2.**

This routine does nothing except use time. The amount of time used depends on the execution time of the various instructions. The maximum length of the delay is limited by the size of the register; however, the entire routine can be placed inside a similar routine that uses another register, etc.

Be careful — **the actual time used depends on the clock rate at which the processor is running, the speed of memory accesses, and operating conditions such as temperature, power supply voltage, and circuit loading which may affect the exact speed of the system clock.**

The following example subroutine uses registers D0 and D1 to produce delays as long as 255 ms. The routine saves the contents of register D0 in the hardware stack so it can be restored. We could use either of the general parameter passing techniques from Chapter 11 to write a completely "transparent" subroutine that would not affect any registers or flags. Of course, we would have to include the extra instructions that transfer parameters, save and restore registers, and adjust the return address in the time budget.

Program Example: A Delay Subroutine

Purpose: This subroutine produces a delay of 1 millisecond times the 16-bit contents of data register D0.

Flowchart:

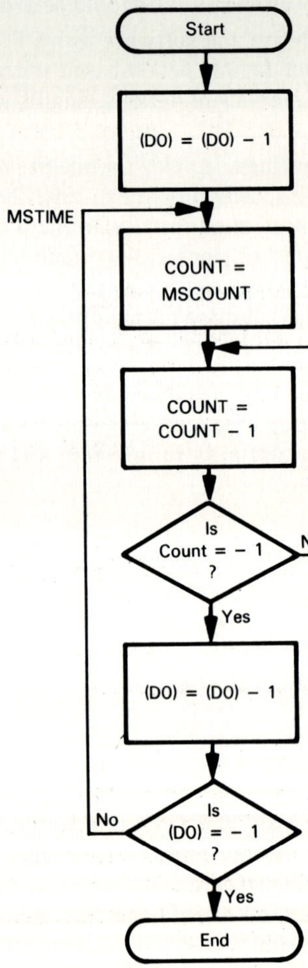

The value of MSCNT depends on the rate at which the CPU executes instructions.

Program 12-1:

```
00004100    PROGRAM  EQU    $4100
0000031E    MSCNT    EQU    797              COUNT FOR 1 MS DELAY
00004100             ORG    PROGRAM
```

```
004100 2F01       PGM12_1  MOVE.L  D1,-(A7)     SAVE REGISTER VALUE
004102 5340                SUBQ.W  #1,D0        DECREMENT FOR DBRA INSTRUCTION
004104 323C031E   MSTIME   MOVE.W  #MSCNT,D1    INITIALIZE 1 MS COUNT
004108 51C9FFFE   MSLOOP   DBRA    D1,MSLOOP    DELAY FOR 1 MS
00410C 51C8FFF6            DBRA    D0,MSTIME    COUNT NUMBER OF MILLISECONDS
004110 221F                MOVE.L  (A7)+,D1     RESTORE REGISTER

004112 4E75                RTS

                           END     PGM12_1
```

Time Budget:

Instruction		Number of Times Executed
MOVE.L	D1,-(A7)	1
SUBQ.W	01,DO	1
MOVE.W	OMSCNT,D1	(DO)
DBRA	D1,MSLOOP	(DO) • MSCNT + 1
DBRA	DO,MSTIME	(DO)
MOVE.L	(A7)+,D1	1

The total time used should be (D0) times 1 MS. If the memory is operating at full speed and *without wait states,* the instructions require the following number of clock cycles (according to Appendix B).

Instruction		Number of Clock Cycles
MOVE.L	D1,-(A7)	16
SUBQ.W	01,DO	4
MOVE.W	OMSCNT,D1	8
DBRA	D1,MSLOOP	10 (14 last time)
DBRA	DO,MSTIME	10 (14 last time)
MOVE.L	(A7)+,D1	12

Therefore, the program takes

$$(DO) \times (8 + 10{*}MSCNT + 14 + 10) + 16 + 4 + 4 + 12 \text{ clock cycles}$$

or

$$(DO) \times (32 + 10 \times MSCNT) + 36 \text{ clock cycles}$$

The 32 is the number of cycles required by MOVE.W OMSCNT,D1; DBRA D0,MSTIME and the 14 cycles required by the last execution of DBRA D1,MSLOOP. The 10 is the number of cycles required by DBRA D1,MSLOOP. Finally, the 36 is the number of cycles required by the two MOVE.L instructions, the SUBQ.W instruction and the four additional cycles required by the last execution of DBRA D0, MSTIME.

So, to make the delay 1 millisecond

$$32 + 10 \times MSCNT = N_c$$

where N_c is the number of clock cycles per millisecond. At an 8MHz MC68000 clock rate, $N_c = 8000$, so

$$10 \times MSCNT = 7968$$
$$MSCNT = 796.8$$

If MSCNT is 796_{10} the time delay will be 1 millisecond minus 1 microsecond (8 cycles). If MSCNT is 797_{10}, the time delay is 1 millisecond plus 0.250 microseconds. The 1 microsecond error represents a 0.1% error in a 1 millisecond time interval. A smaller error is introduced if MSCNT is 797_{10}. To eliminate the small error in the case of MSCNT = 796, we could insert two NOP instructions in the loop as follows:

```
MSTIME    MOVE.W    OMSCNT,D1
MSLOOP    DBRA      D1,MSLOOP
          NOP
          NOP
          DBRA      DO,MSTIME
```

Since each NOP requires four clock cycles, the 1 microsecond error created when MSCNT is 796_{10} will now be eliminated. Before adding these two NOPs you should assure yourself that your clock signal is not introducing larger errors. For example, if your clock is accurate to 0.2%, eliminating smaller errors in a delay loop is not very productive.

Even with the addition of the two NOP instructions and an accurate clock, our program is not yet 100% accurate! The 36 cycles occurring outside both loops occur regardless of the count contained in register D0. These setup instructions could be eliminated if the value of D1 didn't have to be saved and if the count in D0 were initialized with the value "count −1." However, before you go to these limits, don't forget that the call and return instructions as well as others may also contribute to the time delay.

LOGICAL AND PHYSICAL DEVICES[6]

An important goal in writing I/O routines is to make them independent of particular physical hardware. The routines can then transfer data to or from I/O devices, with the actual addresses being supplied as parameters. The I/O device that can actually be accessed through a particular interface is referred to as a *physical device.* The operating system or supervisor program must provide a mapping of logical devices on to physical devices, that is, must assign actual physical I/O addresses and characteristics to be used by the I/O routines.

Note the advantages of this approach:

1. **The operating system can vary the assignments under user control.** Now the user can easily substitute a test panel or a development system interface for the actual I/O devices. This is useful in field maintenance as well as in debugging and testing. Furthermore, the user can change the I/O devices for different situations; typical examples are directing intermediate output to a video display and final output to a printer or obtaining some input from a remote communications line rather than from a local keyboard.
2. **The same I/O routines can handle several identical or similar devices.** The operating system or user need only supply the address of a particular teletypewriter, RS-232 terminal, printer, or other device.
3. **Changes, corrections, or additions to the I/O configuration are easy to make** since only the assignments (or mapping) must be changed. On the MC68000 microprocessor, the I/O routines can use the indirect addressing modes to provide independence of specific physical addresses. Address register indirect

addressing with indexing allows the user to access a physical device through a table.

I/O DEVICE TABLE

If the system has a table of I/O addresses in memory (for example, starting at address IODEV), all an I/O routine needs is an index into the table. It can then access the I/O device using the address register indirect with index mode. If, for example, the device address is table entry DEV, the following program calculates the index and loads the base address of the device into address register A0:

```
MOVEQ.W  #DEV,D0              GET DEVICE NUMBER
LSL.W    #2,D0                MULTIPLY WITH 4 FOR 4 BYTE ADDRESS
MOVEA.L  #IODEV,A0            GET ADDRESS OF I/O DEVICE TABLE
LEA      (A0,D0.W),A0         GET ADDRESS OF DEVICE
```

The program can now transfer data to or from the I/O device using the instructions

```
MOVE.B   DATA,0(A0)           SEND DATA TO LOGICAL I/O DEVICE
```

or

```
MOVE.B   0(A0),DATA           GET DATA FROM LOGICAL I/O DEVICE
```

Using this approach, a single I/O routine can transfer data to or from many different I/O devices. The main program simply supplies the I/O routine with the index for the device table. Compare the flexibility of this approach with the inflexibility of I/O routines that use absolute addressing to transfer data to or from I/O devices and are therefore tied to specific physical addresses.

MC68000 INPUT/OUTPUT CHIPS

Most MC68000 input/output routines will be based on LSI interface chips. These devices combine latches, buffers, flip-flops, and other logic circuits needed for handshaking and other simple interfacing techniques. They contain many logic connections, certain sets of which can be selected according to the contents of programmable registers. Thus the programmer has the equivalent of a Circuit Designer's Casebook under his or her control. The initialization phase of the program places the appropriate values in registers to select the required logic connections. Input or output routines based on programmable LSI interface chips can handle many different applications, and changes or corrections can be made in software rather than by rewiring.

Designers often use the following LSI interface chips with the MC68000 microprocessor:

1. **The 6821 Peripheral Interface Adapter.** We will discuss this device in the next chapter. It contains two 8-bit I/O ports and four control lines.
2. **The 6850 Asynchronous Communications Interface Adapter.** This device transforms data between the 8-bit parallel form and the serial form required in

most communications applications. We will discuss the 6850 ACIA in Chapter 14.

REFERENCES

1. J. Barnes and V. Gregory. "Use Microprocessors to Enhance Performance with Noisy Data," *EDN,* August 20, 1976, pp. 71-72.
2. S. V. Alekar. "M6800 Program Performs Cyclic Redundancy Checks," *Electronics,* December 6, 1979, p. 167.

   J. E. McNamara. *Technical Aspects of Data Communications.* Maynard, Mass.: Digital Equipment Corporation, 1977, Chapter 13.

   R. Swanson. "Understanding Cyclic Redundancy Codes," *Computer Design,* November 1975, pp. 93-99.

   J. Wong et al. "Software Error Checking Procedures for Data Communications Protocols," *Computer Design,* February 1979, pp. 122-25.
3. A. Osborne et al. *An Introduction to Microcomputers: Volume 2 — Some Real Microprocessors.* Berkeley: Osborne/McGraw-Hill, 1978, pp. 9-106 through 9-123.
4. A. Osborne et al. *An Introduction to Microcomputers: Volume 2 — Some Real Microprocessors.* Berkeley: Osborne/McGraw-Hill, 1978, pp. 9-78 through 9-106.
5. A. Osborne et al. *An Introduction to Microcomputers: Volume 2 — Some Real Microprocessors.* Berkeley: Osborne/McGraw-Hill, pp. 9-124 through 9-130.
6. C. W. Gear. *Computer Organization and Programming,* 3rd ed. New York: McGraw-Hill, 1980, Chapter 6.

13

Using the 6821 Peripheral Interface Adapter (PIA)

The 6821 PIA[1,2] is a device which supports many modes of parallel I/O. In this chapter we will discuss the programming of this device in some detail, and give several examples of fundamental I/O routines.

REGISTERS AND CONTROL LINES

Figure 13-1 is the block diagram of a PIA. The device contains two nearly identical 8-bit ports — A, which is usually an input port, and B, which is usually an output port. Each port contains:

- **A data or peripheral register** that holds either input or output data. This register is latched when used for output but unlatched when used for input.
- **A data direction register.** The bits in this register determine whether the corresponding data register bits (and pins) are inputs (0) or outputs (1).
- **A control register** that holds the status signals required for handshaking, and other bits that select logic connections within the PIA.
- **Two control lines** that are configured by the control registers. These lines can be used for the handshaking signals shown in Figures 12-5 and 12-6.

The meanings of the bits in the data direction and control registers are related to the underlying hardware and are entirely arbitrary as far as the assembly language programmer is concerned. You must either memorize them or look them up in the appropriate tables (Tables 13-2 through 13-6).

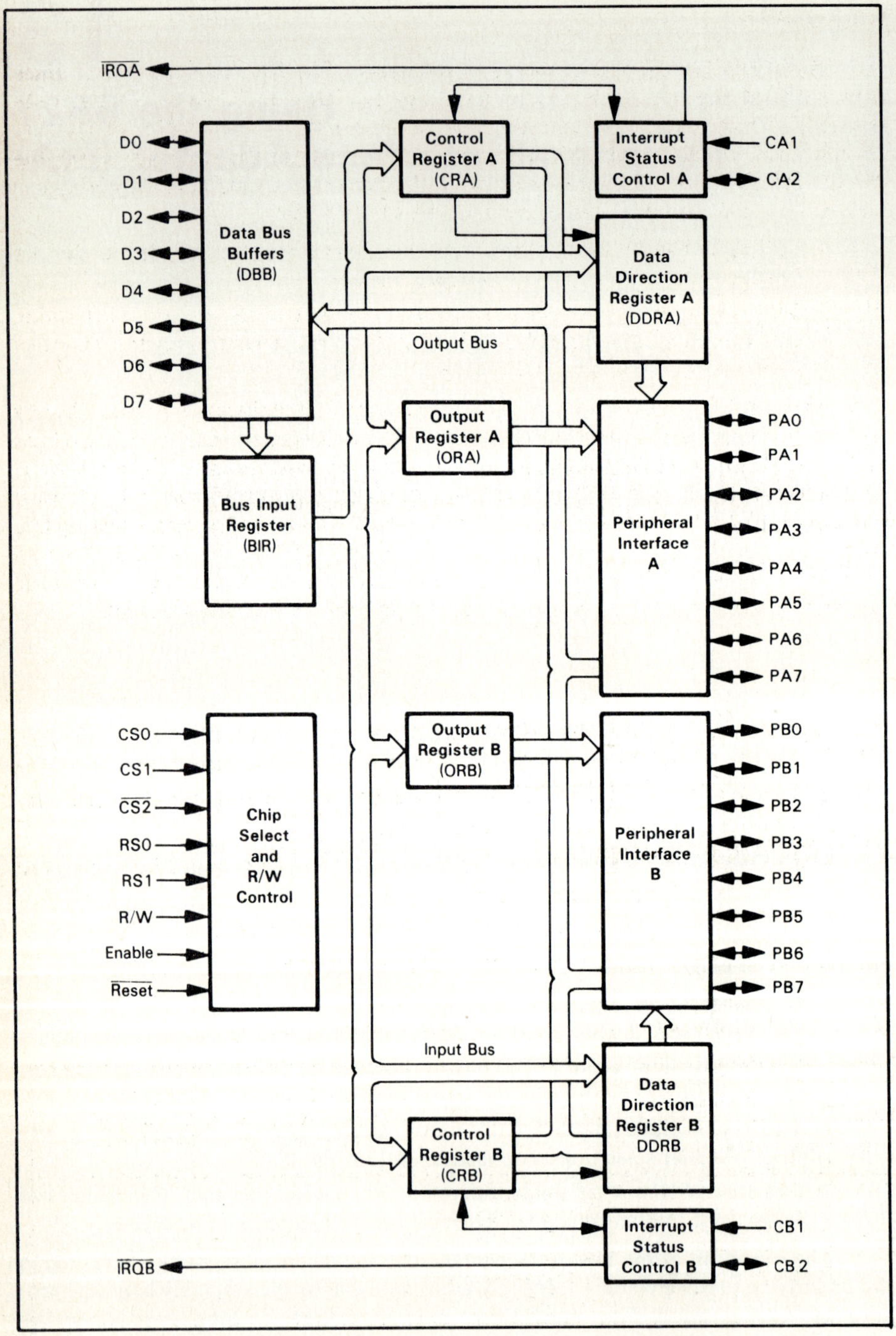

Figure 13-1. Block Diagram of the 6821 Peripheral Interface Adapter

Addresses

Each PIA occupies four memory addresses. The RS (register select) lines choose one of the four registers, as described in Table 13-1. Since there are six registers (two peripheral, two data direction, and two control) in each PIA, one further bit is needed for addressing. **Bit 2 of each control register determines whether the other address on that side refers to the data direction register (0) or to the peripheral register (1).** This sharing of an external address means that

1. A program must change the bit in the control register in order to use the register that is not currently being addressed.
2. The programmer must know the contents of the control register to determine which register is being addressed. RESET clears the control register and thus addresses the data direction register.

Table 13-1 also shows a convenient way to address the registers in the PIA. Usually you will find that the PIA register select lines RS0 and RS1 are tied to the address lines A1 and A2, and the PIA data lines are tied to either the upper or lower eight bits of the data bus. This means that the PIA registers are located at every other memory address; that is, at either odd addresses only, or even addresses only. (We will describe the way this addressing works in detail later in this chapter.) You can thus load one of the MC68000's address registers with the address of data (peripheral) register A and refer to the other registers by using the offsets in the last column of Table 13-1 as displacements.

PIA Control Registers

Table 13-2 shows the organization of the PIA control registers. We may describe the general purpose of each bit as follows:

Bit 7: Status bit set by transitions on control line 1 and cleared by reading the peripheral (data) register

Bit 6: Same as bit 7 except set by transitions on control line 2

Bit 5: Determines whether control line 2 is an input (0) or output (1)

Table 13-1. Addressing 6821 PIA Internal Registers

Address Lines		Control Register Bit		Register Selected	Offset Address (Index Register or Stack Pointer) = Address of Peripheral (Data) Register A
RS1	RS0	CRA-2	CRB-2		
0	0	1	X	Peripheral Register A	0
0	0	0	X	Data Direction Register A	0
0	1	X	X	Control Register A	1
1	0	X	1	Peripheral Register B	2
1	0	X	0	Data Direction Register B	2
1	1	X	X	Control Register B	3

X = Either 0 or 1

Table 13-2. Organization of the PIA Control Registers

<table>
<tr><td rowspan="2">CRA</td><td>7</td><td>6</td><td>5</td><td>4</td><td>3</td><td>2</td><td>1</td><td>0</td></tr>
<tr><td>IRQA1</td><td>IRQA2</td><td colspan="3">CA2 Control</td><td>DDRA Access</td><td colspan="2">CA1 Control</td></tr>
<tr><td rowspan="2">CRB</td><td>7</td><td>6</td><td>5</td><td>4</td><td>3</td><td>2</td><td>1</td><td>0</td></tr>
<tr><td>IRQB1</td><td>IRQB2</td><td colspan="3">CB2 Control</td><td>DDRB Access</td><td colspan="2">CB1 Control</td></tr>
</table>

Table 13-3. Control of 6821 PIA Interrupt Inputs CA1 and CB1

CRA 1 (CRB−1)	CRA−0 (CRB−0)	Interrupt Input CA1 (CB1)	Interrupt Flag CRA−7 (CRB−7)	MPU Interrupt Request $\overline{\text{IRQA}}$ ($\overline{\text{IRQB}}$)
0	0	↓ Active	Set high on ↓ of CA1 (CB1)	Disabled — $\overline{\text{IRQ}}$ remains high
0	1	↓ Active	Set high on ↓ of CA1 (CB1)	Goes low when the interrupt flag bit CRA-7 (CRB-7) goes high
1	0	↑ Active	Set high on ↑ of CA1 (CB1)	Disabled — $\overline{\text{IRQ}}$ remains high
1	1	↑ Active	Set high on ↑ of CA1 (CB1)	Goes low when the interrupt flag bit CRA-7 (CRB-7) goes high

Notes:

1. ↑ indicates positive transition (low to high)
2. ↓ indicates negative transition (high to low)
3. The interrupt flag bit CRA-7 is cleared by an MPU Read of the A Data Register, and CRB-7 is cleared by an MPU Read of the B Data Register
4. If CRA-0 (CRB-0) is low when an interrupt occurs (Interrupt disabled) and is later brought high, $\overline{\text{IRQA}}$ ($\overline{\text{IRQB}}$) occurs after CRA-0 (CRB-0) is written to a "one."

Bit 4: Control line 2 input: determines whether bit 6 is set by high-to-low transitions (0) or low-to-high transitions (1) on control line 2

Control line 2 output: determines whether control line 2 is a pulse (0) or a level (1)

Bit 3: Control line 2 input: if 1, enables interrupt output from bit 6

Control line 2 output: determines ending condition for pulse (0 = handshake acknowledgment lasting until next transition on control line 1, 1 = brief strobe lasting one clock cycle) or value of level

Bit 2: Selects data direction register (0) or data register (1)

Bit 1: Determines whether bit 7 is set by high-to-low transitions (0) or low-to-high transitions (1) on control line 1

Bit 0: If 1, enables interrupt output from bit 7 of control register

Tables 13-3 through 13-6 describe the bits in more detail. You can interpret "E" pulse as "clock pulse."

Table 13-4. Control of 6821 PIA Interrupt Inputs CA2 and CB2 (CRA5 (CRB5) is Low)

CRA−5 (CRB−5)	CRA−4 (CRB−4)	CRA−3 (CRB−3)	Interrupt Input CA2 (CB2)	Interrupt Flag CRA−6 (CRB−6)	MPU Interrupt Request $\overline{IRQA}$ ($\overline{IRQB}$)
0	0	0	↓ Active	Set high on ↓ of CA2 (CB2)	Disabled — $\overline{IRQ}$ remains high
0	0	1	↓ Active	Set high on ↓ of CA2 (CB2)	Goes low when the interrupt flag bit CRA-6 (CRB-6) goes high
0	1	0	↑ Active	Set high on ↑ of CA2 (CB2)	Disabled — $\overline{IRQ}$ remains high
0	1	1	↑ Active	Set high or ↑ of CA2 (CB2)	Goes low when the interrupt flag bit CRA-6 (CRB-6) goes high

Notes

1. ↑ indicates positive transition (low to high)
2. ↓ indicates negative transition (high to low)
3. The Interrupt flag bit CRA-6 is cleared by an MPU Read of the A Data Register and CRB-6 is cleared by an MPU Read of the B Data Register
4. If CRA-3 (CRB-3) is low when an interrupt occurs (Interrupt disabled) and is later brought high, $\overline{IRQA}$ ($\overline{IRQB}$) occurs after CRA-3 (CRB-3) is written to a "one"

Table 13-5. Control of 6821 PIA CB2 Output Line (CRB5 is High)

CRB-5	CRB-4	CRB-3	CB2		Mode
			Cleared	Set	
1	0	0	Low on the positive transition of the first E pulse following an MPU Write "B" Data Register operation.	High when the interrupt flag bit CRB-7 is set by an active transition of the CB1 signal.	Automatic Output Acknowledge
1	0	0	Low on the positive transition of the first E pulse after an MPU Write "B" Data Register operation.	High on the positive edge of the first "E" pulse following an "E" pulse which occurred while the part was deselected.	Automatic Output (Write) Strobe
1	1	0	Low when CRB-3 goes low as a result of an MPU Write in Control Register "B".	Always low as long as CRB-3 is low. Will go high on an MPU Write in Control Register "B" that changes CRB-3 to "one".	Manual Output (Low)
1	1	1	Always high as long as CRB-3 is high. Will be cleared when an MPU Write Control Register "B" results in clearing CRB-3 to "zero."	High when CRB-3 goes high as a result of an MPU Write into Control Register "B".	Manual Output (High)

Table 13-6. Control of 6821 PIA CA2 Output Line (CRA5 is High)

CRA-5	CRA-4	CRA-3	CA2 Cleared	CA2 Set	Mode
1	0	0	Low on negative transition of E after an MPU Read "A" Data operation.	High when the interrupt flag bit CRA-7 is set by an active transition of the CA1 signal.	Automatic Input Acknowledge
1	0	1	Low on negative transition of E after an MPU Read "A" Data operation.	High on the negative edge of the first "E" pulse which occurs during a deselect.	Automatic Input (Read) Strobe
1	1	0	Low when CRA-3 goes low as a result of an MPU Write to Control Register "A".	Always low as long as CRA-3 is low. Will go high on an MPU Write to Control Register "A" that changes CRA-3 to "one".	Manual Output (Low)
1	1	1	Always high as long as CRA-3 is high. Will be cleared on an MPU Write to Control Register "A" that clears CRA-3 to a "zero".	High when CRA-3 goes high as a result of an MPU Write to Control Register "A".	Manual Output (High)

INITIALIZING A PIA

As part of the general system initialization, the program must determine how each PIA will operate. Remember that a PIA contains a large number of logic connections, much as the processor itself does. The data stored in the control and data direction register activates certain connections within the PIA, much as the data loaded into the instruction register of the CPU activates certain connections. The differences are that the PIA contains far fewer connections than the CPU and the program rarely, if ever, changes the active connections in a PIA.

The steps in determining how the PIA will operate are:

1. **Address the data direction registers** by clearing bit 2 of each control register. This allows the program to determine which I/O pins will be inputs and which outputs. Since RESET clears the entire control register, this step is unnecessary in the overall system startup routine.
2. **Determine which I/O pins will be inputs and which outputs** by loading the appropriate combinations of 0's (for inputs) and 1's (for outputs) into the data direction registers.
3. **Determine how the status and control lines will operate** by loading the appropriate values into bit positions 0, 1, 3, 4, and 5 of the control registers. Address the data registers by setting bit 2 of each control register.

The program can address a data direction register as follows:

```
CLR.B    PIACA         CLEAR PIA CONTROL REGISTER (A SIDE)
```

or

```
MOVE.B   #$FB,D0
AND.B    D0,PIACA      ADDRESS DATA DIRECTION REGISTER
```

or

```
BCLR.B   #2,PIACA      SELECT DATA DIRECTION REGISTER
```

The second and third versions are more general, since they do not change any of the other bits in the control register.

After the program has addressed the data direction register, it can select the appropriate combination of inputs and outputs by storing the corresponding pattern of 0's and 1's in that register. Some simple examples are:

```
CLR.B    PIADDA        MAKE ALL DATA LINES INPUTS


MOVE.B   #$FF,PIADDA   MAKE ALL DATA LINES OUTPUTS


MOVE.B   #$F0,PIADDA   DATA LINES 4-7 OUTPUTS, 0-3 INPUTS
```

The third step is clearly the most difficult, since it involves selecting the active logic connections in the PIA and thus determining how the device will operate.

Some factors to remember are:

1. **You cannot change bits 6 and 7 of the control register by writing data into them.** Only transitions on the control lines set these bits and only the reading of the corresponding data registers clears them.
2. **You must set bit 2 of each control register to address the data register and allow the transfer of data** to or from the outside world. As long as bit 2 of a control register is zero, the CPU can only access the corresponding data direction register; it cannot transfer data to or from the I/O pins through the data register.
3. **Bit 1 of the control register determines which edge of a pulse on control line 1 will set bit 7.** If bit 1 is 0, a high-to-low transition (rising edge) on control line 1 will set bit 7; if bit 1 is 1, a low-to-high transition (falling edge) on control line 1 will perform that function. If control line 2 is an input, bit 4 provides the same choice for it.
4. **Bit 0 of the control register is an interrupt enable for control line 1.** Remember that this bit must be *set* to enable interrups. Chapter 15 describes interrupts in more detail. If control line 2 is an input, bit 3 performs the same function for it.
5. **Bit 5 determines whether control line 2 is an output (1) or an input (0).** Bits 3 and 4 determine how control line 2 will operate. In the pulse or automatic strobe mode, ports A and B differ; port A produces a pulse on CA2 only after

the processor reads data register A, while port B produces a pulse on CB2 only after the processor writes into data register B.

6. **You must determine the operating mode of each port of each PIA in your system.** Each port has a separate control register, data direction register, and data register.

PIA OPERATING MODES

We can refer to the operating modes in which CA2 or CB2 are output control signals as follows:

The modes in which the PIA automatically produces a pulse on CA2 after an input operation or on CB2 after an output operation are called automatic modes, since the PIA produces the entire pulse without any explicit CPU intervention. The programmer has no control over the length or polarity of the pulse.

The mode in which bit 3 of the PIA control register determines the level of control line 2 is called a *manual mode,* since the CPU must produce changes by explicitly setting or clearing control register bit 3. The PIA does nothing automatically. This mode requires extra instructions, but gives the programmer complete control over the length and polarity of pulses.

Control line 2 has the following functions in the two automatic modes:

In the mode in which the automatic pulse lasts until the next active transition on control line 1, control line 2 is an *acknowledgment.* The active part of the pulse (the low period) signifies that the CPU has completed its part of the most recent I/O operation; the I/O device may start the next operation by sending data (input) or indicating its readiness (output).

In the mode in which the automatic pulse lasts one clock cycle, control line 2 is a strobe. The pulse indicates that the CPU has performed an I/O operation.

Examples of Selecting a PIA Operating Mode

1. **A simple input port with no control lines** (for example, as needed for a set of switches):

```
CLR.B    PIACA              ADDRESS DATA DIRECTION REGISTER
CLR.B    PIADDA             MAKE ALL DATA LINES INPUTS

BSET.B   #2,PIACA           ADDRESS DATA REGISTER
```

The program first clears bit 2 of the control register to gain access to the data direction register. It then makes all the data lines inputs by storing 0's in all the bits of the data register (and the input port itself). The same sequence of instructions will handle the case in which a high-to-low transition (falling edge) on control line 1 indicates DATA READY or PERIPHERAL READY.

2. **A simple output port with no control lines** (for example, as needed for a set of single LED displays):

```
CLR.B    PIACA              ADDRESS DATA DIRECTION REGISTER

MOVE.B   #$FF,PIADDA        MAKE ALL DATA LINES OUTPUTS

BSET.B   #2,PIACA           ADDRESS DATA REGISTER
```

The only difference from the previous example is that the program makes all the data lines outputs by storing 1's in all the bits of the data direction register.

3. **An input port with a status input that indicates DATA READY with a low-to-high transition (positive transition on control line 1).**

```
CLR.B    PIACA           ADDRESS DATA DIRECTION REGISTER
CLR.B    PIADDA          MAKE ALL DATA LINES INPUTS

MOVE.B   #$06,PIACA      MAKE DATA READY INPUT ACTIVE LOW-TO
```

The only difference from Example 1 is that the program sets bit 1 of the control register. The result is that low-to-high transitions on control line 1 will set bit 7 of the control register. This operating mode is suitable for most encoded keyboards.

4. **An output port that produces a brief strobe to indicate DATA READY or OUTPUT READY.** This strobe could be used to multiplex displays or to provide a DATA AVAILABLE signal to a printer.

```
CLR.B    PIACA           ADDRESS DATA DIRECTION REGISTER

MOVE.B   #$FF,PIADDA     MAKE ALL DATA LINES OUTPUTS

MOVE.B   #$2C,PIACA      MAKE CONTROL LINE 2 A BRIEF STROBE
```

This program selects an operating mode for control line 2 as follows:

Bit 5 = 1 to make control line 2 an output.
Bit 4 = 0 to make control line 2 a pulse, rather than a level.
Bit 3 = 1 to make the pulse one clock period long.

After each instruction that writes data into PIA data register B, control line 2 will go low for one clock cycle. For example, the instruction

```
MOVE.B   D0,PIADB
```

will both send data to the data register (and hence to the output port) and cause a strobe on control line 2. However, the A port of a PIA will produce a strobe only after a read operation. The sequence

```
MOVE.B   D0,PIADA        WRITE DATA
MOVE.B   PIADA,D0        DUMMY READ - PRODUCE OUTPUT STROBE
```

will both send the data to the output port and cause a strobe. The MOVE.B PIADA,DC instruction is a "dummy read;" it has no effect except causing the strobe (and wasting a few clock cycles). Other instruction could serve the same purpose; you should try to name some of them.

5. **An input port with a handshake INPUT ACKNOWLEDGE strobe.** The strobe goes low when the CPU has read the data in the port and can accept more.

```
CLR.B    PIACA           ADDRESS DATA DIRECTION REGISTER
CLR.B    PIADDA          MAKE ALL DATA LINES INPUTS

MOVE.B   #$24,PIACA      CONTROL LINE 2-HANDSHAKE ACKNOWLEDG
```

control register bit 5 = 1 to make control line 2 and output, bit 4 = 0 to make it a pulse, and bit 3 = 0 to make it an active-low acknowledgment that remains low until the next active transition on control line 1. The port operates as follows:

a. A high-to-low transition on control line 1 indicates that the input peripheral has sent the computer new data. Bit 7 of the PIA control register is set and control line 2 goes high.
b. The CPU determines that new data is available by examining bit 7 of the PIA control register. It therefore loads the data from the data register, thus clearing bit 7 of the control register and sending control line 2 low.
c. The input peripheral can determine that the CPU has accepted the most recent data by examining control line 2. It can then repeat step *a* with complete assurance that no data will be lost.

The acknowledgment automatically follows any instruction that reads PIA data register A; for example, the instruction

```
MOVE.B  PIADA,D0
```

will both read the data and cause the acknowledgment. However, the B port will produce an acknowledgment only after an instruction that writes into the data register. The sequence

```
MOVE.B  PIADB,D0        READ DATA
MOVE.B  D0,PIADB        DUMMY WRITE-PRODUCE ACKNOWLEDGEMENT
```

will both read data and produce an acknowledgment. The MOVE.B D0,PIADB instruction is a "dummy write;" it has no effect other than to cause an acknowledgment (that is, to send control line 2 low) and use a few clock cycles. Note that the instructions here are in the opposite order from those in Example 4. This operating mode is suitable for many CRT terminals that require a complete handshake.

6. **An output port with a latched zero control bit** (latched serial output or level output with value 0). The serial output can be used to turn a peripheral on or off, or to determine its mode of operation.

```
CLR.B   PIACA           ADDRESS DATA DIRECTION REGISTER

MOVE.B  #$FF,PIADDA     MAKE ALL DATA LINES OUTPUTS

MOVE.B  #$34,PIACA      CONTROL LINE 2 - LATCHED OUTPUT,
                        INITIAL VALUE 0
```

Bit 5 = 1 to make control line 2 an output, bit 4 = 1 to make it a level or latched bit, and bit 3 = 0 to make the value of the level zero. Operations on the data register do not affect control line 2 in this operating mode, so it will not automatically change value. The only way to change its value is for the program to change the value of bit 3 of the PIA control register; i.e.,

```
MOVE.B  #$08,D0
OR.B    D0,PIADA        MAKE SERIAL OUTPUT ONE
```

or

```
BSET.B  #3,PIACA        MAKE SERIAL OUTPUT ONE
```

```
MOVE.B   #$F3,D0
AND.B    D0,PIACA         MAKE SERIAL OUTPUT ZERO

BCLR.B   #3,PIACA         MAKE SERIAL OUTPUT ZERO
```

You can use this operating mode to produce active-high strobes or tô provide pulses with lengths determined by the program, rather than the hardware.

USING THE PIA TO TRANSFER DATA

Once the program has determined the operating mode of the PIA, you may use its data registers like any other memory locations. **The most straightforward instructions for transferring data from an input device or to an output device are as follows:**

MOVE.B <ea>, Dn transfers 8 bits of data from the specified input pins to a data register.

MOVE.B Dn,<ea> transfers 8 bits of data from a data register to the specifed output pins.

You must be cautious in situations in which input and output ports do not behave like memory locations. For example, it often makes no sense to write data into input ports or read data from output ports. Be particularly careful if the input port is not latched or if the output port is not buffered.

Other instructions that transfer data to or from memory can also serve as I/O instructions. Typical examples are:

Clear places zeros on a set of output pins.

Bit manipulation instructions can set, clear, or test an individual pin. Note, however, that the bit change instruction cannot be used to reference a PIA's data bits.

Compare sets the flags as if the values of a set of input pins had been subtracted from the contents of a data register, and immediate value, or another memory location.

Here also you must be aware of the physical limitations of the I/O ports. Be particularly careful of instructions like the Shift, Complement, and certain Bit manipulation instructions which involve both read and write cycles.

We cannot overemphasize the importance of careful documentation. **Often, complex I/O transfers can be concealed in instructions with no obvious functions. You must describe the purposes of such instructions carefully.** For example, one could easily be tempted to remove the dummy read and write operations mentioned earlier since they do not appear to accomplish anything.

PIA Status Bits

Bit 7 of the PIA control register often serves as a status bit, such as data ready or peripheral ready. You can check its value with any of the following sequences:

```
MOVE.B   PIACA,D0                IS READY FLAG 1?
BMI      DEVRDY1                 ...YES, DEVICE READY

TST.B    PIACA                   IS READY FLAG 1?
BMI      DEVRDY2                 ...YES,DEVICE READY

BTST.B   #7,PIACA                IS READY FLAG 1?
BNE      DEVRDY3                 ...YES, DEVICE READY
```

Note that you should not use the shift instructions, since they will change the contents of the control register. (Why?) The following program will wait for the Ready flag to go high:

```
MOVE.B   PIACA,D0                IS READY FLAG 1?
BPL      WAITR                   ...NO, WAIT
```

How would you change these programs to examine bit 6 instead of bit 7?

The only way to clear bit 7 (or bit 6) is to read the data register. A dummy read will be necessary if a read operation is not normally part of the response to the bit being set. If the port is used for output, the sequence

```
MOVE.B   D0,PIADA                SEND DATA
MOVE.B   PIADA,D0                DUMMY READ - CLEAR READY FLAG
```

will do the job. Note that here the dummy read is necessary on either port of the PIA. The Test instruction can also clear the strobe without changing anything except the flags. Be particularly careful of situations in which the CPU is not ready for input data or has no output data to send.

PROGRAM EXAMPLES

13-1. A PUSHBUTTON

We will interface a pushbutton to an MC68000 microprocessor by means of a 6821 Peripheral Interface Adapter. The pushbutton is a mechanical switch; pressing the button closes the switch and connects the input bit to ground (see Fig. 13-2).

The 6821 PIA acts as a buffer; no latch is needed since the pushbutton remains closed for many CPU clock cycles. Pressing the button grounds one bit of the PIA. The pullup resistor ensures that the input bit is one if the button is not being pressed.

We will perform two tasks with this circuit. They are:

a. Setting a memory location based on the state of the button.

b. Counting the number of times the button is pressed.

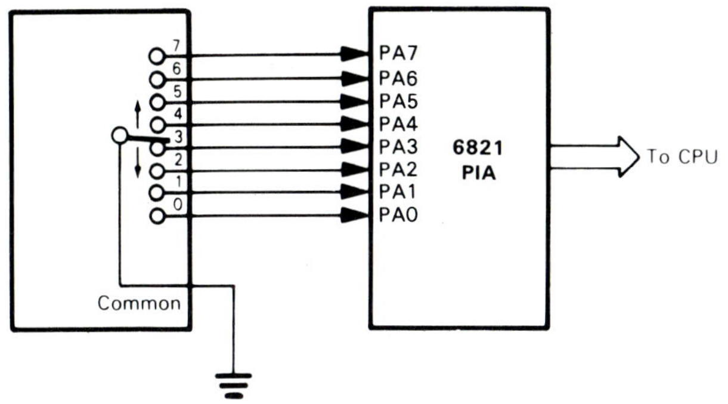

Figure 13-2. A Pushbutton Circuit

Task 13-1a. Determine Switch Closure

Purpose: Set the variable BUTTON at location 6000 to one if the button is not being pressed, and to zero if it is.

Sample Cases:

1. Button open (not pressed)
   BUTTON = (6000) = 01
2. Button closed (pressed)
   BUTTON = (6000) = 00

Program 13-1a:

```
       00004000      PROGRAM  EQU     $4000
       00006000      DATA     EQU     $6000

       0003FF40      PIADDA   EQU     $3FF40           DATA DIRECTION REGISTER A
       0003FF40      PIADA    EQU     $3FF40           DATA REGISTER A
       0003FF44      PIACA    EQU     $3FF44           CONTROL REGISTER A

       00000004      PIADS    EQU     $04              PIA DATA REGISTER SELECT
       00000001      MASKBUT  EQU     $01              MASK FOR BUTTON

       00006000               ORG     DATA

006000 00006000      BUTTON   DS.B    BUTTON           STATUS FLAG

       00004000               ORG     PROGRAM

004000 42390003FF44  PGM13_1A CLR.B   PIACA            ADDRESS DATA DIRECTION REGISTER
004006 42390003FF40           CLR.B   PIADDA           MAKE ALL DATA LINES INPUT
00400C 13FC0004
         0003FF44             MOVE.B  #PIADS,PIACA     ADDRESS DATA REGISTER
004014 42386000               CLR.B   BUTTON           CLEAR BUTTON FLAG
004018 10390003FF40           MOVE.B  PIADA,D0         READ BUTTON POSITION
00401E 02000001               AND.B   #MASKBUT,D0      IS BUTTON CLOSED(LOGICAL ZERO)?
004022 6704                   BEQ.S   DONE             IF YES THEN DONE
004024 52386000               ADDQ.B  #1,BUTTON        ...ELSE SET BUTTON FLAG
004028 4E75          DONE     RTS

                              END     PGM13_1A
```

Flowchart:

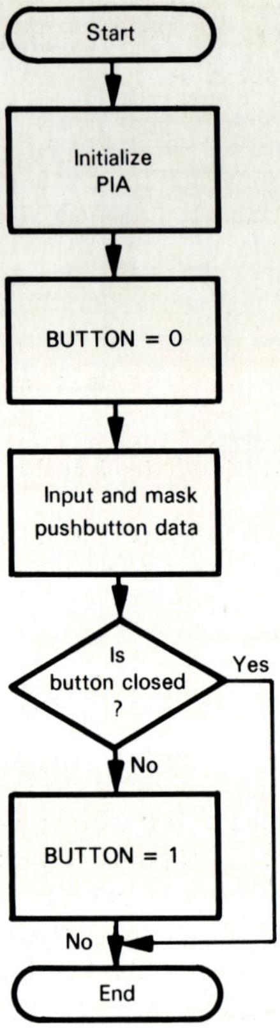

The addresses PIACA (control register A), PIADDA (data direction register A), and PIADA (data register A) depend on how the PIA is connected in your microcomputer. This example does not use the PIA control lines.

MASKBUT depends on the bit to which the pushbutton is connected. It has a one in the button position and zeros elsewhere.

Button Position (Bit Number)	Mask	
	Binary	Hexadecimal
0	00000001	01
1	00000010	02
2	00000100	04
3	00001000	08
4	00010000	10
5	00100000	20
6	01000000	40
7	10000000	80

If the button is attached to bit 7 of the PIA input port, the program can use a MOVE,TST, or BTST instruction to set the Sign (negative) or Equal flag and thereby determine the button's state. For example:

```
MOVE.B  PIADA,D0        IS BUTTON CLOSED (LOGIC ZERO)?
BPL     DONE            ...YES, DONE

TST.B   PIADA           IS BUTTON CLOSED (LOGIC ZERO)?
BPL     DONE            ...YES, DONE

BTST.B  #7,PIADA        IS BUTTON CLOSED (LOGIC ZERO)?
BNE     DONE            ...YES, DONE
```

The BTST instruction can test any bit in the data register.

Task 13-1b. Count Switch Closures

Purpose: Count the number of button closures by incrementing the variable count at memory location 6000 after each closure.

Sample Case:

Pressing the button ten times after the start of the program should result in

BUTTON = (6000)

In order to count the number of times the button has been pressed, we must be sure that each closure causes a single transition. However, a mechanical pushbutton does not produce a single transition for each closure, because the mechanical contacts bounce back and forth before settling into their final positions. We can use a one-shot to eliminate the bounce or we can handle it in software.

The program can debounce the pushbutton by waiting after it finds a closure. The required delay is called the debouncing time and is part of the specifications of the pushbutton. It is typically a few milliseconds long. The program should not examine the pushbutton during this period because it might mistake the bounces for new closures. The program may either enter a delay routine like the one described previously or simply perform other tasks for the specified amount of time.

Even after debouncing, the program must wait for the present closure to end before looking for a new closure. In addition, the opening of the switch must be debounced. This procedure avoids double counting. The following program uses a software delay of 10 ms to debounce the pushbutton. You may want to try varying the delay or eliminating it entirely to see what happens. To run this program, you must also enter the delay subroutine into memory starting at location 4100.

Program 13-1b:

```
00004000    PROGRAM  EQU    $4000
00006000    DATA     EQU    $6000
00004100    DELAY    EQU    $4100         ADDRESS OF DELAY ROUTINE

0003FF40    PIA      EQU    $3FF40        PIA BASE ADDRESS

00000000    PIADDA   EQU    $0            OFFSET DATA DIRECTION REGISTER A
00000000    PIADA    EQU    $0            OFFSET DATA REGISTER A
00000004    PIACA    EQU    $4            OFFSET CONTROL REGISTER A

00000000    A_DATDIR EQU    $00           ALL LINES INPUT ON A SIDE
```

```
                00000004    A_CNTRL   EQU      04                     SELECT DATA REGISTER

                00000000    BUTBIT    EQU      $0                     BUTTON BIT POSITION IN PIA
                0000000A    BOUNCE    EQU      10                     TIME IN MS REQUIRED TO DEBOUNCE BUT

                00006000              ORG      DATA

         006000 00000001    COUNT     DS.B     1                      BUTTON DEPRESSED COUNT

                00004000              ORG      PROGRAM

         004000 207C0003FF40 PGM13_1B MOVEA.L  #PIA,A0                GET PIA BASE ADDRESS
         004006 42280004              CLR.B    PIACA(A0)              INITIALIZE A SIDE
         00400A 117C00000000          MOVE.B   #A_DATDIR,PIADDA(A0)
         004010 117C00040004          MOVE.B   #A_CNTRL,PIACA(A0)

         004016 42386000              CLR.B    COUNT                  CLEAR BUTTON COUNT
         00401A 082800000000 CHKCLOSE BTST.B   #BUTBIT,PIADA(A0)      IS BUTTON PRESSED?
         004020 66F8                  BNE      CHKCLOSE               IF NO THEN WAIT UNTIL IT IS

         004022 52386000              ADD.B    #1,COUNT               ...ELSE INCREMENT CLOSURE COUNT
         004026 700A                  MOVEQ    #BOUNCE,D0             WAIT FOR A WHILE TO DEBOUNCE CLOSUR
         004028 4EB84100              JSR      DELAY
         00402C 082800000000 CHKOPEN  BTST.B   #BUTBIT,PIADA(A0)      IS BUTTON STILL BEING PRESSED?
         004032 67F8                  BEQ      CHKOPEN                IF YES THEN WAIT FOR RELEASE

         004034 700A                  MOVEQ    #BOUNCE,D0             WAIT FOR A WHILE TO DEBOUNCE OPENIN
         004036 4EB84100              JSR      DELAY
         00403A 60DE                  BRA      CHKCLOSE               ... ELSE LOOK FOR NEXT CLOSURE

                                      END      PGM13_1B
```

Flowchart:

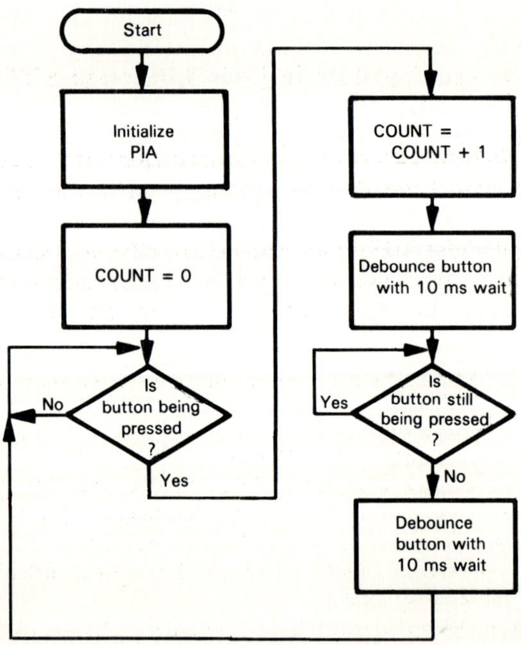

Note that the use of the symbol BOUNCE lets you change all bounce delays at one time. You do not have to search for them in the program; just change the symbol value for BOUNCE and reassemble.

The initialization instructions used here look a little different from those in Program 13-1*a*. This procedure — clear the control register, move a byte to the data direction register, and then a byte to the control register — is very general. You can always use the same sequence; just change the variables A-DATDIR and A-CNTRL to what you want. It is good programming style to make initializations generalized and easy to change. This is especially true in I/O programs which are usually subject to changes during program testing.

We have chosen another addressing mode for the PIA — address register indirect with displacement instead of absolute long, as in the previous program. The advantage obtained is that address register indirect with displacement requires fewer bytes of memory and thus will result in a shorter program. It is also the only addressing mode permitted with the MOVEP instruction, a very useful instruction for I/O programs which we will describe later in this chapter. A third reason for using this addressing mode is to reduce the number of separate addresses you must provide; if you have many PIAs in your system and use absolute long addressing, you must specify the address of each register in each PIA. With indirect addressing with displacement, you only have to specify one address for each PIA and, beyond that, only one set of displacements for the PIA registers.

Now that we have written these programs, it should be obvious that we do not need a PIA for this simple interface. An addressable tristate buffer would do the job at far lower cost.

13-2. A MULTIPLE-POSITION (ROTARY, SELECTOR, OR THUMBWHEEL) SWITCH

We will interface a multiple-position switch to an MC68000 microprocessor. The lead corresponding to the switch position is grounded, while the other leads are high (logic ones).

Figure 13-3 shows the circuitry required to interface an 8-position switch. The switch uses all eight data bits of one port of a PIA. Typical tasks are to determine the position of the switch and to check if that position has changed. The program must handle two special conditions:

1. The switch is temporarily between positions so no leads are grounded.
2. The switch has not reached its final position.

The first condition can be handled by waiting until the input is not all ones, i.e., until a switch lead is grounded. We can handle the second condition by examining the switch again after a delay (such as 1 or 2 seconds) and only accepting the input when it remains the same. This delay will not affect the responsiveness of the system to the switch. Alternatively, we could use another switch (i.e., a load switch) to tell the processor when to read the selector switch.

We will perform two tasks involving the circuit of Figure 13-3. These are:

a. Monitor the switch until it is in a definite position, then determine the position and store its binary value in a memory location.

b. Wait for the position of the switch to change, then store the new position in a memory location.

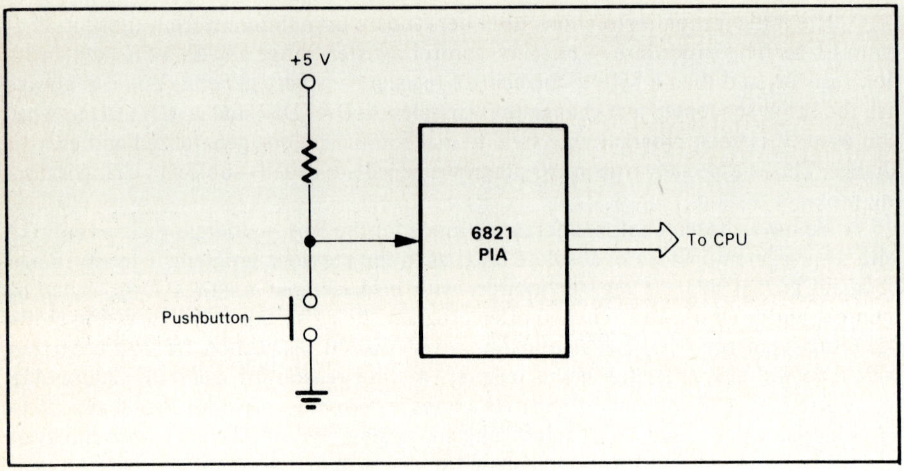

Figure 13-3. A Multiple-Position Switch

If the switch is in a position, the lead from that position is grounded through the common line. Pullup resistors on the input lines avoid problems caused by noise.

Task 13-2a. Determine Switch Position

Purpose: The program waits for the switch to be in a specific position and then stores the position number in the variable POSITION at memory location 6000.

Table 13-7 contains the data inputs corresponding to the various switch positions. This scheme is inefficient, since it requires eight bits to distinguish among eight different positions.

We have arranged the loop that identifies the switch position for somewhat increased efficiency. The program initializes the position to −1 and then increments the position (with ADDQ#1) before shifting the input (with LSR). What happens if you initialize the switch position to zero and shift and check the input before incrementing the position? The approach in which you start the program one step backward often increases execution speed because it lets you handle the first iteration in the same way as the subsequent ones.

Program 13-2a:

```
00004000        PROGRAM  EQU      $4000
00006000        DATA     EQU      $6000

0003FF40        PIA      EQU      $3FF40                PIA BASE ADDRESS

00000000        PIADDA   EQU      $0                    OFFSET DATA DIRECTION REGISTER A
00000000        PIADA    EQU      $0                    OFFSET DATA REGISTER A
00000004        PIACA    EQU      $4                    OFFSET CONTROL REGISTER A

00000000        A_DATDIR EQU      $00                   MAKE ALL LINES INPUT ON A SIDE
00000004        A_CNTRL  EQU      $04                   SELECT DATA REGISTER

000000FF        MASKNS   EQU      $FF                   MASK FOR NO SWITCH SELECTED
```

```
        00006000               ORG       DATA

006000  00000001      POSITION DS.B      1                          SWITCH POSITION

        00004000               ORG       PROGRAM

004000  207C0003FF40  PGM13_2A MOVEA.L   #PIA,A0                    GET PIA BASE ADDRESS
004006  42280004               CLR.B     PIACA(A0)                  INITIALIZE A SIDE
00400A  117C00000000           MOVE.B    #A_DATDIR,PIADDA(A0)
004010  117C00040004           MOVE.B    #A_CNTRL,PIACA(A0)

004016  10280000      CHKSW    MOVE.B    PIADA(A0),D0               READ SWITCH POSITION
00401A  0C0000FF               CMP.B     #MASKNS,D0                 IS SWITCH IN A POSITION?
00401E  67F6                   BEQ       CHKSW                      IF NO THEN WAIT TIL IT IS

004020  11FCFFFF6000           MOVE.B    #-1,POSITION               ...ELSE SET INITIAL SWITCH POSITION
004026  52386000      CHKPOS   ADDQ.B    #1,POSITION                INCREMENT SWITCH POSITION
00402A  E208                   LSR.B     #1,D0                      IS NEXT BIT GROUNDED POSITION?
00402C  65F8                   BCS       CHKPOS                     IF NO THEN KEEP LOOKING

00402E  4E75                   RTS

                               END       PGM13_2A
```

Flowchart:

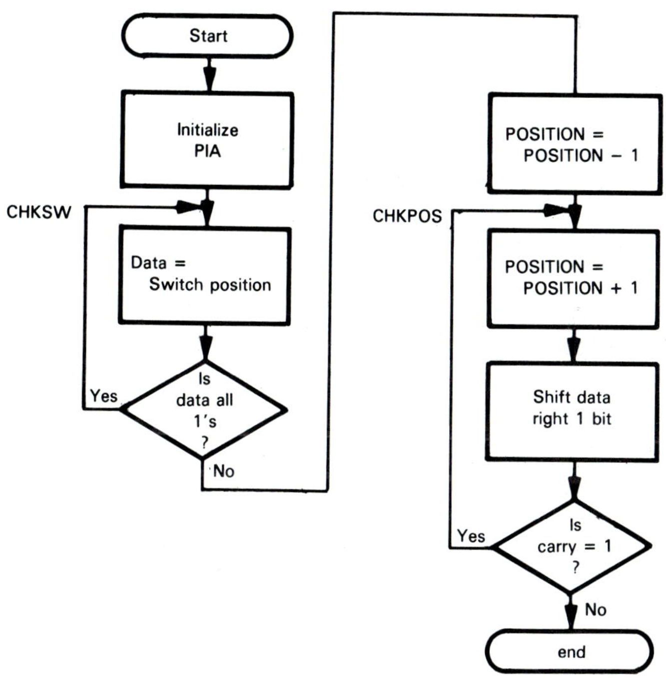

A short quick way to determine if the switch is in a position is:

```
004142  52280000      CHKSW    ADDQ.B    #1,PIADA(A0)               IS SWITCH IN A POSITION?
004146  67FA                   BEQ       CHKSW                      ...NO,WAIT UNTIL IT IS
```

Why does this approach work? Do the contents of the PIA data register actually change? Could you use the Carry flag instead of the Zero flag? Explain your answers.

Table 13-7. Data Input vs Switch Position

Switch Position	Date Input	
	Binary	Hex
0	11111110	FE
1	11111101	FD
2	11111011	FB
3	11110111	F7
4	11101111	EF
5	11011111	DF
6	10111111	BF
7	01111111	7F
This scheme is inefficient, since it requires eight bits to distinguish among eight different positions		

This example assumes that the switch is debounced in hardware. How would you change the program to debounce the switch in software?

A TTL or MOS encoder could reduce the number of input bits needed. Figure 13-4 shows a circuit using the 74LS148 TTL 8-to-3 encoder.[3] We attach the switch outputs in inverse order, since the 74LS148 device has active-low inputs and outputs. The output of the encoder circuit is a 3-bit representation of the switch position. Many switches include encoders so their outputs are coded, usually as a BCD digit (in negative logic).

The encoder produces active-low outputs, so, for example, switch position 5, which is attached to input 2, produces an output of 2 in negative logic (or 5 in positive logic). You may wish to verify the double negative for yourself.

Suppose that a faulty switch or defective PIA results in the input always being FF_{16}. How could you change the program so it would detect this situation?

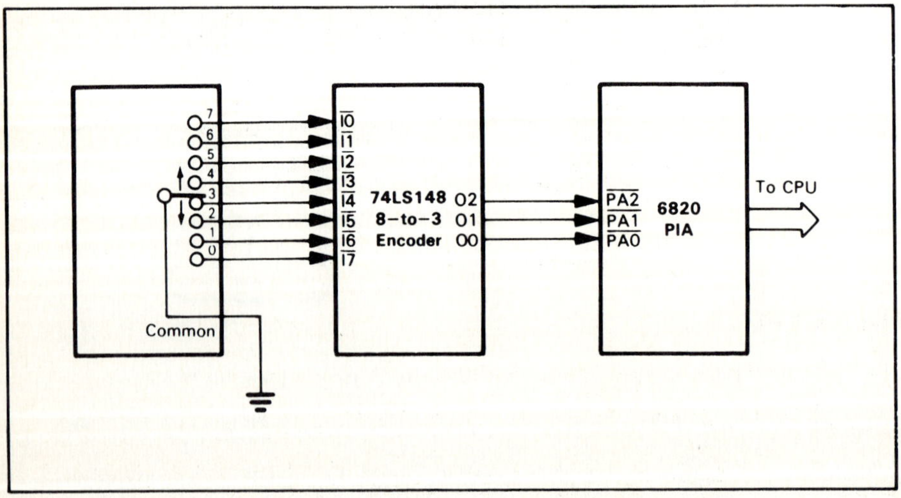

Figure 13-4. A Multiple-Position Switch with an Encoder

Task 13-2b. Wait for Switch Position to Change

Purpose: The program waits for the switch position to change and places the new position (decoded) into the variable POSITION at memory location 6000. The program waits until the switch reaches its new position.

Flowchart:

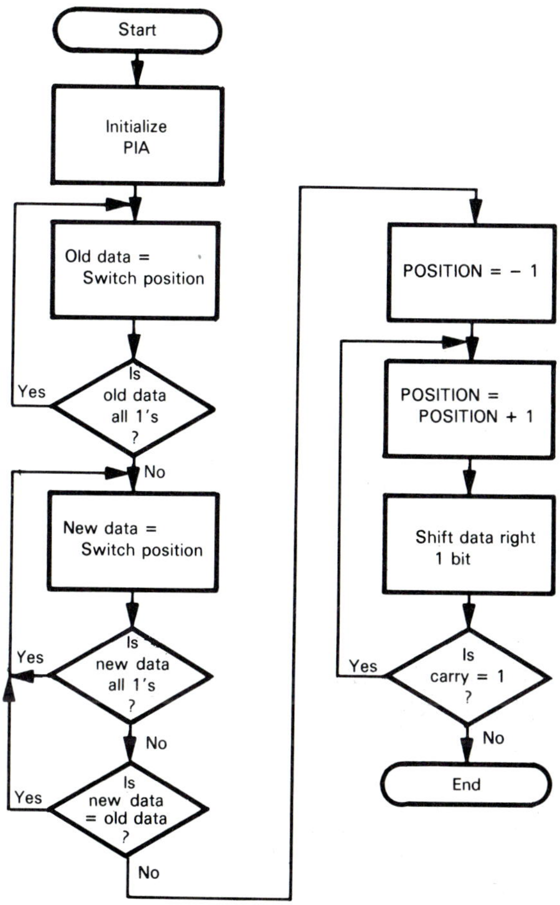

Program 13-2b:

```
00004000        PROGRAM  EQU     $4000
00006000        DATA     EQU     $6000

0003FF40        PIA      EQU     $3FF40                 PIA BASE ADDRESS

00000000        PIADDA   EQU     $0                     OFFSET DATA DIRECTION REGISTER A
00000000        PIADA    EQU     $0                     OFFSET DATA REGISTER A
00000004        PIACA    EQU     $4                     OFFSET CONTROL REGISTER A

00000000        A_DATDIR EQU     $00                    MAKE ALL LINES INPUT ON A SIDE
```

```
         00000004        A_CNTRL  EQU      $04                   SELECT DATA REGISTER

         000000FF        MASKNS   EQU      $FF                   MASK FOR NO SWITCH SELECTED

         00006000                 ORG      DATA

006000   00000001        POSITION DS.B     1                     SWITCH POSITION

         00004000                 ORG      PROGRAM

004000   207C0003FF40    PGM13_2B MOVEA.L  #PIA,A0               GET PIA BASE ADDRESS
004006   42280004                 CLR.B    PIACA(A0)             INITIALIZE A SIDE
00400A   117C00000000             MOVE.B   #A_DATDIR,PIADDA(A0)
004010   117C00040004             MOVE.B   #A_CNTRL,PIACA(A0)

004016   10280000        CHKSW1   MOVE.B   PIADA(A0),D0          READ SWITCH POSITION
00401A   0C0000FF                 CMP.B    #MASKNS,D0            IS SWITCH IN A POSITION?
00401E   67F6                     BEQ      CHKSW1                IF NO THEN WAIT TILL IT IS

004020   12280000        CHKSW2   MOVE.B   PIADA(A0),D1          READ NEW SWITCH DATA
004024   0C0100FF                 CMP.B    #MASKNS,D1            IS SWITCH IN A POSITION
004028   67F6                     BEQ      CHKSW2                IF NO THEN WAIT TILL IT IS

00402A   B200                     CMP.B    D0,D1                 IS POSITION THE SAME AS BEFORE?
00402C   67F2                     BEQ      CHKSW2                IF YES THEN WAIT FOR POSITION TO CH

00402E   11FCFFFF6000             MOVE.B   #-1,POSITION          ...ELSE SET INITIAL SWITCH POSITION
004034   52386000        CHKPOS   ADDQ.B   #1,POSITION           INCREMENT SWITCH POSITION
004038   E209                     LSR.B    #1,D1                 IS NEXT BIT GROUNDED POSITION?
00403A   65F8                     BCS      CHKPOS                IF NO THEN KEEP LOOKING

00403C   4E75                     RTS
```

13-3. A SINGLE LED

We will interface a single light-emitting diode to an MC68000 microprocessor, providing separate interfaces and programs to handle positive logic (a '1' turns it off).

Figure 13-5 shows the circuitry required to interface an LED. The LED lights when its anode is positive with respect to its cathode (Figure 13-5*a*). Therefore, you can light the LED either by grounding the cathode and having the computer supply one to the anode (Figure 13-5*b*) or by connecting the anode to +5 volts and having the computer supply a zero to the cathode (Figure 13-5*c*). Controlling the cathode is the more common approach, since most MOS or TTL I/O ports perform better in this mode. The LED is brightest when it operates from pulsed currents of about 10 or 50 mA applied a few hundred times per second. LEDs have a very short turn-on time (in the microsecond range) so they are well suited to multiplexing (operating several from a single port). LED circuits usually need peripheral or transistor drivers and current-limiting resistors. MOS devices normally cannot drive LEDs directly and make them bright enough for easy viewing.

The PIA has an output latch on each port. However, the B port is normally used for output, since it has somewhat more drive capability. In particular, the B port outputs are capable of driving Darlington transistors (providing 3.2 mA minimum at 1.5V). Darlington transistors are high-gain transistors capable of switching large amounts of current at high speed; they are useful in driving solenoids, relays, and other devices.

Task 13-3. Turn the Light On or Off

Purpose: The program turns a single LED either on or off.

Send a Logic One to the LED (light a display that operates in positive logic or turn off a display that operates in negative logic).

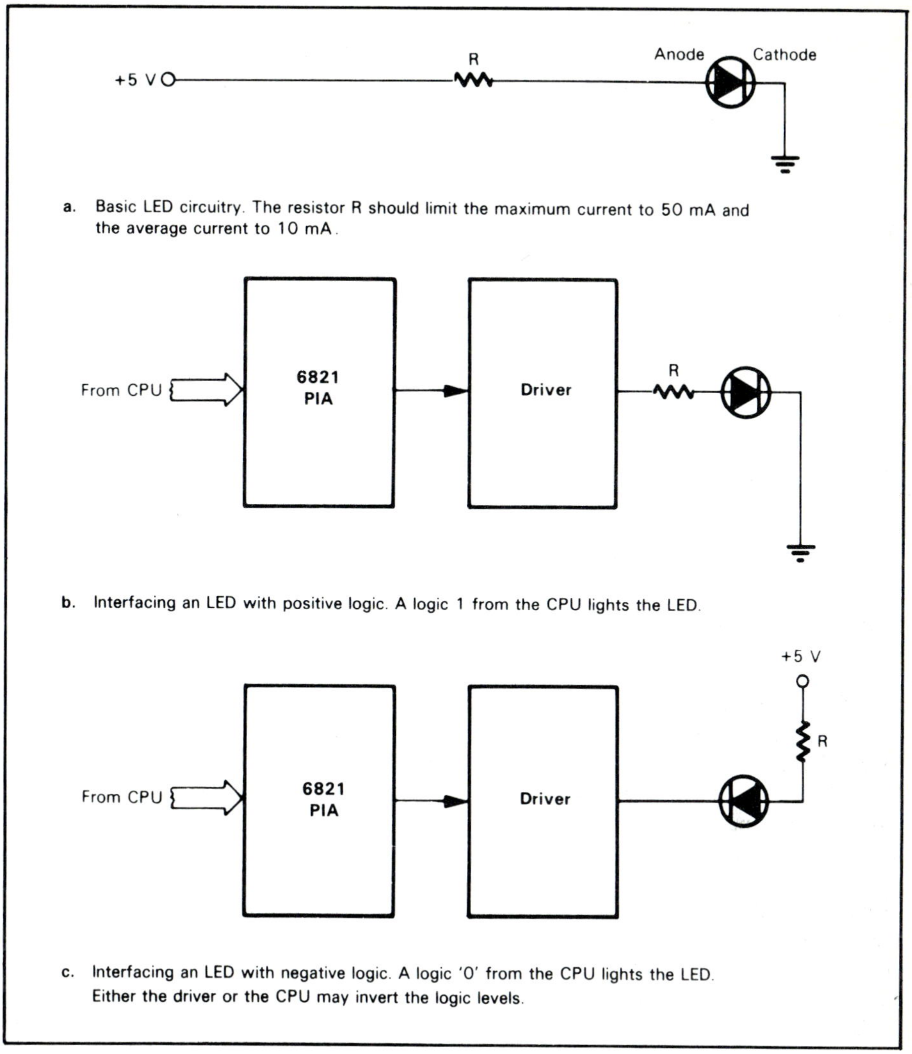

Figure 13-5. Interfacing an LED

Program 13-3: (form data initially)

```
00004000      PROGRAM  EQU     $4000
00006000      DATA     EQU     $6000

0003FF40      PIA      EQU     $3FF40             PIA.BASE ADDRESS

00000002      PIADDB   EQU     $2                 OFFSET DATA DIRECTION REGISTER B
00000002      PIADB    EQU     $2                 OFFSET DATA REGISTER B
00000006      PIACB    EQU     $6                 OFFSET CONTROL REGISTER B

00000080      B_DATDIR EQU     $80                MAKE BIT 7 OUTPUT ON B SIDE
```

```
         00000004      B_CNTRL  EQU      $04                    DATA REGISTER SELECT

         00000007      LEDBIT   EQU      7                      LED BIT POSITION IN PIA

         00004000               ORG      PROGRAM

004000 207C0003FF40 PGM13_3  MOVEA.L  #PIA,A0                GET PIA BASE ADDRESS
004006 42280006              CLR.B    PIACB(A0)              INITIALIZE B SIDE
00400A 117C00800002          MOVE.B   #B_DATDIR,PIADDB(A0)
004010 117C00040006          MOVE.B   #B_CNTRL,PIACB(A0)

004016 08E800070002          BSET.B   #LEDBIT,PIADB(A0)      SET UP LED

00401C 4E75                  RTS

                    * (UPDATE DATA)


00401E 08E800070002          BSET.B   #LEDBIT,PIADB(A0)      SET LED OUTPUT BIT TO 1

004024 4E75                  RTS

                             END      PGM13_3
```

We use the B side of the PIA because of the buffering. This allows the CPU to read the data back (if necessary) without any difficulty.

13-4. SEVEN-SEGMENT LED DISPLAY

We will interface a seven-segment LED display to an MC68000 microprocessor. The display may be either common-anode (negative logic) or common-cathode (positive logic).

Figure 13-6 shows the circuitry required to interface a seven-segment display. Each segment may have one, two, or more LEDs attached in the same way. There are two ways of connecting the displays. One is **tying all the cathodes together to ground** (see Figure 13-7*a*); this **is a "common-cathode display," and a logic one at an anode lights a segment.** The other is **tying all the anodes together to a positive voltage supply** (see Figure 13-7*b*); this **is a "common-anode display," and a logic zero at a cathode lights a segment.** So the common-cathode display uses positive logic and the common-anode display negative logic. Either display requires appropriate drivers and resistors.

The common line from the display is tied either to ground or to +5 volts. The display segments are customarily labelled:

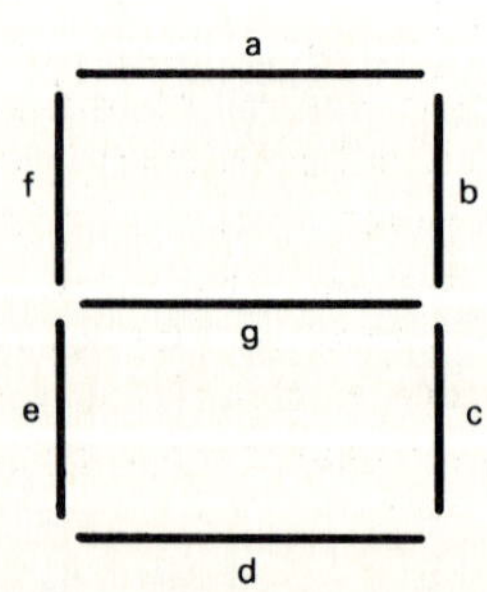

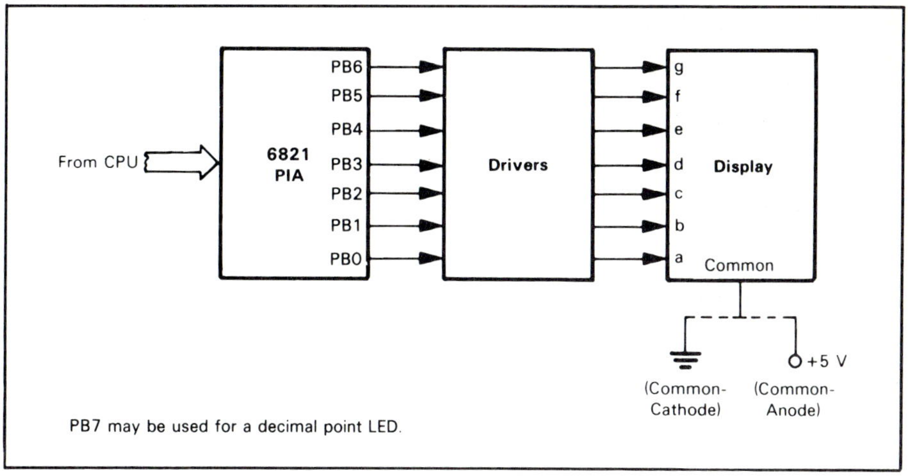

Figure 13-6. Interfacing a Seven-Segment Display

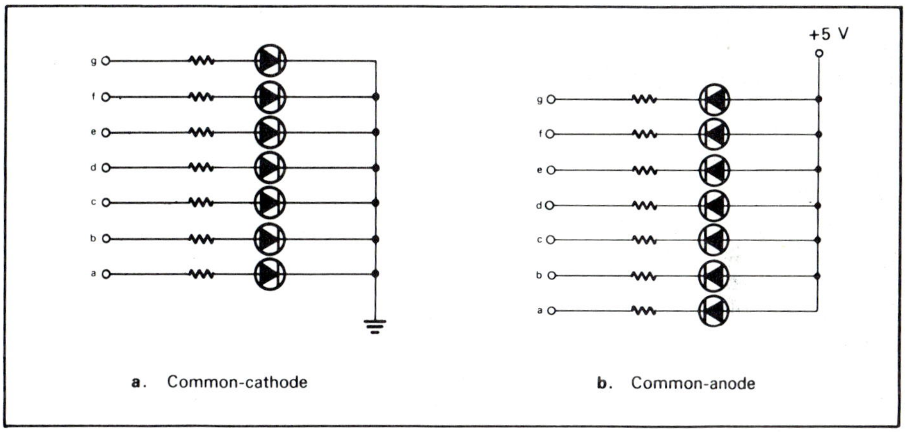

Figure 13-7. Seven-Segment Display Organization

The seven-segment display is widely used because it contains the smallest number of separately controlled segments that can provide recognizable representations of all the decimal digits (see Figure 13-8 and Table 13-8). Seven-segment displays can also produce some letters and other characters (see Table 13-9). Better representations require a substantially larger number of segments and more circuitry.[4] **Since seven-segment displays are so popular, inexpensive seven-segment decoder/drivers have become widely available.** The most popular devices are the 7447 common- anode driver and the 7448 common-cathode driver;[5] these devices have Lamp Test inputs (that turn all the segments on) and blanking inputs and outputs (for blanking leading or trailing zeros).

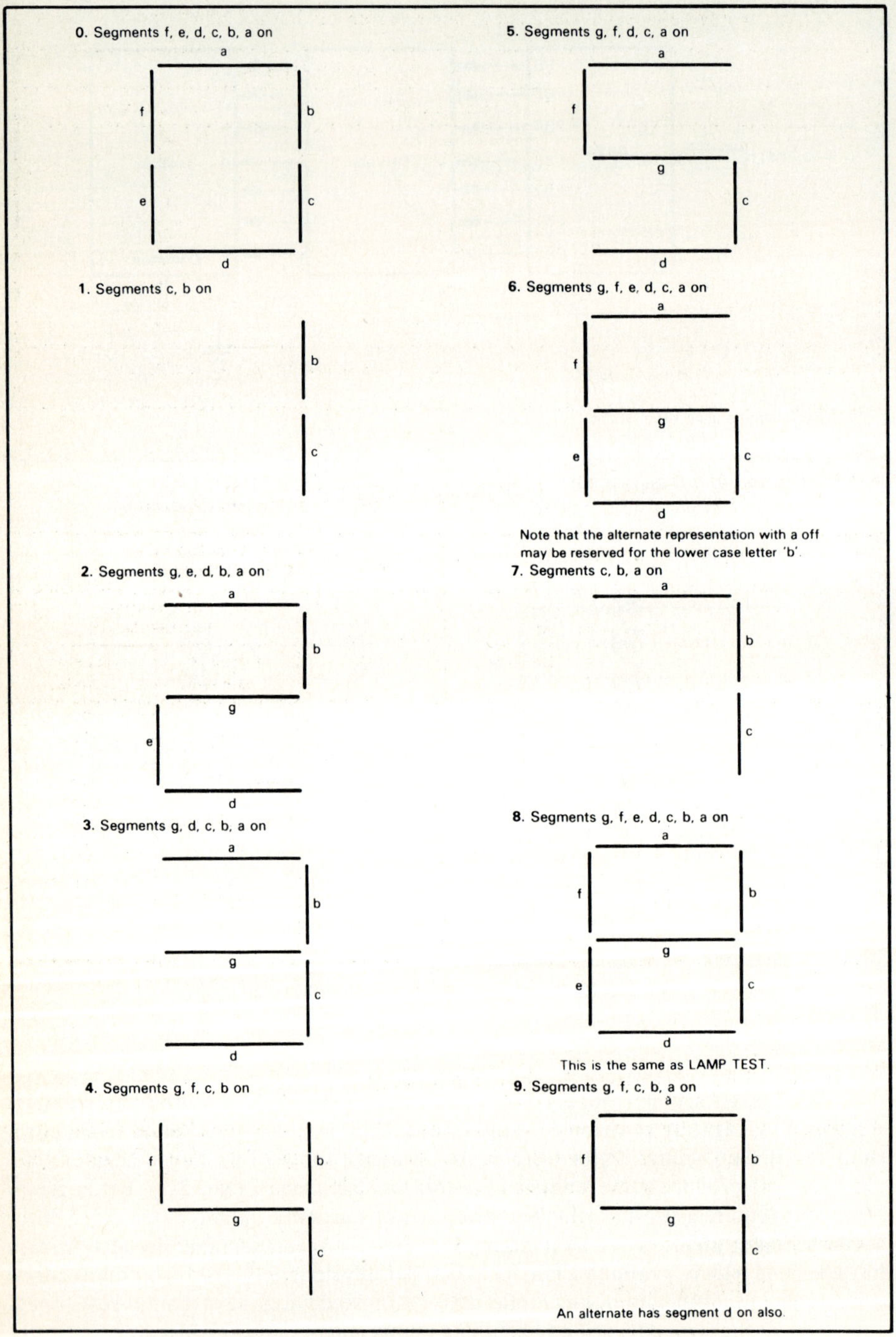

Figure 13-8. Seven-Segment Representation of Decimal Digits

Table 13-8. Seven-Segment Representations of Decimal Numbers

Number	Hexadecimal Representation	
	Common-cathode	Common-anode
0	3F	40
1	06	79
2	5B	24
3	4F	30
4	66	19
5	6D	12
6	7D	02
7	07	78
8	7F	00
9	67	18

Bit 7 is always zero and the others are g, f, e, d, c, b, and a in decreasing order of significance.

Table 13-9. Seven-Segment Representations of Letters and Symbols

Upper-case Letters			Lower-case Letters and Special Characters		
Letter	Hexadecimal Representation		Character	Hexadecimal Representation	
	Common-cathode	Common-anode		Common-cathode	Common-anode
A	77	08	b	7C	03
C	39	46	c	58	27
E	79	06	d	5E	21
F	71	0E	h	74	0B
H	76	09	n	54	2B
I	06	79	o	5C	23
J	1E	61	r	50	2F
L	38	47	u	1C	63
O	3F	40	-	40	3F
P	73	0C	?	53	2C
U	3E	41			
Y	66	19			

Task 13-4a. Display a Decimal Digit

Purpose: Display the contents of the variable DIGIT at memory location 6000 on a seven-segment display if it contains a decimal digit. Otherwise, blank the display. The display is of the common-cathode type.

Sample Problems:

a. DIGIT = (6000) = 05
   Result is 5 on display

b. DIGIT = (6000) = 66
   Result is a blank display

Flowchart:

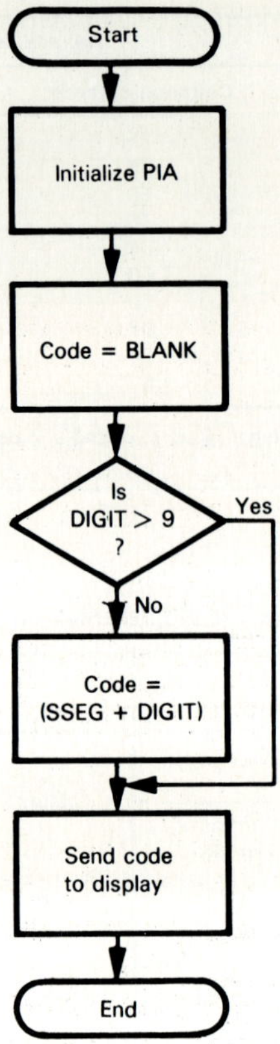

Source Program:

```
        00004000     PROGRAM   EQU      $4000
        00006000     DATA      EQU      $6000

        0003FF40     PIA       EQU      $3FF40                    PIA BASE ADDRESS

        00000002     PIADDB    EQU      $2                        OFFSET DATA DIRECTION REGISTER B
        00000002     PIADB     EQU      $2                        OFFSET DATA REGISTER B
        00000006     PIACB     EQU      $6                        OFFSET CONTROL REGISTER B

        000000FF     B_DATDIR  EQU      $FF                       MAKE ALL LINES OUTPUT ON B SIDE
        00000004     B_CNTRL   EQU      $04                       SELECT DATA REGISTER

        00006000               ORG      DATA

006000  00000001     DIGIT     DS.B     1                         DATA TO BE DISPLAYED

006001  3F           SSEG      DC.B     $3F,$06,$5B,$4F,$66       CODE FOR SEVEN SEGMENT DIGITS
006006  6D                     DC.B     $6D,$7D,$07,$7F,$67       ..ON A COMMON CATHODE DISPLAY
        00000000     BLANK     EQU      $00                       BLANK FOR COMMON CATHODE DISPLAY

        00004000               ORG      PROGRAM

004000  207C0003FF40 PGM13_4A  MOVEA.L  #PIA,A0                   GET PIA BASE ADDRESS
004006  42280006               CLR.B    PIACB(A0)                 INITIALIZE B SIDE
00400A  117C00FF0002           MOVE.B   #B_DATDIR,PIADDB(A0)
004010  117C00040006           MOVE.B   #B_CNTRL,PIACB(A0)
```

```
004016 103C0000              MOVE.B   #BLANK,D0           GET BLANK CODE
00401A 4241                  CLR.W    D1                  CLEAR INDEX (D1.W)
00401C 12386000              MOVE.B   DIGIT,D1            GET DATA
004020 0C010009              CMPI.B   #9,D1               IS DATA A DECIMAL DIGIT (9 OR LESS)
004024 620A                  BHI.S    DSPLY               IF NO THEN DISPLAY BLANK

004026 227C00006001          MOVEA.L  #SSEG,A1            ADDRESS OF SEGMENT TABLE
00402C 10311000              MOVE.B   0(A1,D1.W),D0       CONVERT DATA TO DISPLAY DIGIT
004030 11400002      DSPLY   MOVE.B   D0,PIADB(A0)        SEND CODE TO DISPLAY

004034 4E75                  RTS

                             END      PGM13_4A
```

You should note two things about this program. First, if you want to use a common-anode display, the only thing you must change is the contents of the table SSEG and the symbol BLANK. Second, remember the BLANK is a symbol — it is not stored in memory as the SSEG table is. An alternate solution is to put BLANK in memory as the last entry in the SSEG table. Then replace all improper data values with 10; that is, the instructions after MOVE.B #B.CNTRL,PIACB(A0) are:

```
       00006000      SSEG:    EQU      DATA

004148 12386000               MOVE.B   DATA,D1            GET DATA
00414C 0C010009               CMPI.B   #9,D1              IS DATA A DECIMAL DIGIT (9 OR LESS)
004150 63000006               BLS      CNVRT              ...YES, CONVERT

004154 123C000A               MOVE.B   #10,D1             ...ELSE INDEX IS FOR BLANK CODE
004158 207C00006000 CNVRT:    MOVEA.L  #SSEG,A0           CONVERT DATA TO SEVEN-SEGMENT CODE
00415E 117010000002           MOVE.B   0(A0,D1),PIADB(A0) SEND CODE TO DISPLAY
```

Figure 13-9 shows how to multiplex displays (i.e., drive several displays from the same port).[6] A brief pulse on control CB2 automatically clocks the decade counter after each output operation, thus directing the data to the next display. RESET initializes the decade counter to 9 so that the first output operation clears the counter and directs data to the first (actually, the zeroth) display.

The next program uses a transparent 1 ms delay routine (described in Chapter 12) to pulse each of ten common-cathode displays for 1 ms. An observer will see a continuous ten-digit display much like the ones typical of electronic calculators, watches, and point-of-sale terminals.

Task 13-4b. Display Ten Decimal Digits

Purpose: Continuously display the contents of the digit array DIGIT which starts at memory location 6000 on ten seven-segment displays that are multiplexed with a counter and a decoder. The most significant (leftmost) digit is in memory location 6000.

Sample Problem:

DIGIT = (6000) = 66
(6001) = 3F
(6002) = 7F
(6003) = 7F
(6004) = 06
(6005) = 5B
(6006) = 07
(6007) = 4F
(6008) = 6D
(6009) = 7D

The number on the displays is 4088127356.

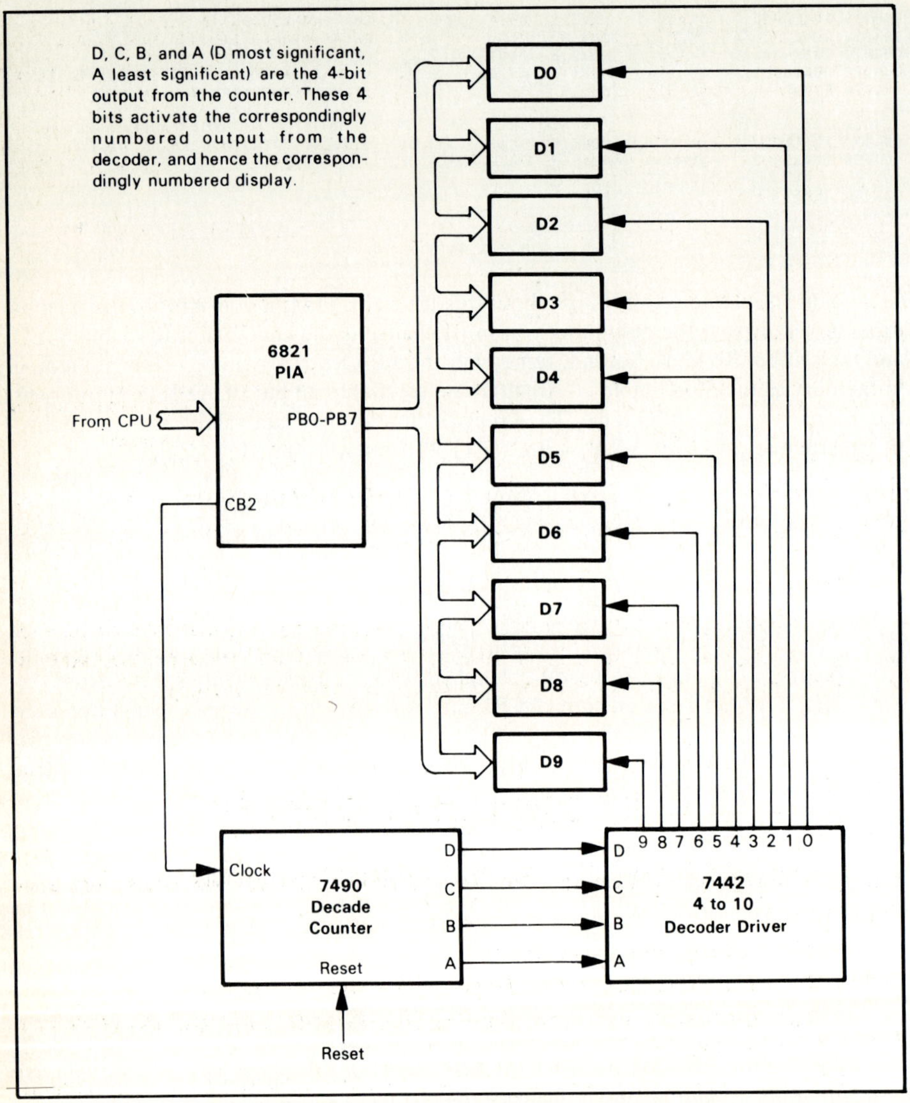

Figure 13-9. Multiplexed Seven-Segment Displays

Program 13-4b:

```
00004000     PROGRAM  EQU    $4000
00006000     DATA     EQU    $6000
00004100     DELAY    EQU    $4100                ADDRESS OF  DELAY ROUTINE

0003FF40     PIA      EQU    $3FF40               PIA BASE ADDRESS

00000002     PIADDB   EQU    $2                   OFFSET DATA DIRECTION REGISTER B
```

```
        00000002        PIADB     EQU      $2                    OFFSET DATA REGISTER B
        00000006        PIACB     EQU      $6                    OFFSET CONTROL REGISTER B

        000000FF        B_DATDIR  EQU      $FF                   MAKE ALL LINES OUTPUT ON B SIDE
        0000002C        B_CNTRL   EQU      $2C                   DATA REGISTER SELECT, CB2 OUTPUT
                        *                                        STROBE WHEN WRITING TO REG B

        00000001        DELAYTIM  EQU      1                     TIME IN MS THAT EACH DIGIT IS LIT
        0000000A        NUMDIGIT  EQU      10                    NUMBER OF DIGITS TO DISPLAY

        00006000                  ORG      DATA

006000  0000000A        DIGIT     DS.B     NUMDIGIT              DATA TO BE DISPLAYED

        00004000                  ORG      PROGRAM

004000  207C0003FF40    PGM13_4B  MOVEA.L  #PIA,A0               GET PIA BASE ADDRESS
004006  42280006                  CLR.B    PIACB(A0)             INITIALIZE B SIDE
00400A  117C00FF0002              MOVE.B   #B_DATDIR,PIADDB(A0)
004010  117C002C0006              MOVE.B   #B_CNTRL,PIACB(A0)

004016  227C00006000    SCAN      MOVEA.L  #DIGIT,A1             POINTER TO DATA START
00401C  7209                      MOVEQ    #NUMDIGIT-1,D1        LOOP COUNTER ADJUSTED FOR DBRA

00401E  11590002        DISPLAY   MOVE.B   (A1)+,PIADB(A0)       MOVE DATA TO DISPLAY
004022  7001                      MOVEQ    #DELAYTIM,D0          WAIT FOR A WHILE
004024  4EB84100                  JSR      DELAY
004028  51C9FFF4                  DBRA     D1,DISPLAY            CONTINUE FOR ALL DIGITS

00402C  60E8                      BRA      SCAN                  REPEAT SCAN

                                  END      PGM13_4B
```

Control register bit 5 = 1 to make CB2 an output, bit 4 = 0 to make it a pulse, and bit 3 = 1 to make it a brief pulse lasting one clock cycle. What changes are necessary if you want to display a different number of digits — for example, 8 digits?

MORE COMPLEX I/O DEVICES

More complex I/O devices differ from simple keyboards, switches, and displays in that:

1. **They transfer data at higher rates.**
2. **They may have their own internal clocks and timing.**
3. **They produce status information and require control information, as well as transferring data.**

Because of their high data rates, you cannot handle these I/O devices casually. If the processor does not provide the appropriate service, the system may miss input data or produce erroneous output data. You are therefore working under much more exacting constraints than when dealing with simpler devices. Interrupts are a convenient method for handling complex I/O devices, as we shall see in Chapter 15.

SYNCHRONIZATION

Peripherals such as keyboards, teletypewriters, cassettes, and floppy disks produce their own internal timing. These devices provide streams of data separated by specific timing intervals. **The computer must synchronize the initial input or output**

operation with the peripheral clock and then provide the proper interval between subsequent operations. A simple delay loop like the one shown previously can produce the time interval. The synchronization may require one or more of the following procedures:

1. **Looking for a transition on a clock or strobe line by the peripheral for timing purposes.** The simplest method is to tie the strobe to a PIA control line and wait until the appropriate bit of the PIA control register is set.
2. **Finding the center of the time interval during which the data is stable.** We would prefer to determine the value of the data at the center of the pulse rather than at the edges, where the data may be changing. Finding the center requires a delay of one half of a transmission interval (bit time) after the edge. Sampling the data at the center also means that small timing errors have little effect on the accuracy of the reception.
3. **Recognizing a special starting code.** This is easy if the code is a single bit or if we have some timing information. The procedure is more complex if the code is long and could start at any time. Shifting will be necessary to determine where the transmitter is starting its bits, characters, or messages. (This is often called a search for the correct "framing.")
4. **Sampling the data several times.** This reduces the probability of receiving data incorrectly from noisy lines. Majority logic (such as best 3 out of 5 or 5 out of 8) can be used to decide on the actual data value.

Reception is, of course, much more difficult than transmission, since the peripheral controls the reception and the computer must interpret timing information generated by the peripheral. In transmission, the computer provides the proper timing and formatting for a specified peripheral.

CONTROL AND STATUS INFORMATION

Peripherals may require or provide other information besides data and timing. We refer to other information transmitted by the computer as "control information;" it may select modes of operation, start or stop processes, clock registers, enable buffers, choose formats or protocols, provide operator displays, count operations, or identify the type and priority of the operation. **We refer to other information transmitted by the peripheral as "status information;"** it may indicate the mode of operation, the readiness of devices, the presence of error conditions, the format of protocol in use, and other states or conditions.

The computer handles control and status information just like data. This information seldom changes, even though actual data may be transferred at a high rate. The control or status information may be single bits, digits, bytes, or multiple bytes. Often single bits or short fields are combined and handled by a single input or output port.

Separating Status Information

Combining status and control information into bytes reduces the total number of I/O port addresses required by the peripherals. However, the combination does mean that individual status input bits must be separately interpreted and control output bits must be separately determined. **The procedure for isolating status bits is as follows:**

Step 1. Read status data from the peripheral.

Step 2. Logical AND with a mask (the mask has ones in bit positions that must be examined, and zeros elsewhere).

Step 3. Shift the separated bits to the least significant positions.

Step 3 is unnecessary if the field is a single bit, since the zero flag will contain the complement of that bit after Step 2. (Try it!) A shift or load instruction can replace Step 2 if the field is a single bit and occupies the least significant, most significant, or next to most significant bit position (positions 0, 7, or 6). These positions are often reserved for the most frequently used status information. You should try to write the required instruction sequences for the 68000 processor. Note, in particular, the use of the bit test instruction. This instruction performs a logical test of the individual bit specified without affecting the bit; the Zero status flag is set as follows:

Zero flag = 1 if the bit is a zero
Zero flag = 0 if the bit is a one.

Combining Control Information

This is the procedure for setting and clearing control bits:

Step 1. Read prior control information.

Step 2. Logical AND with mask to clear bits (mask has zeros in bit positions to be cleared, ones elsewhere).

Step 3. Logically OR with mask to set bits (mask has ones in bit positions to be set, zeros elsewhere).

Step 4. Send new control information to peripheral.

Here again the procedure is simpler if the field is a single bit and occupies a position at either end of a data byte.

Some examples of separating and combining status bits are:

1. A 3-bit field in bit positions 2 through 4 of a PIA data register is a scaling factor. Place that factor in data register D0.

```
                             *
                             *  READ STATUS DATA FROM INPUT PORT
                             *

004164 10280000                      MOVE.B  PIADA(A0),D0           READ STATUS DATA

                             *
                             *  MASK OFF UNWANTED BITS AND SHIFT RESULTS
                             *

004168 0200001C                      ANDI.B  #$1C,D0                SAVE SCALING FACTOR
00416C E408                          LSR.B   #2,D0                  SHIFT TWICE TO NORMALIZE
```

2. Data register D0 contains a 2-bit field that must be placed in bit positions 3 and 4 of a PIA data register.

```
                             *
                             *  MOVE DATA TO FIELD POSITION
                             *
```

```
00416E E708                 LSL.B    #3,D0              SHIFT DATA TO POSITIONS 3 AND 4
004170 02000018             ANDI.B   #$18,D0            CLEAR OTHER BITS
                      *
                      *  COMBINE NEW FIELD POSITION WITH OTHER DATA
                      *
004174 022800E70000         ANDI.B   #$E7,PIADA(A0)     CLEAR OLD FIELD VALUE
00417A 81280000             OR.B     D0,PIADA(A0)       INSERT NEW FIELD VALUE
```

Documenting Status and Control Transfers

Documentation is a serious problem in handling control and status information. **The meanings of status inputs or control outputs are seldom obvious. The programmer should clearly indicate the purposes of input and output operations in the comments,** for example, "CHECK IF READER IS ON," "CHOOSE EVEN PARITY OPTION," or "ACTIVATE BIT RATE COUNTER." The logical and shift instructions will otherwise be very difficult to remember, understand, or debug.

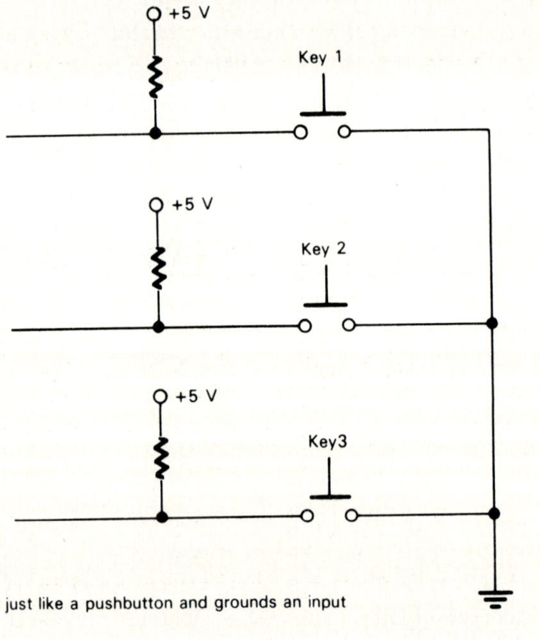

Each key is a switch just like a pushbutton and grounds an input bit if it is pressed.

Figure 13-10. A Small Keyboard

13-5. AN UNENCODED KEYBOARD

The processor will recognize a key closure from an unencoded 3 × 3 keyboard and place the number of the key that was pressed in data register D0.

Keyboards are just collections of switches (see Figure 13-10). Small numbers of keys are easiest to handle if each key is attached separately to a bit of an input port. Interfacing the keyboard is then the same as interfacing a set of switches.

Matrix Keyboard

Keyboards with more than eight keys require more than one input port and therefore multibyte operations. This is particularly wasteful if the keys are logically separate, as in a calculator or terminal keyboard where the user will only strike one at a time. **The number of input lines required may be reduced by connecting the keys into a matrix, as shown in Figure 13-11. Now each key represents a potential connection between a row and a column.** The keyboard matrix requires n + m external lines, where n is the number of rows and m is the number of columns. This compares to n × m external lines if each key is separate. Table 13-10 compares the number of keys required by typical configurations.

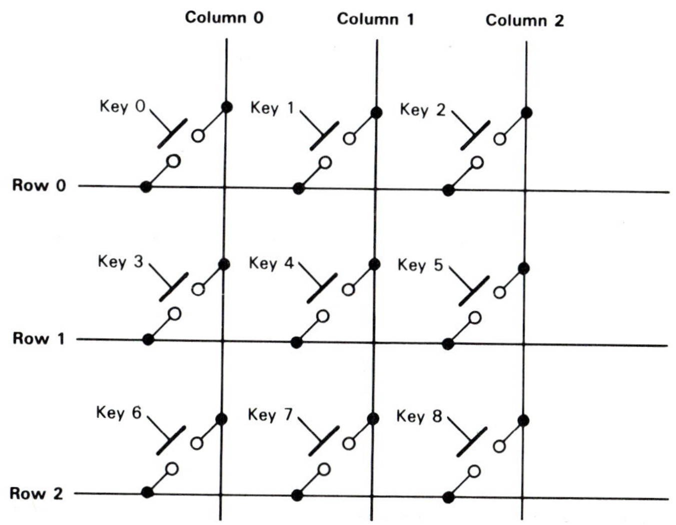

Pressing a key connects a row to a column. For example, pressing key 2 connects row 0 to column 2.

Figure 13-11. A Keyboard Matrix

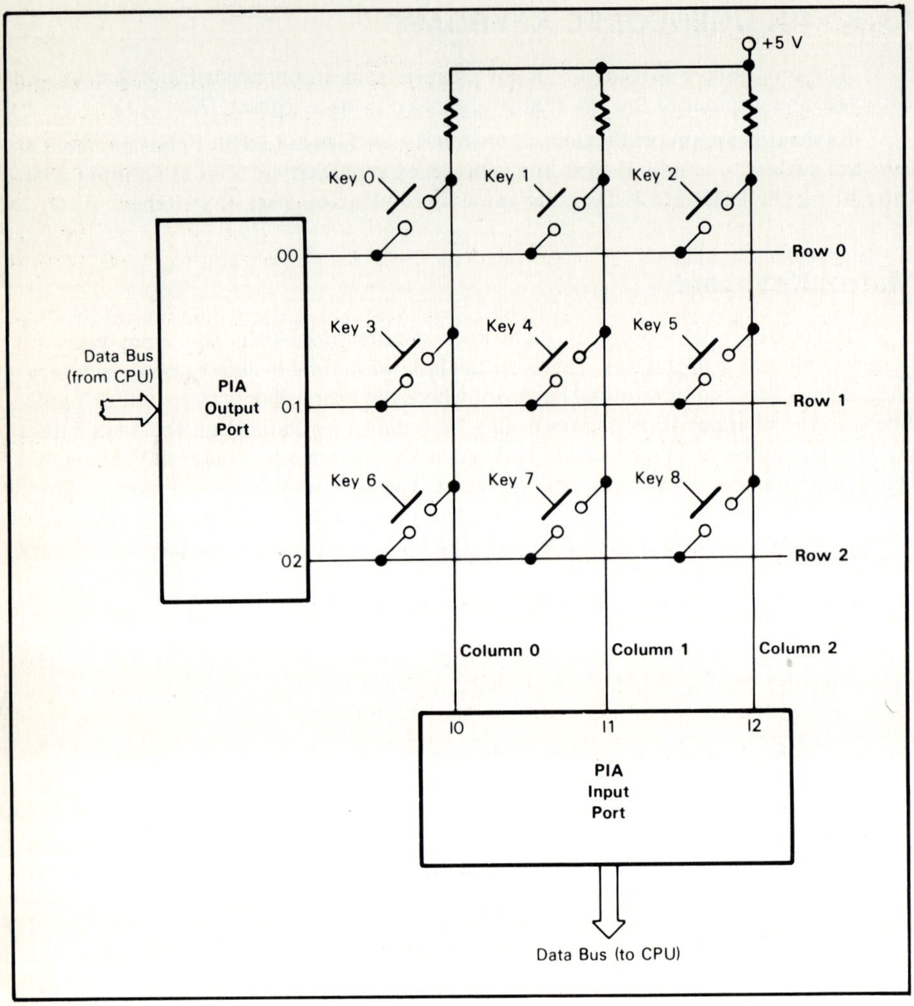

Figure 13-12. I/O Arrangement for a Keyboard Scan

Table 13-10. Comparison Between Independent Connections and Matrix Connections for Keyboards

Keyboard Size	Number of Lines with Independent Connections	Number of Lines with Matrix Connections
3 × 3	9	6
4 × 4	16	8
4 × 6	24	10
5 × 5	25	10
6 × 6	36	12
6 × 8	48	14
8 × 8	64	16

Keyboard Scan

A program can determine which key has been pressed by using the external lines from the matrix. The usual procedure is a "keyboard scan." We ground Row 0 and examine the column lines. If any lines are grounded, a key in that row has been pressed, causing a row-to-column connection. We can determine which key was pressed by determining which column line is grounded; that is, which bit of the input port is zero. If no column line is grounded, we proceed to Row 1 and repeat the scan. Note that **we can check to see if any keys at all have been pressed by grounding all the rows at once and examining the columns.**

The keyboard scan requires that the row lines be tied to an output port and the column lines to an input port. Figure 13-12 shows the arrangement. The CPU can ground a particular row by placing a zero in the appropriate bit of the output port and ones in the other bits.

The CPU can determine the stack of a particular column by examining the appropriate bit of the input port.

Task 13-5a. Wait for Key Closure

Purpose: Wait for a key to be pressed

The procedure is as follows:

1. Ground all the rows by clearing all the output bits.
2. Fetch the column inputs by reading the input port.
3. Return to Step 1 if all the column inputs are ones.

Flowchart:

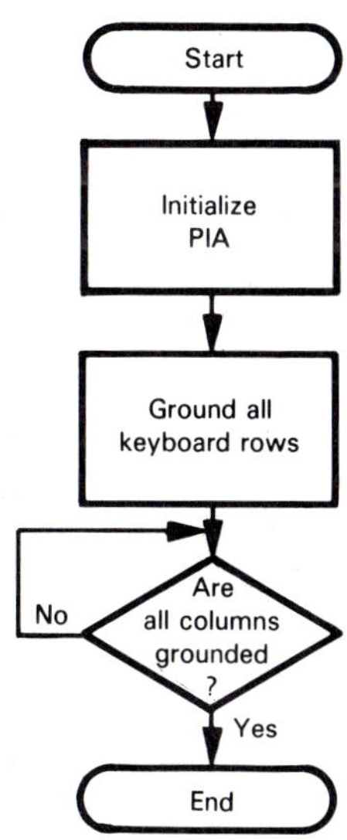

Program 13-5a:

```
          00004000       PROGRAM  EQU      $4000
          00006000       DATA     EQU      $6000

          0003FF40       PIA      EQU      $3FF40                    PIA BASE ADDRESS

          00000000       PIADDA   EQU      $0                        OFFSET DATA DIRECTION REGISTER A
          00000000       PIADA    EQU      $0                        OFFSET DATA REGISTER A
          00000004       PIACA    EQU      $4                        OFFSET CONTROL REGISTER A
          00000002       PIADDB   EQU      $2                        OFFSET DATA DIRECTION REGISTER B
          00000002       PIADB    EQU      $2                        OFFSET DATA REGISTER B
          00000006       PIACB    EQU      $6                        OFFSET CONTROL REGISTER B
          00000000       A_DATDIR EQU      $00                       MAKE ALL LINES INPUTS ON A SIDE
          00000004       A_CNTRL  EQU      $04                       SELECT DATA REGISTER
          00000007       B_DATDIR EQU      $07                       LINES 0-2 OUTPUT ON B SIDE (ROWS)
          00000004       B_CNTRL  EQU      $04                       SELECT DATA REGISTER

          00000007       COL_MASK EQU      $07                       COLUMNS CONNECTED TO BIT 0-2
          00000000       ROWGRND  EQU      $00                       MASK TO GROUND ALL KEYBOARD ROWS

          00004000                ORG      PROGRAM

004000 207C0003FF40 PGM13_5A MOVEA.L #PIA,A0                        GET PIA BASE ADDRESS
004006 42280004              CLR.B    PIACA(A0)                     INITIALIZE A SIDE
00400A 117C00000000          MOVE.B   #A_DATDIR,PIADDA(A0)
004010 117C00040004          MOVE.B   #A_CNTRL,PIACA(A0)
004016 42280006              CLR.B    PIACB(A0)                     INITIALIZE B SIDE
00401A 117C00070002          MOVE.B   #B_DATDIR,PIADDB(A0)
004020 117C00040006          MOVE.B   #B_CNTRL,PIACB(A0)

004026 117800000002          MOVE.B   ROWGRND,PIADB(A0)             GROUND ALL KEYBOARD ROWS

00402C 10280000     WAIT     MOVE.B   PIADA(A0),D0                  GET DATA FROM KEYBOARD COLUMNS
004030 02000007              ANDI.B   #COL_MASK,D0                  MASK COLUMN BITS
004034 0C000007              CMPI.B   #COL_MASK,D0                  ARE ANY KEYS CLOSED?
004038 67F2                  BEQ      WAIT                          IF NO THEN WAIT

00403A 4E75                  RTS

                             END      PGM13_5A
```

Masking off the column bits eliminates any problems that could be caused by the states of the unused input lines.

Using the RESET and MOVEP Instructions in I/O Applications

The MC68000 uses memory-mapped I/O; you can address I/O peripherals simply as memory locations. With this technique, no special I/O instructions are necessary. Nonetheless, the MC68000 provides two unique instructions, RESET and MOVEP, which can be useful in I/O communications.

The RESET instruction causes the processor to output a pulse on its reset pin. Thus, execution of this instruction would affect *all* external devices connected to the reset signal generated by the MC68000. Execution of the RESET instruction does not affect the internal state of the processor — it simply continues and executes the instruction following the RESET instruction. The RESET instruction is one of several special or 'privileged' instructions and can only be executed while the MC68000 is in supervisor mode. We shall discuss this mode in detail in Chapter 15.

The MOVEP (Move Peripheral) instruction is similar to the standard MOVE instruction except that data is transferred between a data register and alternate byte

addresses. For example, if 16 bits of data are being transferred and the specified transfer address is odd, data flow is as follows:

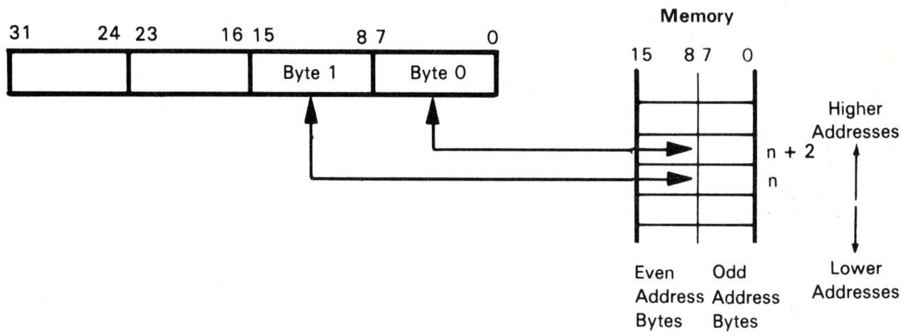

The first byte is transferred from bits 8-15 of the data register to the specified starting address and then the low-order byte of the data register is transferred to the starting address +2. A data transfer with a beginning address that is even is as follows:

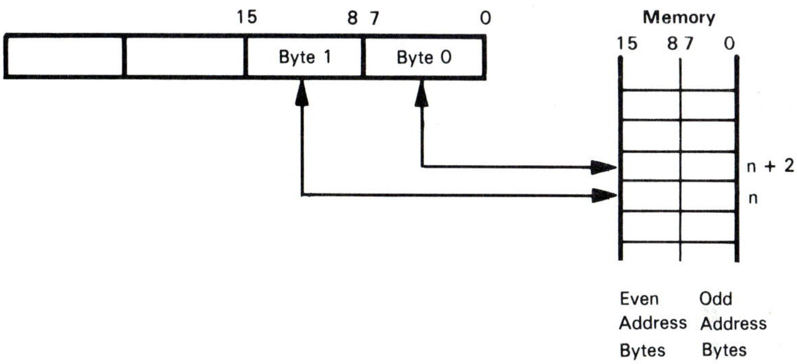

Long word or 32-bit transfers operate similarly. Here is one with an odd address specified:

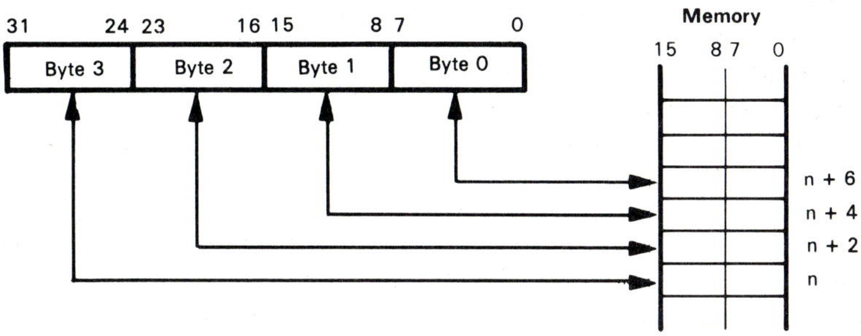

Here is a 32-bit transfer to even byte addresses:

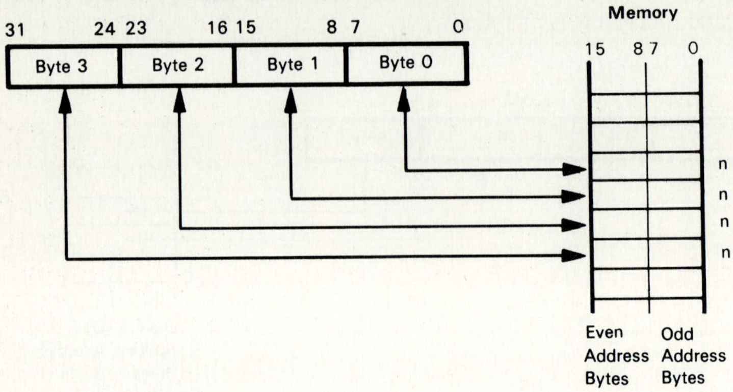

In each case, the more significant byte(s) is transferred first and subsequent bytes are transferred to ascending locations with the address incremented by two each time.

Thus far, the MOVEP instruction may not appear to be very useful; why would you want to transfer bytes of data to or from alternate rather than contiguous bytes of memory? The answer is that this instruction is intended to accomplish data transfers between the MC68000 and 8-bit peripheral devices (such as a PIA). It would obviously make sense to have the data lines of such a device connected to either the high-order eight lines of the system data bus or the low-order lines of the bus. Thus, because of the way the processor addresses memory (and any other devices connected to the system bus) an 8-bit device will always be connected to the odd address portion of the data bus (bits 0-7) or to the even portion (bits 8-15). Now, **if we want to transfer multiple bytes of data to or from the 8-bit device, we must make sure that we always make the transfer on the appropriate half (odd or even) of the bus. This is precisely what the MOVEP instruction does for us.**

Program 13-5*b* uses both the RESET and MOVEP instructions to accomplish the same task as Program 13-5*a*. The RESET instruction causes the PIA to be reset. (Remember, however, that this would also affect all other devices connected to the reset signal.) When the PIA is reset, its data direction register will be selected and all data lines will be input lines. The MOVEP instructions then cause the data registers to be selected for both sides of the PIA.

Program 13-5b:

```
00004000        PROGRAM  EQU      $4000
00006000        DATA     EQU      $6000

0003FF40        PIA      EQU      $3FF40                ADDRESS OF PIA

00000000        PIADDA   EQU      $0                    OFFSET DATA DIRECTION REGISTER A
00000000        PIADA    EQU      $0                    OFFSET DATA REGISTER A
00000004        PIACA    EQU      $4                    OFFSET CONTROL REGISTER A
00000002        PIADDB   EQU      $2                    OFFSET DATA DIRECTION REGISTER B
00000002        PIADB    EQU      $2                    OFFSET DATA REGISTER B
00000006        PIACB    EQU      $6                    OFFSET CONTROL REGISTER B

00000007        B_DATDIR EQU      $07                   MAKE LINES 0-2 OUTPUT ON B SIDE
00000404        AB_CNTRL EQU      $0404                 PIA A&B DATA REGISTER SELECT
```

```
         00000007         COL_MASK EQU      $07                    DATA INPUT BIT MASK
         00000000         ROWGRND  EQU      $00                    MASK TO GROUND KEYBOARD ROWS

         00004000                  ORG      PROGRAM

004000 4E70               PGM13_5B RESET    .                      RESET ALL EXTERNAL DEVICES
004002 207C0003FF40                MOVEA.L #PIA,A0                 ADDRESS OF PIA
004008 117C00070002                MOVE.B  #B_DATDIR,PIADDB(A0)    MAKE B SIDE DATA LINES OUTPUTS
00400E 303C0404                    MOVE.W  #AB_CNTRL,D0            OUPUT CONTROL WORDS TO BOTH
004012 01880004                    MOVEP.W D0,PIACA(A0)            ..PIA-CONTROL REGISTERS

004016 117C00000002                MOVE.B  #ROWGRND,PIADB(A0)      GROUND ALL KEYBOARD ROWS

00401C 10280000           WAIT     MOVE.B  PIADA(A0),D0            GET DATA FORM KEYBOARD COLUMNS
004020 02000007                    ANDI.B  #COL_MASK,D0            MASK COLUMN BITS
004024 0C000007                    CMPI.B  #COL_MASK,D0            ARE ANY KEYS CLOSED?
004028 67F2                        BEQ     WAIT                    IF NO THEN WAIT

00402A 4E75                        RTS

                                   END     PGM13_5B
```

Of course, a 3 × 3 or 4 × 4 keyboard only needs one port of a PIA. Rewrite the program to use only port A.

Task 13-5b. Identify Key

Purpose: Identify a key closure by placing the number of the key in data register D0.

The procedure is as follows:

1. Set key number to 1, keyboard output port to all ones except for a zero in bit 0, and row counter to number of rows.
2. Fetch the column inputs by reading the input port.
3. If any column inputs are zero, proceed to Step 7.
4. Add the number of columns to the key number to reach next row.
5. Update the contents of the output port by rotating output left one position.
6. Decrement row counter. Go to Step 2 if any rows have not been scanned; otherwise, go to Step 9.
7. Add 1 to key number. Shift column inputs right one bit.
8. If carry = 1, return to Step 7.
9. End of program.

This program does not wait for the operator to press a key, so the key must be pressed before the program is executed. How would you modify the program to wait for at least one key to be pressed?

Program 13-5c:

```
00004000    PROGRAM   EQU    $4000

0003FF40    PIA       EQU    $3FF40           PIA BASE ADDRESS

00000000    PIADDA    EQU    $0               OFFSET DATA DIRECTION REGISTER A
00000000    PIADA     EQU    $0               OFFSET DATA REGISTER A
00000004    PIACA     EQU    $4               OFFSET CONTROL REGISTER A
00000002    PIADDB    EQU    $2               OFFSET DATA DIRECTION REGISTER B
00000002    PIADB     EQU    $2               OFFSET DATA REGISTER B
```

Flowchart:

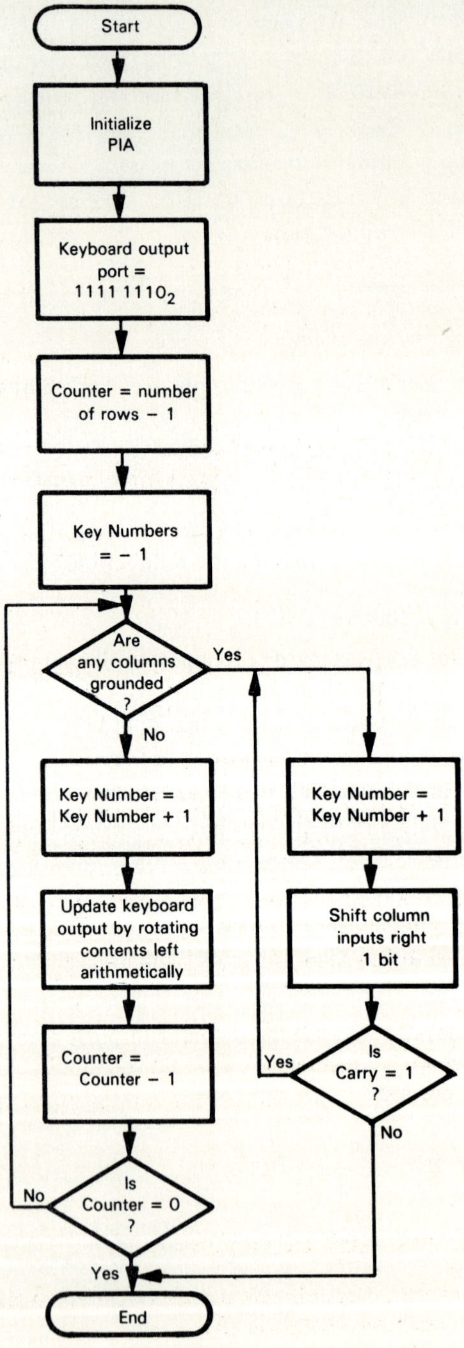
Start
Initialize PIA
Keyboard output port = $1111\ 1110_2$
Counter = number of rows − 1
Key Numbers = − 1
Are any columns grounded ?
Yes
No
Key Number = Key Number + 1
Update keyboard output by rotating contents left arithmetically
Counter = Counter − 1
Is Counter = 0 ?
No
Yes
Key Number = Key Number + 1
Shift column inputs right 1 bit
Is Carry = 1 ?
Yes
No
End

```
         00000006        PIACB      EQU      $6              OFFSET CONTROL REGISTER B

         00000000        A_DATDIR   EQU      $00             ALL LINES INPUT ON A SIDE
         00000007        B_DATDIR   EQU      $07             BIT 0-2 OUTPUT ON B SIDE
         00000004        A_CNTRL    EQU      $04             SELECT DATA REGISTER
         00000004        B_CNTRL    EQU      $04             SELECT DATA REGISTER

         00000007        COL_MASK   EQU      $07             COLUMNS CONNECTED TO BIT 0-2
         00000003        COLCOUNT   EQU      $03             NUMBER OF COLUMNS ON KEYBOARD
         00000003        ROWCOUNT   EQU      $03             NUMBER OF ROWS ON KEYBOARD
         000000FE        ROWGRND    EQU      $FE             MASK TO GROUND FIRST ROW

         00004000                   ORG      PROGRAM

004000 207C0003FF40 PGM13_5C MOVEA.L #PIA,A0                 GET PIA BASE ADDRESS
004006 42280004              CLR.B    PIACA(A0)              INITIALIZE A SIDE
00400A 117C00000000          MOVE.B   #A_DATDIR,PIADDA(A0)
004010 117C00040004          MOVE.B   #A_CNTRL,PIACA(A0)
004016 42280006              CLR.B    PIACB(A0)              INITIALIZE B SIDE
00401A 117C00070002          MOVE.B   #B_DATDIR,PIADDB(A0)
004020 117C00040006          MOVE.B   #B_CNTRL,PIACB(A0)

004026 163C00FE              MOVE.B   #ROWGRND,D3            GET ROWGROUNDING MASK
00402A 70FF                  MOVEQ    #-1,D0                 KEY NUMBER COUNTER
00402C 7202                  MOVEQ    #ROWCOUNT-1,D1         ROWSCANCOUNTER ADJUSTED FOR DBRA

00402E 11430002     ROW      MOVE.B   D3,PIADB(A0)           GROUND ONE ROW
004032 14280000              MOVE.B   PIADA(A0),D2           GET COLUMN BITS
004036 02020007              ANDI.B   #COL_MASK,D2           MASK OF THE COLUMN BITS
00403A 0C020007              CMPI.B   #COL_MASK,D2           ARE ANY KEYS CLOSED IN THIS ROW
00403E 660C                  BNE.S    COLUMN                 .. THEN SCAN COLUMNS

004040 5600                  ADDQ.B   #COLCOUNT,D0           .. ELSE SCAN NEXT ROW
004042 E31B                  ROL.B    #1,D3                  UPDATE SCAN PATTERN
004044 51C9FFE8              DBRA     D1,ROW                 CONTINUE IF NOT ALL ROWS CHECKED

004048 70FF                  MOVEQ    #-1,D0                 CODE FOR NO KEY CLOSED
00404A 6006                  BRA.S    DONE                   FINI, RETURN WITH -1 IN D0

00404C 5200         COLUMN   ADDQ.B   #1,D0                  KEY NUMBER := KEY NUMBER + 1
00404E E20A                  LSR.B    #1,D2                  IS THIS COLUMN GROUNDED ?
004050 65FA                  BCS      COLUMN

004052 4E75         DONE     RTS

                             END      PGM_13_5C
```

Each time a row scan fails, we must add the number of columns (3 in the example) to the key number to move to the next row (try the procedure on the keyboard in Figure 13-12).

What result does the program produce in data register D0 if no keys are being pressed? Change the program so that it starts the scan over again in that case.

An alternative approach is to use the bidirectional capability of the PIA.[7] The procedure would be:

1. Ground all columns and save the row inputs.
2. Ground all rows and save the column inputs.
3. Use both the row and the column inputs to determine the key number from a table.

Write a program to implement this procedure.

13-6. AN ENCODED KEYBOARD[8]

The processor will fetch data, when it is available, from an encoded keyboard that provides a strobe along with each data transfer.

An encoded keyboard provides a unique code for each key. It has internal electronics that perform the scanning and identification procedure of the previous example. The tradeoff is between the simpler software required by the encoded keyboard and the lower cost of the unencoded keyboard.

Encoded keyboards may use diode matrices, TTL encoders, or MOS encoders. The codes may be ASCII, EBCDIC, or a custom code. PROMs are often part of the encoding circuitry.

The encoding circuitry may do more than just encode key closures. It may also debounce the keys and handle "rollover," the problem of more than one key being struck at the same time. Common ways of handling rollover are "2-key rollover," in which two keys (but not more) struck at the same time are resolved into separate closures, and "n-key rollover," in which any number of keys struck at the same time are resolved into separate closures.

The encoded keyboard also provides a strobe with each data transfer. The strobe indicates that another key has been pressed. Figure 13-13 shows the interface between an encoded keyboard and the MC68000 microprocessor. We tie the keyboard strobe line to input CA1; a pulse on the strobe line sets bit 7 of the PIA control register. Bit 1 of the control register determines which edge (leading or trailing) of the pulse the PIA recognizes. Bit 1 = 0 to recognize the trailing edge (high-to-low transition), and 1 to recognize the leading edge (low-to-high transition).

The PIA thus contains an edge-sensitive latched serial status port as well as a parallel data port. It also contains an inverter that allows it to recognize either edge of a pulse. A PIA can therefore replace many simple circuit elements, such as flip-flops, gates, inverters, and buffers. The designer can correct errors by changing the contents of the PIA control register (a simple software change) rather than by rewiring a breadboard. For example, changing the active edge on the strobe line requires the changing of one bit in a program, whereas it might require additional parts and rewiring on a breadboard.

Be careful, however, of the fact that the PIA does not contain an input latch. An actual interface may require a latch if the keyboard is not guaranteed to hold its data. The latch can also be controlled by the strobe signal.

Task: Wait for an active-low strobe on control line CA1 and then load the keyboard data into data register D0.

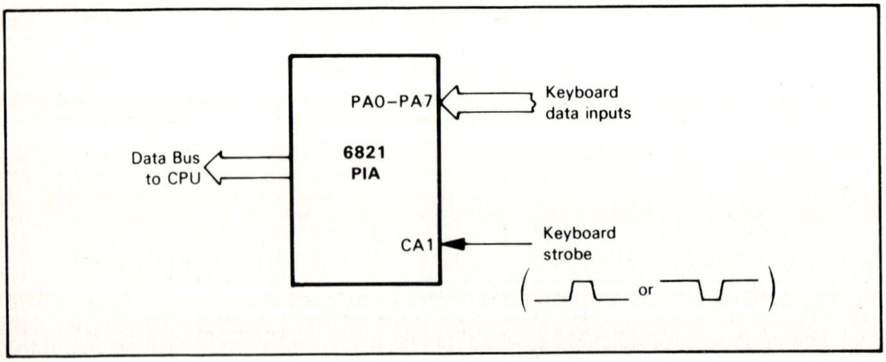

Figure 13-13. I/O Interface for an Encoded Keyboard

Note that reading the data from the data register clears the status bit. (This circuitry is part of the PIA).

Flowchart:

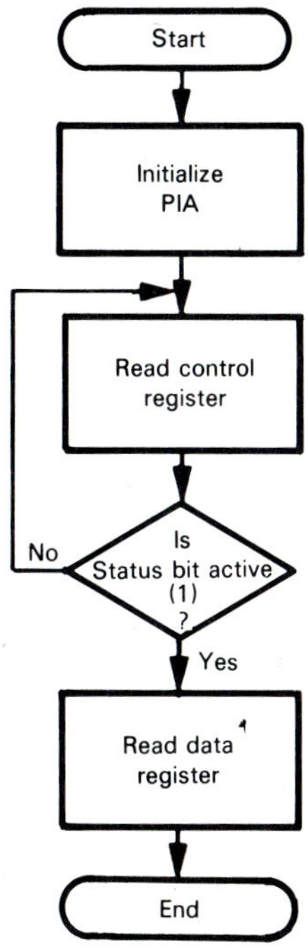

Note the "dummy" read in the initialization portion. The function of this first read is to clear bit 7 in control register A so that we are sure that accidental settings of flags do not cause problems.

Program 13-6:

```
         00004000     PROGRAM   EQU       $4000
         0003FF40     PIA       EQU       $3FF40                  PIA BASE ADDRESS
         00000000     PIADDA    EQU       $0                      OFFSET DATA DIRECTION REGISTER A
         00000000     PIADA     EQU       $0                      OFFSET DATA REGISTER A
         00000004     PIACA     EQU       $4                      OFFSET CONTROL REGISTER A
         00000000     A_DATDIR  EQU       $00                     MAKE ALL LINES INPUT
         00000004     A_CNTRL   EQU       $04                     SELECT DATA REGISTER, USE CA1
                      :                                           AS INPUT ACTIVE LOW
         00004000               ORG       PROGRAM
004000   207C0003FF40 PGM13_6   MOVEA.L   #PIA,A0                 GET PIA BASE ADDRESS
004006   42280004               CLR.B     PIACA(A0)               INITIALIZE A SIDE
00400A   117C00000000           MOVE.B    #A_DATDIR,PIADDA(A0)
004010   117C00040004           MOVE.B    #A_CNTRL,PIACA(A0)
004016   10280000               MOVE.B    PIADA(A0),D0            DUMMY READ-CLEARS STATUS BITS IN RE
00401A   10280004     WAIT      MOVE.B    PIACA(A0),D0            HAS KEY BEEN PRESSED ?
00401E   6AFA                   BPL       WAIT                    IF NO THEN WAIT
```

```
004020 10280000          MOVE.B  PIADA(A0),D0          ..ELSE FETCH KEYBOARD DATA
004024 4E75              RTS
                         END     PGM13_6
```

To set control register bit 7 on low-to-high transitions of the keyboard strobe line, simply replace A_CNTRL EQU $04 with A_CNTRL EQU $06.

If we tied the keyboard strobe line to CA2, control register bit 6 would then serve as the status latch.

Show that reading the data register clears the status bit, indicating that the CPU has read the most recent data and allowing the next input operation to occur. Hint: save the contents of the PIA control register in memory before and after the instruction MOVE.B D0, PIADA(A0),D0 is executed. What happens if you replace MOVE.B PIADA(A0),D0 with MOVE.B D0,PIADA(A0)? Remember that writing data into the data register does not clear the status bit, nor does writing data into or reading data from the control register. What happens if you replace MOVE.B PIADA(A0),D0 with MOVE.B PIACA(A0),D0 or MOVE.B D0,PIACA(A0)?

One reason why we are concerned with the effects of instructions on PIA registers is that we may want to use the control lines for purposes that have nothing to do with the data ports. For example, we may be using a PIA to interface a simple peripheral (e.g., a set of switches of single LEDs) that does not require any status of control lines. The control lines are then available as serial I/O lines at no additional hardware cost. The only problem is that we must manipulate these lines using facilities that are provided on the assumption of a direct connection between the serial lines and the parallel data port.

13-7. A DIGITAL-TO-ANALOG CONVERTER[10-13]

The processor sends data to an 8-bit digital-to-analog converter, which has an active-low latch enable.

Digital-to-analog converters produce the continuous signals required by solenoids, relays, actuators, and other electrical and mechanical output devices. Typical converters consist of switches and resistor ladders with the appropriate resistance values. The user must generally provide a reference voltage and some other digital and analog circuitry, although complete units are becoming available at low cost.

Figure 13-14 describes the 8-bit Signetics NE5018 D/A converter, which contains an on-chip 8-bit parallel data input latch. A low level on the LE (Latch Enable) input gates the input data into the latches, where it remains after LE goes high.

D/A Converter Interface

Figure 13-15 illustrates the interfacing of the NE5018 to an MC68000 system. Note that port B of the PIA automatically produces the active-low pulse required to latch the data into the D/A converter; CB2 acts as an OUTPUT READY signal, indicating that the CPU has sent data to the output port. Remember that in the brief pulse mode, CB2 goes low automatically on the clock pulse following a write operation on data register B, and remains low until the next clock pulse (see Table 13-5). The control

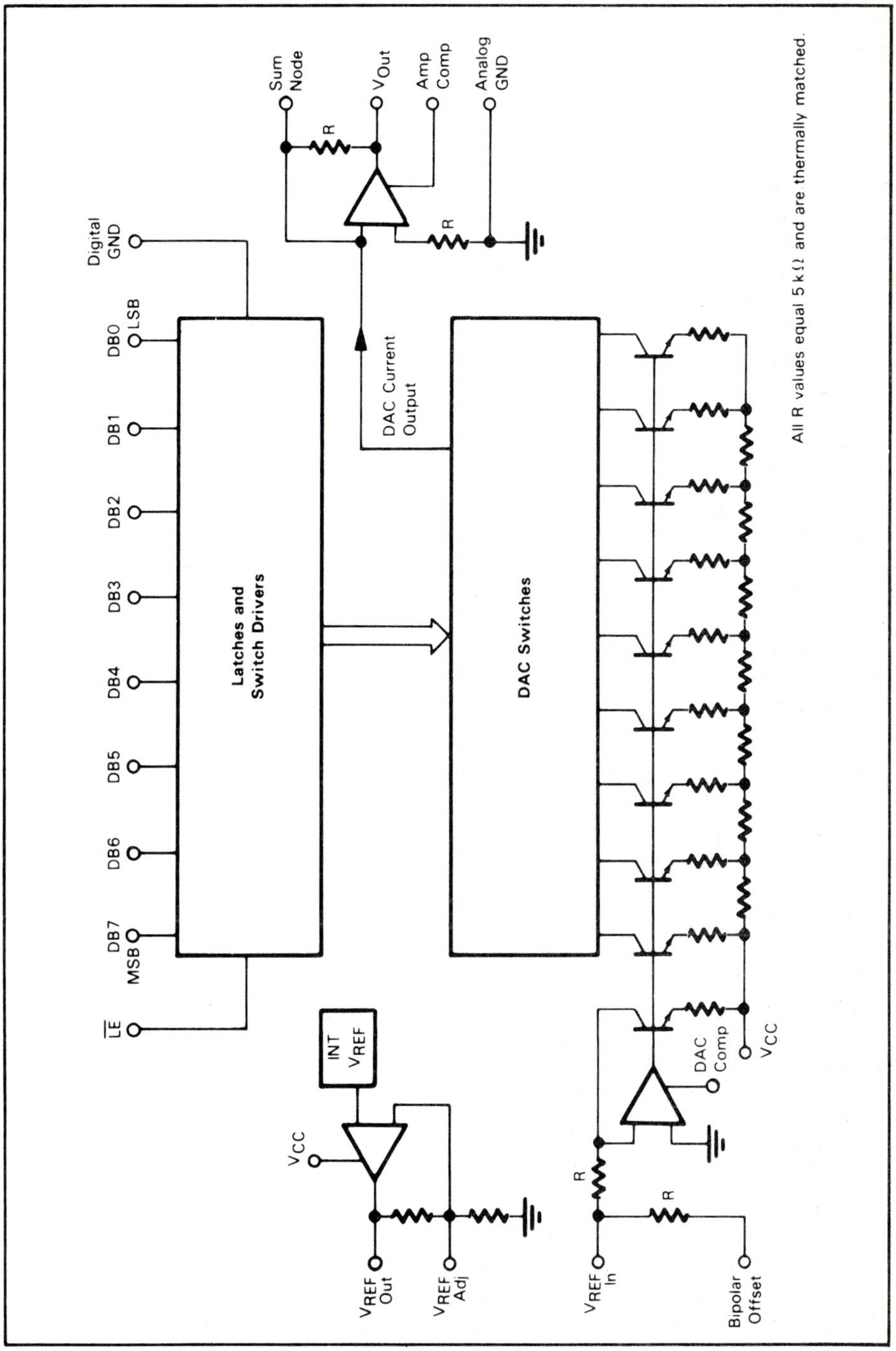

Figure 13-14. Signetics NE5018 D/A Converter

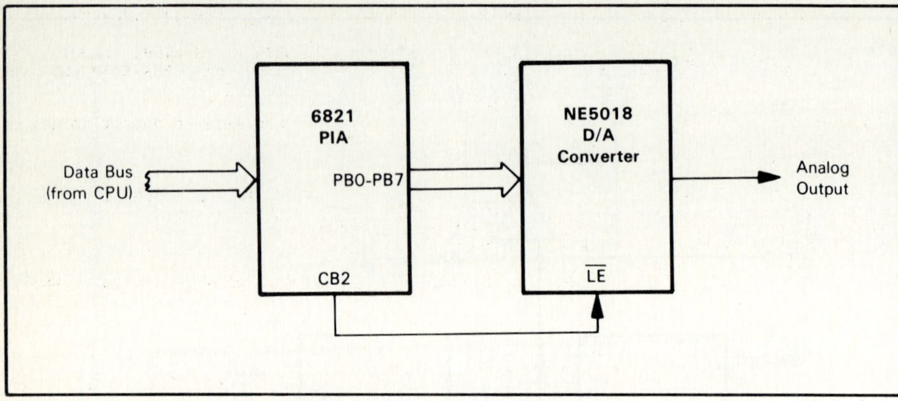

Figure 13-15. I/O Interface for an 8-Bit Digital-to-Analog Converter

register bits that cause the PIA to operate this way are:

Bit 5 = 1 to make CB2 an output
Bit 4 = 0 to make CB2 a pulse
Bit 3 = 1 to make CB2 a brief pulse that typically lasts one clock cycle.

Note that the PIA contains an output latch. The data therefore remains stable during and after conversion, even though the processor only leaves it on the data bus for one clock cycle. Output latches are essential in microcomputer systems, since the processor uses its data bus constantly to transfer data and instructions to and from memory. The converter typically requires only a few microseconds to produce analog outputs, but other peripherals may need the data for much longer periods.

In applications where eight bits of resolution are not enough, you can use the widely available 10-to 16-bit converters. Ones that are advertised as "microprocessor-compatible" usually have separate data ports for the most and least significant bytes. Such devices are much easier to interface than devices that only accept all the data at one time through a single port.

The PIA serves as both a parallel data port and a serial control port. CB2 provides a pulse that lasts one clock cycle after the CPU latches output data into the PIA. This pulse is long enough to meet the requirements (typically 400 ns) of the NE5018 converter.

Task 13-7. Send Data to D/A Converter

Purpose: Send data from the variable BYTE at memory location 6000 to the D/A converter.

Program 13-7:

```
00004000     PROGRAM   EQU     $4000
00006000     DATA      EQU     $6000

0003FF40     PIA       EQU     $3FF40                  PIA BASE ADDRESS

00000002     PIADDB    EQU     $2                      OFFSET DATA DIRECTION REGISTER B
00000002     PIADB     EQU     $2                      OFFSET DATA REGISTER B
```

```
        00000006      PIACB     EQU      $6                OFFSET CONTROL REGISTER B

        000000FF      B_DATDIR  EQU      $FF               MAKE ALL B LINES OUTPUT
        0000002C      B_CNTRL   EQU      $2C               SELECT DATA REGISTER AND STROBE CB2

        00006000                ORG      DATA
006000  00000001      BYTE      DS.B     1                 DATA BYTE TO OUTPUT TO D/A CONV.

        00004000                ORG      PROGRAM

004000  207C0003FF40  PGM13_7A  MOVEA.L  #PIA,A0           GET PIA BASE ADDRESS
004006  42280006                CLR.B    PIACB(A0)         INITIALIZE B SIDE
00400A  117C00FF0002            MOVE.B   #B_DATDIR,PIADDB(A0)
004010  117C002C0006            MOVE.B   #B_CNTRL,PIACB(A0)

004016  117860000002            MOVE.B   BYTE,PIADB(A0)    SEND DATA TO D/A CONV. AND LATCH

00401C  4E75                    RTS

                                END      PGM13_7A
```

Flowchart:

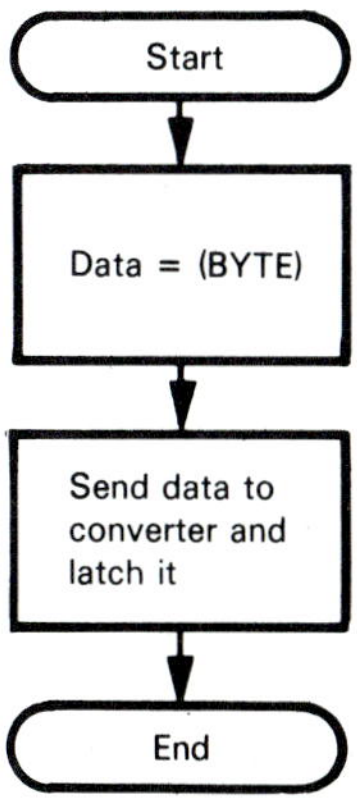

The PIA produces the load pulse automatically after the CPU stores the data in the data register. No explicit instructions are necessary. Although automatic operations like this save time and memory, they also result in documentation problems since there is no record in the program of when they occur. To understand the operations of this interface, you would need a detailed understanding of the 6821 device as well as a hardware schematic and a program listing. Such requirements make maintenance and updating difficult.

The automatic pulse lasts only one clock cycle. If this is not enough (or if an active-high pulse is necessary), we could use the level output from CB2. This operating mode is often called a manual mode, since the PIA does not produce any pulses automatically. The program to use the mode would be:

```
00004000    PROGRAM   EQU    $4000
00006000    DATA      EQU    $6000

0003FF40    PIA       EQU    $3FF40          PIA BASE ADDRESS

00000002    PIADDB    EQU    $2              OFFSET DATA DIRECTION REGISTER B
00000002    PIADB     EQU    $2              OFFSET DATA REGISTER B
00000006    PIACB     EQU    $6              OFFSET CONTROL REGISTER B

000000FF    B_DATDIR  EQU    $FF             MAKE ALL B LINES OUTPUT
00000034    B_CNTRL   EQU    $34             SELECT DATA REGISTER,
                                             CB2 "MANUAL" STROBE
```

```
       00000003      DASTABIT EQU      $03                    CB2 CONNECTED TO LATCH ENABLE

       00006000               ORG      DATA
006000 00000001      BYTE     DS.B     1                      DATA BYTE TO OUTPUT TO D/A CONV.

       00004000               ORG      PROGRAM

004000 207C0003FF40  PGM13_7B MOVEA.L  #PIA,A0                GET PIA BASE ADDRESS
004006 42280006               CLR.B    PIACB(A0)              INITIALIZE B SIDE
00400A 117C00FF0002           MOVE.B   #B_DATDIR,PIADDB(A0)
004010 117C00340006           MOVE.B   #B_CNTRL,PIACB(A0)

004016 117860000002           MOVE.B   BYTE,PIADB(A0)         SEND DATA TO D/A CONV.
00401C 08E800030006           BSET.B   #DASTABIT,PIACB(A0)    OPEN DAC LATCH
004022 08A800030006           BCLR.B   #DASTABIT,PIACB(A0)    LATCH DATA

004028 4E75                   RTS

                              END      PGM13_7B
```

This approach requires more instructions, but it produces a longer pulse and is easier to understand. Here bit 4 of the PIA control register is set to make CB2 a level with the value of bit 3. We can then set and clear bit 3 using the instructions BSET and BCLR.

In the level or manual mode, CB2 is completely independent of operations on the parallel data port. It is simply a serial output that is available for any purpose. The only precaution one must take in using it is to avoid changing any of the other bits in the PIA control register, since they have unrelated functions. Using the BTST and BCLR instructions makes the procedure independent of the contents of the PIA control register, since only bit 3 is changed.

13-8. ANALOG-TO-DIGITAL CONVERTER[14-19]

The processor fetches data from an 8-bit analog-to-digital converter that requires a start conversion pulse to start the conversion process and provides an end of conversion output to indicate the completion of the process and the availability of valid data.

Analog-to-digital converters handle the continuous signals produced by various types of sensors and transducers. The converter produces the digital input that the computer requires.

One form of analog-to-digital converter is the successive approximation device, which makes a direct 1-bit comparison during each clock cycle. Such converters are fast but have little noise immunity. Dual slope integrating converters are another form of analog-to-digital converter. These devices take longer to convert data but are more resistant to noise. Other techniques, such as the incremental charge balancing technique, are also used.

Analog-to-digital converters usually require some external analog and digital circuitry, although complete units are becoming available at low cost.

Figure 13-16 contains a general description and a timing diagram for the National MM5357 8-bit A/D converter. The device contains output latches and tristate data outputs. A pulse on the start conversion (STRT CONV) line starts conversion of the analog input; after about 40 clock cycles (the converter requires a TTL level clock with a minimum pulse width of 400 ns), the result will go to the output latches and the end of conversion (EOC) output will indicate this by going high. Data is read from the latches by applying a '1' to the OUTPUT ENABLE input. Figure 13- 17 shows the connections for the device and some typical applications circuits.

NATIONAL
MM5357 8-bit A/D converter

General Description

The MM5357 is an 8-bit monolithic A/D converter using P-channel ion-implemented MOS technology. It contains a high input impedance comparator, 256 series resistors and analog switches, control logic and output latches. Conversion is performed using a successive approximation technique where the unknown analog voltage is compared to the resistor tie points using analog switches. When the appropriate tie point voltage matches the unknown voltage, conversion is complete and the digital outputs contain an 8-bit complementary binary word corresponding to the unknown. The binary output is tri-state to permit bussing on common data lines.

Features

- Low cost
- +5 V, 10 V input ranges
- No missing codes
- Ratiometric conversion
- Tri-state outputs
- Contains output latches
- TTL compatible

Key Specs

• Resolution	8 bits
• Linearity	+ 1/2 LSB
• Conversion speed	40μs
• Input impedance	>100 MΦ
• Supply voltages	+5 V, −12 V, GND
• Clock range	5.0 kHz to 2.0 MHz

Timing Diagram:

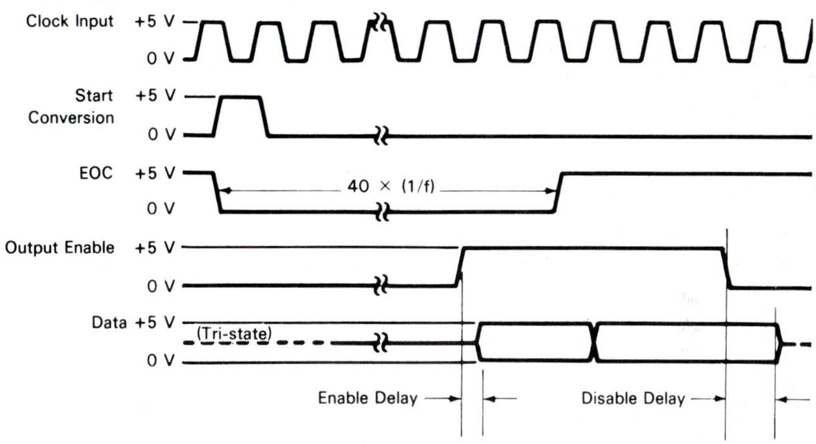

Data is complementary binary (Full scale is "0s" output).

Figure 13-16. General Description and Timing Diagram for the National 5357 A/D Converter

A/D Converter Interface

Figure 13-18 shows the interface between the MC68000 microprocessor and the 5357 A/D converter. Control line CA2 is used in the level (manual) output mode to provide an active-high start conversion pulse of sufficient length. The end of conversion signal is tied to control line CA1 so bit 7 of PIA control register A is set when EOC goes high. The important transition on the end of conversion line is the leading edge (low-to-high transition), which indicates the completion of the conversion. Here we are using

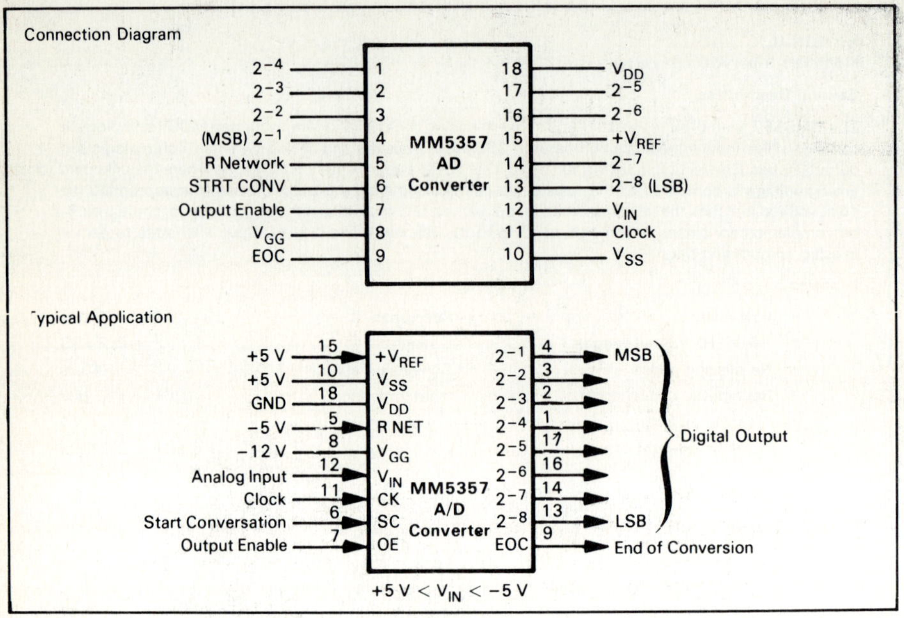

Figure 13-17. Connection Diagram and Typical Application for the National 5357 A/D Converter

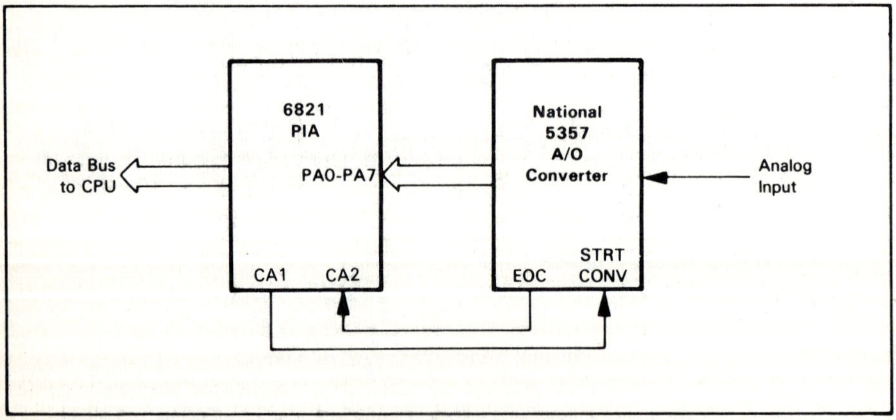

Figure 13-18. Interface for an 8-Bit Analog-to-Digital Converter

the 6820 PIA to handle parallel input, serial input, and serial output, since the A/D converter requires a complete handshake. The OUTPUT ENABLE pin on the converter is tied high, since we are not placing the data directly on the microprocessor's tristate data bus. Note (see Fig. 13-16) that the converter's data outputs are complementary binary. (An all zeros output is full scale.)

Task 13-8. Input from Converter

Purpose: Start the conversion process, wait for end of conversion (OEC) to go high, then read the data and store it in the variable BYTE at memory location 6000.

Flowchart:

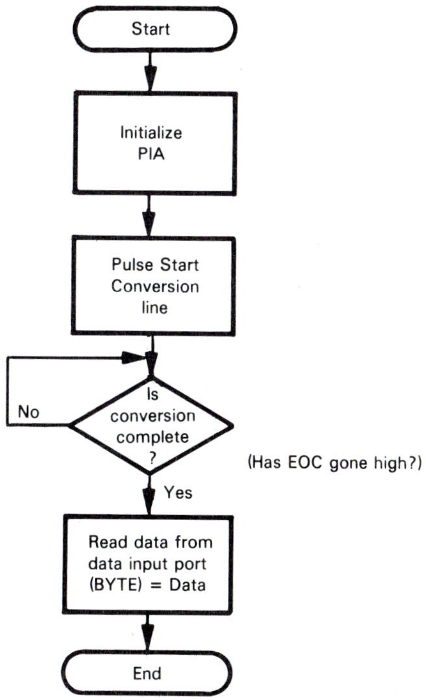

The PIA control register bits are determined as follows:

Bit 5 = 1 to make CA2 an output.
Bit 4 = 1 to make CA2 a level (i.e., to operate in the manual mode).
Bit 3 = 0 to bring start conversion low initially.
Bit 1 = 1 to set bit 7 on a low-to-high transition (leading edge) on the end of conversion line.

A delay routine of appropriate length (longer than the maximum guaranteed conversion time) could replace the examination of the status bit.

Program 13-8:

```
00004000        PROGRAM  EQU      $4000
00006000        DATA     EQU      $6000

0003FF40        PIA      EQU      $3FF40                  PIA BASE ADDRESS

00000000        PIADDA   EQU      $0                      OFFSET DATA DIRECTION REGISTER A
00000000        PIADA    EQU      $0                      OFFSET DATA REGISTER A
00000004        PIACA    EQU      $4                      OFFSET CONTROL REGISTER A
```

```
        00000000       A_DATDIR EQU      $00           ALL LINES INPUT ON A SIDE
        00000036       A_CNTRL  EQU      $36           CA2 OUTPUT LOW,SELECT DATA REGISTER
                       *                               CA1 TRIG ON LOW-TO-HIGH

        00000003       ADSTABIT EQU      $03           CA2 CONNECTED TO A/D START CONV.
        00000007       ADENDBIT EQU      $07           CA1 CONNECTED TO A/D END OF CONV.

        00006000                ORG      DATA
006000  00000001       BYTE     DS.B     1             VALUE TO BE OUTPUT TO A/D CONV.

        00004000                ORG      PROGRAM

004000  207C0003FF40   PGM13_8  MOVEA.L  #PIA,A0       GET PIA BASE ADDRESS
004006  42280004                CLR.B    PIACA(A0)     INITIALIZE A SIDE
00400A  117C00000000            MOVE.B   #A_DATDIR,PIADDA(A0)
004010  117C00360004            MOVE.B   #A_CNTRL,PIACA(A0)

004016  08E800030004            BSET.B   #ADSTABIT,PIACA(A0)  START CONVERSION HIGH
00401C  08A800030004            BCLR.B   #ADSTABIT,PIACA(A0)  START CONVERSION LOW
004022  082800070004   WAIT     BTST.B   #ADENDBIT,PIACA(A0)  HAS CONVERSION BEEN COMPLETE?
004028  67F8                    BEQ      WAIT                 IF NOT THEN WAIT

00402A  11E800006000            MOVE.B   PIADA(A0),BYTE       ...ELSE SAVE A/D VALUE

004030  4E75                    RTS

                                END      PGM13_8
```

There is one subtle problem that we encounter in this application which will also apply to other applications: spurious pulses caused by the initialization can start up undesired processes.

Here is an example. When you first apply power to the system, everything is in a indeterminate state; that is, registers contain random numbers, A/D converters may spontaneously begin conversion proceses, LEDs can be turned on or off, and so on. Then you reset and initialize the system to bring it to a "known state." During this initialization itself, however, you may create pulses or changes in signal levels that could, for example, start up an A/D conversion. Now, to be sure that everything has reached the desired "known state," you may have to wait for a while and perhaps perform dummy read operations to clear status bits and so one. This requires an intimate knowledge of the hardware in your system and makes the initialization process more complicated. But you are more likely to have assurance that your system operates properly under all conditions if you make this extra effort.

In our example with the A/D converter you can insert a loop like this after the MOVE.B #A_CNTRL, PIACA(A0) instruction to ensure that the converter is not performing a conversion after the initialization is complete:

```
MOVEQ    #MAXCONV,D0      WAIT FOR A WHILE TO MAKE SURE THAT
JSR      DELAY            ..EVENTUAL CONVERSION IS COMPLETE
TST.B    PIADA(A0)        DUMMY READ-CLEAR STATUS BITS IN CTR
```

The symbol MAXCONV should be set to the maximum number of milliseconds a conversion can take. The delay routine used is the one described in Chapter 12.

Why is it necessary to wait? Can't we just check the status of bit 7 in the control register? No, because bit 7 does not reflect a level, but rather a change in level on CA1. That is, it is set to 1 by the low-to-high transition when the conversion is complete and not by the low-level output from the converter while it is performing a conversion. How would this have changed if we had used a level sensitive input such as CA2 for the same purpose?

13-9. A TELETYPEWRITER (TTY)

We will transfer data to and from a standard 10-character-per-second serial teletypewriter.

Standard TTY Character Format

The common teletypewriter transfers data in an asynchronous serial mode. The procedure is as follows:

1. The line is normally in the mark state (logic '1').
2. A start bit (space state or logic '0').
3. The character is usually 7-bit ASCII with the least significant bit transmitted first.
4. The most significant bit is a parity bit, which may be even, odd, or fixed at zero or one.
5. Two stop bits (logic '1's) follow each character to provide a minimum separation between characters.

Figure 13-19 shows the format. Note that each character requires the transmission of eleven bits, of which only seven contain information. Since the data rate is ten characters per second, the bit rate is 10 x 11, or 110 Baud. Each bit therefore has a width of 1/110 of a second, or 9.1 milliseconds. This width is an average; the teletypewriter does not maintain it to any high level of accuracy.

TTY Receive Mode

This is the receive procedure, flowcharted in Figure 13-20:

Step 1. Look for a start bit (a logic zero) on the data line.

Step 2. Center the reception by waiting one-half bit time, or 4.55 milliseconds.

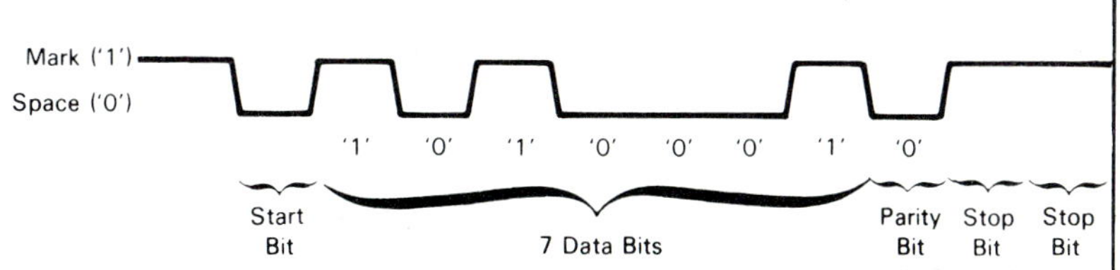

Character is ASCII 'E' with odd parity (45 hex).

The transmission order is: Start bit ('0'), bit 0, bit 1, bit 2, bit 3, bit 4, bit 5, bit 6, Parity bit, Stop bit ('1'), Stop bit ('1').

Figure 13-19. Teletypewriter Data Format

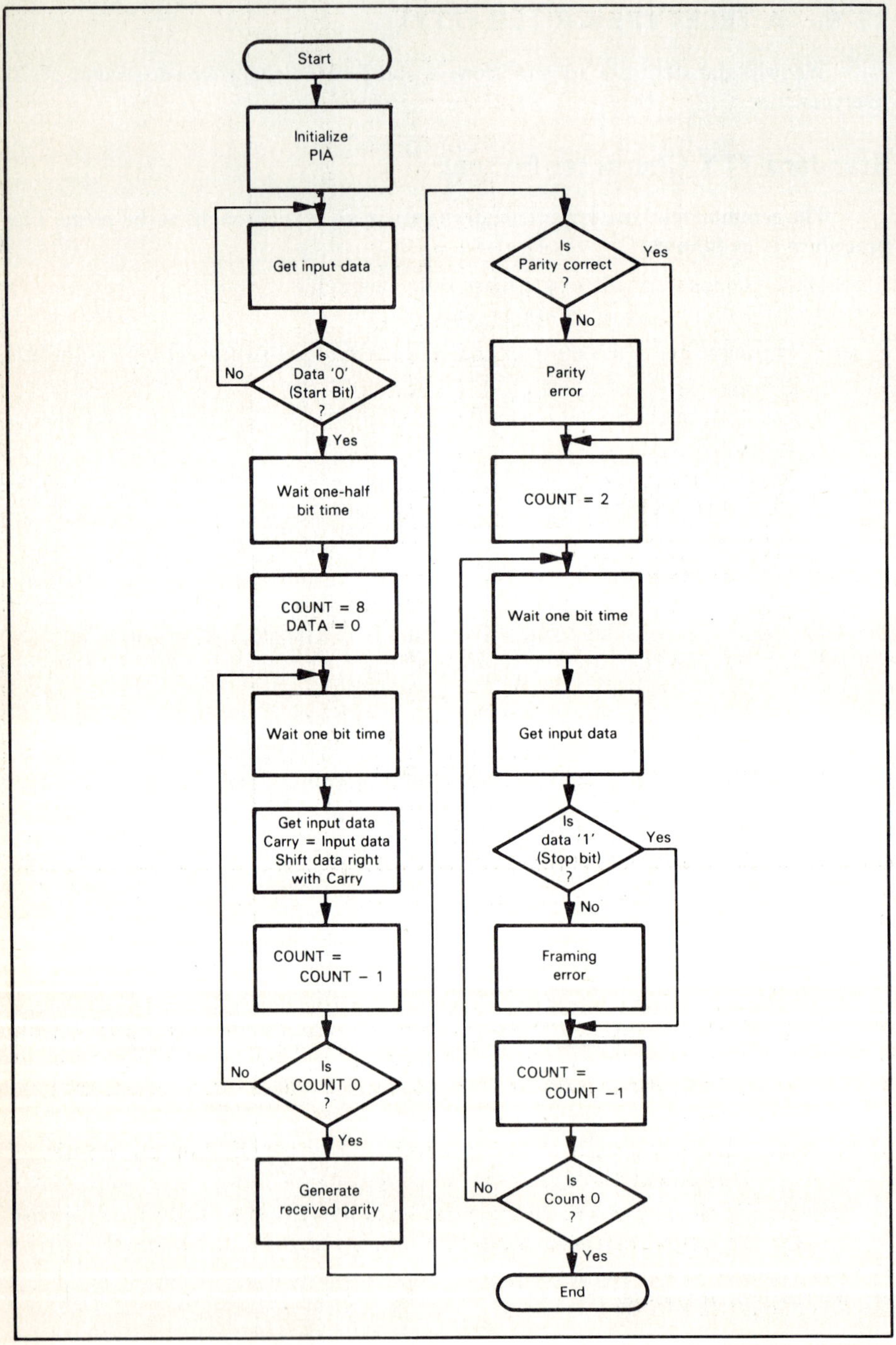

Figure 13-20. Flowchart for Receive Procedure

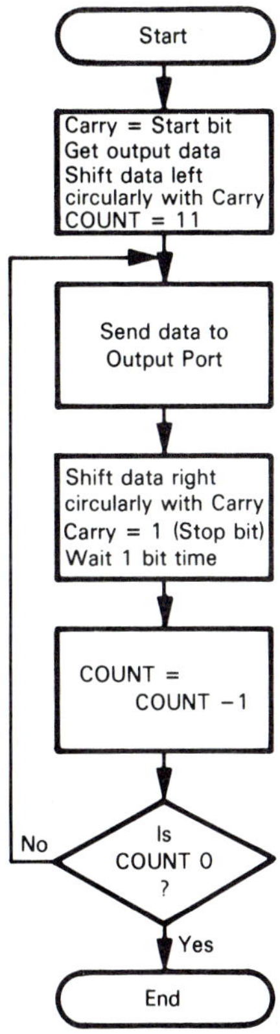

Figure 13-21. Flowchart for Transmit Procedure

Step 3. Fetch the data bits, waiting one bit time before each one. Assemble the data bits into a word by first shifting the bit to the carry and then circularly shifting the data with the carry. Remember that the least significant bit is received first.

Step 4. Generate the received parity and check it against the transmitted parity. If they do not match, indicate a "parity error."

Step 5. Fetch the stop bits (waiting one bit time between inputs). If they are not correct (if both stop bits are not one), indicate a "framing error."

TTY Transmit Mode

This is the transmit procedure, flowcharted in Figure 13-21.

Step 1. Transmit a start bit (i.e., a logic zero).

Step 2. Transmit the seven data bits, starting with the least significant bit.

Step 3. Generate and transmit the parity bit.

Step 4. Transmit two stop bits (i.e., logic ones).

The transmission routine must wait one bit time between output operations.

Task 13-9a. Read Data from TTY

Purpose: Fetch data from a teletypewriter using bit 7 of a PIA data port and place the data in the variable CHAR at memory location 6000. Figure 13-20 describes the procedure.

Program 13-9a:

Assume that the serial port is bit 7 of the PIA and that no parity or framing check is necessary.

```
       00004000     PROGRAM   EQU      $4000
       00006000     DATA      EQU      $6000

       0003FF40     PIA       EQU      $3FF40                PIA BASE ADDRESS

       00000000     PIADDA    EQU      $0                    OFFSET DATA DIRECTION REGISTER A
       00000000     PIADA     EQU      $0                    OFFSET DATA REGISTER A
       00000004     PIACA     EQU      $4                    OFFSET CONTROL REGISTER A

       00000000     A_DATDIR  EQU      $00                   ALL BITS INPUT
       00000004     A_CNTRL   EQU      $04                   SELECT DATA REGISTER

       00000007     TTYBIT    EQU      $7                    TTY CONNECTED TO BIT 7

       00001C70     DCNT1     EQU      7280                  DELAY COUNT FOR 9.1 MS
       00000E38     DCNT2     EQU      3640                  DELAY COUNT FOR 4.55 MS

       00006000               ORG      DATA

006000 00000001     CHAR      DS.B     1                     TTY INPUT CHAR

       00004000               ORG      PROGRAM

004000 207C0003FF40 PGM13_9A  MOVEA.L  #PIA,A0               GET PIA BASE ADDRESS
004006 42280004               CLR.B    PIACA(A0)             INITIAIZE A SIDE
00400A 117C00000000           MOVE.B   #A_DATDIR,PIADDA(A0)
004010 117C00040004           MOVE.B   #A_CNTRL,PIACA(A0)

004016 082800070000 WAIT      BTST.B   #TTYBIT,PIADA(A0)     IS THERE A START BIT?
00401C 66F8                   BNE      WAIT                  IF NOT THEN WAIT
00401E 611C                   BSR.S    DLY4_55               ...ELSE WAIT HALF BIT TIME
004020 103C0080               MOVE.B   #$80,D0               INITIALIZE WITH COUNT BIT

004024 6110         TTYIN     BSR.S    DLY9_1                WAIT ONE BIT TIME
004026 12280000               MOVE.B   PIADA(A0),D1          GET NEXT DATA BIT
00402A E311                   ROXL.B   #1,D1                 EXT.FLAG = BIT VALUE
00402C E210                   ROXR.B   #1,D0                 COMBINE WITH PREVIOUS DATA
00402E 64F4                   BCC      TTYIN                 CONTINUE UNTIL COUNT BIT
004030 11C06000               MOVE.B   D0,CHAR               SAVE INPUT CHAR

004034 4E75                   RTS

                    *  DELAY ROUTINES

004036 323C1C70     DLY9_1    MOVE.W   #DCNT1,D1             DELAY FOR 9.1 MS
00403A 6004                   BRA.S    DELAY
00403C 323C0E38     DLY4_55   MOVE.W   #DCNT2,D1             DELAY FOR 4.55 MS
004040 51C9FFFE     DELAY     DBRA     D1,DELAY
004044 4E75                   RTS

                              END      PGM13_9A
```

Remember that bit 0 of the data is received first.

We obtained the constants for the delay routine as described earlier in this chapter, assuming a clock rate of 8 MHz and no extra wait states. You may want to check them for yourself. The delay times do not have to be highly accurate because the routine centers the reception, each character is handled separately, the bit rate is low, and the teletypewriter itself is not highly accurate.

Note the use of the ROXL and ROXR instructions in this program. If you are used to other Motorola microprocessors, such as the 6800 and 6809, you may have to think twice in situations like this. Remember that none of the MC68000 shift or rotate instructions can shift the Carry bit *into* a register; only the Extend (X) bit from the status register can be shifted into a register. But remember also that most MC68000 instructions can shift *out* to both the Carry and Extend bits.

How would you extend this program to check parity?

Task 13-9b. Write Data to TTY

Purpose: Transmit data to a teletypewriter using bit 0 of a PIA data port. The data is the variable CHAR at memory location 6000. Assume that parity need not be generated.

Program 13-9b:

```
       00004000     PROGRAM  EQU      $4000
       00006000     DATA     EQU      $6000

       0003FF40     PIA      EQU      $3FF40                      PIA BASE ADDRESS

       00000000     PIADDA   EQU      $0                          OFFSET DATA DIRECTION REGISTER A
       00000000     PIADA    EQU      $0                          OFFSET DATA REGISTER A
       00000004     PIACA    EQU      $4                          OFFSET CONTROL REGISTER A

       00000080     A_DATDIR EQU      $80                         MAKE LINE 7 OUTPUT
       00000004     A_CNTRL  EQU      $04                         SELECT DATA REGISTER

       00000007     TTYBIT   EQU      $07                         TTY CONNECTED TO BIT 7

       00001C70     DCNT1    EQU      7280                        DELAY COUNT FOR 9,1 MS

       00000008     CHRBIT   EQU      $08                         NUMBER OF DATA BITS IN CHARACTER
       00000002     STPBIT   EQU      $02                         NUMBER OF STOPBITS TO TRANSMIT

       00006000              ORG      DATA
006000 00000001     CHAR     DS.B     1                           TTY OUTPUT CHAR

       00004000              ORG      PROGRAM

004000 207C0003FF40 PGM13_9B MOVEA.L  #PIA,A0                     GET PIA BASE ADDRESS
004006 42280004              CLR.B    PIACA(A0)                   INITIALIZE A SIDE
00400A 117C00800000          MOVE.B   #A_DATDIR,PIADDA(A0)
004010 117C00040004          MOVE.B   #A_CNTRL,PIACA(A0)

004016 70FF                  MOVEQ    #-1,D0                      FORM STOP BITS
004018 10386000              MOVE.B   CHAR,D0                     GET TTY OUTPUT DATA
00401C 740A                  MOVEQ    #1+CHRBIT+STPBIT-1,D2       BIT COUNTER ADJUSTED FOR DBRA
00401E 08A800070000          BCLR.B   #TTYBIT,PIADA(A0)           SEND START BIT

004024 6100001A     SNDBIT   BSR      DLY9_1                      WAIT 1 BIT TIME
004028 E258                  ROR.W    #1,D0                       CARRY = NEXT DATA BIT
00402A 6508                  BCS.S    SNDONE                      IF DATA = 1 THEN SEND A ONE

00402C 08A800070000          BCLR.B   #TTYBIT,PIADA(A0)           SEND '0' AS DATA BIT
004032 6006                  BRA.S    NEXT

004034 08E800070000 SNDONE   BSET.B   #TTYBIT,PIADA(A0)           SEND '1' AS DATA
00403A 51CAFFE8     NEXT     DBRA     D2,SNDBIT                   CONTINUE UNTIL ALL BIT SENT
```

```
00403E 4E75                        RTS


                      *  DELAY ROUTINE

004040 323C1C70       DLY9_1     MOVE.W   #DCNT1,D1                 DELAY FOR 9.1 MS
004044 51C9FFFE       DELAY      DBRA     D1,DELAY
004048 4E75                      RTS

                                 END      PGM13_9B
```

Remember that bit 0 of the data must be transmitted first.

In actual applications, you should place a logic '1' on the teletypewriter line as part of the startup routine, since that line should normally be in the mark (1) state. Each character consists of 11 bits, beginning with a start bit ('0') and ending with two stop bits ('1's).

How would you rewrite both of these TTY programs so that they use CA2 or CB2 as outputs?

UART

These procedures are sufficiently common and complex to merit a special LSI device: the UART, or Universal Asynchronous Receiver/Transmitter.[20] The UART will perform the reception procedure and provide the data in parallel form and a data ready signal. It will also accept data in parallel form, perform the transmission procedure, and provide a peripheral ready signal when it can handle more data. UARTs may have many other features, including:

1. Ability to handle various bit lengths (usually 5 to 8), parity options, and numbers of stop bits (usually 1, 1-1/2, and 2).
2. Indicators for framing errors, parity errors, and "overrun errors" (failure to read a character before another one is received).
3. RS-232[21] compatibility; i.e., a request-to-send (RTS) output signal that indicates the presence of data to communications equipment and a clear-to-send (CTS) input signal that indicates, in response to RTS, the readiness of the communications equipment. There may be provisions for other RS-232 signals, such as received signal quality, data set ready, or data terminal ready.
4. Tristate outputs and control compatibility with a microprocessor.
5. Clock options that allow the UART to sample incoming data several times in order to detect false start bits and other errors.
6. Interrupt facilities and controls.

UARTs act as four parallel ports: an input data port, an output data port, an input status port, and an output control port. The status bits include error indicators as well as ready flags. The control bits select various options. **UARTs are inexpensive ($5 to $50, depending on features) and easy to use.**

SOME FINAL TIPS ON I/O

Now that we have seen some real examples of I/O routines, let's point out some of the most important things to remember.

I/O programs tend to be fairly intricate and are likely to be subject to a lot of changes during testing. Therefore, it is more important than ever that you use symbols instead of actual values as much as possible. Such symbols as ROWCOUNT, BITDLY, and GROUNDMASK give us much more useful information than 13, $07, and 5 = $03. Use different symbols where applicable even if they have the same actual values as other symbols. For example, define both ROWCOUNT and COLCOUNT for a 3x3 keyboard. Using a symbol that happens to have the value that you need at the moment but which has an inappropriate name will often result in errors the next time you have to make a change to the program. Remember that using a lot of symbols will not increase anything except the time it takes to assemble the program.

Make sure you know the state of your I/O devices before you start a process of some kind. I/O devices such as data converters and, perhaps, even other microcomputers connected to your system may need some time to finish a task you incidentally activated during initialization.

Use the RESET instruction with care: remember that it will reset every device connected to the MC68000's reset signal — not just the particular device you have in mind.

If you have a monitoring system (which we discuss thoroughly in Chapter 19) that allows you to print out the contents of memory, you must be careful if it accesses the PIA. If you print the contents of a PIA's data register, the monitor program must read the data register and this automatically clears status bits 6 and 7 in the PIA's control register. This can sometimes lead to very confusing results.

PROBLEMS

13-1. AN ON-OFF PUSHBUTTON

Purpose: Each closure of the pushbutton complements (inverts) all the bits in the variable SWITCH at memory location 6000. The location initially contains zero. The program should continuously examine the pushbutton and complement the contents of SWITCH with each closure. You may wish to complement a display output port instead, so as to make the results easier to see.

Sample Case:

SWITCH initially contains zero.

The first pushbutton closure changes SWITCH to FF_{16}, the second changes it back to zero, the third back to FF_{16}, etc. Assume that the pushbutton is debounced in hardware. How would you include debouncing in your program?

13-2. DEBOUNCING A SWITCH IN SOFTWARE

Purpose: Debounce a mechanical switch by waiting until two readings, taken a debounce time apart, give the same result. Assume that the debounce time (in ms) is in the variable TIME at memory location 6000 and store the switch position in the variable SWITCH at memory location 6002.

Sample Problem:

SWITCH = 0003 causes the program to wait 3 ms between readings

13-3. CONTROL FOR A ROTARY SWITCH

Purpose: Another switch serves as a load switch for a four-position unencoded rotary switch. The CPU waits for the load switch to close (be zero), and then reads the position of the rotary switch. This procedure allows the operator to move the rotary switch to its final position before the CPU tries to read it. The program should place the position of the rotary switch into the variable SWITCH at memory location 6000. Debounce the load switch in software.

Sample Problem:

Place rotary switch in position 2. Close load switch.

Result: SWITCH – (6000) = 02

13-4. RECORD SWITCH POSITIONS ON LIGHTS

Purpose: A set of eight switches should have their positions reflected on eight LEDs. That is to say, if the switch is closed (zero), the LED should be on; otherwise, the LED should be off. Assume that the CPU output port is connected to the cathodes of the LEDs.

Sample Problem:

SWITCH 0 CLOSED	Result:	LED 0 ON
SWITCH 1 OPEN		LED 1 OFF
SWITCH 2 CLOSED		LED 2 ON
SWITCH 3 OPEN		LED 3 OFF
SWITCH 4 CLOSED		LED 4 OFF
SWITCH 5 OPEN		LED 5 ON
SWITCH 6 OPEN		LED 6 ON
SWITCH 7 OPEN		LED 7 OFF

How would you change the program so that a switch attached to bit 7 of port A on PIA #2 determines whether the displays are active (i.e., if the control switch is closed, the displays attached to Port B reflect the switches attached to Port A; if the control switch is open, the displays are always off)? A control switch is useful when the displays may distract the operator, as in an airplane.

How would you change the program to make the control switch an on-off pushbutton; that is, each closure inverts the previous state of the displays? Assume that the displays start in the active state and that the program examines and debounces the pushbutton before sending data to the displays.

13-5. COUNT ON A SEVEN-SEGMENT DISPLAY

Purpose: The program should count from 0 to 9 continuously on a seven-segment display, starting with zero.

Hint: Try different timing lengths for the displays and see what happens. When does the count become visible? What happens if the display is blanked part of the time?

13-6. SEPARATING CLOSURES FROM AN UNENCODED KEYBOARD

Purpose: The program should read entries from an unencoded 3 x 3 keyboard and save them in an array. The number of entries required is in the variable COUNT at memory location 6000 and the array is defined by the variable KEY at memory location 6001.

Sample Problem:

```
COUNT - (6000) = 04
Entries are 7,2,2,4

Results: KEY - (6001) = 07
               (6002) = 02
               (6003) = 02
               (6004) = 04
```

13-7. READ A SENTENCE FROM AN ENCODED KEYBOARD

Purpose: The program should read entries from an ASCII keyboard (7 bits with a zero parity bit) and place them in an array until it receives an ASCII period (hex 2E). The array is defined by the variable KEY at memory location 6001. Each entry is marked by a strobe as in Example 13-6.

Sample Problem:

Entries are HELLO.

```
Results: KEY - (6001) = 48  'H'
               (6002) = 45  'E'
               (6003) = 4C  'L'
               (6004) = 4C  'L'
               (6005) = 4F  'O'
               (6006) = 2E  '.'
```

13-8. A VARIABLE AMPLITUDE SQUARE WAVE GENERATOR

Purpose: The program should generate a square wave, as shown in the next figure, using a D/A converter. The variable SCALE at memory location 6000 contains the scaled amplitude of the wave. The variable LENGTH at memory location 6001 contains the length of a half cycle in milliseconds. The variable CYCLES at memory location 6002 contains the number of cycles.

Assume that a digital output of 80_{16} to the converter results in an analog output of zero volts. In general, a digital output of D results in an analog output of $(D-80)/80 \times -V_{REF}/4$ volts.

Sample Problem:

SCALE – (6000) = $A0_{16}$
LENGTH – (6001) = 04
CYCLES – (6002) = 03

(0040) = $A0_{16}$
(0041) = 04
(0042) = 03

Result:

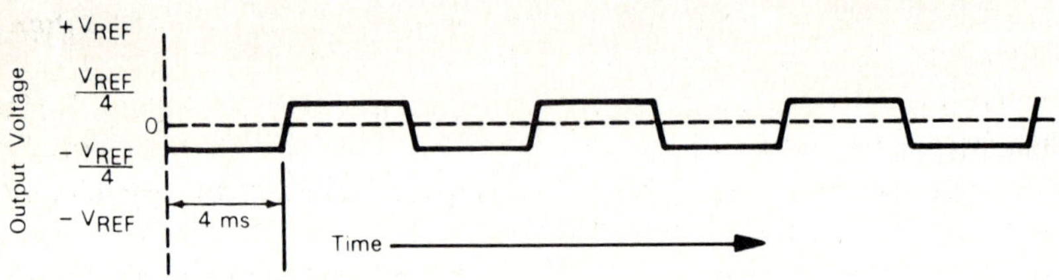

The base voltage is 80_{16} = 0 volts.
Full scale is $100_{16} = -V_{REF}$ volts.
So $A0_{16} = (A0-80)/80 \times (-V_{REF}) = -V_{REF}/4$

The program produces three pulses of amplitude $V_{REF}/4$ with a half cycle length of four milliseconds.

13-9. AVERAGING ANALOG READINGS

Purpose: The program should take four readings from an A/D converter 10 milliseconds apart and place the average in the variable DATA at memory location 6000. Assume that the A/D conversion time can be ignored.

Sample Problem:

Hexadecimal readings are 86, 89, 81, 84

Result: DATA – (6000) = 85_{16}

13-10. A 30 CHARACTER-PER-SECOND TERMINAL

Purpose: Modify the transmit and receive routines of Example 13-9 to handle a 30 cps terminal that transfers ASCII data with one stop bit and even parity. How could you write the routines to handle either terminal depending on a flag in the variable TTYTYPE at memory location 6000; e.g., TTYTYPE = 0 for the 30 cps terminal, and TTYTYPE = 1 for the 10 cps terminal?

REFERENCES

1. A. Osborne et al. *4 & 8 Bit Microprocessor Handbook.* Berkeley: Osborne/McGraw-Hill, 1981, pp. 9-45 through 9-54.
2. J. Gilmore and R. Huntington. "Designing with the 6820 Peripheral Interface Adapter," *Electronics,* December 23, 1976, pp. 85-86.
3. *The TTL Data Book for Design Engineers,* Texas Instruments, Inc., P.O. Box 5012, Dallas, TX 75222, pp. 7-151 through 7-156.
4. E. Dilatush. "Special Report; Numeric and Alphanumeric Displays," *EDN,* January 5, 1978, pp. 26-35.
5. *The TTL Data Book for Design Engineers,* Texas Instruments, Inc., P.O. Box 5012, Dallas, TX 75222, pp. 7-22 through 7-34.
6. A. Pshaenich. "Interface Considerations for Numeric Display Systems," Motorola Semiconductor Products, Inc., Application Note AN-741, Phoenix, Ariz. 1975.
7. Motorola Semiconductor Products Inc., *Microprocessor Applications Manual,* New York: McGraw-Hill, 1975, pp. 5-6 through 5-11 .
8. Motorola Semiconductor Products, Inc., *Microprocessor Applications Manual,* New York: McGraw-Hill, 1975, pp. 5-1 through 5-5.
9. See Reference 2.
10. G. Kane et al. *An Introduction to Microcomputers; Volume 3 — Some Real Support Devices,* Section E1. Berkeley: Osborne/McGraw-Hill, 1979.
11. E.R. Hnatek. *A User's Handbook of D/A and A/D Converters,* New York: Wiley, 1976.
12. P.H. Garrett. *Analog Systems for Microprocessors and Minicomputers,* Reston, Va.: Reston Publishing Co. (Prentice-Hall), 1978.
13. B. Amazeen. "Monolithic D-A Converter Operates on Single Supply," *Electronics,* February 28, 1980, pp. 125-31.
14. See Reference 11.
15. See Reference 12.
16. G. Kane et al. *An Introduction to Microcomputers: Volume 3 — Some Real Support Devices,* Section E2. Berkeley: Osborne/McGraw-Hill, 1979.
17. D. Aldridge. "Analog to Digital Conversion Techniques with the M6800 Microprocessor System," Motorola Semiconductor Products, Inc. Application Note AN-757, Phoenix, Ariz., 1975.
18. P. Bradshaw. "Two-Chip A/D Converter," *Electronic Design,* March 29, 1979, pp. 128-36.
19. M. Tuthill and D. P. Burton. "Low-Cost A/D Converter Links Easily with Microprocessors," *Electronics,* August 30, 1979, pp. 149-55.
20. For a discussion of UARTs, see P. Rony et al. "The Bugbook IIa," E and L Instruments Inc., 61 First Street, Derby, CT 06418, or D. G. Larsen et al. "INWAS: Interfacing with Asynchronous Serial Mode," *IEEE Transactions on Industrial Electronics and Control Instrumentation,* February 1977, pp. 2-12.
21. "Interface Between Data Terminal Equipment and Data Communications Equip-

ment Employing Serial Binary Data Interchange," EIA RS-232C, Electronic Industries Association, 2001 I Street N.W., Washington, D.C. 20006, August 1969.

G. Kane et al. *An Introduction to Microcomputers: Volume 3 — Some Real Support Devices,* Berkeley: Osborne/McGraw-Hill, 1978, pp. J5-9 through J5-14.

G. Pickles. "Who's Afraid of RS-232?", *Kilobaud,* May 1977, pp. 50-54.

C. A. Ogdin. "Microcomputer Buses — Part II," *Mini-Micro Systems,* July 1978, pp. 76-80.

14

Using the 6850 ACIA

The 6850 ACIA, or Asynchronous Communications Interface Adapter (see Figure 14-1), **is a UART specifically designed for use in MC68000, 6800, 6809, and 6502-based microcomputers. It occupies two memory addresses and contains two read-only registers (received data and status) and two write-only registers (transmitted data and control).** Tables 14-1 and 14-2 describe the contents of these registers.

ADDRESSING THE 6850 ACIA

The internal registers of the ACIA are addressed by means of the RS (register select) and R/W (read/write) lines (see Table 14-3). If, as is usual, RS is tied to the least significant bit of the MC68000's address bus, then the address of the data registers is one larger than the address of the control and status registers. The use of R/W for addressing means that read and write cycles access different registers, so the program can neither read the transmitted data or control registers nor write into the received data or status registers. If the program must recall what it stored in the write-only registers, it must retain a copy in RAM. **We will refer to the addresses as ACIADR (the receive data register when reading, the transmitted data register when writing), ACIASR (the read-only status register), and ACIACR (the write-only control register). ACIASR and ACIACR are the same physical address.**

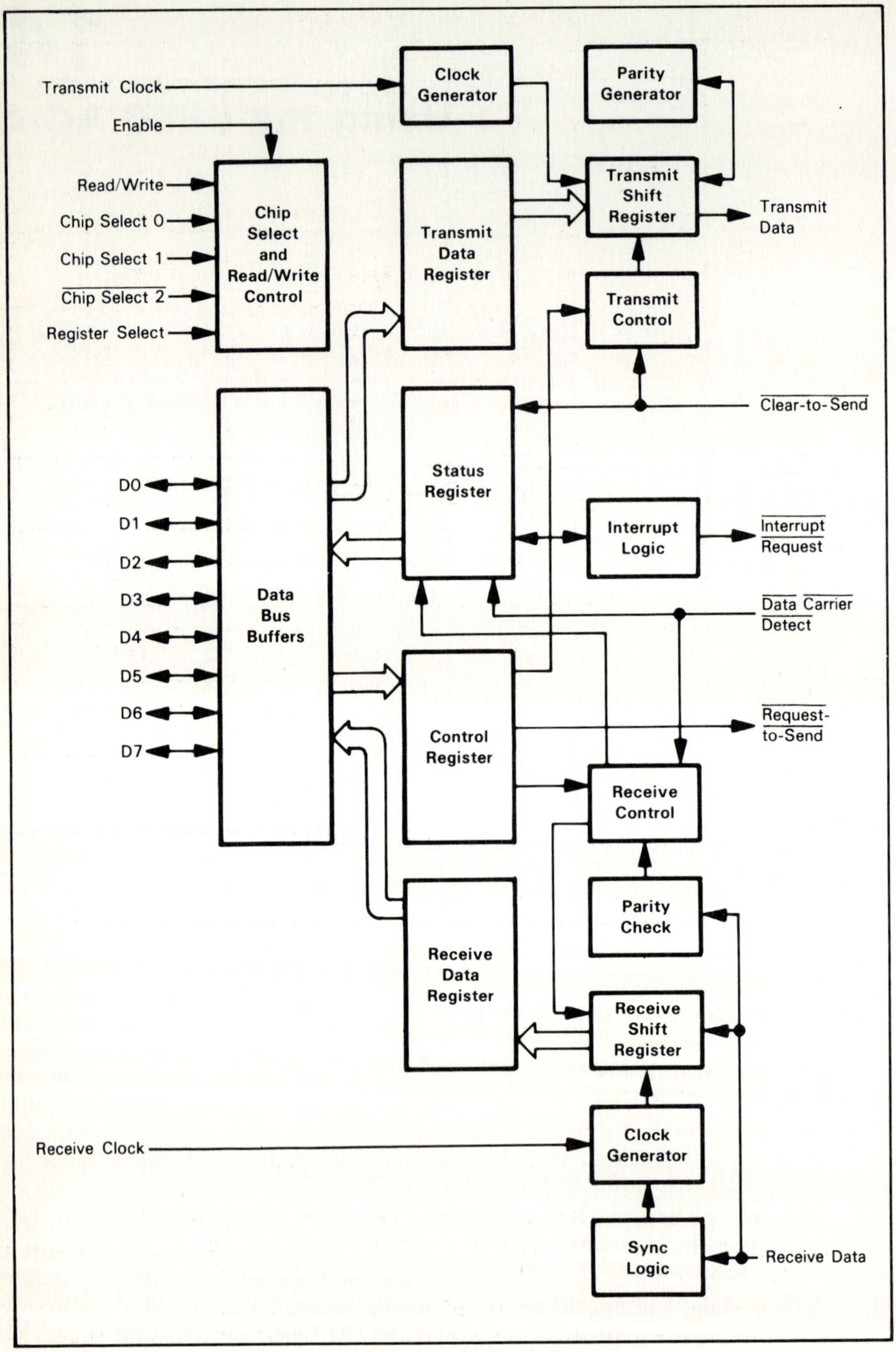

Figure 14-1. Block Diagram of the 6850 ACIA

Table 14-1. Definition of 6850 ACIA Register Contents

Data Bus Line Number	Buffer Address			
	$RS \cdot \overline{R/W}$ Transmit Data Register	$RS \cdot R/W$ Receive Data Register	$\overline{RS} \cdot \overline{R/W}$ Control Register	$\overline{RS} \cdot R/W$ Status Register
	(Write Only)	(Read Only)	(Write Only)	(Read Only)
0	Data Bit 0*	Data Bit 0	Counter Divide Select 1 (CR0)	Receive Data Register Full (RDRF)
1	Data Bit 1	Data Bit 1	Counter Divide Select 2 (CR1)	Transmit Data Register Empty (TDRE)
2	Data Bit 2	Data Bit 2	Word Select 1 (CR2)	Data Carrier Detect ($\overline{DCD}$)
3	Data Bit 3	Data Bit 3	Word Select 2 (CR3)	Clear-to-Send ($\overline{CTS}$)
4	Data Bit 4	Data Bit 4	Word Select 3 (CR4)	Framing Error (FE)
5	Data Bit 5	Data Bit 5	Transmit Control 1 (CR5)	Receiver Overrun (OVRN)
6	Data Bit 6	Data Bit 6	Transmit Control 2 (CR6)	Parity Error (PE)
7	Data Bit 7***	Data Bit 7**	Receive Interrupt Enable (CR7)	Interrupt Request (IRQ)

* Leading bit = LSB = Bit 0
** Data bit will be zero in 7-bit plus parity modes
*** Data bit is "don't care" in 7-bit plus parity modes

SPECIAL FEATURES

Note the following special features of the 6850 ACIA:

1. **Read and write cycles address physically distinct registers.** Therefore, you cannot use the ACIA registers as addresses for instructions which perform memory-to-memory operations such as OR to memory.
2. **The ACIA control register cannot be read by the CPU.** You will have to save a copy of the control register in memory if the program needs its value.
3. **The ACIA** has no reset input. It **can be reset only by placing ones in control**

Table 14-2. Meaning of the 6850 ACIA Control Register Bits

CR6	CR5	Function
0	0	$\overline{RTS}$ = low. Transmitting Interrupt Disabled
0	1	$\overline{RTS}$ = low. Transmitting Interrupt Enabled
1	0	$\overline{RTS}$ = high. Transmitting Interrupt Disabled
1	1	$\overline{RTS}$ = low. Transmits a Break level on the Transmit Data Output. Transmitting Interrupt Disabled

CR4	CR3	CR2	Function
0	0	0	7 Bits + Even Parity + 2 Stop Bits
0	0	1	7 Bits + Odd Parity + 2 Stop Bits
0	1	0	7 Bits + Even Parity + 1 Stop Bit
0	1	1	7 Bits + Odd Parity + 1 Stop Bit
1	0	0	8 Bits + 2 Stop Bits
1	0	1	8 Bits + 1 Stop Bit
1	1	0	8 Bits + Even Parity + 1 Stop Bit
1	1	1	8 Bits + Odd Parity + 1 Stop Bit

CR1	CR0	Function
0	0	÷1
0	1	÷16
1	0	÷64
1	1	Master Reset

Table 14-3. Internal Addressing for the 6850 ACIA

RS (Register Select)	R/W (Read/Write) 1 = Read, 0 = Write	Register Addressed	Indexed Offset from ACIA Control Register
0	0	Control Register (write-only)	0
0	1	Status Register (read-only)	0
1	0	Transmit Data Register (write-only)	1
1	1	Receive Data Register (read-only)	1

register bits 0 and 1. This procedure (called Master Reset) is necessary before the ACIA is used, in order to avoid having a random starting character.

4. **The RS-232 signals are all active-low.** Request-to-Send (RTS), in particular, should be brought high to make it inactive if it is not in use.
5. **The ACIA requires an external clock.** Typically, 4800 Hz is supplied and the 16 mode (control register bit 1 = 0, bit 0 = 1) is used. The ACIA will use the clock to center receiving in the middle of the bit time and to avoid false start bits caused by noise on the lines.
6. **The Data Ready (receive data register full, or RDRF) flag is bit 0 of the status register. The Peripheral Ready (transmit data register empty, or TDRE) flag is bit 1 of the status register.**

PROGRAM EXAMPLES

14-1. RECEIVE DATA FROM TTY

Purpose: Receive data from a teletypewriter using a 6850 ACIA and store the data in the string variable STRING starting at memory location 6000. Terminate input after a carriage return character is received.

Program 14-1:

```
       00006000      DATA     EQU      $6000
       00004000      PROGRAM  EQU      $4000

       0003FF01      ACIA     EQU      $3FF01                   ACIA BASE ADDRESS
       00000000      ACIACR   EQU      $0                       ACIA CONTROL REGISTER
       00000000      ACIASR   EQU      $0                       ACIA STATUS REGISTER
       00000002      ACIADR   EQU      $2                       ACIA DATA REGISTER
       00000015      AMODE    EQU      $45                      ACIA OPERATING MODE
       00000003      MRESET   EQU      $03                      ACIA MASTER RESET
       0000000D      CR       EQU      $0D                      ASCII CARRIAGE RETURN

       00006000               ORG      DATA

006000 00000050      STRING   DS.B     80                       STRING STORAGE

       00004000               ORG      PROGRAM

004000 207C0003FF01  PGM14_1  MOVEA.L  #ACIA,A0                 ADDRESS OF ACIA
004006 117C00030000           MOVE.B   #MRESET,ACIACR(A0)       ACIA MASTER RESET
00400C 117C00150000           MOVE.B   #AMODE,ACIACR(A0)        ACIA OPERATING MODE

004012 327C00006000           MOVEA.W  #STRING,A1               ADDRESS OF INPUT STRING
004018 6108          LOOP     BSR.S    INCH                     READ CHARACTER
00401A 0C19000D               CMPI.B   #CR,(A1)+                CHECK FOR CARRIAGE RETURN
00401E 66F8                   BNE.S    LOOP                     NOT CR, CONTINUE STRING INPUT

004020 4E75                   RTS


004022 10280000      INCH     MOVE.B   ACIASR(A0),D0            READ ACIA STATUS REGISTER
004026 E208                   LSR.B    #1,D0                    TEST FOR RECEIVE REGISTER EMPTY
004028 64F8                   BCC.S    INCH                     NO, CONTINUE CHECKING
00402A 12A80002               MOVE.B   ACIADR(A0),(A1)          READ CHARACTER
00402E 4E75                   RTS

                              END      PGM14_1
```

The program must reset the ACIA initially by placing ones in control register bits 0 and 1. The ACIA does have an internal power-on reset which holds the ACIA in an inoperative state until master reset is applied.

The program determines the operating mode of the ACIA by setting the bits in the control register as follows:

Bit 7 = 0 to disable the receiver interrupt
Bit 6 = 1, Bit 5 = 0 to make Request-to-Send (RTS) high (inactive) and to disable the transmitter interrupt
Bit 4 = 0 for 7-bit words
Bit 3 = 0, Bit 2 = 1 for odd parity with 2 stop bits
Bit 1 = 0, Bit 0 = 1 for 16 clock (4800 Hz must be supplied)

The received data status flag is bit 0 of the ACIA status register. What would happen if we tried to replace

```
MOVE.B   ACIASR(A0),D0
LSR.B    #1,D0
```

with the single instruction

```
LSR      ACIASR(A0)
```

Remember that the status and control registers share an address but are physically distinct, and are selected by the R/W (read/write) line.

Try adding an error-checking routine to the program. Set

```
(STATUS) = 0 if no errors occurred
         = 1 if a parity error occurred
           (Status register bit 6 = 1)
         = 2 if an overrun error occurred
           (Status register bit 5 = 1)
         = 3 if a framing error occurred
           (Status register bit 4 = 1)
```

Assume that the priority of the errors is from higher order bits to lower order bits in the ACIA status register (i.e., parity errors have priority over overrun errors which, in turn, have priority over framing errors if more than one error has occurred).

14-2. SEND DATA TO TTY

Purpose: Send data from the string variable STRING at memory location 6000 to a teletypewriter using a 6850 ACIA. The string is terminated by a carriage return character.

Program 14-2:

```
       00006000       DATA     EQU      $6000
       00004000       PROGRAM  EQU      $4000

       0003FF01       ACIA     EQU      $3FF01              ACIA BASE ADDRESS
       00000000       ACIACR   EQU      $0                  ACIA CONTROL REGISTER
       00000000       ACIASR   EQU      $0                  ACIA STATUS REGISTER
       00000002       ACIADR   EQU      $2                  ACIA DATA REGISTER
       00000015       AMODE    EQU      $45                 ACIA OPERATING MODE
       00000003       MRESET   EQU      $03                 ACIA MASTER RESET
       00000001       TDRE     EQU      $1                  ACIA TRANSMIT DATA REGISTER EMPTY
       0000000D       CR       EQU      $0D                 ASCII CARRIAGE RETURN

       00006000                ORG      DATA

006000 00000050       STRING   DS.B     80                  STRING STORAGE

       00004000                ORG      PROGRAM

004000 207C0003FF01   PGM14_2  MOVEA.L  #ACIA,A0            ADDRESS OF ACIA
004006 117C00030000            MOVE.B   #MRESET,ACIACR(A0)  ACIA MASTER RESET
00400C 117C00150000            MOVE.B   #AMODE,ACIACR(A0)   ACIA OPERATING MODE

004012 327C00006000            MOVEA.W  #STRING,A1          ADDRESS OF OUTPUT STRING
004018 6108           LOOP     BSR.S    OUTCH               OUTPUT CHARACTER
00401A 0C19000D                CMPI.B   #CR,(A1)+           CHECK FOR CARRIAGE RETURN
00401E 66F8                    BNE      LOOP                NOT CR, CONTINUE STRING OUTPUT

004020 4E75                    RTS

004022 082800010000   OUTCH    BTST.B   #TDRE,ACIASR(A0)    READY TO SEND
```

```
004028 67F8              BEQ.S    OUTCH                 NO, CONTINUE CHECKING
00402A 11510002          MOVE.B   (A1),ACIADR(A0)       SEND CHARACTER
00402E 4E75              RTS

                         END      PGM14_2
```

The transmitter status flag is bit 1 of the ACIA status register. The bit test instruction is convenient here, since it tests a specific bit without changing the contents of the ACIA status register. How could you modify the receive program to use the Bit Test instruction?

REFERENCES

1. A. Osborne and Gerry Kane. *4 & 8-Bit Microprocessor Handbook,* Berkeley: Osborne/McGraw-Hill, 1981, pp. 9-55 through 9-61.
2. K. Fronheiser. "Device Operation and System Implementation of the Asynchronous Communications Interface Adapter," Motorola Semiconductor Products, Inc. Application Note AN-754, Phoenix, AZ, 1975.
3. J. Volp. "Software Switches Baud Rate," *EDN,* November 5, 1979, p. 83.

15
Interrupts And Other Exceptions

Interrupts are inputs that the CPU examines as part of each instruction cycle. These inputs allow the CPU to react to asynchronous events more efficiently than by polling devices. The use of interrupts generally involves more hardware than does ordinary (programmed) I/O, but interrupts provide a faster and more direct response.[1]

In the MC68000, interrupts are but one category of events described as *exceptions.* Although this nomenclature is not used in other microprocessors, it is rather appropriate with the MC68000 since the number and types of events that can initiate *exception processing* extend well beyond the typical external interrupt requests. Nonetheless, before proceeding to describe the complete exception processing system provided by MC68000, let us discuss some general characteristics and considerations of interrupts since these are the most commonly encountered exceptions.

Why use interrupts? **Interrupts allow events such as alarms, power failure, the passage of a certain amount of time, and peripherals having data or being ready to accept data to get the immediate attention of the CPU. The program does not have to examine (poll) every potential source, nor need the programmer worry about the system missing events.**

An interrupt system is like the bell on a telephone — it rings when a call comes in so that you don't have to pick up the receiver occasionally to see if someone is on the line. The CPU can go about its normal business (and get a lot more done). When something happens, the interrupt alerts the CPU and forces it to service the input before resuming normal operations. Of course, this simple description becomes more complicated (just like a telephone switchboard) when there are many interrupts of varying importance and when there are tasks that cannot be interrupted.

CHARACTERISTICS OF INTERRUPT SYSTEMS

The implementation of interrupt systems varies greatly. Among the questions that characterize a particular system are:

1. How many interrupt inputs are there?
2. How does the CPU respond to an interrupt?
3. How does the CPU determine the source of an interrupt if the number of sources exceeds the number of inputs?
4. Can the CPU differentiate between important and unimportant interrupts?
5. How and when is the interrupt system enabled and disabled?

There are many different answers to these questions. The aim of all the implementations, however, is to have the CPU respond rapidly to interrupts and resume normal activity afterwards.

The number of interrupt inputs on the CPU chip determines the number of different responses that the CPU can produce without any additional hardware or software. Each input can produce a different internal response.

The ultimate response of the CPU to an interrupt must be to transfer control to the correct interrupt service routine and to save the current value of the program counter. The CPU must therefore execute the equivalent of a Jump-to-Subroutine or Call instruction with the beginning of the interrupt service routine as its address. This action will save the return address in the stack and transfer control to the interrupt service routine. The amount of external hardware required to produce this response varies greatly. Some CPUs internally generate the instruction and the address; others require external hardware to form them. The CPU can generate a different instruction or address only for each different input.

Polling and Vectoring

If the number of interrupting devices exceeds the number of inputs, the CPU will need extra hardware or software to identify the source of the interrupt. In the simplest case, the software can be a polling routine which checks the status of the devices that may be interrupting. The only advantage of such a system over normal polling is that the CPU knows that at least one device is active. **The alternative solution is for additional hardware to provide a unique data input (or "vector") for each source.** The two alternatives can be mixed; the vectors can identify groups of inputs from which the CPU can identify a particular one by polling.

Priority

An interrupt system that can differentiate between important and unimportant interrupts is called a "priority interrupt system." Internal hardware can provide as many priority levels as there are inputs. External hardware can provide additional levels through the use of a priority register and comparator. The external hardware does not allow the interrupt to reach the CPU unless its priority is higher than the contents of the priority register. A priority interrupt system may need a special way to handle low priority interrupts that may be ignored for long periods of time.

Enabling and Disabling

Most interrupt systems can be enabled or disabled. In fact, most CPUs automatically disable interrupts when a RESET is performed (so the startup routine can initialize the interrupt system) and when they accept an interrupt (so that another interrupt will not interrupt the same service routine). The programmer may wish to disable interrupts while preparing or processing data, performing a timing loop, or executing a multibyte operation.

An interrupt that cannot be disabled (sometimes called a "nonmaskable interrupt") may be useful to warn of power failure, an event that obviously must take precedence over all other activities.

Disadvantages of Interrupts

The advantages of interrupts are obvious, but there are also disadvantages. These include:

1. Interrupt systems may require a large amount of extra hardware.
2. Interrupts still require data transfers under program control through the CPU. There is no speed advantage as there is with DMA.
3. Interrupts are random inputs, which make debugging and testing difficult. Errors may occur sporadically, and therefore may be very hard to locate and correct.[2]
4. Interrupts may involve a large amount of overhead if many registers must be saved and the source must be determined by polling.

THE MC68000 EXCEPTION PROCESSING SYSTEM

The MC68000 provides extensive exception processing logic including a very complete set of external interrupts as well as internally initiated exceptions upon detection of various faults, traps, and so on.

OPERATING MODES

Before proceeding to describe the exception processing system, let us discuss the operating modes of the MC68000, since these affect exception processing. As we mentioned previously, **the MC68000 can operate in either a supervisor mode or a user mode. When the MC68000 is reset** using the RESET input, it starts operating in the supervisor mode. **The processor operates in supervisor mode until one of the following instructions is executed:** Return from Exception **(RTE)**, Move to status register **(MOVE word to SR)**, AND Immediate to status register **(ANDI word to SR)**, and Exclusive OR Immediate to status register **(EORI word to SR)**. None of these instructions automatically causes the transition to the user mode of operation — rather, they are capable of changing the state of the S-bit in the status register. **If one of these instructions resets the S-bit, the MC68000 will begin operating in the user mode.**

Once the MC68000 is operating in the user mode, the only thing that can cause a transition back to the supervisor mode is an exception. All initial exception processing is performed in supervisor mode regardless of the current setting of the S-bit of the status register at the time of the exceptions. When the exception processing has been completed, the Return from Exception (RTE) instruction allows return to the User mode.

A number of instructions, designated as "privileged," are reserved for the supervisor mode. An attempt to execute one of these instructions in the user mode results in a "privilege violation" which is one type of exception. We will discuss these instructions and the privilege violation response later in this chapter.

EXCEPTION TYPES

The response of the MC68000 to the various types of exceptions is similar. Before we describe this response, let us look at the sources of exceptions since they go well beyond those provided by other microprocessors.

Exceptions originate in a variety of ways which can be divided into two general categories:

1. **Internally generated exceptions** that result from the execution of certain instructions, or from internally detected errors.
2. **Externally generated exceptions** which include bus errors, reset, and interrupt requests.

Internally Generated Exceptions

The internally generated exceptions to which the MC68000 responds can be further subdivided into three categories: internally detected errors, instruction traps, and the trace function.

The following are the internally detected errors which will cause the MC68000 to initiate exception processing:

1. **Addressing errors.** Any attempt by the MC68000 attempts to access word data, long word data, or an instruction at an odd address is an address error, since all such accesses must be on even address boundaries.
2. **Privilege violations.** Again, some instructions are reserved for use only in the supervisor mode. Exception processing will be initiated if you attempt to execute any of the following instructions when in the User mode: STOP, RESET, RTE, MOVE to SR, AND (word) Immediate to SR, EOR (word) Immediate to SR, OR (word) Immediate to SR, MOVE USP.
3. **Illegal and unimplemented opcodes.** If an instruction is fetched whose bit pattern is not one of the defined instruction bit patterns for the MC68000, exception processing will be initiated. Two bit patterns are defined as unimplemented rather than illegal; if bits 15-12 are 1010 or 1111, these are treated as unimplemented instruction opcodes. If these opcodes are fetched, special exception processing is initiated which can allow you to simulate unimplemented instructions in your own software.

Instruction traps are exceptions which are caused by the execution of instruc-

tions in your program. There is a standard TRAP instruction which is similar to the Z8000 System Call instruction. **There are four other instructions — TRAPV, CHK, DIVS, and DIVU — which will cause exception processing to be initiated** if certain conditions, such as arithmetic overflows or divide by zero, are detected.

The third type of internally generated exception occurs when the MC68000 is operating with the trace function. If the T-bit in the Status register is set, exception processing will be performed after each instruction. The Trace function is used for program debugging since you can analyze, by stepping through the program, the results of each instruction's execution.

Externally Generated Exceptions

There are three different types of externally generated exceptions:

1. **Bus errors.** When the BERR signal is asserted by external logic (and the processor is not halted), exception processing is initiated.
2. **Reset.** When the RESET signal is asserted by external logic, exception processing is initiated.
3. **Interrupt request.** This is the most familiar form of exception processing and is initiated by external logic via the three interrupt request lines (IPL0, IPL1, and IPL2).

Exception Priorities

The different types of exceptions have different priorities, and processing of an exception depends on its priority. The following table lists the types of exceptions according to their relative priorities, and also defines when processing of each type begins.

Group	Priority	Exception Source	Exception Processing Response
0	Highest	Reset Bus Error Address Error	Abort current cycle, then process exception
1		Trace Interrupt Request Illegal/Unimplemented Opcode Privilege Violation	Complete current instruction, then process exception
2	Lowest	TRAP, TRAPV CHK Divide-by-zero	Instruction execution initiates exception processing

The highest priority types of exceptions are Reset, Bus Error, and Address Error. Any of these exceptions will cause immediate termination of the current instruction, even within a bus cycle. The next group of exceptions — trace, interrupt requests, illegal/unimplemented instructions, and privilege violations — allow completion of the current instruction before initiating exception processing. Note that interrupt requests include an additional prioritization which we will discuss later. The lowest priority of exceptions are those that are caused by trap-type instructions. These instructions can initiate exception processing as part of their formal execution. All of the instruction trap exceptions have equal priority since it is impossible for two instructions to be executed at the same time.

Exception Vector Table

Central to the MC68000 exception processing sequence is a vector table that occupies 1024 bytes (512 sixteen-bit words) of memory. This table occupies memory addresses 000000_{16} through $0003FF_{16}$. **Figure 15-1 illustrates the exception vector table.** The table is organized as 256 four-byte vectors. Each vector is a 32-bit address which will be loaded into the program counter as part of the exception processing sequence.

As you can see, a number of the vector table entries serve the defined types of exceptions which we have discussed. Other entries of the vector table are reserved for use by Motorola and should not be used by your program if compatibility with future Motorola software and hardware is desired. The first 64 exception vectors have predefined uses; this leaves 192 vectors available to user defined external interrupt requests — this should be more than enough for most applications. (Of course, in this case, "user" means the microcomputer designer, not the assembly language programmer.) However, the first 64 vector locations are not protected by the MC68000; thus they can be used by external interrupts if a system requires it.

EXCEPTION PROCESSING SEQUENCES

The general sequence of events performed by the MC68000 in response to an exception is the same regardless of the source of the exception. There are, however, some differences. Let us begin by examining the response to internally generated exceptions.

Internally Generated Exception Processing

If exception processing is initiated as a result of either the trace function, a TRAP instruction, an illegal or unimplemented opcode, or a privilege violation, the following steps occur:

1. The status register contents are copied into an internal register.
2. The S-bit in the status register is set, thus placing the MC68000 in the supervisor mode of operation.
3. The T-bit in the status register is reset to disable tracing to allow for continuous execution of the interrupt service routine when debugging using TRACE.
4. The program counter contents are pushed onto the supervisor stack.
5. The previously copied status register contents are pushed onto the supervisor stack.
6. The new program counter contents are taken from the appropriate location in the interrupt vector table.

Memory Addresses (Hex)	16 Bits	
000000	SSP (High)	Reset - Initial SSP
000002	SSP (Low)	
000004	PC0 (High)	Reset - Initial PC
000006	PC0 (Low)	
000008	PC2 (High)	Vector 2 - Bus Error
00000A	PC2 (Low)	
00000C	PC3 (High)	Vector 3 - Address Error
00000E	PC3 (Low)	
000010	PC4 (High)	Vector 4 - Illegal Instruction
000012	PC4 (Low)	
000014	PC5 (High)	Vector 5 - Divide by 0
000016	PC5 (Low)	
000018	PC6 (High)	Vector 6 - CHK Instruction
00001A	PC6 (Low)	
00001C	PC7 (High)	Vector 7 - TRAPV Instruction
00001E	PC7 (Low)	
000020	PC8 (High)	Vector 8 - Privilege Violation
000022	PC8 (Low)	
000024	PC9 (High)	Vector 9 - Trace
000026	PC9 (Low)	
000028	PC10 (High)	Vector 10_{10} - Opcode 1010 Emulation
00002A	PC10 (Low)	
00002C	PC11 (High)	Vector 11_{10} - Opcode 1111 Emulation
00002E	PC11 (Low)	
000030	PC12 (High)	Vector 12_{10} (Vectors 12_{10}–23_{10}: Reserved by Motorola)
000032	PC12 (Low)	
⋮	⋮	
00005C	PC23 (High)	Vector 23_{10}
00005E	PC23 (Low)	
000060	PC24 (High)	Vector 24_{10} - Spurious Interrupt
000062	PC24 (Low)	
000064	PC25 (High)	Vector 25_{10} - Level 1 Interrupt (Vectors 25_{10}–31_{10}: Auto-Vector Interrupts)
000066	PC25 (Low)	
000068	PC26 (High)	Vector 26_{10} - Level 2 Interrupt
00006A	PC26 (Low)	
00006C	PC27 (High)	Vector 27_{10} - Level 3 Interrupt
00006E	PC27 (Low)	
000070	PC28 (High)	Vector 28_{10} - Level 4 Interrupt
000072	PC28 (Low)	
000074	PC29 (High)	Vector 29_{10} - Level 5 Interrupt
000076	PC29 (Low)	
000078	PC30 (High)	Vector 30_{10} - Level 6 Interrupt
00007A	PC30 (Low)	
00007C	PC31 (High)	Vector 31_{10} - Level 7 Interrupt
00007E	PC31 (Low)	
000080	PC32 (High)	Vector 32_{10} (Vectors 32_{10}–47_{10}: TRAP Instruction Vectors)
000082	PC32 (Low)	
⋮	⋮	
0000BC	PC47 (High)	Vector 47_{10}
0000BE	PC47 (Low)	
0000C0	PC48 (High)	Vector 48_{10} (Vectors 48_{10}–63: Reserved by Motorola)
0000C2	PC48 (Low)	
⋮	⋮	
0000FC	PC63 (High)	Vector 63
0000FE	PC63 (Low)	
000100	PC64 (High)	Vector 64 (Vectors 64–255: User Interrupt Vectors)
000102	PC64 (Low)	
⋮	⋮	
0003FC	PC255 (High)	Vector 255
0003FE	PC255 (Low)	

Figure 15-1. Exception Vector Table

7. Instruction execution then begins at the location indicated by the new contents of the program counter; this will be the first instruction of the exception processing program you have provided for that particular type of exception.

Bus and Address Error Exception Processing

The way in which the MC68000 responds to an exception caused by a bus error or address error includes several steps in addition to those described in the preceding paragraphs. First, either of these errors causes immediate termination of the bus cycle in progress. The next steps are the following:

1. The contents of the status register are copied into an internal register.
2. The S-bit in the status register is set, placing the MC68000 in the supervisor mode.
3. The T-bit in the status register is reset to disable trace operations.
4. The contents of the program counter are pushed onto the supervisor stack.
5. The previously copied contents of the status register are pushed onto the supervisor stack.
6. The contents of the MC68000's instruction register, which constitute the first word of the instruction that was in progress when the bus error occurred, are pushed onto the supervisor stack.
7. The 32-bit address that was being used for the bus cycle which was terminated is also pushed onto the supervisor stack.
8. A word which provides information as the the type of cycle that was in progress at the time of the error is pushed onto the supervisor stack.
9. The program counter contents are taken from the appropriate interrupt vector — either the bus error vector or address error vector of the exception vector table.
10. Instruction execution resumes at the location indicated by the new contents of the program counter.

Figure 15-2 shows the order in which information is pushed onto the supervisor stack as part of the exception processing for bus and address errors. The value saved for the program counter is advanced two to ten bytes beyond the address of the first word of the instruction where the error occurred according to the length of that instruction and its addressing information, if any.

If the error occurs during the fetch of the next instruction, the value saved for the program counter is near the current instruction, even if the current instruction is a jump, branch or return instruction. This feature, missing from most computers, will make the detection of many errors easier.

As you can see in Figure 15-2, **the five least significant bits of the last word pushed onto the stack provide information as to the type of access that was in progress when the bus error or address error occurred.** The three least significant bits are a copy of the function code outputs during the aborted bus cycle. Bit 3 indicates the type of processing that was in progress when the error occurred. This bit is set for Group 0 or 1 exception processing and reset for Group 2 exception and normal instruction processing (see the exception priority table shown earlier). Bit 4 indicates whether a read

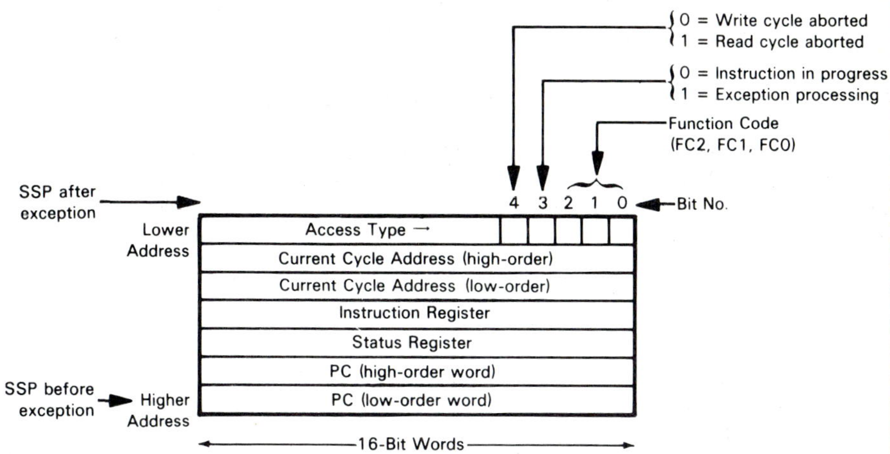

Function Code	Type of Cycle
0	Unassigned
1	User Data
2	User Program
3	Unassigned
4	Unassigned
5	Supervisor Data
6	Supervisor Program
7	Interrupt Acknowledgment

Figure 15-2. System Stack After Bus Error or Address Error Exception

(bit 4 set) or write (bit 4 reset) cycle was in progress when the error occurred. If an error occurs during the exception processing of a preceding bus error, address error, or reset operation, the MC68000 will enter the Halt state and remain there.

All of the information that is pushed onto the supervisor stack as part of the bus and address error exception processing sequence is intended to aid you in analyzing possible sources of the error. Either of these errors implies a serious system failure and it is not likely that you will be able to return to normal program execution.

Reset Exception Processing

An external reset causes a special type of exception processing. After an external RESET has been signalled the following steps occur:

1. The S-bit in the status register is set, placing the MC68000 in the supervisor mode.
2. The T-bit in the status register is reset to disable the trace function.

3. All three interrupt mask bits in the status register are set, thus specifying the interrupt priority mask at level seven.
4. The supervisor stack pointer is loaded with the contents of the first four bytes of memory (addresses 000000-000003).
5. The program counter is loaded from the next four bytes of memory (addresses 00004-00007).
6. Instruction execution commences at the address indicated by the new contents of the program counter, which should reference your power-up/reset initialization program.

Interrupt Request Exception Processing

The last type of exception processing we will discuss is the sequence initiated by the standard interrupt request. An external device requests an interrupt by encoding an interrupt request level on the interrupt inputs. The MC68000 compares these inputs to the interrupt mask bits in the status register. If the encoded priority level is less than or equal to the one specified by the three-bit mask, the interrupt request will not be recognized by the MC68000. **If the encoded interrupt level is higher priority than the level established by the interrupt mask (or if a level seven interrupt request is input) then the interrupt will be processed.** The MC68000 responds to the allowed interrupt request as soon as it completes the instruction execution currently in progress. **Upon completion of the current instruction, the following steps occur:**

1. The contents of the status register are saved internally.
2. The S-bit in the status register is set, placing the MC68000 in the supervisor mode.
3. The T-bit in the status register is reset to disable the trace function.
4. The interrupt mask bits in the status register are changed to the level of the interrupt request that is encoded on the interrupt inputs. This allows the current interrupt to be processed without being interrupted by lower priority events or events at the same level.
5. The MC68000 then performs an interrupt acknowledgement bus cycle. This cycle serves two functions; first, the processor lets the requesting device know that its interrupt request is being serviced, and second, the processor fetches an exception vector byte from the requesting device. After the vector byte has been read from the interupting device, the MC68000 proceeds with the following exception processing steps.
6. The contents of the program counter are pushed onto the supervisor stack.
7. The contents of the previously saved status register are pushed onto the supervisor stack.
8. The program counter is loaded with four bytes of data from the appropriate location in the exception vector table as defined by the exception vector byte.

After the program counter has been loaded with the new value from the exception vector table, instruction execution commences at the location indicated by the new contents of the program counter; this will be the first instruction of your interrupt processing routine for the particular device requesting the interrupt.

Autovector Interrupt Response

A variation on interrupt request processing is the autovector response. If you refer back to Figure 15-1, you will see that seven vector locations are provided in the exception vector table for autovectors, corresponding to the seven interrupt priority levels. These vectors will be used if the device requesting an interrupt responds to the interrupt acknowledge bus cycle by asserting the Valid Peripheral Address (VPA) signal to the CPU instead of supplying a byte of vector data. The processor will then use the autovector from the exception vector table which corresponds to the interrupt level to obtain a new program counter value. This autovector response was provided specifically to emulate the interrupt sequence expected by 6800 family peripheral devices. Of course a non-6800 family device in the system could also exploit this autovector capability should it be advantageous.

PROGRAM EXAMPLE

15-1. STARTUP

Purpose: Power up the computer and wait for a PIA interrupt to occur before starting actual operation.

When power is applied to an MC68000 system, the processor is reset and starts its initialization process. On RESET, the processor is placed in supervisor state and the interrupt priority mask is set to inhibit all interrupts except level seven. The supervisor stack pointer is loaded with the first two words of the reset exception vector at memory location 0. The program counter is loaded with the next two words from low memory and execution then starts at the instruction whose address is contained in the program counter.

Flowchart:

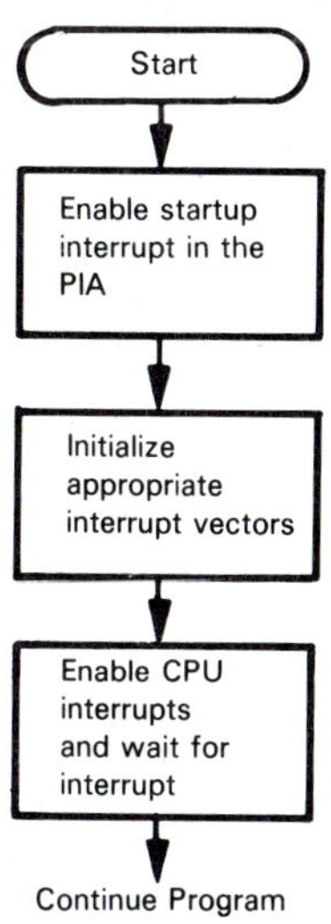

Program 15-1:

```
                00004000         POWER:      EQU       $4000
                00004600         SERVICE:    EQU       $4600
                00005100         STACK:      EQU       $5100
                00006000         DATA:       EQU       $6000

                0003FF40         PIADDA:     EQU       $3FF40            DATA DIRECTION REGISTER A
                0003FF40         PIADA:      EQU       $3FF40            DATA REGISTER A
                0003FF44         PIACA:      EQU       $3FF44            CONTROL REGISTER A
                00000005         PIA_EN:     EQU       $05               PIA INTERRUPT ENABLE
                00002000         IMSKO:      EQU       $2000             SUPERVISOR/INTERRUPT LEVEL 0
                00000064         SVECTOR:    EQU       $64               ADDRESS OF INTERRUPT VECTOR

                00000000                     ORG       0

000000          00005100                     DC.L      STACK             ADDRESS OF STACK
000004          00004000                     DC.L      PGM15_1           ADDRESS OF RESET PROGRAM

                00004000                     ORG       POWER

004000          13FC0005
                    00003FF44 PGM15_1:       MOVE.B    #PIA_EN,PIACA     ENABLE INTERRUPT FROM STARTUP PIA
004008          21FC00004600
                    0064                     MOVE.L    #STARTUP,SVECTOR  INITIALIZE PIA VECTOR
004010          4E722000                     STOP      #IMSKO            ENABLE INTERRUPTS AND WAIT FOR INTE

                             * STARTUP INTERRUPT SERVICE ROUTINE

                00004600                     ORG       SERVICE
004600          4A390003FF40 STARTUP:        TST.B     PIADA             CLEAR STARTUP INTERRUPT
004606          4E73                         RTE                         RETURN TO INTERRUPTED ROUTINE

                                             END       PGM15_1
```

If this program is stored in Read Only Memory (ROM) or Programmable ROM (PROM), when a power on RESET occurs, the supervisor stack will be loaded with 5100 and the program counter with 4000, the address of the startup program. The status register will have its supervisor and interrupt level bits set. Once these three registers have been set up, program execution commences at location 4000 just as in the examples in previous chapters.

Unlike other exception vectors, the reset vector must be in ROM or PROM. The same is true for the initial program to be executed. You must ensure that valid RAM and ROM addresses are referenced by the stack pointer and program counter entries in the reset vector.

All other exception vectors may be located in either RAM or ROM. The design of your system determines which is best for you. In our example, the exception vectors are in RAM. Therefore, they must be initialized with the addresses of the associated service routines prior to the occurrance of any exception.

The instruction MOVE.L #STARTUP,SVECTOR initializes the exception vector associated with the PIA. In our example, interrupts from the PIA are of low priority and have been assigned a priority of level 1. Since the PIA (and also the ACIA) do not support vector numbers, their interrupts are handled by the MC68000's autovectoring. As shown in Figure 15-1, the autovectors start at address 64. Address 64 is the location of Level 1 autovector interrupts and this is the vector in which we store the address of our service routine.

If you forget to initialize an exception vector, the processor will still use the contents of the vector to determine the starting address of the exception handler. However, this address will be invalid and the processor would continue execution at this invalid address. **You must initialize exception vectors, just as you initialize certain program data before use.**

In addition to setting up the exception vector, the program's only other action is to enable the interrupt from the startup PIA. The program enables that interrupt by setting bit 0 of the PIA control register and then enabling processor interrupts.

Finally, the program is ready to wait for the start-up interrupt. Instead of waiting for the interrupt by executing an endless loop such as jump-to-self (LOOP: JMP LOOP), the instruction STOP could be executed. STOP causes the processor to stop executing instructions and wait for an interrupt or exception (TRACE or RESET). The STOP instruction also allows you to change the processor's interrupt level, since the data word following the STOP is loaded into the status register. In order to allow interrupts, the interrupt level must be changed from level 7 (set during RESET) to level 0 (one level less than the startup PIA's level 1). Priority level 0 allows the processor to recognize interrupts at any level. The data word must also have the bit corresponding to the status register's Supervisor Mode (S) bit set.

The STOP instruction is one of the few MC68000 instructions which can only be executed in supervisor mode. If executed in user mode, a privilege violation exception will occur. (Generally, instructions which attempt to change the processor's interrupt level, supervisor/user state, or user stack pointer are privileged instructions.)

When an interrupt is generated from the PIA, the exception process is initiated. First, the contents of the full status register are saved on top of the supervisor stack followed by the contents of the program counter. The program counter is pointing to the next instruction to be executed, in this example the address of the instruction following the STOP instruction. The processor is set to supervisor state and the priority interrupt level is set to the level of the interrupt being processed. Next the processor fetches the address of the interrupt handler from the associated interrupt vector. Since we are expecting an autovector level 1 interrupt, the associated vector is located at address 64.

Upon entry to the interrupt service routine at location STARTUP, the priority level will be 1 and the processor will be in supervisor mode. Since the priority level has now changed, other interrupts of level 1 priority will be masked from interrupting the processor. What would happen if the STOP instruction had set the priority level to 1?

The service routine clears the startup interrupt by reading the appropriate PIA data register. This operation is necessary, even though no data transfer is required. Otherwise the startup interrupt would remain active and would interrupt again as soon as level 1 interrupts were reenabled.

The TST instruction is used to clear the interrupt since it does not modify any registers except the condition code register. **The exception process does not save any data or address registers. If the exception service routine needs to use any registers, they must be saved upon entry and restored upon exit from the routine.**

RTE restores control to the interrupted program sequence at the instruction following the STOP. As part of the restoration process, the supervisor/user state and interrupt priority level are reset to their states prior to the interrupt by pulling the previously copied status register contents from the stack. Next, the previous value of the program counter is pulled from the stack and loaded into the program counter. No other registers except the program counter and status register are modified by RTE. Like STOP, RTE is a privileged instruction and can only be executed in supervisor state.

This program assumes that there are no other level 1 interrupts being generated. If other level 1 interrupts can occur, a polling routine would have to be added to the interrupt handler and the main program would have to be modified. How would you do this?

15-2. A KEYBOARD INTERRUPT

Purpose: The main program clears the variable FLAG at memory location 6000 and waits for a keyboard interrupt. The interrupt service routine sets FLAG to 1 and places the data from the keyboard in the variable KEY at memory location 6001.

Sample Problem:

	Keyboard data = 43	
Result:	FLAG - (6000) = 01	Flag indicating new keyboard data
	KEY - (6001) = 43	Keyboard data

Flowchart:

Main Program:

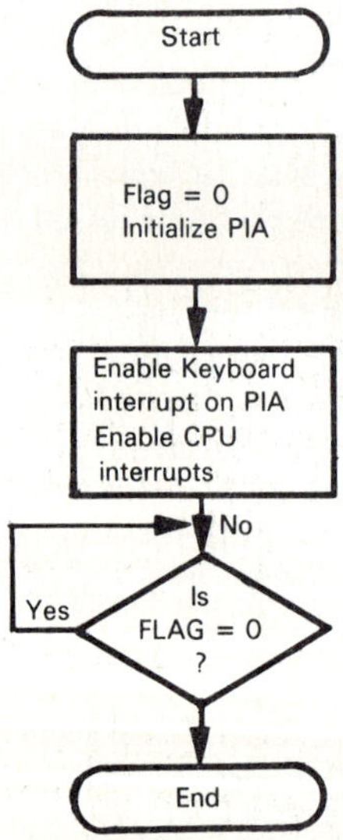

Interrupt Service Routine:

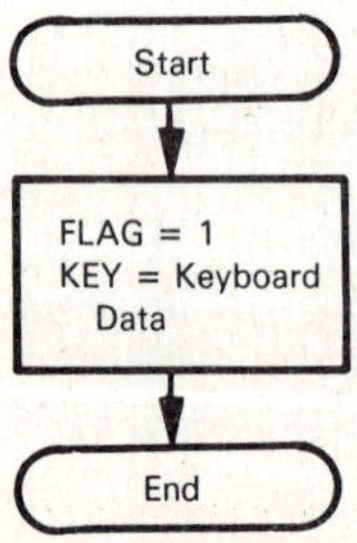

Program 15-2a:

```
            00004000     PROGRAM:  EQU      $4000
            00004600     INT_25:   EQU      $4600
            00006000     DATA:     EQU      $6000

            0003FF40     PIADDA:   EQU      $3FF40            DATA DIRECTION REGISTER A
            0003FF40     PIADA:    EQU      $3FF40            DATA REGISTER A
            0003FF44     PIACA:    EQU      $3FF44            CONTROL REGISTER A
            00000005     PIA_EN:   EQU      $05               PIA INTERRUPT ENABLE
            00002000     IMSKO:    EQU      $2000             SUPERVISOR/INTERRUPT LEVEL 0

            00006000               ORG      DATA
006000      00000001     FLAG:     DS.B     1                 DATA READY FLAG
006001      00000001     KEY:      DS.B     1                 INPUT KEY DATA

            00004000               ORG      PROGRAM

004000      42386000     PGM15_2A: CLR.B    FLAG              CLEAR DATA READY FLAG
004004      42390003FF44           CLR.B    PIACA             ADDRESS DATA DIRECTION REGISTER
00400A      42390003FF40           CLR.B    PIADDA            MAKE ALL DATA LINES INPUTS
004010      13FC0005
                0003FF44           MOVE.B   #PIA_EN,PIACA     ENABLE INTERRUPT FROM KEYBOARD PIA
004018      46FC2000               MOVE     #IMSKO,SR         ENABLE ALL INTERRUPTS
00401C      4A386000     WTRDY:    TST.B    FLAG              IS THERE DATA FROM THE KEYBOARD
004020      67FA                   BEQ      WTRDY             NO, WAIT

004022      4E75                   RTS

                         *  INTERRUPT SERVICE ROUTINE

            00004600               ORG      INT_25

004600      11FC00016000           MOVE.B   #1,FLAG           SET DATA READY FLAG
004606      11F90003FF40
                6001               MOVE.B   PIADA,KEY         SAVE KEYBOARD DATA
00460E      4E73                   RTE                        RETURN TO INTERRUPTED ROUTINE

                                   END      PGM15_2A
```

You must initialize the PIA completely before enabling interrupts. This includes establishing the directions of ports and control lines and determining the transitions to be recognized on input strobes.

The main program clears the Data Ready flag (FLAG) and then simply waits for the interrupt service routine to set it. The main program and the service routine communicate through two fixed memory addresses:

The variable FLAG indicates whether new data has been received from the keyboard.

The variable KEY is a single-location data buffer used to hold the value received from the keyboard.

Note the similarity between the Data Ready flag in memory and the status bit in the control register of the keyboard PIA. The program does not have to test bit 7 of the PIA control register, because there is a direct hardware (interrupt) connection between that bit and the CPU. Of course, we have also assumed that the keyboard is the only source of interrupts.

Unlike our previous example, we don't use the privileged instruction STOP. Instead, we monitor the variable FLAG to determine when an interrupt has occurred. Remember, however, that the STOP instruction, besides waiting for an interrupt to occur, also sets the desired interrupt priority level in the status register. In program 15-*2a,* we use the MOVE to Status Register instruction (MOVE#IMSK0,SR) to set the desired interrupt level. The data word ($2000 in this program) following the instruction opcode word defines the new interrupt priority level. Note that this instruction also defines the state of all condition codes in the status register. The MOVE to Status Register instruction is a privileged instruction.

Sometimes you may want to temporarily accept interrupts of a lower level than are currently being permitted by the status register interrupt mask. If you do this, you would probably want to save the current interrupt mask before enabling lower level interrupts. You could then restore the previous mask after the lower level interrupts have been processed. The MOVE from Status Register instruction can be used to save the current interrupt mask (along with the rest of the status register contents) and it is not a privileged instruction.

Remember that upon entry to the interrupt service routine, the interrupt mask in the status register has already been set automatically by the CPU to the level associated with the interrupt being processed. This inhibits additional interrupts at this level or lower. Only interrupts of a higher level can interrupt the CPU.

The RTE instruction at the end of the service routine transfers control back to the main program. If you want to transfer control somewhere else (perhaps to an error routine), you can change the program counter in the supervisor stack using the methods outlined earlier. RTE also restores the interrupt priority mask to the level that existed prior to the interrupt.

We do not use the registers to pass parameters and results. If we were to change the register values, we could interfere with the execution of the main program. In most applications, the main program is using the registers and random changes will cause havoc. At the very least, changing the registers lacks generality, since modifications to the main program surely could result in the use of registers that are currently available.

The service routine does not have to explicitly reenable the interrupts. The reason is that RTE automatically restores the old status register with the priority level in its original state. In fact, you will have to change the priority level on the stack if you do not want the interrupts to be reenabled to their prior levels.

You can save and restore other data (such as the contents of a memory location) by using the stack. This method can be expanded indefinitely (as long as there is RAM available for the stack), since nested service routines will not destroy the data saved by earlier routines.

Filling a Buffer via Interrupts

An alternative approach would be for the interrupt service routine to set FLAG only after receiving an entire line of text (such as a string of characters ending with a carriage return). Here we use FLAG as an end-of-line flag and memory locations 6002 and 6003 as a buffer pointer, POINTER. We will assume that the buffer starts in memory location 6004.

Program 15-2b:

```
        00004000    PROGRAM:  EQU     $4000
        00004600    INT_25:   EQU     $4600
        00006000    DATA:     EQU     $6000

        0003FF40    PIADDA:   EQU     $3FF40      DATA DIRECTION REGISTER A
        0003FF40    PIADA:    EQU     $3FF40      DATA REGISTER A
        0003FF44    PIACA:    EQU     $3FF44      CONTROL REGISTER A
        00000005    PIA_EN:   EQU     $05         PIA INTERRUPT ENABLE
        00002000    IMSK0:    EQU     $2000       SUPERVISOR/INTERRUPT LEVEL 0
        0000000D    CR:       EQU     $0D         CARRIAGE RETURN

        00006000              ORG     DATA
006000  00000001    FLAG:     DS.B    1           END OF LINE FLAG
```

```
006001   00000001                  DS.B     1
006002   00000002      POINTER:    DS.W     1                 POINTER TO BUFFER END + 1
006004   00000050      BUFFER:     DS.B     80                INPUT BUFFER

         00004000                  ORG      PROGRAM

004000   42386000      PGM15_2B:   CLR.B    FLAG              CLEAR DATA READY FLAG
004004   31FC60046002              MOVE.W   #BUFFER,POINTER   INITIALIZE POINTER
00400A   42390003FF44              CLR.B    PIACA             ADDRESS DATA DIRECTION REGISTER
004010   42390003FF40              CLR.B    PIADDA            MAKE ALL DATA LINES INPUTS
004016   13FC0005
             0003FF44              MOVE.B   #PIA_EN,PIACA     ENABLE INTERRUPT FROM KEYBOARD PIA
00401E   46FC2000                  MOVE     #IMSK0,SR         ENABLE ALL INTERRUPTS
004022   4A386000      WTRDY:      TST.B    FLAG              HAS A LINE BEEN RECEIVED FROM KEYBO
004026   67FA                      BEQ      WTRDY             NO, WAIT

004028   4E75                      RTS

                       *  INTERRUPT SERVICE ROUTINE

         00004600                  ORG      INT_25

004600   2F08                      MOVE.L   A0,-(SP)          PUSH A0 ON SUPERVISOR STACK
004602   30786002                  MOVE.W   POINTER,A0        GET POINTER TO NEXT BUFFER ENTRY
004606   10F90003FF40              MOVE.B   PIADA,(A0)+       SAVE KEY DATA IN BUFFER
00460C   0C28000DFFF               CMPI.B   #CR,-1(A0)        IS KEY INPUT A CARRIAGE RETURN?
004612   6606                      BNE.S    DONE              NO, RETURN
004614   11FC00016000              MOVE.B   #1,FLAG           SET END OF LINE FLAG
00461A   31C86002      DONE:       MOVE.W   A0,POINTER        UPDATE BUFFER POINTER
00461E   205F                      MOVE.L   (SP)+,A0          RESTORE REGISTER A0
004620   4E73                      RTE                        RETURN TO INTERRUPTED ROUTINE

                                   END      PGM15_2B
```

This program fills a buffer starting at memory location 6004 until it receives a carriage return character (CR). POINTER holds the current buffer pointer. The interrupt service routine increments that pointer (with autoincrementing) after each use.

In a real application, the CPU could perform other tasks between interrupts. It could, for example, edit, move, or transmit a line from one buffer while the interrupt service routine was filling another buffer. This is the double buffering approach. The main program only has to ensure that the interrupt service routine doesn't run out of buffers.

An alternative approach would be for FLAG to contain a counter rather than a flag. The contents of that location would then indicate to the main program how many bytes of data had been received. The main program would then know how many characters were in the buffer without counting them. It could even deal with the buffer whenever a certain number of new data bytes were in it. The service routine would simply increment the counter as well as the buffer pointer as part of each input operation.

Interrupt service routines are invoked randomly because of the nature of interrupts. Therefore, you can't know which registers the interrupt program may have been using. **To prevent accidental modification of registers that may be in use by an interrupted program, you should always save and restore the contents of all registers used by the interrupt service routine.** The MOVEM instruction, which we have previously discussed, provides a simple means of saving and restoring registers.

15-3. A PRINTER INTERRUPT

Purpose: The main program clears a variable FLAG at memory location 6000 and waits for a ready interrupt from a printer. This interrupt service routine sets FLAG to 1 and sends the contents of the variable CHAR at memory location 6001 to the printer.

Sample Problem:

CHAR - (6001) = 51
Result: FLAG - (6000) = 01 Flag indicating last data item has been sent

Printer receives a 51_{16} (ASCII Q) when it is ready.

Flowchart:

Main Program:

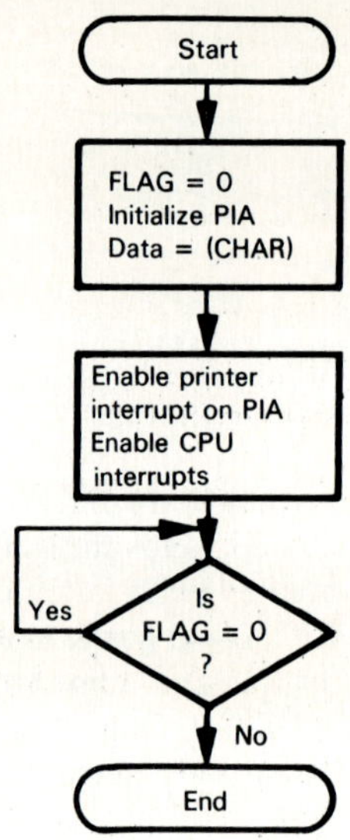

Interrupt Service Routine:

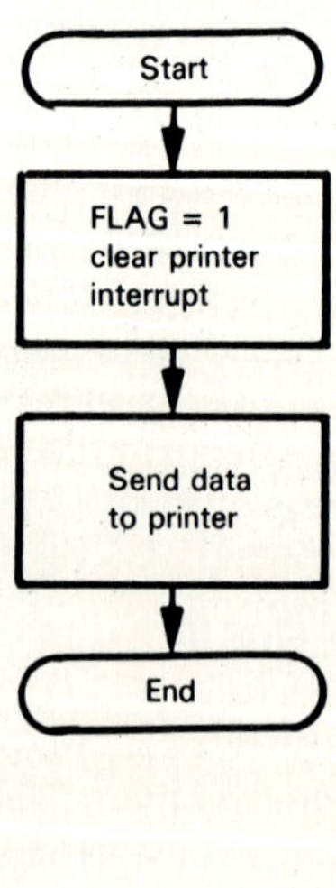

Program 15-3a:

```
00004000        PROGRAM:  EQU        $4000
00004600        INT_25:   EQU        $4600
```

```
        00006000      DATA:      EQU      $6000

        0003FF40      PIADDA:    EQU      $3FF40             DATA DIRECTION REGISTER A
        000000FF      DLOUT:     EQU      $FF                PIA DATA LINES AS OUTPUTS
        0003FF40      PIADA:     EQU      $3FF40             DATA REGISTER A
        0003FF44      PIACA:     EQU      $3FF44             CONTROL REGISTER A
        00000005      PIA_EN:    EQU      $05                PIA INTERRUPT ENABLE
        00002000      IMSK0:     EQU      $2000              SUPERVISOR/INTERRUPT LEVEL 0

        00006000                 ORG      DATA
006000  00000001      FLAG:      DS.B     1                  DATA ACCEPT FLAG
006001  00000001      CHAR:      DS.B     1                  PRINTER OUTPUT DATA

        00004000                 ORG      PROGRAM

004000  42386000      PGM15_3A:  CLR.B    FLAG               CLEAR DATA ACCEPT FLAG
004004  42390003FF44             CLR.B    PIACA              ADDRESS DATA DIRECTION REGISTER
00400A  13FC00FF
            0003FF40             MOVE.B   #DLOUT,PIADDA      MAKE ALL DATA LINES OUTPUTS
004012  13FC0005
            0003FF44             MOVE.B   #PIA_EN,PIACA      ENABLE INTERRUPT FROM PRINTER PIA
00401A  46FC2000                 MOVE     #IMSK0,SR          ENABLE ALL INTERRUPTS
00401E  4A386000      WTACK:     TST.B    FLAG               HAS DATA BEEN OUTPUTTED TO PRINTER?
004022  67FA                     BEQ      WTACK              NO, WAIT

004024  4E75                     RTS

                      *  INTERRUPT SERVICE ROUTINE

        00004600                 ORG      INT_25

004600  11FC00016000             MOVE.B   #1,FLAG            SET DATA ACCEPT FLAG
004606  4A390003FF40             TST.B    PIADA              CLEAR PRINTER INTERRUPT
00460C  13F86001
            0003FF40             MOVE.B   CHAR,PIADA         OUTPUT DATA TO PRINTER
004614  4E73                     RTE                         RETURN TO INTERRUPTED ROUTINE

                                 END      PGM15_3A
```

The only differences from the keyboard interrupt routines are the meaning of the flag, the direction of the data transfer, and the need for the instruction TST.B PIADA to clear bit 7 of the PIA control register. Remember that an input operation automatically clears that bit, but an output operation does not.

Here a cleared FLAG indicates that the CPU has data available that has not yet been sent to the printer. When the interrupt service routine sets the flag, the main program knows the data has been sent. The flag acts as an acknowledgment from the printer or a data accepted indicator.

Remember that you may find it necessary to place a read at the start of the main program to clear stray interrupts. MOVE.B PIADA,D0 or TST.B PIADA will do the job, as long as you place it after the instruction that addresses the data register but before the instruction that enables CPU interrupts.

Emptying a Buffer with Interrupts

As in the keyboard example, **we could have the interrupt service routine set the Data Accepted flag after it sends the printer an entire line of data** ending with a carriage return. Here again we use FLAG as an end-of-line flag and memory locations 6002 and 6003 as a buffer pointer. We will assume that the buffer starts in memory location 6004.

Program 15-3b:

Main Program:

```
00004000      PROGRAM:   EQU      $4000
00004600      INT_25:    EQU      $4600
00006000      DATA:      EQU      $6000
```

```
         0003FF40     PIADDA:   EQU      $3FF40              DATA DIRECTION REGISTER A
         000000FF     DLOUT:    EQU      $FF                 DATA LINES AS ALL OUTPUTS
         0003FF40     PIADA:    EQU      $3FF40              DATA REGISTER A
         0003FF44     PIACA:    EQU      $3FF44              CONTROL REGISTER A
         00000005     PIA_EN:   EQU      $05                 PIA INTERRUPT ENABLE
         00002000     IMSK0:    EQU      $2000               SUPERVISOR/INTERRUPT LEVEL 0
         0000000D     CR:       EQU      $0D                 CARRIAGE RETURN

         00006000               ORG      DATA
006000   00000001     FLAG:     DS.B     1                   END OF LINE FLAG
006001   00000001               DS.B     1
006002   00000002     POINTER:  DS.W     1                   POINTER TO BUFFER END + 1
006004   00000050     BUFFER:   DS.B     80                  INPUT BUFFER

         00004000               ORG      PROGRAM

004000   42386000     PGM15_3B: CLR.B    FLAG                CLEAR END OF LINE FLAG
004004   31FC60046002           MOVE.W   #BUFFER,POINTER     INITIALIZE POINTER
00400A   42390003FF44           CLR.B    PIACA               ADDRESS DATA DIRECTION REGISTER
004010   13FC00FF
             0003FF40           MOVE.B   #DLOUT,PIADDA       MAKE ALL DATA LINES OUTPUTS
004018   13FC0005
             0003FF44           MOVE.B   #PIA_EN,PIACA       ENABLE INTERRUPT FROM PRINTER PIA
004020   46FC2000               MOVE     #IMSK0,SR           ENABLE ALL INTERRUPTS
004024   4A386000     WTEOL:    TST.B    FLAG                HAS ALL OF LINE BEEN PRINTED?
004028   67FA                   BEQ      WTEOL               NO, WAIT

00402A   4E75                   RTS

                      *  INTERRUPT SERVICE ROUTINE

         00004600               ORG      INT_25

004600   2F08                   MOVE.L   A0,-(SP)            PUSH A0 ON SUPERVISOR STACK
004602   4A390003FF40           TST.B    PIADA               CLEAR PRINTER INTERRUPT
004608   30786002               MOVE.W   POINTER,A0          GET POINTER TO NEXT BUFFER ENTRY
00460C   13D80003FF40           MOVE.B   (A0)+,PIADA         SEND NEXT CHARACTER TO PRINTER
004612   0C28000DFFFF           CMPI.B   #CR,-1(A0)          WAS LAST CHARACTER A CARRIAGE RETURN
004618   6606                   BNE.S    DONE                NO,RETURN
00461A   11FC00016000           MOVE.B   #1,FLAG             SET END OF LINE FLAG
004620   31C86002     DONE:     MOVE.W   A0,POINTER          UPDATE BUFFER POINTER
004624   205F                   MOVE.L   (SP)+,A0            RESTORE REGISTER A0
004626   4E73                   RTE                          RETURN TO INTERRUPTED ROUTINE

                                END      PGM15_3B
```

We could use double buffering to allow I/O and processing to occur independently without ever halting the CPU to wait for the printer.

Fixed-Length Buffer

Still another approach uses FLAG as a buffer counter. For example, the following program waits for 20 characters to be sent to the printer.

Program 15-3c:

```
         00004000     PROGRAM:  EQU      $4000
         00004600     INT_25:   EQU      $4600
         00006000     DATA:     EQU      $6000

         0003FF40     PIADDA:   EQU      $3FF40              DATA DIRECTION REGISTER A
         000000FF     DLOUT:    EQU      $FF                 DATA LINES AS ALL OUTPUTS
         0003FF40     PIADA:    EQU      $3FF40              DATA REGISTER A
         0003FF44     PIACA:    EQU      $3FF44              CONTROL REGISTER A
         00000005     PIA_EN:   EQU      $05                 PIA INTERRUPT ENABLE
         00002000     IMSK0:    EQU      $2000               SUPERVISOR/INTERRUPT LEVEL 0
         0000000D     CR:       EQU      $0D                 CARRIAGE RETURN

         00006000               ORG      DATA
006000   00000001     FLAG:     DS.B     1                   BUFFER COUNTER
006001   00000001               DS.B     1
006002   00000002     POINTER:  DS.W     1                   POINTER TO BUFFER END + 1
006004   00000050     BUFFER:   DS.B     80                  INPUT BUFFER

         00004000               ORG      PROGRAM

004000   42386000     PGM15_3C: CLR.B    FLAG                CLEAR BUFFER COUNTER
004004   31FC60046002           MOVE.W   #BUFFER,POINTER     INITIALIZE POINTER
```

```
00400A  42390003FF44            CLR.B    PIACA            ADDRESS DATA DIRECTION REGISTER
004010  13FC00FF
          0003FF40              MOVE.B   #DLOUT,PIADDA    MAKE ALL DATA LINES OUTPUTS
004018  13FC0005
          0003FF44              MOVE.B   #PIA_EN,PIACA    ENABLE INTERRUPT FROM PRINTER PIA
004020  46FC2000                MOVE     #IMSK0,SR        ENABLE ALL INTERRUPTS
004024  0C3800146000    WTEOL:  CMP.B    #20,FLAG         HAVE 20 CHARACTERS BEEN SENT?
00402A  66F8                    BNE      WTEOL            NO, WAIT

00402C  4E75                    RTS

                        :: INTERRUPT SERVICE ROUTINE

        00004600                ORG      INT_25

004600  2F08                    MOVE.L   A0,-(SP)         PUSH A0 ON SUPERVISOR STACK
004602  4A390003FF40            TST.B    PIADA            CLEAR PRINTER INTERRUPT
004608  30786002                MOVE.W   POINTER,A0       GET POINTER TO NEXT BUFFER ENTRY
00460C  13D80003FF40            MOVE.B   (A0)+,PIADA      SEND NEXT CHARACTER TO PRINTER
004612  0C28000DFFFF            CMPI.B   #CR,-(A0)        WAS LAST CHARACTER A CARRIAGE RETURN
004618  6604                    BNE.S    DONE             NO,RETURN
00461A  52786000                ADDQ     #1,FLAG          INCREMENT BUFFER COUNTER
00461E  31C86002        DONE:   MOVE.W   A0,POINTER       UPDATE BUFFER POINTER
004622  205F                    MOVE.L   A0,POINTER       RESTORE REGISTOR A0
004624  4E73                    RTE                       RETURN TO INTERRUPTED ROUTINE

                                END      PGM15_3C
```

15-4. A REAL-TIME CLOCK INTERRUPT

Purpose: The computer waits for an interrupt from a real-time clock.

Real-Time Clock

A real-time clock simply provides a regular series of pulses. The interval between the pulses can be used as a time reference. Real-time clock interrupts can be counted to give any multiple of the basic time interval. A real-time clock can be produced by dividing down the CPU clock, by using a timer like the 6840 device or the one included in the 6846 multifunction support device,or by using external sources such as the AC line frequency.

Note the tradeoffs involved in determining the frequency of the real-time clock. A high frequency (say 10 kHz) allows the creation of a wide range of time intervals of high accuracy. On the other hand, the overhead involved in counting real-time clock interrupts may be considerable. **The choice of frequency depends on the precision and timing requirements of your application. The clock may, of course, consist partly of hardware; a counter may count high frequency pulses and interrupt the processor only occasionally. A program will have to read the counter to measure time to high accuracy.**

One problem is synchronizing operations with the real-time clock. Clearly, there will be some effect on the precision of the timing interval if the CPU starts the measurement randomly during a clock period, rather than exactly at the beginning. **Some ways to synchronize operations are:**

1. **Start the CPU and clock together.** RESET or a startup interrupt can start the clock as well as the CPU.
2. **Allow the CPU to start and stop the clock under program control.**
3. **Use a high-frequency clock** so that an error of less than one clock period will be small.

4. **Line up the clock** (by waiting for an edge or interrupt) **before starting the measurement.**

A real-time clock interrupt should have very high priority, since the precision of the timing intervals will be affected by any delay in servicing the interrupt. **The usual practice is to make the real-time clock the highest priority interrupt except for power failure.** The clock interrupt service routine is generally kept extremely short so that it does not interfere with other CPU activities.

In the following programs we assume a clock has been connected to a PIA interrupt. An interrupt will occur once each clock cycle.

15-4a. Wait for Real-Time Clock

Program 15-4a:

```
        00004000        PROGRAM:  EQU      $4000
        00004600        INT_26:   EQU      $4600
        00006000        DATA:     EQU      $6000

        0003FF40        TPIADA:   EQU      $3FF40              DATA REGISTER A FOR TIMER PIA
        0003FF44        TPIACA:   EQU      $3FF44              CONTROL REGISTER A FOR TIMER PIA
        00000005        PIA_EN:   EQU      $05                 PIA INTERRUPT ENABLE
        00002000        IMSK0:    EQU      $2000               SUPERVISOR/INTERRUPT LEVEL 0

        00006000                  ORG      DATA

006000  00000001        COUNTER:  DS.B     1                   TIMER COUNTER

        00004000                  ORG      PROGRAM

004000  42386000        PGM15_4A: CLR.B    COUNTER             CLEAR TIMER COUNTER
004004  13FC0005
          0003FF44                MOVE.B   #PIA_EN,TPIACA      ENABLE INTERRUPT FROM TIMER PIA
00400C  46FC2000                  MOVE     #IMSK0,SR           ENABLE ALL INTERRUPTS
004010  4A386000        TWAIT:    TST.B    COUNTER             HAS TIMER COUNTER BEEN INCREMENTED?
004014  67FA                      BEQ      TWAIT               NO, WAIT

004016  4E75                      RTS

                        *  TIMER INTERRUPT SERVICE ROUTINE

        00004600                  ORG      INT_26

004600  4A390003FF40              TST.B    TPIADA              CLEAR TIMER INTERRUPT
004606  52386000                  ADDQ.B   #1,COUNTER          INCREMENT TIMER COUNTER
00460A  4E73                      RTE                          RETURN TO INTERRUPTED ROUTINE

                                  END      PGM15_4A
```

The variable COUNTER at memory location 6000 contains the clock counter.

If bit 1 of the PIA control register is 0, the interrupt will occur on the high-to-low (falling) edge of the clock. If that bit is 1, the interrupt will occur on the low-to-high (rising) edge of the clock.

The interrupt service routine must explicitly clear bit 7 of the PIA control register since no data transfer is necessary.

You could still use the PIA data port as long as you did not accidentally clear the status bit from the real-time clock before it was recognized. This would be no problem if the port were used for output to a simple peripheral (such as a set of LEDs), since output operations do not affect the status bits anyway.

Clearly, **we can easily extend this routine to handle more counts and provide greater precision by using more memory locations for the clock counter** and a different test in the main program.

15-4b. Wait for 10 Clock Interrupts

Program 15-4b:

```
         00004000     PROGRAM:  EQU      $4000
         00004600     INT_26:   EQU      $4600
         00006000     DATA:     EQU      $6000

         0003FF40     TPIADA:   EQU      $3FF40            DATA REGISTER A FOR TIMER PIA
         0003FF44     TPIACA:   EQU      $3FF44            CONTROL REGISTER A FOR TIMER PIA
         00000005     PIA_EN:   EQU      $05               PIA INTERRUPT ENABLE
         00002000     IMSK0:    EQU      $2000             SUPERVISOR/INTERRUPT LEVEL 0
         0000000A     TDELAY:   EQU      10                TIMER DELAY

         00006000               ORG      DATA

006000   00000001     COUNTER:  DS.B     1                 TIMER COUNTER

         00004000               ORG      PROGRAM

004000   42386000     PGM15_4B: CLR.B    COUNTER           CLEAR TIMER COUNTER
004004   13FC0005
           0003FF44             MOVE.B   #PIA_EN,TPIACA    ENABLE INTERRUPT FROM TIMER PIA
00400C   46FC2000               MOVE     #IMSK0,SR         ENABLE ALL INTERRUPTS
004010   103C000A               MOVE.B   #TDELAY,D0        TIMER COUNT DELAY
004014   B0386000     TWAIT:    CMP.B    COUNTER,D0        HAS DESIRED DELAY BEEN ACHIEVED?
004018   67FA                   BEQ      TWAIT             NO, WAIT

00401A   4E75                   RTS

                      *  TIMER INTERRUPT SERVICE ROUTINE

         00004600               ORG      INT_26

004600   4A390003FF40           TST.B    TPIADA            CLEAR TIMER INTERRUPT
004606   52386000               ADDQ.B   #1,COUNTER        INCREMENT TIMER COUNTER
00460A   4E73                   RTE                        RETURN TO INTERRUPTED ROUTINE

                                END      PGM15_4B
```

15-4c. Maintaining Real Time

A more realistic real-time clock interrupt routine could keep track of the passage of time using several memory locations. For example, the following routine uses addresses 6000 through 6003 to maintain clock time as follows:

6000 - hundredths of seconds
6001 - seconds
6002 - minutes
6003 - hours

We assume that a 100Hz input provides the regular source of interrupts.

Program 15-4c:

```
         00004000     PROGRAM:  EQU      $4000
         00004600     INT_26:   EQU      $4600
         00006000     DATA:     EQU      $6000

         0003FF40     TPIADA:   EQU      $3FF40            DATA REGISTER A FOR TIMER PIA
         0003FF44     TPIACA:   EQU      $3FF44            CONTROL REGISTER A FOR TIMER PIA
         00000005     PIA_EN:   EQU      $05               PIA INTERRUPT ENABLE
         00002000     IMSK0:    EQU      $2000             SUPERVISOR/INTERRUPT LEVEL 0
         0000001E     TDELAY:   EQU      30                300 DELAY (DELAY MUST BE < 1 SECOND

         00006000               ORG      DATA

006000   00000001     HUNDSEC:  DS.B     1                 HUNDREDTHS OF SECONDS
006001   00000001     SECONDS:  DS.B     1                 SECONDS
006002   00000001     MINUTES:  DS.B     1                 MINUTES
006003   00000001     HOURS:    DS.B     1                 HOURS

         00004000               ORG      PROGRAM
```

```
004000   13FC0005
             0003FF44  PGM15_4C: MOVE.B    #PIA_EN,TPIACA      ENABLE INTERRUPT FROM TIMER PIA
004008   46FC2000                MOVE      #IMSK0,SR           ENABLE ALL INTERRUPTS
00400C   10386000                MOVE.B    HUNDSEC,D0          GET CURRENT HUNDREDTHS OF SECOND TI
004010   0600001E                ADDI.B    #TDELAY,D0          ADD DELAY TIME
004014   0C000064                CMPI.B    #100,D0             MOD 100
004018   65000006                BCS       TWAIT
00401C   04000064                SUBI.B    #100,D0
004020   B0386000      TWAIT:    CMP.B     HUNDSEC,D0          HAS DESIRED DELAY BEEN ACHIEVED?
004024   67FA                    BEQ       TWAIT               NO, WAIT

004026   4E75                    RTS

                       *  TIMER INTERRUPT SERVICE ROUTINE

         00004600                ORG       INT_26

004600   48E78000                MOVEM.L   D0,-(SP)            SAVE D0
004604   4A390003FF40            TST.B     TPIADA              CLEAR TIMER INTERRUPT
00460A   52386000                ADDQ.B    #1,HUNDSEC          UPDATE HUNDREDTHS OF SECONDS
00460E   103C0064                MOVE.B    #100,D0
004612   B0386000                CMP.B     HUNDSEC,D0          IS THERE A CARRY FROM HUNDREDTHS?
004616   6628                    BNE.S     TDONE               NO, DONE
004618   42386000                CLR.B     HUNDSEC             YES, CLEAR HUNDREDTHS OF SECONDS
00461C   52386001                ADDQ.B    #1,SECONDS          UPDATE SECONDS
004620   103C003C                MOVE.B    #60,D0
004624   B0386001                CMP.B     SECONDS,D0          IS THERE A CARRY TO MINUTES
004628   6616                    BNE.S     TDONE               NO, DONE
00462A   42386001                CLR.B     SECONDS             YES, CLEAR SECONDS
004632   B0386002                CPM.B     MINUTES,D0          IS THERE A CARRY TO HOURS
004636   6608                    BNE.S     TDONE               NO, DONE
004638   42386002                CLR.B     MINUTES             YES, MAKE MINUTES ZERO
00463C   52386003                ADDQ.B    #1, HOURS           UPDATE HOURS
00462E   52386002                ADDQ.B    #1,MINUTES          UPDATE MINUTES
004640   4CDF0001      TDONE:    MOVEM.L   (SP)+,D0            RESTORE D0
004644   4E73                    RTE                           RETURN TO INTERRUPTED ROUTINE

                                 END       PGM15_4C
```

The main program produces a delay of 300 milliseconds. The longest delay that can be handled by this routine is 990 milliseconds. How would you modify this program to handle longer delays?

This approach is the same one you would take if you had to let something cook for 20 minutes. You must determine the current time by reading your watch (the counter), calculate the target time by adding 20 (mod 60, so 20 minutes past 6:50 is 7:10), and wait for your watch to reach the target time. Notice that if the delay is less than one hour, you can ignore the hour hand and wait until the minute hand comes around to ten minutes after the hour. This is the method the program uses. (If your watch doesn't have hands, just wait until the minutes numbers display 10.)

Change the program so it produces a 20 minute delay (an obvious requirement for a microprocessor-controlled microwave oven).

Of course, the program could perform other tasks and only check the elapsed time occasionally. How would you produce a delay of seven seconds? of three minutes? Many applications do not require long delays to be highly accurate; for example, the operator of a microwave oven does not care if intervals in minutes are off by a few seconds.

Sometimes you may want to keep time either as BCD digits or as ASCII characters. How would you revise the last interrupt service routine to handle these alternatives?

Assuming that the clock PIA generates level 2 interrupts, its interrupts are then handled by the level 2 autovector at address 68. If the MC68000 has its interrupt priority mask set at level 0 and simultaneous interrupts are received from both the clock PIA

Flowchart 15-4c:

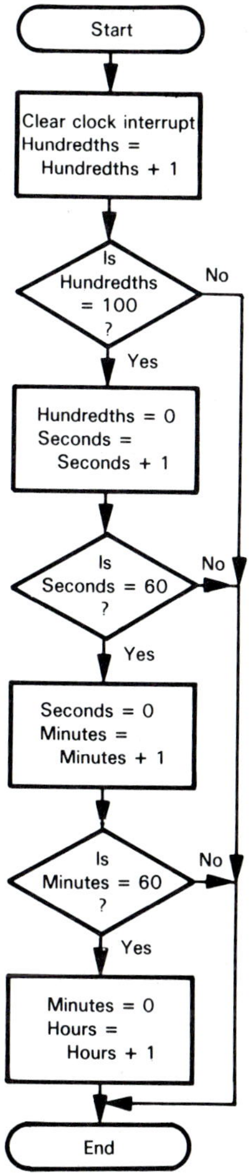

and the printer PIA in example 15-3, here is what happens. Since the printer PIA generates a level 1 interrupt, the clock PIA is serviced first. The interrupt from the printer PIA would be inhibited until the priority mask was reset to zero. If the printer interrupt occurs first and service of this interrupt has begun, this service would be interrupted by the occurrence of a clock PIA interrupt. After the clock service routine has been completed, control would be returned to the printer service routine at the point where it was interrupted.

High-Frequency Clock

Even a high-frequency real-time clock can be handled without much processor intervention. The usual method is to have the clock increment a set of counters which then interrupt the processor at a much lower frequency. For example, the input frequency could be 1 MHz; that input frequency would then be passed through 3 decimal counters and the output of the last one would be tied to the PIA. The PIA would recive a single clock pulse for every 1000 input pulses (that is, when the 3 decimal counters overflow). The processor can determine the time to greater precision than 1 ms by reading the counters, since they contain the less significant digits. As usual, some additional hardware (counters and input ports) is necessary to reduce the burden on the CPU. This is a typical tradeoff; the additional hardware is worthwhile only if the application requires precise timing.

15-5. A TELETYPEWRITER INTERRUPT

15-5a. ACIA Interrupt Routine

Purpose: The main program clears a flag represented by the variable FLAG at memory location 6000 and waits for an interrupt from a 6850 ACIA. The interrupt service routine sets FLAG to 1 and places the data from the ACIA in the variable CHAR at memory location 6001. The characters are 7 bits in length with odd parity and 2 stop bits.

Program 15-5a:

```
        00004000    PROGRAM:   EQU     $4000
        00004600    INT_25:    EQU     $4600
        00006000    DATA:      EQU     $6000

        0003FF01    ACIACR:    EQU     $3FF01           ACIA CONTROL REGISTER
        000EFF03    ACIADR:    EQU     $EFF03           ACIA DATA REGISTER
        000000C5    AMODE:     EQU     $C5              ACIA OPERATING MODE
        00000003    MRESET:    EQU     $03              ACIA MASTER RESET
        00002000    IMSK0:     EQU     $2000            SUPERVISOR/INTERRUPT LEVEL 0

        00006000               ORG     DATA
006000  00000001    FLAG:      DS.B    1                DATA ACCEPT FLAG
006001  00000001    CHAR:      DS.B    1                CHARACTER FROM TTY

        00004000               ORG     PROGRAM

004000  42386000    FGM15_5A:  CLR.B   FLAG             CLEAR DATA ACCEPT FLAG
004004  13FC0003
          0003FF01             MOVE.B  #MRSET,ACIACR    MASTER RESET ACIA
00400C  13FC00C5
          0003FF01             MOVE.B  #AMODE,ACIACR    ENABLE ACIA INTERRUPT/SET MODE
004014  46FC2000               MOVE    #IMSK0,SR        ENABLE ALL INTERRUPTS
004018  4A386000    WAIT:      TST.B   FLAG             IS THERE DATA FROM ACIA?
00401C  67FA                   BEQ     WAIT             NO, WAIT

00401E  4E75                   RTS

                    *  INTERRUPT SERVICE ROUTINE

        00004600               ORG     INT_25

004600  11FC00016000           MOVE.B  #1,FLAG          SET DATA ACCEPT FLAG
004606  11F9000EFF03
          6001                 MOVE.B  ACIADR,CHAR      SAVE TTY CHARACTER INPUT
00460E  4E73                   RTE                      RETURN TO INTERRUPTED ROUTINE
00460E  4E73                   RTE                      RETURN TO INTERRUPTED ROUTINE
                               END     PGM15_5A
```

Since the 6850 ACIA has no RESET input, a master reset (setting control register bits 0 and 1 to one simultaneously) is necessary before the ACIA is initialized.

We then initialize the bits in the ACIA control register as follows:

Bit 7 = 1 to enable the receiver interrupt
Bit 6 = 1 and Bit 5 = 0 to disable the transmitter interrupt
Bit 4 = 0, Bit 3 = 0, and Bit 2 = 1 to select 7-bit data with odd parity and two stop bits
Bit 1 = 0 and Bit 0 = 1 to select the divide by 16 clock mode (a 1760 Hz clock must be supplied for a 110 Baud data rate).

To determine if a particular 6850 ACIA is the source of an interrupt, the program must examine the interrupt request bit (bit 7 of the status register)in each ACIA. To differentiate between receiver and transmitter interrupts, the program must examine the Receive Data Register Full bit (bit 0 of the status register). Either reading the receive data register or writing into the transmit data register clears the ACIA's interrupt request bit.

15-5b. PIA Start Bit Interrupt

Teletypewriter data can also be received with a PIA. In this case, the serial input line from the teletypewriter is connected to both data bit 7 and control line 1 of the PIA.

Purpose: The main program clears a flag represented by the variable FLAG at memory location 6000 and waits for a teletypewriter interrupt. The interrupt service routine sets FLAG to 1 and places the data from the teletypewriter in the variable CHAR at memory location 6001.

Program 15-5b:

```
        00004000    PROGRAM:   EQU     $4000
        00004600    INT_25:    EQU     $4600
        00006000    DATA:      EQU     $6000
        00004800    TTYRCV:    EQU     $4800

        0003FF40    PIADDA:    EQU     $3FF40          DATA DIRECTION REGISTER A
        00000000    DATIN:     EQU     $0              PIA DATA LINES AS INPUTS
        0003FF40    PIADA:     EQU     $3FF40          DATA REGISTER A
        0003FF44    PIACA:     EQU     $3FF44          CONTROL REGISTER A
        00000005    PIA_EN:    EQU     $05             PIA INTERRUPT ENABLE
        00000004    PIA_DIS:   EQU     $04             PIA INTERRUPT DISABLE
        00002000    IMSK0:     EQU     $2000           SUPERVISOR/INTERRUPT LEVEL 0

        00006000               ORG     DATA
006000  00000001    FLAG:      DS.B    1               DATA ACCEPT FLAG
006001  00000001    CHAR:      DS.B    1               CHARACTER INPUT FROM TTY

        00004000               ORG     PROGRAM

004000  42386000    PGM15_5B:  CLR.B   FLAG            CLEAR DATA ACCEPT FLAG
004004  42390003FF44           CLR.B   PIACA           ADDRESS DATA DIRECTION REGISTER
00400A  13FC0000
            0003FF40           MOVE.B  #DATIN,PIADDA   MAKE ALL DATA LINES INPUTS
004012  13FC0005
            0003FF44           MOVE.B  #PIA_EN,PIACA   ENABLE INTERRUPT FROM TTY PIA
00401A  46FC2000               MOVE    #IMSK0,SR       ENABLE ALL INTERRUPTS
00401E  4A386000    WAIT:      TST.B   FLAG            HAS START BIT BEEN RECEIVED?
004022  67FA                   BEQ     WAIT            NO, WAIT
004024  4EB84800               JSR     TTYRCV          YES, FETCH DATA FROM TTY
004028  11C06001               MOVE.B  D0,CHAR         SAVE TTY INPUT CHARACTER

00402C  4E75                   RTS

                    *   INTERRUPT SERVICE ROUTINE
```

```
          00004600                    ORG       INT_25

004600    11FC00016000                MOVE.B    #1,FLAG            SET DATA ACCEPT FLAG
004606    4A390003FF40                TST.B     PIADA              CLEAR START BIT INTERRUPT
00460C    13FC0004
              0003FF44                MOVE.B    #PIA_DIS,PIACA     DISABLE START BIT INTERRUPT
004614    4E73                        RTE                          RETURN TO INTERRUPTED ROUTINE

                                      END       PGM15_5B
```

Subroutine TTYRCV called by Program 15-5*b* is similar to the teletypewriter receive routine shown in Chapter 13, example 9, except that we have assumed a version that leaves the data in data register DO. The edge used to cause the interrupt is very important here. The transition from the normal '1' (MARK) state to the '0' (SPACE) state must cause the interrupt, since this transition signifies the start of the transmission. No '0' to '1' transition will occur until a non-zero data bit is received.

The service routine must disable the PIA interrupt, since otherwise each '1' to '0' transition in the character will cause an interrupt. Note that reading the data bits will clear any status flags set by the ignored transitions. Of course, the program must reenable the PIA interrupt (by setting bit 0 of the control register) to allow receipt of the next character, but this should be done after the current character has been read.

15-6. A Supervisor Call

Purpose: Allowing programs in the user state to access utility routines in the supervisor state.

In the design of systems which include monitors or operating systems, it is good programming practice to make utility routines out of frequently used sequences of instructions. These routines may provide simple functions such as determining time-of-day or they may provide much more complex functions such as memory management in a multi-user system or logical input/output on a disk-based system. The two-state architecture of the MC68000 prevents application programs in the user state from performing certain privileged instructions which are reserved for operation in the supervisor state. In future systems which may provide memory management, programs in the user state may be restricted to using memory only within their own limited address space.

In cases where user state programs must communicate with a monitor or operating system in the supervisor state, you can use the TRAP instructions. Execution of a TRAP instruction causes a processor exception and exception processing is performed in much the same manner as interrupt processing. Programs 15-6*a* and 15-6*b* show typical uses of the TRAP instruction.

Program 15-6a:

```
          00004000    PROGRAM:    EQU       $4000
          00004400    TTYIN:      EQU       $4400
          00004500    PRINT:      EQU       $4500
          00004600    TRAP1:      EQU       $4600
          00005100    USTACK:     EQU       $5100
          00006000    DATA:       EQU       $6000

          00000084                ORG       $84                TRAP 1 VECTOR
000084    00004600                DC.L      TRAP1

          00006000                ORG       DATA

006000    00000050    BUFFER:     DS.B      80                 INPUT/OUTPUT BUFFER

          00004000                ORG       PROGRAM
```

```
                               *  PROGRAM IN USER STATE

004000    3C7C6000          PGM156A:  MOVE.W     #BUFFER,A6
004004    4E41                        TRAP       #1                 POINTER TO INPUT/OUTPUT BUFFER
004006    0001                        DC.W       1                  MONITOR CALL
004008    4E41                        TRAP       #1                 TO READ ONE TTY LINE
00400A    0002                        DC.W       2                  MONITOR CALL
00400C    4E75                        RTS                           TO WRITE ONE PRINTER LINE

                               *  TRAP 1 HANDLER

          00004600                    ORG        TRAP1

004600    48E7FFFE                    MOVEM.L    D0-D7/A0-A6,-(SP)
004604    2A6F003E                    MOVE.L     60+2(SP),A5        SAVE ALL USER REGISTERS
004608    4BED0002                    LEA.L      2(A5),A5           RETURN ADDRESS
00460C    2F4D003E                    MOVE.L     A5,60+2(SP)        ADDRESS OF INSTRUCTION AFTER TRAP
004610    0C6D0001FFFE                CMP.W      #1,-2(A5)          UPDATE STACK VALUE
004616    6606                        BNE.S      PRINTER            READ MONITOR CALL?
004618    4EB84400                    JSR        TTYIN              NO, PRINTER CALL
00461C    6004                        BRA.S      DONE               READ ONE LINE FROM TTY
00461E    4EB84500          PRINTER:  JSR        PRINT
004622    4CDF7FFF          DONE:     MOVEM.L    (SP)+,D0-D7/A0-A6  OUTPUT ONE LINE TO PRINTER
004626    4E73              RTE                                     RESTORE USER REGISTERS
                                                                    RETURN TO USER PROGRAM
                            END       PGM15 6A
```

Each of the processor's two states has its own stack pointer (address register A7). When the MC68000 is reset, all references to address register A7 use the supervisor stack pointer. The supervisor stack pointer is used until the s-bit in the status register is cleared, and the user state is entered. While in the user state, A7 references the user stack pointer.

Program 15-6a demonstrates a typical instruction sequence used to read and write from a TTY device using a monitor such as Motorola's MAC^sBUG.™ The sequence uses the TRAP #1 instruction to perform a call to supervisor function. In this example, address register A6 is used as an input parameter to the function and it points to the TTY input/output buffer. A second parameter to the function is contained in the word immediately following the TRAP instruction. This parameter indicates whether an input or output function is requested. A detailed description of parameter passing is contained in Chapter 10.

As discussed in the beginning of this chapter, the exception processing of the TRAP instruction causes the current processor program counter and status register to be pushed on the supervisor stack. The trap number, 1 in this example, is used to determine the appropriate TRAP vector much as the interrupt vector number is used to calculate the address of the interrupt vector. Since the TRAP vectors start at address \$80, the vector for TRAP #1 is located at

$$\$80 + 1 * 4 = \$84$$

The long word address at location \$84 contains the starting address of the TRAP #1 processing routine at location \$4600. Again, like interrupt processing, initial exception processing is performed in supervisor mode.

Since only the status register and program counter are saved as part of the exception process, the exception handler must save any register which it uses. These registers must be restored prior to returning to the instruction following the exception. In the event that control may not immediately be returned to the application program causing the exception, you may also want to save the user stack register. The instruction MOVE USP,An can be used to accomplish this operation. On completion of processing, a MOVE An,USP is used to restore the user stack pointer. Both instructions are privileged instructions and necessary for systems with more than one task.

Upon completion of exception processing by the exception handler, control must be returned to the instruction following the instruction which caused the exception. This is accomplished by using the RTE instruction which restores the previously saved status register and program counter from the supervisor stack. Since RTE affects the supervisor portion of the status register, it is a privileged instruction.

A variation of program 15-6*a* is shown in 15-6*b*. This variation uses two different TRAP instructions and therefore two exception handlers. Normally, we think of using the TRAP instructions while in user mode to communicate with functions in supervisor mode. However, the TRAP instructions may be used while in supervisor mode.

Program 15-6b:

```
          00004000   PROGRAM:  EQU      $4000
          00004400   TTYIN:    EQU      $4400
          00004500   PRINT:    EQU      $4500
          00004600   TRAPHDLR: EQU      $4600
          00005100   USTACK:   EQU      $5100
          00006000   DATA:     EQU      $6000

          00000084             ORG      $84                  TRAP 1/2 VECTOR
000084    00004600             DC.L     TRAP1
000088    0000460A             DC.L     TRAP2

          00006000             ORG      DATA

006000    00000050   BUFFER:   DS.B     80                   INPUT/OUTPUT BUFFER

          00004000             ORG      PROGRAM

                     * PROGRAM IN USER STATE

004000    3E7C5100   PGM15_6B: MOVEA.W  #USTACK,A7           INITIALIZE USER STACK
004004    3C7C6000             MOVE.W   #BUFFER,A6           POINTER TO INPUT/OUTPUT BUFFER
004008    4E41                 TRAP     #1                   MONITOR CALL TO READ ONE TTY LINE
00400A    4E42                 TRAP     #2                   MONITOR CALL TO PRINT ONE LINE
00400C    4E75                 RTS

                     * TRAP 1 AND 2 HANDLERS

          00004600             ORG      TRAPHDLR

004600    48E7FFFE   TRAP1:    MOVEM.L  D0-D7/A0-A6,-(SP)    SAVE ALL USER REGISTERS
004604    4EB84400             JSR      TTYIN                READ ONE LINE FROM TTY
004608    6008                 BRA.S    RETURN
00460A    48E7FFFE   TRAP2:    MOVEM.L  D0-D7/A0-A6,-(SP)    SAVE ALL USER REGISTERS
00460E    4EB84500             JSR      PRINT                OUTPUT ONE LINE TO PRINTER
004612    4CDF7FFF   RETURN:   MOVEM.L  (SP)+,D0-D7/A0-A6    RESTORE USER REGISTERS
004616    4E73                 RTE                           RETURN TO USER PROGRAM

                               END      PGM15_6B
```

15-7. ENTERING USER MODE

Purpose: Establishing programs in user mode.

Program 15-7:

```
          00004800   RESET:    EQU      $4800
          00005100   STACK:    EQU      $5100
          00005300   USTACK:   EQU      $5300
          00000000   USER:     EQU      $0            USER STATE/PRIORITY LEVEL 0
          00004000   USERPGM:  EQU      $4000         USER PROGRAM

          00000000             ORG      0

000000    00005100             DC.L     STACK         ADDRESS OF STACK
000004    00004800             DC.L     PGM15         ADDRESS OF RESET PROGRAM

          00004800             ORG      RESET

004800    307C5300   PGM15     MOVE.A W #USTACK,A0    ADDRESS OF USER STACK
```

```
004804    4E60                 MOVE.L    A0,USP         INITIALIZE USER STACK
004806    46FC0000             MOVE.W    #USER,SR       SET TO USER MODE
00480A    4EF84000             JMP       USERPGM        JUMP TO USER PROGRAM

                               END       PGM15
```

As mentioned previously, the MC68000 is initialized to operate in supervisor mode. To enter user mode, the Supervisor flag (S-bit) in the status register must be reset. This can be accomplished by any instruction which affects the Supervisor flag such as MOVE to SR, ANDI to SR, EORI to SR or RTE. With the MOVE, ANDI or EORI instructions, only the status register is affected and the instruction following the MOVE, ANDI or EORI is executed next in the user mode. The RTE instruction allows you to switch to user mode at a given address.

MORE GENERAL SERVICE ROUTINES[8]

More general interrupt service routine that are part of a complete interrupt-driven system must handle the following tasks:

1. **Saving any needed data on the stack so that interrupted programs can resume correctly.** The MC68000 saves only the program counter and the status register on the supervisor stack during its response to an interrupt. Therefore, your interrupt service routines must save and restore any additional registers they use.
2. **Restoring data and registers before executing RTE** and returning control to interrupted programs.
3. **Polling of all devices associated with a given interrupt** when more than one device can cause the interrupt. This is generally the case for devices which use autovectoring.
4. **Enabling and disabling interrupts appropriately.** Remember that the CPU automatically disables interrupts of the same or lower level as that of the interrupt just accepted.

REFERENCES

1. A, Osborne. *An Introduction to Microcomputers: Volume 1 — Basic Concepts.* Berkeley: Osborne/McGraw-Hill, 1980, Chapter 5.
2. R. L. Baldridge. "Interrupts Add Power, Complexity to Microcomputer Software Design," *EDN,* August 5, 1977, pp. 67-73.
3. R. Morris. "6800 Routine Supervises Service Requests," *EDN,* October 5, 1979, pp. 73-81.

4. I. P. Breikss. "Nonmaskable Interrupt Saves Processor Register Contents," *Electronics,* July 21, 1977, p. 104.
5. A. Osborne. *An Introduction to Microcomputers: Volume 2 — Some Real Microprocessors.* Berkeley: Osborne/McGraw-Hill, 1980, pp. 9-71 through 9-77.
6. R. Grappel. "Technique Avoids Interrupt Dangers," *EDN,* May 5, 1979, p. 88.
7. G. Horner. "Online Control of a Laboratory Instrument by a Timesharing Computer," *Computer Design,* February 1980, pp. 90-106.
8. For further discussion and some real-life examples of designing systems with interrupt, see the following:

   S. C. Baunach. "An Example of an M6800-based GPIB Interface," *EDN,* September 20, 1977, pp. 125-28.

   L. E. Cannon and P. S. Kreager. "Using a Microprocessor: a Real-Life Application, Part 2 — Software," *Computer Design,* October 1975, pp. 81-89.

   D. Fullager et al. "Interfacing Data Converters and Microprocessors," *Electronics,* December 8, 1976, pp. 81-9.

   S. A. Hill. "Multiprocess Control Interface Makes Remote MP Command Possible," *EDN,* February 5, 1976, pp. 87-9.

   Holderby. "Designing a Microprocessor-based Terminal for Factory Data Collection," *Computer Design,* March 1977, pp. 81-8.

   A. Lange. "OPTACON Interface permits the Blind to 'Read' Digital Instruments," *EDN,* February 5, 1976, pp. 84-6.

   J. D. Logan and P. S. Kreager. "Using a Microprocessor: a Real-Life Application, Part 1 — Hardware," *Computer Design,* September 1975, pp. 69-77.

   A. Moore and M. Eidson. "Printer Control," Application Note available from Motorola Semiconductor Products, Phoenix, Ariz.

   M. C. Mulder and P. P. Fasang. "A Microprocessor Controlled Substation Alarm Logger," IECI '78 Proceedings — Industrial Applications of Microprocessors, March 20-22, 1978, pp. 2-6.

   P. J. Zsombar-Murray et al. "Microprocessor Based Frequency Response Analyzer," IECI '78 Proceedings — Industrial Applications of Microprocessors, March 20-22, 1978, pp. 36-44.

The Proceedings of the IEEE's Industrial Electronics and Control Instrumentation Group's Annual Meeting on "Industrial Applications of Microprocessors" contain many interesting articles. Volumes (starting with 1975) are available from IEEE Service Center, CP Department, 445 Hoes Lane, Piscataway, N. J. 08854.

IV
Software Development

The previous chapters have described how to write short assembly language programs. While this is an important topic, it is only a small part of software development. Although writing assembly language programs is a major task for the beginner, it soon becomes simple. By now you should be familiar with standard methods for programming in assembly language on the MC68000 microprocessor. **The next six chapters will describe how to formulate tasks as programs and how to combine short programs to form a working system.**

THE STAGES OF SOFTWARE DEVELOPMENT

Software development consists of many stages. **Figure IV-1 is a flowchart of the software development process. Its stages are:**

- **Problem definition**
- **Program design**
- **Coding**
- **Debugging**
- **Testing**
- **Documentation**
- **Maintenance and redesign**

Each of these stages is important in the construction of a working system. Coding, the writing of programs in a form that the computer understands, is only one stage in a long process.

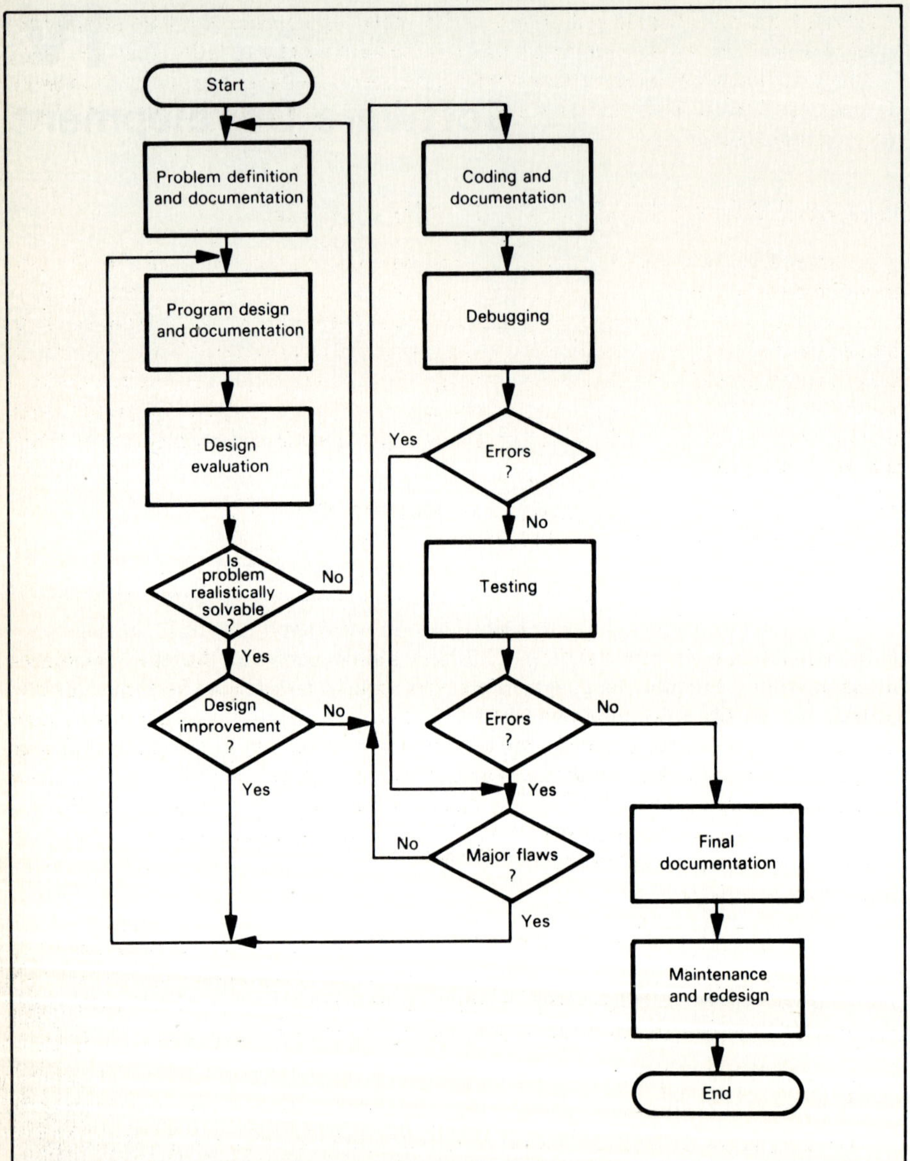

Figure IV-1. Flowchart of Software Development

RELATIVE IMPORTANCE OF CODING

Coding is usually the easiest stage to define and perform. The rules for writing computer programs are easy to learn. They vary somewhat from computer to computer, but the basic techniques remain the same. Few software projects run into trouble because of coding; indeed, coding is not the most time-consuming part of software development. Experts estimate that a programmer can write one to ten fully debugged and documented statements per day. Clearly, the mere coding of one to ten statements is hardly a full day's effort. On most software projects, coding occupies less than 25% of the programmer's time.

MEASURING PROGRESS IN OTHER STAGES

Measuring progress in other stages is difficult. You can say that half of the program has been written, but you can hardly say that half of the errors have been removed or half of the problem has been defined. Timetables for such stages as program design, debugging, and testing are difficult to produce. Many days or weeks of effort may result in no clear progress. Furthermore, an incomplete job in one stage may result in tremendous problems later. For example, poor problem definition or program design can make debugging and testing very difficult. Time saved in one stage may be spent many times over in later stages.

DEFINITION OF THE STAGES

Problem Definition

Problem definition is the formulation of the requirements that the task places on the computer. For example, what is necessary to make a computer control a tool, run a series of electrical tests, or handle communications between a central controller and a remote instrument? Problem definition requires that you determine the forms and rates of inputs and outputs, the amount and speed of processing that is needed, and the types of possible errors and their handling. Problem definition takes a vague idea of building a computer-controlled system and defines the tasks and requirements for the computer.

Program Design

Program design is the outline of the computer program that will meet the requirements. In the design stage, the tasks are described in a way that can easily be converted into a program. **Among the useful techniques in this stage are flowcharting, structured programming, modular programming, and top-down design.**

Coding

Coding is the writing of the program in a form that the computer can either directly understand or translate. The form may be machine language, assembly language, or a high-level language.

Debugging

Debugging, also called program verification, **is making the program perform according to the design.** In this stage, you use such tools as breakpoints, traces, simulators, logic analyzers, and in-circuit emulators. The end of the debugging stage is hard to define, since you never know when you have found the last error.

Testing

Testing, also referred to as program validation, **is ensuring that the program performs the overall system tasks correctly.** The designer uses simulators, exercisers, and statistical techniques to measure the program's performance. This stage is like quality control for hardware.

Documentation

Documentation is the description of the program in the proper form for users and maintenance personnel. Documentation also allows the designer to develop a program library so that subsequent tasks will be far simpler. Flowcharts, comments, memory maps, and library forms are some of the tools used in documentation.

Maintenance and Redesign

Maintenance and redesign are the servicing, improvement, and extension of the program. Clearly, the designer must be ready to handle field problems in computer-based equipment. Special diagnostic modes or programs and other maintenance tools may be required. Upgrading or extension of the program may be necessary to meet new requirements or handle new tasks.

16
Problem Definition

Typical microprocessor tasks require a lot of definition. For example, what must a program do to control a scale, a cash register, or a signal generator? Clearly, we have a long way to go just to define the tasks involved.

INPUTS

How do we start the definition? The obvious place to begin is with the inputs. **We should begin by listing all the inputs that the computer may receive in this application.**

Examples of inputs are:

- Data blocks from transmission lines
- Status words from peripherals
- Data from A/D converters

Then we may ask the following questions about each input:

1. What is its form; that is, what signals will the computer actually receive?
2. When is the input available and how does the processor know it is available? Does the processor have to request the input with a strobe signal? Does the input provide its own clock?
3. How long is it available?
4. How often does it change, and how does the processor know that it has changed?
5. Does the input consist of a sequence or block of data? Is the order important?
6. What should be done if the data contains errors? These may include transmission errors, incorrect data, sequencing errors, extra data, etc.
7. Is the input related to other inputs or outputs?

OUTPUTS

The next step to define is the output. **We must list all the outputs that the computer must produce.** Examples of outputs include:

- Data blocks to transmission lines
- Control words to peripherals
- Data to D/A converters

Then we may ask the following questions about each output:

1. What is its form; that is, what signals must the computer produce?
2. When must it be available, and how does the peripheral know it is available?
3. How long must it be available?
4. How often must it change, and how does the peripheral know that it has changed?
5. Is there a sequence of outputs?
6. What should be done to avoid transmission errors or to sense and recover from peripheral failures?
7. How is the output related to other inputs and outputs?

PROCESSING SECTION

Between the reading of input data and the sending of output results is the processing section. Here **we must determine exactly how the computer must process the input data. The questions are:**

1. What is the basic procedure (algorithm) for transforming input data into output results?
2. What time constraints exist? These may include data rates.
3. What memory constraints exist? Do we have limits on the amount of program memory or data memory, or on the size of buffers?
4. What standard programs or tables must be used? What are their requirements?
5. What special cases exist, and how should the program handle them?
6. How accurate must the results be?
7. How should the program handle processing errors or special conditions such as overflow, underflow, or loss of significance?

ERROR HANDLING

An important factor in many applications is the handling of errors. Clearly, the designer must make provisions for recovering from common errors and for diagnosing malfunctions. **Among the questions that the designer must ask at the definition stage are:**

1. What errors could occur?
2. Which errors are most likely? If a person operates the system, human error is the most common. Following human errors, communications or transmission errors are more common than mechanical, electrical, mathematical, or processor errors.
3. Which errors will not be immediately obvious to the system? A special problem is the occurrence of errors that the system or operator may not recognize as incorrect.
4. How can the system recover from errors with a minimum loss of time and data and yet be aware that an error has occurred?
5. Which errors or malfunctions cause the same system behavior? How can these errors or malfunctions be distinguished for diagnostic purposes?
6. Which errors involve special system procedures? For example, do parity errors require retransmission of data?

Another question is: How can the field technician systematically find the source of malfunctions without being an expert? Built-in test programs, special diagnostics, or signature analysis can help.[1]

HUMAN FACTORS/OPERATOR INTERACTION

Many microprocessor-based systems involve human interaction. **Human factors must be considered throughout the development process for such systems. Among the questions that the designer must ask are:**

1. What input procedures are most natural for the human operator?
2. Can the operator easily determine how to begin, continue and end the input operations?
3. How is the operator informed of procedural errors and equipment malfunctions?
4. What errors is the operator most likely to make?
5. How does the operator know that data has been entered correctly?
6. Are displays in a form that the operator can easily read and understand?
7. Is the response of the system adequate for the operator?
8. Is the system easy for the operator to use?
9. Are there guiding features for an inexperienced operator?
10. Are there shortcuts and reasonable options for the experienced operator?
11. Can the operator always determine or reset the state of the system after interruptions or distractions?

Building a system for people to use is difficult. The microprocessor can make the system more powerful, more flexible, and more responsive. However, **the designer** still **must add the human touches that can greatly increase the usefulness and attractiveness of the system and the productivity of the human operator.**[2]

The processor, of course, has no intrinsic preference in situations involving human characteristics or cultural choices. The processor does not prefer left-to-right over right-to-left, forward over backward, increasing order over decreasing order, or decimal numbers over other number systems. Nor does the processor recognize the operator's preference for simplicity, consistency, compatibility with previous experience, and "logical" order of operations. The processor never gets distracted, disoriented, confused, or bored. The designer must allow for all these considerations in the design and development of interactive systems.

EXAMPLES

DEFINING A SWITCH AND LIGHT SYSTEM

Figure 16-1 shows a simple system in which the input is from a single SPST switch and the output is to a single LED display. In response to a switch closure, the processor turns the display on for one second. This system should be easy to define.

Switch Input

Let us first examine the input and answer each of the questions previously presented:

1. The input is a single bit, which may be either '0' (switch closed) or '1' (switch open).
2. The input is always available and need not be requested.
3. The input is available for at least several milliseconds after the closure.
4. The input will seldom change more than once every few seconds. The processor has to handle only the bounce in the switch. The processor must monitor the switch to determine when it is closed.
5. There is no sequence of inputs.
6. The obvious input errors are switch failure, failure in the input circuitry, and the operator attempting to close the switch again before a sufficient amount of time has elapsed. We will discusss the handling of these errors later.
7. The input does not depend on any other inputs or outputs.

Light Output

The next requirement in defining the system is to examine the output. The answers to our questions are:

1. The output is a single bit, which is '0' to turn the display on, '1' to turn it off.
2. There are no time constraints on the output. The peripheral does not need to be informed of the availability of data.

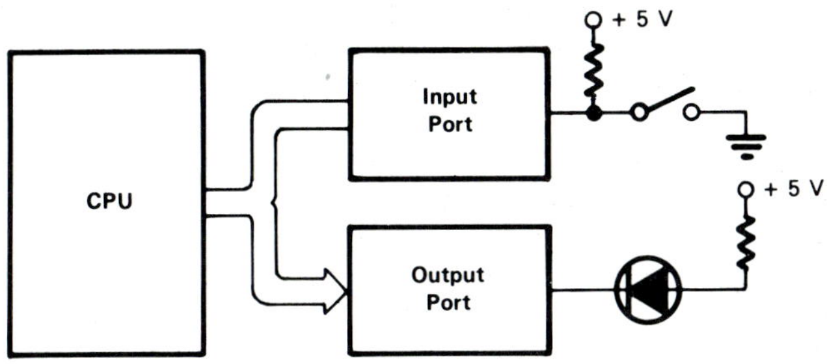

The switch input is a '1' if the switch is open, '0' if the switch is closed.
The CPU applies the output to the cathode of the LED: a '0' lights the display.

Figure 16-1. The Switch and Light System

3. If the display is an LED, the data need be available for only a few milliseconds at a pulse rate of about 100 times per second. The observer will see a continuously lit display.
4. The data must change (go off) after one second.
5. There is no sequence of outputs.
6. The possible output errors are display failure and failure in the output circuitry.
7. The output depends only on the switch input and time.

Processing

The processing section is extremely simple. As soon as the switch input becomes a logic '0', the CPU turns the light on (a logic '0') for one second. No time or memory constraints exist.

Error Handling

Let us now look at the possible errors and malfunctions. These are:

- Another switch closure before one second has elapsed
- Switch failure
- Display failure
- Computer failure

Surely the first error is the most likely. The simplest solution is for the processor to ignore switch closures until one second has elapsed. This brief unresponsive period will hardly be noticeable to the human operator. Furthermore, ignoring the switch during this period means that no debouncing circuitry or software is necessary, since the system will not react to the bounce anyway.

Clearly, the last three failures can produce unpredictable results. The display may stay on, stay off, or change state randomly. Some possible ways to isolate the failures would be:

- Lamp-test hardware to check the display; i.e., a button that turns the light on independently of the processor
- A direct connection to the switch to check its operation
- A diagnostic program that exercises the input and output circuits

If both the display and switch are working, the computer is at fault. A field technician with proper equipment can determine the cause of the failure.

DEFINING A SWITCH-BASED MEMORY LOADER

Figure 16-2 shows a system that allows the user to enter data into any memory location in a microcomputer. One input port, DPORT, reads data from eight toggle switches. The other input port, CPORT, is used to read control information. There are four momentary switches: High Address, Mid Address, Low Address and Data. The output is the value of the last completed entry from the data switches; eight LEDs are used for the display.

The system will also, of course, require resistors, buffers, and drivers.

Inputs

The characteristics of the switches are the same as in the previous example. To simplify the debouncing procedure and force the operator to release the buttons, we have the system respond only after a button is released; this is a common technique that reduces wear on the switches as well, since the operator is less tempted to press a button repeatedly. In this system **there is a distinct sequence of inputs, as follows:**

1. The operator must set the data switches according to the eight most significant bits of an address, then
2. press and release the High Address button. The high address bits will appear on the lights, and the program will interpret the data as the high byte of the address (bits A23-A16).
3. Then the operator must set the data switches with the value of the middle byte of the address (bits A15-A8) and
4. press and release the Mid Address button. The middle address bits will appear on the lights, and the program will consider the data to be the middle byte of the address.
5. Then the operator must set the data switches with the value of the least significant byte of the address bits (A7-A0) and
6. press and releast the Low Address button. The low address bits will appear on the lights, and the program will consider the data to be the low byte of the address.
7. Finally, the operator must set the desired data into the data switches and
8. press and release the Data button. The display will now show the data, and the program stores the data in memory at the previously entered address.

The operator may repeat the process to enter an entire program. Clearly, even in this simplified situation, we will have many possible sequences to consider. How do we cope with erroneous sequences and make the system easy to use?

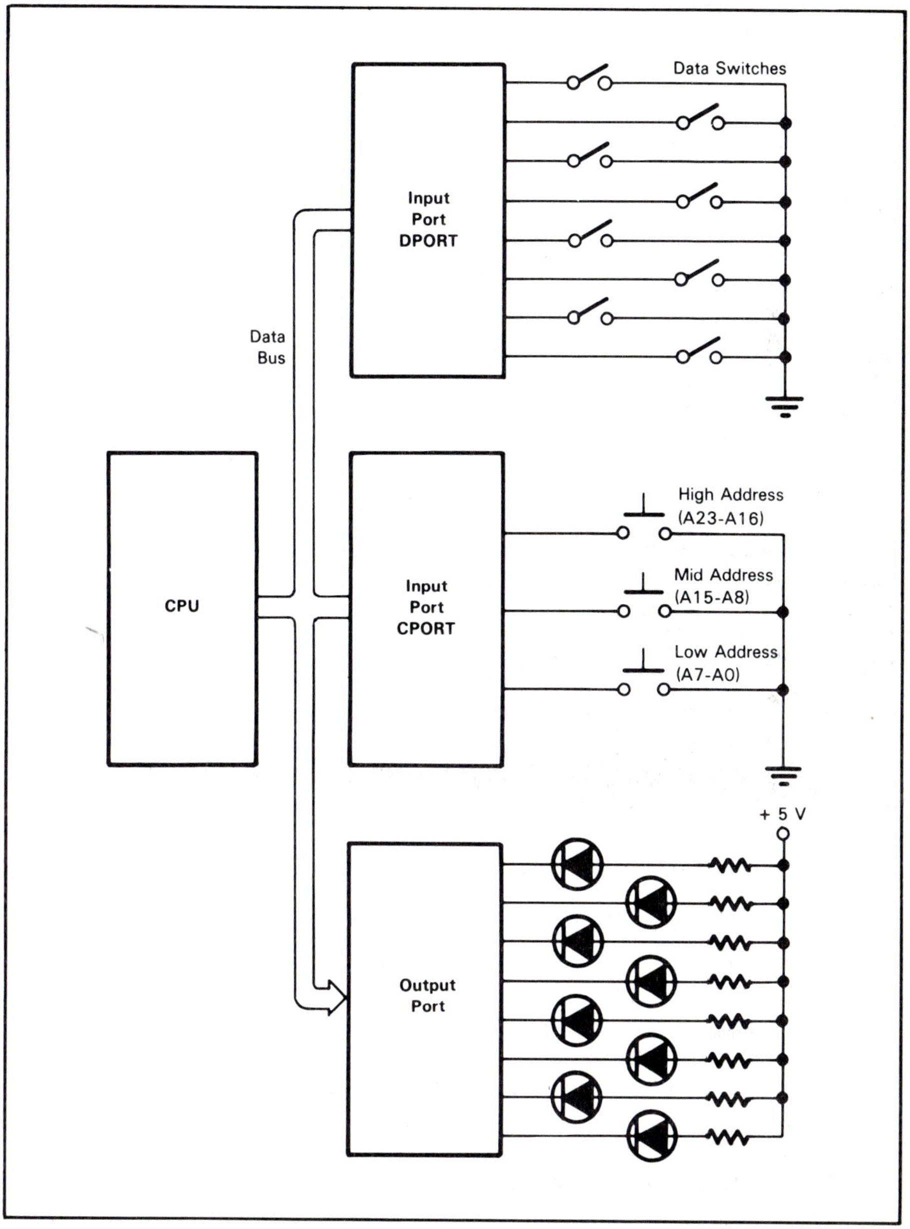

Figure 16-2. The Switch-Based Memory Loader

Output

Output is no problem. After each input, the program sends to the displays the complement (since the displays are active-low) of the input bits. The output data remains the same until the next input operation.

Processing

The processing section remains quite simple. There are no time or memory constraints. The program can debounce the switches by waiting for a few milliseconds, and must provide complemented data to the displays.

Error Handling

The most likely errors are operator mistakes. These include:

- Incorrect entries
- Incorrect order
- Incomplete entries; for example, forgetting the data

The system must be able to handle these problems in a reasonable way, since they are certain to occur in actual operation.

The designer must also consider the effects of equipment failure. Just as before, the possible difficulties are:

- Switch failure
- Display failure
- Computer failure

In this system, however, we must pay more attention to how these failures affect the system. A computer failure will cause a complete system breakdown that will be easy to detect. A display failure may not be immediately noticeable; here a Lamp Test feature will allow the operator to check the operation. Note that we would like to test each LED separately, in order to diagnose the case in which output lines are shorted together. In addition, the operator may not immediately detect switch failure; however, the operator should soon notice it and establish which switch is faulty by a process of elimination.

Operator Error Correction

Let us look at **some of the possible operator errors.** Typical errors **will be:**

- Erroneous data
- Wrong order of entries or switches
- Trying to go on to the next entry without completing the current one

The operator will presumably notice erroneous data as soon as it appears on the displays. **What is a viable recovery procedure? Some options are:**

1. The operator must complete the entry procedure; i.e., enter Mid Address, Low Address and Data if the error occurs in the High Address. Clearly, this

procedure is wasteful and annoying.

2. The operator may restart the entry process by returning to the high address entry steps. This solution is useful if the error was in the High Address, but forces the operator to re-enter earlier data if the error was in the Mid Address, Low Address or Data stage.
3. The operator may enter any part of the sequence at any time simply by setting the Data switches with the desired data and pressing the corresponding button. This procedure allows the operator to make corrections at any point in the sequence.

This type of procedure should always be preferred over one that does not allow immediate error correction, has a variety of concluding steps, or enters data into the system without allowing the operator a final check. Any added complication in hardware or software will be justified in increased operator efficiency. You should always prefer to let the microcomputer do the tedious work and recognize arbitrary sequences; it never gets tired and never forgets the operating procedures.

A further helpful feature would be status lights that would define the meaning of the display. Four status lights, marked "High Address," "Mid Address," "Low Address," and "Data," would let the operator know what had been entered without having to remember which button was pressed. The processor would have to monitor the sequence, but the added complication in software would simplify the operator's task. Clearly, four separate sets of displays plus the ability to examine a memory location would be even more helpful to the operator.

We should note that, although we have emphasized human interaction, machine or system interaction has many of the same characteristics. The microprocessor should do the work. If complicating the microprocessor's task makes error recovery simple and the causes of failure obvious, the entire system will work better and be easier to maintain. Note that you should not wait until after the software has been completed to consider system use and maintenance; instead, you should include these factors in the problem definition stage.

DEFINING A VERIFICATION TERMINAL

Figure 16-3 is a block diagram of a simple credit-verification terminal. One input port derives data from a keyboard (see Figure 16-4); the other input port accepts verification data from a transmission line. One output port sends data to a set of displays (see Figure 16-5); another sends the credit card number to the central computer. A third output port turns on one light whenever the terminal is ready to accept an inquiry, and another light when the operator sends the information. The "busy" light is turned off when the terminal receives a response. Clearly, the input and output of data will be more complex than in the previous case, although the processing is still simple.

Additional displays may be useful to emphasize the meaning of the response. Many terminals use a green light for "Yes," a red light for "No," and a yellow light for "Consult Store Manager." Note that these lights will still have to be clearly marked with their meanings to allow for a color-blind operator.

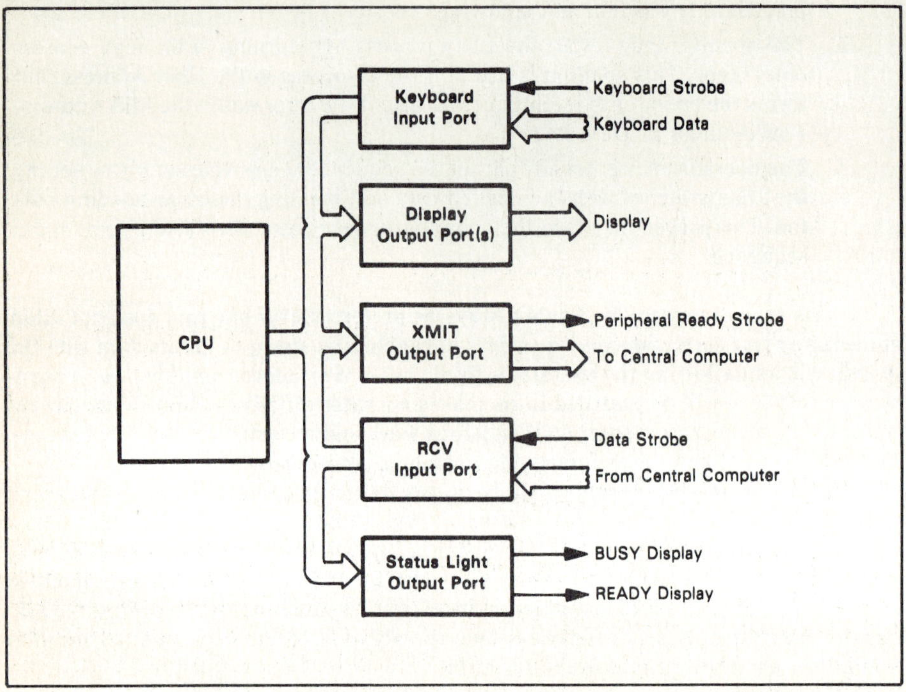

Figure 16-3. Block Diagram of a Verification Terminal

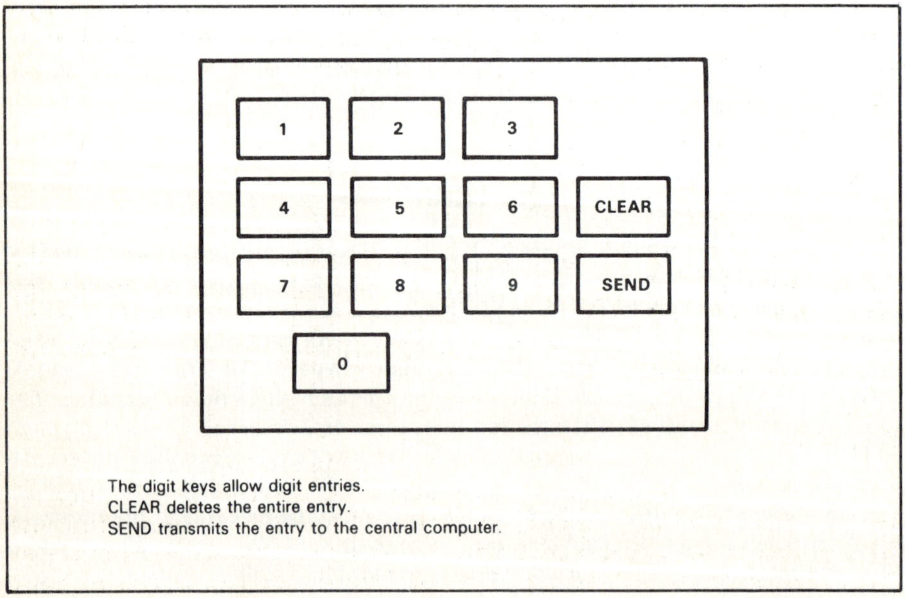

Figure 16-4. Verification Terminal Keyboard

The display consists of ten 7-segment displays, which may be multiplexed, controlled by a shift register, or addressed separately. Two additional lights, READY and BUSY, are also present.

Figure 16-5. Verification Terminal Display

Inputs

Let us first look at the keyboard input. This is, of course, different from the switch input, since the CPU must have some way of distinguishing new data. **We will assume that each key closure provides a unique hexadecimal code (we can code each of the 12 keys into one digit) and a strobe. The program will have to recognize the strobe and fetch the hexadecimal number that identifies the key.** There is a time constraint, since the program cannot miss any data or strobes. The constraint is not serious, since keyboard entries will be at least several milliseconds apart.

The transmission input similarly consists of a series of characters, each identified by a strobe (perhaps from a UART). The program will have to recognize each strobe and fetch the character. The data being sent across the transmission lines is usually organized into messages. A possible message format is:

- Introductory characters, or header
- Terminal destination address
- Coded yes or no
- Ending characters, or trailer

The terminal will check the header, read the destination address, and see if the message is intended for it. If the message is for the terminal, the terminal accepts the data. The address could be (and often is) hard-wired into the terminal so that the terminal receives only messages intended for it. This approach simplifies the software at the cost of some flexibility.

Outputs

The output is also more complex than in the earlier examples. **If the displays are multiplexed, the processor must not only send the data to the display port but must also direct the data to a particular display.** We will need either a separate control port or a counter and decoder to handle this. Note that hardware blanking controls can blank leading zeros as long as the first digit in a multi-digit number is never zero. Software can also handle this task. Time constraints include the pulse length and frequency required to produce a continuous display for the operator.

The communications output will consist of a series of characters with a particular format. The program will also have to consider the time required between characters. A possible format for the output message is:

- Header
- Terminal address
- Credit card number
- Trailer

A central communication computer may poll the terminals, checking for data ready to be sent.

Processing

The processing in this system involves many new tasks, such as:

- Identifying the control keys by number and performing the proper actions
- Adding the header, terminal address, and trailer to the outgoing message
- Recognizing the header and trailer in the returning message
- Checking the incoming terminal address

Note that none of the tasks involves any complex arithmetic or any serious time or memory constraints.

Error Handling

The number of possible errors in this system is, of course, much larger than in the earlier examples. Let us first consider the possible operator errors. These include:

- Entering the credit card number incorrectly
- Trying to send an incomplete credit card number
- Trying to send another number while the central computer is processing one
- Clearing nonexistent entries

Some of these errors can be handled easily by organizing the program correctly. For example, the program should not accept the Send key until the credit card number has been completely entered, and it should ignore any additional keyboard entries until the response comes back from the central computer. Note that the operator will know that the entry has not been sent, since the Busy light will not go on. The operator will also know when the keyboard has been locked out (the program is ignoring keyboard entries), since entries will not appear on the display and the Ready light will be off.

Correcting Keyboard Errors

Incorrect entries are an obvious problem. **If the operator recognizes an error, he or she can use the Clear key to make corrections. The operator would probably find it more convenient to have two Clear keys, one that cleared the most recent key and one**

that cleared the entire entry. This would allow both for the situation in which the operator recognizes the error immediately and for the situation in which the operator recognizes the error late in the procedure. **The operator should be able to correct errors immediately and have to repeat as few keys as possible. The operator will, however, make a certain number of errors without recognizing them. Most credit card numbers include a self-checking digit; the terminal could check the number before permitting it to be sent to the central computer.** This step would save the central computer from wasting processing time checking the number.

This requires, however, that the terminal have some way of informing the operator of the error, perhaps by flashing one of the displays or by providing some other special indicator that the operator is sure to notice.

Still another problem is how the operator knows that an entry has been lost or processed incorrectly. Some terminals simply unlock after a maximum time delay. The operator notes that the Busy light has gone off without an answer being received. The operator is then expected to try the entry again. After one or two further attempts, the operator should report the failure to supervisory personnel.

Many equipment failures are also possible. Besides the displays, keyboard, and processor, there now exist the problems of communications errors or failures and central computer failures.

Correcting Transmission Errors

The data transmission will probably have to include error checking and correcting procedures. Some possibilities are:

1. Parity provides an error detection facility but no correction mechanism. The receiver will need some way of requesting retransmission, and the sender will have to save a copy of the data until proper reception is acknowledged. Parity is, however, very simple to implement.
2. Short messages may use more elaborate schemes. For example, the yes/no response to the terminal could be coded to provide error detection and correction capability.
3. An acknowledgement and a limited number of retries could trigger an indicator that would inform the operator of a communications failure (inability to transfer a message without errors) or central computer failure (no response within a certain period of time). Such a scheme, along with the Lamp Test, would allow simple failure diagnosis.

A communications or central computer failure indicator should also "unlock" the terminal, that is, allow it to accept another entry. This is necessary if the terminal will not accept entries while a verification is in progress. **The terminal may also unlock after a certain maximum time delay. Certain entries could be reserved for diagnostics;** i.e., certain credit card numbers could be used to check the internal operation of the terminal and test the displays.

REVIEW

Problem definition is as important a part of software development as it is of any other engineering task. Note that it does not require any programming or knowledge of the computer; rather, it is based on an understanding of the system and sound engineering judgment. Microprocessors offer flexibility and local intelligence that the designer can use to provide a wide range of features.

Problem definition is independent of any particular computer, computer language, or development system. It should, however, provide guidelines as to what type or speed of computer the application will require and what kind of hardware/software tradeoffs the designer can make. The problem definition stage should not even depend on whether a computer is used, although a knowledge of the capabilities of the computer can help the designer in suggesting possible implementations of procedures.

REFERENCES

1. D. R. Ballard. "Designing Fail-Safe Microprocessor Systems," *Electronics,* January 4, 1979, pp. 139-43.

   "A Designer's Guide to Signature Analysis," Hewlett-Packard Application Note 222, Hewlett-Packard, Inc, Palo Alto, CA, 1977.

   Donn, E. S. and M. D. Lippman. "Efficient and Effective Microcomputer Testing Requires Careful Preplanning," *EDN,* February 20, 1979, pp. 97-107 (includes self-test examples for 6502).

   Gordon, G. and H. Nadig. "Hexadecimal Signatures Identify Troublespots in Microprocessor Systems," *Electronics,* March 3, 1977, pp. 89-96.

   Neil, M. and R. Goodner. "Designing a Serviceman's Needs into Microprocessor-Based Systems," *Electronics,* March 1, 1979, pp. 122-28.

   Schweber, W. and L. Pearce. "Software Signature Analysis Identifies and Checks PROMs," *EDN,* November 5, 1978, pp. 79-81.

   Srini, V. P. "Fault Diagnosis of Microprocessor Systems," *Computer,* January 1977, pp. 60-65.

2. For a brief discussion of human factors considerations, see G. Morris. "Make Your Next Instrument Design Emphasize User Needs and Wants," *EDN,* October 20, 1978, pp. 100-05.

17
Program Design

Program design is the stage in which the problem definition is formulated as a program. If the program is small and simple, this stage may involve little more than the writing of a one-page flowchart. If the program is larger or more complex, the designer should consider more elaborate methods.

We will discuss flowcharting, modular programming, structured programming, and top-down design. We will try to indicate the reasoning behind these methods, and their advantages and disadvantages. We will not, however, advocate any particular method since there is no evidence that one method is always superior to all others. You should remember that the goal is to produce a good working system, not to follow religiously the tenets of one methodology or another.

BASIC PRINCIPLES

All the methodologies are based on common principles, many of which apply to any kind of design. Among these principles are:

1. **Proceed in small steps.** Do not try to do too much at one time.
2. **Divide large jobs into small, logically separate tasks.** Make the sub-tasks as independent of one another as possible, so that they can be tested separately and so that changes can be made in one without affecting the others.
3. **Keep the flow of control simple** to make programs easy to follow and errors easy to locate and correct.
4. **Use pictorial or graphic design descriptions** as much as possible. They are easier to visualize than word descriptions. This is the great advantage of flowcharts.

5. **Emphasize clarity and simplicity at first.** You can improve performance (if necessary) once the system is working.
6. **Proceed in a thorough and systematic manner.** Use checklists and standard procedures.
7. Do not tempt fate. **Either do not use methods that you are not sure of, or use them very carefully. Watch for situations that might cause confusion,** and clarify them as soon as possible.
8. Keep in mind that **the system must be debugged, tested and maintained. Plan for these later stages.**
9. **Use simple and consistent terminology and methods.** Repetitiveness is no fault in program design, nor is complexity a virtue.
10. **Have your design completely formulated before you start coding.** Resist the temptation to start writing down instructions: it makes no more sense than making parts lists or laying out circuit boards before you know exactly what will be in the system.
11. Be particularly careful of factors that may change. **Make the implementation of likely changes as simple as possible.**
12. **Keep the overall task in mind.** Build a total framework in which individual pieces can be defined and tested. Do not leave the entire system integration to the end.
13. If the data is complex or there are numerous relationships between data items, **you must organize your data just as carefully as you organize your program. We will briefly discuss the design of data structures at the end of this chapter.**

FLOWCHARTING

Flowcharting is certainly the best known of all program design methods. Programming textbooks describe how programmers first write complete flowcharts and then start writing the actual program. In fact, few programmers have ever worked this way, and flowcharting has often been more of a joke or a nuisance to programmers than a design method. We will try to describe both the advantages and disadvantages of flowcharts, and show the place of this technique in program design.

ADVANTAGES OF FLOWCHARTING

The basic advantage of the flowchart is that it is a pictorial representation. People find such representations much more meaningful than written descriptions. The designer can visualize the whole system and see the relationships of the various parts. Logical errors and inconsistencies often stand out instead of being hidden in a printed page. At its best, the flowchart is a picture of the entire system.

Some specific advantages of flowcharts are:

1. Standard symbols exist (see Figure 17-1) so that flowcharting forms are widely recognized.

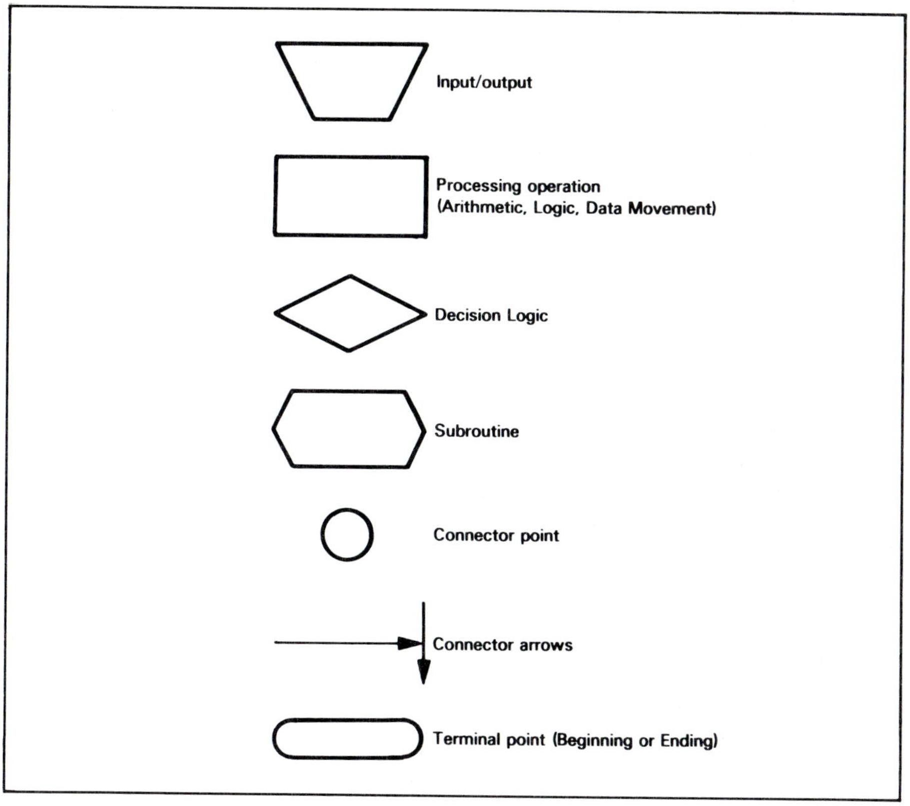

Figure 17-1. Standard Flowchart Symbols

2. Flowcharts can be understood by someone without a programming background.
3. Flowcharts can be used to divide the entire project into sub-tasks. The flowchart can then be examined to measure overall progress.
4. Flowcharts show the sequence of operations and can therefore aid in locating the source of errors.
5. Flowcharting is widely used in other areas besides programming.
6. There are many tools available to aid in flowcharting, including programmer's templates and automated drawing packages.

DISADVANTAGES OF FLOWCHARTING

These advantages are all important. There is no question that flowcharting will continue to be widely used. But **we should note some disadvantages of flowcharting as a program design method:**

1. Flowcharts are difficult to design, draw, or change in all except the simplest situations.

2. There is no easy way to debug or test a flowchart.
3. Flowcharts tend to become cluttered. Designers find it difficult to balance between the amount of detail needed to make the flowchart useful and the amount that makes the flowchart little better that a program listing.
4. Flowcharts show only the program organization. They do not show the organization of the data or the structure of the input/output modules.
5. Flowcharts do not help with hardware or timing problems or give hints as to where these problems might occur.
6. Flowcharts allow unstructured design. There are no rules governing the numbers of entries and exits, the number or type of interconnections, or the logic that may be employed.
7. There is no obvious way to represent the simple repetition of a loop.

MAKING FLOWCHARTS USEFUL

The most useful flowcharts may ignore program variables and ask questions directly. Of course, compromises are often necessary here. **Two versions of the flowchart are sometimes helpful — one general version in layman's language, which will be useful to non-programmers, and one programmer's version in terms of the program variables, which will be useful to other programmers.**

A third type of flowchart, a data flowchart, may also be helpful. This flowchart serves as a cross-reference for the other flowcharts, since it shows how the program handles a particular type of data. Ordinary flowcharts show how the program proceeds, handling different types of data at different points. **Data flowcharts,** on the other hand, **show how particular types of data move through the system, passing from one part of the program to another.** Such flowcharts are very useful in debugging and maintenance, since errors most often show up as a particular type of data being handled incorrectly.

Thus **flowcharting is a helpful technique that you should not try to extend too far. Flowcharts are useful as program documentation, since they have standard forms and are comprehensible to non-programmers.** As a design tool, **however,** flowcharts cannot provide much more than a starting outline; **the programmer cannot debug a detailed flowchart** and the flowchart is often more difficult to design than the program itself.

EXAMPLES

Flowcharting the Switch and Light System

This simple task, in which a single switch turns on a light for one second, is easy to flowchart. In fact, such tasks are typical examples for flowcharting books, although they form a small part of most systems. The data structure here is so simple that it can be safely ignored.

Figure 17-2 is the flowchart. There is little difficulty in deciding on the amount of detail required. The flowchart gives a straightforward picture of the procedure, which anyone could understand.

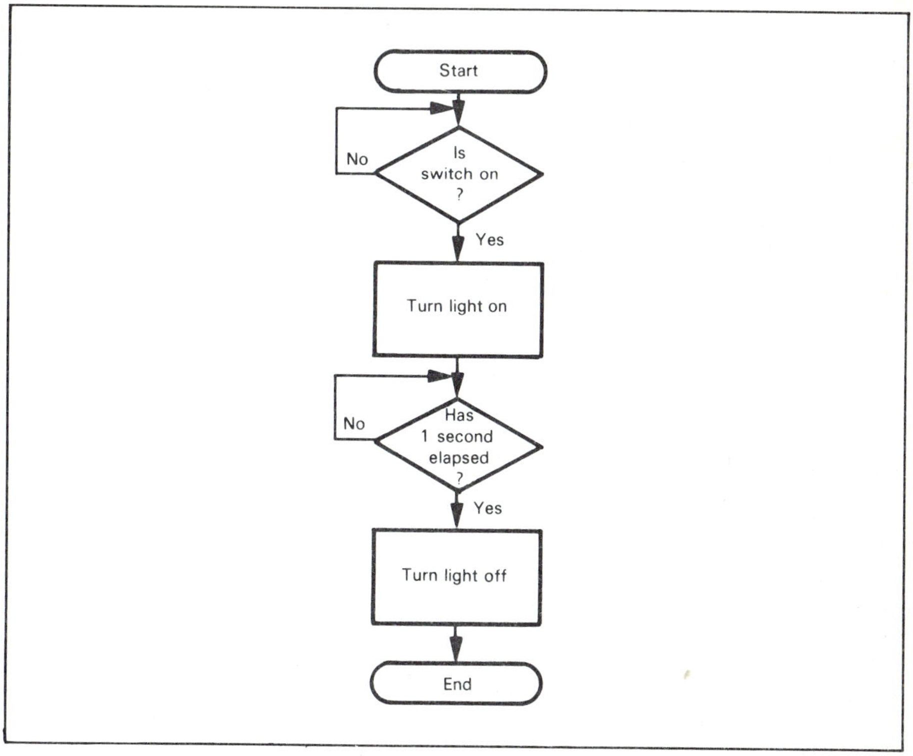

Figure 17-2. Flowchart of One-Second Response to a Switch

Flowcharting the Switch-Based Memory Loader

This system (see Figure 16-2) is considerably more complex than the previous example, and involves many more decisions. **The flowchart (see Figure 17-3) is more difficult to draw and is not as straightforward as the previous example.** In this example, we face the problem that there is no way to debug or test the flowchart.

The flowchart in Figure 17-3 includes the improvements we suggested as part of the problem definition. Clearly, this flowchart is beginning to get cluttered and lose its advantages over a written description. Adding other features that define the meaning of the entry with status lights and allow the operator to check entries after completion would make the flowchart even more complex. Drawing the complete flowchart from scratch could quickly become a formidable task. However, once the program has been written, the flowchart is useful as documentation.

Flowcharting the Verification Terminal

In this application (see Figures 16-3 through 16-5) the flowchart will be even more complex than in the switch-based memory loader case. Here, **the best idea is to flowchart sections separately so that the flowcharts remain manageable.** However, the presence of data structures (as in the multi-digit display and the messages) will make the gap between flowchart and program much wider.

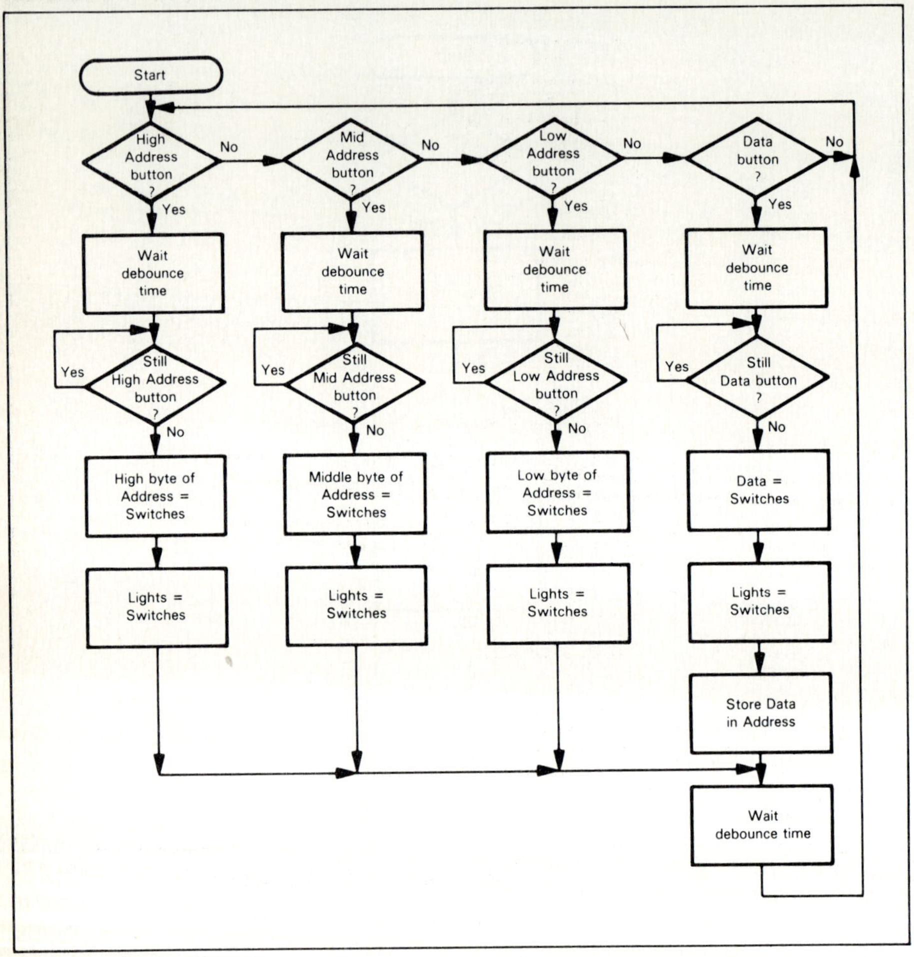

Figure 17-3. Flowchart of a Switch-Based Memory Loader

Let us look at some of the sections. **Figure 17-4 shows the keyboard entry process for the digit keys.** The program must fetch the data after each strobe and place the digit into the display array if there is room for it. If there are already ten digits in the array, the program simply ignores the entry.

The actual program will have to handle the displays at the same time. Note that either software or hardware must de-activate the keyboard strobe after the processor reads a digit.

Figure 17-5 adds the Send key. This key, of course, is optional. The terminal could just send the data as soon as the operator enters a complete number. However, that procedure would not give the operator a chance to check the entire entry. The flowchart with the Send key is more complex because there are two alternatives.

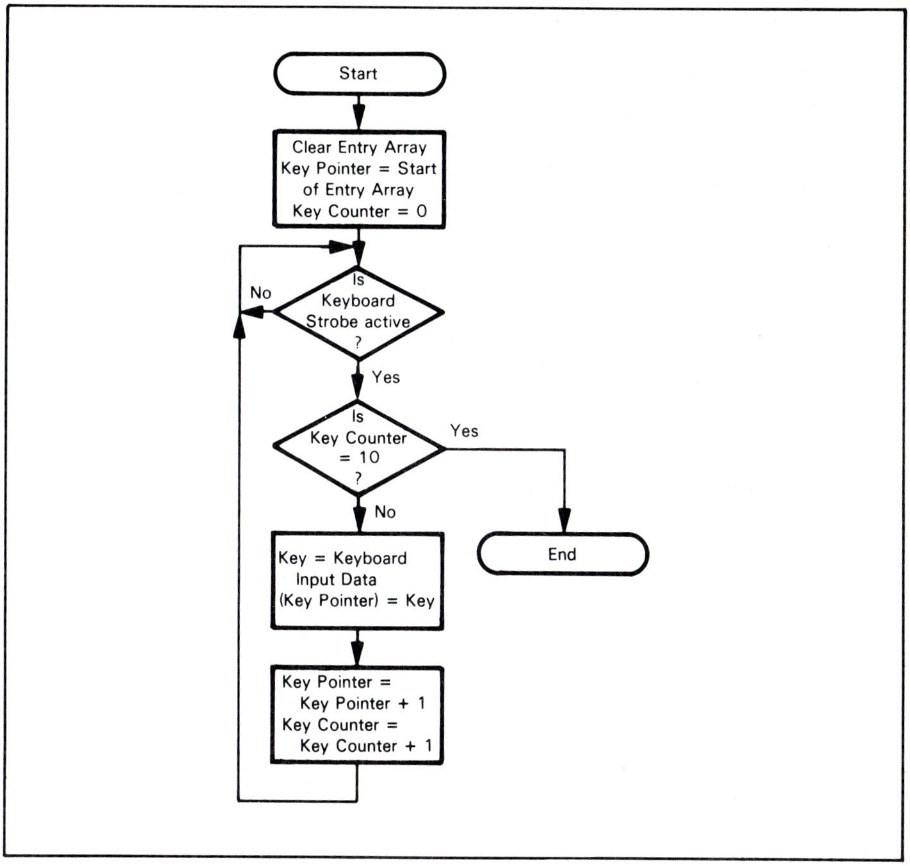

Figure 17-4. Flowchart of Keyboard Entry Process

1. If the operator has not entered ten digits, the program must ignore the Send key and place any other key into the entry.
2. If the operator has entered ten digits, the program must respond to the Send key by transferring control to the Send routine; and ignore all other keys.

Note that the flowchart has become much more difficult to organize and to follow. There is also no obvious way to check the flowchart.

Figure 17-6 shows the flowchart of the keyboard entry process with all the function keys. In this example, the flow of control is not simple. Clearly, some written description is necessary. The organization and layout of complex flowcharts requires careful planning. We have followed the process of adding features to the flowchart one at a time, but this still results in a large amount of redrawing. Again we should remember that throughout the keyboard entry process, the program must also refresh the displays if they are multiplexed and not controlled by shift registers or other hardware.

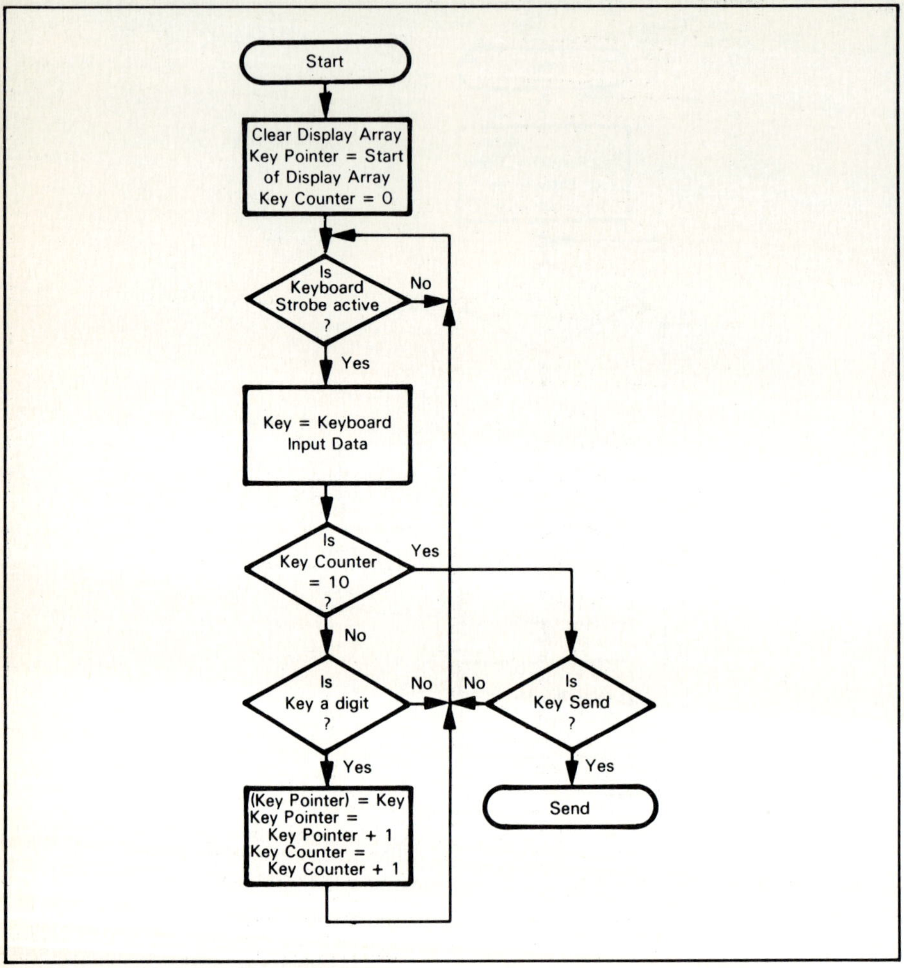

Figure 17-5. Flowchart of Entry Process With Send Key

Figure 17-7 is the flowchart of a receive routine. We assume that the serial/parallel conversion and error checking are done in hardware (e.g., by a UART). The processor must:

1. Look for the header. (We assume that it is a single character.)
2. Read the destination address (we assume that it is three characters long) and see if the message is meant for this terminal; i.e., if the three characters agree with the terminal address.
3. Wait for the trailer character.

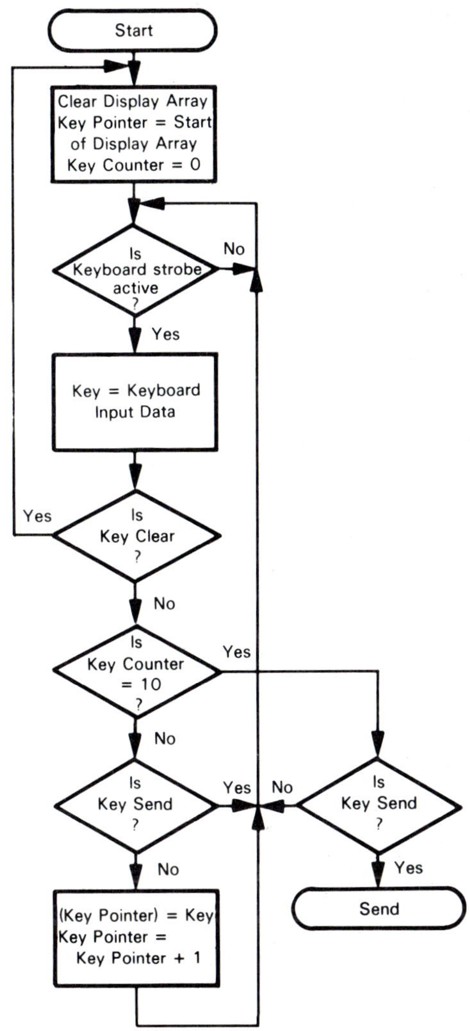

Figure 17-6. Flowchart of Keyboard Entry Process With Function Keys

4. If the message is meant for the terminal, turn off the Busy light and go to Display Answer routine.
5. In the event of any errors, request retransmission by going to the appropriate RTRANS routine.

This routine involves a large number of decisions, and the flowchart is neither simple nor obvious.

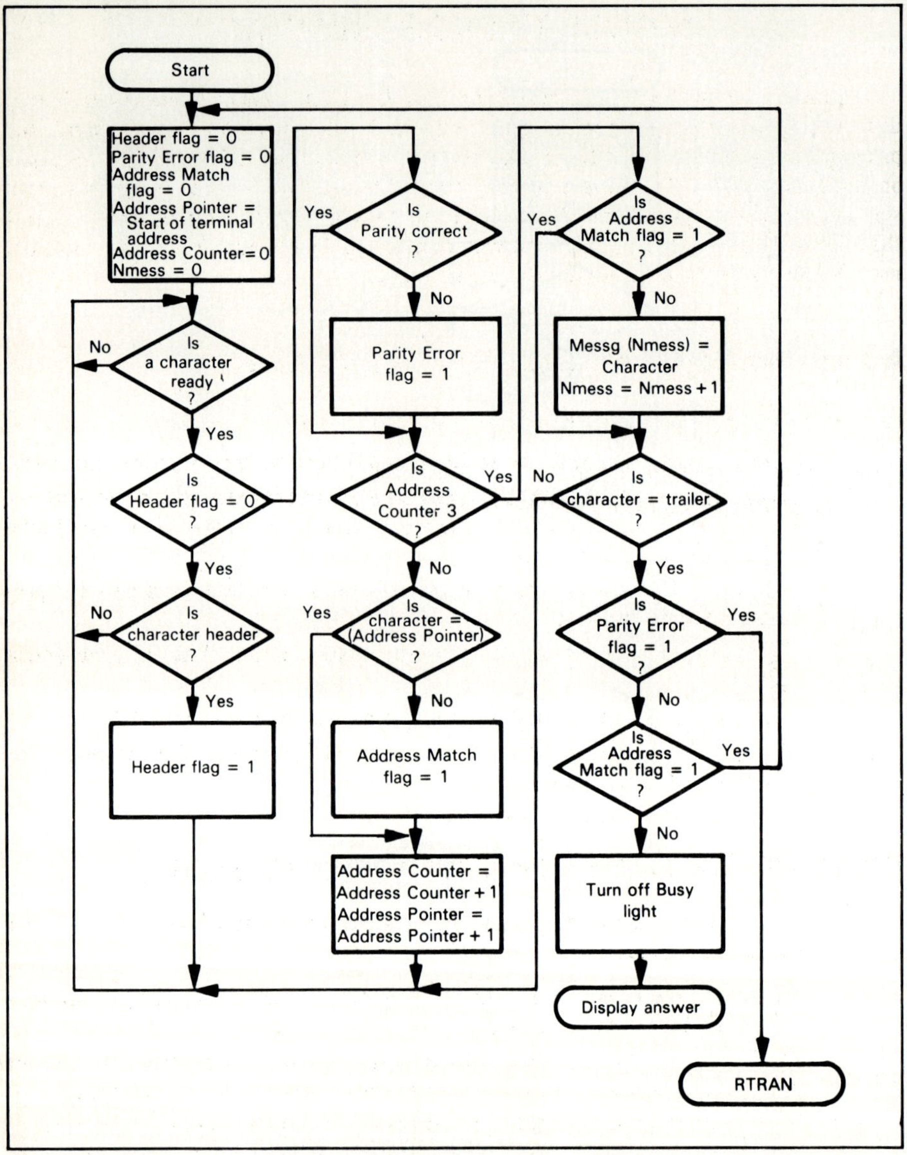

Figure 17-7. Flowchart of Receive Routine

Clearly, we have come a long way from the simple flowchart (Figure 17-2) of the first example. A complete set of flowcharts for the transaction terminal would be a major task. It would consist of several interrelated charts with complex logic, and would require a large amount of effort. Such an effort would be just as difficult as writing a preliminary program, and not as useful, since you could not check the flowcharts on the computer.

MODULAR PROGRAMMING

Once programs become large and complex, flowcharting is no longer a satisfactory design tool. However, the problem definition and the flowchart can help you divide the program into reasonable sub-tasks. **The division of the entire program into sub-tasks or modules is called "modular programming."** Clearly, most of the programs we presented in earlier chapters would typically be modules in a large program. **The problems that the designer faces in modular programming are how to divide the program into modules and how to put the modules together.**

ADVANTAGES OF MODULAR PROGRAMMING

The advantages of modular programming are obvious:

1. A single module is easier to write, debug, and test than an entire program.
2. A module is likely to be useful in many places and in other programs, particularly if it is reasonably general and performs a common task. You can build a library of standard modules.
3. Modular programming allows the programmer to divide tasks and use previously written programs.
4. Changes can be incorporated into one module rather than into the entire system.
5. Errors can often be isolated and then attributed to a single module.
6. Modular programming helps with project management, since it results in obvious goals and milestones.

DISADVANTAGES OF MODULAR PROGRAMMING

The idea of modular programming is so simple that its disadvantages are often ignored. These include:

1. Fitting the modules together can be a major problem, particularly if different people write the modules.
2. Modules require very careful documentation, since they may affect other parts of the program, such as data structures used by all the modules.
3. Testing and debugging modules separately is difficult, since other modules may produce the data used by the module being debugged and still other modules may use the results. You may have to write special programs (called "drivers") just to produce sample data and test the programs. These drivers require extra programming effort that adds nothing to the system.
4. Programs may be very difficult to modularize. If you modularize the program poorly, integration will be very difficult, since almost all errors and changes will involve several modules.
5. Modular programs often require extra time and memory, since the separate modules may repeat functions.

Therefore, while modular programming is certainly an improvement over trying to write the entire program from scratch, it does have some disadvantages as well.

Important considerations include restricting the amount of information shared by modules, limiting design decisions that are subject to change to a single module, and restricting the access of one module to another.[1]

PRINCIPLES OF MODULARIZATION

An obvious problem is that there are no proven, systematic methods for modularizing programs. We should mention the following principles:[2]

1. Modules that reference common data should be parts of the same overall module.
2. Two modules in which the first uses or depends on the second, but not the reverse, should be separate.
3. A module that is used by more than one other module should be part of a different overall module than the others.
4. Two modules in which the first is used by many other modules and the second is used by only a few other modules should be separate.
5. Two modules whose frequencies of usage are significantly different should be part of different modules.
6. The structure or organization of related data should be hidden within a single module.

If a program is difficult to modularize, you may need to redefine the tasks that are involved. Too many special cases or too many variables that require special handling are typical signs of inadequate problem definition.

EXAMPLES

Modularizing the Switch and Light System

This simple program can be divided into two modules:

Module 1 waits for the switch to be turned on and turns the light on in response.

Module 2 provides the one-second delay.

Module 1 is likely to be specific to the system, since it will depend on how the switch and light are attached. Module 2 will be generally useful, since many tasks require delays. Clearly, it would be advantageous to have a standard delay module that could provide delays of varying lengths. The module will require careful documentation so that you will know how to specify the length of the delay, how to call the module, and what registers and memory locations the module affects.

A general version of Module 1 would be far less useful, since it would have to deal with different types and connections of switches and lights.

You would probably find it simpler to write a module for a particular configuration of switches and lights rather than try to use a standard routine. Note the difference between this situation and Module 2.

Modularizing the Switch-Based Memory Loader

The switch-based memory loader is difficult to modularize, since all the programming tasks depend on the hardware configuration and the tasks are so simple that modules hardly seem worthwhile. The flowchart in Figure 17-3 suggests that one module might be the one that waits for the operator to press one of the four pushbuttons.

Some other modules might be:

- A delay module that provides the delay required to debounce the switches
- A switch and display module that reads the data from the switches and sends it to the displays
- A Lamp Test module

Highly system-dependent modules such as the last two are unlikely to be generally useful. This example is not one in which modular programming offers great advantages.

Modularizing the Verification Terminal

The verification terminal, on the other hand, lends itself very well to modular programming. The entire system **can easily be divided into three main modules:**

- **Keyboard and display module**
- **Data transmission module**
- **Data reception module**

A general keyboard and display module could handle many keyboard- and display-based systems. The sub-modules would perform such tasks as:

- Recognizing a new keyboard entry and fetching the data
- Clearing the array in response to a Clear Key
- Entering digits into storage
- Looking for the terminator or Send key
- Displaying the digits

Although the key interpretations and the number of digits will vary, the basic entry, data storage, and data display processes will be the same for many programs. Such function keys as Clear would also be standard. Clearly, **the designer must consider which modules will be useful in other applications, and pay careful attention to those modules.**

The data transmission module could also be divided into such sub-modules as:

1. Adding the header character.
2. Transmitting characters as the output line can handle them.
3. Generating delay times between bits or characters.
4. Adding the trailer character.
5. Checking for transmission failures; i.e., no acknowledgement, or inability to transmit without errors.

The data reception module could include sub-modules which:

1. Look for the header character.
2. Check the message destination address against the terminal address.
3. Store and interpret the message.
4. Look for the trailer character.
5. Generate bit or character delays.

INFORMATION HIDING PRINCIPLE

Note here how important it is that each design decision (such as the bit rate, message format, or error-checking procedure) be implemented in only one module. A change in any of these decisions will then require changes only to that single module. The other modules should be written so that they are totally unaware of the values chosen or the methods used in the implementing module. **An important concept here is the "information-hiding principle,"[3] whereby modules share only information that is absolutely essential to getting the task done. Other information is hidden within a single module.**

Error handling is a typical situation in which information should be hidden. When a module detects a lethal error, it should not try to recover; instead, it should inform the calling module of the error status and allow that module to decide how to proceed. The reason is that the lower level module often lacks sufficient information to establish recovery procedures. For example, suppose that the lower level module is one that accepts numeric input from a user. This module expects a string of numeric digits terminated by a carriage return. Entry of a non-numeric character causes the module to terminate abnormally. Since the module does not know the context (i.e. is the numeric string an operand, a lone number, an I/O unit number, or the length of a file?), it cannot decide how to handle an error. If the module always followed a single error recovery procedure, it would lose its generality and only be usable in those situations where that procedure was required.

REVIEW OF MODULAR PROGRAMMING

Modular programming can be very helpful if you abide by the following rules:

1. **Use modules of 20 to 50 lines.** Shorter modules are usually a waste of time, while longer modules are seldom general and may be difficult to integrate.
2. **Make modules reasonably general.** Differentiate between common features like ASCII code or asynchronous transmission formats, which will be the same for many applications, and key identifications, number of displays, or number of characters in a message, which are likely to be unique to a particular application. Make the changing of the latter parameters simple. Major changes like different character codes should be handled by separate modules.
3. **Take extra time on modules** like delays, display handlers, keyboard handlers, etc. **that will be useful in other projects or in many different places in the present program.**

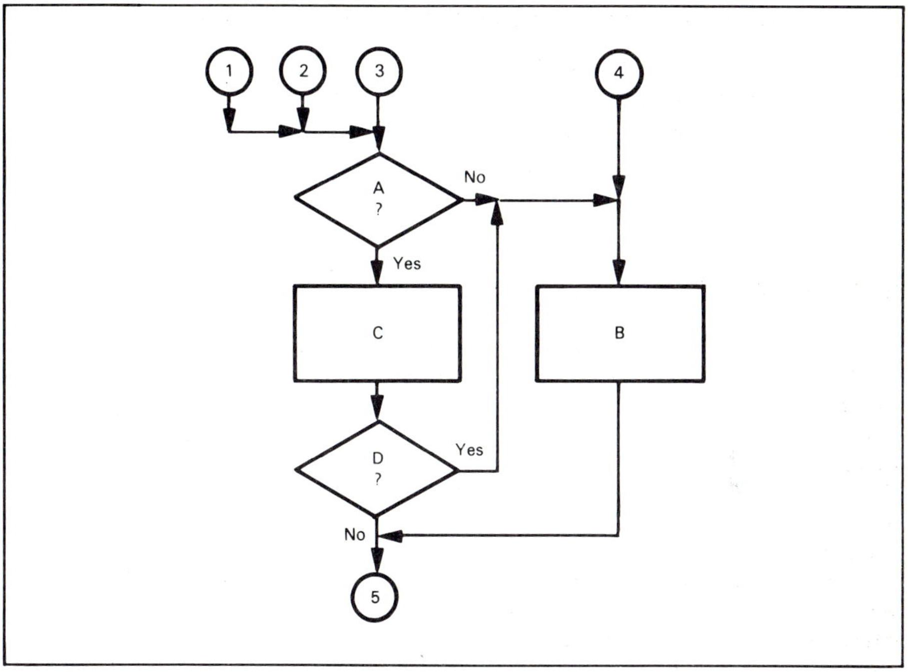

Figure 17-8. Flowchart of an Unstructured Program

4. **Make modules independent of each other.** Restrict the flow of information between modules and implement each design in a single module.
5. **Do not modularize simple tasks** that are already easy to implement.

STRUCTURED PROGRAMMING

How do you keep modules distinct and stop them from interacting? How do you write a program that has a clear sequence of operations so that you can isolate and correct errors? One answer is to use the methods known as "structured programming," whereby each part of the program consists of elements from a limited set of structures and each structure has a single entry and a single exit.

Figure 17-8 shows a flowchart of an unstructured program. If an error occurs in Module B, we have five possible sources for that error. Not only must we check each sequence, but we also have to make sure that corrections do not affect any sequences. The usual result is that debugging becomes like wrestling an octopus. Every time you think the situation is under control, there is another loose tentacle somewhere.

BASIC STRUCTURES

The solution is to **establish a clear sequence of operations so that you can isolate errors. Such a sequence uses single-entry, single-exit structures.** A program consists of a sequence of structures; it may be a single statement or it may consist of structures that are nested within each other to any level of complexity. **The required structures are listed below.**

1. **An ordinary sequence;** that is, a linear structure in which programs are executed consecutively. If the sequence is:

    ```
    P1
    P2
    P3
    ```

    the computer executes P1 first, P2 second, and P3 third. P1, P2, and P3 may be single statements or complex programs.

2. **A conditional structure in which the execution of a program depends on a condition.**

    There are many possible conditional structures, but a common one is "if C then P1 else P2" where C is a condition and P1 and P2 are programs. The computer executes P1 if C is true, and P2 if C is false. Figure 17-9 shows the logic of this structure. Note that it has a single entry and a single exit; the computer cannot enter or leave P1 or P2 other than through the structure.

3. **A loop structure in which a program is repeated until (or as long as) a condition holds.**

    There are many possible loop structures. A common one (called a "do-while" structure) is "while C do P," where C is a condition and P is a program. The computer continually checks C and then executes P as long as C is true.

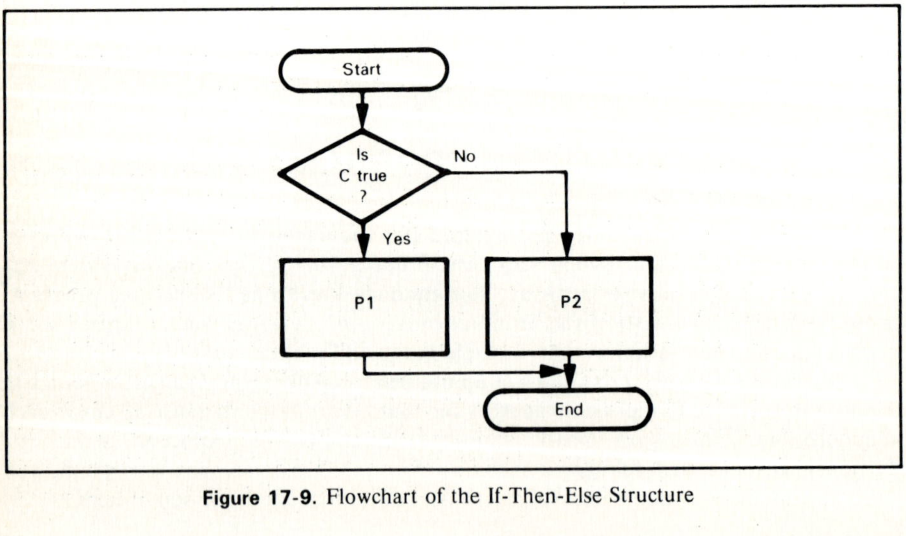

Figure 17-9. Flowchart of the If-Then-Else Structure

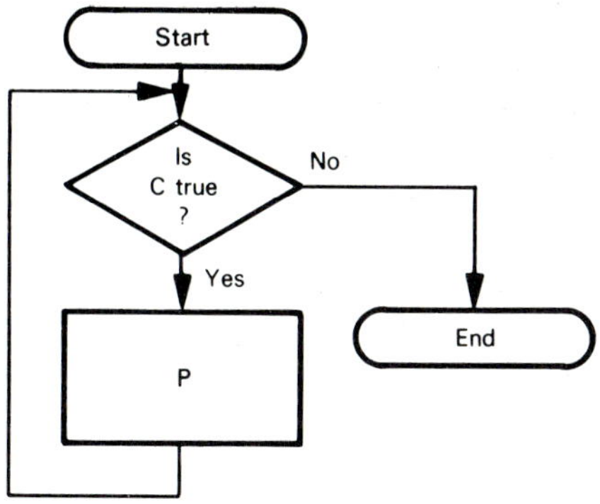

Figure 17-10. Flowchart of the Do-While Structure

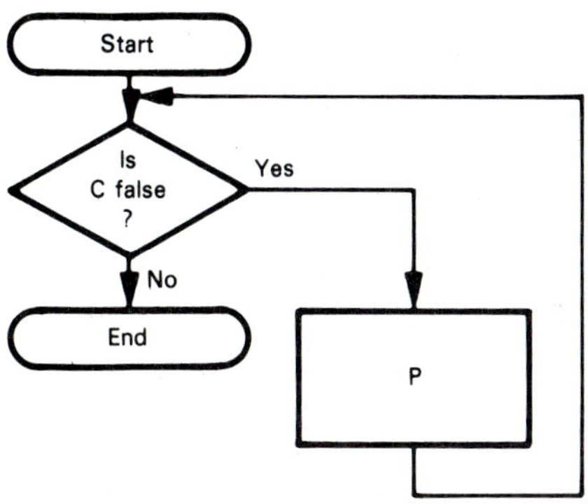

Figure 17-11. Flowchart of the Do-Until Structure

An obvious alternative is "until C do P" in which the computer continually checks C and then executes P as long as C is false. Figures 17-10 and 17-11 show the logic of these alternatives. Both have a single entry and a single exit. The computer will not execute P at all if C is originally in the exit state; thus P is not executed at least once automatically as it is in a FORTRAN DO loop. Alternative structures like "do P while C" or "repeat P until C" produce the FORTRAN implementation in which the computer checks the condition after executing the program (remember Figures 5-1 and 5-2). This approach is often more efficient, but we will use only the form in Figure 17-10 to simplify the discussion. Most high-level structured languages allow all four alternatives to provide flexibility. In most cases, the program P must eventually force C into the exit state; if it does not, the computer will execute P endlessly (the

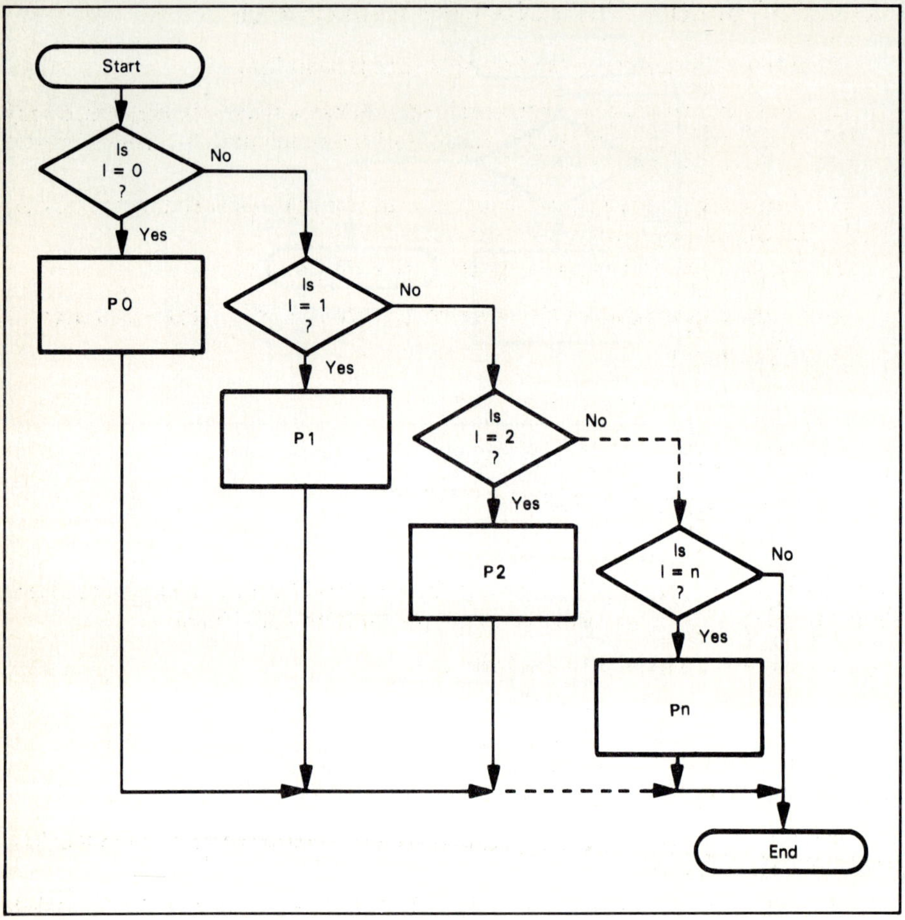

Figure 17-12. Flowchart of the Case Structure

so-called DO FOREVER structure) as it must if P is the overall control program for an instrument, computer peripheral, test system, or electronic game.

4. **A case structure.** Although it is not a primitive structure like our first three, the case structure is so common that it merits a special description. The case structure is "case I of P0, P1, ... , Pn," where I is an index and P0, P1, ... , Pn are programs. The computer executes program P0 if I is 0, P1 if I is 1, and so on; it executes only one of the n programs. If I is greater than n (the number of programs in the case statement) or after execution of one of the programs, the computer then executes the next sequential statement as shown in Figure 17-12. Obviously, we could implement a case structure as a series of conditional structures, much as we could implement a jump table as a series of conditional branches. However, the alternative implementations are long, awkward, and difficult to expand.

FEATURES AND EXAMPLES OF STRUCTURES

Note the following features of structured programming:

1. **Only the three basic structures, and possibly a small number of auxiliary structures, are permitted.** Variations of the conditional and loop structures may be allowed.
2. **Structures may be nested to any level of complexity** since any structure can, in turn, contain any of the structures.
3. **Each structure has a single entry and a single exit.**

Some examples of the conditional structure illustrated in Figure 17-9 are:

1. **P2 included:**

```
IF X > 0 THEN NPOS = NPOS + 1
   ELSE NNEG = NNEG + 1
```

Both P1 and P2 are single statements.

2. **P2 omitted:**

```
IF X = 0 THEN Y = 1/X
```

Here no action is taken if C (X · 0) is false. P2 and "else" can be omitted in this case.
Some examples of the loop structure illustrated in Figure 17-10 are:

1. **Form the sum of integers from 1 to N.**

```
I = 0
SUM = 0
DO WHILE I < N
   I = I + 1
   SUM = SUM + I
END
```

The computer executes the loop as long as I < N. If N=0, the program within the "do-while" is not executed at all.

2. **Count characters in an array SENTENCE until you find an ASCII period.**

```
NCHAR = 0
DO WHILE SENTENCE(NCHAR) ≠ PERIOD
   NCHAR = NCHAR + 1
END
```

The computer executes the loop as long as the character in SENTENCE is not an ASCII period. The count is zero if the first character is a period.

ADVANTAGES OF STRUCTURED PROGRAMMING

The advantages of structured programming are:

1. The sequence of operations is simple to trace. This allows you to test and debug programs easily.
2. The number of structures is limited and the terminology is standardized.
3. The structures can easily be made into modules.
4. Theoreticians have proved that the given set of structures is complete; that is, all programs can be written in terms of the three structures.

5. The structured version of a program is partly self-documenting and fairly easy to read.
6. Structured programs are easy to describe with program outlines.
7. Structured programming has been shown in practice to increase programmer productivity.

Structured programming basically forces much more discipline on the programmer than does modular programming. The result is more systematic and better organized programs.

DISADVANTAGES OF STRUCTURED PROGRAMMING

The disadvantages of structured programming are:

1. Only a few high-level languages (e.g., PL/M, Pascal) will directly accept the structures. The programmer therefore has to go through an extra translation stage to convert the structures to assembly language code. The structured version of the program, however, is often useful as documentation.
2. Structured programs often execute more slowly and use more memory than unstructured programs.
3. Limiting the structures to the three basic forms makes some tasks very awkward to perform. The completeness of the structures only means that all programs can be implemented with them; it does not mean that a given program can be implemented efficiently or conveniently.
4. The standard structures are often quite confusing: e.g., nested "if-then-else" structures may be very difficult to read, since there may be no clear indication of where the inner structures end. A series of nested "do-while" loops can also be difficult to read.
5. Structured programs consider only the sequence of program operations, not the flow of data. Therefore, the structures may handle data awkwardly.
6. Few programmers are accustomed to structured programming. Many find the standard structures awkward and restrictive.

WHEN TO USE STRUCTURED PROGRAMMING

We are neither advocating nor discouraging the use of structured programming. It is one way of systematizing program design. In general, structured programming is most useful in the following situations:

- Larger programs, perhaps exceeding 1000 instructions.
- Applications in which memory usage is not critical.
- Low-volume applications where software development costs, particularly testing and debugging, are important factors.
- Applications involving string manipulation, process control, or other algorithms rather than simple bit manipulations.

In the future, we expect the cost of memory to decrease, the average size of microprocessor programs to increase, and the cost of software development to increase. Therefore, methods like structured programming, which decrease software development costs for larger programs but use more memory, will become more valuable.

Just because structured programming concepts are usually expressed in high-level languages does not mean that structured programming is not applicable to assembly language programming. On the contrary, **the assembly language programmer, with the total freedom of expression that assembly level programming allows, needs the structuring concept provided by structured programming. Creating modules with single entry and exit points, using simple control structures and keeping the complexity of each module minimal increases the productivity of the assembly language programmer.**

EXAMPLES

Structured Program for the Switch and Light System

The structured version of this example is:

```
SWITCH = OFF
DO WHILE SWITCH = OFF
  READ SWITCH
  END
LIGHT = ON
DELAY 1
LIGHT = OFF
```

ON and OFF must have the proper definitions for the switch and light. We assume that DELAY is a module that provides a delay given by its parameter in seconds.

A statement in a structured program may actually be a subroutine. However, in order to conform to the rules of structured programming, the subroutine cannot have any exits other than the one that returns control to the main program.

Since "do-while" checks the condition before executing the loop, we set the variable SWITCH to OFF before starting. The structured program is straightforward, readable, and easy to check by hand. However, it would probably require somewhat more memory than an unstructured program, which would not have to initialize SWITCH and could combine the reading and checking procedures.

Structured Program for the Switch-Based Memory Loader

The switch-based memory loader is a more complex structured programming problem. We may implement the flowchart of Figure 17-3 as follows (a * indicates a comment, and we use "begin" and "end" around a conditionally executed program that consists of more than one line):

```
*
*CLEAR ADDRESS INITIALLY SO ITS STARTING VALUE IS ZERO
*
HIADDRESS = 0
MIDADDRESS = 0
LOADDRESS = 0
*
*CONTINUOUSLY EXAMINE THE SWITCHES AND LOAD DATA INTO MEMORY
```

```
*  NOTE THAT "DO FOREVER" IS JUST "DO WHILE" WITH NO CONDITION
*
DO FOREVER
*
*TEST HIGH ADDRESS BUTTON. IF IT IS BEING PRESSED, DEBOUNCE IT
*  AND WAIT FOR THE OPERATOR TO RELEASE IT. THEN ENTER HIGH
*  ADDRESS FROM THE SWITCHES AND SHOW IT ON THE LIGHTS
*
   IF HIGHADDRBUTTON = 0 THEN
      BEGIN
         DO WHILE HIADDRBUTTON = 0
            DELAY (DEBOUNCE TIME)
            END
         HIADDRESS = SWITCHES
         LIGHTS = SWITCHES
      END
*TEST MID ADDRESS BUTTON. IF IT IS BEING PRESSED, DEBOUNCE IT
*  AND WAIT FOR THE OPERATOR TO RELEASE IT. THEN ENTER MID
*  ADDRESS FROM THE SWITCHES AND SHOW IT ON THE LIGHTS
*
   IF MIDADDRBUTTON.= 0 THEN
      BEGIN
         DO WHILE MIDADDRBUTTON - 0
            DELAY (DEBOUNCE TIME)
            END
         MIDADDRESS = SWITCHES
         LIGHTS = SWITCHES
      END
*TEST LOW ADDRESS BUTTON. IF IT IS BEING PRESSED, DEBOUNCE IT AND
*  WAIT FOR THE OPERATOR TO RELEASE IT. THEN ENTER LOW ADDRESS
*  FROM THE SWITCHES AND SHOW IT ON THE LIGHTS
*
   IF LOADDRBUTTON = 0 THEN
      BEGIN
         DO WHILE LOADDRBUTTON = 0
            DELAY (DEBOUNCE TIME)
            END
         LOADDRESS = SWITCHES
         LIGHTS = SWITCHES
      END
*
*TEST DATA BUTTON. IF IT IS BEING PRESSED, DEBOUNCE IT AND WAIT
*  FOR THE OPERATOR TO RELEASE IT. THEN ENTER DATA FROM THE
*  SWITCHES, SHOW IT ON THE LIGHTS, AND STORE IT IN MEMORY AT
*  (HIGH ADDRESS, MID ADDRESS, LOW ADDRESS)

*
   IF DATABUTTON = 0 THEN
      BEGIN
         DO WHILE DATABUTTON = 0
            DELAY (DEBOUNCE TIME)
            END
         DATA = SWITCHES
         LIGHTS = SWITCHES
         (HIADDRESS, MIDADRESS, LOADDRESS) = DATA
      END
*
*WAIT THE DEBOUNCING TIME BEFORE EXAMINING THE BUTTONS AGAIN.
*  THIS DELAY DEBOUNCES THE RELEASE FOR SURE
*
   DELAY (DEBOUNCE TIME)
END
*
*THE LAST END ABOVE TERMINATES THE
*  DO FOREVER LOOP
*
```

Structured programs are not easy to write, but they can give a great deal of insight into the overall program logic. You can check the logic of the structured program by hand before writing any actual code.

Structured Program for the Verification Terminal

Let us look at the keyboard entry for the transaction terminal. We will assume that the display array is ENTRY, the keyboard strobe is KEYSTROBE, and the keyboard data is KEYIN. **The structured program without the function keys is:**

```
NKEYS = 10
::
::CLEAR ENTRY TO START
::
  DO WHILE NKEYS > 0
    NKEYS = NKEYS - 1
    ENTRY(NKEYS) = 0
  END
::
::FETCH A COMPLETE ENTRY FROM KEYBOARD
::
  DO WHILE NKEYS < 10
    IF KEYSTROBE = ACTIVE THEN
      BEGIN
        KEYSTROBE = INACTIVE
        ENTRY(NKEYS) = KEYIN
        NKEYS = NKEYS + 1
      END
  END
```

Adding the SEND key means that the program must ignore extra digits after it has a complete entry, and must ignore the SEND key until it has a complete entry. The structured program is:

```
NKEYS = 10
::
::CLEAR ENTRY TO START
::
  DO WHILE NKEYS > 0
    NKEYS = NKEYS - 1
    ENTRY(NKEYS) = 0
  END
::
::WAIT FOR COMPLETE ENTRY FOLLOWED BY SEND KEY
::
  DO WHILE KEY ≠ SEND OR NKEYS ≠ 10
    IF KEYSTROBE = ACTIVE THEN
      BEGIN
        KEYSTROBE = INACTIVE
        KEY = KEYIN
        IF NKEYS ≠ 10 AND KEY ≠ SEND THEN
          BEGIN
          ENTRY(NKEYS) = KEY
          NKEYS = NKEYS + 1
        END
      END
  END
```

Note the following features of this structured program.

1. The second if-then is nested within the first one, since the keys are only entered after a strobe is recognized. If the second if-then were on the same level as the first, a single key could fill the entry, since its value would be entered into the array during each iteration of the do-while loop.
2. KEY need not be defined initially, since NKEYS is set to zero as part of the clearing of the entry.

Adding the CLEAR key allows the program to clear the entry originally by

simulating the pressing of CLEAR; i.e., by setting NKEYS to 10 and KEY to CLEAR before starting. The structured program must also only clear digits that have previously been filled. **The new structured program is:**

```
:
: SIMULATE COMPLETE CLEARING
:
NKEYS = 10
KEY = CLEAR
:
:WAIT FOR COMPLETE ENTRY AND SEND KEY
:
DO WHILE KEY = SEND OR NKEYS = 10
:
:CLEAR WHOLE ENTRY IF CLEAR KEY STRUCK
:
    IF KEY = CLEAR THEN
        BEGIN
            KEY = 0
            DO WHILE NKEYS > 0
              NKEYS = NKEYS - 1
              ENTRY(NKEYS) = 0
            END
        END
:
:GET DIGIT IF ENTRY INCOMPLETE
:
    IF KEYSTROBE = ACTIVE THEN
        BEGIN
         KEYSTROBE = INACTIVE
         KEY = KEYIN
         IF KEY < 10 AND NKEYS ≠ 10 THEN
            BEGIN
              ENTRY(NKEYS) = KEY
              NKEYS = NKEYS + 1
            END
        END
END
```

Note that the program resets KEY to zero after clearing the array, so that the operation is not repeated.

We can similarly build a structured program for the receive routine. An initial program could just look for the header and trailer characters. We will assume that RSTB is the indicator that a character is ready. **The structured program is:**

```
:
:CLEAR HEADER FLAG TO START
:
HFLAG = 0
:
:WAIT FOR HEADER AND TRAILER
:
DO WHILE HFLAG = 0 OR CHAR ≠ TRAILER
:
:GET CHARACTER IF READY. LOOK FOR HEADER
:
    IF RSTB = ACTIVE THEN
        BEGIN
            RSTB = INACTIVE
            CHAR = INPUT
            IF CHAR = HEADER THEN HFLAG = 1
        END
END
```

Now we can add the section that checks the message address against the three digits in TERMINAL ADDRESS (TERMADDR). If any of the corresponding digits are not equal, the ADDRESS MATCH flag (ADDRMATCH) is set to 1.

```
:
:CLEAR HEADER FLAG, ADDRESS MATCH FLAG, ADDRESS COUNTER TO START
:
HFLAG = 0
ADDRMATCH = 0
ADDRCTR = 0
```

```
:
:WAIT FOR HEADER, DESTINATION ADDRESS, AND TRAILER
:
DO WHILE HFLAG = 0 OR CHAR = TRAILER OR ADDRCTR = 3
:
:GET CHARACTER IF READY
:
   IF RSTB = ACTIVE THEN
      BEGIN
         RSTB = INACTIVE
         CHAR = INPUT
      END
:
:CHECK FOR TERMINAL ADDRESS AND HEADER
:
   IF HFLAG = 1 AND ADDRCTR = 3 THEN
      BEGIN
         IF CHAR = TERMADDR(ADDRCTR) THEN ADDRMATCH = 1
         ADDRCTR = ADDRCTR + 1
      END
   IF CHAR = HEADER THEN HFLAG = 1
END
```

The program must now wait for a header, a three-digit identification code, and a trailer. You must be careful of what happens during the iteration when the program finds the header, and of what happens if an erroneous identification code character is the same as the trailer.

A further addition can store the message in MESSG. NMESS is the number of characters in the message; if it is not zero at the end, the program knows that the terminal has received a valid message. We have not tried to minimize the logic expressions in this program.

```
:
:CLEAR FLAGS, COUNTERS TO START
:
HFLAG = 0
ADDRMATCH = 0
ADDRCTR = 0
NMESS = 0
:
:WAIT FOR HEADER, DESTINATION ADDRESS, AND TRAILER
:
DO WHILE HFLAG = 0 OR CHAR = TRAILER OR ADDRCTR ≠ 3
:
:GET CHARACTER IF READY
:
   IF RSTB = ACTIVE THEN
      BEGIN
         RSTB = INACTIVE
         CHAR = INPUT
      END
:
:READ MESSAGE IF DESTINATION ADDRESS = TERMINAL ADDRESS
:
   IF HFLAG = 1 AND ADDRCTR = 3 THEN
      IF ADDRMATCH = 0 AND CHAR ≠ TRAILER THEN
         BEGIN
           MESSG(NMESS) = CHAR
           NMESS = NMESS + 1
         END
:
:CHECK FOR TERMINAL ADDRESS
:
   IF HFLAG = 1 AND ADDRCTR ≠ 3 THEN
      BEGIN
        IF CHAR = TERMADDR(ADDRCTR) THEN ADDRMATCH = 1
        ADDRCTR = ADDRCTR + 1
      END
:
:LOOK FOR HEADER
:
   IF CHAR = HEADER THEN HFLAG = 1
END
```

The program checks for the identification code only if it found a header during a previous iteration. It accepts the message only if it has previously found a header and a complete, matching destination address. The program must work properly during the iterations when it finds the header, the trailer and the last digit of the destination address. It must not try to match the header with the terminal address or place the trailer or the final digit of the destination address in the message. **You might try adding the rest of the logic from the flowchart (Figure 17-7) to the structured program. Note that the order of operations is often critical. You must be sure that the program does not complete one phase and start the next one during the same iteration.**

REVIEW OF STRUCTURED PROGRAMMING

Structured programming brings discipline to program design. It forces you to limit the types of structures you use and the sequence of operations. It provides single-entry, single-exit structures, which you can check for logical accuracy. Structured programming often makes the designer aware of inconsistencies or possible combinations of inputs. Structured programming is not a cure-all, but it does bring some order into a process that can be chaotic. The structured program should also aid in debugging, testing, and documentation.

Structured programming is not simple. The programmer must not only define the problem adequately, but must also work through the logic carefully. This is tedious and difficult, but it results in a clearly written, working program.

Terminators

The particular structures we have presented are not ideal and are often awkward. In addition, it can be difficult to determine where one structure ends and another begins, particularly if they are nested. Theorists may provide better structures in the future, or designers may wish to add some of their own. A terminator for each structure seems necessary, since indenting does not always clarify the situation. "End" is a logical terminator for the "do-while" loop. There is no obvious terminator, however, for the "if-then-else" statement; some theorists have suggested "endif" or "fi" ("if" backwards), but these are both awkward and detract from the readability of the program.

RULES FOR STRUCTURED PROGRAMMING

We suggest the following rules for applying structured programming:

1. **Begin by writing a basic flowchart** to help define the logic of the program.
2. **Start with the "sequential," "if-then-else," and "do-while" structures.** They are known to be a complete set, i.e., any program can be written in terms of these structures.
3. **Indent each level** a few spaces from the previous level, so that you will know which statements belong where.
4. **Use terminators for each structure:** e.g., "end" for the "do-while" and "endif" or "fi" for the "if-then-else." The terminators plus the indentation should make the program reasonably clear.

5. **Emphasize simplicity and readability.** Leave lots of spaces, use meaningful names, and make expressions as clear as possible. Do not try to minimize the logic at the cost of clarity.
6. **Comment the program** in an organized manner.
7. **Check the logic.** Try all the extreme cases or special conditions and a few sample cases. Any logical errors you find at this level will not plague you later.

TOP-DOWN DESIGN

The remaining problem is how to check and integrate modules or structures. Certainly we want to divide a large task into sub-tasks. But how do we check the sub-tasks in isolation and put them together? The standard procedure, called "bottom-up design," requires extra work in testing and debugging and leaves the entire integration task to the end. What we need is a method that allows testing and debugging in the actual program environment and modularizes system integration.

This method is "top-down design." Here we start by writing the overall supervisor program. We replace the undefined sub-programs by program "stubs," temporary programs that may either record the entry, provide the answer to a selected test problem, or do nothing. We then test the supervisor program to see that its logic is correct.

We proceed by expanding the stubs. Each stub will often contain sub-tasks, which we will temporarily represent as stubs. This process of expansion, debugging, and testing continues until all the stubs are replaced by working programs. Note that testing and integration occur at each level, rather than all at the end. No special driver or data generation programs are necessary. We get a clear idea of exactly where we are in the design. **Top-down design assumes modular programming, and is compatible with structured programming as well.**

DISADVANTAGES OF TOP-DOWN DESIGN

The disadvantages of top-down design are:

1. The overall design may not mesh well with system hardware.
2. It may not take good advantage of existing software.
3. Stubs may be difficult to write, particularly if they must work correctly in several different places.
4. Top-down design may not result in generally useful modules.
5. Errors at the top level can have catastrophic effects, whereas errors in bottom-up design are usually limited to a particular module.

In large programming projects, top-down design has been shown to greatly improve programmer productivity. However, almost all of these projects have used some bottom-up design in cases where the top-down method would have resulted in a large amount of extra work.

Top-down design is a useful tool that should not be followed to extremes. It provides the same discipline for system testing and integration that structured programming provides for module design. The method, however, has more general applicability, since it does not assume the use of programmed logic. However, top-down design may not result in the most efficient implementation.

EXAMPLES

Top-Down Design of Switch and Light System

The first structured programming example actually demonstrates top-down design as well. The program was:

```
SWITCH = OFF
DO WHILE SWITCH = OFF
  READ SWITCH
END
LIGHT = ON
DELAY 1
LIGHT = OFF
```

These statements are really stubs, since none of them is fully defined. For example, what does READ SWITCH mean? If the switch were one bit of input port SPORT, it really means:

```
SWITCH = SPORT AND SMASK
```

where SMASK has a '1' bit in the appropriate position. The masking may, of course, be implemented with a Bit Test instruction.
Similarly, DELAY 1 actually means (if the processor itself provides the delay):

```
REG = COUNT
DO WHILE REG ≠ 0
  REG = REG - 1
END
```

COUNT is the appropriate number to provide a one-second delay. **The expanded version of the program is:**

```
SWITCH = 0
DO WHILE SWITCH = 0
  SWITCH = SPORT AND MASK
END
LIGHT = ON
REF = COUNT
DO WHILE REG = 0
  REG = REG - 1
END
LIGHT - NOT(LIGHT)
```

Certainly this program is more explicit, and could more easily be translated into actual instructions or statements.

Top-Down Design of the Switch-Based Memory Loader

This example is more complex than the first example, so we must proceed systematically. Here again, **the structured program contains stubs.**

For example, if the HIGH ADDRESS button is one bit of input port CPORT, "if HIADDRBUTTON=0" really means:

1. Input from CPORT
2. Logical AND with HAMASK

where HAMASK has a '1' in the appropriate bit position and '0's elsewhere. Similarly the condition "if DATABUTTON=0" really means:

1. Input from CPORT
2. Logical AND with DAMASK

So, the initial stubs could just assume that no buttons are being pressed:

```
HIADDRBUTTON = 1
MIDADDRBUTTON = 1
LOADDRBUTTON = 1
DATABUTTON = 1
```

A run of the supervisor program should show that it takes the implied "else" path through the "if-then-else" structures, and never reads the switches. Similarly, if the stub were:

```
HIADDRBUTTON = 0
```

the supervisor program should stay in the "do while HIADDRBUTTON=0" loop waiting for the button to be released. These simple runs check the overall logic.

Now we can expand each stub and see if the expansion produces a reasonable overall result. Note how debugging and testing proceed in a straightforward and modular manner. We expand the HIADDRBUTTON=0 stub to:

```
READ CPORT
HIADDRBUTTON = (CPORT) AND HAMASK
```

The program should wait for the HIGH ADDRESS button to be released. The program should then display the values of the switches on the lights. This run checks for the proper response to the HIGH ADDRESS button.

We then expand the MID ADDRESS button module to:

```
READ CPORT
MIDADDRBUTTON = (CPORT) AND MAMASK
```

When the MID ADDRESS button is released, the program should display the value of the switches on the lights. This run checks for the proper response to the MID ADDRESS button.

We then expand the LOW ADDRESS button module to:

```
READ CPORT
LOADDRBUTTON = (CPORT) AND LAMASK
```

When the LOW ADDRESS button is released, the program should display the values of the switches on the lights. This run checks for the proper response to the LOW ADDRESS button.

Similarly, we can expand the DATA button module and check for the proper response to that button. The entire program will then have been tested.

When all the stubs have been expanded, the coding, debugging, and testing stages will all be complete. Of course, we must know exactly what results each stub should produce. However, many logical errors will become obvious at each level without any further expansion.

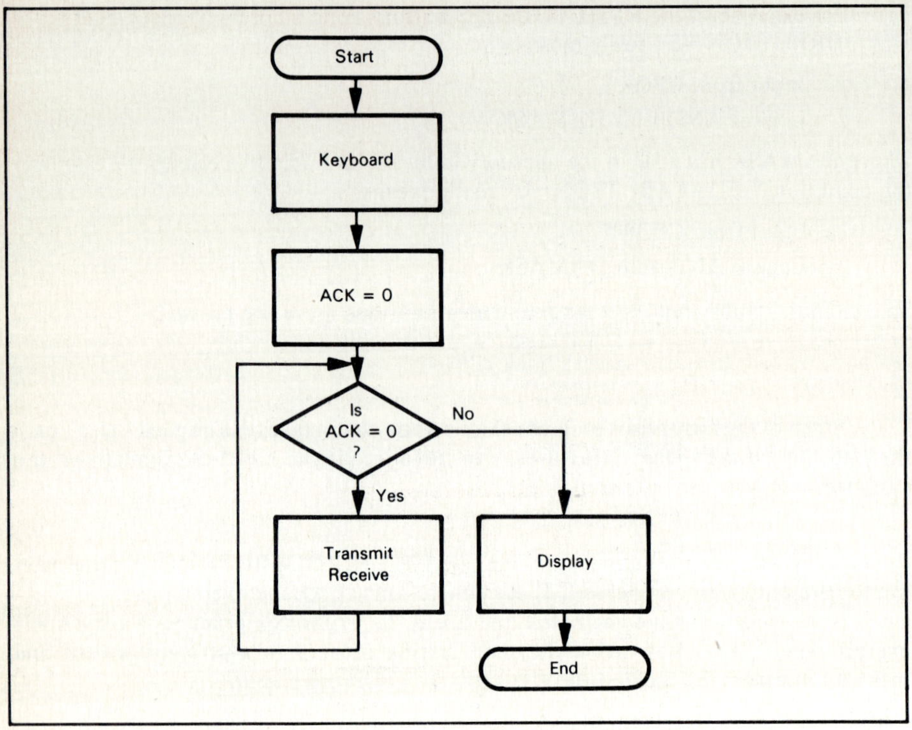

Figure 17-13. Initial Flowchart of Transaction Terminal

Top-Down Design of Verification Terminal

This example, of course, will have more levels of detail. **We could start with the following program** (see Figure 17-13 for a flowchart):

```
KEYBOARD
ACK = 0
DO WHILE ACK = 0
   TRANSMIT
   RECEIVE
END
DISPLAY
```

Here, KEYBOARD, TRANSMIT, RECEIVE, and DISPLAY are program stubs that will be expanded later. KEYBOARD, for example, could simply place a ten-digit verified number into the appropriate buffer.

The next stage of expansion could produce the following program for KEYBOARD (see Figure 17-14):

```
VER = 0
DO WHILE VER = 0
   COMPLETE = 0
   DO WHILE COMPLETE = 0
      KEYIN
      KEYDS
   END
   VERIFY
END
```

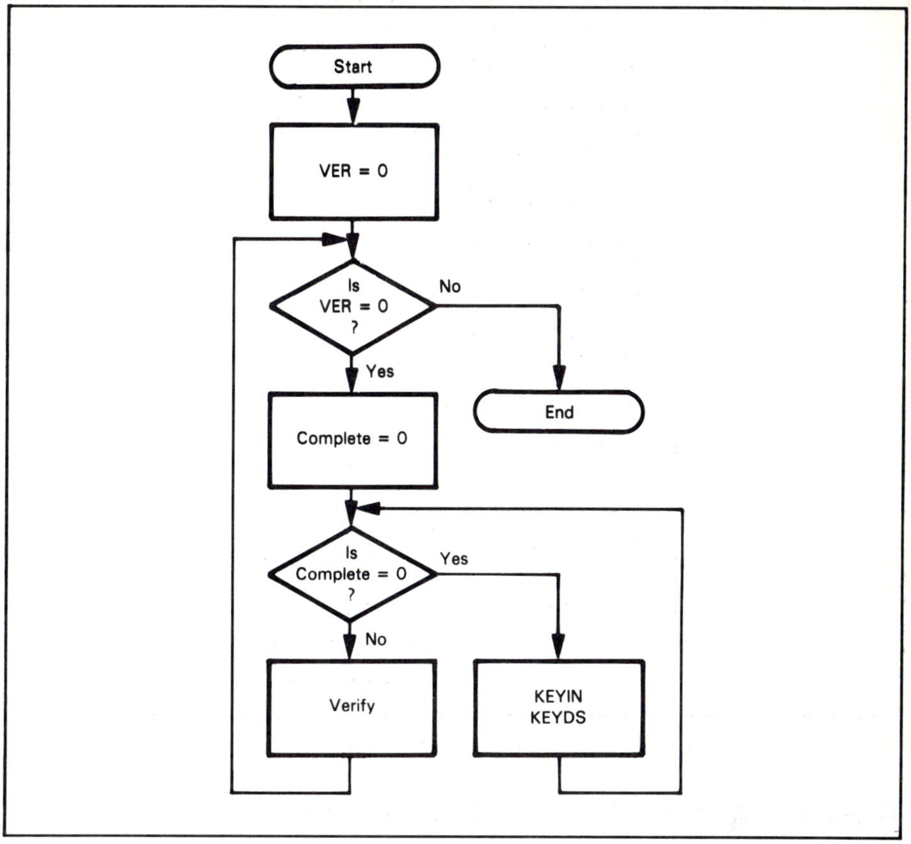

Figure 17-14. Flowchart for Expanded KEYBOARD Routine

Here VER=0 means that an entry has not been verified; COMPLETE=0 means that the entry is incomplete. KEYIN and KEYDS are the keyboard input and display routines respectively. VERIFY checks the entry. A stub for KEYIN would simply place a random entry (from a random number table or generator) into the buffer and set COMPLETE to 1.

We would continue by similarly expanding, debugging, and testing TRANSMIT, RECEIVE, and DISPLAY. Note that you should expand each program by one level so that you do not perform the integration of an entire program at any one time. You must use your judgment in defining levels. Too small a step wastes time, while too large a step gets you back to the problems of system integration that top-down design is supposed to solve.

REVIEW OF TOP-DOWN DESIGN

Top-down design brings discipline to the testing and integration stages of program design. It provides a systematic method for expanding a flowchart or problem

definition to the level required to actually write a program. Together with structured programming, it forms a complete set of design techniques.

Like structured programming, top-down design is not simple. The designer must have defined the problem carefully and must work systematically through each level. Here again the methodology may seem tedious, but the payoff can be substantial if you follow the rules.

We recommend the following approach to top-down design:

1. Start with a basic flowchart.
2. Make the stubs as complete and as separate as possible.
3. Define precisely all the possible outcomes from each stub and select a test set.
4. Check each level carefully and systematically.
5. Use the structures from structured programming.
6. Expand each stub by one level. Do not try to do too much in one step.
7. Watch carefully for common tasks and data structures.
8. Test and debug after each stub expansion. Do not try to do an entire level at a time.
9. Be aware of what the hardware can do. Do not hesitate to stop and do a little bottom-up design where that seems necessary.

DESIGNING DATA STRUCTURES

Beginning programmers seldom think about data structures. They generally assume that the data will be stored somewhere in the computer's memory, much as records are piled into a cabinet or books into a bookcase. Designing data structures seems as far fetched as establishing a complete card catalog for one's books or records; few people take organization to such lengths.

But the fact is that **most computer-based systems involve a surprisingly large amount of data processing.** Numerical algorithms assume that the processor can easily find the element in the next row or next column of an array. Editor programs assume that the processor can easily find the next character, the previous line, a particular string of characters, or the starting point of an entire paragraph or page. An operator interface for a piece of test equipment may assume that the processor can easily find a particular command or data entry and move it from one place to another. **Imagine how difficult the following tasks would be to implement if the data is simply scattered through memory or organized in a long, linear array:**

1. The operator of a machine tool wants to insert two extra cutting steps between steps 14 and 15 of a 40-step pattern.
2. The operator of a chemical processing plant wants to see the last ten values of the temperature at the inlet to tank 05.
3. An accounting clerk wants to enter a new account into an alphabetical list.

The processor may spend most of its time finding the data, moving from one data item to the next, and organizing the data.

SELECTING DATA STRUCTURES

Obviously, we cannot provide a complete description of data structures here.[4,5] Just as clearly, **the design of data structures has great influence on the design of programs if the data is complex. We will briefly mention the following considerations in selecting data structures:**

1. **How are the data items related?** Closely related items should be accessible from each other, since such accesses will be frequent.
2. **What kind of operations will be performed on the data?** Simple linear structures are adequate if the data is always handled in a single, fixed order. However, more complex structures are essential if the tasks involve operations such as searching, editing, or sorting.
3. **Can standard structures be used?** Methods are readily available for handling structures such as queues, stacks, and linked lists. Other arrangements will require special programming.
4. **What kind of access is necessary?** Clearly we need more structure if we must find elements that are identified by a number or a relative position, rather than just the first or last entries. We must organize the data to make the accesses as rapid as possible.

REVIEW OF PROBLEM DEFINITION AND PROGRAM DESIGN

You should note that we have spent two entire chapters without mentioning any specific microprocessor or assembly language, and without writing a single line of actual code. However, you should now know a lot more about the examples than you would if we had just asked you to write the programs at the start. **Although we often think of the writing of computer instructions as a key part of software development, it is actually one of the easiest stages.**

Once you have written a few programs, coding will become simple. You will soon learn the instruction set, recognize which instructions are really useful, and remember the common sequences that make up the largest part of most programs. **You will then find that many of the other stages of software development remain difficult and have few clear rules.**

We have suggested some ways to systematize the important early stages. In the problem definition stage, you must define all the characteristics of the system — its inputs, outputs, processing, time and memory constraints, and error handling. **You must particularly consider how the system will interact with the larger system of which it is a part, and whether that larger system includes electrical equipment, mechanical equipment, or a human operator. You must start at this stage to make the system easy to use and maintain.**

In the program design stage, several techniques can help you to systematically specify and document the logic of your program. Modular programming forces you to divide the total program into small, distinct modules. Structured programming provides a systematic way of defining the logic of those modules, while top-down design

is a systematic method for integrating and testing them. Of course, no one can compel you to follow all of these techniques; they are, in fact, guidelines more than anything else. But they do provide a unified aproach to design, and you should consider them a basis on which to develop your own approach.

REFERENCES

1. D. L. Parnas (see the references below) has been a leader in the area of modular programming.
2. Collected by B. W. Unger (see reference below).
3. Formulated by D. L. Parnas.
4. K. J. Thurber. and P. C. Patton. *Data Structures and Computer Architecture,* Lexington Books, Lexington, Mass., 1977.
5. K. S. Shankar. "Data Structures, Types, and Abstractions," *Computer,* April 1980, pp. 67-77.

The following references provide additional information on problem definition and program design:

Chapin, N. *Flowcharts,* Auerbach, Princeton, N. J., 1971.

Dalton, W. F. "Design Microcomputer Software like Other Systems — Systematically," *Electronics,* January 19, 1978, pp. 97-101.

Dijkstra, E. W. *A Discipline of Programming,* Prentice-Hall, Englewood Cliffs, N. J., 1976.

Halstead, M. H. *Elements of Software Science,* American Elsevier, New York, 1977.

Hughes, J. K. and J. I. Michtom. *A Structured Approach to Programming,* Prentice-Hall, Englewood Cliffs, N. J., 1977.

Morgan, D. E. and D. J. Taylor. "A Survey of Methods for Achieving Reliable Software," *Computer,* February 1977, pp. 44-52.

Myers, W. "The Need for Software Engineering," *Computer,* February 1978, pp. 12-25.

Parnas, D. L. "On the Criteria to be Used in Decomposing Systems into Modules," *Communications of the ACM,* December 1972, pp. 1053-58.

Parnas, D. L. "A Technique for the Specification of Software Modules with Examples," *Communications of the ACM,* May 1973, pp. 330-336.

Phister, M. Jr. *Data Processing Technology and Economics,* Santa Monica Publishing Co., Santa Monica, Ca., 1976.

Schneider, V. "Prediction of Software Effort and Project Duration — Four New Formulas," *SIGPLAN Notices,* June 1978, pp. 49-59.

Schneiderman, B. et al. "Experimental Investigations of the Utility of Detailed Flowcharts in Programming," *Communications of the ACM,* June 1977, pp. 373-381.

Tausworthe, R. C. *Standardized Development of Computer Software.* Prentice-Hall: Englewood Cliffs, N. J., 1977 (Part 1); 1979 (Part 2).

Unger, B. W. "Programming Languages for Computer System Simulation," *Simulation,* April 1978, pp. 101-10.

Wirth, N. *Algorithms + Data Structures = Programs.* Prentice-Hall: Englewood Cliffs, N. J., 1976.

Wirth, N. *Systematic Programming: an Introduction.* Prentice-Hall: Englewood Cliffs, N. J., 1973.

Yourdon, E. U. *Techniques of Program Structure and Design.* Prentice-Hall: Englewood Cliffs, N. J., 1975.

18
Documentation

Software development must yield more than just a working program. A software product must also include the documentation that allows it to be used, maintained, and extended. Adequate documentation is helpful during program debugging and testing, and essential in the later stages of the program's life cycle.

SELF-DOCUMENTING PROGRAMS

Although no program is ever completely self-documenting, some of the rules that we mentioned earlier can help. These include:

- Clear, simple structure with as few transfers of control (jumps) as possible
- Use of meaningful names and labels
- Use of names instead of literal numbers for I/O devices, parameters, numerical factors, subroutine addresses, branch destinations, etc.
- Emphasis on simplicity rather than on minor savings in memory usage, execution time, or typing

For example, the following program sends a character to a teletypewriter:

```
        MOVEQ   -1,D0
        MOVE.B  $6000,D0
        MOVEQ   #10,D2

        BCLR.B  #7,0(A0)
SNDBIT  BSR     DELAY9_1
        ROR.W   #1,D0
        BCS.S   SNDONE

        BCLR.B  #7,0(A0)
        BRA.S   NEXT

SNDONE  BSET.B  #7,0(A0)
NEXT    DBRA    D2,SNDBIT

        RTS
        END
```

CHOOSING USEFUL NAMES

Even without comments we can improve the program as follows:

```
PROGRAM  EQU      $4000
DATA     EQU      $6000

PIADA    EQU      $00                    OFFSET DATA REGISTER A

TTYBIT   EQU      $07                    TTY CONNECTED TO BIT 7
CHRBIT   EQU      $08                    NUMBER OF DATA BITS IN CHARACTER
STPBIT   EQU      $02                    NUMBER OF STOPBITS TO TRANSMIT

TTYOUT   MOVEQ    -1,D0                  FORM STOP BITS
         MOVE.B   CHAR,D0                GET TTY OUTPUT DATA
         MOVEQ    #1+CHRBIT+STPBIT-1,D2  BIT COUNT ADJUSTED FOR DBRA

         BCLR.B   #TTYBIT,PIADA(A0)      SEND START BIT
SNDBIT   BSR      DELAY9_1               WAIT 1 BIT TIME
         ROR.W    #1,D0                  CARRY = NEXT DATA BIT
         BCS.S    SNDONE                 IF DATA = 1 THEN SEND A ONE

         BCLR.B   #TTYBIT,PIADA(A0)      SEND '0' AS DATA BIT
         BRA.S    NEXT

SNDONE   BSET.B   #TTYBIT,PIADA(A0)      SEND '1' AS DATA BIT
NEXT     DBRA     D2,SNDBIT              CONTINUE UNTIL ALL DATA BITS SENT


         RTS
         END
```

This program is undoubtedly easier to understand than the earlier version. **Even without further documentation, you could probably guess at the function of the program and the meanings of most of the variables.** Other documentation techniques cannot substitute for self-documentation.

Some further notes on choosing names:

1. **Use the obvious name** when it is available, like TTY or CRT for output devices, START or RESET for addresses, DELAY or SORT for subroutines, COUNT or LENGTH for data.
2. **Avoid acronyms** like S16BA for SORT 16-BIT ARRAY. These seldom mean anything to anybody.
3. **Use full words** or close to full words when possible, like DONE, PRINT, SEND, etc.
4. **Keep the names** as **distinct** as possible. Avoid names that look alike, such as TEMPI and TEMP1, or those that resemble operation codes or other built-in names.

COMMENTS

Comments are a simple form in which to provide additional documentation. However, few programs (even those used as examples in books) have effective comments. **You should consider the following guidelines for good comments:**

1. **Don't explain the internal effects of the instruction.** Instead, explain the purpose of the instruction in the program. Comments like

```
         SUBQ.W   #1,D0                 D0 := D0 - 1
```

do not help the reader understand the program. A more useful comment is

```
SUBQ.W  #1,D0                 LINE NUMBER := LINE NUMBER - 1
```

Remember that the standard manuals contain descriptions of how the processor executes its instructions. The comments should explain what tasks the program is performing and what methods it is using.

2. **Make the comments as clear as possible.** Do not use abbreviations or acronyms unless they are well known (like ASCII, PIA, or UART) or standard (like "num" for number, "ms" for millisecond, etc.). Avoid comments like

```
SUBQ.W  #1,D0                 L N := L N - 1
```

or

```
SUBQ.W  #1,D0                 DEC. LN BY 1
```

The extra typing required to enter meaningful comments is certainly worthwhile.

3. **Comment every important or obscure point.** Be particularly careful to mark operations that may not have obvious functions, such as

```
MOVEA.L (A0),A0               GET ADDRESS TO NEXT ELEMENT IN QUEUE
```

or

```
ANDI.B  #$FE,PIADA(A0)        TURN OFF LED INDICATOR
```

Clearly, I/O operations often require extensive comments. If you're not exactly sure what an instruction does, or if you have to think about it, add a clarifying comment. The comment will save you time later and will be helpful in documentation.

4. **Don't comment the obvious.** A comment on each line makes it difficult to find the important points. Standard instructions like

```
DBRA    D1,LOOP
```

need not be marked unless you're doing something special. One comment will often suffice for several lines, as in

```
CLR.B   PIACA(A0)             INITIALIZE A SIDE
MOVE.B  #A_DATDIR,PIADDA(A0)
MOVE.B  #A_CNTRL,PIACA(A0)
```

or

```
MOVE.B  (A0)+,D0              EXCHANGE MOST SIGNIFICANT AND
MOVE.B  (A0),-(A0)            .. LEAST SIGNIFICANT BYTES
MOVE.B  D0,1(A0)
```

5. **Place comments on the lines to which they refer or at the start of a sequence.**

6. **Keep your comments up-to-date.** If you change the program, change the comments.

7. **Use standard forms and terms** in commenting. Don't worry about repetition. Varied names for the same things are confusing, even if the variations are just COUNT and COUNTER, START and BEGIN, DISPLAY and LEDS, or PANEL and SWITCHES. You gain nothing from inconsistency. Minor varia-

tions may be obvious to you now, but may not be clear later; others will get confused immediately.

8. **Make comments mingled with instructions brief.** Leave a complete explanation to header comments and other documentation. Otherwise the program gets lost in the comments and you may have a hard time even finding the actual instructions.
9. **Keep improving your comments.** If you come to one that you cannot read or understand, take the time to change it. If you find that the listing is getting crowded, add some blank lines. The comments won't improve themselves; in fact, they will just become worse as you leave the task behind and forget exactly what you did.
10. **Use comments to place a heading in front of every major section, subsection, or subroutine.** The heading should describe the functions of the code that follows it; it should include information about the algorithm employed, the inputs and outputs, and any incidental effects that may be produced.
11. **If you modify a working program, use comments to describe the modifications that you made and identify the date and author of the revision.** This information should go both at the front of the program (so a user can easily tell one version from another) and at the points where changes were actually made.

Remember, **comments are important. Good ones will save you time and effort.** Put some work into comments and try to make them effective.

EXAMPLES

18-1. COMMENTING A TELETYPEWRITER OUTPUT ROUTINE

The basic program is:

```
        MOVEQ   -1,D0
        MOVE.B  $6000,D0
        MOVEQ   #10,D2

        BCLR.B  #7,0(A0)
SNDBIT  BSR     DELAY9_1
        ROR.W   #1,D0
        BCS.S   SNDONE

        BCLR.B  #7,0(A0)
        BRA.S   NEXT

SNDONE  BSET.B  #7,0(A0)
NEXT    DBRA    D2,SNDBIT

        RTS
        END
```

Commenting the important points and adding names for numbers gives:

```
          :         TELETYPEWRITER OUTPUT
          :         THIS PROGRAM SENDS THE CHARACTER IN LOCATION CHAR
          :         TO THE TELETYPE AT THE ADDRESS IN REGISTER A0

PROGRAM   EQU       $4000
DATA      EQU       $6000

PIADA     EQU       $00                        OFFSET FOR DATA REGISTER A OF PIA

TTYBIT    EQU       $07                        TTY CONNECTED TO BIT 7
CHRBIT    EQU       $08                        NUMBER OF DATA BITS IN CHARACTER
STPBIT    EQU       $02                        NUMBER OF STOPBITS TO TRANSMIT


          ORG       DATA

CHAR      DS.B      1                          TTY OUTPUT CHARACTER

          ORG       PROGRAM

TTYOUT    MOVEQ     -1,D0                      FORM STOP BITS
          MOVE.B    CHAR,D0                    GET TTY OUTPUT DATA
          MOVEQ     #1+CHRBIT+STPBIT-1,D2 BIT COUNT ADJUSTED FOR DBRA

          BCLR.B    #TTYBIT,PIADA(A0)          SEND START BIT
SNDBIT    BSR       DELAY9_1                   WAIT 1 BIT TIME
          ROR.W     #1,D0                      CARRY = NEXT DATA BIT
          BCS.S     SNDONE                     IF DATA = 1 THEN SEND A ONE

          BCLR.B    #TTYBIT,PIADA(A0)          SEND '0' AS DATA BIT
          BRA.S     NEXT

SNDONE    BSET.B    #TTYBIT,PIADA(A0)          SEND '1' AS DATA BIT
NEXT      DBRA      D2,SNDBIT                  CONTINUE UNTIL ALL DATA BITS SENT


          RTS
          END
```

Changing the Program

Note how easily we could change this program so that it would transfer a whole string of data, starting at the address in location CHRSTR and ending with an 03 character (ASCII ETX).

```
                    :         PROGRAM    TTYOUT
                    :
                    :         TELETYPEWRITER OUTPUT
                    :
                    :         THIS PROGRAM SENDS A STRING TO A
                    :         TELETYPEWRITER
                    :
                    :         TO USE THIS PROGRAM:
                    :
                    :                   CHRSTR          PUT ADDRESS OF STRING IN
                    :                                   THIS LOCATION
                    :                   A0              PUT ADDRESS OF TELETYPEWRITER
                    :                                   DEVICE IN REGISTER A0
                    :                   ETX             END STRING WITH AN ASCII
                    :                                   ETX CHARACTER
                    :
00004000            PROGRAM   EQU       $4000
00006000            DATA      EQU       $6000

00000000            PIADA     EQU       $00             OFFSET FOR DATA REGISTER A OF PIA

00000007            TTYBIT    EQU       $07             TTY CONNECTED TO BIT 7
00000008            CHRBIT    EQU       $08             NUMBER OF DATA BITS IN CHARACTER
00000002            STPBIT    EQU       $02             NUMBER OF STOPBITS TO TRANSMIT
00000003            ENDMARK   EQU       $03             ASCII ETX'MARKS END OF OUTPUT STRIN


00006000                      ORG       DATA
```

```
006000 00000001     CHRSTR DS.B     1                      TTY OUTPUT CHARACTERSTRING

       00004000            ORG      PROGRAM

004000 227C00006000 TTYOUT MOVEA.L #CHRSTR,A1              GET ADDRESS OF OUTPUT STRING

004006 70FF         OUTCHR MOVEQ    -1,D0                  FORM STOP BITS
004008 1019                MOVE.B   (A1)+,D0               GET TTY OUTPUT DATA
00400A 0C000003            CMPI.B   #ENDMARK,D0            IS IT END OF STRING
00400E 6724                BEQ.S    DONE                   ..THEN DONE

004010 740A                MOVEQ    #1+CHRBIT+STPBIT-1,D2  BIT COUNT ADJUSTED FOR DBRA

004012 08A800070000        BCLR.B   #TTYBIT,PIADA(A0)      SEND START BIT
004018 6100BFE6     SNDBIT BSR      DELAY9_1               WAIT 1 BIT TIME
00401C E258                ROR.W    #1,D0                  CARRY = NEXT DATA BIT
00401E 6508                BCS.S    SNDONE                 IF DATA = 1 THEN SEND A ONE

004020 08A800070000        BCLR.B   #TTYBIT,PIADA(A0)      SEND '0' AS DATA BIT
004026 6006                BRA.S    NEXT

004028 08E800070000 SNDONE BSET.B   #TTYBIT,PIADA(A0)      SEND '1' AS DATA BIT
00402E 51CAFFE8     NEXT   DBRA     D2,SNDBIT              CONTINUE UNTIL ALL DATA BITS SENT

004032 60D2                BRA      OUTCHR                 CONTINUE UNTIL ALL CHARACTERS SENT

004034 4E75         DONE   RTS
```

Good comments will help you change a program to meet new requirements. For example, try changing the last program so that it:

- Starts each message with ASCII STX (02) followed by a two-digit identification code stored in memory location IDCODE.
- Adds no start or stop bits.
- Waits 1 ms between bits.
- Transmits 40 characters, starting with the one located at the address in DPTR.
- Ends each message with two consecutive ASCII ETXs (03).

18-2. COMMENTING A MULTIPLE-PRECISION ADDITION ROUTINE

The basic program is:

```
        ORG      $4000
        MOVE.L   #$6008,A0
        MOVE.L   #$6208,A1
        MOVE     #0,CCR
        MOVEQ    #7,D2
LOOP    MOVE.B   -(A0),D0
        MOVE.B   -(A1),D1
        ADDX.B   D1,D0
        MOVE.B   D0,(A0)
        DBRA     D2,LOOP
        RTS
        END
```

Important Points

First, comment the important points. These are typically initializations, data fetches, and processing operations. Don't bother with standard sequences like updating pointers and counters. Remember that **names are clearer than numbers, so use them freely.**

The new version of the program is:

```
*        MULTIPRECISION ADDITION
*
*        THIS PROGRAM ADDS TWO NUMBERS STORED
*        AT LOCATIONS NUM1 AND NUM2 AND
*        STORES THE RESULT IN LOCATION NUM1
*
*        THE NUMBERS MUST BE EIGHT BYTES LONG
*        (OR CHANGE BYTECOUNT)

PROGRAM  EQU      $4000

NUM1     EQU      $6000
NUM2     EQU      $6200
BYTECOUNT EQU     $8

         ORG      PROGRAM

         MOVEA.L  #NUM1+BYTECOUNT,A0     ADDRESS BEYOND END OF FIRST NUMBER
         MOVEA.L  #NUM2+BYTECOUNT,A1     ADDRESS BEYOND END OF SECOND NUMBER
         MOVE     #0,CCR
         MOVEQ    #BYTECOUNT-1,D2

LOOP     MOVE.B   -(A0),D0               GET BYTES TO ADD, START WITH
         MOVE.B   -(A1),D1               LEAST SIGNIFICANT BYTES
         ADDX.B   D1,D0                  ADD THEM WITH CARRY
         MOVE.B   D0,(A0)                STORE RESULT IN NUM1
         DBRA     D2,LOOP

         RTS
```

Obscure Functions

Second, look for instructions that may not have obvious functions and explain their purposes with comments. Here, the purpose of MOVE #0,CCR is to clear the Extend flag (and other flags) before adding the least significant bytes.

```
*        MULTIPRECISION ADDITION
*
*        THIS PROGRAM ADDS TWO NUMBERS STORED
*        AT LOCATIONS NUM1 AND NUM2 AND
*        STORES THE RESULT IN LOCATION NUM1
*
*        THE NUMBERS MUST BE EIGHT BYTES LONG
*        (OR CHANGE BYTECOUNT)

PROGRAM  EQU      $4000

NUM1     EQU      $6000                  ADDRESS OF FIRST BINARY NUMBER
NUM2     EQU      $6200                  ADDRESS OF SECOND BINARY NUMBER
BYTECOUNT EQU     $8                     NUMBER OF BYTES TO ADD

         ORG      PROGRAM

         MOVEA.L  #NUM1+BYTECOUNT,A0     ADDRESS BEYOND END OF FIRST NUMBER
         MOVEA.L  #NUM2+BYTECOUNT,A1     ADDRESS BEYOND END OF SECOND NUMBER
         MOVE     #0,CCR                 CLEAR EXTEND FLAG (AND OTHER FLAGS)
         MOVEQ    #BYTECOUNT-1,D2        LOOP COUNTER ADJUSTED FOR DBRA

LOOP     MOVE.B   -(A0),D0               GET BYTES TO ADD, START WITH
         MOVE.B   -(A1),D1               LEAST SIGNIFICANT BYTES
         ADDX.B   D1,D0                  ADD THEM WITH CARRY
         MOVE.B   D0,(A0)                STORE RESULT IN NUM1
         DBRA     D2,LOOP

         RTS
```

Questions for Commenting

Third, ask yourself whether the comments tell you what you would need to know to use the program; for example:

1. Where is the program entered? Are there alternative entry points?
2. What parameters are necessary? How and in what form must they be supplied?
3. What operations does the program perform?
4. From where does it get the data?
5. Where does it store the results?
6. What special cases does it consider?
7. What does the program do about errors?
8. How does it exit?

Some questions may be irrelevant and some answers may be obvious. Make sure, however, **that you wouldn't have to dissect the program to answer the important questions. Remember also that too much explanation may be an obstacle to using the program.** Are there any changes you would like to see in the listing? If so, make them — you are the one who has to decide if the commenting is adequate and reasonable.

FLOWCHARTS AS DOCUMENTATION

We have already described the use of flowcharts as a design tool in Chapter 17. Flowcharts are also useful in documentation, particularly if:

- They are not cluttered or too detailed.
- Their decision points are explained and marked clearly.
- They include all branches.
- They correspond to the actual program listings.

Flowcharts are helpful if they give you an overall picture of the program. They are not helpful if they are just as difficult to read as the program listing.

STRUCTURED PROGRAMS AS DOCUMENTATION

A structured program can serve as documentation for an assembly language program if:

- You describe the purpose of each section in the comments.
- You make it clear which statements are included in each conditional or loop structure by using indentation and ending markers.
- You make the total structure as simple as possible.
- You use a consistent, well-defined language.

The structured program can help you check the logic or improve it. Furthermore, since the structured program is machine-independent, it can also help you implement the same task on another computer.

MEMORY MAPS

A memory map is simply a list of all the memory assignments in a program. The map allows you to determine the amount of memory needed, the locations of data or subroutines, and the parts of memory not allocated. The map is a handy reference for finding storage locations and entry points and for dividing memory between different routines or programmers. The map will also give you easy access to data and subroutines if you need them in later extensions or in maintenance. **Sometimes a graphical map is more helpful than a listing.**

A typical map is:

Program Memory

Address	Routine	Purpose
E000 - E1FF	RDKBD	Interrupt Service Routine for Keyboard
E200 - E240	BRKPT	Breakpoint Routine Entered Via Software Interrupt
E241 - E250	DELAY	Generalized Delay Program
E251 - E270	DSPLY	Control Program for Operator Displays
E271 - E3EF	SUPER	Main Supervisor Program
0000 - 03FF		Interrupt and Reset Vectors

Data Memory

Address	Name	Purpose
1000	NKEYS	Number of Keys Pressed by Operator
1001 - 1002	KBPTR	Keyboard Buffer Pointer
1003 - 1041	KBUFFR	Keyboard Buffer
1042 - 1050	DBUFFR	Display Buffer
1051 - 106F	TEMP	Miscellaneous Temporary Storage
1070 - 10FF	STACK	Hardware Stack

The map may also list additional entry points and include a specific description of the unused parts of memory.

PARAMETER AND DEFINITION LISTS

Parameter and definition lists at the start of the main program and each subroutine make understanding and changing the program far simpler. The following rules can help.

1. **Separate data locations, I/O units, parameters, definitions, and fixed memory addresses.**
2. **Arrange lists alphabetically when possible, with a description of each entry.**
3. **Give each parameter that might change a name and include it in the lists.** Such parameters may include time constants, inputs or codes corresponding to particular keys or functions, control or masking patterns, starting or ending characters, thresholds, etc.
4. **List fixed memory addresses separately.** These may include reset and interrupt service addresses, the starting address of the program memory areas, stack areas, etc.

5. **Give each port used by an I/O device a name,** even though devices may share ports in the current system. The separation will make it easier for you to expand or change the I/O section.

A typical list of definitions is:

```
*
* MEMORY SYSTEM CONSTANTS
*
IRQ_1LEV EQU      $21000          LEVEL 1 INTERRUPT SERVICE ROUTINE
IRQ_2LEV EQU      $210AB          LEVEL 2 INTERRUPT SERVICE ROUTINE
IRQ_7LEV EQU      $22000          LEVEL 7 INTERRUPT SERVICE ROUTINE
MEMORY   EQU      $0              STARTING ADDRESS FOR MEMORY
SSTKPNT  EQU      $F000           INITIAL SUPERVISOR STACK POINTER
USTKPNT  EQU      $E000           INITIAL USER STACK POINTER
*
* I/O UNITS
*
PIA1     EQU      $3FF40          BASE ADDRESS PIA 1
PIA2     EQU      $3FF41          BASE ADDRESS PIA 2
ACIA1    EQU      $3FF01          BASE ADDRESS ACIA 1
ACIA2    EQU      $3FF21          BASE ADDRESS ACIA 2
*
* I/O UNITS OFFSETS
*
PIADDA   EQU      $0              OFFSET FOR DATA DIRECTION REGISTER A
PIADA    EQU      $0              OFFSET FOR DATA REGISTER A
PIACA    EQU      $4              OFFSET FOR CONTROL REGISTER A
*
* DATA STORAGE
*
         ORG      RAM
NUMROWS  DS.B     1               NUMBER OF ROWS ON INPUT KEYBOARD
NUMCOL   DS.B     1               NUMBER OF COLUMNS ON INPUT KEYBOARD
INPUTBUF DS.L     1               ADDRESS TO INPUT BUFFER
OUTBUF   DS.L     1               ADDRESS TO OUTPUT BUFFER
TEMP     DS.L     $10             TEMPORARY DATA BUFFER
*
* PARAMETERS
*
BOUNCE1  EQU      $2              BOUNCE TIME IN MS FOR KEYBOARD
OPEN     EQU      $0F             INPUT PATTERN WHEN NO KEYS ARE CLOSED
DISDLY   EQU      $01             PULSE LENGTH FOR DISPLAYS IN MS
*
* DEFINITIONS
*
ALLHI    EQU      $FF             ALL ONES INPUT
STCON    EQU      $80             OUTPUT FOR START OF CONVERSION PULSE
```

Of course, the **data storage entries may not always be in alphabetical order, since the designer may order these differently for various reasons.**

LIBRARY ROUTINES

Standard documentation of subroutines helps you build a library of programs that are easy to use. If you describe each subroutine with a standard form, anyone can see at a glance what the routines do and how to use them. You should organize the forms carefully, defining them, for example, by processor, language, and type of program. Remember, without proper documentation and organization, using the library may be more difficult than writing programs from scratch. If you are going to use subroutines from a library or other outside source, you must know all their effects in order to debug your overall program.

STANDARD PROGRAM LIBRARY FORMS

Among the information that you will need in the standard form is:

- Purpose of the program
- Processor used
- Language used
- Parameters required and how they are passed to the subroutine
- Results produced and how they are passed to the calling program
- Number of bytes of memory used
- Number of clock cycles required. This number may be an average or a typical figure, or it may vary widely. Actual execution time will, of course, depend on the processor clock rate and the memory cycle time.
- Registers affected
- Flags affected
- A typical example
- Error handling
- Special cases
- Documented program listing

If the program is complex, the standard library form should also include a general flowchart or a structured outline of the program. As we have mentioned before, a library program is most likely to be useful if it performs a single function in a general manner.

TOTAL DOCUMENTATION

Complete documentation of microprocessor software will include all or most of the elements that we have mentioned.

DOCUMENTATION PACKAGE

The total documentation package may involve:

- General flowcharts
- A written description of the program
- A list of all parameters and definitions
- A memory map
- A documented listing of the program
- A description of the test plan and test results

The documentation may also include:

- Program flowcharts
- Data flowcharts
- Structured programs

Even this package is sufficient only for non-production software. **Production software also requires the following documents:**

- Program Logic Manual
- User's Guide
- Maintenance Manual

Program Logic Manual

The program logic manual expands the written explanation provided wih the software. It should explain the system's design goals, algorithms, and tradeoffs, assuming a reader who is competent technically but lacks detailed knowledge of the program. It should provide a step-by-step guide to the operations of the program and it should explain the data structures and their manipulation.

User's Guide

The user's guide is the most important single piece of documentation. No matter how well designed the system may be, it will not be useful if no one can understand its operations or take advantage of its features. **The user's guide should explain system features and their use, provide frequent examples that clarify the text, and give tested step-by-step directions. The writing of user's guides requires care and objectivity, since the writer must be able to take an outsider's point of view.**

One problem in writing user's guides is the need to avoid overwhelming the beginner or taxing the patience of the experienced user. Two separate versions can help overcome this problem. **A guide for the beginner can explain the most common features of the program with the aid of simple examples and detailed discussions. A guide for the experienced user can provide more extensive descriptions of features and fewer examples.** Remember that the beginner needs help getting started, whereas the experienced user wants organized reference material.

Maintenance Manual

The maintenance manual is designed for the programmer who has to modify the system. It **should explain the procedures for any changes or expansion that have been designed into the program.**

IMPORTANCE OF DOCUMENTATION

Documentation should not be taken lightly or left to the last minute. Good documentation, combined with proper programming practices, is not only an important part of the final product but can also make development simpler, faster, and more productive. **The designer should make consistent and thorough documentation part of every stage of software development.**

19 Debugging

As we noted at the beginning of this section, debugging and testing are among the most time-consuming stages of software development. **Even though such methods as modular programming, structured programming and top-down design can simplify programs and reduce the frequency of errors, debugging and testing are still difficult** because they are so poorly defined. The selection of an adequate set of test data is seldom a clear or scientific process. Finding errors sometimes seems like a game of pin the tail on the donkey, except that the donkey is moving and the programmer must position the tail by remote control. Few tasks are as frustrating as debugging programs.

This chapter will first describe the tools available to aid in debugging. It will then discuss basic debugging procedures, describe the common types of errors, and present some examples of program debugging. The next chapter will describe how to select test data and test programs.

We will describe only the purposes of most debugging tools. There is little standardization in this area and we cannot discuss all the available products. The examples show the uses, advantages, and limitations of some common tools.

Debugging tools have two major functions. One is to pin the error down to a short section of the program; the other is to provide more detailed information about what the computer is doing than is provided by normal runs, and so make the source of the error obvious. Current debugging tools do not find and correct errors by themselves; you must know enough about what is happening to recognize and correct the error when the debugging tools zero in on it and show its effects in detail.

SIMPLE DEBUGGING TOOLS

The most common simple debugging tools are:

- A breakpoint facility
- A single-step facility
- A trace facility
- A register dump program
- A memory dump program

BREAKPOINT

A breakpoint is a place at which the program will automatically halt or wait so that the user can examine the current status of the system. A program will not continue until the user orders its resumption. Breakpoints allow you either to check or pass over an entire section of a program. To see if an initialization routine is correct, you can place a breakpoint at the end of it and run the program. You can then check memory locations and registers to see if the entire section is correct. However, note that if the section is not correct, you must still pinpoint the error, either with earlier breakpoints or with a single-step mode.

Breakpoints often use the exception processing system (see Chapter 15). You can use any of the 16 trap vectors to act as a breakpoint. Any of the 7 interrupt levels can also be used by external equipment to cause breakpoints. A breakpoint will usually cause a special program to be executed; for example, it might automatically print the contents of specified registers or wait for the user to enter a command.

Inserting Breakpoints

The simplest and best way to insert a breakpoint in a program is to replace the first word of an instruction with a trap instruction. When the trap instruction is executed, program control is transferred to a breakpoint routine specified via a trap vector, the processor is forced into supervisor mode, and the program counter and status register contents are saved.

Don't forget that the value saved for the program counter points to the instruction after the one which caused the trap. If you want the actual breakpoint address displayed, or if you want the program to resume correctly after restoring the original instruction, you will have to subtract two from the stored program counter value. The simplest way to accomplish this would be to execute the instruction SUBQ.L #2,−2(A7). Note that this method assumes that the supervisor stack pointer still points to the data saved at the time of the trap.

Figure 19-1 shows a simple breakpoint routine with its trap vector and a call to the breakpoint routine. This routine causes an endless loop, and the only way to terminate the loop is with a reset or an interrupt.

Setting and Clearing Breakpoints

Many monitors have facilities for automatically inserting (setting) **and remov-**

```
*EXCEPTION VECTORS
          ORG 0
          .
          .
          DS.L      BRKPT                 TRAP 0 = BREAKPOINT
          .
          .
*
* USER PROGRAM
*
          ORG $4000
PGM14_2   MOVEA.L #ACIA,A0                ADDRESS OF ACIA
          .
          .
          TRAP      #0                    BREAKPOINT HERE
          .
          .
          .
*
* BREAKPOINT HANDLER
*
          ORG $10000
BRKPT     BRA BRKPT                       WAIT IN PLACE
          .
          .
          .
```

Figure 19-1. A Simple Breakpoint Routine

ing (clearing) **breakpoints based on one of the TRAP instructions.** Such breakpoints do not affect the timing of the program until one of them is executed. However, you obviously cannot replace instructions that are in ROM or PROM. **Other monitors implement breakpoints by actually checking the address lines or the program counter in hardware or in software.** This method allows the user to set breakpoints on addresses in ROM or PROM, but it may affect system timing if the address must be checked in software. A more powerful facility would allow the user to enter an address to which the processor would transfer control. Another possibility would be a return dependent on a switch as in the following example.

```
BRKPT     BTST #7,PIADR          WAIT FOR SWITCH IN BIT 7 TO CLOSE
          BNE  BRKPT

          RTE
```

Of course, other PIA data or control lines could also be used. Remember that RTE automatically reenables interrupts. If a PIA interrupt is used, the service routine must read the PIA data register to clear the interrupt status bit.

Precautions in Using Breakpoints

When you use breakpoints (whether manually or through monitor facilities), remember the following precautions:

1. **Only set breakpoints at addresses that contain operation codes.** Replacing data or parts of addresses with Trap instructions can result in chaos.

2. **Interpret the results carefully.** Remember that the computer has not yet executed the instruction that was replaced.
3. **Check all conditions before resuming the program.** You may have to change the program counter, correct the contents of registers or memory locations, clear breakpoints that are no longer necessary, and set new breakpoints. Methods for resuming programs vary greatly, so consult your microcomputer's user's guide. Be particularly careful never to resume a program in the middle of an instruction (that is, at an address that does not contain an operation code) or in the middle of an I/O or timing operation (e.g., sending data to a teletypewriter) that cannot logically be resumed after a delay.

REGISTER DUMP

A register dump is a facility that lists the contents of all, or some selected subset, of the processor's registers. A register dump routine is very often a part of a breakpoint handling routine and the debug program that controls the trace facility.

A useful register dump program will let you specify which registers, and even which portion of selected registers, to display. Since the MC68000 allows operations on portions of registers (byte or word operations) it will often be useful to display, for example, just the least significant byte of a register. Similarly, if you are only interested in the contents of a few data registers, it would be most useful simply to display the contents of those registers rather than the contents of all 16 data and address registers. **Figure 19-2 shows the results of a typical register dump program.**

There are a couple of things we must keep in mind when we write a register dump program. First, if we want the program counter contents to be displayed, it is usually possible to find the PC contents somewhere on the stack. However, you have to know how many exceptions and/or subroutine calls may have intervened before the register dump program, since they may have stored additional items on the stack.

Secondly, stack pointer A7 may cause problems if you don't keep track of whether the processor is in the user or supervisor state. Here are some rules to remember:

- In the user state, the user stack pointer is in A7 and it is impossible to reach the supervisor stack pointer.
- In the supervisor state, the supervisor stack pointer is in A7 and you can reach the user stack pointer with the help of the MOVE USP,An instruction.

Thirdly, remember that a subroutine call stores just a program counter value on the stack while an exception (trap, interrupt, and so on) **stores the program counter content and the status register contents.**

Lastly, if you are in the user state and save the status register contents somewhere, don't attempt to restore the entire status register; that is a privileged instruction. It will be sufficient to restore the condition code part of the status register with a MOVE to CCR instruction. Alternately, you can use the RTR instruction which automatically restores the condition code portion of the status register.

Figure 19-3 shows a flowchart of the register dump program REGDUMP. In this program, we assume that the subroutines PRT8HEX and PRT4HEX convert and

```
D0=3FD56709 D1=100002 D2=2430 D4=3C A0=00014000 A1=6000 A7=00056421
```

Figure 19-2. Results of a Typical MC68000 Register Dump

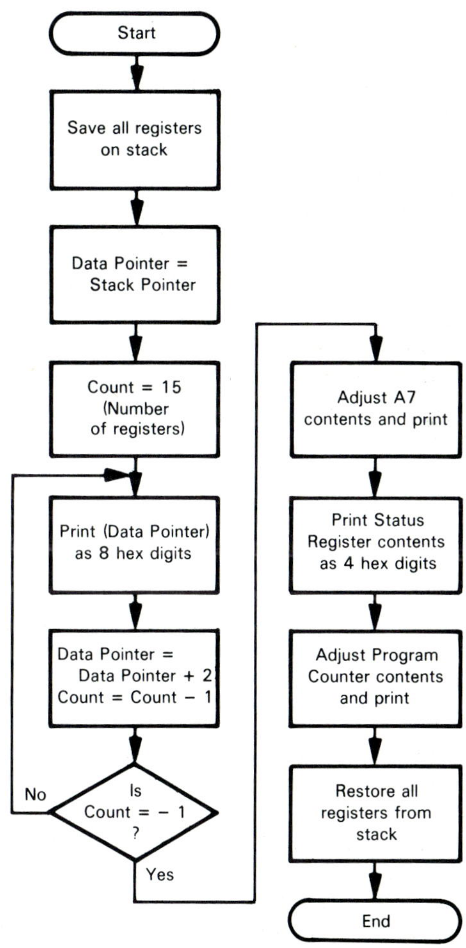

Figure 19-3. Flowchart of a Register Dump Program

print 32 or 16 bits of register D0 as hex digits on the system printer. We also assume that the register dump routine is called by a BSR or JSR instruction and that the system is in the user state.

```
*
*REGISTER DUMP PROGRAM
*

PROGRAM  EQU      $4000
         ORG      PROGRAM

REGDUMP  MOVE.W   SR,-(A7)                 SAVE STATUS REGISTER
         MOVEM.L  D0-D7/A0-A7,-(A7)        SAVE REST OF REGISTERS

         MOVEA.L  A7,A0                    A0 IS LOCAL STACKPOINTER
         MOVEQ    #15-1,D4                 15 REGISTERS TO PRINT-ADJUST FOR DB

LOOP     MOVE.L   (A0)+,D0                 GET PUSHED REGISTER
         BSR      PRT8HEX                  AND PRINT IT
         DBRA     D4,LOOP

         MOVE.L   (A0)+,D0                 GET STACKPOINTER
         ADDI.L   #6,D0                    ADJUST TO VALUE BEFORE CALL
         BSR      PRT8HEX                  PRINT IT

         MOVE.W   (A0)+,D0                 GET STATUS WORD
         BSR      PRT4HEX                  PRINT IT

         MOVE.L   (A0)+,D0                 GET OLD PC
         SUBI.L   #2,D0                    ADJUST IT TO VALUE BEFORE CALL
         BSR      PRT8HEX                  PRINT IT

         MOVEM.L  (A7)+,D0-D7/A0-A7        RESTORE REGISTERS

         RTR      RETURN                   AND  RESTORE THE CONDITION CODES
```

Note that the last instruction is an RTR instruction. If you want to call the register dump program via an exception, you must make some changes to this program. Required changes are shown in the program SYSDUMP.

```
*
*REGISTER DUMP AFTER TRAP OR EXCEPTION
*

PROGRAM  EQU      $4000

         ORG      PROGRAM

SYSDUMP  MOVEM.L  D0-D7/A0-A6,-(A7)        SAVE REGISTERS ON SUPERVISOR STACK

         MOVEA.L  A7,A0                    A0 IS LOCAL STACKPOINTER
         MOVEQ    #15-1,D4                 15 REGISTERS TO PRINT-ADJUST FOR DB.

LOOP     MOVE.L   (A0)+,D0                 GET PUSHED REGISTER
         BSR      PRT8HEX                  AND PRINT IT
         DBRA     D4,LOOP

         MOVE.L   USP,A1                   GET USER STACKPOINTER
         MOVE.L   A1,D0
         BSR      PRT8HEX                  PRINT IT

         MOVE.W   (A0)+,D0                 GET STATUS WORD
         BSR      PRT4HEX                  PRINT IT

         MOVE.L   (A0)+,D0                 GET OLD PC
         SUBI.L   #2,D0                    ADJUST IT TO VALUE BEFORE CALL
         BSR      PRT8HEX                  PRINT IT

         MOVEM.L  (A7)+,D0-D7/A0-A6        RESTORE REGISTERS

         RTE      RETURN                   AND  RESTORE THE CONDITION CODES
```

Make sure you understand the difference between the instructions RTE, RTR, and RTS. Which of them is privileged and why?

SINGLE-STEP

A single-step facility allows you to execute a program one instruction or one memory cycle at a time. After each step you might display some register or memory contents. Usually, single-stepping is associated with some external circuitry which monitors the output lines of the processor. The MC68000, however, provides internal circuitry to accomplish single-stepping via its trace logic.

TRACE

The trace facility allows you to see intermediate results since you can determine the status of the processor's registers after each instruction is executed. A simple trace usually lets you step through your program instruction by instruction and prints all the registers after each instruction is executed. A more useful **trace facility might allow you to execute several instructions before stopping and permit you to specify how much information you want each time you stop.** It might also allow you to print the contents of memory locations you specify. This will result in a reduced volume of information and means that you must decide what you need before instituting the trace, but it should give you the information that is most useful.

Simple instruction tracing may provide you with very detailed information about what happens inside the processor. This information should be sufficient to identify such errors as jump and branch instructions with incorrect conditions and/or destinations, omitted or incorrect addresses, incorrect operation codes, and improper data values.

You must keep in mind, however, **that a single-step trace slows the processor far below its normal speed.** Thus, you cannot check delay loops or I/O operations in real time. Nor can a single-step trace help you find timing errors or errors in the interrupt or DMA systems. In fact, the single-step mode typically operates at less than one millionth of normal processor speed. To single-step through one second of real processor time would require more than ten days. **The single-step trace mode, therefore, is useful only to check the logic of short sequences of instructions.**

The MC68000 has a built-in trace facility not often found on microprocessors. Bit 15 in the status register can be set to force the processor into the trace state. In this state, an exception is forced after each instruction, thus allowing a debug program to have control over program execution. **In the trace mode, it essentially looks as though we had inserted breakpoints (trap instructions) after every instruction.**

The exception processing for the trace operation follows the same general pattern as for the processing of a trap instruction. The contents of the program counter and status register are saved, and control is transferred to the address stored in the trace exception vector which is #9, at memory address 24_{16}.

If you want to implement a very simple trace facility on your MC68000 system, just place the address of the register dump program (SYSDUMP), described previously, in address 24_{16} (the trace exception vector location).

```
ORG     $24
DC.L    SYSDUMP
```

Then set bit 15 in the status register, using one of the instructions that operate on the status register, and start your program. You will get all of the processor's registers (except the supervisor stack pointer) printed after each instruction is executed. Once again, for a more detailed discussion of exception processing, refer to Chapter 15. Note that the program counter printout resulting from SYSDUMP would have to be modified. How would you modify it?

This trace routine will provide you with an enormous amount of information. If you improve on it, or if you have a good trace program already, here is some advice to keep in mind:

1. **Decide what you need before executing the trace.** Otherwise you will not know what to do with the results.
2. **Start by tracing only one or two variables and printing the results infrequently.** This will give you less information to analyze at one time.
3. **Use breakpoints to limit the extent of the trace.** Turn tracing on or off at the breakpoints.
4. **Use whatever facility your computer has to mark the output.** Otherwise you will end up with pages of unidentified numbers and you will spend most of your time just figuring out what they are.
5. **Be careful when you specify that only a portion of a register is to be displayed** (if your trace allows this option). Remember that phenomena like sign-extensions can cause problems that you won't see if you don't display the contents of the entire register.

MEMORY DUMP

A memory dump is a program that lists the contents of memory on an output device (such as a printer). This is a more efficient way of examining data arrays or entire programs than just looking at single locations. However, very large memory dumps are not useful (except to supply scrap paper) because of the sheer mass of information that they produce. They may also take a long time to execute on a slow printer. **Small dumps may,** however, **provide the programmer with a reasonable amount of information that can be examined as a unit. Regular repetitions of data patterns or offsets of entire arrays are easily spotted in a dump.**

A general dump program is often rather difficult to write. Make sure that the ending memory address is not smaller than the starting memory address. A larger starting memory address might be treated as an error, or it may cause no output.

Since the speed of the memory dump depends on the speed of the output device, the efficiency of the routine seldom matters. **The following program will ignore cases where the starting address is larger than the ending address, and will handle memory blocks of any length.**

```
                    *
                    * THIS PROGRAM PRINTS A PIECE OF MEMORY CONTENTS ON THE
                    * SYSTEM PRINTER.
                    *
00004000            PROGRAM  EQU      $4000
00006000            DATA     EQU      $6000

00006000                     ORG      DATA
```

```
006000 00000004     START    DS.L     1
006004 00000004     END      DS.L     1

       00004000              ORG      PROGRAM

004000 20786000     MEMDUMP  MOVEA.L  START,A0      GET START ADDRESS
004004 22786004              MOVEA.L  END,A1        GET THE END ADDRESS

004008 B1C9         LOOP     CMPA.L   A1,A0         IF END > START
00400A 6208                  BHI.S    DONE          ..THEN DONE
00400C 2018                  MOVE.L   (A0)+,D0      ..ELSE GET DATA, INCREMENT START
00400E 61000006              BSR      PRT8HEX       AND PRINT DATA
004012 60F4                  BRA      LOOP

004014 4E75         DONE     RTS
```

A typical result of this memory dump program is shown in Figure 19-4. Note that since we are printing long words, we may print a maximum of three bytes beyond the specified ending address. To illustrate this, try START = 6000,END = 6004.

This memory dump routine correctly handles the case in which the starting and ending locations are the same (try it!). You will have to interpret the results carefully if the dump area includes the stack, since the dump subroutine itself uses the stack. The PRT8HEX subroutine may also change memory and stack locations.

Obviously, these results may sometimes be hard to interpret. They don't tell you which addresses are involved and the results are not output in a very satisfying format. **Figure 19-5 shows a better format that gives you the addresses involved and makes it easier to distinguish between bytes, words, and long words.**

If you are working a lot with ASCII strings, then it will be useful to get the ASCII characters corresponding to the memory locations as shown in Figure 19-6. This is a common and useful format. It will, for example, immediately show you if some unprintable character is intermixed in the string. Thus, if we happen to get a byte with a

```
48415353
45204D41
44452054
48495320
44554D50
```

Figure 19-4. Results of an Unformatted Memory Dump

```
005000  43  48  41  4C   4D  45  52  53   20  53  57  45   44  45  4E  20
```

Figure 19-5. Results of a Formatted Memory Dump

```
005000  54 48 45 20 4D 45 4D 4F 52 59 20 44 55 4D 50 20    THE.MEMORY.DUMP
```

Figure 19-6. Results of a Memory Dump with ASCII Characters

```
005000  54 48 45 20 4D 45 4D 15 4F 52 59 20 44 55 4D 50    THE.MEM.ORY.DUMP
```

Figure 19-7. Results of an ASCII Memory Dump with Unprintable Character

value 15_{16} between M and O in MEMORY the dump would appear as shown in Figure 19-7. A dump program which just shows you printable characters wouldn't have revealed this extra character.

Try to rewrite the memory dump program so that it produces a memory dump that shows you the address and the hexadecimal form as well as the ASCII characters contained in memory.

MORE ADVANCED DEBUGGING TOOLS

The more advanced debugging tools that are most widely used are:

- **Simulator programs to check program logic**
- **Logic analyzers to check signals and timing**

Many variations of both these tools exist, and we will discuss only the standard features.

Software Simulator

The simulator is the computer equivalent of a pencil-and-paper computer. It **is a computer program that goes through the operating cycle of a computer, keeping track of the contents of all the registers, flags, and memory locations.** We could, of course, do this by hand, but it would require a large effort and close attention to the exact effects of each instruction. The simulator program never gets tired or confused, never forgets an instruction or register, and does not run out of paper.

Typical simulator features include:

- **A breakpoint facility.** Usually, breakpoints can be set to occur after a particular number of cycles have been executed; when a memory location or one of a set of memory locations is referenced; when the contents of a location or one of a set of locations is altered, or on other conditions.

- **Register and memory dump facilities** that display the contents of memory locations, registers, and I/O ports.
- **A trace facility** that prints the contents of particular registers or memory locations whenever the program changes or uses them.
- **A load facility** that allows you to set initial register and/or memory location contents, or change them during the simulation.

Some simulators can simulate input/output, interrupts, and even DMA. **The simulator has many advantages:**

1. It can provide a complete description of the status of the computer, since the simulator program is not restricted by microprocessor chip pinout limitations or other characteristics of the underlying circuitry.
2. It can provide breakpoints, dumps, traces, and other facilities, without using any of the simulated processor's memory space or control system. These facilities will therefore not interfere with the user program.
3. Programs, starting points, and other conditions are easy to change.
4. All the facilities of a large computer, including peripherals and software, are available to the microprocessor designer.

On the other hand, the simulator is limited by its software base and its separation from the real microcomputer. The major limitations are:

1. The simulator cannot cope with timing problems, since it operates at less than real-time execution speed. The simulator is usually quite slow. Reproducing one second of actual processor time may require hours of computer time.
2. The simulator cannot model the input/output section exactly since it cannot represent external hardware or interfaces accurately.

The simulator represents the software side of debugging; it has the typical advantages and limitations of a wholly software-based approach. The simulator can provide insight into program logic and other software problems, but often cannot help with timing, I/O, and hardware problems.

Logic Analyzer

The logic, or microprocessor, analyzer is the hardware solution to debugging. Basically, the analyzer is a parallel digital version of the standard oscilloscope. The analyzer displays information in binary, hexadecimal, or mnemonic form on a CRT, and has a variety of triggering events, thresholds, and inputs. Most analyzers also have a memory so that they can display the past contents of the microcomputer busses.

The standard procedure is to set a triggering event, such as the occurrence of a particular address on the address bus or instruction on the data bus. For example, one might trigger the analyzer if the microcomputer tries to store data in a particular address, or execute an input or output instruction. One may then look at the sequence of events that preceded the breakpoint. **Common problems you can find in this way include short noise spikes (or glitches), incorrect signal sequences, overlapping waveforms,**

- **Number of input lines.** At least 40 are necessary to monitor a 16-bit data bus and a 24-bit address bus. Still more are necessary for control signals, clocks, and other important inputs.
- **Amount of memory.** Each previous state that is saved will occupy several bytes of memory.
- **Maximum frequency.** It must be several MHz to handle the fastest processors.
- **Minimum signal width** (important for catching glitches).
- **Type and number of triggering events allowed.** Important features are pre- and post-trigger delays; these allow the user to display events occurring before or after the trigger event.
- **Methods of connecting to the microcomputer.** This may require a rather complex interface.
- **Number of display channels.**
- **Binary, hexadecimal, or mnemonic displays.**
- **Display formats.**
- **Signal hold time requirements.**
- **Probe capacitance.**
- **Single or dual thresholds.**

All of these factors are important in comparing different logic and microprocessor analyzers, since these instruments are new and unstandardized. A tremendous variety of products is already available and this variety will become even greater in the future.[1]

Logic analyzers, of course, **are necessary only for systems with complex timing. Simple applications with low-speed peripherals have few hardware problems that a designer cannot handle with a standard oscilloscope.**

DEBUGGING WITH CHECKLISTS

No one can hope to check an entire program by hand; however, certain trouble spots can be checked. **You can use systematic hand checking to find a large number of errors without resorting to any debugging tools.**

The question is where to place the effort. The answer is on points that can be handled with either a yes-no answer or a simple arithmetic calculation. Do not do complex arithmetic, follow all status flags, or try every conceivable case. Limit your hand-checking to matters that can be settled easily. Leave the complex problems to be solved with the aid of debugging tools. But proceed systematically; build your checklist, and make sure that the program performs all basic operations correctly.

The first step is to compare the flowchart or other program documentation with the actual code. Make sure that everything which appears in one also appears in the other. A simple checklist will do the job. It is easy to omit an entire branch or a processing section.

Next concentrate on the program loops. Make sure that all registers and memory locations used inside the loops are initialized correctly. This is a common source of errors; once again, a simple checklist will suffice.

Now look at each conditional branch. Select a sample case that should produce a branch and one that should not; try both of them. Is the branch correct or reversed? If the branch involves checking whether a number is above or below a threshold, try the equality case. Does the correct branch occur? Make sure that your choice is consistent with the problem definition.

Look at the loops as a whole. Try the first and last iterations by hand; these are often troublesome special cases. What happens if the number of iterations is zero; e.g., there is no data or the table has no elements? Does the program fall through correctly? Programs will often perform one iteration unnecessarily, or, even worse, decrement counters past zero before checking them. Check for other trivial cases where there is nothing for the program to do.

Check off everything down to the last statement. Don't optimistically assume that the first error is the only one in the program. Hand-checking will allow you to get the maximum benefit from debugging runs, since you will get rid of many simple errors ahead of time.

Hand-Checking Questions

Here is a quick review of the hand-checking questions:

1. Does the program include everything that was designed into it (and vice versa for documentation purposes)?
2. Are all registers and memory locations initialized before they are used inside loops?
3. Are all conditional branches logically correct?
4. Do all loops start and end properly?
5. Are equality cases handled correctly?
6. Are trivial cases handled correctly?

LOOKING FOR ERRORS

Of course, despite all these precautions (or if you skip over some of them), programs often still won't work. The designer is left with the problem of how to find the remaining mistakes. The lists that follow may be of some help. We have attempted to categorize the types of errors that you may encounter. However, you must remember that a certain kind of error will not necessarily be limited to just one kind of program. The groupings we have arrived at may make it faster for you to pinpoint the error. But if you don't find the error within the category in which it seems most likely to occur, look under all the other categories.

ERRORS LIKELY TO BE FOUND IN CERTAIN PARTS OF A PROGRAM

The Initialization Section

- **Failure to initialize variables such as counters, pointers, sums, indexes, and so on.** Do not assume that the registers, memory locations, or condition codes necessarily contain zero before they are used. Also make sure that you initialize the correct part of a register. For example, if you are going to use register D0 as an 8-bit counter for a DBRA loop, it is necessary to clear the entire low-order word of D0 since this instruction always operates on the entire 16-bit word.

- **Failure to follow through correctly in trivial cases.** It is usually here where you must decide what to do if there is nothing for the program to do (no data present, no entries in a list, and so on). Do not assume that such cases will never occur unless the program specifically eliminates them.
- **Accidental initializations.** Make sure that no jump or branch instructions transfer control back to the initialization section.

Loops

- **Updating counters, pointers, or indexes in the wrong place or not at all.** Be sure that there are no paths through a loop that either skip or repeat the updating function. Be especially careful when you deal with nested loops, and remember that counters for inner loops must be reinitialized each time they are entered.
- **Confusing postincrement and predecrement operations.** Remember that postincrement increments the address register after using its contents, while predecrement decrements the address register before using its contents. Also remember that it is the "size" of the instruction that determines the amount of the increment or decrement. A long word instruction increments or decrements by 4, a word instruction by 2 and a byte instruction by 1. Did you correctly specify the size?
- **Confusing the use of the DBcc instruction.** The condition specified is the condition that makes the program exit the loop, rather than remaining in the loop by taking the branch. Remember that if the condition is not met, the processor will decrement the counter and test for counter contents exactly equal to -1: the test is not for less than zero. Also remember that if you don't compensate for the -1 (rather than the zero) that is tested for, the loop will be executed one more time than you had expected.
- **Inverting the logic of a conditional jump such as using branch on carry set when you meant branch on carry clear.** Remember that compare and subtraction instructions perform the operations *destination* (second operand) – *source* (first operand), and set the Carry and Zero flags as follows:

  Zero flag (Z) = 1 if destination $\neq$ source
  Zero flag (C) = 0 if destination $>$ source
  Carry flag (C) = 1 if destination $<$ source

  Note that the Carry flag is cleared if destination = source.
- **Changing condition codes before using them or failure to change them.** Remember that the MOVE instruction affects all the condition codes except the Extend (X) flag. Operations using address registers as a destination do not affect the condition codes with the exception of the CMPA instruction. Also refer back to the precautions given with Program 9-2*b* concerning testing of flags that may have been set as a result of more than one instruction.

Subroutines and Macros

- **Ignoring the effects of subroutines and macros.** Subroutine calls and references to macros typically result in the execution of many instructions. These instructions will almost always change the condition code register (CCR) and may change the contents of other registers and memory locations as well. Be sure that you know all the effects of any subroutine or macro you use. Also note the importance of documenting subroutines and macros so that users can determine their effect without examining a long listing.
- **Forgetting that the stack is used in subroutine linkages.** The JSR and BSR instructions save the return address in the hardware stack on top of any parameter you may have placed there. The RTS instruction simply transfers control to the address at the top of the current stack (user or supervisor). If you have not carefully managed the stack, the processor could end up at a completely unexpected location.
- **Using the wrong return instruction.** RTS does not restore condition codes, RTR does. Note that no subroutine calling instructions automatically store the contents of the condition codes; you must explicitly accomplish this function. Remember that RTR fetches the condition codes before it restores the program counter; thus, the sequence

  ```
  MOVE.W SR,-(A7)
  BSR SUBR
  ```

  will not work in conjunction with an RTR instruction. Instead, if you want to save the contents of the condition codes, you must do it at the beginning of the subroutine to which control is transferred.
- **Failure to restore previously saved registers.** This is a very common error. Be sure that you restore the correct number of registers and to the correct locations. Use the MOVEM.L instruction and store on the stack. Remember that if you are moving 16-bit words from memory to address registers, they will be sign-extended to 32 bits, and this may result in problems.
- **Using Link and Unlink instructions improperly.** Don't change the "link-register" during execution of the subroutine. For example, if you use LINK A6,#−16 at the beginning of a subroutine, then A6 must have exactly the same value when you execute the UNLK A6 instruction. Otherwise the stack will go out of phase and the result will probably be disastrous to your system. Also remember that the displacement is interpreted as a two's complement integer; if you have a stack that grows downward (as the system stack does) you have to specify a negative displacement with the link instruction. The displacement must also always be an even number since the stack is organized on a word boundary.

General Processing Sections

- **Reversing order of operands.** Remember that MOVE D1,D2 moves the contents of D1 to D2. (This is the opposite of the way the Z8000 and 8086 work.) Also remember that SUB src,dst and CMP src,dst perform the operation dst - src. The DIV src,Dn instruction performs the operation Dn ÷ src (and stores the result in Dn).

- **Confusing addressing modes**
  - **Data versus addresses** (immediate and absolute). Remember that MOVE.W #$2000,D0 loads register D0 with the number 2000_{16}, whereas MOVE.W $2000,D0 loads register D0 with the contents of memory locations 2000_{16} and 2001_{16}.
  - **Address register direct and indirect.** Remember that CLR.L A0 loads register A0 with zeros, whereas CLR.L (A0) loads the memory word pointed to by A0 with zeros.
  - **Forgetting that addressing modes operate differently on jump instructions than on other instructions.** Jump instructions (JMP or JSR) are executed as if one level of indirection had been removed. For example, JMP $1000 loads 1000_{16} into the program counter, whereas MOVE $1000,A0 loads the contents of memory location 1000_{16} into register D0.
- **Ignoring the fact that certain instructions only operate in one size format**

  Examples: DBcc subtracts 1 from the low-order 16 bits of the specified data register.

  MOVEQ affects all 32 bits of the specified data register.

  MOVE ea,−(A7) and MOVE (A7)+,ea must always be performed on a word boundary (even address).

  MOVE to CCR is a word instruction but only the low-order byte of the status register is affected.

  DIVS and DIVU affect all 32 bits of the destination data register but use only 16 bits of the source. The same is true of MULS and MULU.

  When an address register is used as a destination, the entire register is affected regardless of what size you specify. If the source operand is specified as a word, it is sign-extended to 32 bits in the address register.
- **Forgetting that the MC68000 sign-extends your 16-bit addresses.** This may cause trouble if you work in the memory space between 32K and 64K (addresses 8000_{16} through $FFFF_{16}$). Also be careful when you load immediate values into an address register and when you use the absolute short addressing mode. In both of these cases, strange results can be obtained if the size is word and if the MSB of the word is a 1: the automatic sign-extension will propagate 1's through the most significant 16 bits of the long word address.
- **Forgetting the details of sign extension of data.** MOVEQ treats the operand as a signed value and extends the sign. ADDQ and SUBQ work only with positive numbers. MOVEM sign extends to 32 bits when moving words from memory registers.
- **Using the shift instructions improperly.** Remember the difference between arithmetic shifts, logical shifts, and rotates. They will all affect the condition codes even if they are operating on data in a memory location. If you specify that a shift count is to be found in a data register, remember that the count is interpreted modulo 64.

- **Confusing 8, 16, and 32-bit quantities.** Remember that the processor doesn't keep track of whether the variable you stored in a register was an 8-, 16-, or 32-bit value. You must specify the size in each instruction. Here are some size-related points to keep in mind:
  - A byte can hold two BCD numbers and the BCD instructions (ABCD, SBCD) are byte-sized.
  - A 16-bit word occupies two bytes and therefore "two addresses in memory." In other words, a 16-bit word stored in memory location 1000_{16} occupies location 1001_{16} also.
  - A long word (32 bits) occupies 4 bytes; this may be a common source of errors if you are used to 8-bit microprocessors.
- **Ignoring the limitations of read-only memory.** Obviously, instructions that both read from and write to memory locations make little sense when applied to an address occupied by a read-only memory (ROM) device. A sorting program that has been given data located in ROM will run forever!
- **Using the wrong register.** The MC68000 has a large number of data and address registers. While this is one of the sources of the power and flexibility of the processor, it demands that you very carefully keep track of what you put where. Note the specifications for two data registers may differ by only one character (e.g. D1, D2). The same is true of address and data registers (e.g. A1, D1). Typing errors are easy to make and often difficult to find.
- **Confusing BCD, binary, hexadecimal, and decimal numbers.** In the BCD representation, each decimal digit is coded separately into binary, using four binary digits (0 or 1). In hexadecimal representation, four binary digits are grouped together and represented with a hex digit (0 through F). For example, the decimal number 54_{10} is equal to 110110_2 in binary, 36_{16} in hexadecimal, and 54_{16} in the standard BCD representation.
- **Forgetting to transfer control past sections of the program that should not be executed.** Remember that the processor proceeds sequentially unless you tell it to do otherwise. You may need some unconditional branches to avoid routines that should not be executed.
- **Confusing the stack and its pointers.** The contents of the stack are always addressed with one of the indirect modes and the stack pointer is addressed using register direct mode.
- **Confusing the bit positions in the bit operate instructions.** Bits are numbered from 31 down through zero. The least significant bit is zero, bit 7 is the most significant bit (MSB) in a byte, bit 15 is the MSB in a word, and bit 31 is the MSB in a long word.

String Manipulation Errors

- **Counting the length of an array incorrectly.** Remember that the addresses 1000_{16} through 1004_{16} include five (not four) memory locations. Thus, the number of elements in an array is *ending address — starting address* + 1.

- **Confusing numbers and characters.** Remember that the ASCII representation of a digit is not the same as the binary or BCD representation. For example, the ASCII representation of the number seven is 37_{16}; 07_{16} is the ASCII BELL character which rings the bell on a teletypewriter.
- **Forgetting that word operations don't work on odd addresses.** String operations are often byte-sized. Be careful if you are using word or long word operations to move strings or append characters to a string. For example, if register A4 holds the address of the current position within a string and you want to append the text "The End" to the string, the instruction sequence

```
MOVE.L #"THE ", (A4)+
MOVE.L # "END", (A4)+
```

  will cause an address error exception if A4 points to an odd address before execution of the first instruction.

Input/Output Errors

- **Ignoring the physical limitations of I/O and interface chips.** While we address interface chips as if they were memory locations, they may not behave like memory devices. Storing data in an input port seldom makes sense, nor does loading data from an output port unless the port is latched and buffered. Some I/O devices have two different registers (one read-only and one write-only) at the same address. The 6850 ACIA control and status registers are an example of this case. Be careful of instructions like shift, negate, and so on, which read from and then write back to the "same" location; they will produce strange errors with register combinations like those provided by the 6850.
- **Using incorrect bits in status and control registers.** The order of bits in these kinds of registers may appear to be random. Are you sure you used the right combination?
- **Misusing the MOVEP instruction.** Remember that MOVEP uses every other address, all even addresses or all odd addresses.
- **Forgetting to reset or initialize I/O devices.** For example, the 6850 ACIA requires a software reset sequence.

Assembler-Related Errors

The use of an assembler is the only practical way to convert source programs into object code, but it can introduce a few annoying errors. In particular,

- **Be careful of what your assembler may use as defaults. For example, the standard MC68000 assembler will make the following assumptions:**
  - **Default instruction size is word if no size is specified.** Remember that it is good programming style always to specify the size with every instruction, even though it is obviously not necessary with instructions where the size is word.

- **Unmarked numbers are assumed to be decimal.** If you want hexadecimal numbers, ASCII characters, and so on, you must explicitly specify such numbers.
- **The default addressing modes are register direct and absolute.** That is, A1 specifies address register A1, not the memory location pointed to by A1. The value $1000 will specify memory location 1000_{16}, and #$1000 will specify the number 1000_{16}.

- **Be careful with absolute short addresses.** If you have used the ORG directive, the assembler assumes that any reference to an absolute address can be achieved using the short absolute addressing form of the instruction. The processor will then sign-extend this address. You should note that this condition may be remedied with later versions of assemblers.
- **Remember that the assembler chooses the quick form of instructions where possible, regardless of whether you have specified the quick version.** Thus, ADD #2,D0 will cause the object code for the ADDQ instruction to be generated.
- **Watch for simple typing errors. The register numbers are close to each other on the keyboard and no assembler can detect a typing error if the erroneous result is a legal instruction.** Also, some assemblers get confused if you insert extra spaces where it didn't expect them, or if you accidentally use meaningless characters such as 1/2. In fact, the assembler may object to a minor error, but accept a totally illogical entry that its developer never considered.
- **Remember, the assembler can print a reassuring message like TOTAL ERRORS 0 even when the program is wrong. All the message means is that the assembler found no errors according to its interpretations of the rules of the language. This does not exclude errors that produce legal instructions or that are beyond the assembler's comprehension. Most of all, it does not exclude logical errors that may be present in your program and does not necessarily mean that the program does what you intended.**

Exception Processing

Exception processing can, from the trouble-shooter's point of view, be divided into two groups: interrupts, and all the other types of exceptions. This is because, in general, interrupts are controlled by external devices and therefore appear to occur at random occasions. Other kinds of exceptions, illegal instructions, address errors, and so on, are often possible to pinpoint a specific instruction or sequence. If your microcomputer doesn't have an exception processing software system, it will be most useful to write one that at least tells you which exception caused a trap (address error, bus error, and so on), and gives you the address where the trap occurred.

Some errors that may be found when you deal with exceptions of any kind are:

- **Forgetting the general facts about exceptions.** The processor is put in the supervisor state, and some information (usually the program counter and status register) is saved on the supervisor stack.
- **Using the wrong return instruction.** RTE and RTR are not the same, so you cannot be clever and use your subroutines just as they are, as part of exception

processing. RTE restores the entire status register while RTR restores just the condition code portion of the status register. RTE is a privileged instruction.

- **Causing multiple bus or addressing errors.** If the processor recognizes an address or bus error while it is processing a previous address or bus error, it will halt. For example, assume that you have an odd value in the supervisor stack pointer for some reason. You try to use the stack pointer with this odd address value and thereby cause an address trap. But the trap handler also uses the supervisor stack and this causes a new address error which will then halt the processor.

Interrupt-Driven Programs

Interrupt-driven programs are particularly difficult to debug, since errors may show up only when an interrupt occurs at a particular time. If, for example, the program enables the interrupts a few instructions too early, an error will appear only if an interrupt occurs while the processor is executing those few instructions. In fact, you can usually assume that sporadic or randomly occuring errors are caused by the interrupt system.[2,3]

Since the MC68000 has an interrupt priority mask in the status register, it may be possible to mask off some of the interrupts and pinpoint the error. Sometimes a breakpoint placed at the start of the interrupt routine may give you a hint as to the cause of the problem, although this may be impossible in real-time systems. Another approach is to save the return addresses every time you get an interrupt, and in this way you may locate the section of the system that causes the problem.

Here are some typical errors in interrupt-driven programs:

- **Incorrect value of the interrupt priority level.** When the processor is reset, it sets its interrupt priority mask to level 7. Upon acknowledging an interrupt, the priority mask is set to the level of the interrupt being acknowledged. RTE will restore the status register, and thus the interrupt priority level, as it was before the interrupt occurred. Make sure that no path through a program fails to set the interrupt priority level to its desired value.
- **Allowing interrupts on a certain level before the system is ready to handle it.** System parameters such as condition codes, flags, pointers, and counters must be initialized first. A checklist might give some help here.
- **Forgetting to store and restore registers.** Interrupts are much like subroutines. Use the same precautions when storing and restoring registers or allocating space on the stack.
- **Forgetting that the interrupt leaves the old program counter and status register contents on the stack whether you use them or not.**
- **Forgetting to clear the source of the interrupt before exiting from the service routine.** For example, if the interrupt comes from a PIA, the interrupt service routine must read the PIA's data register in order to clear the interrupt flag. The read operation is necessary even if the interrupt is from an output device or a real-time clock; otherwise, the interrupt will remain active and will be recognized again as soon as the processor reenables interrupts on this level.

- **Failing to disable certain interrupts during multiword transfers and other critical sequences.** For example, assume that you have a real-time clock with six digits stored in six consecutive bytes of memory. If the clock contains 115959 and you are reading the digits from memory one at a time without disabling the interrupt that updates the clock, here is what could happen. If a clock-updating interrupt occurs after you have read the second digit, it will cause the four last digits to be 0000 and you will think the time is 110000. Such an error may be hard to find because it occurs so seldom and because some very special coincidences are required to create the error. Another area where you must be very cautious of interrupts is in delay routines.
- **Failing to reenable the interrupt after executing a routine that requires interrupts to be disabled.**
- **Ignoring the possibility that the interrupt routine may get reentered.** An interrupt routine might have to be reentered just like a subroutine (see Chapter 11).

A list of possible errors can be endless and the purpose of the preceding list is to give you some ideas as to where you might start looking for errors. Unfortunately, no one has found the algorithm which describes how to be one hundred percent sure that you have found all errors; you may be left with errors no matter how systematic you are. Sometimes the following approach may be your best bet: turn off the computer, have a beer, and let your brain rest. Perhaps let the problem sit overnight or have someone with a fresh viewpoint look at it. Often, when you are explaining a problem to someone else, you will see the answer yourself.

PROGRAM EXAMPLES

19-1. DEBUGGING A CODE CONVERSION PROGRAM

The purpose of this program is to convert a decimal number in memory location DIGIT to a 7-segment code in memory location CODE. The program should blank the display if DIGIT does not contain a decimal number. This appears to be a simple task and we start off with the flowchart shown in Figure 19-8. Our first coding attempt looks like this:

Initial Program: (from flowchart in Figure 19-8)

```
*
*BCD TO SEVEN SEGMENT DISPLAY CONVERSION
*
*INPUT--BCD NUMBER IN DIGIT
*OUTPUT--BIT PATTERN FOR SEVEN SEGMENT DISPLAY IN CODE
*
DATA      EQU     $8000
PROGRAM   EQU     $4200


          ORG     DATA

DIGIT     DS.B    1
CODE      DS.B    1
```

```
SSEG       DC.B      $3F,$06,$5B,$4F,$66
           DC.B      $6D,$7F,$07,$7F

BCD_7SEG MOVEA.W SSEG,A0                    GET BASE ADDRESS OF TABLE
           MOVE      DIGIT,D0               GET DIGIT TO CONVERT
           CMP.B     #9,D0                  IF GREATER THEN 9
           BCS.S     DONE                      THEN DONE

           EXT.W     D0                     ELSE MAKE LOOK LIKE A WORD
           MOVE.B    0(A0,D0),D1               GET CODE FROM TABLE

           MOVE.B    D0,CODE

 DONE      RTS
```

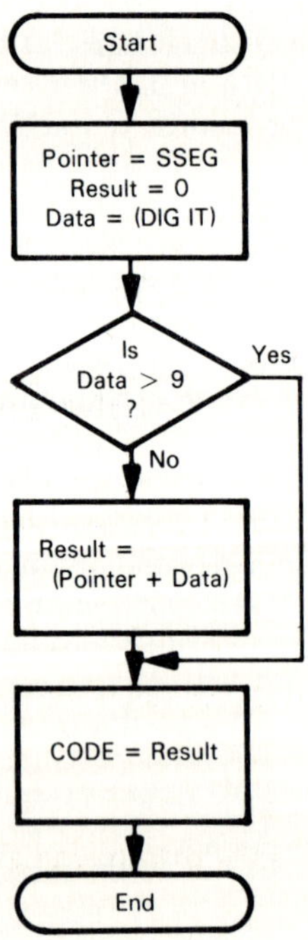

Figure 19-8. Flowchart of Decimal to Seven-Segment Conversion

Using the Checklist

Let us use the checklist we described earlier in this chapter to evaluate this program.

1. Every element of the design in the program? No! We forgot the section that clears the display if the data was not a decimal digit.
2. Initialization? Okay.
3. Conditional branches correct? No! Branch on carry set (BCS) will not handle the equality case correctly. (Try it!). BHI.S DONE is the correct instruction.
4. No loops.
5. Equality cases? Yes, they are now handled correctly.
6. Trivial cases? Yes, (DIGIT) = 0 is handled in the same way as other digits.(Since zero is just another digit in this example, this isn't really a trivial case.)

We also forgot to specify the suffix for the second MOVE instruction. Our second version of the program looks like this:

Second program:

```
DATA      EQU       $8000
PROGRAM   EQU       $4200


          ORG       DATA

DIGIT     DS.B      1
CODE      DS.B      1
SSEG      DC.B      $3F,$06,$5B,$4F,$66
          DC.B      $6D,$7F,$07,$7F

BCD_7SEG  MOVEA.W SSEG,A0                    GET BASE ADDRESS OF TABLE


          MOVEQ     #0,D1
          MOVE.B    DIGIT,D0                 GET DIGIT TO CONVERT
          CMP.B     #9,D0                    IF GREATER THEN 9
          BHI.S     DONE                       THEN DONE

          EXT.W     D0                       ELSE MAKE LOOK LIKE A WORD
          MOVE.B    0(A0,D0.W),D1              GET CODE FROM TABLE

          MOVE.B    D0,CODE

DONE      RTS
```

The hand check did not uncover any errors in this version.

Assembling

The next step is to key in the program and assemble it.

Third Program:

```
00008000        DATA      EQU      $8000
00004200        PROGRAM   EQU      $4200


00008000                  ORG      DATA
```

```
008000 00000001      DIGIT    DS.B     1
008001 00000001      CODE     DS.B     1
008002 3F            SSEG     DC.B     $3F,$06,$5B,$4F,$66
008007 6D                     DC.B     $6D,$7F,$07,$7F

       00004200               ORG      PROGRAM

004200 307900008002 BCD_7SEG MOVEA.W  SSEG,A0          GET BASE ADDRESS OF TABLE
004206 7200                   MOVEQ    #0,D1
004208 103900008000           MOVE.B   DIGIT,D0          GET DIGIT TO CONVERT
00420E 0C000009               CMP.B    #9,D0             IF GREATER THEN 9
004212 620C                   BHI.S    DONE                THEN DONE

004214 4880                   EXT.W    D0                ELSE MAKE LOOK LIKE A WORD
004216 12300000               MOVE.B   0(A0,D0.W),D1       GET CODE FROM TABLE

00421A 13C000008001           MOVE.B   D0,CODE

004220 4E75          DONE     RTS

                              END      BCD_7SEG
```

Single-Step

It is now time to single-step through this program (this can be done quickly because it's a short program). If you have the ability to specify which registers to display after each step, choose PC, D0, D1, SR, and A0.

We chose the following test data for the trials:

0	The smallest decimal digit
9	The lagest decimal digit
10	A boundary case
6B	A randomly selected case

For the first trial, we place zero in memory location DIGIT. After executing the first instruction, MOVE.W SSEG,A0 we find the value $3F06_{16}$ in register A0. That doesn't sound familiar; we expected to have 8000_{16} in A0. The first thing to check here is whether we selected the correct addressing mode. In this case, the answer is no; we confused the immediate and absolute addressing modes. Replace SSEG with #SSEG and try again. This time, we find $FFFF8000_{16}$ in register A0. Again, not the expected result. However, all of the F's must have come from sign-extension (provided that A0 contained zero when we first started). We have specified a word address to be loaded into A0 and the most significant bit in the word is 1. When this address is sign-extended, it produces all ones (FFFF) in the most significant word of the register. The solution is to specify the long word form of the MOVEA instruction. All of this trouble has showed us that the correct first instruction is MOVEA.L #SSEG,A0. (Once again, this is a weakness in the version of the assembler we are using and will probably be handled by later assemblers.)

After correcting this problem, we continue single-stepping through the program. Everything seems to work fine. The branch is not taken and we get $3F_{16}$ as we had expected in register D1. But when we check memory position CODE, we find the BCD digit which we used as the input test data, zero. Something is wrong. To find the problem, ask the question: which instruction(s) affects memory location CODE. In this case it is the last instruction: MOVE D0,CODE. What do we have in register D0? The BCD code. Where is the 7-segment code? In register D1. Aha! It appears that we have a typing error. We change D0,CODE to D1,CODE and make another try. This time we find $3F_{16}$ in memory location CODE. The program now looks like this:

Fourth Program:

```
       00008000     DATA      EQU      $8000
       00004200     PROGRAM   EQU      $4200

       00008000               ORG      DATA

008000 00000001     DIGIT     DS.B     1
008001 00000001     CODE      DS.B     1
008002 3F           SSEG      DC.B     $3F,$06,$5B,$4F,$66
008007 6D                     DC.B     $6D,$7F,$07,$7F

       00004200               ORG      PROGRAM

004200 207C00008002 BCD_7SEG  MOVEA.L  #SSEG,A0           GET BASE ADDRESS OF TABLE
004206 7200                   MOVEQ    #0,D1
004208 103900008000           MOVE.B   DIGIT,D0           GET DIGIT TO CONVERT
00420E 0C000009               CMP.B    #9,D0              IF GREATER THEN 9
004212 620C                   BHI.S    DONE                 THEN DONE

004214 4880                   EXT.W    D0                 ELSE MAKE LOOK LIKE A WORD
004216 12300000               MOVE.B   0(A0,D0.W),D1        GET CODE FROM TABLE

00421A 13C100008001           MOVE.B   D1,CODE

004220 4E75         DONE      RTS

                              END      BCD_7SEG
```

Run Test

This time we run the entire program with the second test value, 9. A check of memory location CODE shows that it does not contain $7D_{16}$, which is the last value in the 7-segment code table. The input test value 9 should cause the program to follow the same path as for the value 0. To see what has happened, we make another single-step pass through the program. Everything works fine until we reach the MOVE.B 0(A0,D0.W),D1 instruction. We expected $7D_{16}$ to be loaded into D1 but this was not the case. A memory dump of the table and its environment shows that the value we get comes from the byte immediately following the 7-segment table. Did we miss an entry in the table? We have nine bytes in the table. The values 0 through 9 require ...ten bytes! A check shows that we forgot the last entry, $6F_{16}$, for the digit 9. After adding this value to the table the run test works with both 0 and 9.

The test result after the two last runs were

Digit	Code
10	6F
6B	6F

The code has not been changed since we tested with the digit equal to 9. Both of the values are invalid data so the error can probably be found in the neighborhood of the branch. To what location does the branch transfer control? Aha!, directly to the RTS instruction! We must execute the MOVE D1,CODE instruction and store the cleared results. The label DONE should be moved up one statement.

Exhaustive Test

Since the program is simple, it can be tested for all the decimal digits. The results are

Digit	Code
0	3F
1	06
2	5B
3	4F
4	66
5	6D
6	7F
7	07
8	7F
9	6F

The result for number 6 is wrong; it should be 7D. Since everything else seems to be correct, the error is almost surely in the table. Entry 6 in the table had been typed incorrectly.

Final Program:

```
*
*BCD TO SEVEN SEGMENT DISPLAY CONVERSION
*
*INPUT--BCD NUMBER 0-9 IN LOCATION DIGIT
*OUTPUT--BIT PATTERN FOR SEVEN SEGMENT DISPLAY
*         IN LOCATION CODE. DISPLAY CLEARED IF
*         DIGIT OUT OF RANGE
*
DATA      EQU      $8000
PROGRAM   EQU      $4200

          ORG      DATA

DIGIT     DS.B     1
CODE      DS.B     1
SSEG      DC.B     $3F,$06,$5B,$4F,$66
          DC.B     $6D,$7D,$07,$7F,$6F

          ORG      PROGRAM

BCD_7SEG  MOVEA.L  #SSEG,A0                GET BASE ADDRESS OF TABLE
          MOVEQ    #0,D1
          MOVE.B   DIGIT,D0                GET DIGIT TO CONVERT
          CMP.B    #9,D0                   IF GREATER THEN 9
          BHI.S    DONE                      THEN DONE

          EXT.W    D0                      ELSE MAKE LOOK LIKE A WORD
          MOVE.B   0(A0,D0.W),D1             GET CODE FROM TABLE

FINI      MOVE.B   D1,CODE

          RTS

          END      BCD_7SEG
```

Notice that we have also improved the comments.

Summary of Errors Discovered

The errors that we found in this example are typical of the ones that MC68000 assembly language programmers should expect. They include:

1. **Failing to initialize registers or memory locations.**
2. **Inverting the logic on conditional branches.**
3. **Misalignment of data when dealing with byte values (although the assembler will usually tell you that something is wrong in this case).**
4. **Confusing the immediate and absolute addressing modes (i.e., data and addresses).**
5. **Forgetting when sign-extension occurs and when it does not (especially when dealing with addresses).**
6. **Failing to keep track of which register is used for what, or typing the wrong digit for a register number.**
7. **Copying lists of numbers, characters, or instructions incorrectly.**
8. **Branching to the wrong place.**

19-2. DEBUGGING A SORT PROGRAM

This program sorts a list of unsigned 16-bit numbers into decreasing order. The address of the beginning of the list is in memory location LISTADDR and the first byte in the list contains the length of the list.

Initial Program: (from flowchart in Figure 19-9)

```
        00006000    DATA     EQU      $6000
        00004000    PROGRAM  EQU      $4000

        00006000             ORG      DATA

006000  00000004    LISTADDR DS.L     1                 ADDRESS OF START OF LIST

        00004000             ORG      PROGRAM

004000  22786000    BUB_SORT MOVEA.L  LISTADDR,A1       GET START OF LIST
004004  7200                 MOVEQ    #0,D1
004006  1219                 MOVE.B   (A1)+,D1          GET LENGTH OF LIST

004008  5341                 SUBQ     #1,D1             N ENTRIES REQUIRES N-1 COMPARES

00400A  45E90002             LEA      2(A1),A2          GET ADDRESS TO SECOND ELEMENT
00400E  08820000             BCLR.B   #0,D2             CLEAR INTERCHANGE FLAG

004012  B549        NEXT     CMPM.W   (A1)+,(A2)+       IF (A1) <= (A2)
004014  6506                 BCS.S    NSWITCH           THEN TEST NEXT PAIR IF ANY

004016  3611                 MOVE.W   (A1),D3           ELSE INTERCHANGE THE
004018  3292                 MOVE.W   (A2),(A1)         ADJACENT ENTRIES
00401A  3483                 MOVE.W   D3,(A2)


00401C  51C9FFF4    NSWITCH  DBRA     D1,NEXT

004020  08020000             BTST.B   #0,D2             INTERCHANGE DURING THIS PASS ?
004024  66EC                 BNE      NEXT              IF YES, START NEW PASS

004026  4E75        DONE     RTS                        ELSE DONE

                             END      BUB_SORT
```

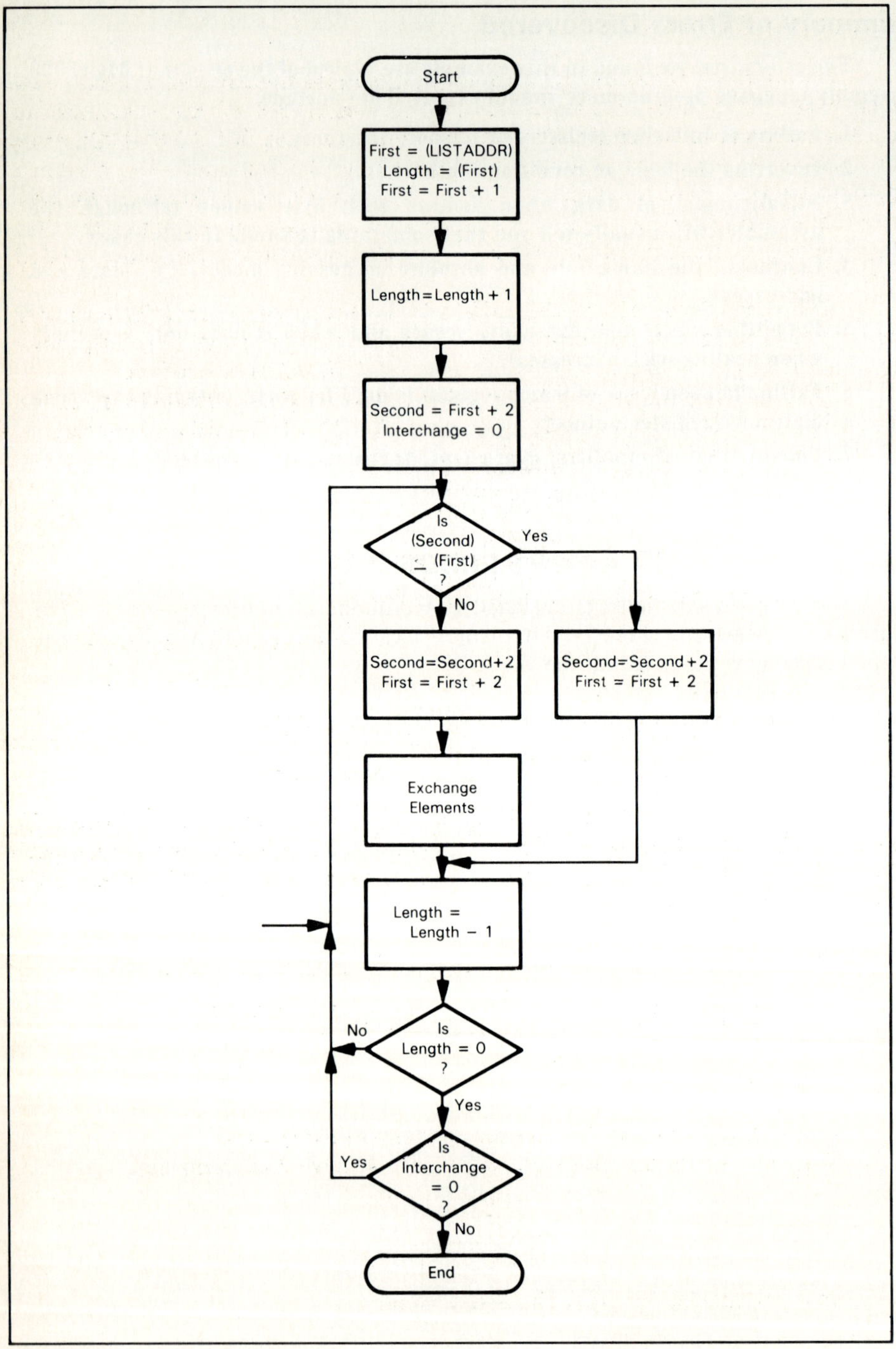

Figure 19-9. Flowchart of a Sort Program

Initial Hand Check

A hand check shows us that all of the blocks in the flowchart have been implemented and the registers used in the loop have been initialized. We must examine two conditional branches carefully. The branch in the inner loop BCS.S NSWITCH must be taken if the second entry is less than or equal to the first entry. The operation peformed is (A2)−(A1). If (A2)≠(A1), the Carry flag will be set because of the borrow. The equality condition (A2)=(A1) will not set the Carry flag but will set the Zero flag. The BCS instruction will not handle the equality case correctly; we must use BLS instead.

The second condition branch is BNE NEXT which is supposed to force another pass through the loop if an interchange occurred. We clear the interchange flag before the inner loop so a set flag means interchange and BNE will work fine here.

The next thing to check is the loop. Let us test the first iteration by hand. We assume that memory location LISTADDR contains 5000_{16}. The initialization section — the first six instructions — causes the following result:

```
A1 = 5001
A2 = 5003
D1 = count
D2 bit#0 = 0
```

The effect of the loop instructions is as follows:

```
NEXT      CMPM.W   (A1)+,(A2)+          (5001) - (5003) AND AUTOINCREMENT
          BLS.S    NSWITCH

          MOVE.W   (A1),D3              D3 := (5003)
          MOVE.W   (A2),(A1)            (5003) := (5005)
          MOVE.W   D3,(A2)              (5005) := (5003)

NSWITCH   DBRA     D1,NEXT              COUNT := COUNT - 1
```

There is something weird here. The contents of memory locations 5001 and 5003 were compared and then location 5005 somehow got involved in the interchange. Clearly, we forgot that the CMPM instruction autoincremented both A1 and A2. Let's try this code for the loop:

```
NEXT      CMPM.W   (A1)+,(A2)+          IF (A1) >= (A2)
          BLS.S    NSWITCH              THEN TEST NEXT PAIR IF ANY

          MOVE.W   -(A1),D3             ELSE INTERCHANGE THE
          MOVE.W   -(A2),(A1)+          ADJACENT ENTRIES
          MOVE.W   D3,(A2)+

NSWITCH   DBRA     D1,NEXT
```

A new check shows us that this code performs what we want.

Now let us check the last iteration. Suppose we have three elements:

```
(5000) = 03
(5001) = 2015
(5003) = 1B11
(5005) = 000A
```

This is what happens. After the first iteration:

```
D1 = 02
A1 = 5003
A2 = 5005
```

DBRA subtracts 1 from D1 and branches to NEXT.
After the second iteration:

```
D1 = 1
A1 = 5005
A2 = 5007
```

Now A2 points beyond the list and things should stop here. But when DBRA subtracts 1 from D1, the result becomes 0 and DBRA tests for −1. The branch will be taken and the loop executes one more time — one time too many. We must adjust D1 by subtracting 1 from it before we enter the loop.

The next checkpoint in our list is the equality cases. We checked what happened with two equal entries when we discussed the conditional branches, and that is the only equality case that exists in this program.

Checking Trivial Cases

What happens in the trivial cases? First, which are the trivial cases — zero entries in the list? Yes, but another trivial case is when there is only one entry in the list — it doesn't make much sense to try to sort a single element. Remember that trivial cases are not only zero entries, zero objects, and so on. What happens if we have one entry? The answer is that the program tries to sort 64K of memory (if there is read-only memory in this area, the program will run forever). A few instructions added to handle trivial cases will save you from a lot of trouble and they can usually be positioned outside of the loop so that they don't increase the execution time very much. The BLS.S DONE instruction is the only one required in our program to handle the trivial cases. The program now looks like this:

```
       00006000    DATA     EQU      $6000
       00004000    PROGRAM  EQU      $4000

       00006000             ORG      DATA

006000 00000004    LISTADDR DS.L     1                 ADDRESS OF START OF LIST

       00004000             ORG      PROGRAM

004000 22786000    BUB_SORT MOVEA.L  LISTADDR,A1       GET START OF LIST
004004 7200                 MOVEQ    #0,D1
004006 1219                 MOVE.B   (A1)+,D1          GET LENGTH OF LIST

004008 5341                 SUBQ     #1,D1             N ENTRIES REQUIRES N-1 COMPARES
00400A 631E                 BLS.S    DONE              IF 0 OR 1 ENTRY THEN DONE

00400C 45E90002             LEA      2(A1),A2          GET ADDRESS TO SECOND ELEMENT
004010 08820000             BCLR.B   #0,D2             CLEAR INTERCHANGE FLAG
004014 5341                 SUBQ.W   #1,D1             ADJUST FOR DBCC

004016 B549        NEXT     CMPM.W   (A1)+,(A2)+       IF (A1) <= (A2)
004018 6506                 BCS.S    NSWITCH           THEN TEST NEXT PAIR IF ANY

00401A 3621                 MOVE.W   -(A1),D3          ELSE INTERCHANGE THE
00401C 32E2                 MOVE.W   -(A2),(A1)+       ADJACENT ENTRIES
00401E 34C3                 MOVE.W   D3,(A2)+

004020 51C9FFF4    NSWITCH  DBRA     D1,NEXT

004024 08020000             BTST.B   #0,D2             INTERCHANGE DURING THIS PASS ?
004028 66EC                 BNE      NEXT              IF YES, START NEW PASS

00402A 4E75        DONE     RTS                        ELSE DONE

                            END      BUB_SORT
```

Run Test with Breakpoints

Now it is time to check the program on a computer or on a simulator. A simple set of test data is:

```
(6000) = 00005000     Address of array
(5000) = 02           Length of array
(5001) = 0100
(5003) = 0A00         Array to be stored
```

This set consists of two elements in the wrong order. The program should require two passes. The first pass should exchange the elements, producing:

```
(5001) = 0A00
(5003) = 0100

D2b#0 = 1             Interchange flag
```

The second pass should just find the elements already in the proper (descending) order and produce:

```
D2bit#0 = 0           Interchange flag
```

This program is too long for single-stepping, so we will use breakpoints instead. Each breakpoint will halt the computer and print contents of key registers. We will use four breakpoints and we position them as follows:

1. After SUBQ.W #1,D1 to check the initialization.
2. After CMPM.W (A1)+,(A2)+ to check the comparison and the branch.
3. After MOVE.W D3,(A2)+ to check the interchange.
4. After BTST.B #0,D2 to check the completion of a pass through the list.

Assuming that our trace facility allows us to display just the contents of those registers we select, we select registers PC, D1, D2, A1, A2, and the condition codes of the status register.

After the first breakpoint these are our results:

```
PC = 004016
CCR = 04
D1 = 0000
D2 bit#0 = 0
```

These are all correct, so the program is performing the initialization properly in this case.

When we start up our program again, we get a trap. (At this point the less intrepid travelers of the marvelous world of computer programming simply throw up their hands in dismay and consternation and cry, ''Damn this noise!'') The trap handler tells us that it is an address error and the instruction code that caused it was B549 (the program counter is not reliable in this case). This instruction code is the CMPM.W (A1)+,A2+ instruction. The size is word. A1 contains 5001, and A3 contains 5003 — both odd values! The list length is a byte value and this causes A1 and A3 to get odd values. This is a serious problem and the solution is far from trivial.

One solution is to rewrite the program so that it reads byte by byte instead but that is a lot of unnecessary work. A second alternative is to realign the entire list so that the words are on even boundaries. A third and simpler (for us) alternative is to decide that the first entry in the list (the length) should be a word. This alternative means that we only have to change the suffix after the MOVE instruction that obtains the length. But be careful. This is a change in the "specifications" and it may not fit with other parts of your system. However, in this case we assume that it is possible to make this change and the third instruction of the program is changed to:

```
MOVE. W (A1)+,D1
```

Note that this error would not have been discovered if the list had started in memory location 4FFF. Why?

Notice also that our program does not have any comments at the beginning to tell users how to specify the location and length of the list.

We must change the list to look like this before we can start our second trial:

```
(5000) = 0002
(5002) = 0100
(5004) = 0A00
```

This time the initialization gives us the same results, and after the second breakpoint these are the results:

```
PC = 004018
CCR = 00
D1 = 0000
D2 bit#0 = 0
A1 = 005004
A2 = 005006
```

These are the correct results, and we proceed to the third breakpoint:

```
PC = 004020
CCR = 00
D1 = 00
D2 bit#0 = 0
A1 = 005004
A2 = 005006
```

A check of memory locations shows:

```
(5002) = 0A00
(5004) = 0100
```

Exactly what we expected. We proceed to the fourth breakpoint:

```
PC = 004028
CCR = 04
D1 = FFFF
D2 bit#0 = 0
A1 = 005004
A2 = 005006
```

Something is wrong. The bit that should indicate that an interchange occurred is still 0. A quick look in the loop-de-loop shows that no instruction ever changes this bit. The solution is to insert BSET #0,D2 after MOVE.W D3,(A2)+.

At this point in the debugging procedure, the easiest thing to do is simply to set the interchange bit ourselves and proceed with the second pass. The next breakpoint we reach is the one at address 4016 following the SUBQ.W #1,D1 instruction:

```
PC = 004016
SR = 00
D1 = FFFF
D2 bit#0 = 1
A1 = 005004
A2 = 005006
```

There is still something wrong: the registers are not reinitialized. For this pass, we must be sure that we branch all the way to the start of the program to reinitialize.

We change BNE NEXT to BNE BUB SORT and this time everything works correctly.

Final Program:

```
         00006000        DATA      EQU      $6000
         00004000        PROGRAM   EQU      $4000

         00006000                  ORG      DATA

006000 ·00000004         LISTADDR  DS.L     1                      ADDRESS OF START OF LIST

         00004000                  ORG      PROGRAM

004000 22786000        BUB_SORT MOVEA.L LISTADDR,A1     GET START OF LIST
004004 7200                     MOVEQ   #0,D1
004006 3219                     MOVE.W  (A1)+,D1        GET LENGTH OF LIST

004008 5341                     SUBQ    #1,D1           N ENTRIES REQUIRES N-1 COMPARES
00400A 6322                     BLS.S   DONE            IF <= 0  THEN DONE

00400C 45E90002                 LEA     2(A1),A2        GET ADDRESS TO SECOND ELEMENT
004010 08820000                 BCLR.B  #0,D2           CLEAR INTERCHANGE FLAG
004014 5341                     SUBQ.W  #1,D1           ADJUST COUNTER FOR DBCC

004016 B549            NEXT     CMPM.W  (A1)+,(A2)+     IF (A1) <= (A2)
004018 630A                     BLS.S   NSWITCH         THEN TEST NEXT PAIR IF ANY

00401A 3621                     MOVE.W  -(A1),D3        ELSE INTERCHANGE THE
00401C 32E2                     MOVE.W  -(A2),(A1)+     ADJACENT ENTRIES
00401E 34C3                     MOVE.W  D3,(A2)+

004020 08C20000                 BSET.B  #0,D2           SET INTERCHANGE FLAG

004024 51C9FFF0        NSWITCH  DBRA    D1,NEXT

004028 08020000                 BTST.B  #0,D2           INTERCHANGE DURING THIS PASS ?
00402C 66D2                     BNE     BUB_SORT        IF YES, START NEW PASS

00402E 4E75            DONE     RTS                     ELSE DONE

                                END     BUB_SORT
```

This program still needs some comments at the start for documentation.

Other Test Cases

Clearly, we cannot test all possible cases for this program. Some other simple test cases we could use for debugging are:

1. No elements in list

(6000) = 00005000
(5000) = 0000

2. One element in list:

(6000) = 00005000
(5000) = 0001

3. A "random case" with two equal elements:

```
(6000) = 00008200
(8200) = 0004          Number of elements in list
(8202) = 8345
(8204) = 0001          Array to be stored
(8206) = 0001
(8208) = 4657
```

Summary of Errors Discovered

With this program, we have become acquainted with some other errors which you certainly will encounter in your career as an MC68000 programmer. They included:

1. **Specifying the wrong condition in conditional branches** (again, but this is a very common error).
2. **Forgetting the effects of autoincrements/autodecrements or forgetting the values of pointers.**
3. **Forgetting that DBcc tests for −1 or incorrectly calculating the length of an array** (length = end-start + 1).
4. **Failure to handle trivial cases and equality cases or perhaps even missing some of the trivial cases.**
5. **Trying to address words and long words at odd addresses.** This is very easy to do with poorly defined data structures that require a mixture of byte and word instructions.
6. **Forgetting to set and/or reset flags.**
7. **Forgetting to reinitialize the inner loops in nested structures.**

REFERENCES

1. For more information about logic analyzers, see:

   Brock, G. "Logic-State Analyzers Seek Out Microprocessor-System Faults," *EDN,* January 5, 1980, pp. 137-40.

   Lorentzen, R. "Logic Analyzers Finish What Development Systems Start," *Electronic Design,* March 29, 1980, pp. 81-85.

   Marshall, J. "Digital Analysis Instruments," *EDN,* January 20, 1980, pp. 141-43.

   Ogdin, C.A. "Setting up a Microcomputer Design Laboratory," *Mini-Micro Systems,* May 1979, pp. 87-94.

   Spector, I.H., and Muething, R. "Logic Analyzer Deploys Its Full Strength," *Electronic Design,* March 29, 1980, pp. 177-214.

2. Weller, W.J. *Assembly Level Programming for Small Computers.* Lexington, Mass.: Lexington Books, 1975, Chapter 23.
3. Baldridge, R.L. "Interrupts Add Power, Complexity to Microcomputer System Design," *EDN,* August 5, 1977, pp. 67-73.

20

Testing

Program testing[1] is closely related to program debugging. We must test the program on the data that we used to debug it; for example,

- **Trivial cases** such as no data or a single statement
- **Special cases** that the program singles out for some reason
- **Simple cases** that exercise particular parts of the program

For the decimal to seven-segment conversion program in Chapter 19, these cases cover all possible situations. The test data consists of:

- The numbers 0 through 9
- The boundary case 10
- The random case $6B_{16}$

The program does not distinguish any other cases. **Here debugging and testing are virtually the same.**

In the sorting program, the problem is more difficult. The number of elements could range from 0 to 255, and each of the elements could lie anywhere in that range. The number of possible cases is therefore enormous. Furthermore, the program is moderately complex. How do we select test data that will give us a degree of confidence in that program? **Here testing requires some design decisions.** The testing problem is particularly difficult if the program depends on sequences of real-time data. How do we select the data, generate it, and present it to the microcomputer in a realistic manner?

TESTING AIDS

Most of the tools mentioned earlier for debugging are helpful in testing also. Logic or microprocessor analyzers can help check the hardware; simulators[2] can help check the software. Other tools can also be of assistance:

1. **I/O simulations** that can simulate many devices from a single input and a single output device.
2. **In-circuit emulators** that allow you to attach the prototype to a development system or control panel and test it.[3]
3. **ROM simulators** that can be changed like RAM but otherwise behave like the ROM or PROM that will be used in the final system.
4. **Real-time operating systems** that can provide inputs or interrupts at specific times (or perhaps randomly) and mark the occurrence of outputs. Real-time breakpoints and traces may also be included.
5. **Emulations** (often on microprogrammable computers) that may provide real-time execution speed and programmable I/O.[4]
6. **Interfaces** that allow another computer to control the I/O system and test the microcomputer program.
7. **Testing programs** that check each branch in a program for logical errors.
8. **Test generation programs** that can generate random data or other distributions.

Formal testing theorems exist, but are only practical for verifying short programs. You must be careful that the test equipment does not invalidate the test by modifying the environment. Often test equipment may buffer, latch, or condition input and output signals. The actual system may not do this and may therefore behave differently.

Furthermore, extra software in the test environment may use some of the memory space or part of the interrupt system. It may also provide error recovery and other features that will not exist in the final system. A software test bed must be just as realistic as a hardware test bed since software failure can be just as critical as hardware failure.

Emulations and simulations are, of course, never precise. They are usually adequate for checking logic, but can seldom help test interfaces or timing. On the other hand, real-time test equipment does not provide much of an overview of the program logic and may affect the interfacing and timing.

SELECTING TEST DATA[5]

Few real programs can be checked for all cases. The designer must choose a sample set that is in some sense representative.

Structured Testing

Testing should, of course, be part of the total development procedure. **Top-down design and structured programming provide for testing as part of the design. This is**

called structured testing. Each module within a structured program should be checked separately. **Testing, as well as design, should be modular, structured, and top-down.**

Special Cases

But that leaves the question of selecting test data for a module. The designer must first list all special cases that a program recognizes. These may include:

- Trivial cases
- Equality cases
- Special situations

The test data should include all of these.

Forming Classes of Data

You must next identify each class of data that statements within the program may distinguish. These may include:

- Positive or negative numbers
- Numbers above or below a particular threshold
- Data that does or does not include a particular sequence or character
- Data that is or is not present at a particular time

Be careful; **each two-way decision doubles the number of classes** since you must test both paths. Thus three conditional branches will result in $2 \times 2 \times 2 = 8$ classes if the computer always executes each branch. **Limiting the size of test sets is another important reason to keep modules short and general.**

Selecting Data from Classes

You must now separate the classes according to whether the program produces a different result for each entry in the class (as in a table) or produces the same result for each entry (such as a warning that a parameter is above a threshold). In the discrete case, one may include each element if the total number is small or sample if the number is large. The sample should include all boundary cases and at least one case selected randomly. Random number tables are available in books, and random number generators are part of most computer facilities.[6]

You must be careful of distinctions that may not be obvious. For example, the MC68000 microprocessor will regard an 8-bit unsigned number greater than 127 as negative; you must consider this when using the branch instructions that depend on the Negative (Sign) flag.

EXAMPLES

20-1. TESTING A SORT PROGRAM

The special cases here are obvious:

- **No elements in the array**
- **One element,** magnitude may be selected randomly

The other special case to be considered is one in which elements are equal.

There may be some problem here with signs and data length. Note that the array itself must contain fewer than 256 elements.

We could check to see if the sign of the number of elements has any effect by choosing half the test cases with elements between 128 and 255 and half with elements between 2 and 127. We should choose the magnitudes of the elements randomly to avoid unconscious bias which might favor small numbers, decimal (rather than hexadecimal) digits, or regular patterns.

20-2. TESTING AN ARITHMETIC PROGRAM

Here we will presume that a prior validity check has ensured that the number has the right length and consists of valid digits. Since the program makes no other distinctions, test data should be selected randomly. Here a random number table or random number generator will prove ideal; the range of the random numbers is 0 to 255 for each byte in each number.

RULES FOR TESTING

Sensible design simplifies testing. The following rules can help:

1. **Eliminate trivial cases early** without introducing unnecessary distinctions.
2. **Avoid special cases,** since they increase debugging and testing time.
3. **Perform validity or error checks on the data before it is processed.**
4. **Avoid inadvertent distinctions,** particularly in handling signed numbers or in using instructions that are intended to handle signed numbers.
5. **Check boundary cases by hand.** Be sure to define what should happen in these es.
6. **Emphasize generality.** Each distinction and separate routine leads to more testing.
7. **Use top-down design and modular programming to modularize testing.**

CONCLUSIONS

Debugging and testing are the stepchildren of the software development process. Most projects leave far too little time for them and most textbooks neglect them. But designers and managers often find that these stages are the most expensive and time-consuming. Progress may be difficult to measure or produce. Debugging and testing microprocessor software is particularly difficult because the powerful hardware and software tools that can be used on larger computers are seldom available for microcomputers.

The designer should plan debugging and testing carefully. We recommend the following guidelines:

1. **Try to write programs that are easy to debug and test.** Modular programming, structured programming, and top-down design are useful techniques.
2. **Prepare a debugging and testing plan as part of the problem definition.** Decide early what data you must generate and what equipment you will need.
3. **Debug and test each module using top-down design.**
4. **Debug each module's logic systematically.** Use checklists, breakpoints, and the single-step mode. If the program logic is complex, consider using the software simulator.
5. **Check each module's timing systematically if this timing is a problem.** An oscilloscope can solve many problems if you plan the test properly. If the timing is complex, consider using a logic or microprocessor analyzer.
6. **Be sure that the test data is representative.** Watch for any classes of data that the program may distinguish. Include all special and trivial cases.
7. **If the program handles each element differently or the number of cases is large, select the test data randomly.**
8. **Document all tests.** If errors are found later, you will not have to repeat tests you have already run.

REFERENCES

1. G. J. Myers. *The Art of Software Testing,* Wiley, New York, 1979.

   R. C. Tausworthe. *Standardized Development of Computer Software,* Prentice-Hall, Englewood Cliffs, N.J., Vol. 1, 1977, Chapter 9; Vol. 2, 1979, Chapters 14 and 15.

   E. Yourdon. *Techniques of Program Structure and Design,* Prentice-Hall, Englewood Cliffs, N.J., 1975, Chapter 7.

2. F. J. Langley. "Simulating Modular Microcomputers," *Simulation,* May 1979, pp. 141-54.

   L. A. Leventhal. "Design Tools for Multiprocessor Systems," *Digital Design,* October 1979, pp. 24-26.

   F. I. Parke et al. "An Introduction to the N.mPc Design Environment," *Proceedings of the 1979 Design Automation Conference,* San Diego, Ca., pp. 513-19.

3. R. Francis and R. Teitzel. "Realtime Analyzer Aids Hardware/Software Integration," *Computer Design,* January 1980, pp. 140-50.
4. H. R. Burris. "Time-Scaled Emulations of the 8080 Microprocessor," *Proceedings of the 1977 National Computer Conference,* pp. 937-46.
5. R. A. DeMillo et al. "Hints on Test Data Selection: Help for the Practicing Programmer," *Computer,* April, 1978, pp. 34-41.

   W. F. Dalton. "Design Microcomputer Software," *Electronics,* January 19, 1978, pp. 97-101.
6. R. D. Grappel and J. Hemenway. "EDN Software Tutorial: Pseudorandom Generators," *EDN,* May 20, 1980, pp. 119-23.

   T. G. Lewis. *Distribution Sampling for Computer Simulation,* Lexington Books, Lexington, Mass., 1975.

   R. A. Mueller et al. "A Random Number Generator for Microprocessors," *Simulation,* April 1977, pp. 123-27.

21
Maintenance and Redesign

Program maintenance always involves elements of redesign. A program may not work correctly in the field because of a flaw which was not discovered during the debugging and testing phases of development. Sometimes, however, a program works correctly but inefficiently — taking too long to respond, for example, or requiring an awkward sequence of actions by the operator. A manufacturer may decide to adapt a control program to run in a different hardware configuration. Inevitably, someone will find a use for a microcomputer that never occurred to the system designer; a user's needs often change in unanticipated ways. Thus **it may become necessary to change a program or system even if it works correctly.**

Sometimes the designer may have to squeeze the last microsecond of speed or the last byte of extra memory out of a program. As larger single-chip memories have become available, the memory problem has become less serious. The time problem, of course, is serious only if the application is time-critical. In many applications the microprocessor spends most of its time waiting for external devices and program speed is not a major factor.

COST OF REDESIGN

Squeezing the last bit of performance out of a program is seldom as important as some writers would have you believe. In the first place, the practice **is expensive for the following reasons:**

1. It requires extra programmer time, which is often the single largest cost in software development.
2. It sacrifices structure and simplicity with a resulting increase in debugging and testing time.
3. The programs require extra documentation.
4. The resulting programs will be difficult to extend, maintain, or re-use.

In the second place, the lower per-unit cost and higher performance may not really be important. Will the lower cost and higher performance really sell more units? Or would you do better with more user-oriented features? **The only applications that would seem to justify the extra effort and time are very high-volume, low-cost and low-performance applications, where the cost of an extra memory chip will far outweigh the cost of the extra software development.** For other applications, you will find that you are playing an expensive game for no reason.

MAJOR OR MINOR REORGANIZATION

However, if you must redesign a program, the following hints will help. First, determine how much more performance or how much less memory usage is necessary. If the required improvement is 25% or less, you may be able to achieve it by reorganizing the program. If it is more than 25% you have made a basic design error; you will need to consider drastic changes in hardware or software. We will deal first with reorganization and later with drastic changes. Reducing memory usage is particularly important if it results in a program that fits in the ROM and RAM provided by a simple one or two-chip microcomputer. The use of such stand-alone microcomputers can reduce hardware costs substantially in limited applications.

SAVING MEMORY

The following procedures will reduce memory usage for assembly language programs:

1. **Replace repetitious in-line code with subroutines.** Be sure, however, that the JSR (Jump to Subroutine) and RTS (Return from Subroutine) instructions do not offset most of the gain. Note that this replacement usually results in slower programs because of the time spent in transferring control back and forth.
2. **Load data into registers whenever possible.** Register pointers use less memory than direct and indexed addresses, unless the setup offsets the gain.
3. **Use the stack or the auto-decrement modes of addressing whenever possible.** The stack pointer or the addresses are automatically updated after each use so that no explicit updating instructions are necessary.
4. **Eliminate jump instructions.** Try to reorganize the program instead.
5. **Use leftover results from previous selections of the program.**
6. **Use the shift instructions to operate on bit positions at either end of a byte, word, or long word.**
7. **Watch for special short forms of instructions such as ADDQ, MOVEQ, and so on.**
8. **Use relative jumps rather than jumps with direct addressing.**
9. **When you must use absolute direct addressing use the short version rather than the long version.**

10. **Use algorithms rather than tables to calculate arithmetic or logical expressions and to perform code conversions.** Note that this replacement may result in slower programs.
11. **Reduce the size of mathematical table by interpolating between entrys.** Here again, we are saving memory at the cost of execution time.
12. **Take advantage of the LEA instruction** to perform arithmetic as well as to calcuate indirect, indexed, and relative addresses for repeated use later.
13. **Use indexed addressing rather than absolute addressing to handle** PIAs and other situations involving **several addresses that are close together.**
14. **Try to replace sequences of branch instructions with single branches.** You may be able to eliminate sequences by rearranging computations or by using the conditional branches that depend on combinations of flags. Examine the precise effects of branches like BGE, BGT, BHI, BLE, BLS, and BLT; they may be useful in situations that differ greatly from those suggested by their mnemonics.
15. **Use instructions such as BTST and CMP that affect the flags without changing any registers or memory locations.** You may be able to retain data for later use.
16. **Inspect complex tables for redundant information.** Large tables are often the most rewarding place to start looking for wasted memory space.
17. **Two separate parts of a program may be able to share a data area,** such as an I/O buffer, especially when neither depends on the contents of the other.

SAVING EXECUTION TIME

Although some of the methods that reduce memory usage also save time, you can generally save an appreciable amount of time only by concentrating on frequently executed loops. Even completely eliminating an instruction that is executed only once can save at most a few microseconds. But a savings in a loop that is executed frequently will be multiplied many times over.

So, **if you must reduce execution time, proceed as follows:**

1. **Determine how frequently each program loop is executed.** You can do this by hand or by using the software simulator or other testing methods.
2. **Examine the loops in the order determined by their frequency of execution,** starting with the most frequent. Continue through the list until you achieve the required reduction.
3. **First, see if there are any operations that can be moved outside the loop,** such as repetitive calculations, data that can be stored in a register or in the stack, data or addresses that can be stored on the direct page, special cases or errors that can be handled elsewhere, etc. Note that this may require extra initialization and memory but will save time.
4. **Try to eliminate Jump statements.** These are very time-consuming. Sometimes changing the initial conditions helps, particularly if the changes allow you to perform tests at the end of a loop rather than at the beginning.

5. **Replace subroutines with in-line code.** This will save at least a BSR and a RTS instruction.
6. **Use the stack for temporary data storage** if you can take advantage of the automatic ordering it provides.
7. **Use any of the hints mentioned in saving memory that also decrease execution time.**
8. **Do not even look at instructions that are executed only once.** Any changes that you make in such instructions only invite errors for no appreciable gain.
9. **Avoid indexed and indirect addressing whenever possible** because they take extra time.
10. **Use tables rather than algorithms;** make the tables handle as much of the tasks as possible even if many entries must be repeated.

MAJOR REORGANIZATION

If you need more than a 25% increase in speed or decrease in memory usage do not try reorganizing the code. Your chances of getting that much of an improvement are small unless you call in an outside expert. **You are generally better off making a major change.**

BETTER ALGORITHMS

The most obvious change is a better algorithm. Particularly if you are doing sorts, searches, or mathematical calculations, you may be able to find a faster or shorter method in the literature. Libraries of algorithms are available in some journals and from professional groups. See the references at the end of this chapter for some important sources.

OTHER MAJOR CHANGES

Hardware can replace software. Counters, shift registers, arithmetic units, hardware multipliers, and other fast add-ons can save both time and memory. Calculators, UARTs, keyboards, encoders, and other slower add-ons may save memory even though they operate slowly. Compatible parallel and serial interfaces, and other devices specially designed for use with the 6809 or 6502 may save time by taking some of the burden off the CPU.

Other changes may help as well:

1. **A CPU with a longer word will be faster** if the data is long enough. Such a CPU will use less total memory. 16-bit processors, for example, use memory more efficiently than 8-bit processors, since more of their instructions are one word long.
2. **Versions of the CPU may exist that operate at higher clock rates.** But remember that you will need faster memory and I/O ports, and you will have to adjust any delay loops.

3. **Two CPUs may be able to do the job in parallel** or separately if you can divide the job and solve the communications problem.
4. **A specially microprogrammed processor may be able to execute the same program much faster.** The cost, however, will be much higher even if you use an off-the-shelf emulation.
5. **You can make tradeoffs between time and memory.** Lookup tables and function ROMs will be faster than algorithms, but will occupy more memory.

Deciding on a Major Change

This kind of problem, in which a large improvement is necessary, usually results from lack of adequate planning in the definition and design stages. In the problem definition stage you should determine which processor and methods will handle the problem. If you misjudge, the cost later will be high. A cheap solution may result in an unwarranted expenditure of expensive development time. Do not try to just get by; the best solution is usually to do the proper design and chalk a failure up to experience. **If you have followed such methods as flowcharting, modular programming, structured programming, top-down design, and proper documentation, you can salvage a lot of your effort even if you have to make a major change.**

REFERENCES

Carnahan, B., et al. *Applied Numerical Methods,* Wiley, New York, 1969.

Chen, T. C. "Automatic Computation of Exponentials, Logarithms, Ratios, and Square Roots," *IBM Journal of Research and Development,* Volume 18, pp. 380-388, July 1972.

Collected Algorithms from ACM, ACM Inc., P.O. Box 12105, Church Street Station, New York, 10249.

Despain, A. M. "Fourier Transform Computers Using CORDIC Iterations," *IEEE Transactions on Computers,* October 1974, pp. 993-1001.

Edgar, A. D. and S. C. Lee. "FOCUS Microcomputer Number System," *Communications of the ACM,* March 1979, pp. 166-177.

Hwang, K. *Computer Arithmetic,* Wiley, New York, 1978.

Knuth, D. E. *The Art of Computer Programming, Volume 1: Fundamental Algorithms; The Art of Computer Programming, Volume 2: Seminumerical Algorithms; The Art of Computer Programming, Volume 3: Sorting and Searching,* Addison-Wesley, Reading, Mass. 1967-1969.

Luke, Y. L. *Algorithms for the Computation of Mathematical Functions,* Academic Press, New York, 1977.

Schmid, H. *Decimal Computation,* Wiley-Interscience, New York, 1974.

New methods for performing arithmetic operations on computers are often discussed in the triennial Symposium on Computer Arithmetic. The Proceedings (starting with 1969) are available from the IEEE Computer Society, 10662 Los Vaqueros Circle, Los Alamitos, Calif. 90720.

V
MC68000 Instruction Set

Chapter 22 and the appendices that follow it comprise a total reference for the MC68000 instruction set. Chapter 22 describes each instruction in some detail; the appendices summarize that information.

22 Descriptions of Individual MC68000 Instructions

In this chapter we present instructions in alphabetical order and describe them in great detail. The information contained here is summarized in Appendices A, B, and C. Each instruction description includes, or refers to, a diagram of the execution of the instruction. Since the MC68000 has so many addressing modes, we have not attempted to describe all the modes for each instruction. As part of each instruction's description, however, we do indicate which addressing modes can be used with the instruction.

ABCD — Add Decimal with Extend Register to Register

This instruction adds the contents of the source data register and the value of the extend (X) flag to the contents of the destination data register. The result is stored in the destination data register. The addition is performed using binary-coded decimal (BCD) arithmetic. Only the least significant eight bits of the data registers are involved.

The object code for this instruction is:

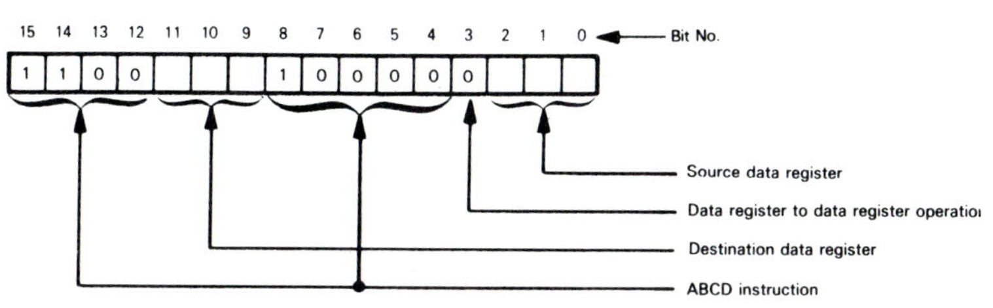

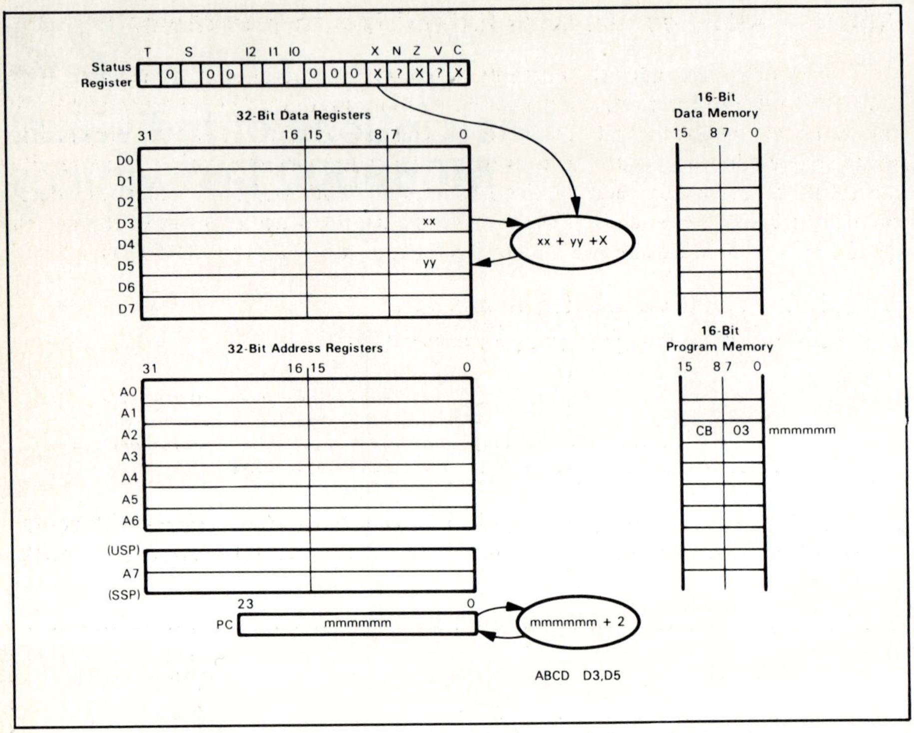

Figure 22-1. Execution of the ABCD Instruction with Operands in Data Registers

Figure 22-1 illustrates execution of the ABCD instruction with register D3 as the source register and D5 as the destination register. Suppose that $xx=43_{10}$, extend=1, and $yy=57_{10}$. After the processor executes the instruction ADCD D3,D5 the contents of D5 will be 01_{10}.

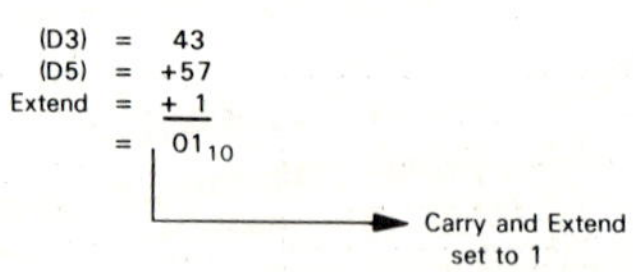

Bits 8 through 31 of the data registers are unaffected by this instruction.

The Carry (C) and Extend (X) flags are set if a decimal carry is generated as a result of the operation and are cleared otherwise. The Zero (Z) flag is cleared if the result is nonzero and is unchanged if the result is zero. The N and V flags are undefined.

Note that the Zero flag is not changed if the result is zero. To perform multiple-precision arithmetic, first set the Zero flag (using MOVE to CCR), then perform the operation. If any part of the result is nonzero, the Zero flag will be cleared; otherwise, the result is zero and the Zero flag remains set.

ABCD — Add Decimal with Extend Memory to Memory

This instruction adds the contents of one memory location and the value of the Extend (X) flag to the contents of another memory location. The memory address for the source operand is taken from the source address register, and the memory address for the destination operand is taken from the destination address register. The result is stored at the destination address. The contents of both address registers are decremented before the operation. The addition is performed using binary-coded decimal (BCD) arithmetic. The object code for this form of the ABCD instruction is:

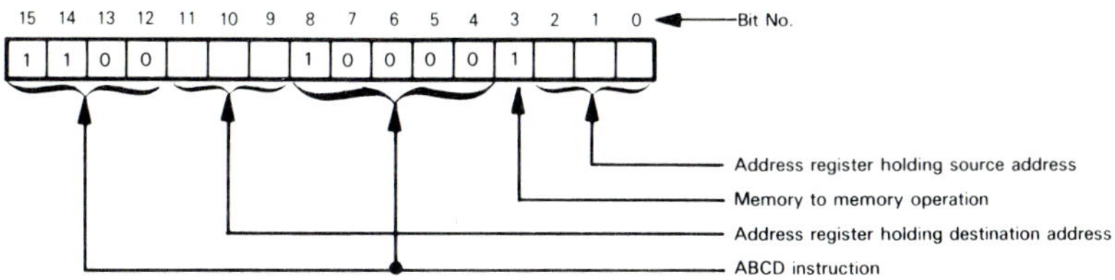

Figure 22-2 illustrates execution of the ABCD instruction where register A1 holds the address of the source operand in memory and register A4 holds the address of the

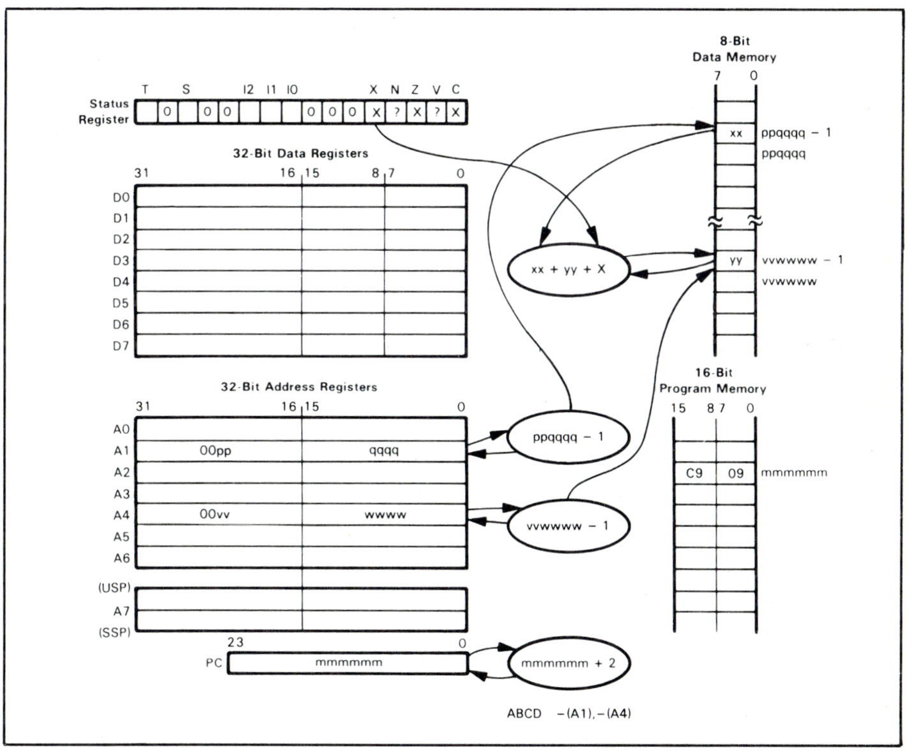

Figure 22-2. Execution of the ABCD Instruction with Memory Operands

destination operand in memory. As you can see, the contents of both address registers are decremented before the operands are accessed for the add operation. This is done to facilitate multibyte BCD addition, since a string of BCD digits representing a decimal number would normally be stored with the least significant digit right-justified at the higher memory address. Refer to Chapter 8 for a discussion of multibyte BCD addition.

The status flags are affected in the same way by the ABCD register instruction.

ADD — Add Binary

This instruction adds the contents of the source operand to the destination operand and stores the result in the destination.

There are two general forms for this instruction. In the first form, a data register provides one of the operands and is the destination for the ADD. In this form, all addressing modes are allowed:

Addressing Modes Allowed	Operand		Source ea Field	
	Source	Destination	Mode	Register No.
Data register direct	X	X	000	rrr
Address register direct	X*		001	rrr
Address register indirect	X		010	rrr
Postincrement register indirect	X		011	rrr
Predecrement register indirect	X		100	rrr
Register indirect with displacement	X		101	rrr
Register indirect with index	X		110	rrr
Absolute short	X		111	000
Absolute long	X		111	001
Program counter relative with displacement	X		111	010
Program counter relative with index	X		111	011
Immediate	X		111	100

*Not allowed if operation size is byte.

The only limitation on addressing modes for this form is that address register direct addressing cannot provide the source if the operand size specification is byte, since the address registers cannot handle data on a byte basis.

In the other general form of the ADD instruction, a data register must provide the source operand; the second operand and destination can be specified using any of the addressing modes shown:

Addressing Modes Allowed	Operand		Source ea Field	
	Source	Destination	Mode	Register No.
Data register direct	X	X	000	rrr
Address register direct			001	rrr
Address register indirect		X	010	rrr
Postincrement register indirect		X	011	rrr
Predecrement register indirect		X	100	rrr
Register indirect with displacement		X	101	rrr
Register indirect with index		X	110	rrr
Absolute short		X	111	000
Absolute long		X	111	001
Program counter relative with displacement				
Program counter relative with index				
Immediate				

The address mode limitations for this form are logical, since both programs and immediate data will frequently be stored in read-only memory and thus these locations cannot serve as destinations.

The ADD instruction's object code is:

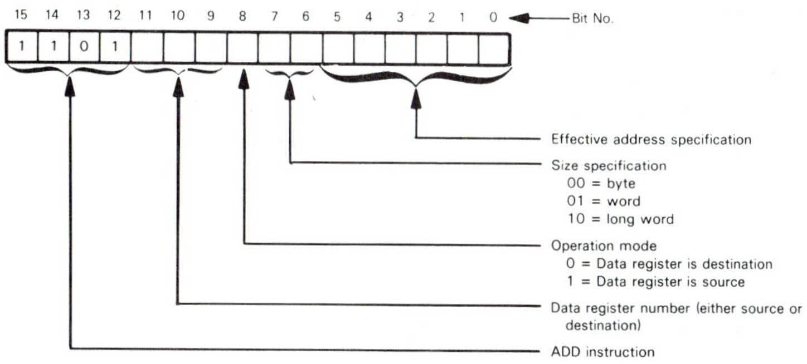

Figure 22-3 illustrates the execution of an ADD instruction using the absolute long addressing mode with D3 serving as the destination register.

The Carry (C) and Extend (X) flags are set if a carry is generated as a result of the operation and cleared otherwise. The Zero (Z) flag is set if the result is zero and cleared otherwise. The Negative (N) flag is set if the result is negative and cleared otherwise. The Overflow (V) flag is set if an overflow is generated and cleared otherwise. For a discussion of the interaction of these flags in unsigned and two's complement arithmetic, see Chapter 8.

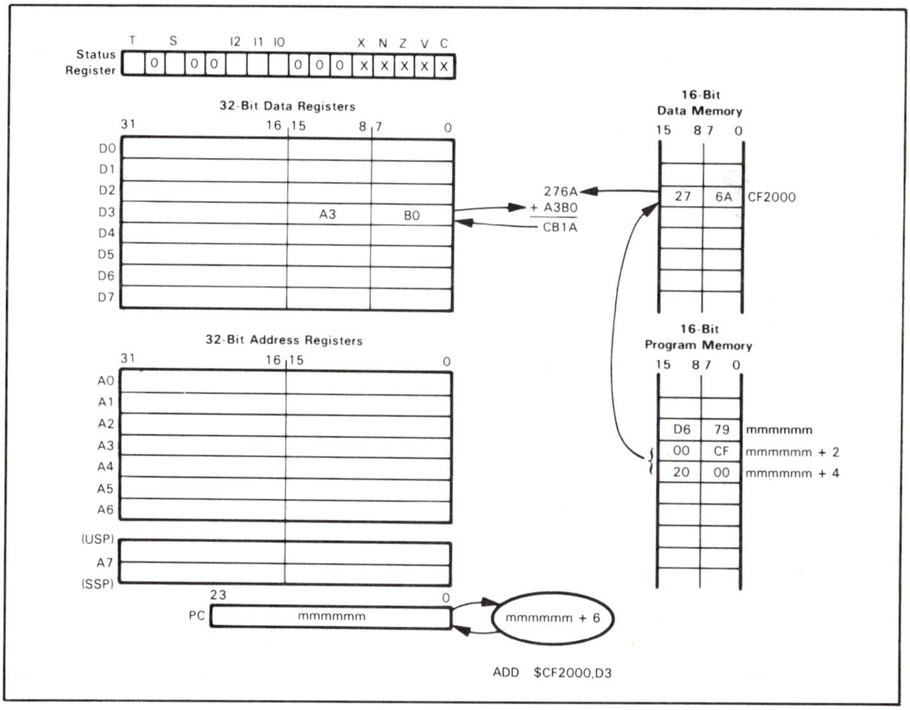

Figure 22-3. Execution of the ADD Instruction Using Absolute Long Addressing

Using the operands illustrated in Figure 22-3, this is what happens when the ADD $CF2000,D3 instruction is executed:

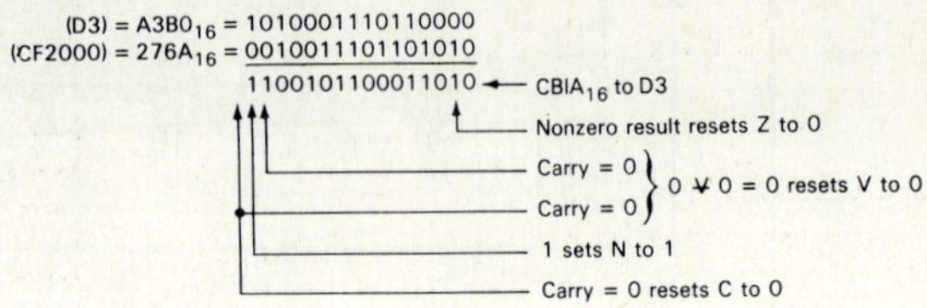

ADDA — Add Address

This instruction is a special case of the ADD instruction and adds a source operand to a specified address register. All addressing modes are permitted for the source operand:

Addressing Modes Allowed	Operand		Source ea Field	
	Source	Destination	Mode	Register No.
Data register direct	X		000	rrr
Address register direct	X	X	001	rrr
Address register indirect	X		010	rrr
Postincrement register indirect	X		011	rrr
Predecrement register indirect	X		100	rrr
Register indirect with displacement	X		101	rrr
Register indirect with index	X		110	rrr
Absolute short	X		111	000
Absolute long	X		111	001
Program counter relative with displacement	X		111	010
Program counter relative with index	X		111	011
Immediate	X		111	100

The ADDA instruction's object code is:

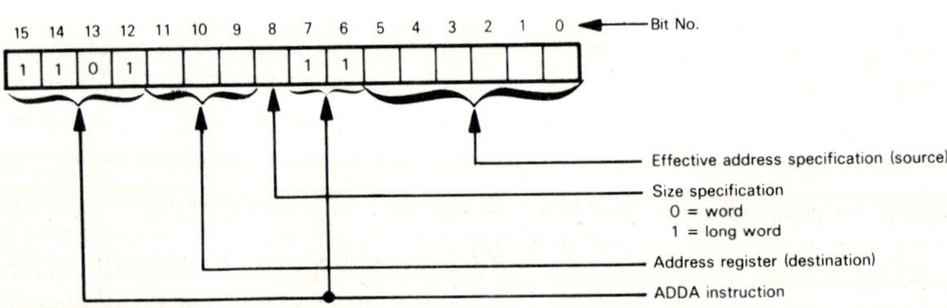

If you compare this object code to that of the ADD instruction, you will see that they are identical except for the size field: the 2-bit pattern that was not used with the ADD instruction is used to indicate an ADDA instruction.

Figure 22-4 illustrates the execution of the ADDA instruction with register D3 providing the 32-bit source operand and register A3 serving as the destination.

If you specify a 16-bit word source operand instead of a long word, the source operand is sign-extended to a long operand and the ADD operation is performed on the specified address register using all 32 bits.

A significant difference between this ADD Address operation and the standard ADD instruction is that none of the status flags is affected by the ADDA instruction.

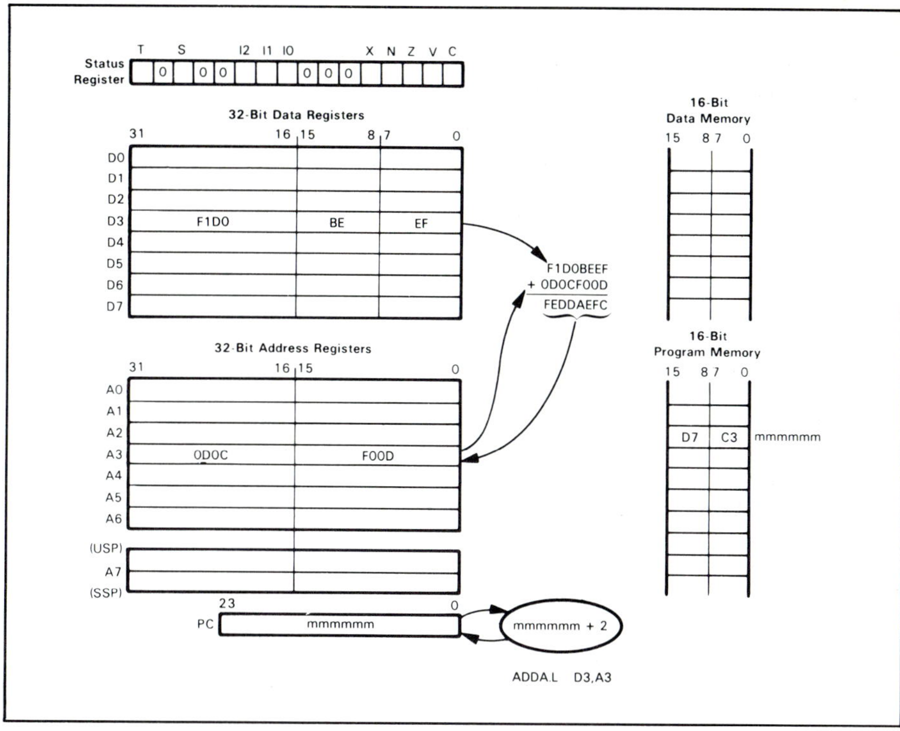

Figure 22-4. Execution of the ADDA Instruction Using Register Direct Addressing

ADDI — Add Immediate

This instruction is used to add the immediate data present in the succeeding program memory byte(s) to a specified destination operand. The result is stored in the destination. The addressing modes that can be used are:

Addressing Modes Allowed	Operand		Source ea Field	
	Source	Destination	Mode	Register No.
Data register direct		X	000	rrr
Address register direct			001	rrr
Address register indirect		X	010	rrr
Postincrement register indirect		X	011	rrr
Predecrement register indirect		X	100	rrr
Register indirect with displacement		X	101	rrr
Register indirect with index		X	110	rrr
Absolute short		X	111	000
Absolute long		X	111	001
Program counter relative with displacement				
Program counter relative with index				
Immediate	X			

The object code for this instruction is:

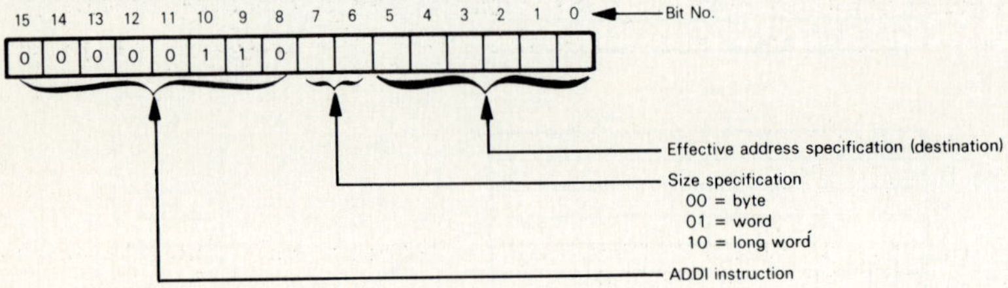

The size of the ADDI operation can be specified as byte, word, or long word. The immediate data follows the instruction word in memory and must match the specified operation size. Thus, either one or two words of immediate data must follow the instruction operation code in program memory. If the instruction specifies a byte operand, the low-order (second) byte of the immediate data word is used. The assembler automatically places this byte correctly.

Figure 22-5 illustrates the execution of the ADDI instruction with an operation size of word (16 bits) using absolute short addressing. As you can see, the word following the instruction operation code contains the immediate data ($A3B0_{16}$ in this example). The absolute short address, which is sign-extended to designate the destination

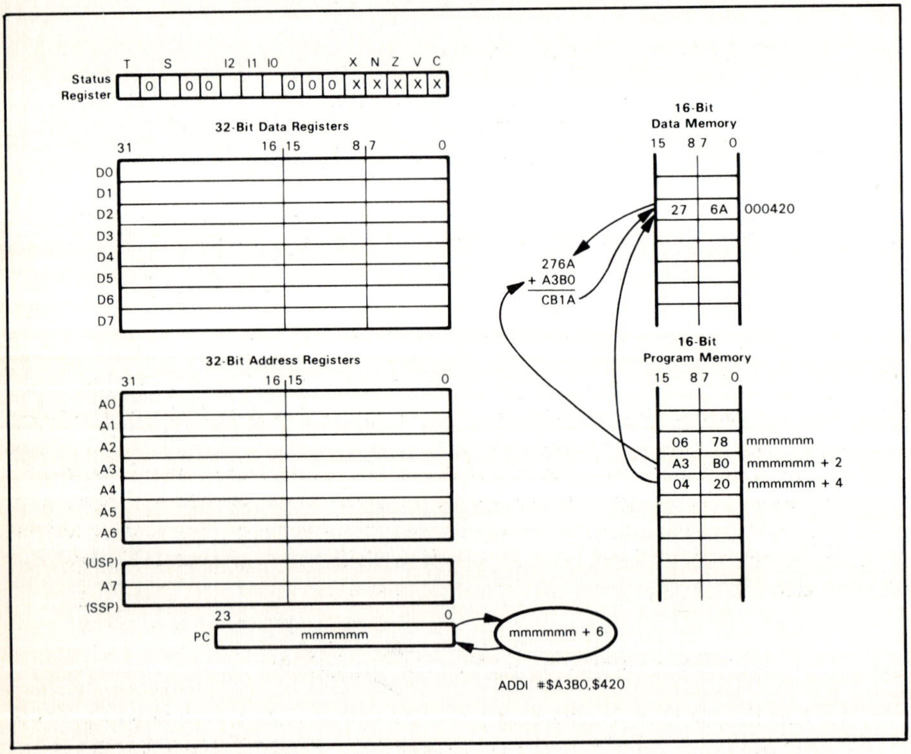

Figure 22-5. Execution of the ADDI Instruction Using Absolute Short Addressing

operand, follows the immediate data in program memory. The immediate data is added to the contents of location 000420_{16} and the result is stored in location 000420_{16}.

The X, N, Z, V, and C status flags are all affected in the same way as by the ADD instruction.

ADDQ — Add Quick

This instruction adds the immediate data contained within the instruction object code word to the destination operand and stores the result in the destination. The addressing modes that can be used are:

Addressing Modes Allowed	Operand		Source ea Field	
	Source	Destination	Mode	Register No.
Data register direct		X	000	rrr
Address register direct		X*	001	rrr
Address register indirect		X	010	rrr
Postincrement register indirect		X	011	rrr
Predecrement register indirect		X	100	rrr
Register indirect with displacement		X	101	rrr
Register indirect with index		X	110	rrr
Absolute short		X	111	000
Absolute long		X	111	001
Program counter relative with displacement				
Program counter relative with index				
Immediate	X			

*Not allowed if operation size is byte.

The ADDQ instruction object code is:

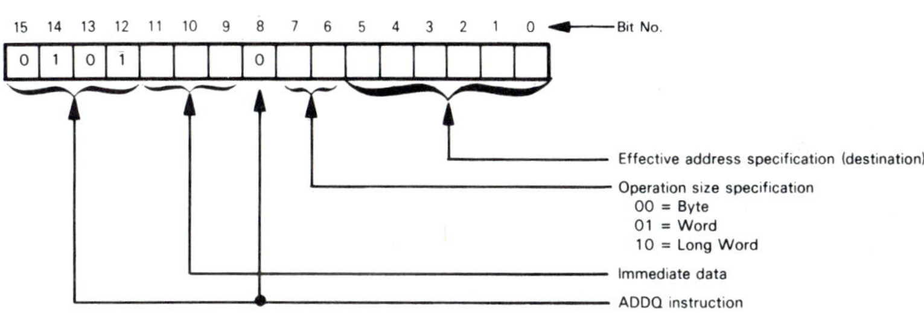

Three bits of immediate data are contained in bits 9, 10 and 11 of the instruction's object code. Thus, immediate operands in the range 1 through 8 can be represented: immediate data of all zeros is interpreted as 8.

Figure 22-6 illustrates execution of the ADDQ instruction using data register direct addressing. When the ADDQ.B #6,D4 instruction is executed, the immediate value of 6 (110_2) is added to the least significant byte of register D4, and the result is stored in D4. Bits 8-31 of the register are not affected. The X, N, Z, V and C status flags are all affected in the same way as by the ADD instruction.

ADDX — Add Extended Register to Register

This instruction adds the contents of the source data register and the value of the Extend (X) flag to the contents of the destination data register. The result is stored in the destination data register. The operation size can be byte, word, or long word.

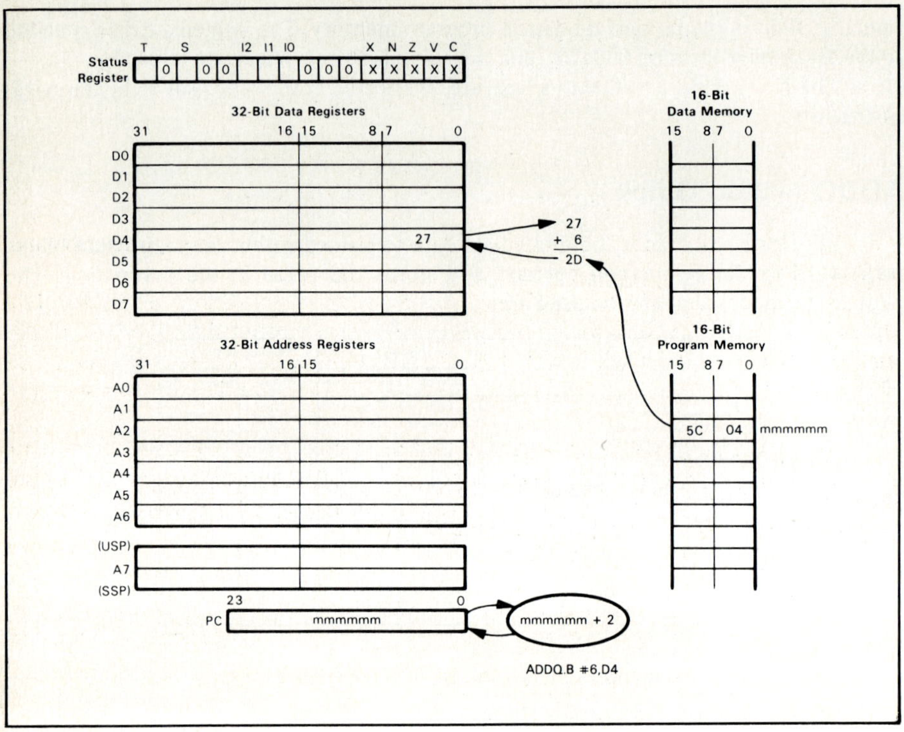

Figure 22-6. Execution of the ADDQ Instruction Using Data Register Direct Addressing

The object code for this instruction is:

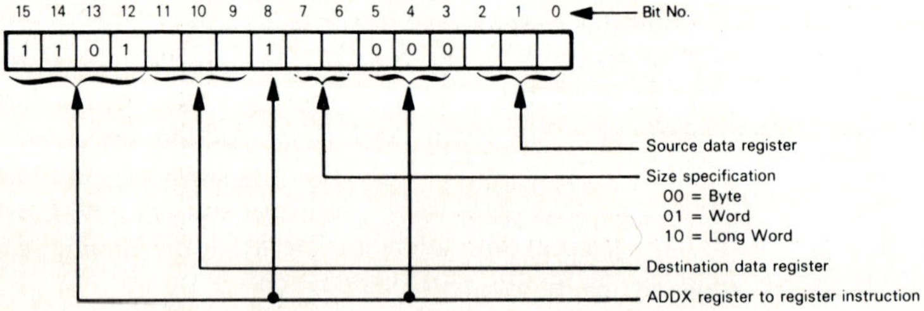

Figure 22-7 illustrates execution of the ADDX instruction with register D3 as the source register and D5 as the destination register. Suppose that xxxx=$276A_{16}$, extend=1, and yyyy=$A3B0_{16}$. After the processor executes the instruction ADDX D3,D5 the contents of D5 will be $CB1B_{16}$.

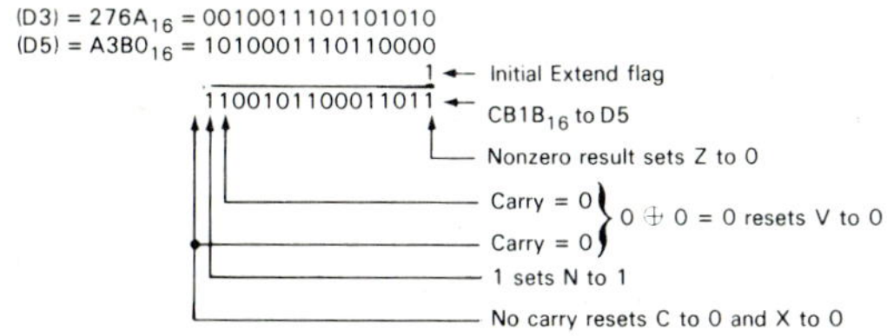

Since this instruction is using a data size of word, only bits 0 through 15 of the data registers are involved in the addition.

The Carry (C) and Extend (X) flags are set if a carry is generated as a result of the operation and are cleared otherwise. The Zero (Z) flag is cleared if the result is nonzero and is unchanged if the result is zero. The Negative (N) flag is set if the result is zero and cleared otherwise. The Overflow (V) flag is set if there is an overflow and cleared otherwise.

Note that the Zero flag is not changed if the result is zero. To perform multiple-precision arithmetic, first set the Zero flag (using MOVE to CCR), then perform the operation. If any part of the result is nonzero, the Zero flag will be cleared; otherwise, the result is zero and the Zero flag remains set.

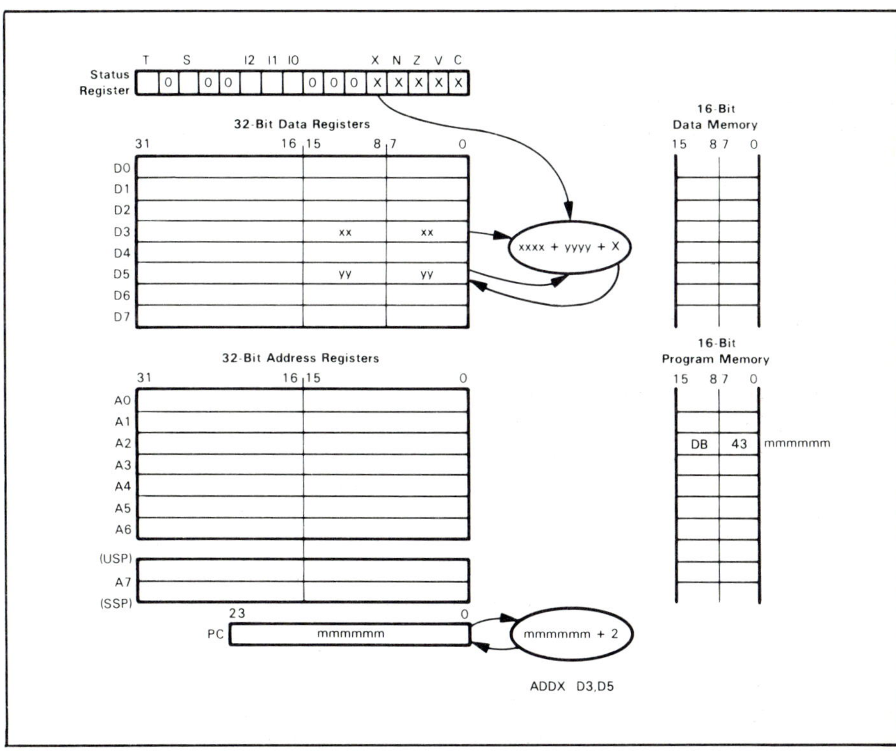

Figure 22-7. Execution of the ADDX Register to Register Instruction

ADDX — Add Extended Memory to Memory

This instruction adds the contents of one memory location and the value of the Extend (X) flag to the contents of another memory location. The memory address for the source operand is held in one address register and the memory address for the destination operand is held in another address register. The contents of both address registers are decremented before the operation.

The object code for this form of the ADDX instruction is:

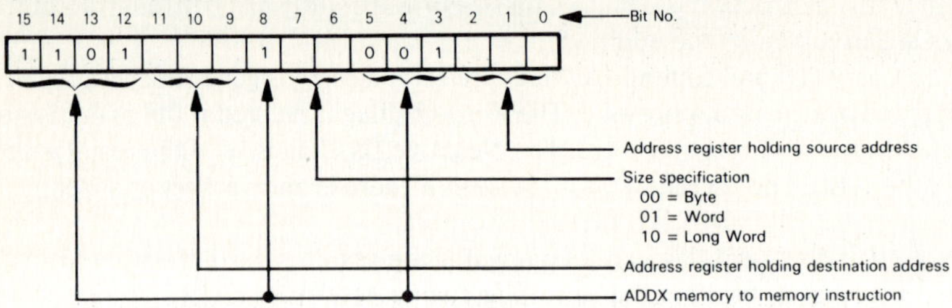

The data size for the ADDX instruction can be byte, word, or long word.

Figure 22-8 illustrates execution of the ADDX instruction where register A1

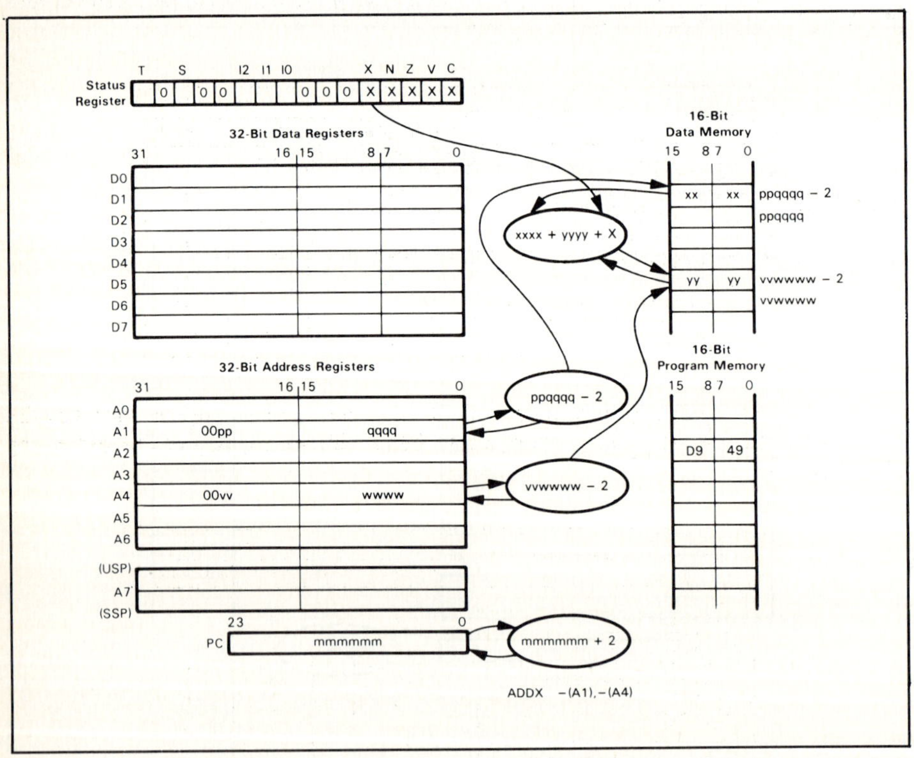

Figure 22-8. Execution of the ADDX Memory to Memory Instruction

holds the address of the source operand in memory and register A4 holds the address of the destination operand in memory. As you can see, the contents of both address registers are decremented by 2 before the operands are accessed for the ADDX operation. If a data size of byte had been specified, then the address registers would have been decremented by 1, and if a data size of a long word had been specified, the address registers would be decremented by 4. This predecrement mode of operation facilitates multiple-precision binary arithmetic, since the address registers are automatically modified to access the next byte, word, or long word to be used. Refer to Chapter 8 for a discussion of multiple-precision arithmetic.

The status flags are affected in the same way as by the ADDX register instruction.

AND — AND Logical

This instruction performs a bitwise logical AND of the contents of the source operand with the contents of the destination operand, and stores the result in the destination.

There are two general forms for this instruction. In the first form, a data register provides the destination operand, and all addressing modes except address register direct are permitted for the source operand:

Addressing Modes Allowed	Operand		Source ea Field	
	Source	Destination	Mode	Register No.
Data register direct	X	X	000	rrr
Address register direct				
Address register indirect	X		010	rrr
Postincrement register indirect	X		011	rrr
Predecrement register indirect	X		100	rrr
Register indirect with displacement	X		101	rrr
Register indirect with index	X		110	rrr
Absolute short	X		111	000
Absolute long	X		111	001
Program counter relative with displacement	X		111	010
Program counter relative with index	X		111	011
Immediate	X		111	100

In the other general form of the AND instruction, a data register provides the source operand; the destination operand can be specified using any of the addressing modes shown:

Addressing Modes Allowed	Operand		Source ea Field	
	Source	Destination	Mode	Register No.
Data register direct	X	X	000	rrr
Address register direct			001	rrr
Address register indirect		X	010	rrr
Postincrement register indirect		X	011	rrr
Predecrement register indirect		X	100	rrr
Register indirect with displacement		X	101	rrr
Register indirect with index		X	110	rrr
Absolute short		X	111	000
Absolute long		X	111	001
Program counter relative with displacement				
Program counter relative with index				
Immediate				

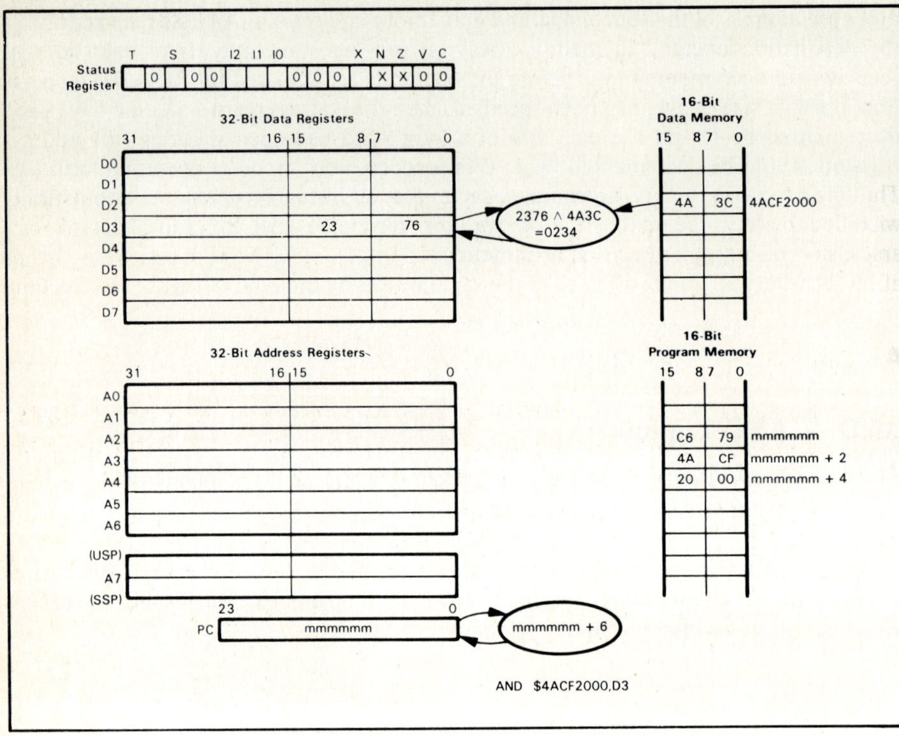

Figure 22-9. Execution of the AND Instruction Using Absolute Long Addressing

The object code for the AND instruction is:

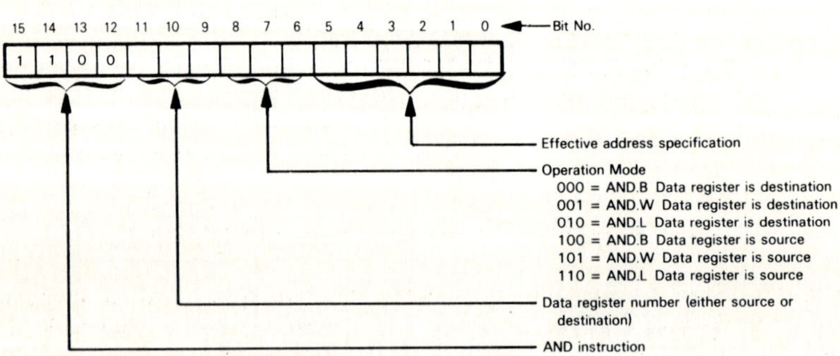

Figure 22-9 illustrates execution of the AND instruction using the absolute long addressing mode with D3 serving as the destination register. Using the operands illustrated in Figure 22-9, this is what happens when the AND $4ACF2000,D3 instruction is

executed:

```
      (D3) = 2376₁₆ = 0010001101110110
(4ACF2000) = 4A3C₁₆ = 0100101000111100
             AND    = 0000001000110100  ◄— 0234₁₆ to D3
                      ↑           ↑
                      |           └—— Nonzero result resets Z to 0
                      └—————————————— 0 resets N to 0
```

The N flag will be set if the most significant bit of the result is 1 and will be cleared otherwise. The Z status flag will be set if the result is zero and will be cleared otherwise. The V and C status flags are always cleared by the AND instruction. The X status flag is not affected by this instruction.

ANDI — AND Immediate

This instruction is used to AND the immediate data present in the succeeding program memory locations to the destination operand. The result is stored in the destination. The addressing modes that can be used are:

Addressing Modes Allowed	Operand		Source ea Field	
	Source	Destination	Mode	Register No.
Data register direct		X	000	rrr
Address register direct				
Address register indirect		X	010	rrr
Postincrement register indirect		X	011	rrr
Predecrement register indirect		X	100	rrr
Register indirect with displacement		X	101	rrr
Register indirect with index		X	110	rrr
Absolute short		X	111	000
Absolute long		X	111	001
Program counter relative with displacement				
Program counter relative with index				
Immediate	X			
Status Register		X	111	100

Note that the destination operand may be the condition codes or the entire status register. **If the destination is the entire status register, this is a privileged instruction and can only be executed while the processor is in the supervisor mode.**

The opcode for the ANDI instruction is:

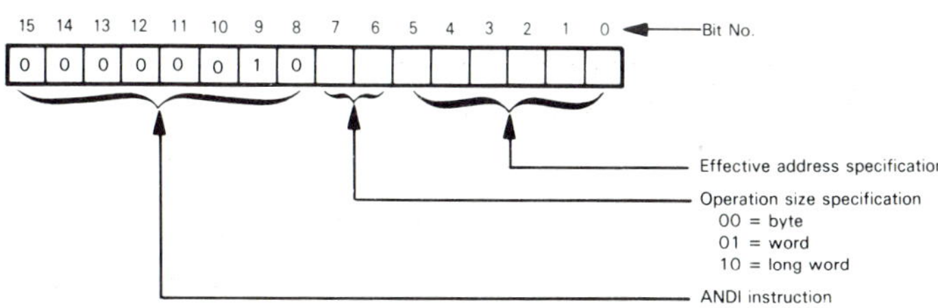

The size of the AND operation can be specified as byte, word, or long word. The immediate data follows the instruction word in memory and must match the specified operation size. Thus, either one or two words of immediate data must follow the instruction operation code in program memory. If the instruction specifies a byte operand, the low-order (second) byte of the immediate data word is used. The assembler automatically places the byte correctly. If the instruction refers to the status register and the operation size is byte, the destination is the low-order byte of the status register and only

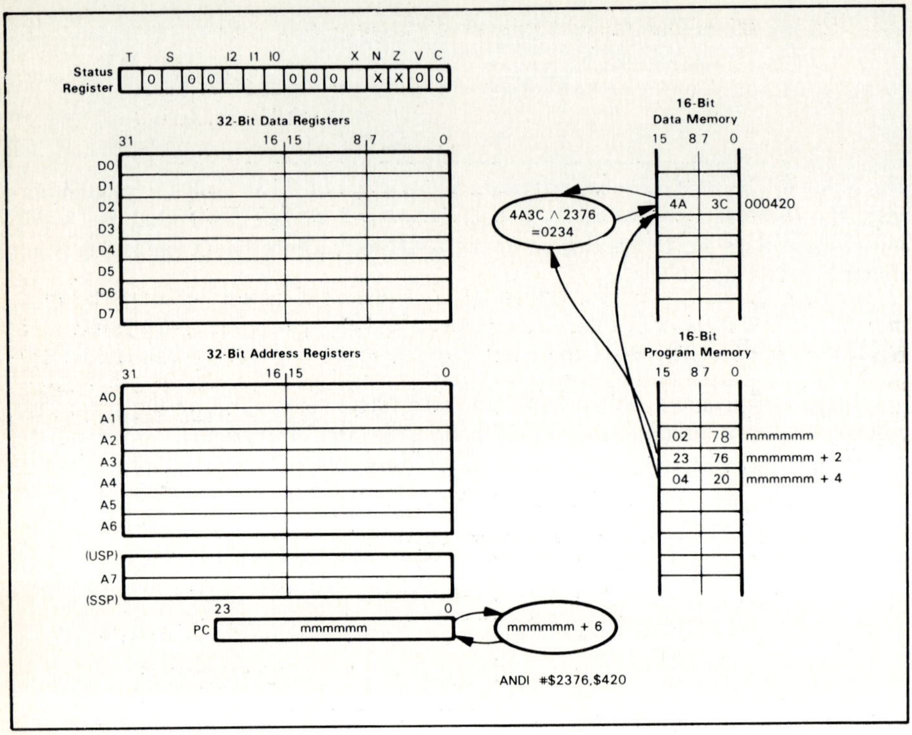

Figure 22-10. Execution of the ANDI Instruction Using Absolute Short Addressing

the condition codes are affected. If the operation size is word, the entire status register is the destination and the instruction is privileged.

Figure 22-10 illustrates execution of the ANDI instruction with an operation size of word (16 bits) using absolute short addressing. As you can see, the word following the instruction operation code contains the immediate data (2376_{16} in this example). The absolute short address, which is sign-extended to designate the destination operand, follows the immediate data in program memory. The immediate data is bitwise ANDed with the contents of location 000420_{16} and the result (0234_{16}) will be returned to location 000420_{16}.

The N and Z status flags are modified by the ANDI instruction according to the results obtained. The V and C status flags are always cleared. The X status flag is not affected. Of course, if the destination of the instruction is the condition codes or the entire status register, then the condition codes are affected according to the result of the operation.

ASL — Arithmetic Shift Left in Data Register

This instruction arithmetically shifts to the left the contents of a specified data register. The Carry and Extend flags receive the last bit shifted out of the data register, and zeros are shifted into the low-order bit of the register as shown:

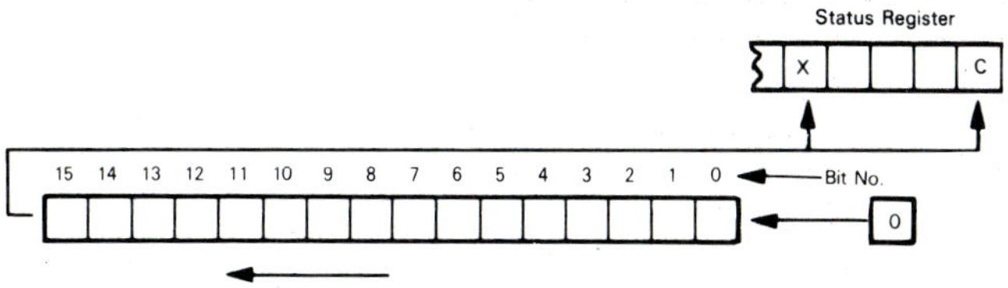

The shift count may be specified by the contents of another data register or by immediate data. If the shift count is contained in a data register, the least significant six bits of that data register specify the count in the range from 0 to 63. If immediate data is used, shift counts in the range of 1 to 8 can be specified as part of the instruction operation code. A value of 0 specifies a shift of 8. The object code for the ASL register instruction is:

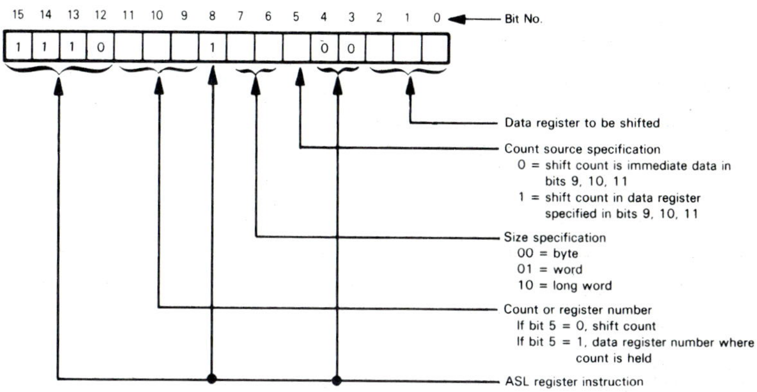

Bit 5 of the instruction operation code determines whether the count is to be specified using immediate data held in bits 9, 10, or 11, or whether the count is to be contained in another data register whose number is specified in bits 9, 10, and 11.

Figure 22-11 illustrates execution of an ASL instruction with register D0 specified as the destination operand and with the shift count specified in register D3. If register D0 initially contains $C23A_{16}$ and D3 contains 03, the following 3-bit left shift would be performed.

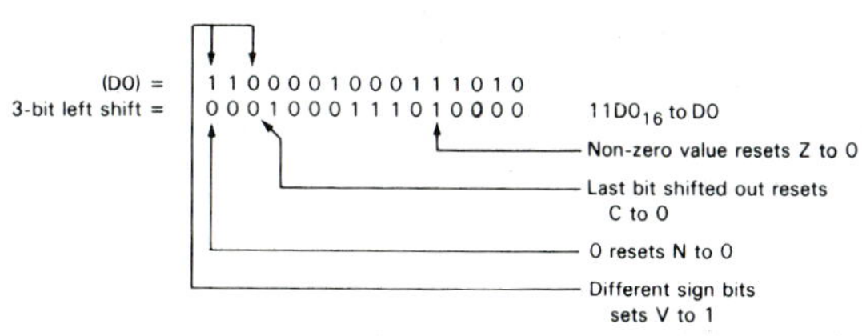

Bits shifted out of the high-order bit go to both the Carry and Extend status flags in the status register. If the shift count is zero, the Carry flag is cleared and the Extend flag is unaffected. Zeros are shifted into the low-order bit of the data register. The Over-

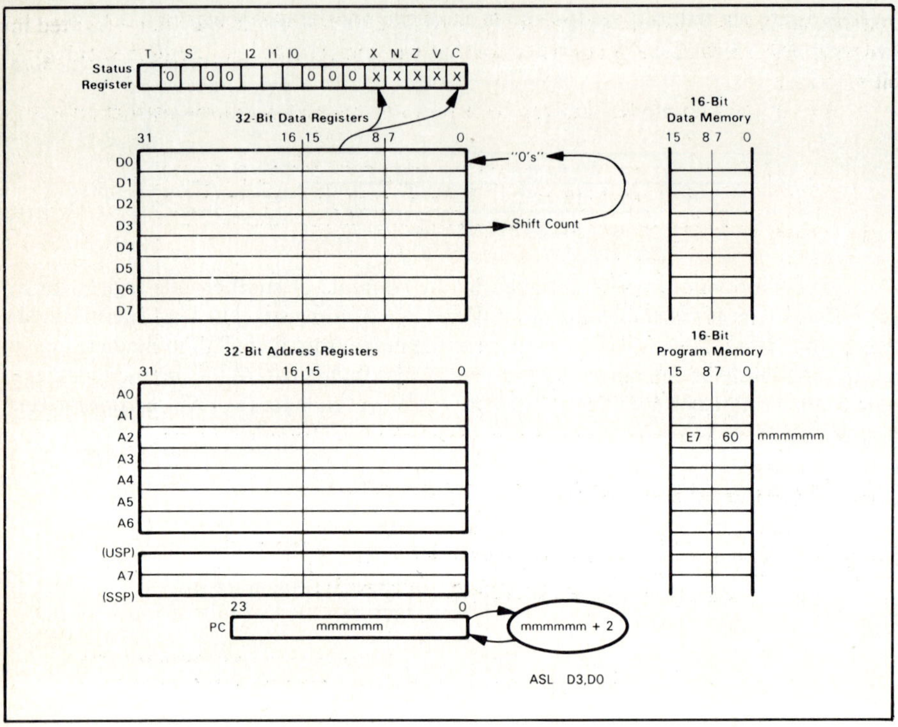

Figure 22-11. Execution of the ASL Instruction with Operand and Shift Count in Data Registers

flow (V) status flag indicates if any sign changes occur during the shift. The N and Z flags are modified according to the value of the result.

Figure 22-11 illustrated an ASL operation with an operand size of word in the data register. Only bits 0 through 15 of the data register were affected; bits 16-31 remained unchanged. The ASL instruction can also operate on byte and long word operands in the data register. Note that for the instruction illustrated in Figure 22-11, the same results could have been obtained by executing the following instruction:

```
ASL #3,D0
```

This instruction uses an immediate data value of 3 to indicate the shift count instead of using the contents of another data register (D3) as was illustrated earlier. The advantage of using a data register to indicate the shift count is that you may alter the contents of the data register dynamically under program control, whereas an immediate data value is contained in program memory and will usually be unchangeable.

ASL — Arithmetic Shift Left Memory

This instruction performs the same operation as the ASL register instruction described in preceding pages, but performs that operation on an operand contained in memory rather than in a data register. This version of the ASL instruction is limited in two ways: the operand size is restricted to word and the operand may be shifted only one bit position.

The addressing modes that can be used with the ASL memory instruction are:

Addressing Modes Allowed	Operand		Source ea Field	
	Source	Destination	Mode	Register No.
Data register direct				
Address register direct				
Address register indirect		X	010	rrr
Postincrement register indirect		X	011	rrr
Predecrement register indirect		X	100	rrr
Register indirect with displacement		X	101	rrr
Register indirect with index		X	110	rrr
Absolute short		X	111	000
Absolute long		X	111	001
Program counter relative with displacement				
Program counter relative with index				
Immediate				

The object code for the ASL memory instruction is:

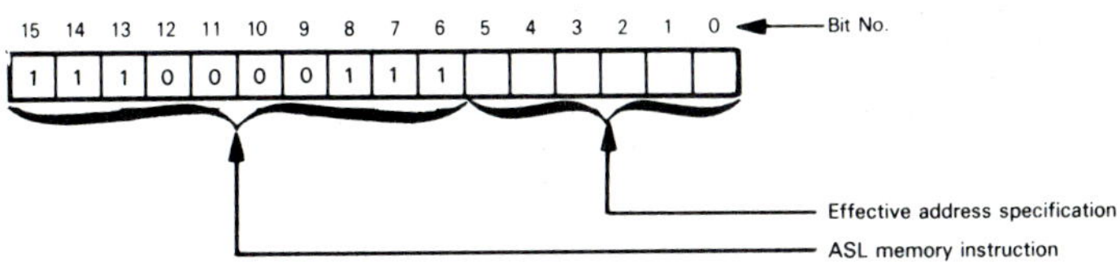

The execution of this ASL instruction is the same as was illustrated for the ASL data register version. The operand in memory is shifted left one bit, and the bit shifted out of the high-order bit (bit 15) goes to both the Carry and Extend flags in the status register. A zero is shifted into the low-order bit of the memory word. The Overflow (V) bit will indicate if any sign change occurs as a result of the shift.

ASR — Arithmetic Shift Right

This instruction arithmetically shifts the bits of the operand to the right. Just as was the case with the ASL instructions described in the preceding pages, there are two general versions of this instruction. One version allows an operand contained in a data register to be shifted a number of bit positions specified either by the contents of another data register or by an immediate value indicated in the instruction word itself. The second version of the ASR instruction allows a 1-bit shift of a word operand contained in memory. The addressing modes allowed for the ASR instruction are the same as were illustrated for the ASL register and ASL memory instructions.

The object code for the ASR register instruction is:

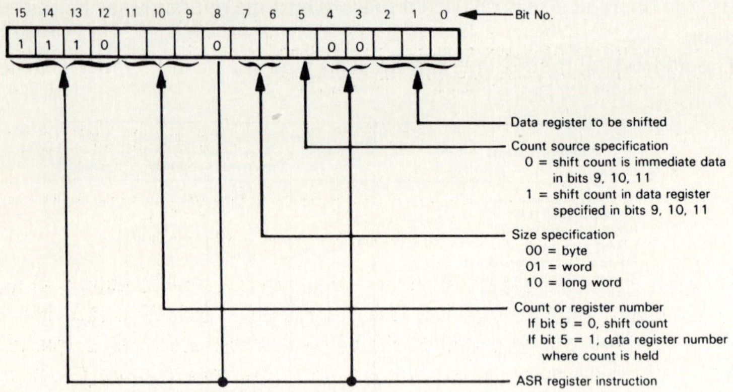

When the ASR instruction is executed, the operand is shifted right, the number of positions indicated, and the bits shifted out of the low-order bit go to both the Carry and Extend status flags in the status register. If the shift count is zero, the Carry flag is cleared and the Extend flag is unaffected. The high-order (sign bit) is shifted right and is also duplicated in the high-order bit here:

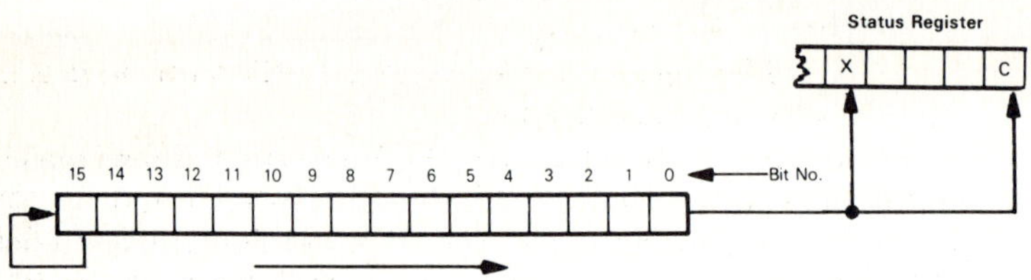

As was the case with the ASL instruction, the differences between the register and memory versions of this instruction are that the memory version must have an operand size of word and the bit shift can only be one position. The object code for the ASR memory instruction is:

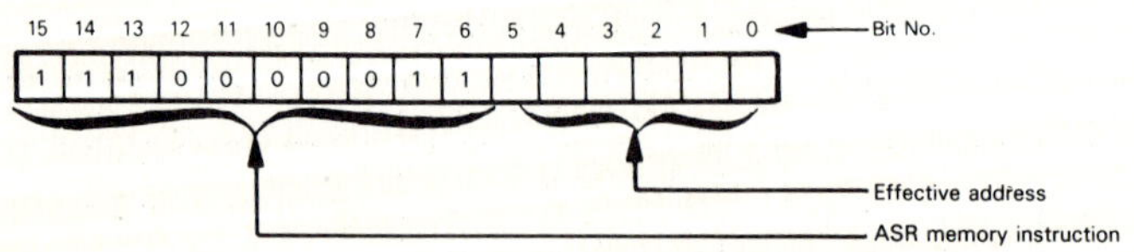

B_{cc} — Branch Conditionally

This instruction causes a transfer of program control to an address relative to the value of the program counter is the condition specified by cc is met. The only addressing mode used by this instruction is the program counter relative addressing mode. The displacement from the location of the instruction can be either from −126 to +128 or from −32766 to +32768. The object for this instruction is:

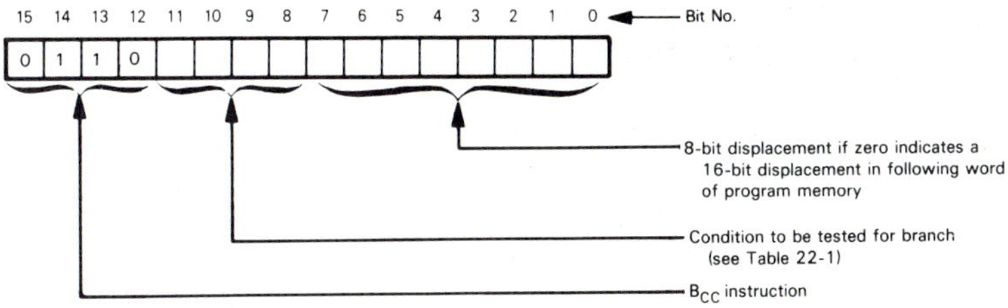

Bits 8 through 11 of the instruction word specify the condition which is to be tested to determine whether the branch is to be taken. **Table 22-1 lists the conditions that can be used with this instruction and the values that are computed from the values of the flags in the status register to determine whether the test is successful.**

If the value computed for the test is one, then the specified condition is met. A new program counter value is computed by adding the sign-extended contents of the 8-bit displacement field from the instruction word to the program counter contents, after the program counter has been incremented by two. If the least significant eight bits of the B_{cc} instruction word are zero, then the sign-extended contents of the 16-bit displacement word following the instruction word are added to the program counter contents to obtain the new program counter value. Program execution continues at the location specified by the new program counter value.

If the value computed for the test is zero, then the specified condition is not met and execution continues with the next instruction.

Figure 22-12 illustrates execution of the BVC instruction. If the Overflow (V) flag in the status register is set, program execution simply continues with the next consecutive instruction in program memory. However, if the Overflow (V) flag in the status register is cleared, then the 8-bit, two's complement displacement provided in the instruction code is added to the program counter contents after the program counter has been incremented by two. Using the object code displacement of 40_{16} illustrated in Figure 22-12, a branch, if taken, will advance program execution to memory word mmmmmm + 42_{16}.

Table 22-1. B_{cc}Conditional Tests

Mnemonic(cc)	Condition	Condition Field	Test
HI	High	0010	$\overline{C} \wedge \overline{Z}$
LS	Low or same	0011	$C \vee Z$
CC	Carry clear	0100	$\overline{C}$
CS	Carry set	0101	C
NE	Not equal	0110	$\overline{Z}$
EQ	Equal	0111	Z
VC	Overflow clear	1000	$\overline{V}$
VS	Overflow set	1001	V
PL	Plus	1010	$\overline{N}$
MI	Minus	1011	N
GE	Greater or equal	1100	$(N \wedge V) \vee (\overline{N} \wedge \overline{V})$
LT	Less than	1101	$(N \wedge \overline{V}) \vee (\overline{N} \wedge V)$
GT	Greater than	1110	$(N \wedge V \wedge \overline{Z}) \vee (\overline{N} \wedge \overline{V} \wedge \overline{Z})$
LE	Less or equal	1111	$Z \vee (N \wedge \overline{V}) \vee (\overline{N} \wedge V)$

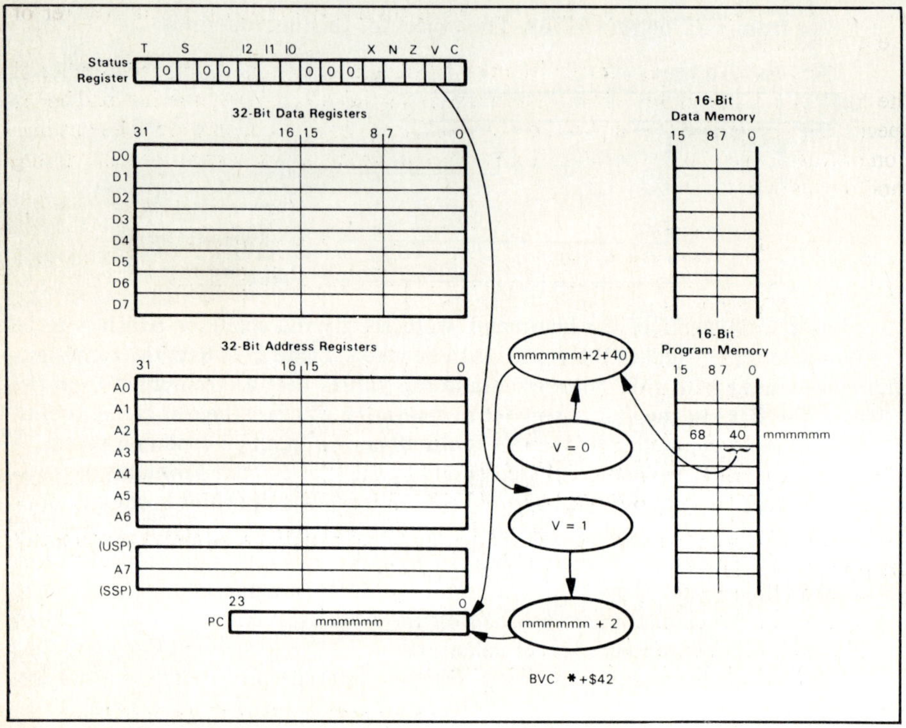

Figure 22-12. Execution of the BVC Instruction

Note that the displacement in the object code is added to the program counter value after the program counter is incremented by two. However, in the assembly language, the asterisk symbol refers to the location of the instruction in which the asterisk occurs. Therefore **the number given as the displacement in the assembly language is relative to the location of the instruction.** The assembler automatically reduces this by two when generating the object code. **Of course, use of absolute displacements is bad programming practice. Use labels instead.**

Typically, you will not use the form of the instruction shown in Figure 22-12 (BVC *+$42). Instead, you will simply provide a label indicating the point where program execution is to continue if the condition you have specified is met. The assembler will then determine the displacement required to reach the label, and provide the appropriate 8-bit or 16-bit displacement value to accompany the instruction object code.

The B_{cc} instruction does not affect any status flags. The previous value of the program counter is lost.

BCHG — Test a Bit and Change

This instruction tests the state of a specified bit in a memory location or data register, and the state of the specified bit is reflected in the Zero (Z) status flag. After the test operation, the state of the specified bit is complemented in the data register or memory location.

There are two general forms for this instruction. In the first form, the number of the bit to be tested is held in a data register. In the other form, the bit number is specified using immediate data in the word following the instruction word. The destination operand which holds the bit to be tested can be specified using any of the addressing modes shown:

Addressing Modes Allowed	Operand		Destination ea Field	
	Bit No.	Destination	Mode	Register No.
Data register direct	X	X	000	rrr
Address register direct				
Address register indirect		X	010	rrr
Postincrement register indirect		X	011	rrr
Predecrement register indirect		X	100	rrr
Register indirect with displacement		X	101	rrr
Register indirect with index		X	110	rrr
Absolute short		X	111	000
Absolute long		X	111	001
Program counter relative with displacement				
Program counter relative with index				
Immediate	X			

The object code for the BCHG instruction when a data register is used to specify the bit number is:

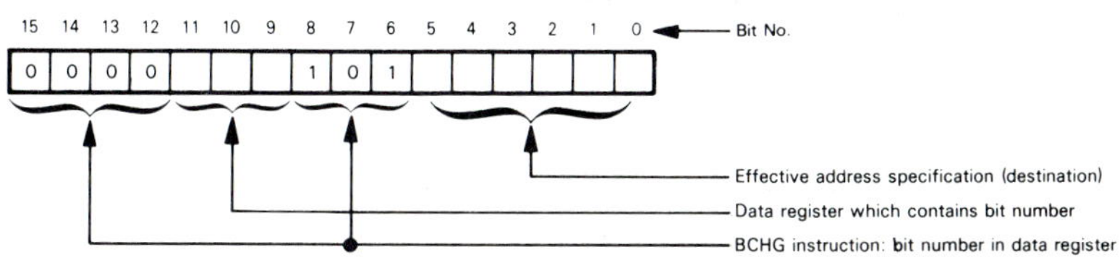

Bits 9, 10 and 11 of the instruction word specify the data register which holds the number of the bit to be tested. If the bit that is to be tested is contained in another data register, then any of the 32 bits in that register can be tested. In this case, the bit number is specified using the six least significant bits (modulo 32) of the first data register. If the bit to be tested is in memory, then the BCHG operation is limited to a data size of byte. In this case, the bit number to be tested in the memory byte is specified by the three least significant bits (modulo 8) of the data register.

Figure 22-13 illustrates execution of a BCHG instruction using data register direct addressing. In this figure, data register D4 is used to hold the number of the bit to be tested (bit number 3) and the bit to be tested is held in data register D1. After this instruction executes, data register D1 would hold all zeros since bit 3 would be complemented after the test operation.

In the second form of this instruction, the number of the bit to be tested is specified using immediate data. The instruction object code for this form of the BCHG instruction is:

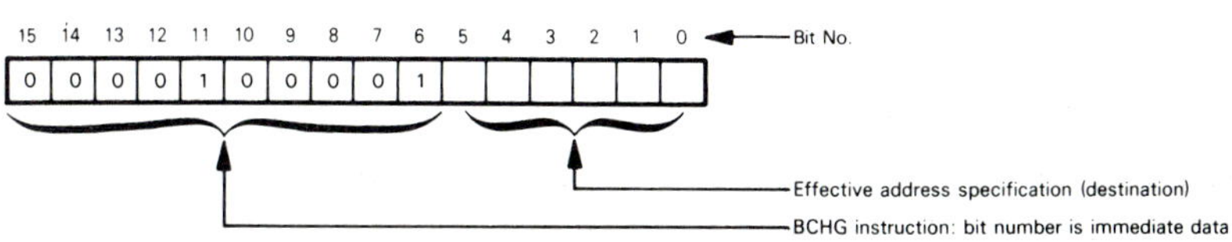

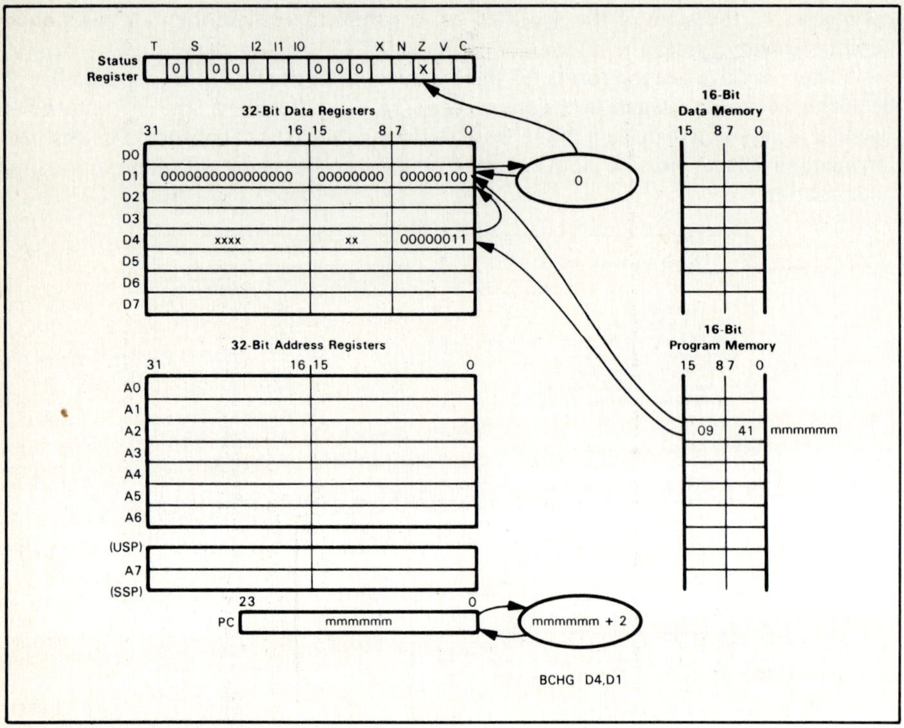

Figure 22-13. Execution of the BCHG Instruction Using Data Register Direct Addressing

In this case, the bit number to be tested is specified using immediate data provided in the word which follows the instruction word in program memory. The destination operand which contains the bit to be tested can be either a 32-bit data register or an 8-bit byte in memory just as was the case with the first form of the BCHG instruction. Thus, for the instruction illustrated in Figure 22-13, the same results could have been obtained by executing the following instruction:

```
BCHG #3,D1
```

This instruction uses an immediate data value of 3 to indicate the bit to be tested, instead of using the contents of another data register (D4) as was illustrated earlier. The advantage of using a data register to indicate the bit to be tested is that you can dynamically alter the contents of the data register under program control, whereas an immediate data value will usually be unchangeable since it is contained in program memory. The only status flag affected by the BCHG instruction is the Zero (Z) flag: this bit is set if the bit that was tested is 0, and is cleared if the bit that was tested is 1.

BCLR — Test a Bit and Clear

This instruction tests a bit in a specified data register or memory location and modifies the Zero (Z) status flag to reflect the state of that bit. After the test, the specified bit is cleared (set to 0). Thus, this instruction is identical to the BCHG instruction except that instead of complementing the bit after testing, the bit will always be cleared to zero after the test.

The addressing modes that can be used to specify the destination operand are the same as for the BCHG instruction:

Addressing Modes Allowed	Operand		Destination ea Field	
	Bit No.	Destination	Mode	Register No.
Data register direct	X	X	000	rrr
Address register direct				
Address register indirect		X	010	rrr
Postincrement register indirect		X	011	rrr
Predecrement register indirect		X	100	rrr
Register indirect with displacement		X	101	rrr
Register indirect with index		X	110	rrr
Absolute short		X	111	000
Absolute long		X	111	001
Program counter relative with displacement				
Program counter relative with index				
Immediate	X			

As was the case with the BCHG instruction, there are two forms of the BCLR instruction. In the first form the bit number to be tested is contained in a data register. The instruction object code for this form is:

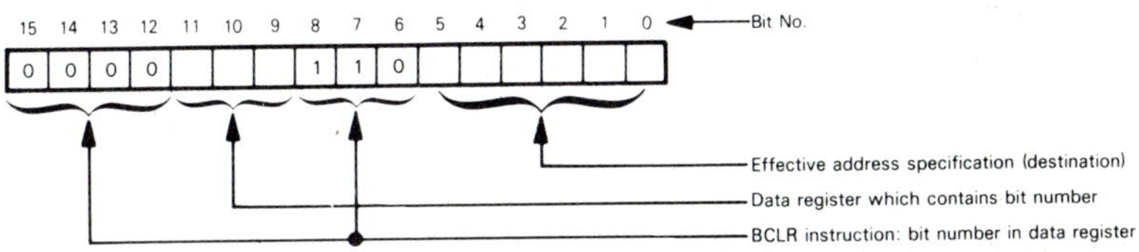

In the second form of the BCLR instruction, immediate data contained in the word following the instruction word is used to indicate the bit number to be tested:

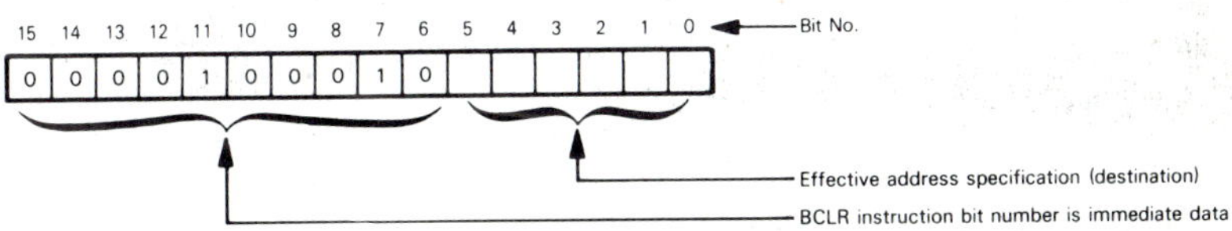

Both of these forms are identical to those of the BCHG instruction and you should refer to that instruction description for additional discussion.

Only the Zero (Z) flag in the status register is affected by the BCLR instruction. The Z flag will be set if the bit tested is 0 and will be cleared if the bit tested is 1.

BRA — Branch Always

This instruction always causes a branch to the specified address by placing that address in the program counter. The specified address is the sum of the current value of the program counter, after it has been incremented by two, and a displacement value. The displacement is the sign-extended value of a two's complement number which is contained either in the least significant byte of the instruction word or, if this byte contains all zeros, in the 16-bit word which follows the instruction object code in memory.

The object code for the BRA instruction is:

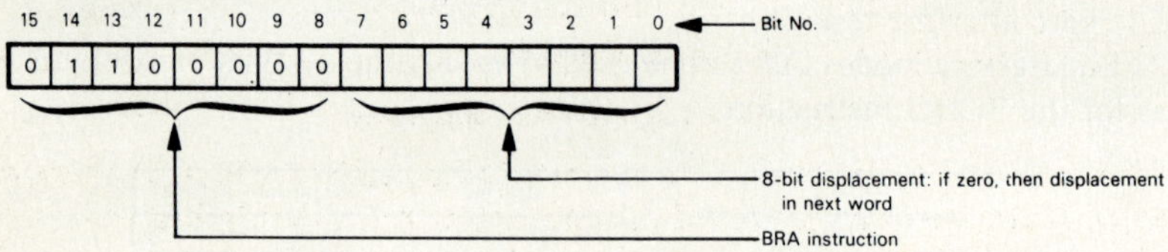

Figure 22-14 illustrates execution of the BRA instruction.

Note that the displacement in the object code is added to the program counter value after the program counter is incremented by two. However, in the assembly language, the asterisk symbol refers to the location of the instruction in which the asterisk occurs. Therefore **the number given as the displacement in the assembly language is relative to the location of the instruction.** The assembler automatically reduces this by two when generating the object code. **Of course, use of absolute displacements is bad programming practice. Use labels instead.** Consider the following section of a program:

```
        BRA   NEXT
        LSL   #1,D0
         -
         -
         -
NEXT    NOT   D0
```

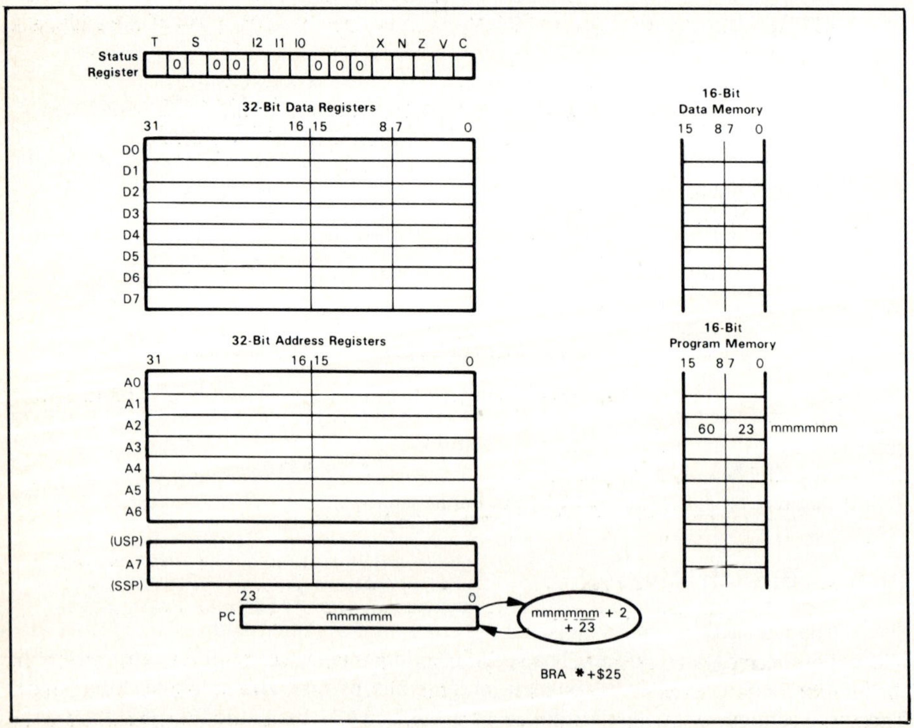

Figure 22-14. Execution of the BRA Instruction

After executing BRA, the processor always executes the NOT instruction next. It will never execute the LSL instruction unless a branch or jump instruction elsewhere in the program transfers control to that LSL instruction.

The overall effect of a BRA instruction is:

PC = PC + 2 + object code displacement

The extra two is the result of the two bytes occupied by the BRA instruction itself. The program counter is incremented as soon as the instruction is fetched.

The BRA instruction does not affect any status flags. The previous value of the program counter is lost.

BSET — Test a Bit and Set

This instruction tests the state of a specified bit in a memory location or data register, and the state of the specified bit is reflected in the Zero (Z) status flag. After the test operation, the bit that was tested is set to 1.

This instruction is identical to the BCHG instruction, which we described earlier, except that the tested bit is always set in this case instead of being complemented as was the case with BCHG.

There are two general forms for this instruction. In the first form, the number of the bit to be tested is held in a data register. In the other form, the bit number is specified using immediate data in the word following the instruction word. The destination operand which holds the bit to be tested can be specified using any of the addressing modes shown:

Addressing Modes Allowed	Operand		Destination ea Field	
	Bit No.	Destination	Mode	Register No.
Data register direct	X	X	000	rrr
Address register direct				
Address register indirect		X	010	rrr
Postincrement register indirect		X	011	rrr
Predecrement register indirect		X	100	rrr
Register indirect with displacement		X	101	rrr
Register indirect with index		X	110	rrr
Absolute short		X	111	000
Absolute long		X	111	001
Program counter relative with displacement				
Program counter relative with index				
Immediate	X			

The object code for the BSET instruction when a data register is used to specify the bit number is:

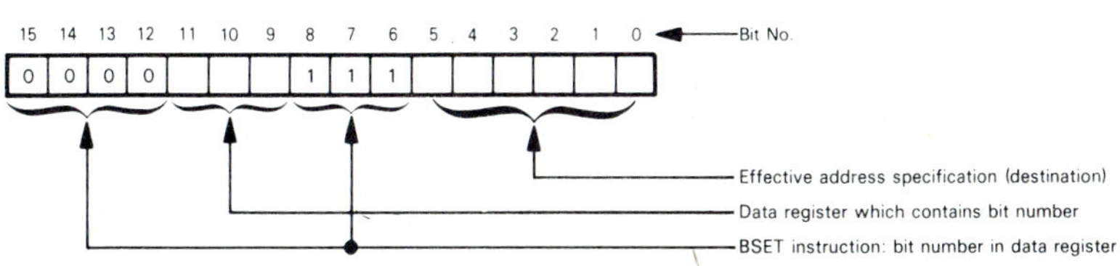

The execution is essentially the same as that which we described earlier for the BCHG instruction except that the tested bit is always set in the operand. You should refer to that instruction description and to Figure 22-13 for an illustration of how the instruction operates.

In the second form of the BSET instruction, the number of the bit to be tested is specified using immediate data. The instruction object code for this form of the BSET instruction can be illustrated as follows:

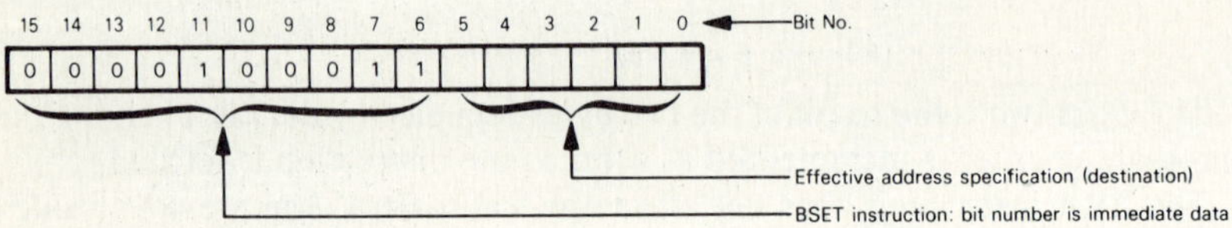

Once again, the execution is essentially the same as was illustrated for the BCHG instruction except that the tested bit is always set in the operand. Refer to that instruction description for a discussion of how the instruction operates. The only status flag affected by the BSET instruction is the Zero (Z) flag; this flag is set if the bit that was tested is 0 and cleared if the bit that was tested is 1.

BSR — Branch to Subroutine

This instruction pushes the address of the instruction immediately following the BSR instruction on the system stack. The displacement provided as part of the BSR instruction is then added to the current value of the program counter after it has been incremented by two, and program execution will continue at this new location.

The object code for the BSR instruction is:

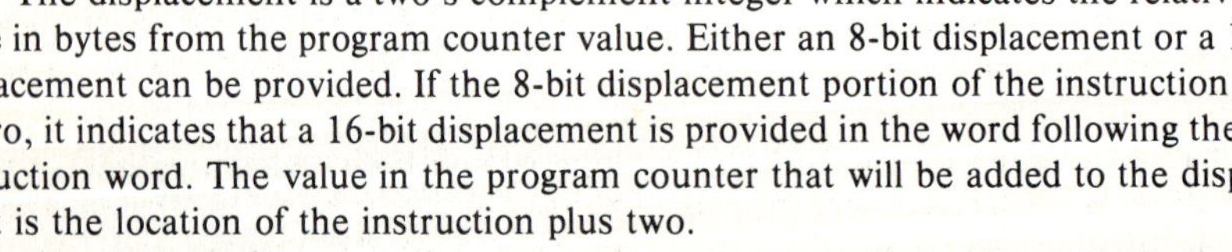

The displacement is a two's complement integer which indicates the relative distance in bytes from the program counter value. Either an 8-bit displacement or a 16-bit displacement can be provided. If the 8-bit displacement portion of the instruction word is zero, it indicates that a 16-bit displacement is provided in the word following the BSR instruction word. The value in the program counter that will be added to the displacement is the location of the instruction plus two.

Figure 22-15 illustrates execution of the BSR instruction using a 16-bit displacement (110_{16}). In Figure 22-15 it is assumed that the program is being executed in user mode and therefore the stack pointer used will be the user stack pointer (USP) in register A7. After the program counter has been incremented to access the instruction and the 16-bit displacement, the new program counter value (mmmmmm+4) is pushed onto the user stack. Note that the contents of the stack pointer (wwvvvv) are first decremented by two to store the low-order half of a program counter and then decremented by two again to store the high-order half of the program counter. Thus, the value contained in the user stack pointer after the instruction is executed will be wwvvvv−4.

After the incremented program counter contents have been pushed onto the stack, the subroutine execution address is loaded into the program counter.

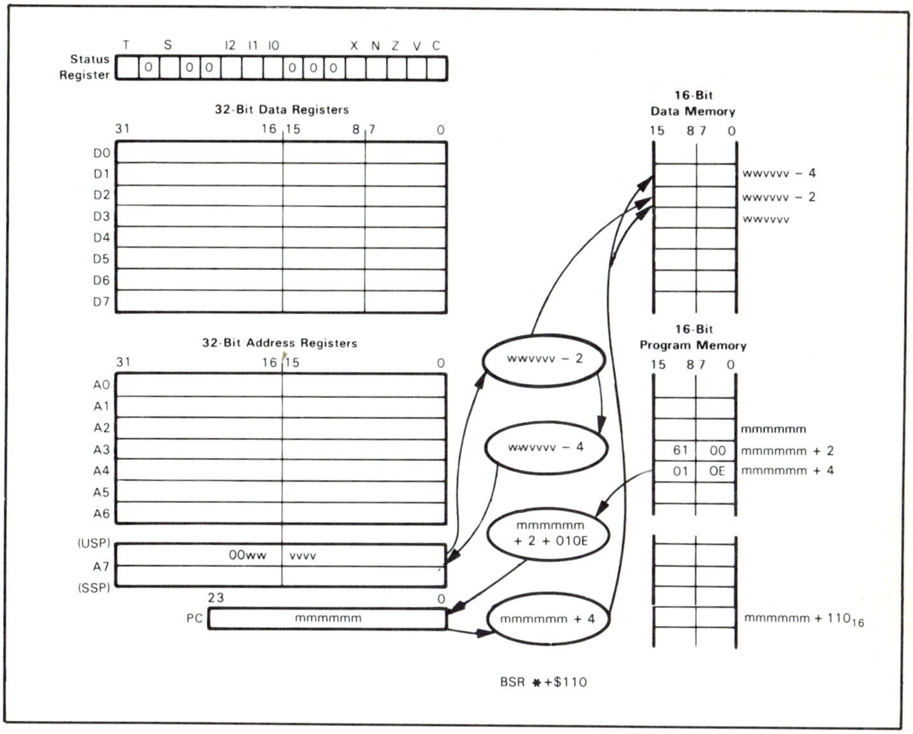

Figure 22-15. Execution of the BSR Instruction

BSR is the same as BRA, except that BSR saves the old value of the program counter on the stack, thus providing a subroutine linkage. An RTS instruction at the end of the subroutine can transfer control back to the instruction immediately following BSR, provided that the subroutine has not changed the return address or the stack pointer contents. BSR provides an unconditional relative jump-to-subroutine capability provided by JSR. However, note that JSR *+300 has exactly the same effect as BSR *+300.

Note that the displacement in the object code is added to the program counter value after the program counter is incremented by two. However, in the assembly language, the asterisk symbol refers to the location of the instruction in which the asterisk occurs. Therefore **the number given as the displacement in the assembly language is relative to the location of the instruction.** The assembler automatically reduces this by two when generating the object code. **Of course, use of absolute displacements is bad programming practice. Use labels instead.**

No status flags are affected by the BSR instruction.

BTST — Test a Bit

This instruction tests the state of a specified bit in a memory location or data register and the state of the specified bit is reflected in the Zero (Z) status flag. The bit tested is not changed. This instruction is thus the functional equivalent of the first portion of the other bit manipulation instructions (BCHG, BCLR, and BSET) that we have described in preceding pages.

There are two general forms for this instruction. In the first form, the number of the bit to be tested is held in a data register. In the other form, the bit number is specified using immediate data in the word following the instruction word. The destination operand which holds the bit to be tested can be specified using any of the addressing modes shown:

Addressing Modes Allowed	Operand		Destination ea Field	
	Bit No.	Destination	Mode	Register No.
Data register direct	X	X	000	rrr
Address register direct				
Address register indirect		X	010	rrr
Postincrement register indirect		X	011	rrr
Predecrement register indirect		X	100	rrr
Register indirect with displacement		X	101	rrr
Register indirect with index		X	110	rrr
Absolute short		X	111	000
Absolute long		X	111	001
Program counter relative with displacement		X	111	010
Program counter relative with index		X	111	011
Immediate	X			

The object code for the BTST instruction when a data register is used to specify the bit number is:

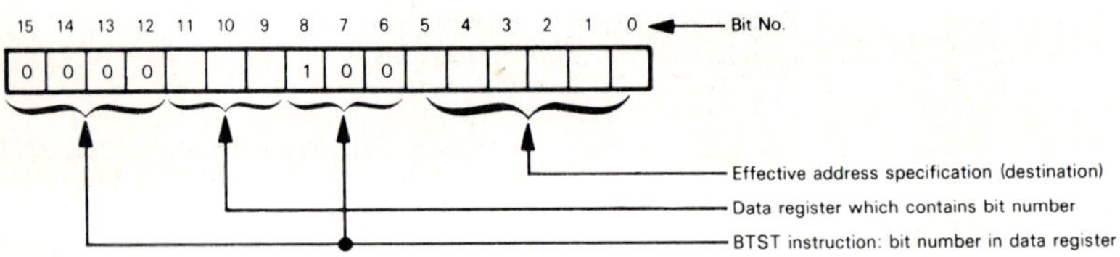

This format is essentially the same as for the other bit test and manipulation instructions we have described.

In the second form of the BTST instruction, the number of the bit to be tested is specified using immediate data. The instruction object code for this form of the BTST instruction is:

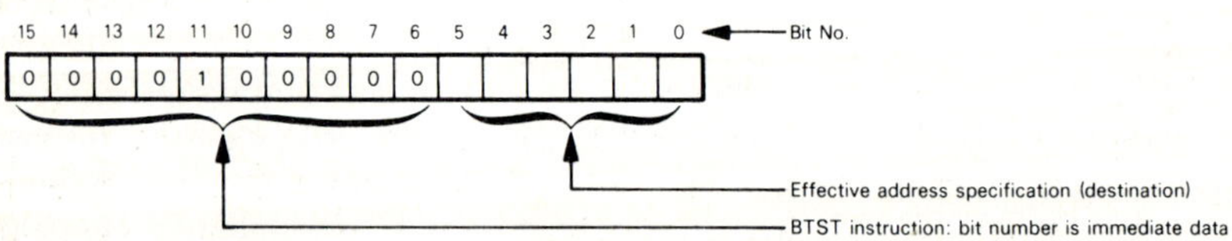

The format for this version of the BTST instruction is also essentially the same as we described for BCHG and the other bit test instructions. Refer to the description of the BCHG instruction for a more detailed discussion of instruction execution, noting that BTST does not change the tested bit.

The only status flag affected by the BTST instruction is the Zero (Z) flag: this flag is set if the bit that was tested is 0 and cleared if the bit that was tested is 1.

CHK — Check Register Against Boundaries

This instruction compares the contents of a data register to the contents of a source operand. If the contents of the data register are less than zero or if the contents of the data register are greater than the contents of the source operand, a TRAP is generated and the processor initiates exception processing.

The source operand which holds the value to be compared to the data register contents can be specified using any of the addressing modes except address register direct:

Addressing Modes Allowed	Operand		Source ea Field	
	Source	Destination	Mode	Register No.
Data register direct	X	X	000	rrr
Address register direct				
Address register indirect	X		010	rrr
Postincrement register indirect	X		011	rrr
Predecrement register indirect	X		100	rrr
Register indirect with displacement	X		101	rrr
Register indirect with index	X		110	rrr
Absolute short	X		111	000
Absolute long	X		111	001
Program counter relative with displacement	X		111	010
Program counter relative with index	X		111	011
Immediate	X		111	100

The object code for the CHK instruction is:

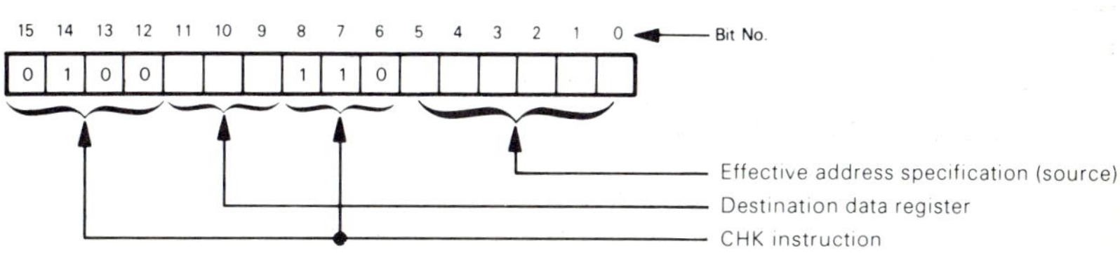

Figure 22-16 illustrates execution of the CHK instruction using address register indirect addressing. In this figure, the contents of the register D3 (xxxx) are compared to (yyyy), the contents of the memory location (wwvvvv) pointed to by A3. If xxxx is greater than yyyy, or if xxxx is less than zero, a TRAP is generated. When the processor initiates exception processing for this TRAP, it will use the CHK vector from the exception vector table located at memory address 018_{16}. For a complete discussion of the sequence that occurs when a TRAP is generated, refer to the TRAP instruction description later in this chapter and to Chapter 15.

In Figure 22-16, if xxxx is greater than zero and less than or equal to yyyy, then no TRAP is generated and the next instruction in sequence is executed. Note that the value compared to the data register contents is a two's complement integer and that only the least significant 16-bits of the data register are used in the comparison; there is no byte or long word version. The Negative (N) status flag will be set if the contents of the data register are less than zero, and will be cleared if the contents of the data register are greater than the upper bound to which it is compared. The Z, V, and C status flags are affected by this instruction but their state is undefined. The X status flag is not affected.

The purpose of the CHK instruction is to allow simple boundary checking by seeing if the contents of a data register are in the range from zero to an upper limit. This bounds-testing operation is useful for maintaining arrays since you can simply set the upper limit used in the instruction equal to the length of the array (less the length of

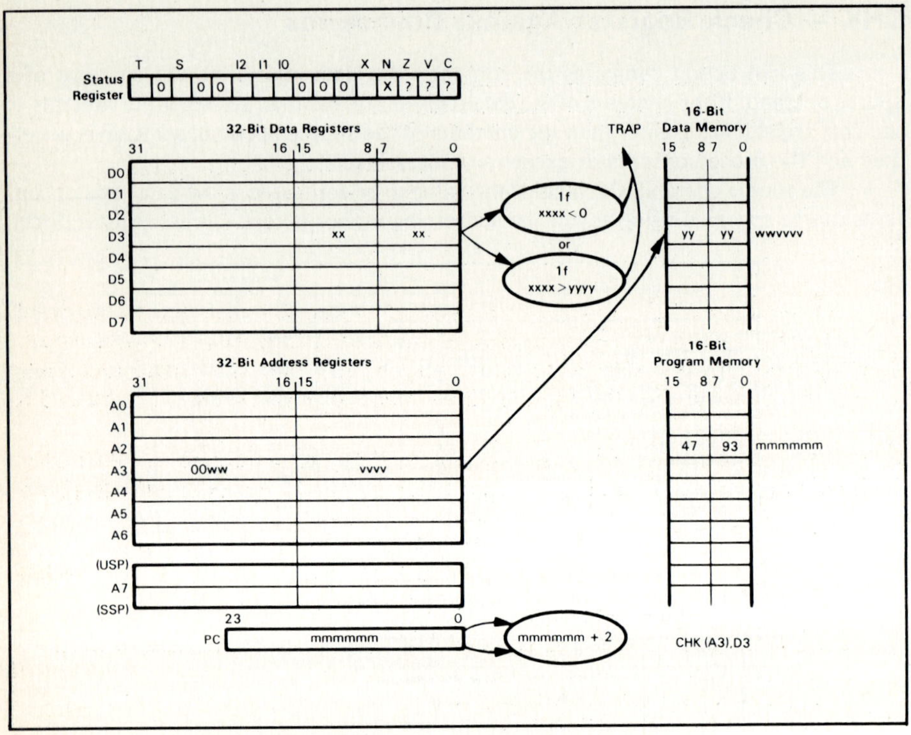

Figure 22-16. Execution of the CHK Instruction Using Address Register Indirect Addressing

one element if the array is considered to start at zero). Then, each time you need to access the array you execute the CHK instruction to ensure that the array bounds have not been violated.

CLR — Clear an Operand

This instruction clears a specified data register or memory location — that is, it loads the data register or memory location with binary zero. The addressing modes that can be used are:

Addressing Modes Allowed	Operand		Destination ea Field	
	Source	Destination	Mode	Register No.
Data register direct		X	000	rrr
Address register direct				
Address register indirect		X	010	rrr
Postincrement register indirect		X	011	rrr
Predecrement register indirect		X	100	rrr
Register indirect with displacement		X	101	rrr
Register indirect with index		X	110	rrr
Absolute short		X	111	000
Absolute long		X	111	001
Program counter relative with displacement				
Program counter relative with index				
Immediate				

The object code format for the CLR instruction is:

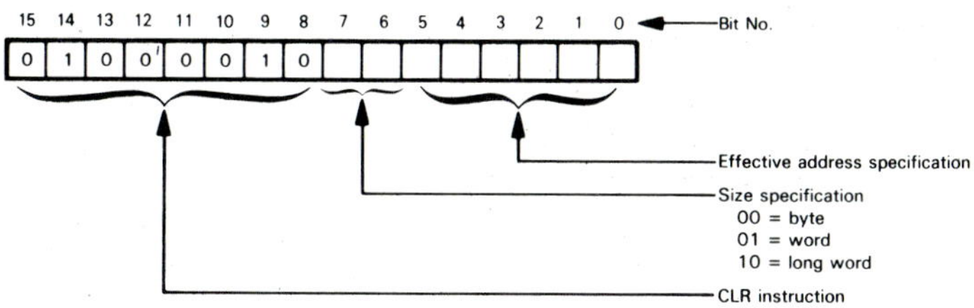

As you can see, the data size for this instruction can be byte, word, or long word.

Figure 22-17 illustrates execution of the CLR instruction with data register direct addressing used to specify the destination. In this figure, an operand size of long word is specified and thus the entire 32-bit contents of register D3 will be cleared to zero.

The CLR instruction always sets the Zero (Z) flag and always clears the Negative (N), Overflow (V), and Carry (C) flags in the status register. The Extend (X) flag is not affected.

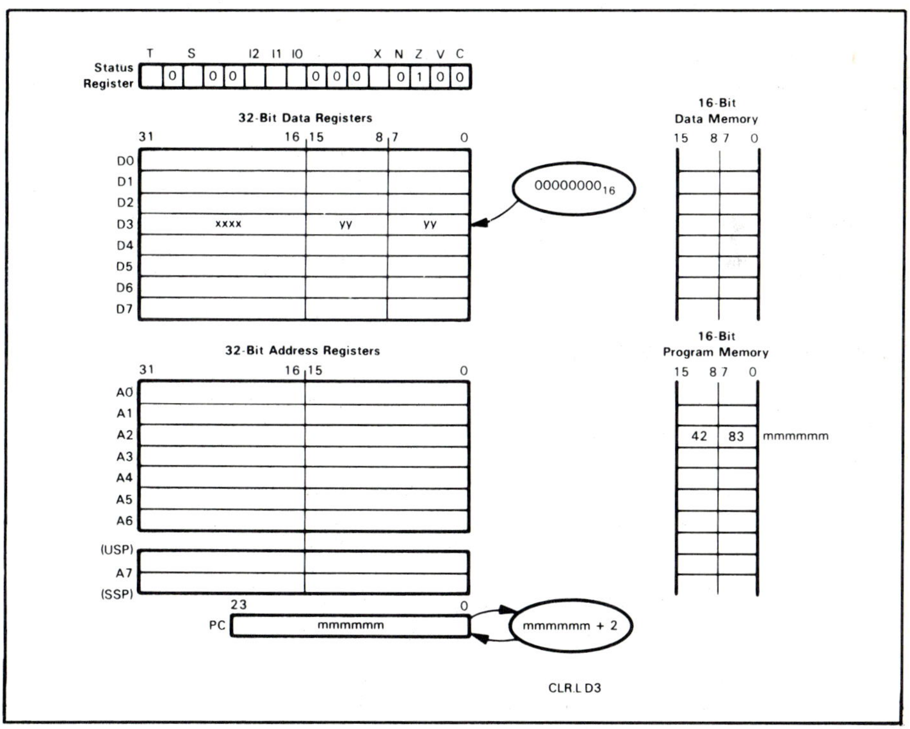

Figure 22-17. Execution of the CLR Instruction Using Data Register Direct Addressing

CMP — Compare

This instruction subtracts the contents of a register or memory location from the contents of a data register and sets the status flags accordingly. Neither the contents of the source operand nor the contents of destination data register are changed. The Carry (C) flag represents a borrow for this instruction.

The addressing modes that can be used to specify the source operand are:

Addressing Modes Allowed	Operand		Source ea Field	
	Source	Destination	Mode	Register No.
Data register direct	X	X	000	rrr
Address register direct	X*		001	rrr
Address register indirect	X		010	rrr
Postincrement register indirect	X		011	rrr
Predecrement register indirect	X		100	rrr
Register indirect with displacement	X		101	rrr
Register indirect with index	X		110	rrr
Absolute short	X		111	000
Absolute long	X		111	001
Program counter relative with displacement	X		111	010
Program counter relative with index	X		111	011
Immediate	X		111	100

*Not allowed if operation size is byte.

The object code format for the CMP instruction is:

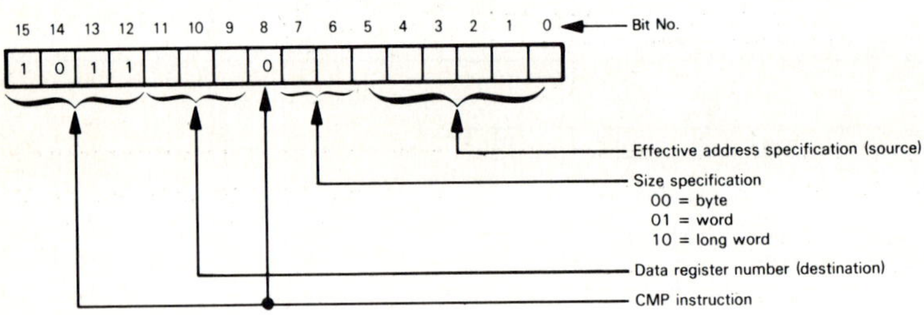

Figure 22-18 illustrates execution of the CMP instruction using the absolute long addressing mode with D3 serving as the destination register. The N, Z, V, and C status flags are all modified by the CMP instruction. The X status is not affected. Using the operands illustrated in Figure 22-18, this is what happens when the CMP $CF2000,D3 instruction is executed:

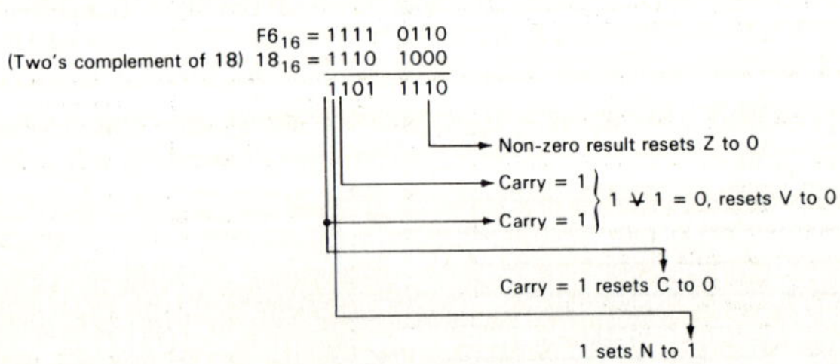

Note that C is the complement of the resultant carry since this is a subtraction and it represents a borrow. Compare instructions are most frequently used to set flags before the execution of conditional branch instructions.

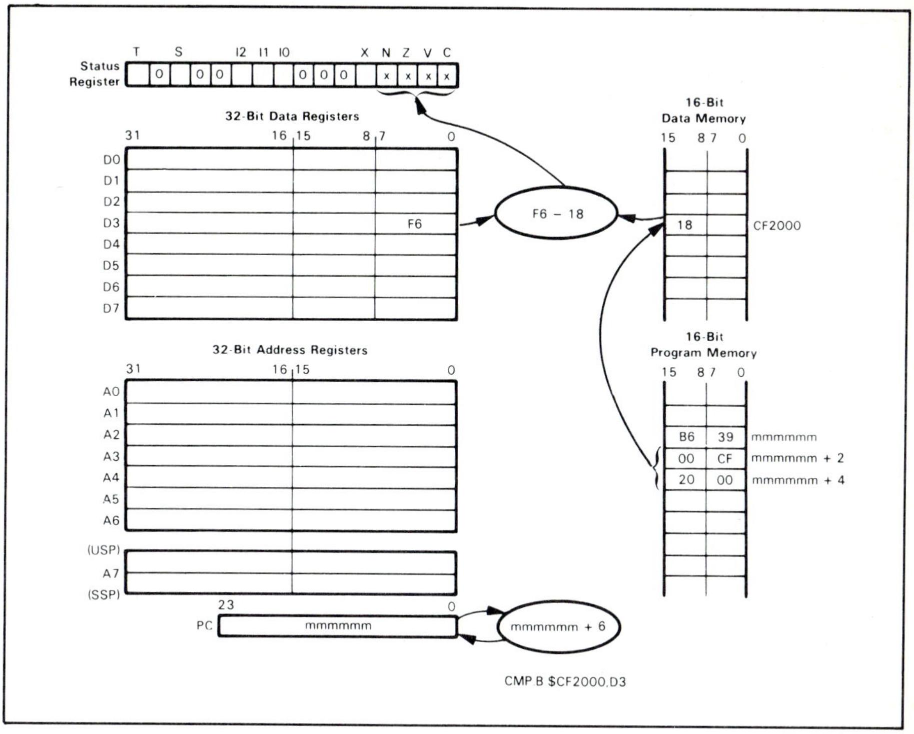

Figure 22-18. Execution of the CMP Instruction Using Absolute Long Addressing

CMPA — Compare Address

This instruction is a special case of the CMP instruction and subtracts the contents of a register or memory location from the contents of an address register and sets the status flags accordingly. Neither the contents of the source operand nor the contents of the destination address register are changed. The Carry (C) flag represents a borrow for this instruction. All addressing modes can be used to specify the source operand:

Addressing Modes Allowed	Operand		Source ea Field	
	Source	Destination	Mode	Register No.
Data register direct	X		000	rrr
Address register direct	X	X	001	rrr
Address register indirect	X		010	rrr
Postincrement register indirect	X		011	rrr
Predecrement register indirect	X		100	rrr
Register indirect with displacement	X		101	rrr
Register indirect with index	X		110	rrr
Absolute short	X		111	000
Absolute long	X		111	001
Program counter relative with displacement	X		111	010
Program counter relative with index	X		111	011
Immediate	X		111	100

The destination must be an address register.

The CMPA instruction's object code is:

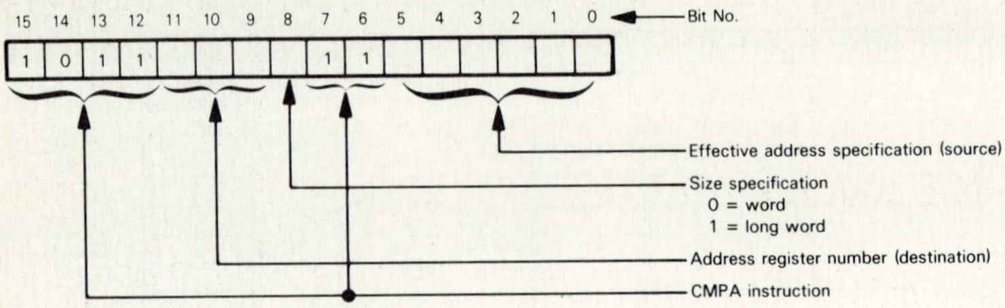

If you compare this object code to that of the CMP instruction, you will see that it is identical except for the size field: the 2-bit pattern that was not used with the CMP instruction is used to indicate a CMPA instruction. Only 16-bit words or 32-bit long words are permitted since the address registers are not capable of handling byte data.

Figure 22-19 illustrates execution of the CMPA instruction with register D3 providing the 32-bit source operand and register A3 serving as the destination.

If you specify a 16-bit word source operand instead of a long word, the source operand is sign-extended to a long word operand and the compare is performed on the specified address register using all 32 bits.

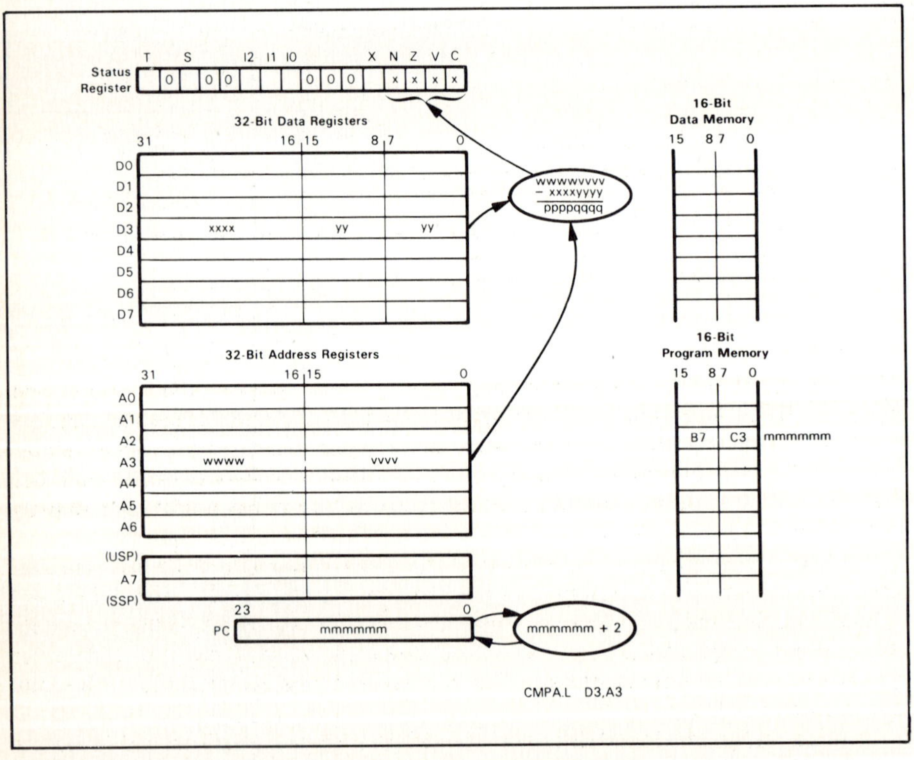

Figure 22-19. Execution of the CMPA Instruction Using Data Register Direct Addressing

The status flags are affected in the same way by the CMPA instruction as they were by the CMP instruction. The Negative (N), Zero (Z), Overflow (V), and Carry (C) flags are all affected. The Extend (X) status flag is not affected.

CMPI — Compare Immediate

This instruction subtracts the immediate data present in the succeeding program memory location from a destination operand and sets the status flags accordingly. The contents of the destination are not changed.

The addressing modes that can be used to specify the destination operand are:

Addressing Modes Allowed	Operand		Destination ea Field	
	Source	Destination	Mode	Register No.
Data register direct		X	000	rrr
Address register direct				
Address register indirect		X	010	rrr
Postincrement register indirect		X	011	rrr
Predecrement register indirect		X	100	rrr
Register indirect with displacement		X	101	rrr
Register indirect with index		X	110	rrr
Absolute short		X	111	000
Absolute long		X	111	001
Program counter relative with displacement				
Program counter relative with index				
Immediate	X			

The object code for the CMPI instruction is:

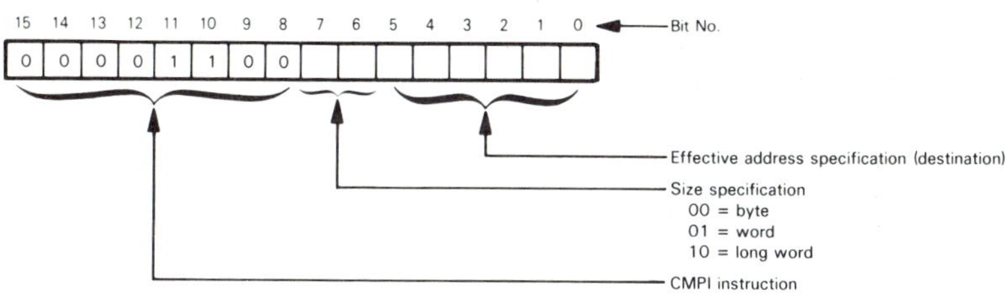

The size of the CMPI operation can be specified as byte, word, or long word. The immediate data follows the instruction word in memory and must match the specified operation size. Thus, either one or two words of immediate data must follow the instruction operation code in program memory. If the instruction specifies a byte operand, the low-order (second) byte of the immediate data word is used. The assembler automatically places the byte correctly.

Figure 22-20 illustrates execution of the CMPI instruction with an operation size of word (16 bits) using absolute short addressing. As you can see, the word following the instruction operation code contains the immediate data (4544_{16} in this example). The absolute short address, which is sign-extended to designate the destination operand, follows the immediate data. The immediate data is subtracted from the contents of location 0420_{16}.

After the instruction CMPI #$4544,$420 is executed, the flags will be set as described in the following illustration.

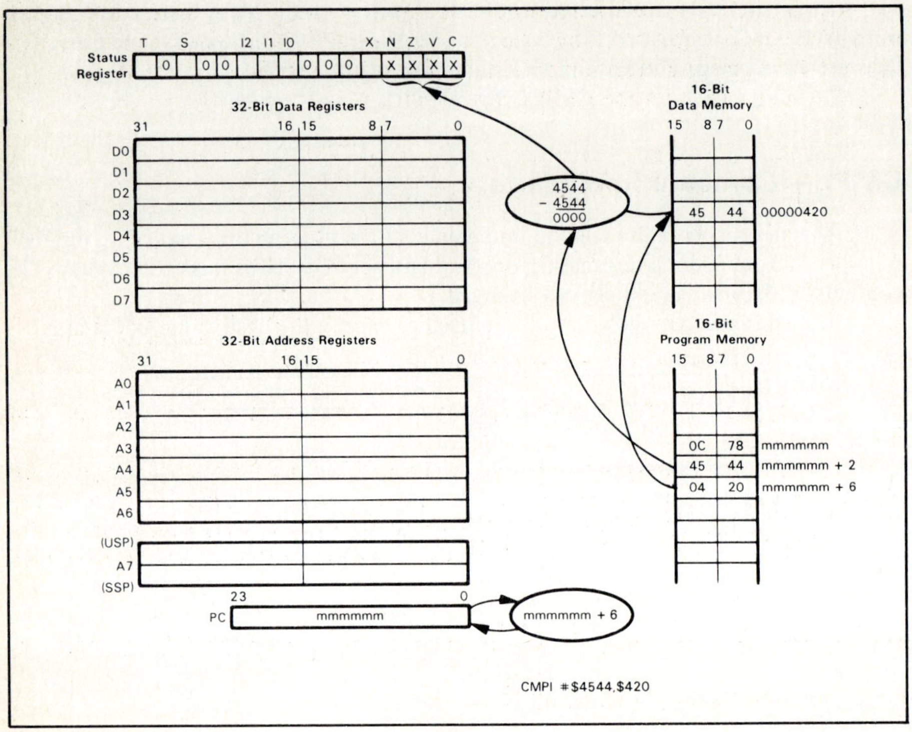

Figure 22-20. Execution of the CMPI Instruction Using Absolute Short Addressing

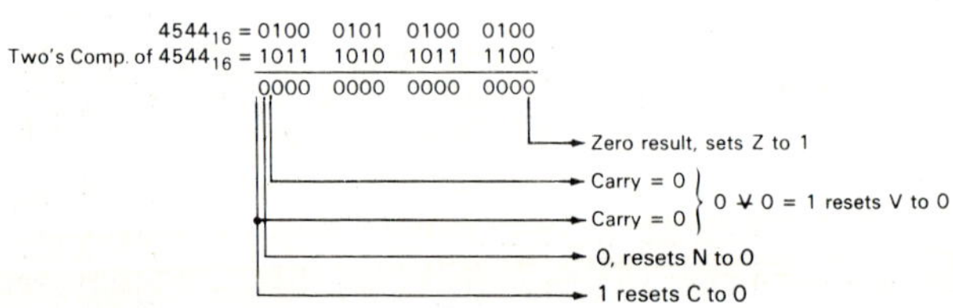

Note that C is the complement of the resultant carry since this is a subtraction and it represents a borrow.

The contents of the destination operand are not affected by the comparison. The Negative (N), Zero (Z), Overflow (V), and Carry (C) status flags are set to reflect the results of the subtraction, with C being set if a borrow is generated. The Extend (X) status flag is not affected.

CMPM — Compare Memory

This instruction compares the contents of two memory locations and sets the status flags according to the results of the comparison. Both the source and destination operands and addresses are held in address registers and the postincrement register indirect addressing mode is always used. The contents of the source memory location and destination memory location remain unchanged by the comparison operation.

The object code for the CMPM instruction is:

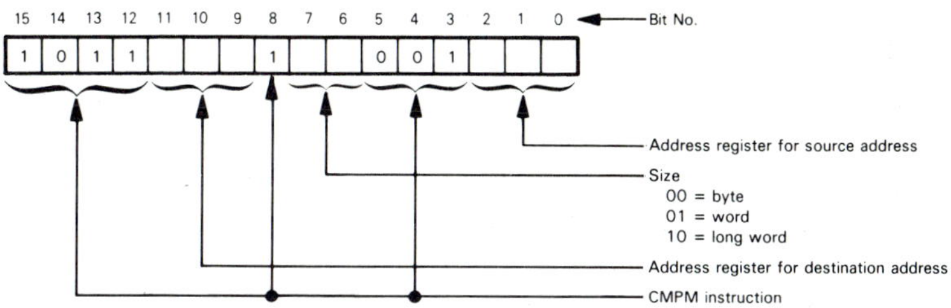

The CMPM instruction can compare bytes, words, or long words of data from memory.

Figure 22-21 illustrates execution of the CMPM instruction with register A4 providing the address of the source operand and register A1 providing the address of the destination operand. The contents of these two address registers are used to access the operands in memory. After the operands have been accessed and the comparisons

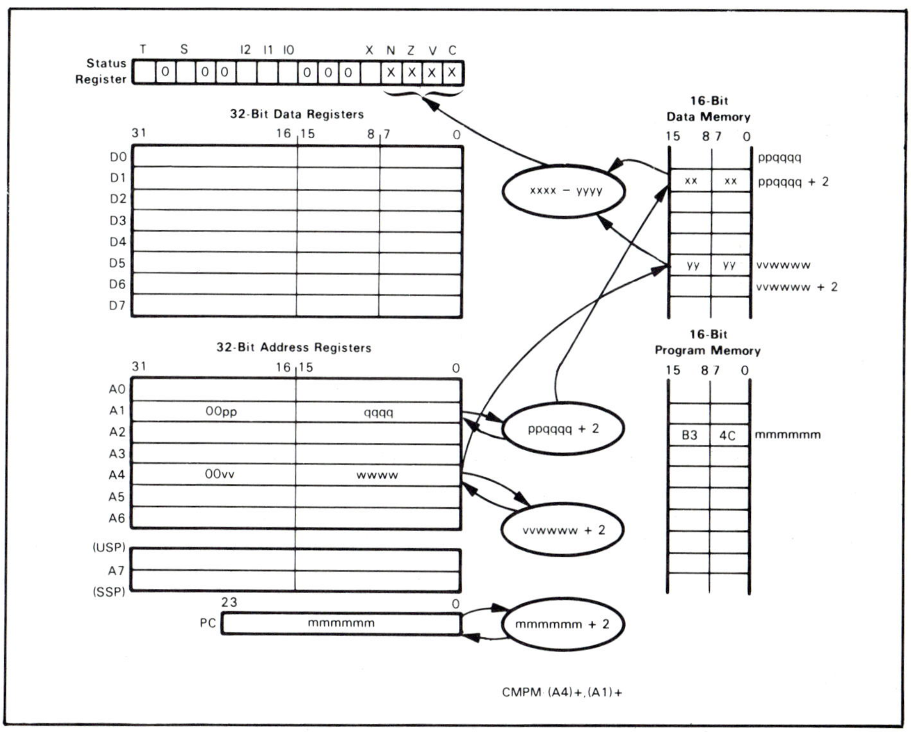

Figure 22-21. Execution of the CMPM Instruction

made, the contents of both address registers are incremented. In Figure 22-21, an operand size of word is being used and thus the address registers will be incremented by two at the conclusion of the instruction. If you specify an operand size of byte, then the address registers will be incremented by 1, and if a long word size were specified, the address register contents would be incremented by 4.

The contents of neither memory location are modified by the comparison but the Negative (N), Zero (Z), Overflow (V), and Carry (C) flags in the status register are affected by the CMPM instruction. The Extend (X) status flag is not affected.

This version of the Compare instruction could be used to implement a string search. It could serve as one step of an instruction loop that searches a string, beginning with the lowest string address and ending with the highest string address. For each step of the search, the destination operand is compared to the source operand. The Z8000 microprocessor provides several similar compare and increment instructions, although that processor's versions are more sophisticated; they also maintain a counter which modifies a status bit that can be tested to determine when the entire string has been compared. The MC68000 CMPM instruction provides no such capabilities and this function would have to be provided separately using the Decrement and Branch (DB_{cc}) instruction.

DB_{CC} — Test Condition, Decrement and Branch

This instruction tests both the status flags and the value in a data register. It first tests to determine if the condition specified by cc is met. If the condition is met, then the next instruction in sequence is executed. If the condition specified is not met, then the contents of the specified data register are decremented by 1. If that data register contains −1, the next instruction in sequence is executed.

If the condition is not met and the specified data register does not contain −1 after being decremented, then program control is transferred to an address relative to the current value of the program counter. The displacement from the location of the instruction can be from −32766 to +32769. The object code for the DB_{cc} instruction is:

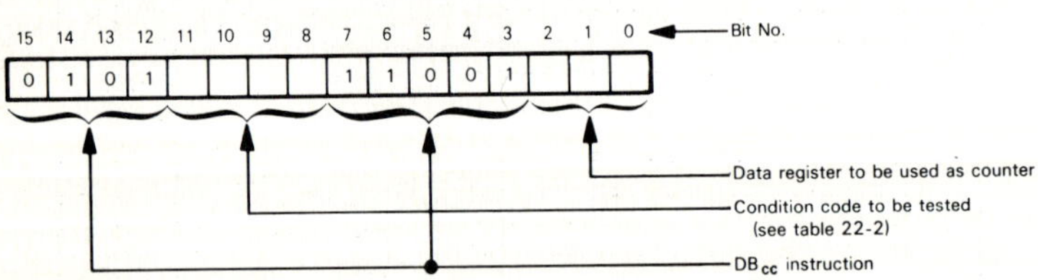

The DB_{cc} instruction always consists of two 16-bit words: the first is the instruction word and the second, the 16-bit displacement. Bits 8 through 11 of the instruction word specify the condition which is to be tested. **Table 22-2 lists the conditions that can be used with this instruction** and the values that are computed from the values of the flags in the status register to determine whether the test is successful.

Figure 22-22 illustrates the execution of the DBNE instruction. If the Zero (Z) status flag is equal to 0, the program counter contents are simply incremented by 4 and the next instruction in sequence is executed. If the Zero (Z) flag is set to 1, the low-order 16 bits of data register D0 are decremented by 1. If the low-order 16 bits of D0

Table 22-2. DB_{cc} Conditional Tests

Mnemonics(cc)	Condition	Condition Field	Test
T	True	0000	1
F	False	0001	0
HI	High	0010	$\overline{C} \wedge \overline{Z}$
LS	Low or same	0011	$C \vee Z$
CC	Carry clear	0100	$\overline{C}$
CS	Carry set	0101	C
NE	Not equal	0110	$\overline{Z}$
EQ	Equal	0111	Z
VC	Overflow clear	1000	$\overline{V}$
VS	Overflow set	1001	V
PL	Plus	1010	$\overline{N}$
MI	Minus	1011	N
GE	Greater or equal	1100	$(N \wedge V) \vee (\overline{N} \wedge \overline{V})$
LT	Less than	1101	$(N \wedge \overline{V}) \vee (\overline{N} \wedge V)$
GT	Greater than	1110	$(N \wedge V \wedge \overline{Z}) \vee (\overline{N} \wedge \overline{V} \wedge \overline{Z})$
LE	Less or equal	1111	$Z \vee (N \wedge \overline{V}) \vee (\overline{N} \wedge V)$

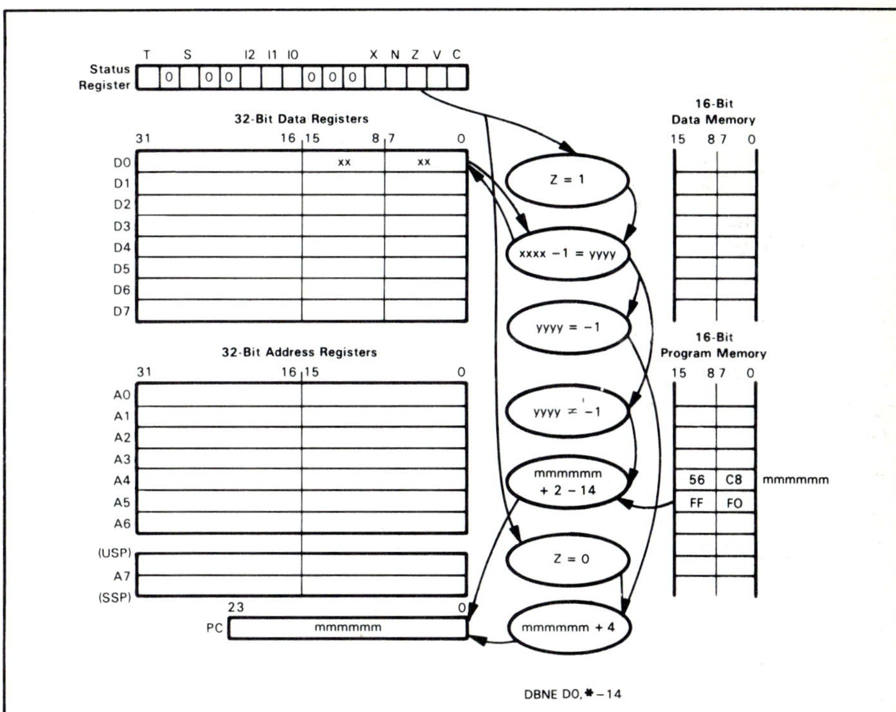

Figure 22-22. Execution of the DBNE Instruction

contain −1 after being decremented, then the program counter contents are simply incremented by 4 and the next instruction in sequence is executed.

If the Zero (Z) status flag is equal to 0 and the results obtained after decrementing the contents of register D0 do not = −1, this indicates that the loop is not complete and a branch is executed by adding the sign-extended 16-bit displacement to the value contained in the program counter after it has been incremented by two. Thus, **this branch logic is the reverse of that used with the conditional branch instruction (B_{cc}):** with B_{cc} the displacement value was added to the program counter when the condition specified (cc) was met, while **with the DB_{cc} the branch is taken if the condition (cc) is not met and if a sufficient number of iterations through the loop have not been performed.**

The DB_{cc} instruction eases the implementation of repetitive loops since it both tests the condition code register and provides a loop counter in one of the data registers. For a thorough discussion of this instruction and its use refer to Chapter 6.

No status flags are affected by the DB_{cc} instruction.

DIVS — Signed Divide

This instruction divides a 32-bit operand in the destination data register by a 16-bit operand in the source operand. The operation is performed using two's complement binary arithmetic. A 32-bit result is obtained in the destination data register.

The source operand can be specified using any address modes except address register direct:

Addressing Modes Allowed	Operand		Source ea Field	
	Source	Destination	Mode	Register No.
Data register direct	X	X	000	rrr
Address register direct				
Address register indirect	X		010	rrr
Postincrement register indirect	X		011	rrr
Predecrement register indirect	X		100	rrr
Register indirect with displacement	X		101	rrr
Register indirect with index	X		110	rrr
Absolute short	X		111	000
Absolute long	X		111	001
Program counter relative with displacement	X		111	010
Program counter relative with index	X		111	011
Immediate	X		111	100

The 32-bit result that is obtained by the DIVS instruction consists of the quotient in the least significant 16 bits of the destination data register and the remainder in the most significant 16 bits. The sign of the remainder is always the same as the sign of the dividend unless the remainder is equal to zero.

The object code for the DIVS instruction is:

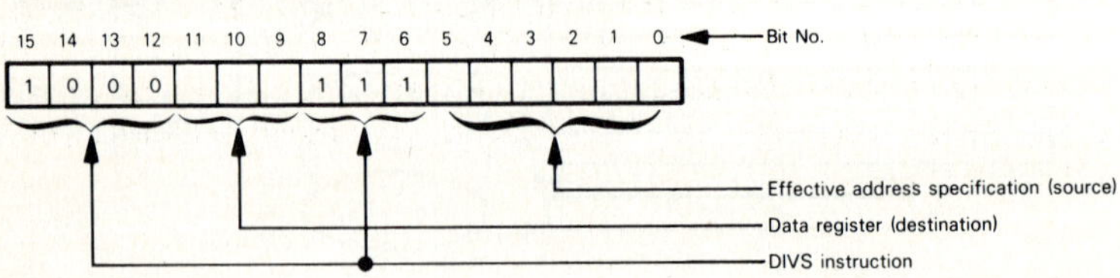

Figure 22-23 illustrates execution of the DIVS instruction using address register indirect addressing to specify the source operand. After the instruction illustrated has

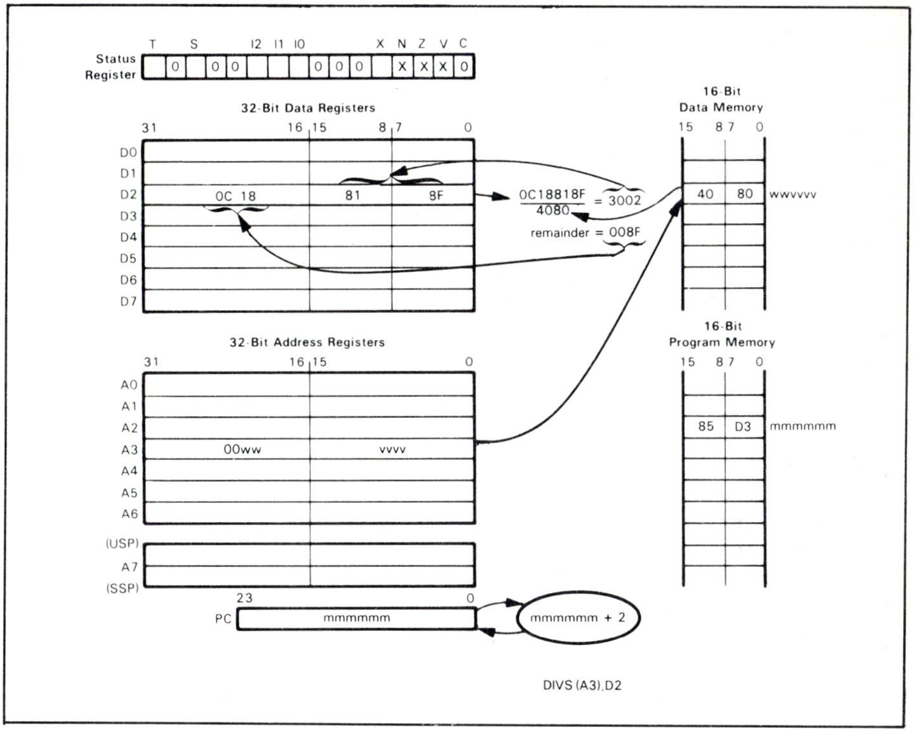

Figure 22-23. Execution of the DIVS Instruction Using Address Register Indirect Addressing

been executed, register D2 will hold the remainder ($008F_{16}$) in the most significant 16 bits and the quotient (3002_{16}) in the least significant 16 bits.

The Negative (N) flag in the status register will be set if the quotient is negative and cleared otherwise. If an overflow occurs, the state of the N flag is undefined. The Zero (Z) flag will be set if the quotient is zero and cleared otherwise. Its state is also undefined if an overflow occurs. Overflow will occur if the source operand is larger than the destination operand. This will be detected before the division begins. The Overflow (V) flag will be set and the operands will be unchanged. The Carry (C) flag is always cleared. The Extend (X) flag is not affected.

If division by zero is attempted, the division instruction is aborted, a TRAP is generated, and exception processing is automatically initiated by the processor. The exception vector generated during this processing will be 014_{16} (vector #5) which is assigned to zero divide traps. Refer to the TRAP instruction for a description of the sequence of events that occur during a TRAP and see the discussion of exception processing in Chapter 15.

DIVU — Unsigned Divide

This instruction divides a 32-bit operand in the destination data register by a 16-bit source operand. The division is performed using unsigned binary arithmetic. A

32-bit result is produced and is held in the destination data register. The source operand can be specified using any addressing mode except address register direct:

Addressing Modes Allowed	Operand		Source ea Field	
	Source	Destination	Mode	Register No.
Data register direct	X	X	000	rrr
Address register direct				
Address register indirect	X		010	rrr
Postincrement register indirect	X		011	rrr
Predecrement register indirect	X		100	rrr
Register indirect with displacement	X		101	rrr
Register indirect with index	X		110	rrr
Absolute short	X		111	000
Absolute long	X		111	001
Program counter relative with displacement	X		111	010
Program counter relative with index	X		111	011
Immediate	X		111	100

The 32-bit result obtained from the DIVU instruction is stored in the specified destination register with the remainder in the most significant 16 bits and the quotient in the least significant 16 bits of the register.

The object code for the DIVU instruction is:

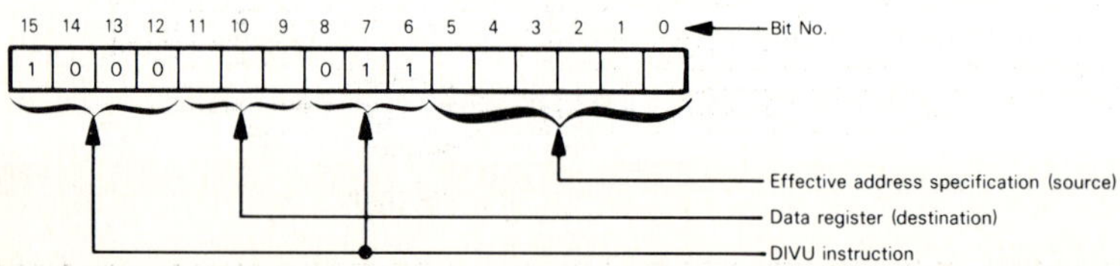

Figure 22-24 illustrates execution of the DIVU instruction with address register indirect addressing used to specify the source operand. Using the operands shown in Figure 22-24, after the DIVU instruction is executed the remainder value ($004C_{16}$) will be held in the most significant 16 bits of register D2, and the quotient ($5D25_{16}$) will be held in the least significant 16 bits of register D2.

The Negative (N) status flag is set if the most significant bit of the quotient is set and is cleared otherwise. If an overflow occurs, the state of the N flag is undefined. The other status flags are affected in the same way as by the DIV instruction.

If a divide by zero is attempted, a TRAP is generated and exception processing is automatically initiated by the processor. The exception vector generated will be 014_{16} (vector #5) which is the vector assigned to the zero divide trap. Refer to the TRAP instruction for a description of the sequence of events that occurs during a TRAP and see the discussion of exception processing in Chapter 15.

EOR — Exclusive OR Logical

This instruction performs a bitwise exclusive-OR of the contents of a data register with the contents of the destination operand and stores the results in the destination. The destination operand can be specified using the addressing modes shown below.

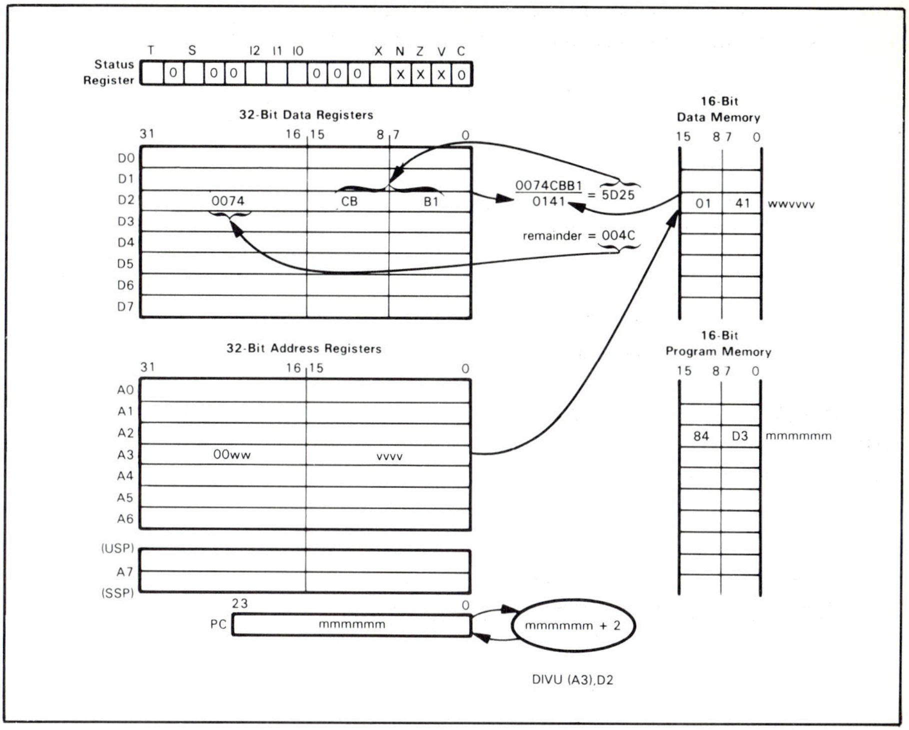

Figure 22-24. Execution of the DIVU Instruction Using Address Register Indirect Addressing

Addressing Modes Allowed	Operand		Destination ea Field	
	Source	Destination	Mode	Register No.
Data register direct	X	X	000	rrr
Address register direct				
Address register indirect		X	010	rrr
Postincrement register indirect		X	011	rrr
Predecrement register indirect		X	100	rrr
Register indirect with displacement		X	101	rrr
Register indirect with index		X	110	rrr
Absolute short		X	111	000
Absolute long		X	111	001
Program counter relative with displacement				
Program counter relative with index				
Immediate				

The object code for the EOR instruction is:

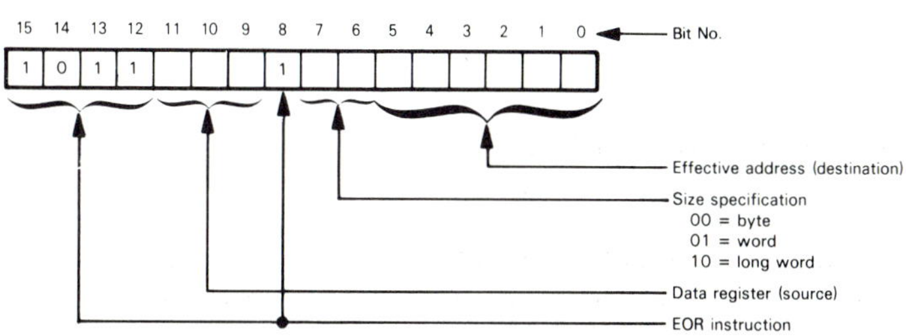

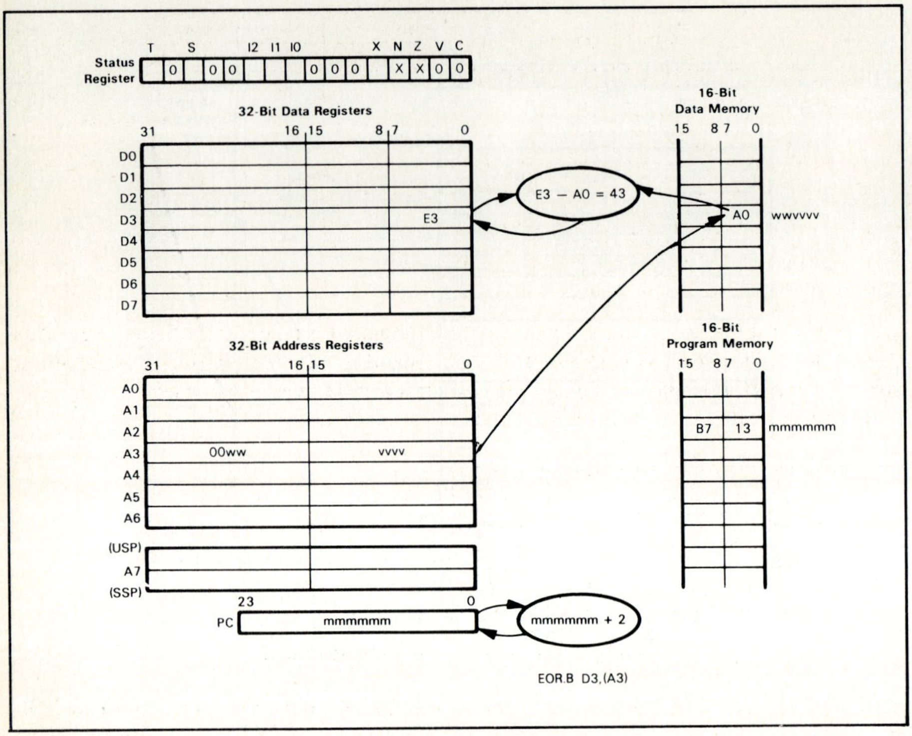

Figure 22-25. Execution of the EOR Instruction Using Address Register Indirect Addressing

Figure 22-25 illustrates execution of the EOR instruction using address register indirect addressing. Using the operand values shown in this figure, the least significant 8 bits of register D3 will contain 43_{16} after the EOR.B instruction is executed.

Note that the logical exclusive-OR is the same as a bit-by-bit "not equal" operation; that is, the output is 1 if and only if the inputs are not equal. **EOR is used to test for changes in bit status and to calculate parity and other error-detecting and correcting codes.**

The Negative (N) status flag is set if the most significant bit of the result is set. It is cleared otherwise. The Zero (Z) flag is set if the result is 0 and is cleared otherwise. The Overflow (V) and Carry (C) status flags are always cleared. The Extend (X) status flag is not affected.

EORI — Exclusive or Immediate

This instruction performs a bitwise exclusive-OR of the immediate data present in the succeeding program memory locations with the destination operand. The result is stored in the destination. The addressing modes that follow can be used to specify the destination location.

Addressing Modes Allowed	Operand		Destination ea Field	
	Source	Destination	Mode	Register No.
Data register direct		X	000	rrr
Address register direct				
Address register indirect		X	010	rrr
Postincrement register indirect		X	011	rrr
Predecrement register indirect		X	100	rrr
Register indirect with displacement		X	101	rrr
Register indirect with index		X	110	rrr
Absolute short		X	111	000
Absolute long		X	111	001
Program counter relative with displacement				
Program counter relative with index				
Immediate	X			
Status Register		X	111	100

Note that the destination operand may be the condition codes or the entire status register. **If the destination is the entire status register, this is a privileged instruction and can only be executed while the processor is in the supervisor mode.**

The object code for the EORI instruction is:

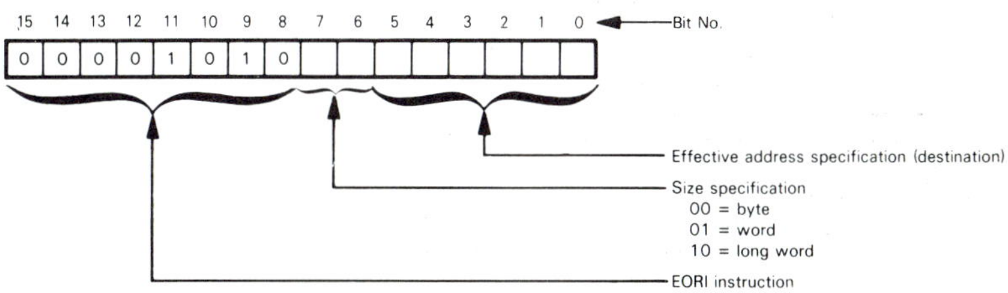

The size of the EORI operation can be specified as byte, word, or long word. The immediate data follows the instruction word in memory and must match the specified operation size. Thus, either one or two words of immediate data must follow the instruction operation code in program memory. If the instruction specifies a byte operand, the low-order (second) byte of the immediate data word is used. The assembler automatically places the byte correctly. If the instruction refers to the status register and the operation size is byte, the destination is the low-order byte of the status register and only the condition codes are affected. If the operation size is word, the entire status register is the destination and the instruction is privileged.

Figure 22-26 illustrates the execution of the EORI instruction with an operation size of word (16 bits) using absolute short addressing. As you can see, the word following the instruction operation code contains the immediate data ($B31C_{16}$ in this example). The absolute short address, which is sign-extended to designate the destination operand, follows the immediate data in program memory. The immediate data is exclusive ORed to the contents of the memory location 420_{16}.

The Negative (N) and Zero (Z) status flags will be modified by the EORI instruction according to the results obtained. The Overflow (V) and Carry (C) status flags will be cleared by the EOR instruction. The Extend (X) status flag is not affected. Of course, if the destination of the instruction is the condition codes, or the entire status register, then the condition codes are affected according to the result of the operation.

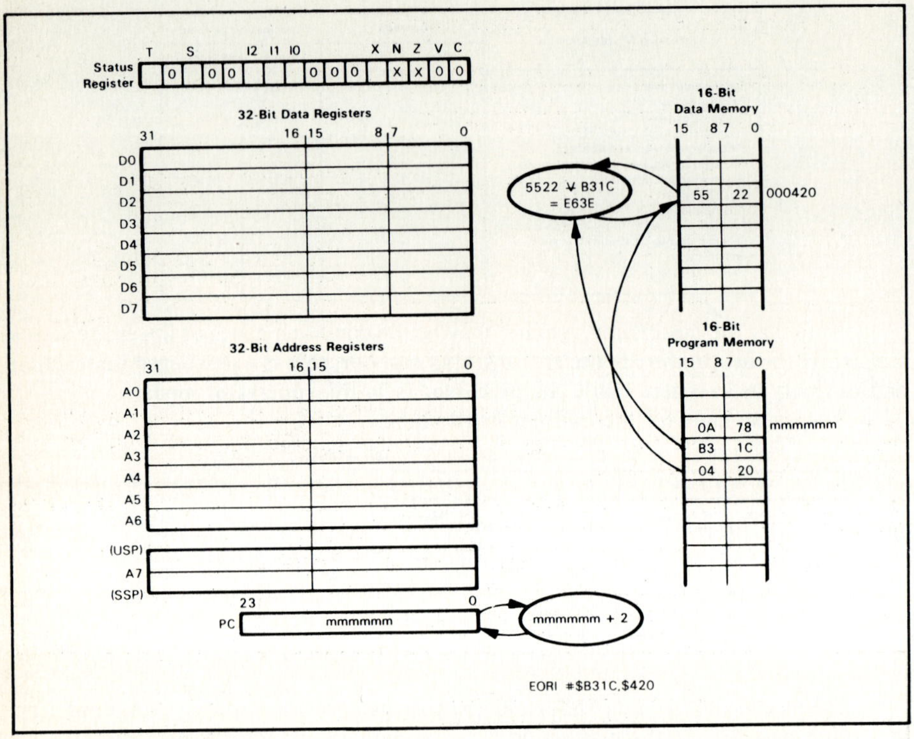

Figure 22-26. Execution of the EORI Instruction Using Absolute Short Addressing

EXG — Exchange Registers

This instruction exchanges the contents of one 32-bit register with another. The registers involved can be either two data registers, two address registers, or an address register and a data register.

Only register direct addressing modes are allowed:

Addressing Modes Allowed	Operand		Source ea Field	
	Source	Destination	Mode	Register No.
Data register direct	X	X	000	rrr
Address register direct	X	X	001	rrr
Address register indirect				
Postincrement register indirect				
Predecrement register indirect				
Register indirect with displacement				
Register indirect with index				
Absolute short				
Absolute long				
Program counter relative with displacement				
Program counter relative with index				
Immediate				

The object code for this EXG instruction is:

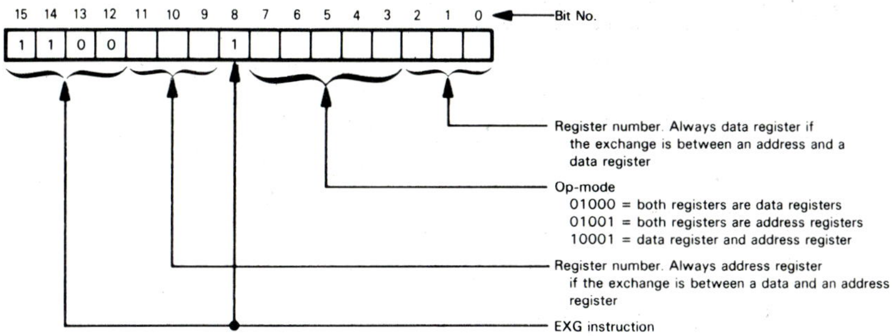

Figure 22-27 illustrates execution of the EXG instruction with the contents of registers D2 and A1 being exchanged. Note that the entire 32-bit contents of both registers are always exchanged.

EXG is, of course, symmetrical — for instance, EXG A1,D2 and EXG D2,A1 are the same operation.

None of the status flags is affected by the EXG instruction.

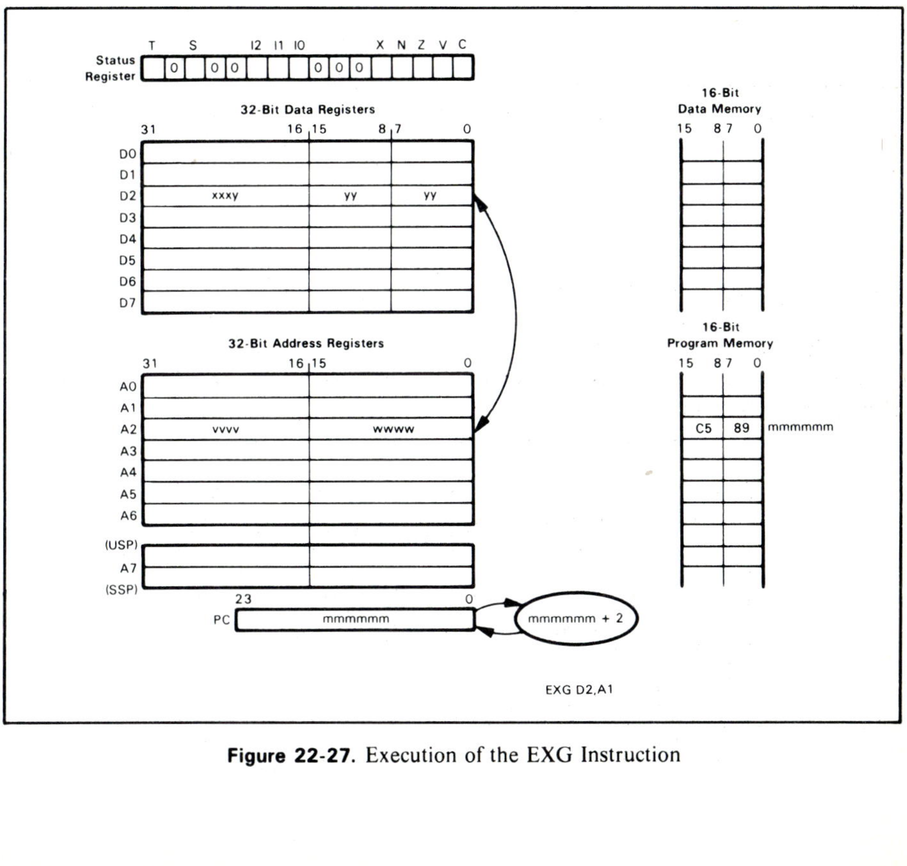

Figure 22-27. Execution of the EXG Instruction

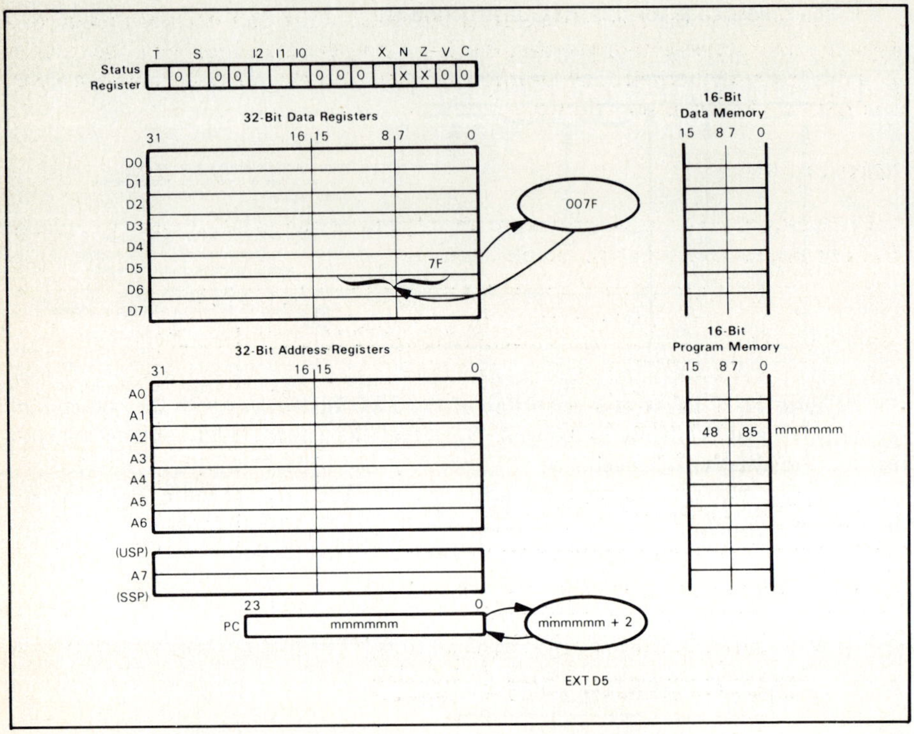

Figure 22-28. Execution of the EXT Instruction

EXT — Sign Extend

This instruction causes the sign-bit (bit 7) of a byte to be extended through bits 8-15 of a data register word, or the sign bit of a word (bit 15) to be extended through bits 16-32 of a data register. The object code for the EXT instruction is:

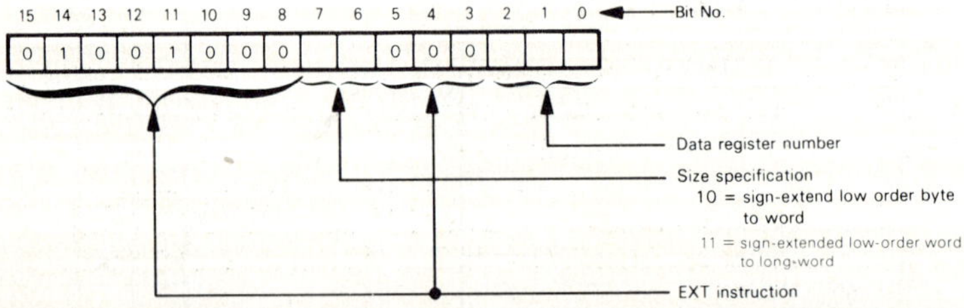

Figure 22-28 illustrates execution of the EXT instruction with an operation size of word. Since bit 7 in register D5 is 0, bits 8 through 15 will all be set to 0 by execution of the EXT instruction. If an operation size of long word is specified, bits 16 through 31 will be set to the value of bit 15. Thus, if the instruction illustrated in Figure 22-28 were followed by the instruction EXT.L D5, it would cause bits 16 through 31 of register D5 also to be set to 0.

The Negative (N) status flag is set if the result of the EXT operation produces a negative number and is cleared otherwise. The Zero (Z) status flag is set if the result is 0, and is cleared otherwise. The Overflow (V) and Carry (C) flags are always cleared. The Extend (X) flag is not affected.

JMP — Jump

This instruction causes an unconditional jump to the specified memory address. The addressing modes that can be used are:

Addressing Modes Allowed	Operand		Destination ea Field	
	Source	Destination	Mode	Register No.
Data register direct				
Address register direct				
Address register indirect		X	010	rrr
Postincrement register indirect				
Predecrement register indirect				
Register indirect with displacement		X	101	rrr
Register indirect with index		X	110	rrr
Absolute short		X	111	000
Absolute long		X	111	001
Program counter relative with displacement		X	111	010
Program counter relative with index		X	111	011
Immediate				

The object code for the JMP instruction is:

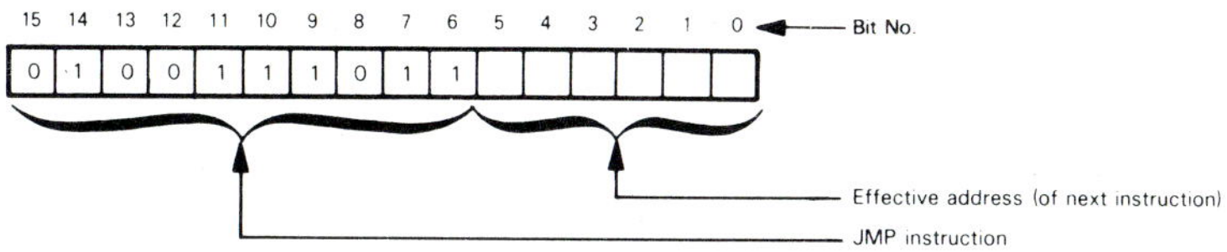

Figure 22-29 illustrates execution of the Jump instruction using address register indirect adressing. When the JMP (A5) instruction is executed, the program counter will be loaded with the address held in register A5.

None of the status flags is affected by the JMP. The previous value of the program counter is lost.

JSR — Jump to Subroutine

This instruction causes an unconditional jump to the specified memory address, saving the old value of the program counter on the system stack. The addressing modes that can be used with the JSR instruction are:

Addressing Modes Allowed	Operand		Destination ea Field	
	Source	Destination	Mode	Register No.
Data register direct				
Address register direct				
Address register indirect		X	010	rrr
Postincrement register indirect				
Predecrement register indirect				
Register indirect with displacement		X	101	rrr
Register indirect with index		X	110	rrr
Absolute short		X	111	000
Absolute long		X	111	001
Program counter relative with displacement		X	111	010
Program counter relative with index		X	111	011
Immediate				

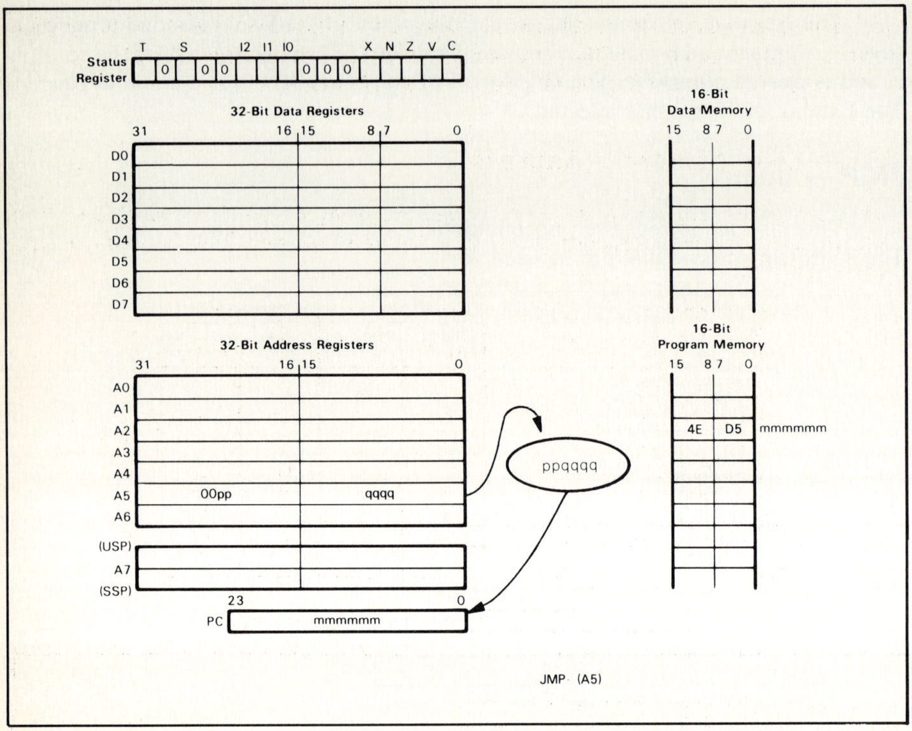

Figure 22-29. Execution of the JMP Instruction Using Address Register Indirect Addressing

The object code for the JSR instruction is:

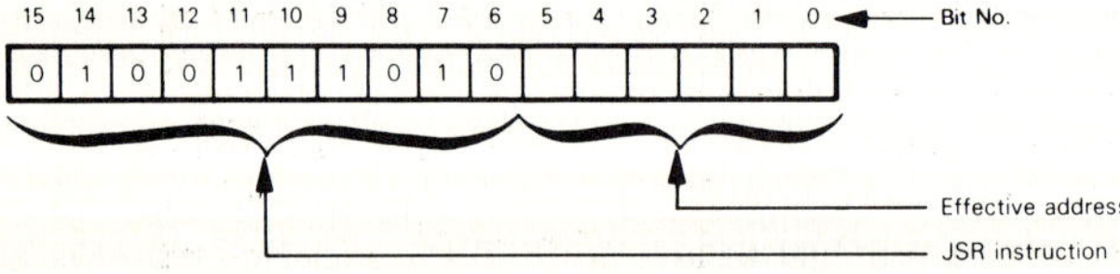

Figure 22-30 illustrates execution of the JSR instruction using absolute short addressing. After the instruction illustrated in Figure 22-30 is executed, program execution will continue beginning at memory location 000400_{16}. The value of the program counter at the end of the JSR instruction (mmmmmm+4) will have been saved on the user stack. The final value of the user stack pointer (USP) will be 4 less than its original value.

JSR is the same as JMP, except that JSR saves the old value of the program counter on the stack, thus providing a subroutine linkage. An RTS instruction at the end of the subroutine can transfer control back to the instruction immediately following JSR, provided that the subroutine has not changed the return address or the stack pointer contents. JSR provides an unconditional, absolute jump-to-subroutine capability, as compared to the relative jump-to-subroutine capability provided by BSR. However, note that JSR *+300 has exactly the same effect as BSR *+300.

None of the status flags is affected by the JSR instruction.

LEA — Load Effective Address

This instruction forms an effective address using one of the available address modes and loads that address into the specified address register. The addressing modes that can be used are:

Addressing Modes Allowed	Operand		Source ea Field	
	Source	Destination	Mode	Register No.
Data register direct				
Address register direct		X		
Address register indirect	X		010	rrr
Postincrement register indirect				
Predecrement register indirect				
Register indirect with displacement	X		101	rrr
Register indirect with index	X		110	rrr
Absolute short	X		111	000
Absolute long	X		111	001
Program counter relative with displacement	X		111	010
Program counter relative with index	X		111	011
Immediate				

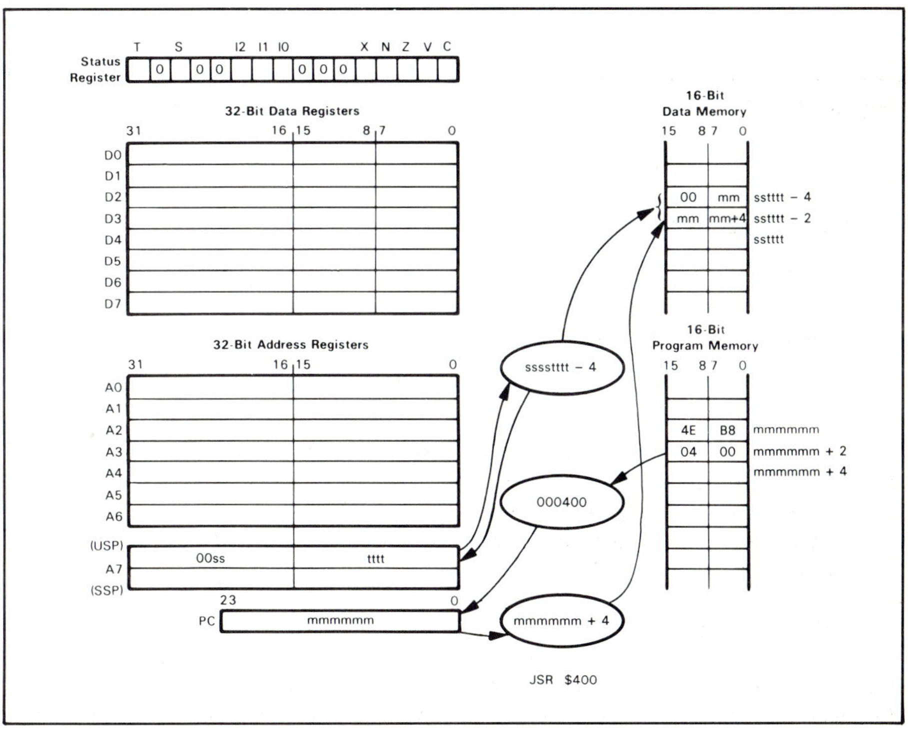

Figure 22-30. Execution of the JSR Instruction Using Absolute Short Addressing

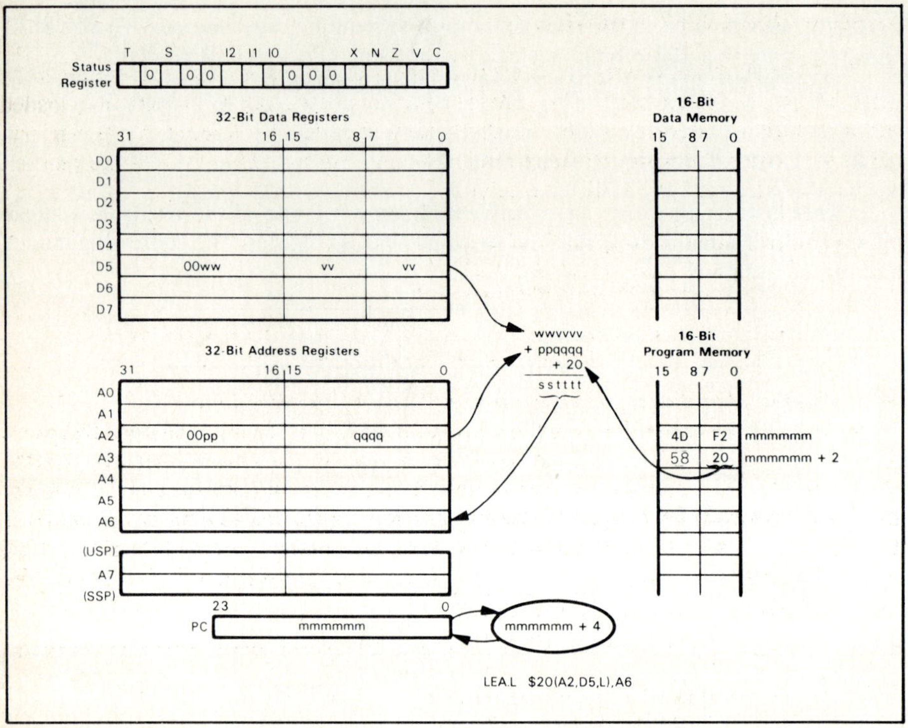

Figure 22-31. Execution of the LEA Instruction Using Address Register Indirect with Long Index Addressing

The object code for the LEA instruction is:

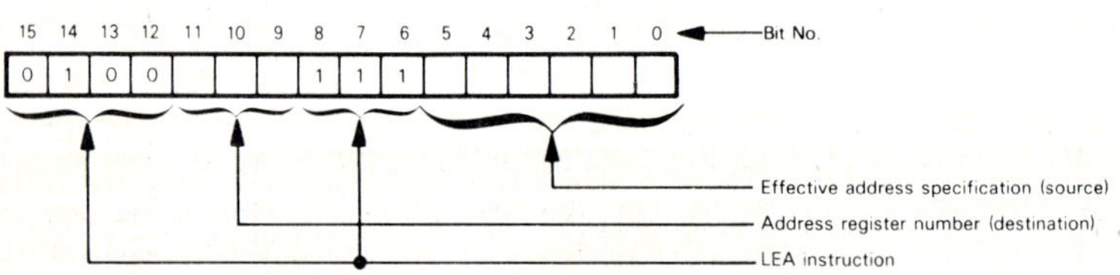

Figure 22-31 illustrates execution of the LEA instruction using address register indirect with index addressing. In this figure, the contents of register D5 are added to the contents of register A2 and then the displacement value (20_{16}) included after the instruction word is added to those two 32-bit values. The resultant 32-bit address (sstttt) is then loaded into register A6.

As you can see, when the LEA instruction is executed, the computed address is loaded into the destination register. That is to say, the memory address, rather than the contents of the addressed memory word, is loaded into the destination register.

None of the status flags is affected by execution of the LEA instruction.

LINK — Link and Allocate

This instruction causes the current contents of a specified address register to be pushed onto the system stack. The updated contents of the stack pointer are then loaded into the specified address register. Finally, a sign-extended two's complement displacement value from the word following the instruction word is added to the stack pointer. The object code for the LINK instruction is:

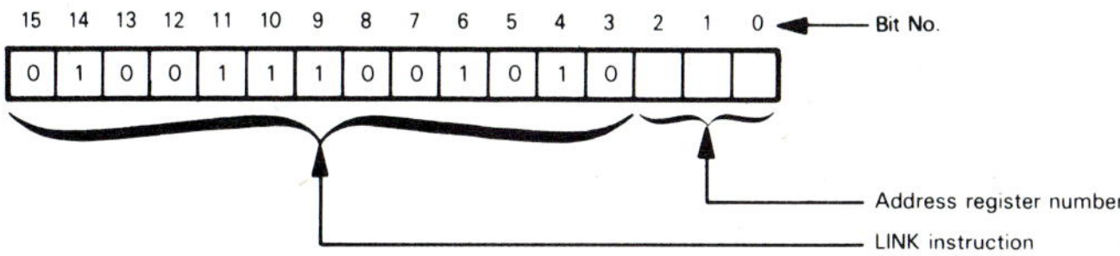

Figure 22-32 illustrates execution of the LINK instruction.

The LINK instruction uses the stack pointer, one of the other address registers, as a "frame pointer" and a displacement value. This instruction will typically be used at the beginning of a subroutine. The LINK instruction first pushes the current value of the frame pointer onto the system stack. The decremented value of the stack pointer is then loaded into the frame pointer so that it now points to the new top of the stack which will become the top of the current frame. Finally, the displacement included with the

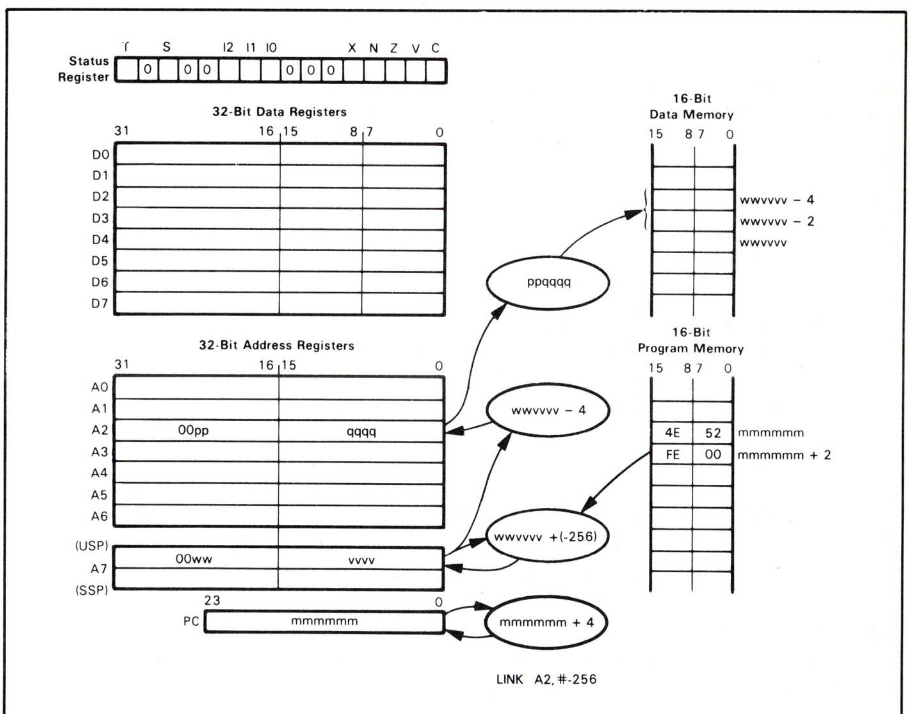

Figure 22-32. Execution of the LINK Instruction

LINK instruction is used to decrement the stack pointer so that it is displaced to clear a space ("frame") in memory for storage of such things as local variables and parameters. These variables can then be accessed via the frame pointer by the subroutine that is executing. Upon completion of a subroutine, the Unlink (UNLK) instruction is used to clear up the stack.

Consider the following sequence. In the illustration that follows, the stack pointer contains an address of bb after procedure A executes a JSR to procedure B. The stack pointer points to a stack location containing the address in procedure A to which procedure B is to return. At that point, the frame pointer contains address aa which points to the top of Procedure A's frame. When the LINK instruction is executed, the following sequence is performed: First, (1) address aa in the frame pointer (FP) is pushed onto the stack using the predecrement mode of addressing and is thus stored at address bb−4. Next, (2) the contents of SP, in this case bb−4, are loaded into the frame pointer (FP). Finally, (3) the displacement that was included as part of the LINK instruction is added to the contents of the stack pointer. Thus, after the LINK instruction has been executed, SP will contain a new value (cc in the following illustration), and the frame pointer will contain an address of bb−4. Thus, an area of the stack equal to the displacement value provided as part of the LINK instruction is set aside to store local variables for procedure B. The stack beginning at address cc is available for use as a stack by procedure B.

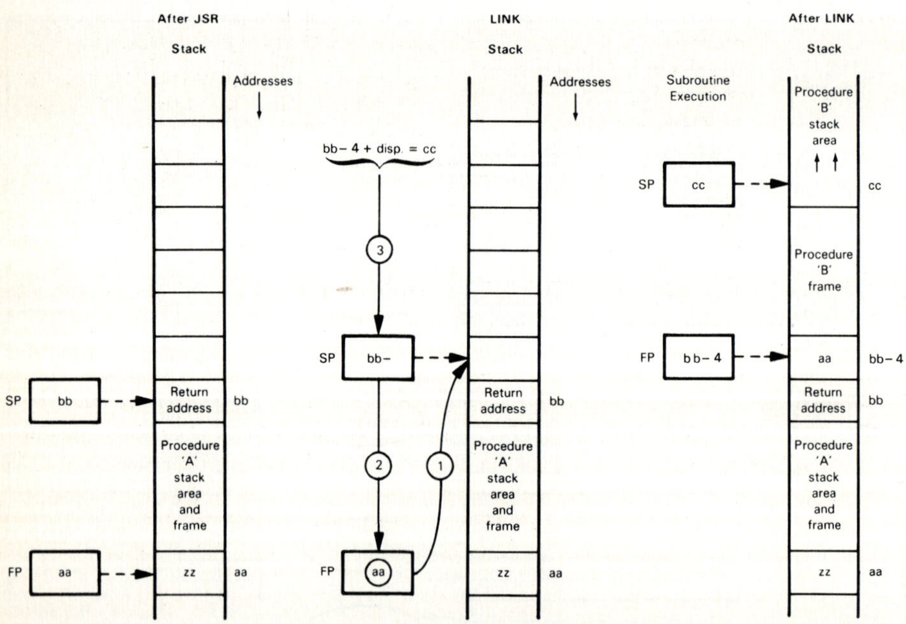

Upon completion of the procedure B which executed the LINK instruction, an UNLK instruction can be executed to restore conditions that existed prior to the JSR to procedure B. The following illustration shows the sequence of events that occur during the UNLK instruction.

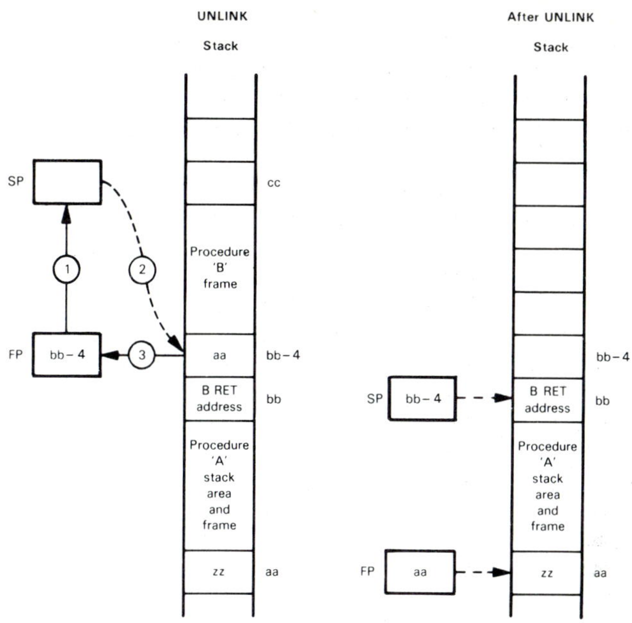

First, (1) the contents of the frame pointer are loaded into the stack pointer. Then, (2) the stack pointer is used to access the stack and the contents of that stack location are loaded into the frame pointer using postincrement addressing of the stack pointer. If you compare this illustration with the preceding illustration you will see that after the UNLK instruction is executed, the conditions that existed prior to executing the LINK instruction have been restored: the frame pointer (FP) contains the address aa and the stack pointer (SP) contains the address bb. Note that the SP originally contained bb. When the expected return from subroutine (RTS) instruction is executed, the postincrement mode of accessing the stack will obtain the return address for procedure B from address bb.

The LINK instruction does not affect any status flags.

The LINK instruction allows a 16-bit displacement which is sign-extended prior to being added to the stack pointer. **When the LINK instruction is used to create stack frames, be sure that a** ***negative*** **displacement is used.** A positive displacement overwrites the stack and thus may cause current variables stored on the stack to be destroyed.

LSL — Logical Shift Left In Data Register

This instruction shifts left the contents of a specified data register. This instruction is exactly the same as the arithmetic shift left or ASL instruction; consult ASL for a detailed description of its execution. The shift is performed as shown:

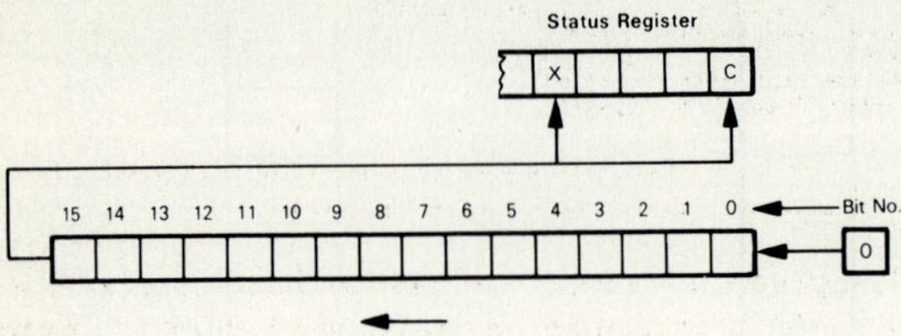

The object code for the LSL instruction is:

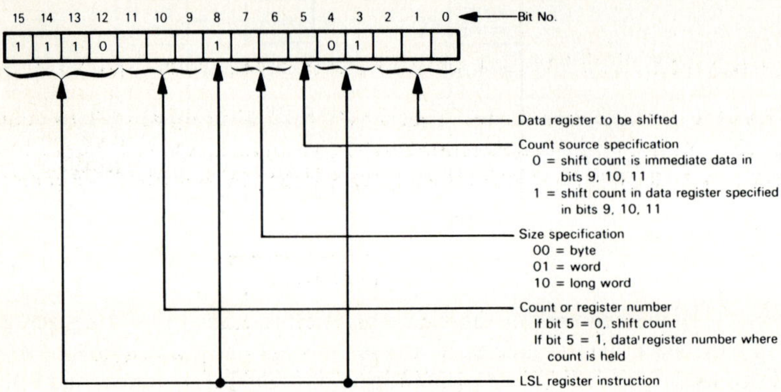

LSL — Logical Shift Left in Memory

This instruction performs a 1-bit logical left shift of the contents of a specified memory location. The addressing modes that can be used to specify the memory location are:

Addressing Modes Allowed	Operand		Destination ea Field	
		Destination	Mode	Register No.
Data register direct				
Address register direct				
Address register indirect		X	010	rrr
Postincrement register indirect		X	011	rrr
Predecrement register indirect		X	100	rrr
Register indirect with displacement		X	101	rrr
Register indirect with index		X	110	rrr
Absolute short		X	111	000
Absolute long		X	111	001
Program counter relative with displacement				
Program counter relative with index				
Immediate				

The object code for the LSL memory instruction is:

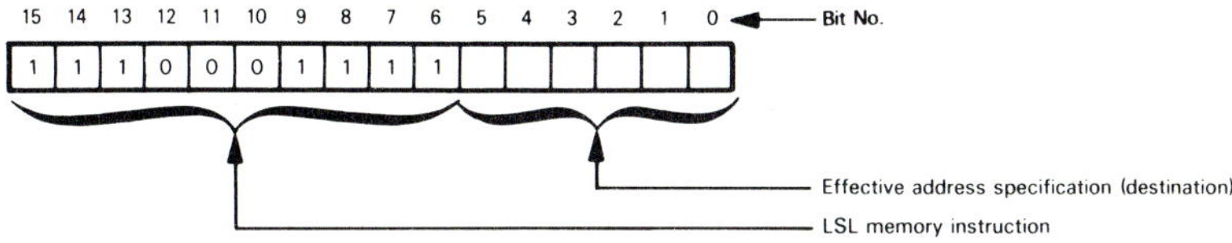

This version of the LSL instruction is exactly the same as the arithmetic shift left or ASL instruction; consult the ASL instruction for a detailed description of its execution. The shift is performed as shown above for the LSL register instruction.

LSR — Logical Shift Right of a Data Register or Memory

The LSR instruction performs a logical right shift of the operand. This instruction is identical to the ASR instruction except that LSR causes a zero to be shifted into the most significant bit position instead of keeping it intact, as does the ASR instruction:

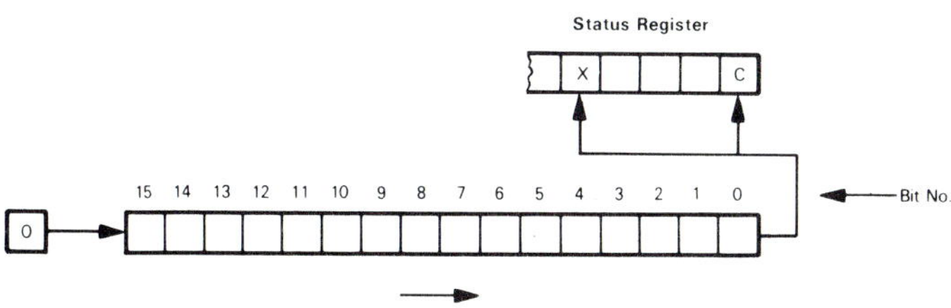

Status flags are affected the same way as in the ASR instruction. Of course, in the LSR instruction, the negative (N) flag is cleared since the most significant bit is cleared by execution of the instruction. Consult the ASR instructions for more details on LSR.

The addressing modes that can be used with the LSR instruction are identical to those described for the LSL instruction.

The object code for the LSR register instruction is:

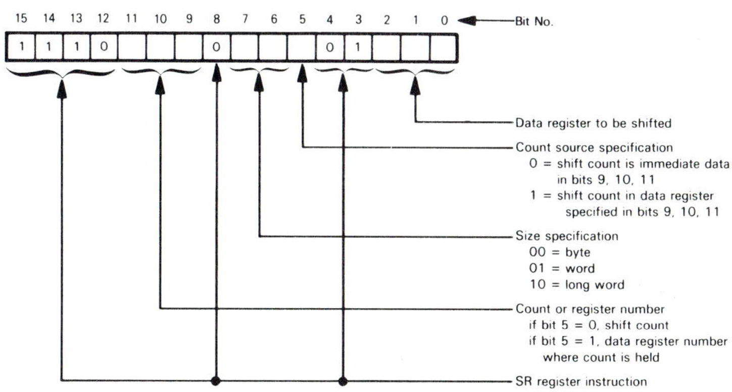

The object code for the LSR memory instruction is:

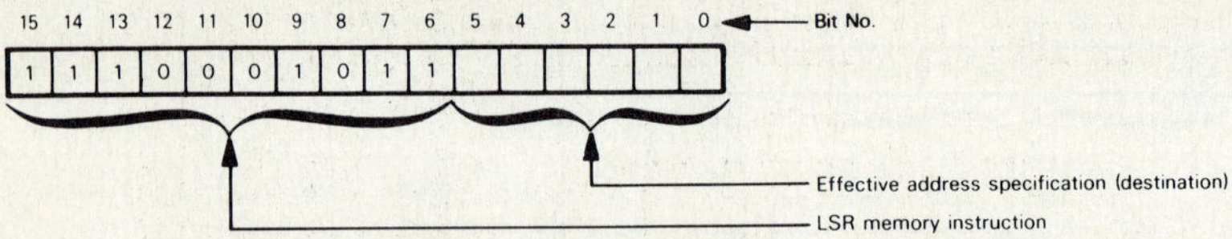

MOVE — Move Data from Source to Destination

This instruction can be used to move data from registers to memory, from memory to registers, or between registers. It is thus the equivalent of the LOAD and STORE instructions provided by many other microprocessors. There are very few limitations on the ways in which source and destination operands can be specified for the MOVE instruction:

Addressing Modes Allowed	Operand		Source ea Field	
	Source	Destination	Mode	Register No.
Data register direct	X	X	000	rrr
Address register direct	X*		001	rrr
Address register indirect	X	X	010	rrr
Postincrement register indirect	X	X	011	rrr
Predecrement register indirect	X	X	100	rrr
Register indirect with displacement	X	X	101	rrr
Register indirect with index	X	X	110	rrr
Absolute short	X	X	111	000
Absolute long	X	X	111	001
Program counter relative with displacement			111	010
Program counter relative with index			111	011
Immediate	X		111	100

*Not allowed if operation size is byte.

The object code for the MOVE instruction is:

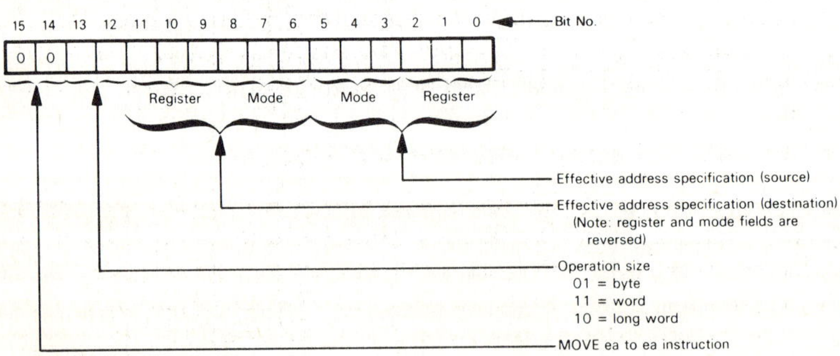

Note that the register number and mode fields are reversed in the destination effective address specification. Of course, the assembler will handle this automatically.

Figure 22-33 illustrates execution of the MOVE instruction using address register indirect addressing to specify the source operand and data register direct for the destination operand. In this figure, register A3 holds the memory address of the data word to be transferred to register D2. After the instruction illustrated is executed, the least significant 16 bits of register D2 will hold the value xxxx.

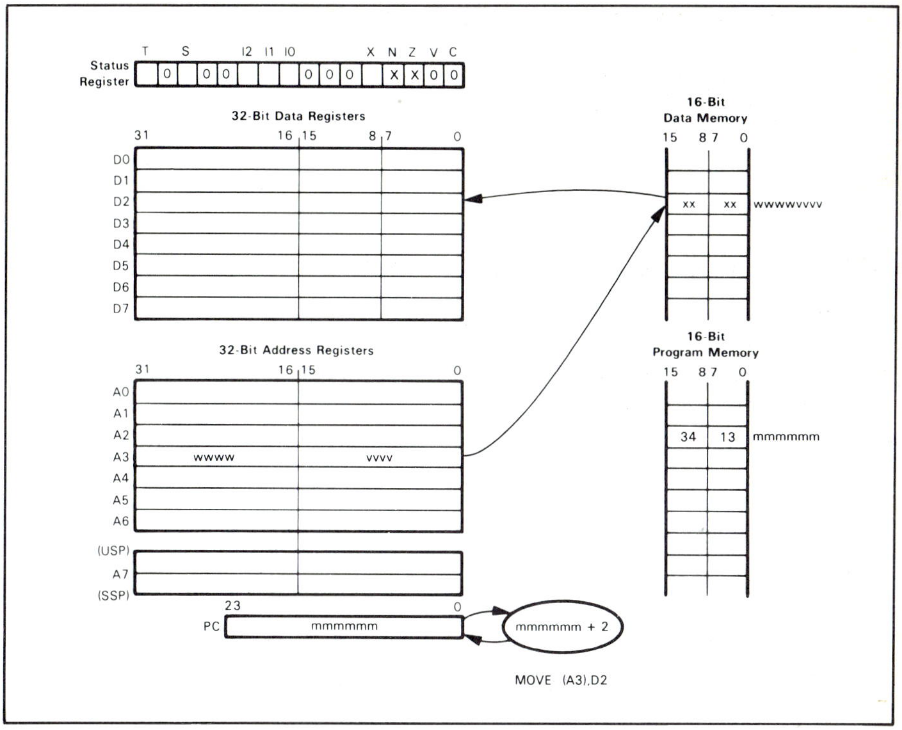

Figure 22-33. Execution of the MOVE Instruction Using Address Register Indirect Addressing

Transfer of data in the opposite direction could be accomplished by executing the instruction MOVE D2,(A3).

As the data is transferred, it is examined by the processor and the Negative (N) and Zero (Z) status flags are set accordingly. The Overflow (V) and Carry (C) status flags are always cleared by the MOVE instruction. The Extend (X) flag is not affected.

MOVE to CCR — Move to Condition Codes

This is a special form of the MOVE instruction which moves the contents of the specified source operand to the condition code portion (the low-order byte) of the status register. The addressing modes that can be used to specify the source operand are:

Addressing Modes Allowed	Operand		Source ea Field	
	Source		Mode	Register No.
Data register direct	X		000	rrr
Address register direct				
Address register indirect	X		010	rrr
Postincrement register indirect	X		011	rrr
Predecrement register indirect	X		100	rrr
Register indirect with displacement	X		101	rrr
Register indirect with index	X		110	rrr
Absolute short	X		111	000
Absolute long	X		111	001
Program counter relative with displacement	X		111	010
Program counter relative with index	X		111	011
Immediate	X		111	100

The object code for the MOVE to CCR instruction is:

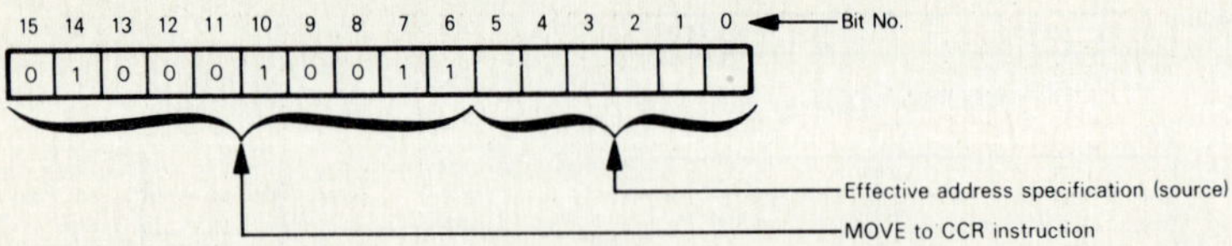

The source operand for this instruction is a word, but only the low-order byte of that word is moved to the status register.

Obviously, the X, N, Z, V, and C flags are all affected by this instruction.

MOVE to SR — Move to the Status Register

This instruction is a special case of the MOVE instruction used to move the contents of a source operand to the status register. **This instruction is a privileged instruction and can only be executed when the processor is in the supervisor mode.** The addressing modes that can be used to specify the source operand are:

Addressing Modes Allowed	Operand		Source ea Field	
	Source		Mode	Register No.
Data register direct	X		000	rrr
Address register direct				
Address register indirect	X		010	rrr
Postincrement register indirect	X		011	rrr
Predecrement register indirect	X		100	rrr
Register indirect with displacement	X		101	rrr
Register indirect with index	X		110	rrr
Absolute short	X		111	000
Absolute long	X		111	001
Program counter relative with displacement	X		111	010
Program counter relative with index	X		111	011
Immediate	X		111	100

The object code for the MOVE to SR instruction is:

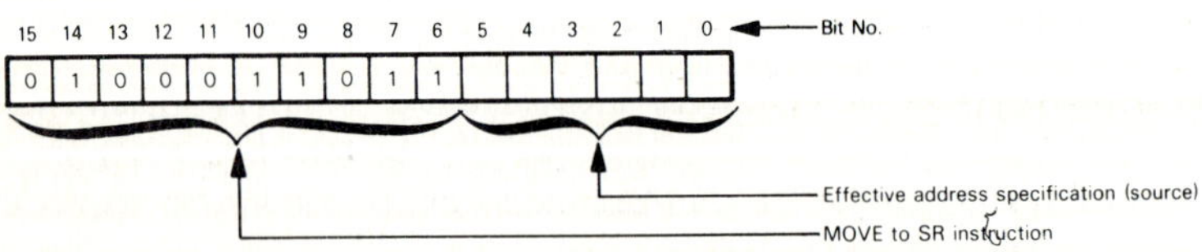

Obviously, this instruction affects all bits of the status register.

MOVE from SR — Move from the Status Register

This instruction causes the contents of the 16-bit status register to be moved to the destination. The destination operand can be specified using the following modes.

Addressing Modes Allowed	Operand		Destination ea Field	
	Source	Destination	Mode	Register No.
Data register direct		X	000	rrr
Address register direct				
Address register indirect		X	010	rrr
Postincrement register indirect		X	011	rrr
Predecrement register indirect		X	100	rrr
Register indirect with displacement		X	101	rrr
Register indirect with index		X	110	rrr
Absolute short		X	111	000
Absolute long		X	111	001
Program counter relative with displacement				
Program counter relative with index				
Immediate				

The object code for the MOVE from SR instruction is:

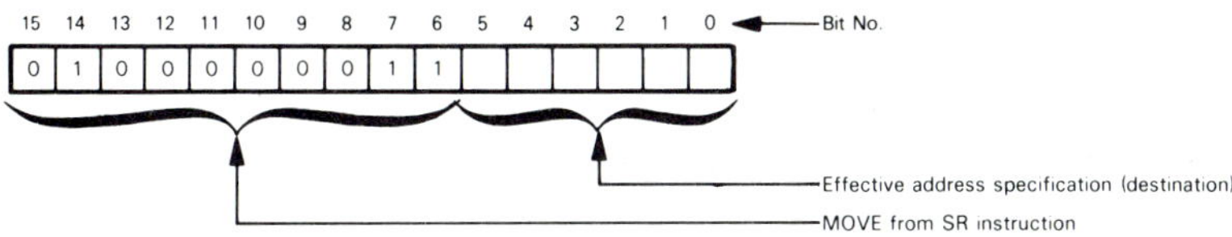

Unlike the MOVE to SR, this instruction can be executed in both the supervisor and user modes. Execution of this instruction does not affect the contents of the status register; it simply saves them in the specified location.

MOVE USP — Move User Stack Pointer

This instruction transfers the contents of the user stack pointer (A7) to or from a specified address register. **This instruction is a privileged instruction and can only be executed while the processor is in the supervisor mode.**

The object code for the MOVE USP instruction is:

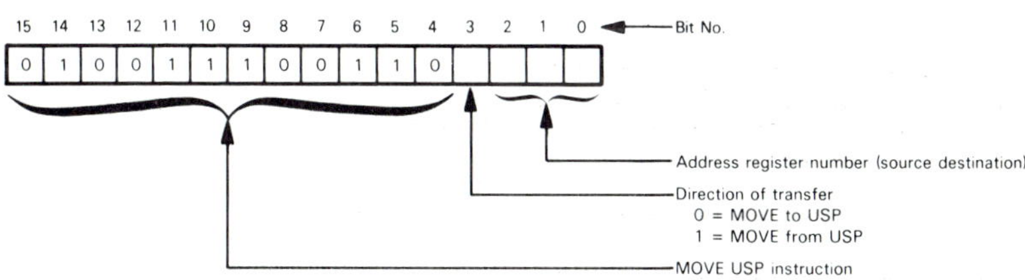

MOVEA — Move Address

This instruction is a special version of the MOVE instruction which moves the contents of a specified source operand to an address register. The source operand may be specified using the address modes shown:

Addressing Modes Allowed	Operand		Source ea Field	
	Source	Destination	Mode	Register No.
Data register direct	X		000	rrr
Address register direct	X	X	001	rrr
Address register indirect	X		010	rrr
Postincrement register indirect	X		011	rrr
Predecrement register indirect	X		100	rrr
Register indirect with displacement	X		101	rrr
Register indirect with index	X		110	rrr
Absolute short	X		111	000
Absolute long	X		111	001
Program counter relative with displacement	X		111	010
Program counter relative with index	X		111	011
Immediate	X		111	100

The object code for the MOVEA instruction is:

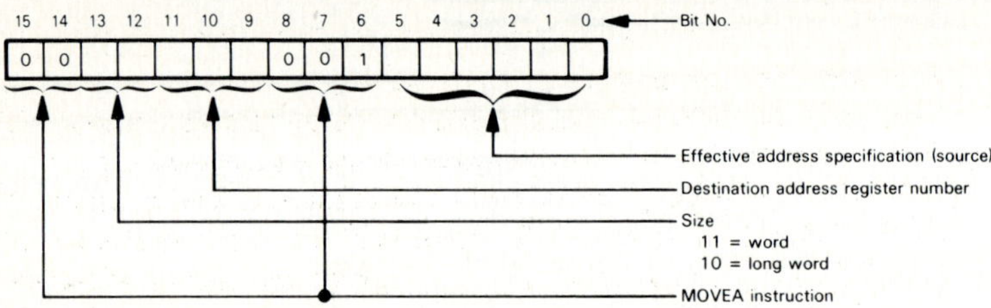

The only limitation on this version of the MOVE instruction is that only word or long word operands can be specified since the address registers cannot handle byte-size data. If a word operand is specified, it is sign-extended prior to being moved to the address register.

None of the flags in the status register is affected by the MOVEA instruction.

MOVEM — Move Multiple Registers from Memory

This instruction causes specified registers to be loaded from consecutive memory locations beginning at the location specified by the effective address. The address of the source memory locations can be specified using the address modes shown:

Addressing Modes Allowed	Operand		Source ea Field	
	Source	Destination	Mode	Register No.
Data register direct				
Address register direct				
Address register indirect	X		010	rrr
Postincrement register indirect	X		011	rrr
Predecrement register indirect				
Register indirect with displacement	X		101	rrr
Register indirect with index	X		110	rrr
Absolute short	X		111	000
Absolute long	X		111	001
Program counter relative with displacement	X		111	010
Program counter relative with index	X		111	011
Immediate				

The object code for the MOVEM-from-memory instruction is:

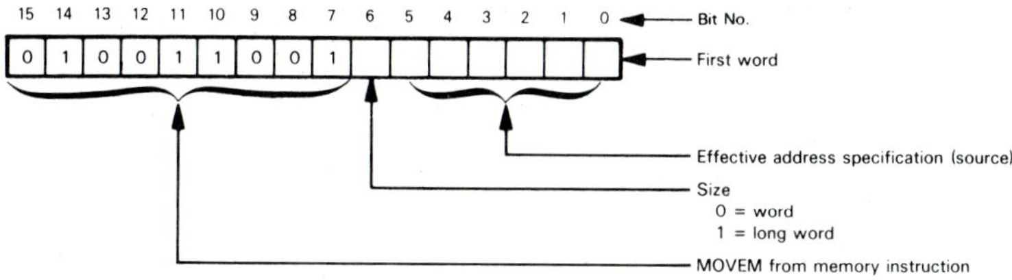

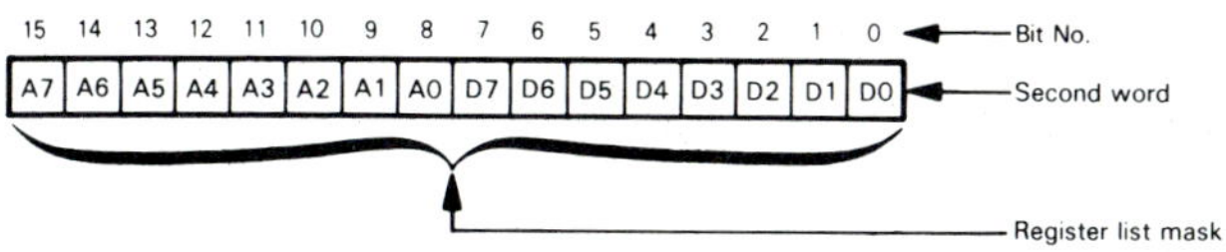

This instruction always consists of at least two words: the first word contains the instruction object code for MOVEM and the effective address specification, while the second word is the register list mask which specifies those registers whose contents are to be loaded from memory. Each bit in the mask word that is set indicates that the corresponding register contents are to be loaded from memory. **The registers are loaded starting at the specified source address and up through the higher addresses. The order of transfer is from data register D0 (or the lowest number data register specified) through data register D7 and on up to address register A7.** In other words, registers are loaded in the order they appear in the mask, starting at bit 0 and going up to bit 15.

Figure 22-34 illustrates execution of the MOVEM-from-memory instruction using address register indirect with postincrement addressing. In this figure, the contents of registers D1, D3, and A1 through A3 are loaded from five consecutive words of data memory beginning at address ppqqqq. When a data size of word is specified with this instruction, each word is sign-extended to 32 bits and the resulting long word is loaded into the associated register. Thus, using the operands in Figure 22-34, register D1 would contain 00000101_{16} after the instruction is executed while register A2 would contain $FFFFF000_{16}$. If a data size of long word is specified, then four bytes of memory will be used to load each specified register.

Note that the registers to be loaded are specified to the assembler using a special notation. The character slash, (/), is used to separate the names of registers to be loaded. The character minus, (−), is used to indicate a group of registers to be loaded. Thus D1/D3 loads D1 and D3; while A1-A3 loads A1, A2, and A3.

Note also that if you use the postincrement register indirect mode of addressing, as was shown in Figure 22-34, the incremented address register is updated to contain the address of the last word loaded plus 2 upon completion of the instruction.

Execution of the MOVEM instruction does not affect any of the status flags.

The MOVEM instruction can be used to quickly and efficiently restore the context of the processor and thus will be quite useful in implementing high-level languages.

MOVEM — Move Multiple Registers to Memory

This instruction stores the contents of specified registers in consecutive memory locations. It is thus the complement of the MOVEM-from-memory instruction de-

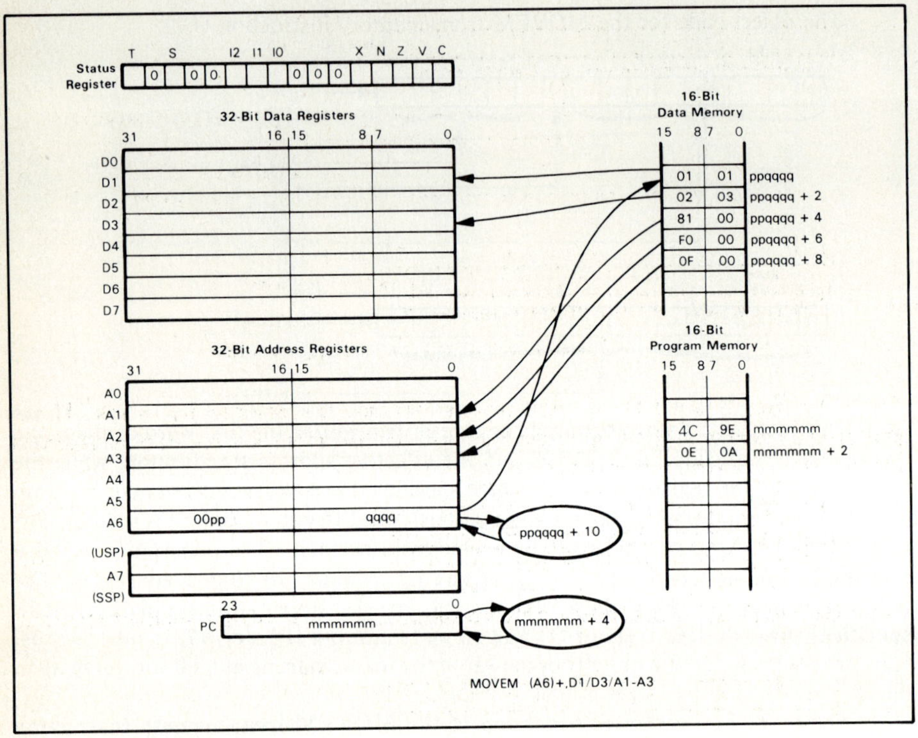

Figure 22-34. Execution of the MOVEM (From Memory) Instruction Using Address Register Postincrement Addressing

scribed in preceding paragraphs. The addressing modes that can be used with this version of the MOVEM instruction are:

Addressing Modes Allowed	Operand		Source ea Field	
	Source	Destination	Mode	Register No.
Data register direct				
Address register direct				
Address register indirect		X	010	rrr
Postincrement register indirect				
Predecrement register indirect		X	100	rrr
Register indirect with displacement		X	101	rrr
Register indirect with index		X	110	rrr
Absolute short		X	111	000
Absolute long		X	111	001
Immediate				

The only difference between addressing modes allowed with this version and those allowed with the "from memory" version is that this "to memory" version can utilize predecrement register indirect addressing (but not postincrement) while the "from memory" version could use postincrement register indirect addressing (but not predecrement).

The object code for this version of the MOVEM instruction can be illustrated as follows below.

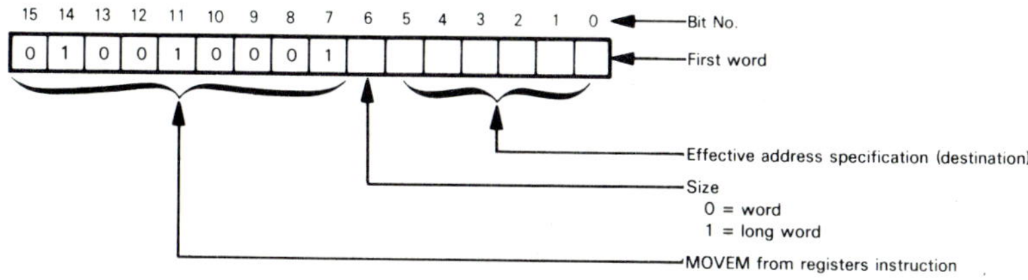

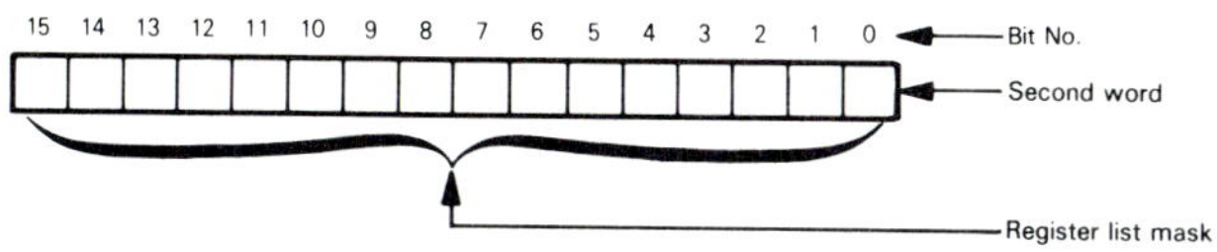

The second word of the instruction provides the register list mask. If any addressing mode except predecrement is used, the mask is the same as was described for the MOVEM-from-memory version:

Bit No.	15	14	13	12	11	10	9	8	7	6	5	4	3	2	1	0
	A7	A6	A5	A4	A3	A2	A1	A0	D7	D6	D5	D4	D3	D2	D1	D0

However, if the predecrement addressing mode is used, the register mask is:

Bit No.	15	14	13	12	11	10	9	8	7	6	5	4	3	2	1	0
	D0	D1	D2	D3	D4	D5	D6	D7	A0	A1	A2	A3	A4	A5	A6	A7

In this case, the registers are stored starting at the specified address −2 and down through the lower addresses. The order of storing is from address register A7 through address register A0 and then from data register D7 through data register D0. This is logical, since the other addressing modes use increasing addresses, while the predecrement mode uses decreasing addresses. In any case, the assembler generates the masks automatically.

Just as was the case with the register mask described for the other version of the MOVEM instruction, only those registers whose corresponding bits are set to 1 will be transferred. If the predecrement addressing mode is used, the decremented address register will be updated to contain the address of the last word stored upon completion of the instruction.

No status flags are affected by the MOVEM instruction.

MOVEP — Move Peripheral Data

This instruction is a special version of the MOVE instruction and causes two or four bytes of data to be transferred between a specified data register and alternate byte locations in memory. **This instruction is intended to simplify data transfers between the processor and 8-bit devices. The only addressing mode is address register indirect with displacement.**

The object code for the MOVEP instruction is:

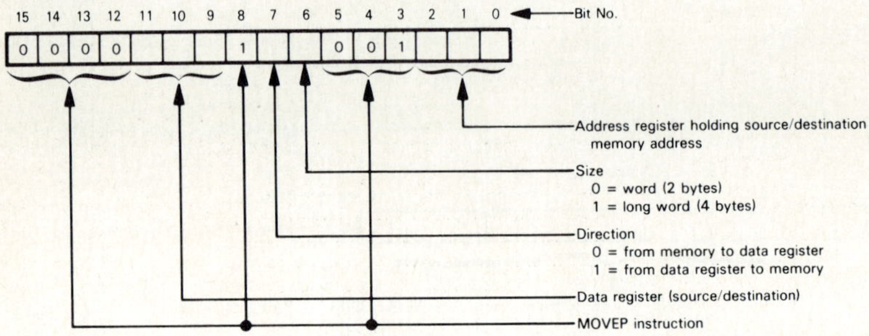

As you can see, the direction of the data transfer can be either from memory to a data register or from a data register to memory. The instruction object code is followed by a 16-bit displacement which will be added to the contents of the specified address register to generate the address of the memory source or destination.

If an operation size of long word is specified, then four 8-bit bytes of data will be transferred. For example, if the MOVEP instruction is being used to transfer data from a data register to memory and a long word size is specified, the transfer of data is as shown:

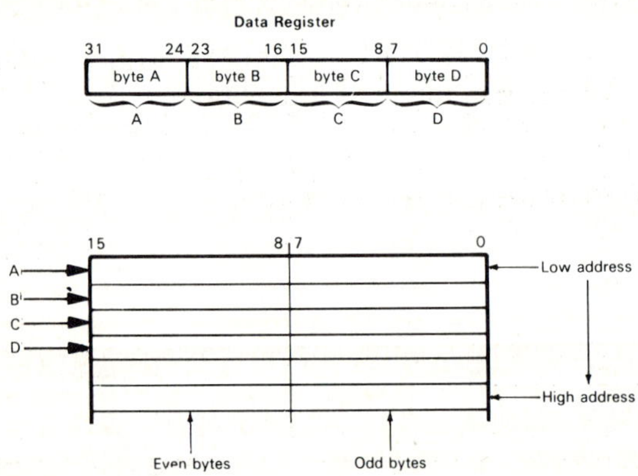

The high-order byte of the data register is transferred first, and the low-order byte is transferred last. **As each byte of data is transferred, the address is incremented by 2. (Note that the contents of the address register itself are not incremented.)** Thus, if the specified starting address is an even number (as shown in the preceding illustration) all of the transfers are made on the high-order half of the data bus. If the starting address is an odd number, all of the transfers will be accomplished on the low-order half of the data bus.

If an operation size of word is specified with the MOVEP instruction, the

low-order half of the register is transferred, high-order byte first, as shown:

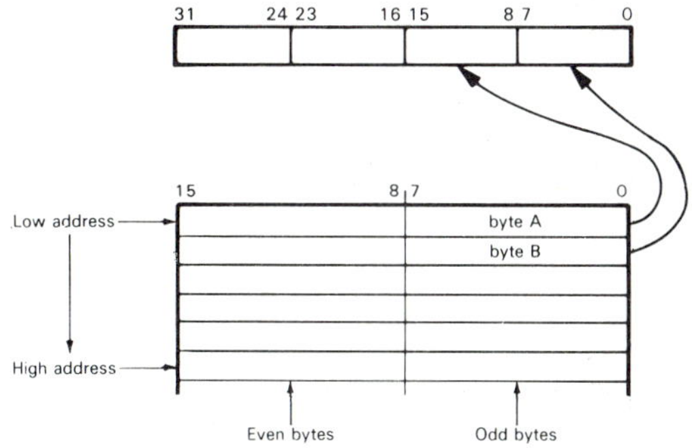

This illustration shows transfer of data from memory to a data register. The first byte will be loaded into bits 8 through 15 of the data register and the second byte transferred will be loaded into bits 0 through 7 of the data register. In this case, an odd memory address has been specified.

Figure 22-35 illustrates execution of the MOVEP instruction with data being transferred from even memory bytes to data register D4. In Figure 22-35, the contents

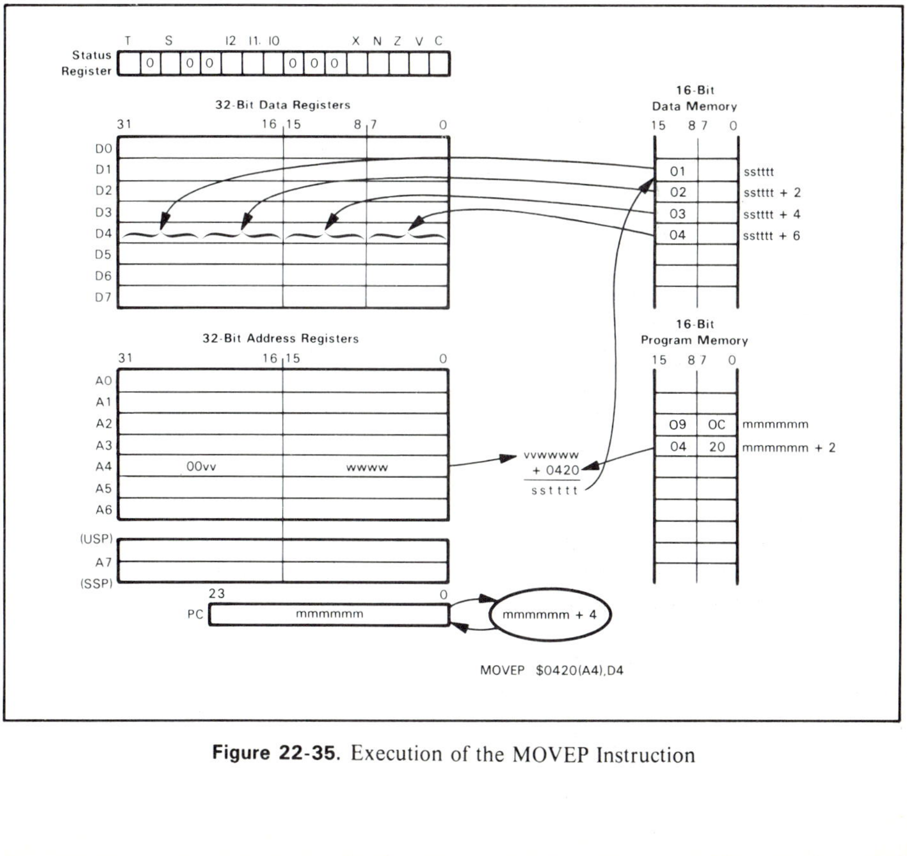

Figure 22-35. Execution of the MOVEP Instruction

of register A4 are added to the 16-bit displacement value (0420_{16}) that follows the instruction word in program memory. The resultant address (sstttt) is assumed to be an even address in this figure and points to the first byte of data that is to be transferred. That byte and the three bytes at the subsequent even addresses are transferred to register D4.

None of the status flags is affected by the MOVEP instruction.

MOVEQ — Move Quick

This instruction moves the immediate data contained within the instruction object code to a specified data register. The object code for this instruction is:

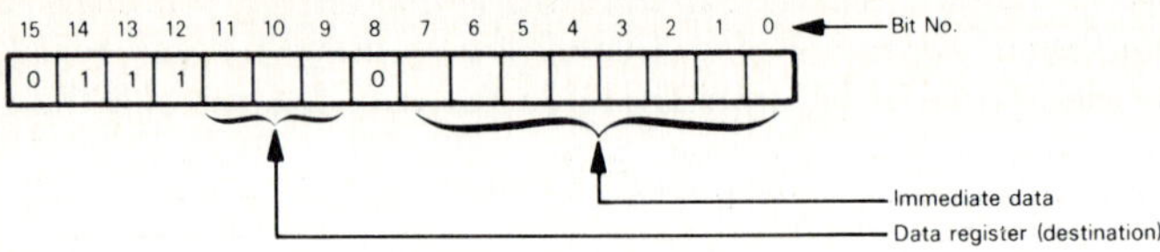

The least significant eight bits of the instruction word contain the immediate data. This data is sign-extended to a long operand, and all 32 bits are transferred to the data register.

Figure 22-36 illustrates execution of the MOVEQ instruction. In this figure, the immediate data ($7F_{16}$) is sign-extended and then loaded into register D3. Thus, after the instruction is executed D3 will hold $0000007F_{16}$.

The Negative (N) flag will be set if the value loaded into the data register is negative and will be cleared otherwise. The Zero (Z) flag will be set if a zero value is loaded into the data register and cleared otherwise. The Overflow (V) and Carry (C) status flags are always cleared. The Extend (X) flag is not affected.

MULS — Signed Multiply

This instruction multiplies two signed 16-bit operands yielding a 32-bit signed result. The multiplication is performed using two's complement binary arithmetic. A data register always serves as the destination operand and the source operand can be specified using these addressing modes:

Addressing Modes Allowed	Operand		Source ea Field	
	Source	Destination	Mode	Register No.
Data register direct	X	X	000	rrr
Address register direct				
Address register indirect	X		010	rrr
Postincrement register indirect	X		011	rrr
Predecrement register indirect	X		100	rrr
Register indirect with displacement	X		101	rrr
Register indirect with index	X		110	rrr
Absolute short	X		111	000
Absolute long	X		111	001
Program counter relative with displacement	X		111	010
Program counter relative with index	X		111	011
Immediate	X		111	100

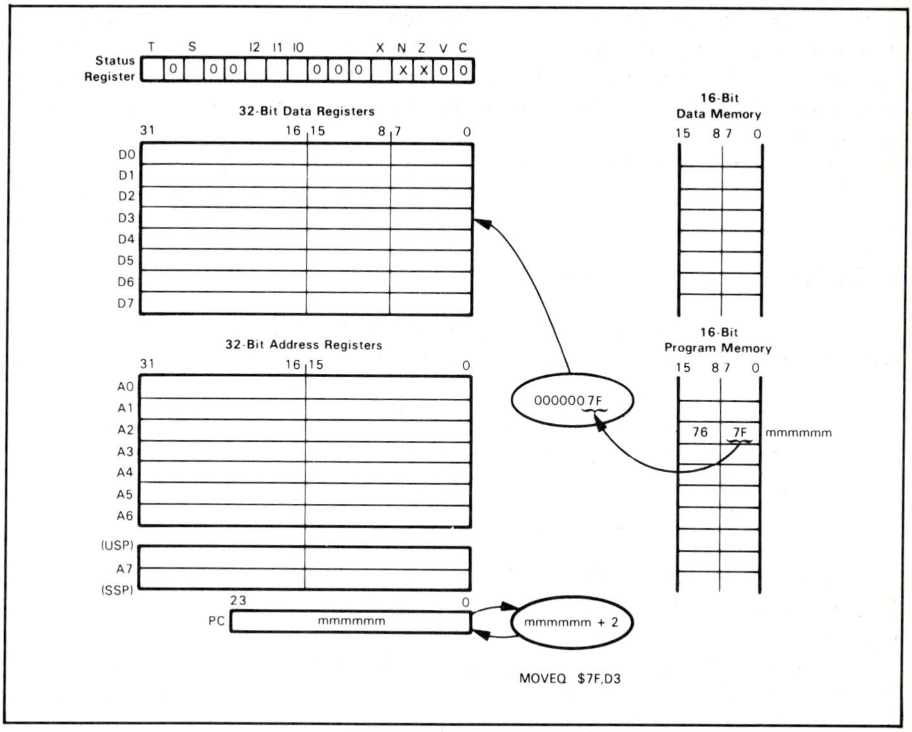

Figure 22-36. Execution of the MOVEQ Instruction

The object code for the MULS instruction is:

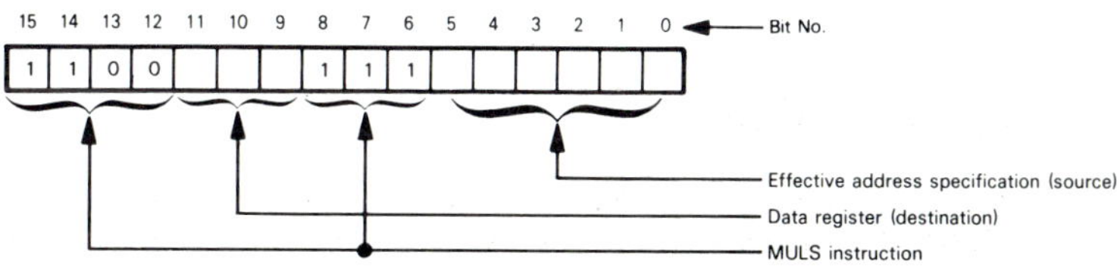

Figure 22-37 illustrates execution of the MULS instruction using address register indirect addressing to specify the source operand. After the instruction illustrated has been executed, register D2 will hold the product (00800000_{16}).

The Negative (N) status flag will be set if the result is negative and will be cleared otherwise. The Zero (Z) status flag will be set if the result is zero and will be cleared otherwise. The Overflow (V) and Carry (C) status flags are always cleared. The Extend (X) status flag is not affected.

Note that the operand taken from the data register to perform the multiplication is taken from the low-order word of the register; the high-order half of the destination register does not participate in the multiplication and its contents are overwritten when the 32-bit product is returned to the register after the multiplication.

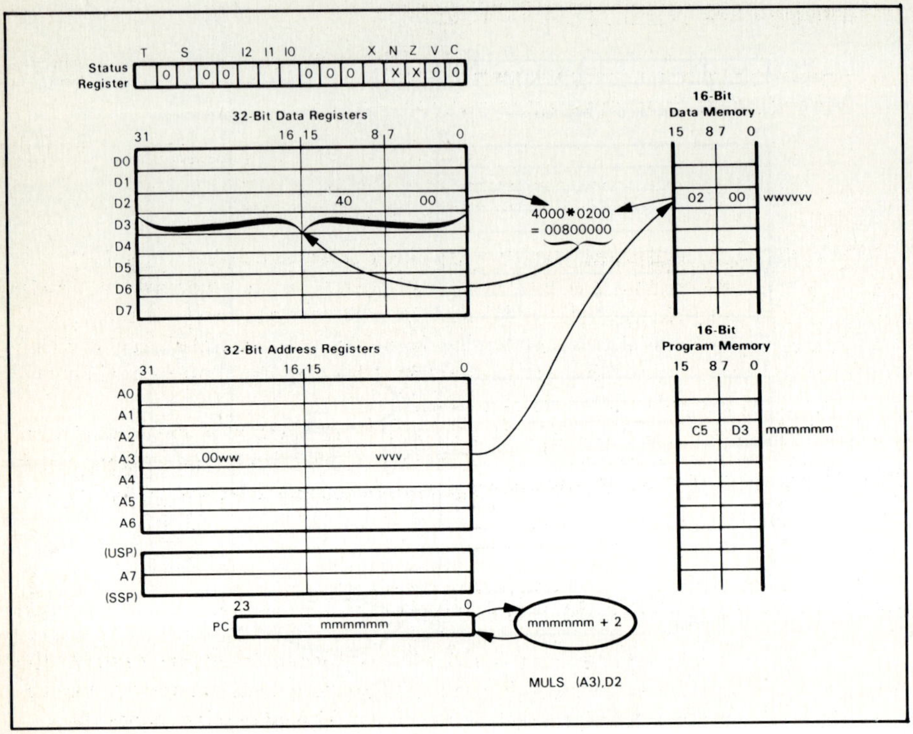

Figure 22-37. Execution of the MULS Instruction Using Address Register Indirect Addressing

MULU — Multiply Unsigned

This instruction multiplies two unsigned 16-bit operands yielding a 32-bit unsigned result. The operation is performed using unsigned binary arithmetic. A data register always provides one for the operands and serves as the destination for the resultant product. The source operand to be used can be specified using these addressing modes:

Addressing Modes Allowed	Operand		Source ea Field	
	Source	Destination	Mode	Register No.
Data register direct	X	X	000	rrr
Address register direct				
Address register indirect	X		010	rrr
Postincrement register indirect	X		011	rrr
Predecrement register indirect	X		100	rrr
Register indirect with displacement	X		101	rrr
Register indirect with index	X		110	rrr
Absolute short	X		111	000
Absolute long	X		111	001
Program counter relative with displacement	X		111	010
Program counter relative with index	X		111	011
Immediate	X		111	100

The object code for the MULU instruction is:

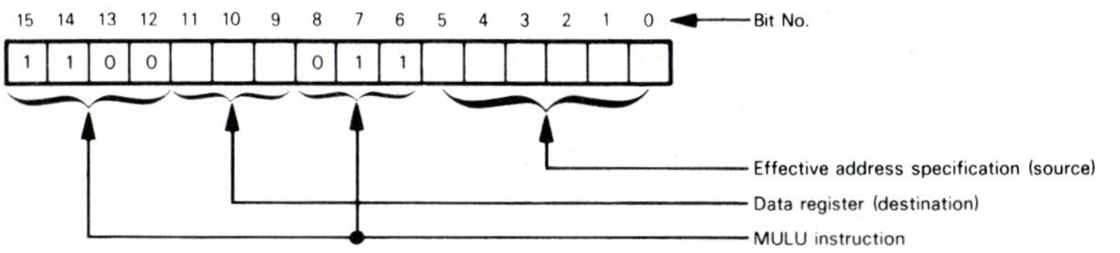

The 16-bit operand taken from the data register for use in the multiplication is taken from the low-order word of the register; the upper word is not used in the multiplication and is overwritten when the 32-bit product is returned to the data register.

Execution of the MULU instruction is identical to that illustrated for the MULS instruction except, of course, that unsigned arithmetic is used. Refer to Figure 22-37 for an illustration of execution of the MULS instruction.

The Negative (N) status flag is set if the most significant bit of the product is set and is cleared otherwise. The Zero (Z) status flag is set if the product is zero and is cleared otherwise. The Overflow (V) and Carry (C) status flags are always cleared. The Extend (X) status flag is not affected.

NBCD — Negate Decimal with Extend

This instruction subtracts both the destination operand and the value of the Extend (X) flag from zero. The result is saved in the destination. The operation is performed using binary-coded decimal (BCD) arithmetic. The addressing modes that can be used to specify the destination are:

Addressing Modes Allowed	Operand		Destination ea Field	
	Source	Destination	Mode	Register No.
Data register direct		X	000	rrr
Address register direct				
Address register indirect		X	010	rrr
Postincrement register indirect		X	011	rrr
Predecrement register indirect		X	100	rrr
Register indirect with displacement		X	101	rrr
Register indirect with index		X	110	rrr
Absolute short		X	111	000
Absolute long		X	111	001
Program counter relative with displacement				
Program counter relative with index				
Immediate				

The object code for the NBCD instruction is:

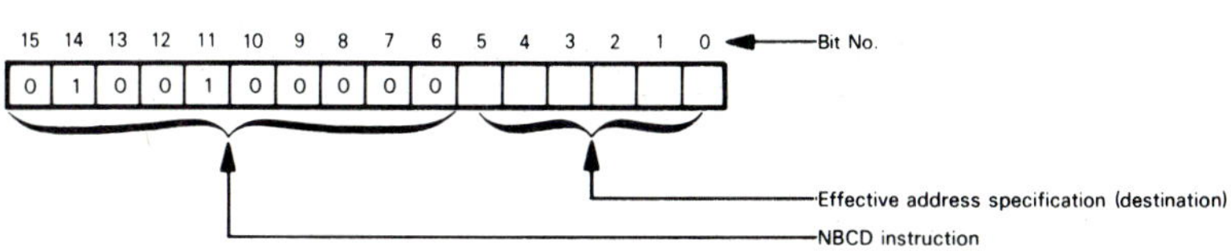

Figure 22-38 illustrates execution of the NBCD instruction using address register indirect addressing. The NBCD instruction always operates only on one byte of data.

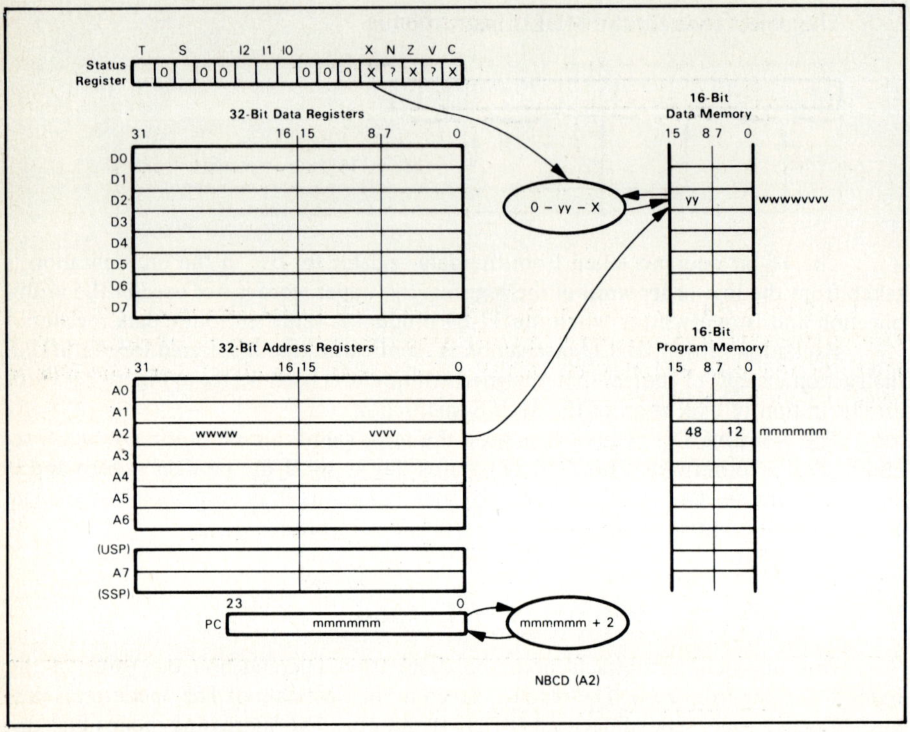

Figure 22-38. Execution of the NBCD Instruction Using Address Register Indirect Addressing

This instruction can be used in multibyte BCD operations to easily compute the negative of BCD data. Refer to Chapter 8 for a discussion of multibyte BCD arithmetic. The status flags are affected in the same way as for the SBCD instruction.

NEG — Negate

This instruction subtracts the contents of the destination operand from zero using two's complement binary arithmetic. The result is stored in the destination. The operand that is to be negated can be specified using these addressing modes:

Addressing Modes Allowed	Operand		Destination ea Field	
	Source	Destination	Mode	Register No.
Data register direct		X	000	rrr
Address register direct				
Address register indirect		X	010	rrr
Postincrement register indirect		X	011	rrr
Predecrement register indirect		X	100	rrr
Register indirect with displacement		X	101	rrr
Register indirect with index		X	110	rrr
Absolute short		X	111	000
Absolute long		X	111	001
Program counter relative with displacement				
Program counter relative with index				
Immediate				

The object code for the NEG instruction is:

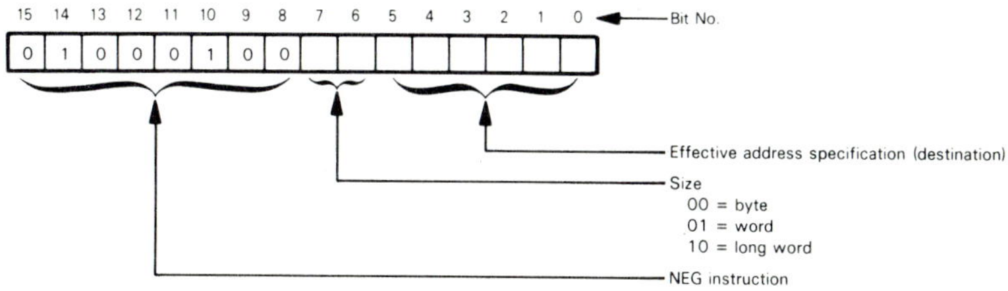

Figure 22-39 illustrates execution of the NEG instruction using data register direct addressing. If, for example, the least significant byte of register D3 contains $3A_{16}$, after the processor executes the NEG.B D3 instruction, the least significant byte of register D3 will contain $C6_{16}$.

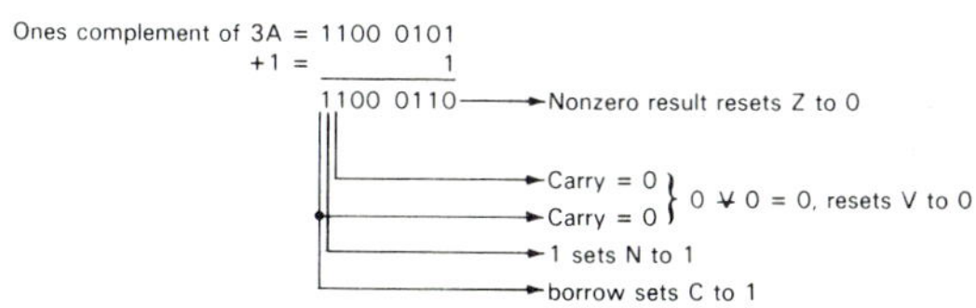

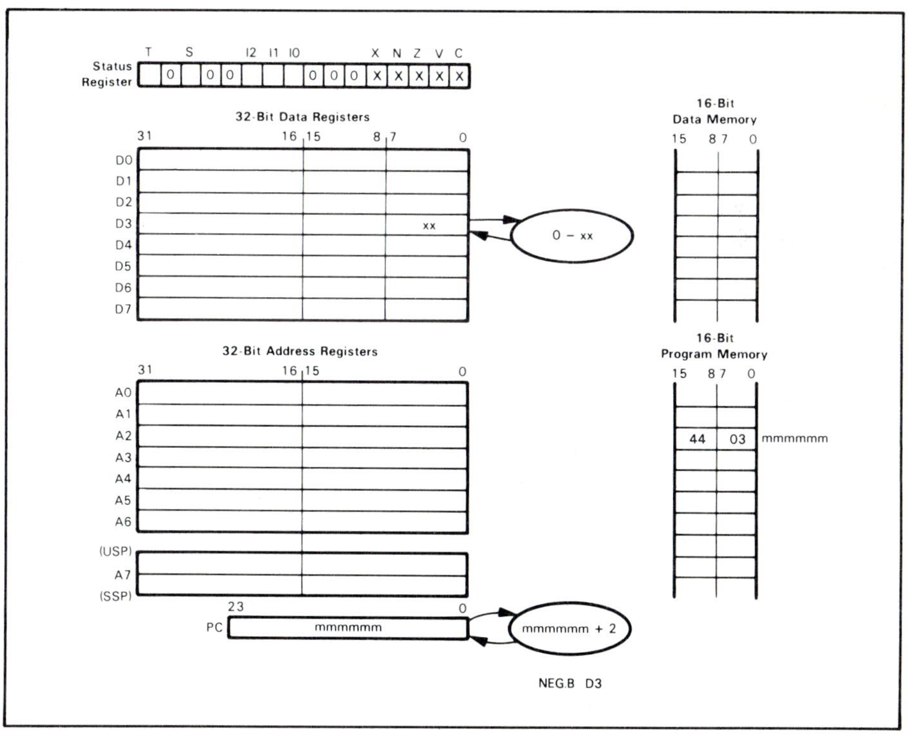

Figure 22-39. Execution of the NEG Instruction Using Data Register Direct Addressing

The Status flags (N, Z, V, C, X) are affected in the same way as by the SUB instruction.

NEGX — Negate with Extend

This instruction subtracts both the contents of the destination operand and the value of the Extend (X) flag from zero. The result is stored in the destination. The addressing modes that can be used to specify the destination are:

Addressing Modes Allowed	Operand		Destination ea Field	
	Source	Destination	Mode	Register No.
Data register direct		X	000	rrr
Address register direct				
Address register indirect		X	010	rrr
Postincrement register indirect		X	011	rrr
Predecrement register indirect		X	100	rrr
Register indirect with displacement		X	101	rrr
Register indirect with index		X	110	rrr
Absolute short		X	111	000
Absolute long		X	111	001
Program counter relative with displacement				
Program counter relative with index				
Immediate				

The object code for the NEGX instruction is:

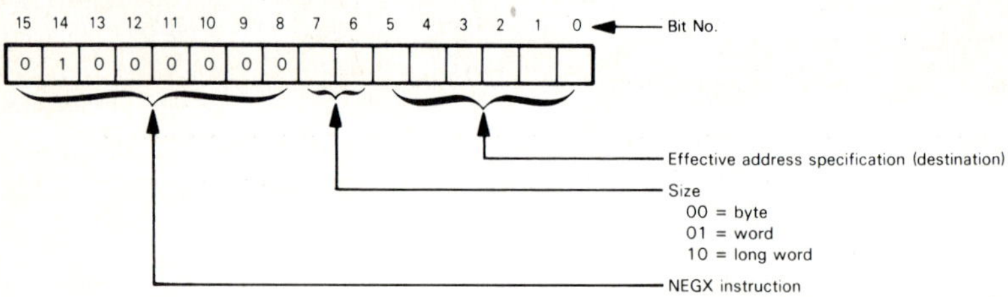

This instruction operates exactly as the NEG instruction except that the contents of the X flag are also subtracted from zero to obtain the negated value. Thus, this instruction is for use in multiple-precision operations. See Chapter 8 for a discussion of multiple-precision arithmetic.

The status flags are all set in the same way as by the SUBX instruction.

NOP — No Operation

NOP is an instruction that does nothing except increment the program counter. The object code for the NOP instruction is:

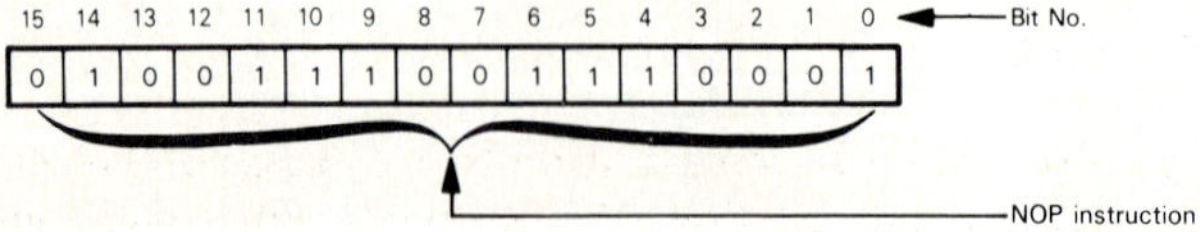

Execution of the NOP instruction is illustrated in Figure 22-40.

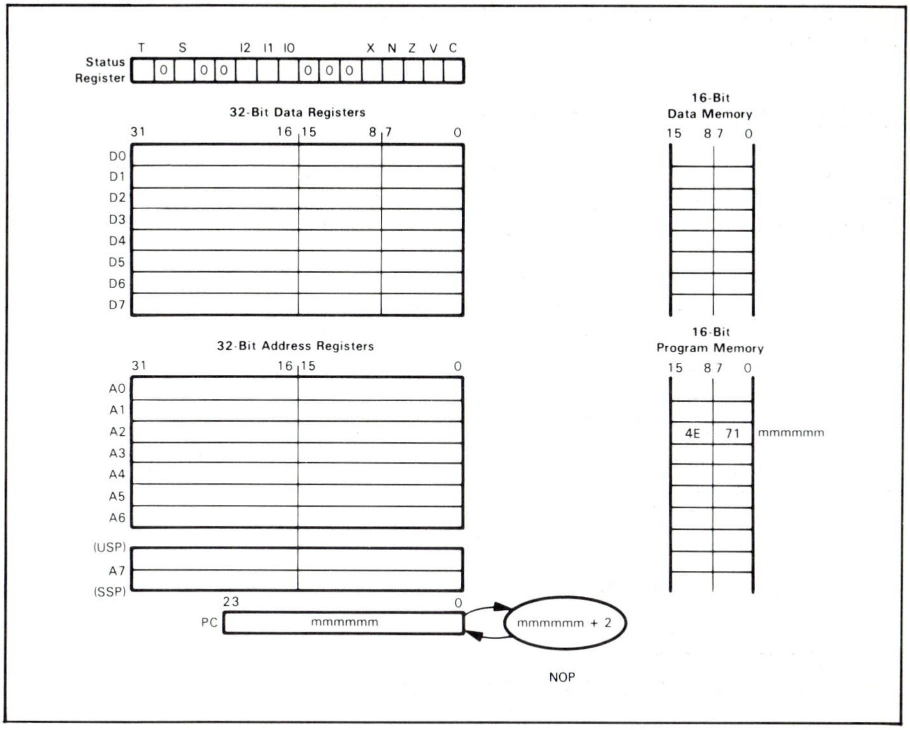

Figure 22-40. Execution of the NOP Instruction

Typical uses of NOP are the following:

1. To provide a position for a label without affecting the object program.
2. To produce a precise delay time.
3. To replace instructions that are no longer needed because of corrections or changes.
4. To replace instructions (such as subroutine calls) that you may not want to include in debugging runs.

The NOP instruction is seldom used in completed programs, but is often quite handy in debugging and testing stages.

NOT — Logical Complement

This instruction performs a bitwise complement of the contents of the destination operand. The result is stored in the destination. This is a one's complement operation, which replaces each 1 in the operand with a 0, and each 0 with a 1. Extraneous complements are disregarded.

The addressing modes that can be used to specify the destination operand are:

Addressing Modes Allowed	Operand		Destination ea Field	
	Source	Destination	Mode	Register No.
Data register direct		X	000	rrr
Address register direct				
Address register indirect		X	010	rrr
Postincrement register indirect		X	011	rrr
Predecrement register indirect		X	100	rrr
Register indirect with displacement		X	101	rrr
Register indirect with index		X	110	rrr
Absolute short		X	111	000
Absolute long		X	111	001
Program counter relative with displacement				
Program counter relative with index				
Immediate				

The object code for the NOT instruction is:

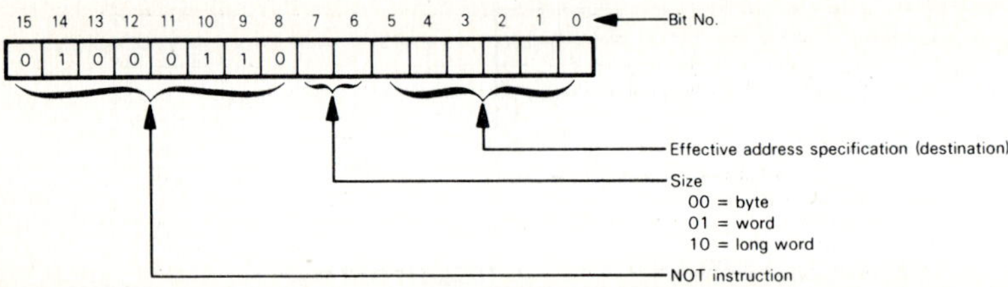

Figure 22-41 illustrates execution of the NOT instruction using address register indirect addressing.

The Negative (N) status flag is set if the result is negative and is cleared otherwise. The Zero (Z) flag is set if the result is zero and is cleared otherwise. The Overflow (V) and Carry (C) flags are always cleared. The Extend (X) flag is not affected.

OR — Inclusive OR Logical

This instruction performs a bitwise (inclusive) logical OR of the contents of the source operand with the contents of the destination operand, and stores the result in the destination.

There are two general forms for this instruction. In the first form, a data register provides one of the operands and is the destination location for the OR operation. In this form, all addressing modes except address register direct are permitted:

Addressing Modes Allowed	Operand		Source ea Field	
	Source	Destination	Mode	Register No.
Data register direct	X	X	000	rrr
Address register direct				
Address register indirect	X		010	rrr
Postincrement register indirect	X		011	rrr
Predecrement register indirect	X		100	rrr
Register indirect with displacement	X		101	rrr
Register indirect with index	X		110	rrr
Absolute short	X		111	000
Absolute long	X		111	001
Program counter relative with displacement	X		111	010
Program counter relative with index	X		111	011
Immediate	X		111	100

In the other general form of the OR instruction, a data register must provide the source operand and the destination operand may be specified using any of the addressing modes shown:

Addressing Modes Allowed	Operand		Destination ea Field	
	Source	Destination	Mode	Register No.
Data register direct	X	X	000	rrr
Address register direct			001	rrr
Address register indirect		X	010	rrr
Postincrement register indirect		X	011	rrr
Predecrement register indirect		X	100	rrr
Register indirect with displacement		X	101	rrr
Register indirect with index		X	110	rrr
Absolute short		X	111	000
Absolute long		X	111	001
Program counter relative with displacement				
Program counter relative with index				
Immediate				

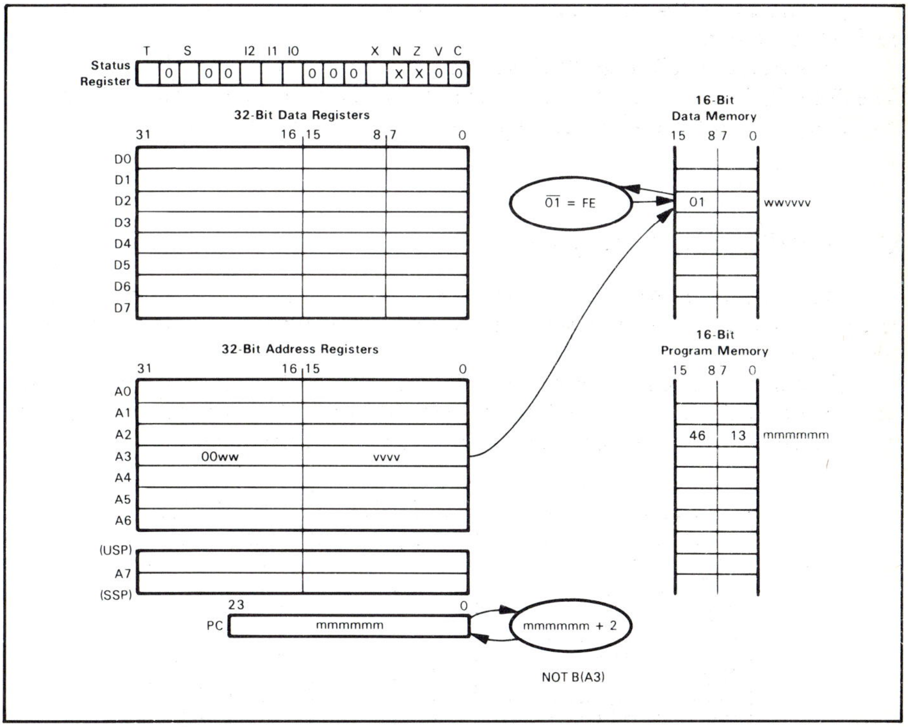

Figure 22-41. Execution of the NOT Instruction Using Address Register Indirect Addressing

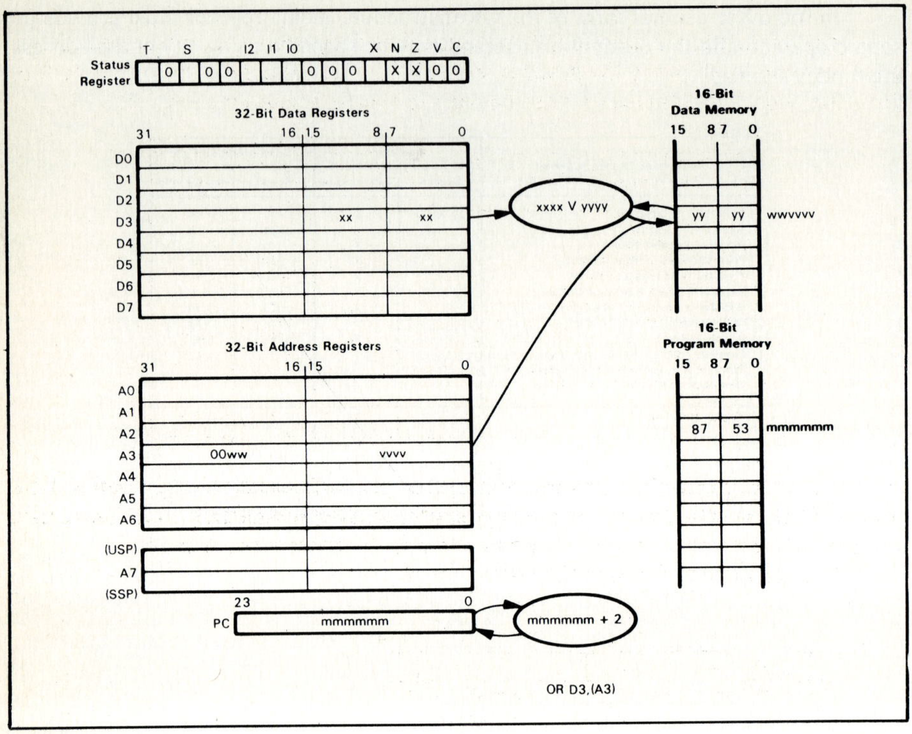

Figure 22-42. Execution of the OR Instruction Using Address Register Indirect Addressing

The object code for the OR instruction is:

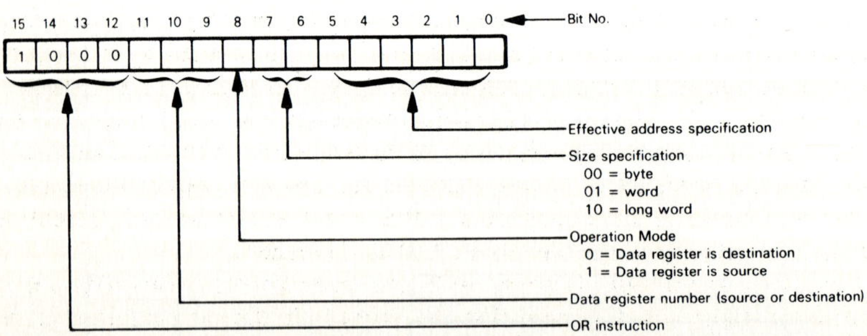

Figure 22-42 illustrates execution of the OR instruction using address register indirect addressing. In this figure, address register A3 indicates the operand location (wwvvvv) and the source location is the least significant 16 bits of register D3.

OR is a common logical instruction, most often used to set bits to a 1. Note that logically ORing a bit position with 1 produces a result of 1 while logically ORing a bit position with 0 leaves the value unchanged.

ORI — Inclusive OR Immediate

This instruction is used to OR the immediate data present in the succeeding program memory locations to the destination operand. The result is stored in the destination. The addressing modes that can be used to specify the destination are:

Addressing Modes Allowed	Operand		Destination ea Field	
	Source	Destination	Mode	Register No.
Data register direct		X	000	rrr
Address register direct				
Address register indirect		X	010	rrr
Postincrement register indirect		X	011	rrr
Predecrement register indirect		X	100	rrr
Register indirect with displacement		X	101	rrr
Register indirect with index		X	110	rrr
Absolute short		X	111	000
Absolute long		X	111	001
Program counter relative with displacement				
Program counter relative with index				
Immediate	X			
Status Register		X	111	100

Note that the destination operand may be the condition codes or the entire status register. **If the destination is the entire status register, this is a privileged instruction and can only be executed while the processor is in the supervisor mode.**

The object code for the ORI instruction is:

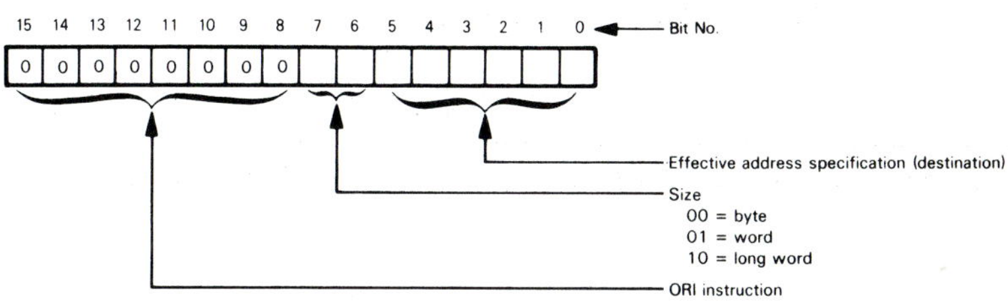

The size of the ORI instruction can be specified to be byte, word, or long word. The immediate data follows the instruction word in memory and must match the specified operation size. Thus, either one or two words of immediate data must follow the instruction operation code in program memory. If the instruction specifies a byte operand, the low-order (second) byte of the immediate data word is used. The assembler automatically places the byte correctly. If the instruction refers to the status register and the operation size is byte, the destination is the low-order byte of the status register and only the condition codes are affected. If the operation size is word, the entire status register is the destination, and the instruction is privileged.

Execution of the ORI instruction is the same as that illustrated for the OR instruction in Figure 22-42 except that the immediate data is contained in program memory following the instruction word.

The N and Z flags are modified by the ORI instruction according to the results obtained. The Overflow (V) and Carry (C) flags will always be cleared. The Extend (X) status flag is not affected. Of course, if the destination of the instruction is the condition codes, or the entire status register, then the condition codes are affected according to the result of the operation.

PEA — Push Effective Address

This instruction forms an effective address using one of the control addressing modes and then pushes that calculated address onto the stack. The addressing modes that can be used are:

Addressing Modes Allowed	Operand		Source ea Field	
	Source	Destination	Mode	Register No.
Data register direct				
Address register direct				
Address register indirect	X		010	rrr
Postincrement register indirect				
Predecrement register indirect				
Register indirect with displacement	X		101	rrr
Register indirect with index	X		110	rrr
Absolute short	X		111	000
Absolute long	X		111	001
Program counter relative with displacement	X		111	010
Program counter relative with index	X		111	011
Immediate				

The object code for the PEA instruction is:

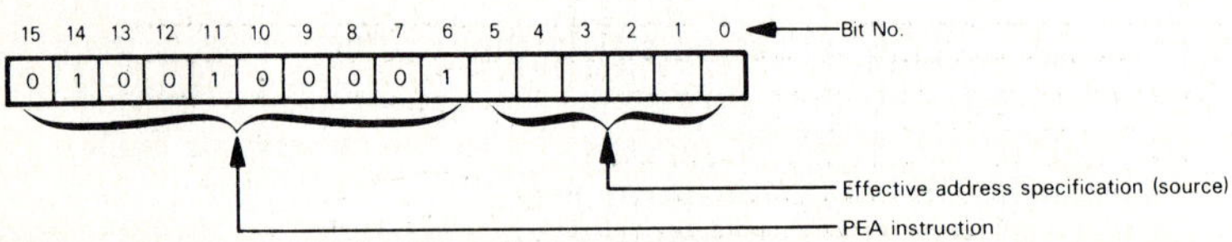

Figure 22-43 illustrates execution of the PEA instruction using absolute short addressing. The 16-bit short address (420_{16}) is sign-extended to 32 bits. That 32-bit address is then pushed onto the system stack. In Figure 22-43 the user stack pointer (USP) is used during this push operation. The least significant bits of the effective address (0420_{16}) will be stored at memory word wwwwvvvv−2. The stack pointer is then decremented by 2 and the most significant 16 bits of the address are pushed onto the stack. The final value of the stack pointer will be four less than when instruction execution began.

Of course, a more complex address calculation may be performed if other addressing modes are used. None of the status flags is affected by the PEA instruction.

The address that is pushed onto the stack by PEA is always a 32-bit address regardless of the addressing mode used to specify the effective address.

RESET — Reset External Devices

This instruction causes a pulse to be output on the RESET pin from the processor. This instruction is therefore used to cause reset of external devices. The state of the processor itself is unaffected except that the program counter is incremented by 2. Program execution thus continues with the next consecutive instruction. The object code for the RESET instruction follows.

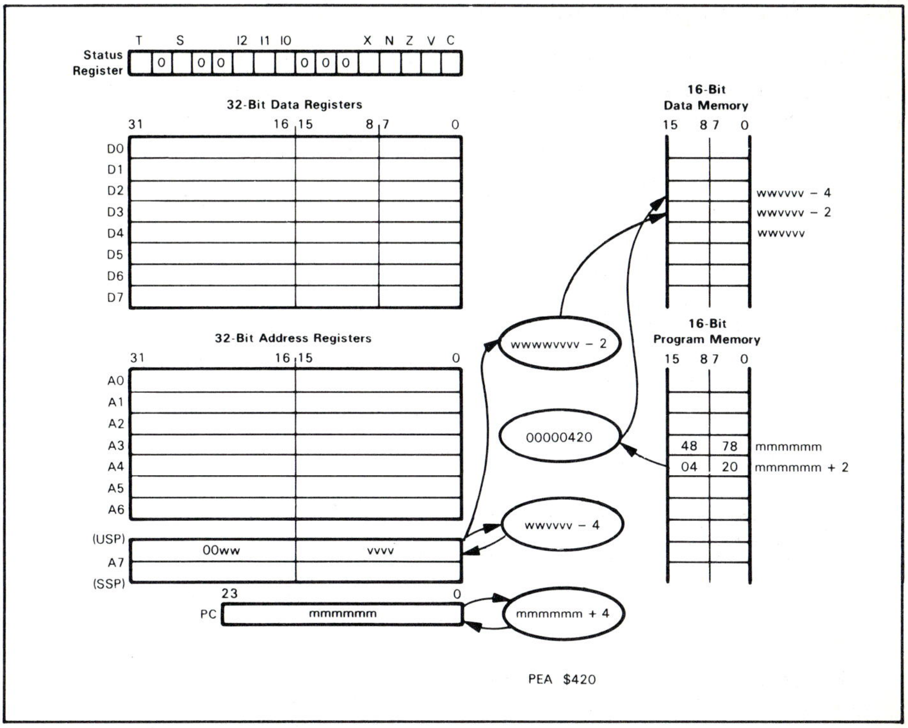

Figure 22-43. Execution of the PEA Instruction Using Absolute Short Addressing

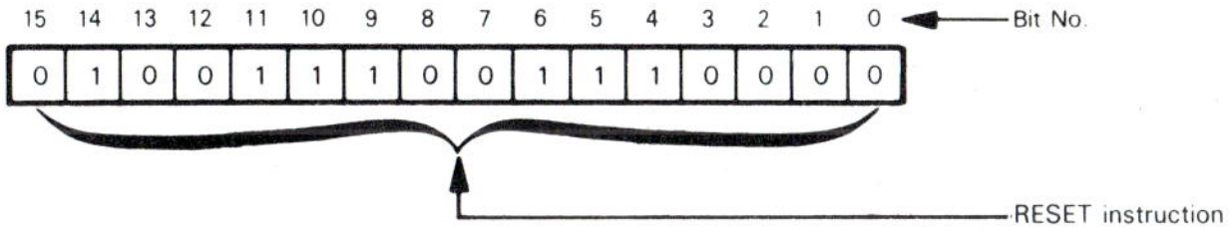

None of the status flags is affected by the RESET instruction.

ROL — Rotate Data Register Left

This instruction causes the contents of a specified data register to be rotated left. The Carry flag receives the last bit shifted out of the most significant bit of the data register and that bit is also shifted into the low-order bit of the data register. The shift count may be specified by the contents of another data register or by immediate data.

If the rotate count is contained in a data register, the least significant six bits of that data register specify the count in the range from 0 to 63 (modulo 64).

If immediate data is used, shift count in the range of 1 to 8 can be specified as part of the instruction operation code.

The object code for the ROL instruction is:

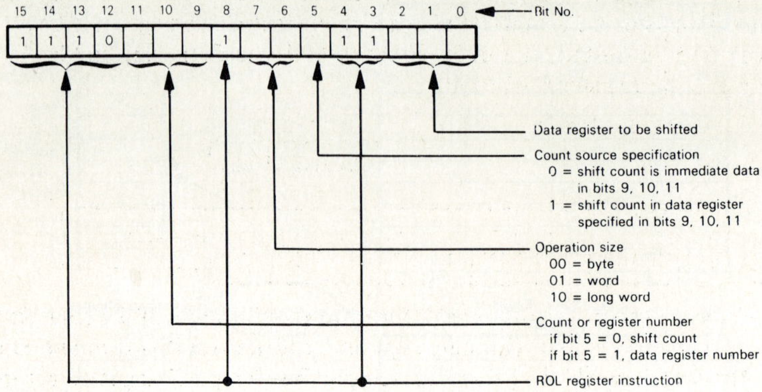

Bit 5 of the instruction operation code determines whether the count is specified using immediate data held in bits 9, 10, or 11 or whether the count is contained in the data register specified in bits 9, 10, and 11.

Figure 22-44 illustrates an ROL instruction with register D0 specified as the destination operand and with the shift count contained in register D3. If register D0

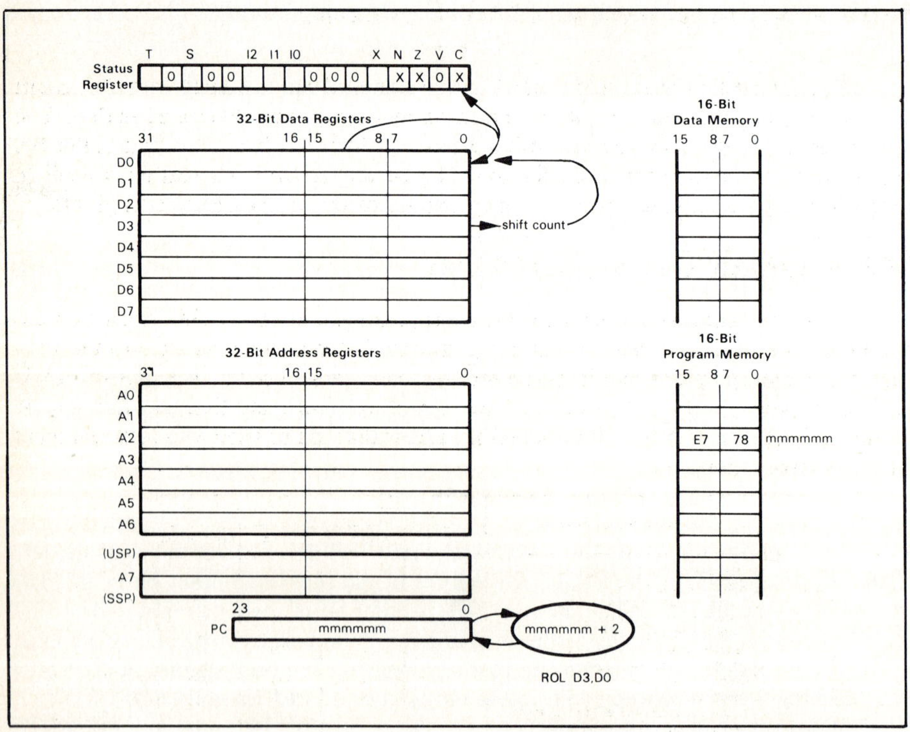

Figure 22-44. Execution of ROL Instruction with Operand and Shift Count in Data Registers

initially contains $AD1F_{16}$ and register D3 contains 03_{16}, the contents of register D0 would be rotated three bit positions to the left. After the instruction ROL D3,D0 has been executed, register D0 would contain $68FD_{16}$ and the Carry flag would be set to 1.

Bits shifted out of the high-order bit go to both the Carry flag and back into the low-order bit of the register as shown:

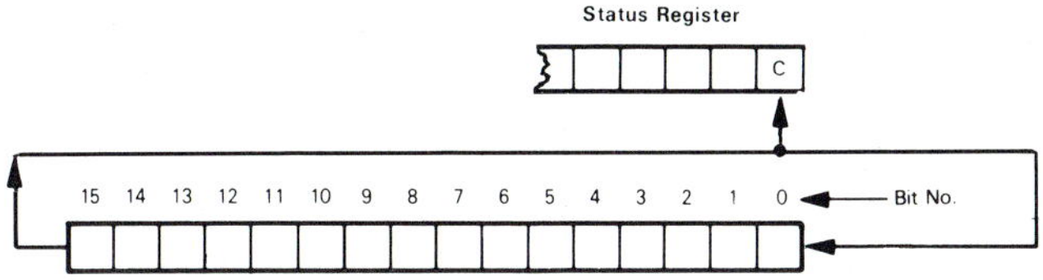

The Negative (N) status flag is set if the most significant bit of the result is set and is cleared otherwise. The Zero (Z) status flag is set if the result is zero and is cleared otherwise. The Overflow (V) flag is always cleared. The Carry (C) flag is set according to the last bit shifted out of the operand. C is cleared if a shift count of 0 is specified. The Extend (X) flag is not affected.

Figure 22-44 illustrated an ROL operation with an operand size of word in the data register. Only bits 0 through 15 of the data register were affected; bits 16-31 remain unchanged. The ROL instruction can also operate on byte and long word operands in the data register.

Note that for the instruction illustrated in Figure 22-44, the same results could have been obtained by executing the following instruction:

```
ROL#3,DO
```

This instruction uses an immediate data value of three to indicate the shift count instead of using the contents of another data register as was illustrated earlier. The advantage of using a data register to indicate the shift count is that you may alter the contents of the data register dynamically under program control, whereas an immediate data value will be contained in program memory and will usually be unchangeable.

ROL — Rotate Memory Word Left

This instruction performs the same operation as the ROL register instruction described in the preceding paragraphs but performs that operation on an operand contained in memory rather than in a data register. This version of the ROL instruction is limited in two ways: the operand size is restricted to a word and that operand may be shifted only one bit position. The addressing modes that can be used with this version of the ROL instruction are:

Addressing Modes Allowed	Operand		Destination ea Field	
	Source	Destination	Mode	Register No.
Data register direct				
Address register direct				
Address register indirect		X	010	rrr
Postincrement register indirect		X	011	rrr
Predecrement register indirect		X	100	rrr
Register indirect with displacement		X	101	rrr
Register indirect with index		X	110	rrr
Absolute short		X	111	000
Absolute long		X	111	001
Program counter relative with displacement				
Program counter relative with index				
Immediate				

The object code for this version of the ROL instruction is:

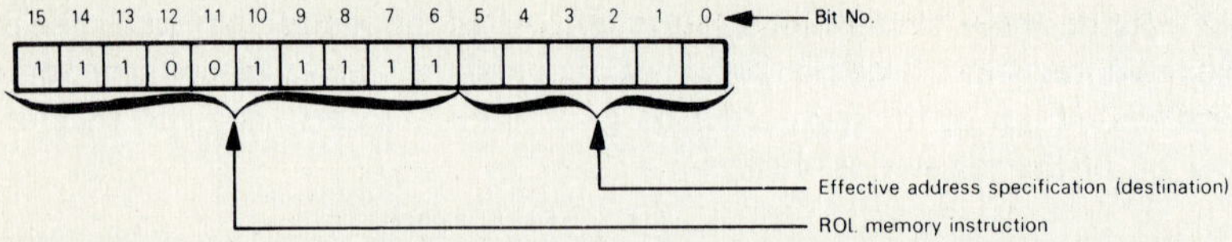

The execution of this ROL instruction is the same as was illustrated for the ROL data register version. The operand in memory is rotated left one bit and the bit shifted out of the high-order bit goes to both the Carry (C) flag in the status register and to bit zero of the memory word.

Refer to the ROL register instruction for a description of the effect that this instruction has on the status flags.

ROR — Rotate Right

This instruction rotates the bits of a specified operand to the right. Just as was the case with the ROL instructions described in the preceding pages, there are two general versions of this instruction: one version allows an operand contained in a data register to be shifted a number of bit positions specified either by the contents of another data register or by an immediate value indicated in the instruction word itself. The second version of the ROR instruction allows a 1-bit shift of a word operand contained in memory. The addressing modes allowed for the ROR instructions are the same as for the ROL register and ROL memory instructions.

The object code for the ROR register instruction can be illustrated as follows:

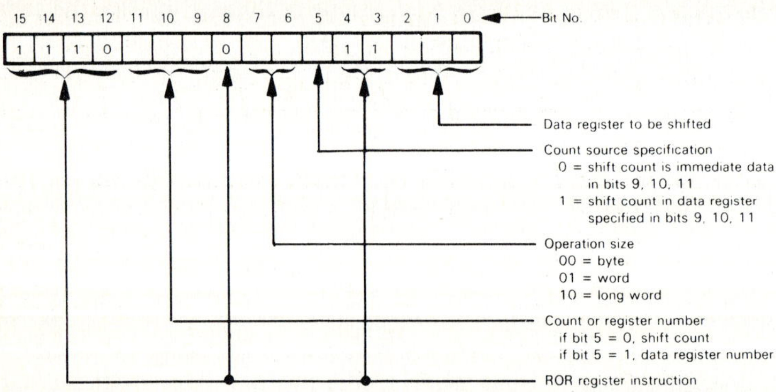

When the ROR instruction is executed, the operand is shifted right the number of bit positions indicated and the bits shifted out of the low-order bit go to both the Carry (C) flag in the status register and to the high-order bit of the operand as shown:

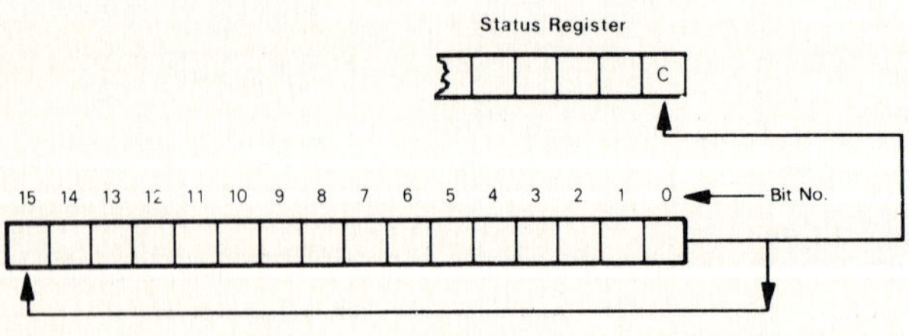

As was the case with the ROL instruction, the only differences between the register and memory version of this instruction are that the memory version must have an operand size of word and that the bit shift can only be one position. The addressing modes allowed are:

Addressing Modes Allowed	Operand		Destination ea Field	
	Source	Destination	Mode	Register No.
Data register direct				
Address register direct				
Address register indirect		X	010	rrr
Postincrement register indirect		X	011	rrr
Predecrement register indirect		X	100	rrr
Register indirect with displacement		X	101	rrr
Register indirect with index		X	110	rrr
Absolute short		X	111	000
Absolute long		X	111	001
Program counter relative with displacement				
Program counter relative with index				
Immediate				

The object code for the memory version of the ROR instruction is:

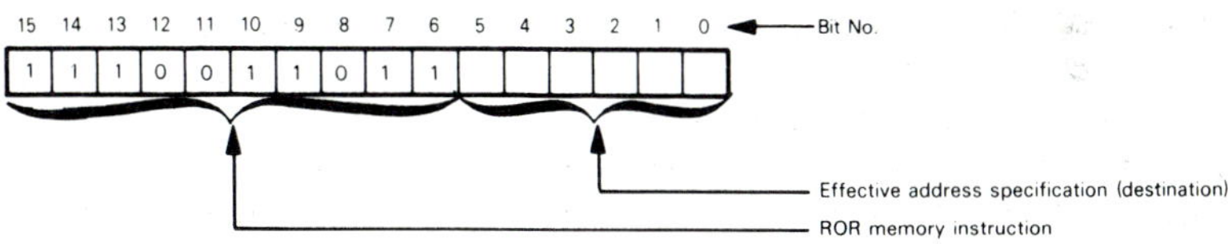

ROXL — Rotate Left with Extend

This instruction, like the ROL instruction, rotates the bits of a specified operand to the left. However, bits shifted out of the high-order bit go to both the Carry (C) and Extend (X) status flags. The previous value of the Extend flag is shifted into the low-order bit. Thus, **this version of the rotate instruction can be used in multiprecision operations.**

The versions and addressing modes that can be used with the ROXL instruction are the same as those that may be used with the ROL instruction described in the preceding pages. You should refer to the descriptions of the ROL register and ROL memory instructions to determine the available addressing modes.

The object code for the rotate register version of the ROXL instruction is:

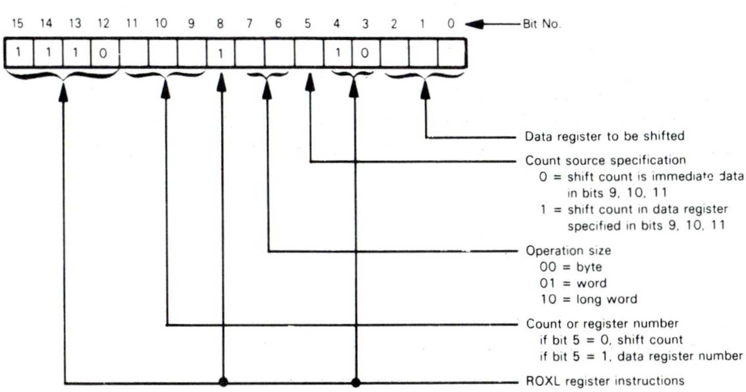

The object code for the rotate memory version of ROXL is:

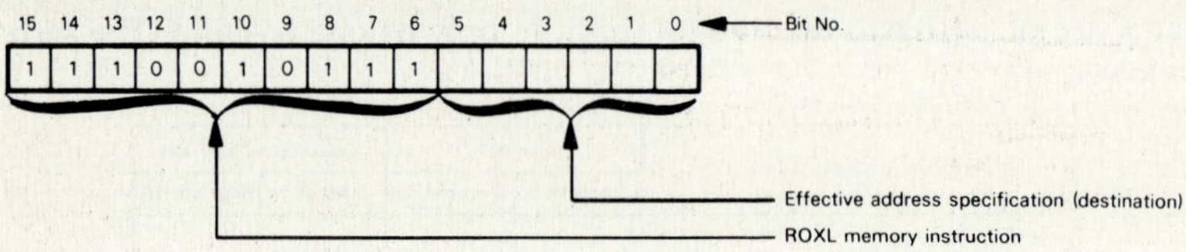

For a detailed discussion of the operation of the ROXL instruction, refer to our earlier description of the ROL instruction, noting the following differences. First, the Extend (X) flag is affected and will be set according to the last bit shifted out of the operand. Thus the Carry (C) and Extend flags will be set the same. Second, the low-order bit of the operand will be set according to the prior value of the Extend flag. If the register D0 initially contains $AD1F_{16}$ and register D3 contains 03_{16} as in the ROL example, the execution of the instruction ROXL D3,D0 would set both the Carry and Extend flags to 1. Register D0 would contain $68FD_{16}$ if the value of the Extend flag was 1 prior to the execution of the ROXL instruction. If the prior value of the Extend flag was 0, register D0 would contain $68F9_{16}$. The effect of the ROXL instruction is:

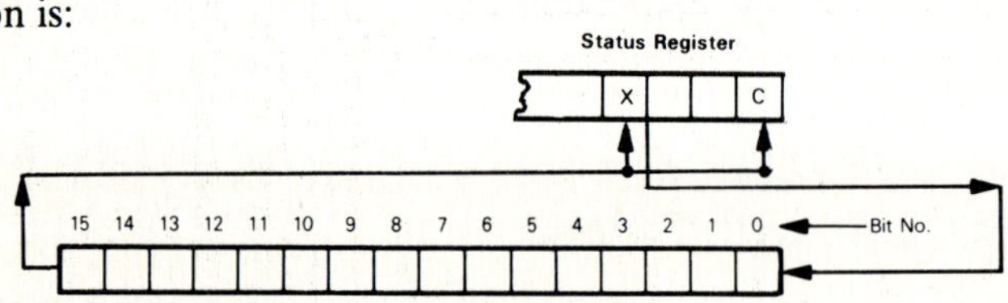

ROXR — Rotate Right with Extend

This instruction operates in exactly the same manner as the ROXL instruction except the bits are shifted out of the low-order bit of the operand into the Carry (C) and Extend (X) flags. The previous value of the Extend flag is shifted into the high-order bit of the operand. Thus, **this version of the rotate instruction can be used in multiprecision operations.**

The versions and addressing modes that can be used with the ROXR instruction are the same as those available with the ROR instruction and you should refer to those descriptions to determine the modes available.

The object code for the data register version of the ROXR instruction is:

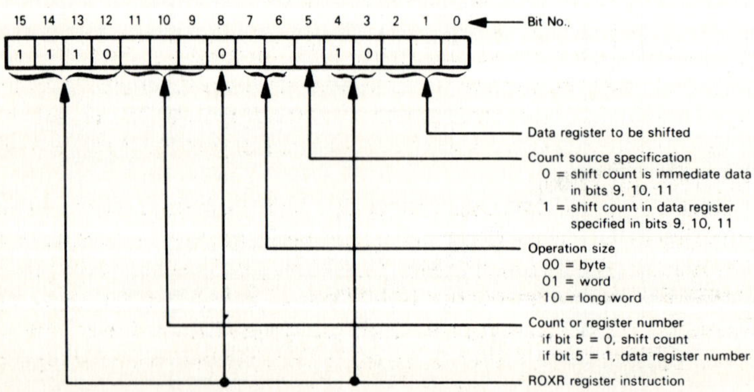

The object code for the rotate memory version of the ROXR instruction is:

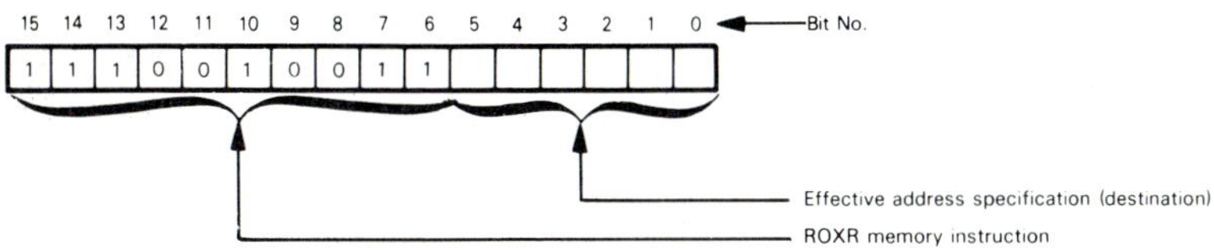

When the ROXR instruction is executed, the operand is shifted right the number of bit positions indicated, and bits shifted out of the low-order bit go to both the Carry and Extend flags. The previous value of the Extend flag goes to the high-order bit of the operand, as shown below.

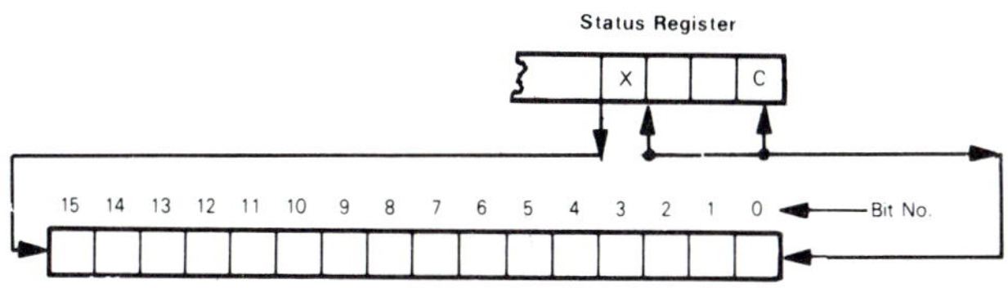

RTE — Return from Exception

This instruction restores the state of a program that was interrupted by exception processing by loading the status register and program counter from the system stack. **RTE should be the last instruction executed by an exception processing service routine.**

The object code for the RTE instruction is:

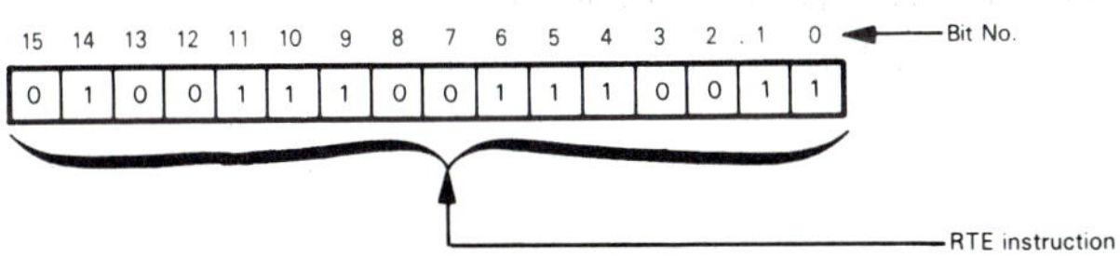

Figure 22-45 illustrates execution of the RTE instruction. First the top word pulled from the stack is loaded into the status register replacing the previous contents of the status register. The next two words pulled from the stack are then loaded into the program counter. Program execution will then continue beginning at the new address loaded into the program counter.

Note that the stack pointer used during the RTE instruction is the supervisor stack pointer (SSP) since all exception processing is performed in the supervisor mode. After the RTE instruction is executed, the processor may be in either the supervisor or user mode depending on the state of the S-bit that was loaded into the status register. Obviously, all 16 bits of the status register, both the system byte and user byte, will be affected by the RTE instruction except for those bits not yet used which always remain set to 0.

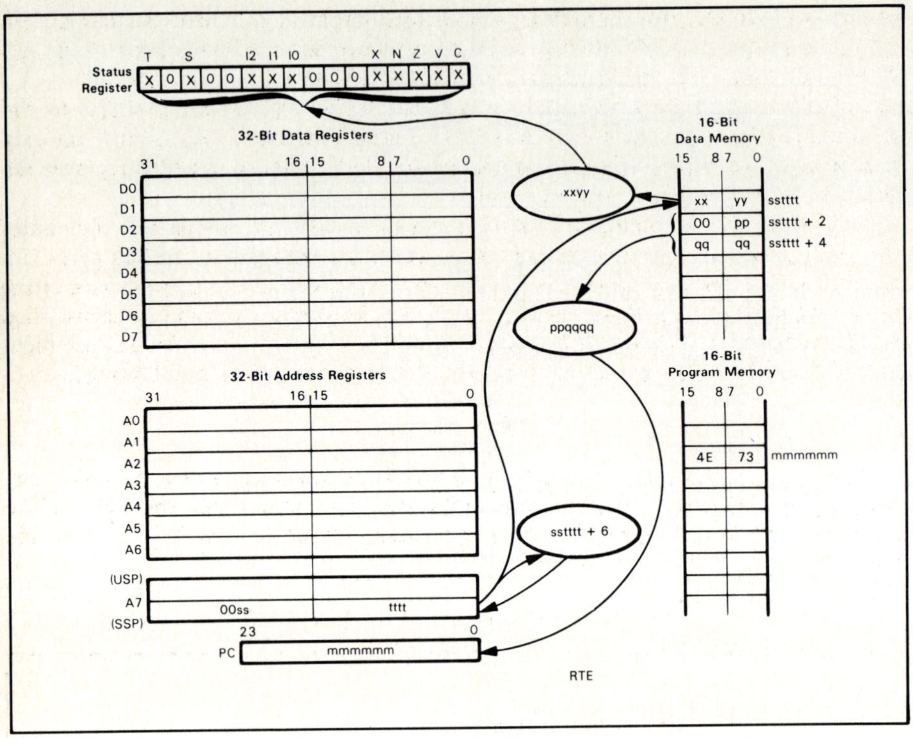

Figure 22-45. Execution of the RTE Instruction

RTR — Return and Restore Condition Codes

This instruction restores the condition code portion of the status register by pulling a word from the stack and placing the five least significant bits into the status register. It returns program control from a subroutine to the calling program by pulling a return address from the stack and placing it in the program counter.

The object code for the RTR instruction is:

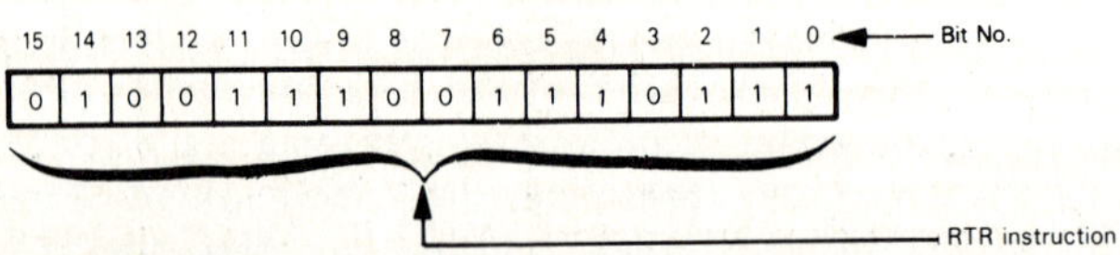

Figure 22-46 illustrates execution of the RTR instruction. The five least significant bits of the first word pulled from the system stack are used to replace the previous contents of the condition code portion of the status register (the X, N, Z, V, and C flags). The next two words pulled from the system stack are loaded into the program counter and the previous contents of the program counter are lost. The processor increments the stack pointer after pulling each word from the stack, so the final value of that pointer is six greater than its starting value. Note that in Figure 22-45 we have shown the user stack pointer (USP) being used. Had the processor been operating in the supervisor mode, the supervisor stack pointer (SSP) would have been used instead.

Only the five least significant bits of the status register are modified by the RTR instruction; the system byte of the status register is unaffected. This is the only difference between the RTR instruction and the RTE instruction which replaces the entire 16-bit contents of the status register.

The MC68000 provides no special jump-to-subroutine instruction which automatically saves the condition codes from the status register on the stack as part of its execution. Therefore, if you are going to use the RTR instruction, your subroutine must save the contents of the condition codes on the stack. This can be accomplished by executing the MOVE from SR instruction using register indirect with predecrement addressing and specifying that A7 serve as the register as shown in the following instruction:

```
MOVE SR,-(A7)
```

Note that this instruction must be executed before your subroutine makes any other use of the system stack since the RTR instruction expects the saved value of the condition codes and the program counter to occupy three consecutive words on the stack.

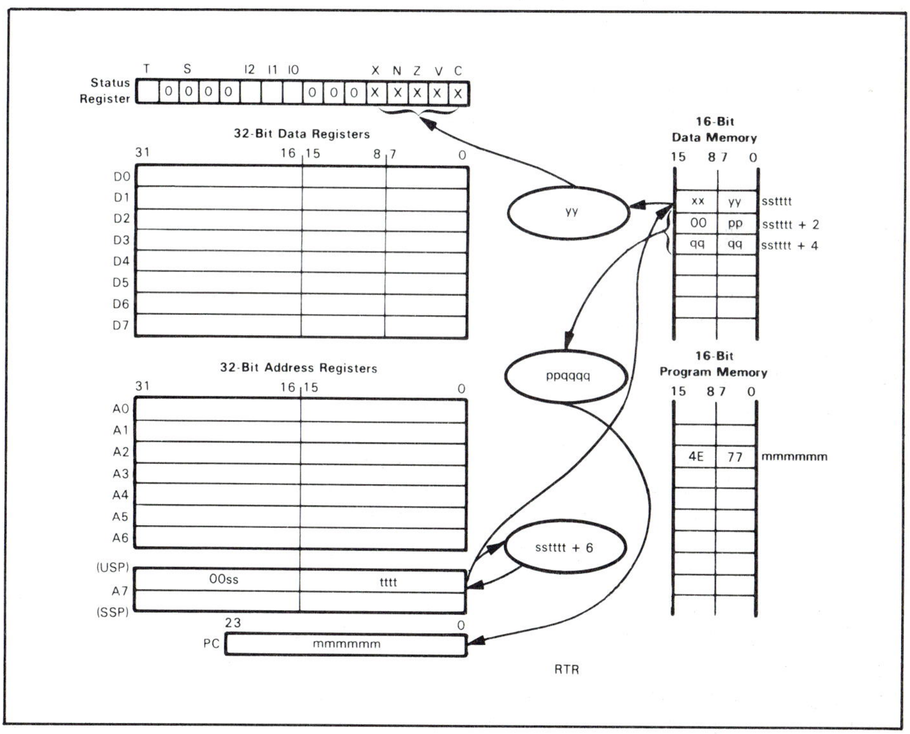

Figure 22-46. Execution of the RTR Instruction

RTS — Return from Subroutine

This instruction causes program control to be returned from a subroutine to the calling program by pulling the return address from the stack and placing it into the program counter.

The object code for the RTS instruction is:

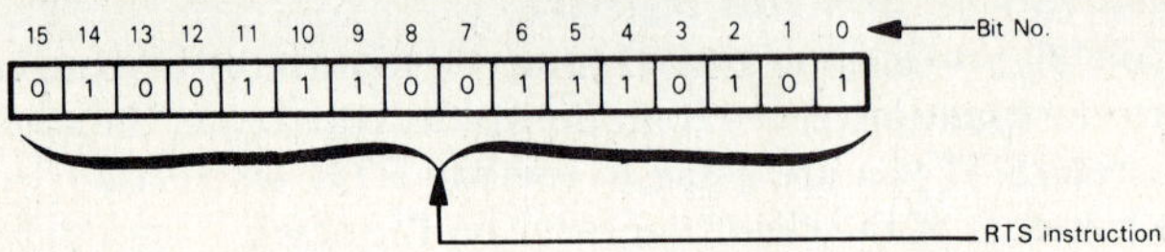

Figure 22-47 illustrates execution of the RTS instruction. The previous contents of the program counter are lost. The processor increments the stack pointer by 2 after pulling each word, so the final value of that pointer is four larger than its starting value. Each subroutine normally contains at least one RTS instruction; this is the last instruction executed within the subroutine and causes control to return to the calling program. RTS does affect any of the status flags.

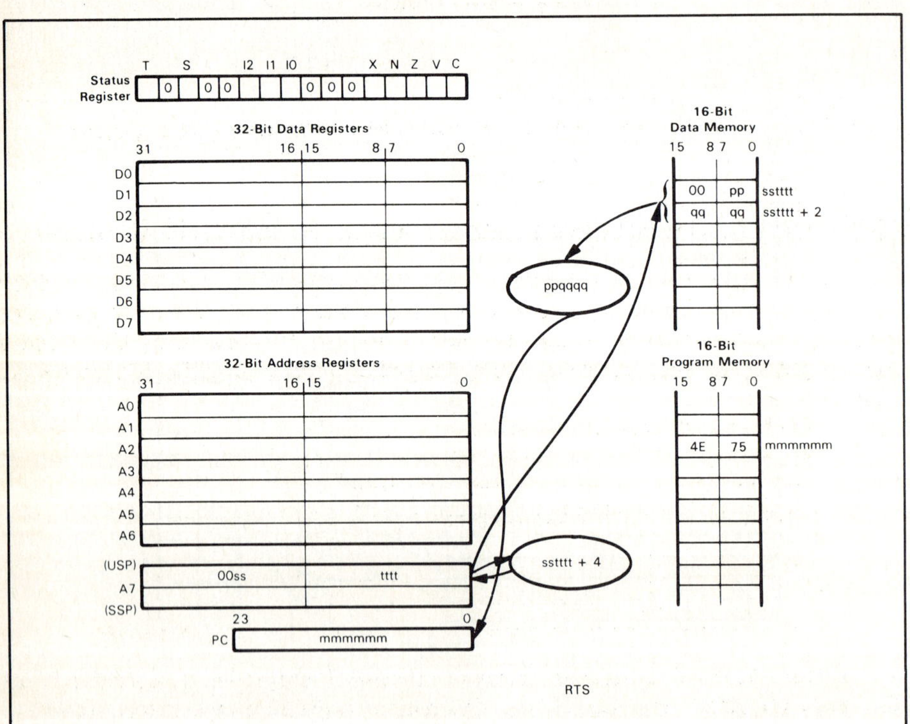

Figure 22-47. Execution of the RTS Instruction

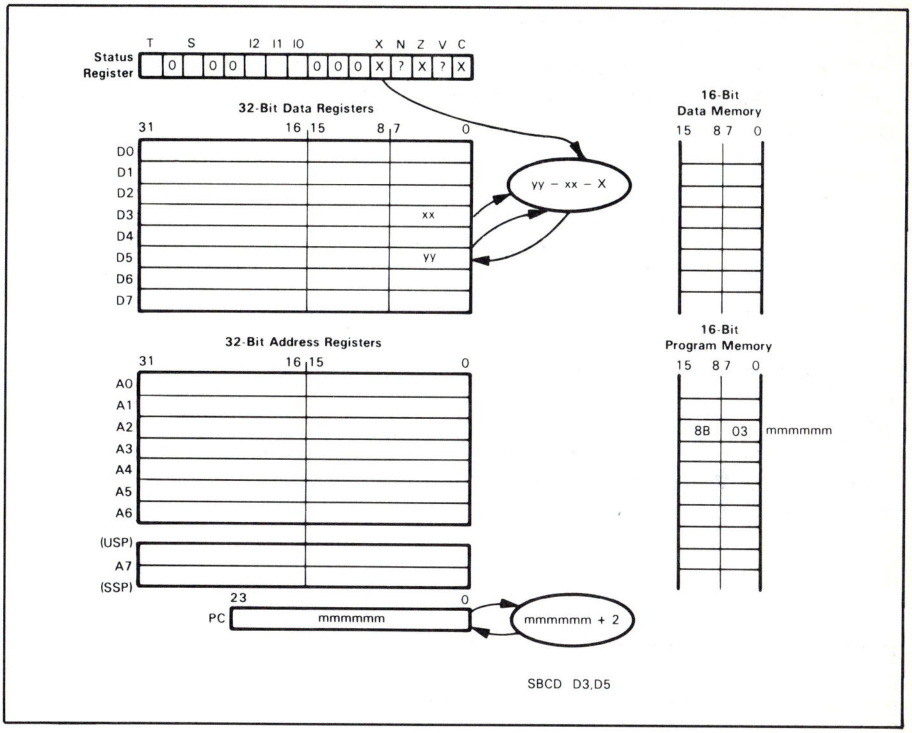

Figure 22-48. Execution of the SBCD Instruction with Operands in Data Registers

SBCD — Subtract Decimal with Extend Register to Register

This instruction subtracts both the contents of the source data register and the value of the Extend (X) flag from the contents of the destination data register. The result is stored in the destination. The subtraction is performed using binary-coded decimal (BCD) arithmetic and only the least significant eight bits of the data register are involved.

The object code for this instruction is:

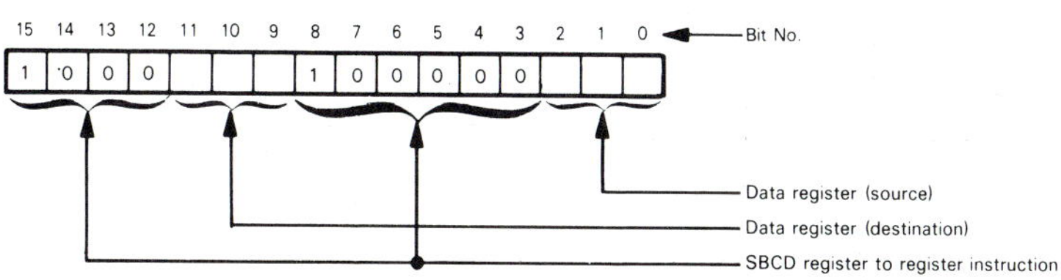

Figure 22-48 illustrates execution of the SBCD instruction with register D3 as the source register and D5 as the destination register. Suppose that $xx=43_{10}$, Extend=1, and $yy=57_{10}$. After the processor executes the instruction SBCD D3,D5 the contents of D5 will be 13_{10}.

```
  (D5)  =  57
  (D3)  =  43
           14
Extend  =  -1
  (D5)  =  13
           └──────→ No borrow, Carry and Extend cleared to 0
```

Bits 8 through 31 of the data registers are unaffected by this instruction.

The Carry (C) and Extend (X) flags are set if a borrow is generated as a result of the operation and are cleared otherwise. The Zero (Z) flag is cleared if the result is non-zero and is unchanged if the result is zero. The N and V flags are undefined.

Note that the Zero flag is not changed if the result is zero. To perform multiple precision arithmetic, first set the Zero flag (using MOVE to CCR), then perform the operation. If any part of the result is non-zero, the Zero flag will be cleared; otherwise, the result is zero and the Zero flag remains set.

SBCD – Subtract Decimal with Extend Memory to Memory

This instruction subtracts both the contents of the source memory location and the value of the Extend (X) flag from the contents of the destination memory location. The result is stored in the destination. The memory address of the source operand is held in one address register and the memory address of the destination operand is held in another address register. The contents of both address registers are decremented before the operation. The subtraction is performed using binary-coded decimal (BCD) arithmetic.

The object code for this form of the SBCD instruction is:

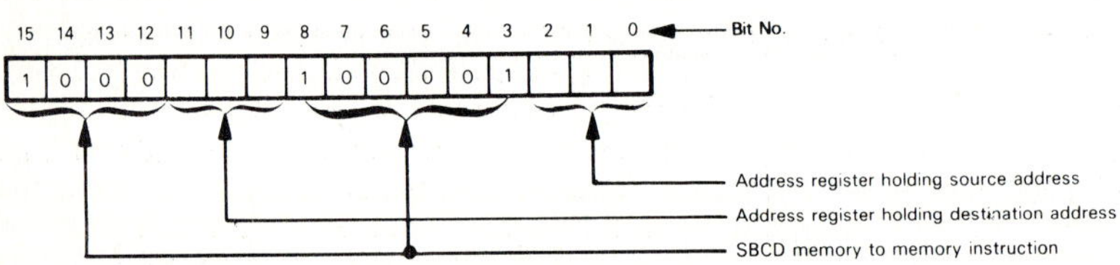

Figure 22-49 illustrates execution of the SBCD instruction where register A1 holds the address of the source operand in memory and register A4 holds the address of the destination operand in memory. As you can see, the contents of both address registers are decremented before the operands are accessed for the SBCD operation. This is done to facilitate multibyte BCD subtraction, since a string of BCD digits representing a decimal number would normally be stored with the least significant digits right justified at the higher memory address. Refer to Chapter 8 for a discussion of multibyte BCD subtraction.

The effect of this version of the SBCD instruction on status flags is the same as described for the SBCD register instruction.

S_{CC} – Set According to Condition

This instruction tests the state of a specified condition code (cc). If the specified condition is met, then the contents of a byte specified in the destination operand are set

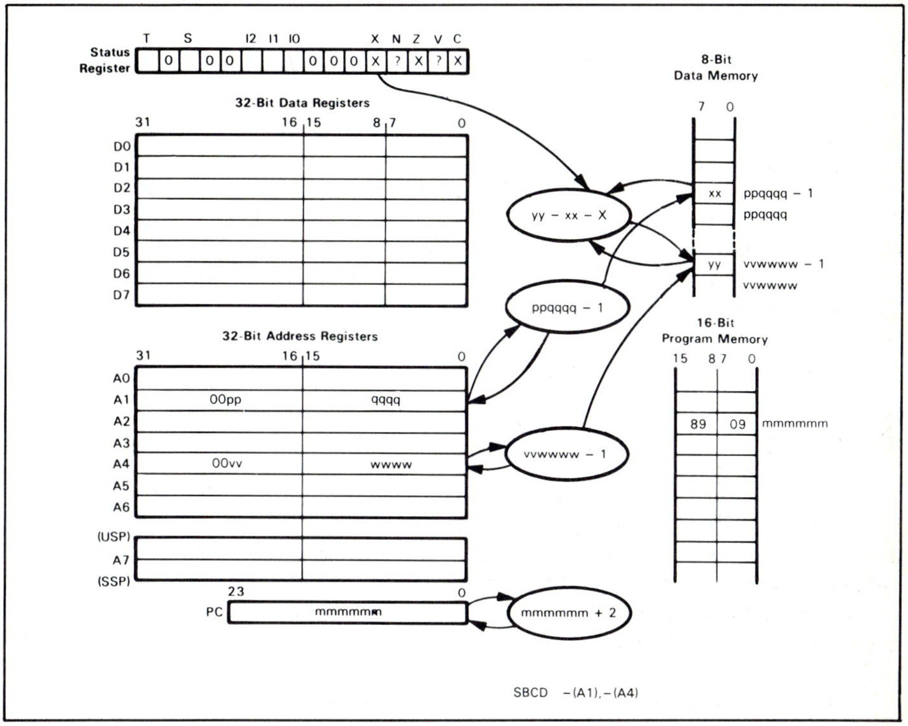

Figure 22-49. Execution of the SBCD Instruction with Memory Operands

to all ones. If the condition is not met, the byte is set to all zeros. The addressing modes that can be used to specify the destination are:

Addressing Modes Allowed	Operand		Destination ea Field	
	Source	Destination	Mode	Register No.
Data register direct		X	000	rrr
Address register direct				
Address register indirect		X	010	rrr
Postincrement register indirect		X	011	rrr
Predecrement register indirect		X	100	rrr
Register indirect with displacement		X	101	rrr
Register indirect with index		X	110	rrr
Absolute short		X	111	000
Absolute long		X	111	001
Program counter relative with displacement				
Program counter relative with index				
Immediate				

The object code for the S_{cc} instruction is:

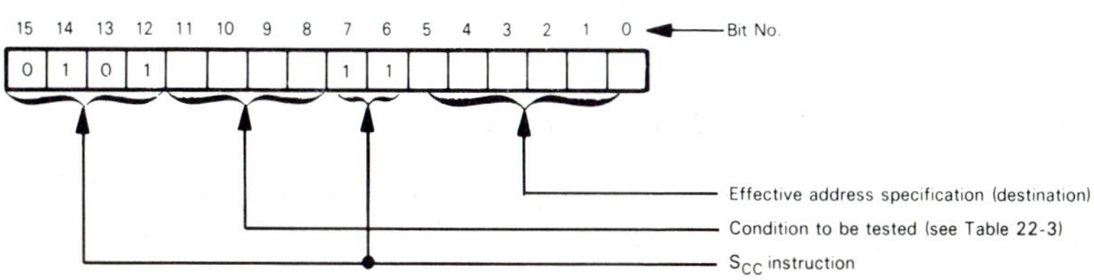

Table 22-3. CC Conditional Tests

Mnemonic(cc)	Condition	Condition Field	Test
T	True	0000	1
F	False	0001	0
HI	High	0010	$\overline{C} \wedge \overline{Z}$
LS	Low or same	0011	$C \vee Z$
CC	Carry clear	0100	$\overline{C}$
CS	Carry set	0101	C
NE	Not equal	0110	$\overline{Z}$
EQ	Equal	0111	Z
VC	Overflow clear	1000	$\overline{V}$
VS	Overflow set	1001	V
PL	Plus	1010	$\overline{N}$
MI	Minus	1001	N
GE	Greater or equal	1100	$(N \wedge V) \vee (\overline{N} \wedge \overline{V})$
LT	Less than	1101	$(N \wedge \overline{V}) \vee (\overline{N} \wedge V)$
GT	Greater than	1110	$(N \wedge V \wedge \overline{Z}) \vee (\overline{N} \wedge V \wedge \overline{Z})$
LE	Less or equal	1111	$Z \vee (N \wedge \overline{V}) \vee (\overline{N} \wedge V)$

Bits 8 through 11 of the instruction word specify the condition code which is to be tested. **Table 22-3 lists the conditions that can be used with this instruction** and the values that are computed from the values of the flags in the status register to determine whether the test is successful.

Figure 22-50 illustrates execution of the SPL instruction using address register indirect addressing to specify the byte that is to be modified. The specified condition (PL) is true if the Negative flag (N) is cleared. In this case, the specified byte in memory will be set to all ones. If N=1, the plus condition is not met and the specified memory byte will be cleared to all zeros.

None of the status flags is affected by the S_{cc} instruction.

STOP — Load Status Register and Stop

This instruction loads a 16-bit immediate value contained in program memory into the status register and the processor then stops fetching and executing instructions. Execution of instructions will not resume until a trace, interrupt, or reset exception occurs.

The object code for the STOP instruction is:

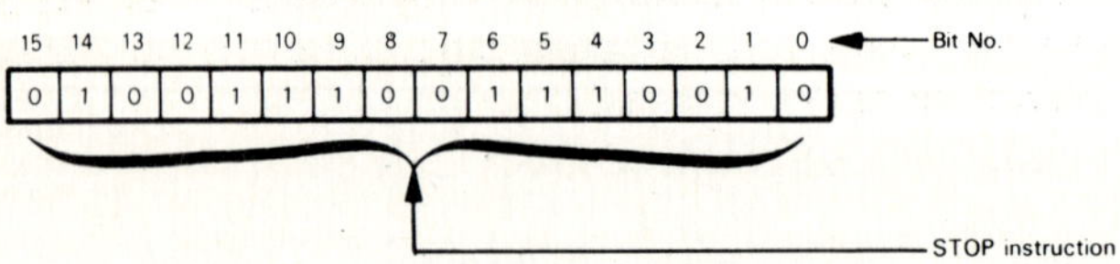

The 16 bits of immediate data following the instruction word are moved into the entire status register. The program counter contents will be advanced by four to point to the next instruction. The processor then simply waits for a trace, interrupt, or reset exception to occur.

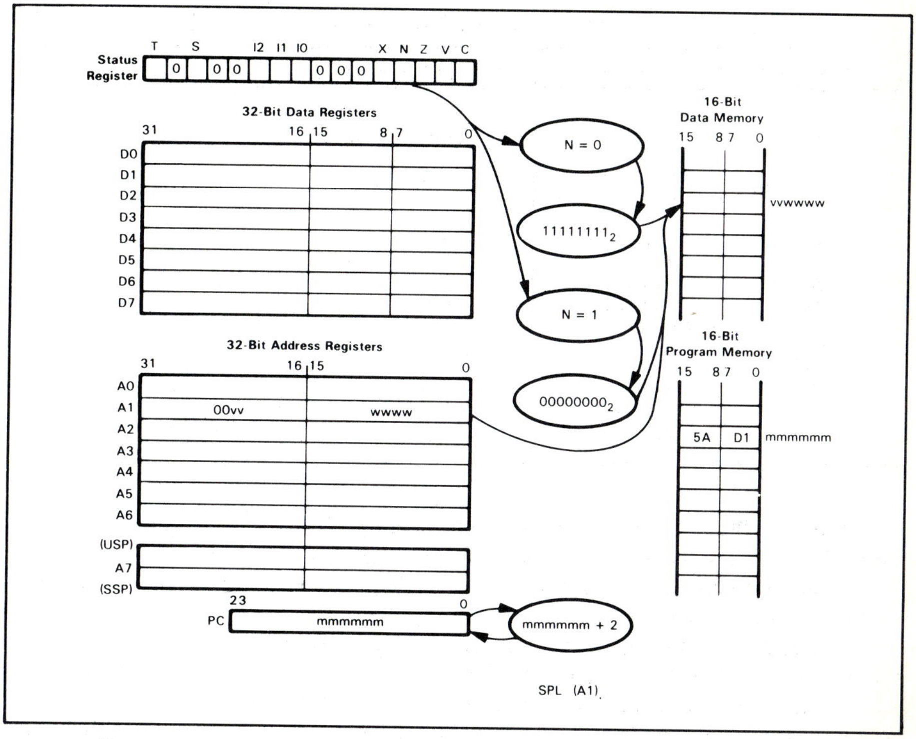

Figure 22-50. Execution of the SPL Instruction Using Address Register Indirect Addressing

A trace exception will occur immediately if the trace state is on (T-bit in the status register=1) when the STOP instruction is executed.

Exception processing in response to an interrupt request will be initiated if an interrupt request is detected whose priority is higher than the current value allowed by the interrupt mask in the status register.

If the RESET signal is pulsed low, this will always initiate reset exception processing and terminate the STOP instruction.

The STOP instruction is a privileged instruction and can only be executed while the processor is in the supervisor mode of operation. If you attempt to execute this instruction while in the user mode of operation, it will cause a privilege violation and exception processing will be initiated.

SUB — Subtract Binary

This instruction subtracts the contents of the source operand from the destination operand and stores the result in the destination.

There are two general forms for this instruction. In the first form, a data register provides one of the operands and is the destination for the subtraction. In this form, all addressing modes are allowed:

Addressing Modes Allowed	Operand		Source ea Field	
	Source	Destination	Mode	Register No.
Data register direct	X	X	000	rrr
Address register direct	X*		001	rrr
Address register indirect	X		010	rrr
Postincrement register indirect	X		011	rrr
Predecrement register indirect	X		100	rrr
Register indirect with displacement	X		101	rrr
Register indirect with index	X		110	rrr
Absolute short	X		111	000
Absolute long	X		111	001
Program counter relative with displacement	X		111	010
Program counter relative with index	X		111	011
Immediate	X		111	100

*Not allowed if operation size is byte.

The only limitation on addressing modes for this form is that address register direct addressing cannot provide the source if the operand size specification is byte, since the address registers cannot handle data on a byte basis.

In the other general form of the SUB instruction, a data register must provide the source operand and the destination operand can be specified using any of the addressing modes shown:

Addressing Modes Allowed	Operand		Destination ea Field	
	Source	Destination	Mode	Register No.
Data register direct	X			
Address register direct				
Address register indirect		X	010	rrr
Postincrement register indirect		X	011	rrr
Predecrement register indirect		X	100	rrr
Register indirect with displacement		X	101	rrr
Register indirect with index		X	110	rrr
Absolute short		X	111	000
Absolute long		X	111	001
Program counter relative with displacement				
Program counter relative with index				
Immediate				

The object code for the SUB instruction is:

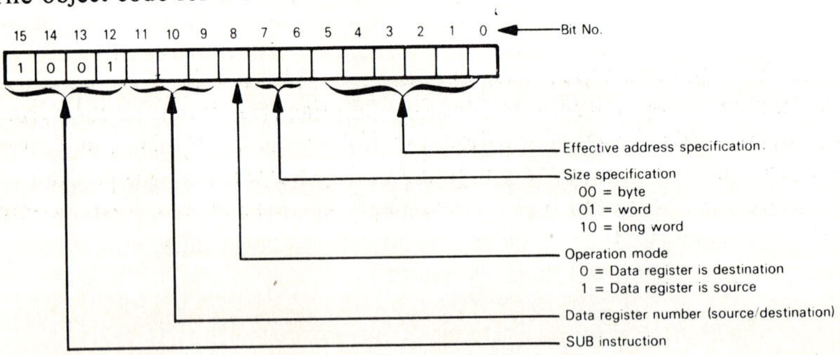

Figure 22-51 illustrates execution of the SUB instruction using address register indirect addressing; register A2 provides the address of the source operand in memory and register D3 serves as the destination register. The contents of memory location wwvvvv will be subtracted from the contents of register D3 and the result will be returned to register D3.

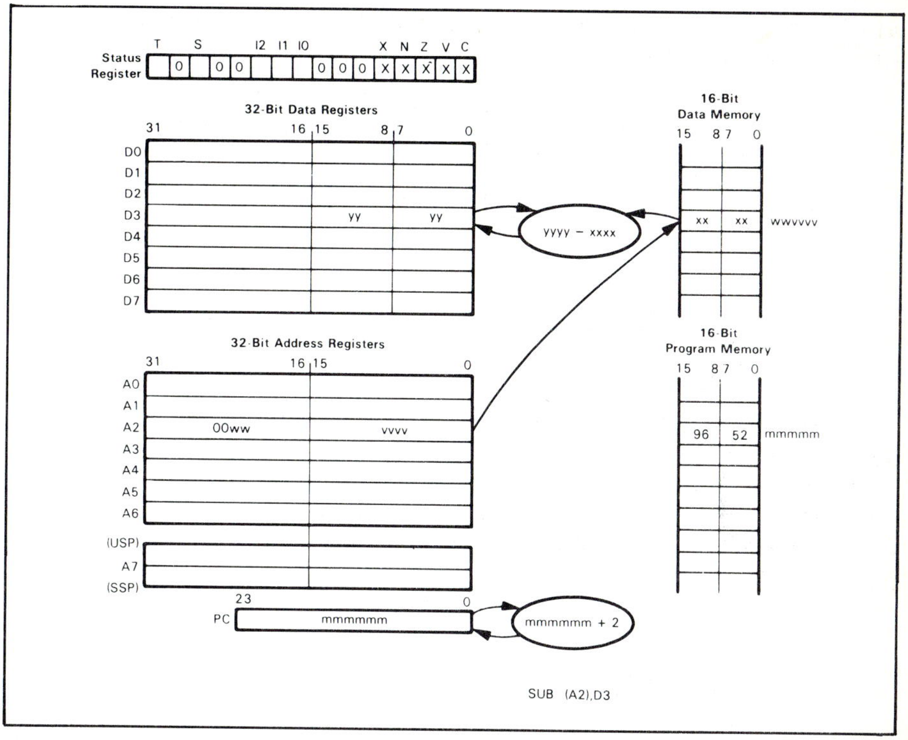

Figure 22-51. Execution of the SUB Instruction Using Address Register Indirect Addressing

The Carry (C) and Extend (X) flags are set if a borrow is generated as a result of the operation and cleared otherwise. The Zero (Z) flag is set if the result is negative and cleared otherwise. The Negative (N) flag is set if the result is negative and cleared otherwise. The Overflow (V) flag is set if an overflow is generated and cleared otherwise. For a discussion of the interaction of these flags in unsigned and two's complement arithmetic, see Chapter 8.

SUBA — Subtract Address

This instruction is a special case of the SUB instruction and subtracts a source operand from a destination address register. The result is stored in the destination address register.

All addressing modes are permitted:

Addressing Modes Allowed	Operand		Source ea Field	
	Source	Destination	Mode	Register No.
Data register direct	X		000	rrr
Address register direct	X	X	001	rrr
Address register indirect	X		010	rrr
Postincrement register indirect	X		011	rrr
Predecrement register indirect	X		100	rrr
Register indirect with displacement	X		101	rrr
Register indirect with index	X		110	rrr
Absolute short	X		111	000
Absolute long	X		111	001
Program counter relative with displacement	X		111	010
Program counter relative with index	X		111	011
Immediate	X		111	100

The object code for the SUBA instruction is:

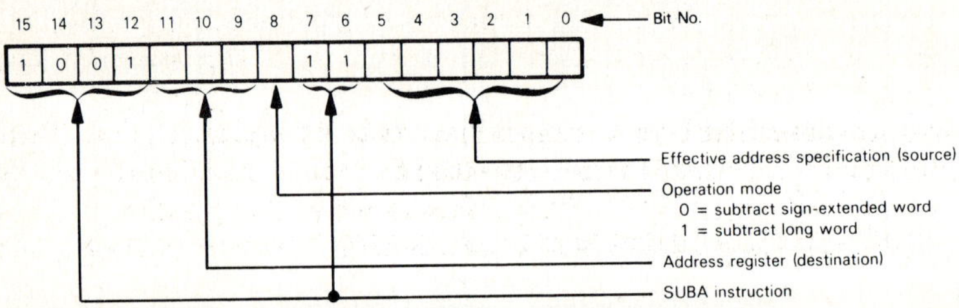

If you specify a 16-bit word source operand instead of a long word, the source is sign-extended to a long word operand and the SUBA operation is performed on a specified address register using all 32 bits.

A significant difference between this subtraction operation and the standard SUB instruction is that none of the status flags is affected by the SUBA instruction.

SUBI – Subtract Immediate

This instruction subtracts the immediate data present in the succeeding program memory locations from the destination operand. The result is stored in the destination. The addressing modes that can be used with this instruction are:

Addressing Modes Allowed	Operand		Destination ea Field	
	Source	Destination	Mode	Register No.
Data register direct		X	000	rrr
Address register direct				
Address register indirect		X	010	rrr
Postincrement register indirect		X	011	rrr
Predecrement register indirect		X	100	rrr
Register indirect with displacement		X	101	rrr
Register indirect with index		X	110	rrr
Absolute short		X	111	000
Absolute long		X	111	001
Program counter relative with displacement				
Program counter relative with index				
Immediate	X			

The object code for this instruction is:

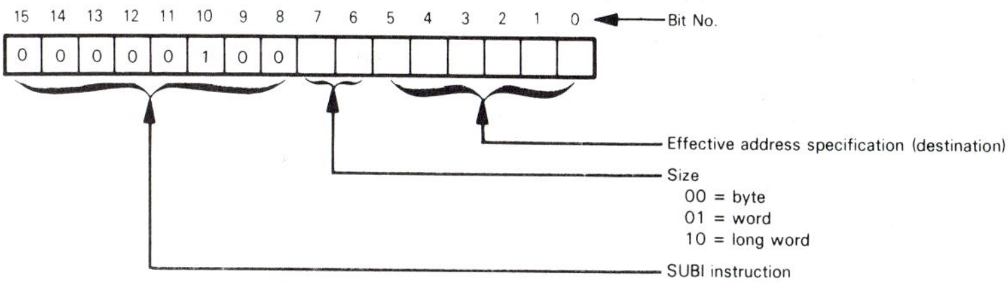

The size of the SUBI operation can be specified as byte, word, or long word. The immediate data follows the instruction word in memory and must match the specified operation size. Thus, either one or two words of immediate data must follow the instruction operation code in program memory. If the instruction specifies a byte operand, the low-order (second) byte of the immediate data word is used. The assembler automatically places the byte correctly.

Operation of the SUBI instruction is essentially the same as that illustrated earlier for the ADDI instruction and you should refer to that instruction and its accompanying figure (Figure 22- 5) for an illustration of its operation.

The X, N, Z, V, and C status bits are all affected in the same way as by the SUB instruction.

SUBQ — Subtract Quick

This instruction subtracts the immediate data contained within the instruction object code word from the destination operand. The result is stored in the destination. The addressing modes that can be used are:

Addressing Modes Allowed	Operand		Destination ea Field	
	Source	Destination	Mode	Register No.
Data register direct		X	000	rrr
Address register direct		X*	001	rrr
Address register indirect		X	010	rrr
Postincrement register indirect		X	011	rrr
Predecrement register indirect		X	100	rrr
Register indirect with displacement		X	101	rrr
Register indirect with index		X	110	rrr
Absolute short		X	111	000
Absolute long		X	111	001
Program counter relative with displacement				
Program counter relative with index				
Immediate	X			

*Not allowed if operation size is byte

Note that address register direct addressing cannot serve as the source if the size specification is byte.

The object code for the SUBQ instruction is:

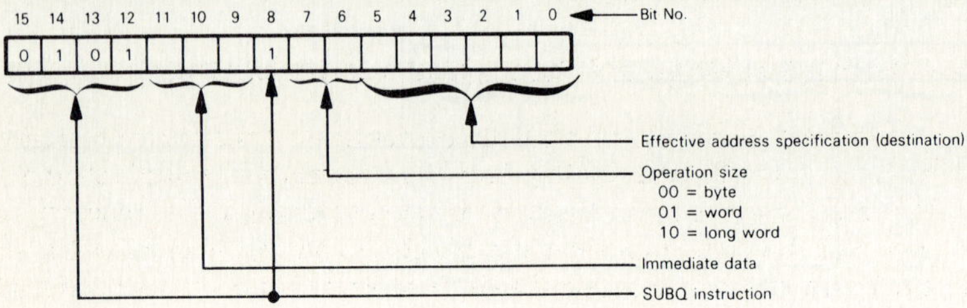

Three bits of immediate data are contained in bits 9, 10, and 11 of the instruction's object code. Thus, immediate operands in the range 1 through 8 can be represented. Immediate data of all zeros is interpreted as 8.

Operation of the SUBQ instruction is essentially the same as that illustrated earlier for the ADDQ instruction. You should refer to that instruction's description and Figure 22-6 for illustration of the instruction's execution.

The N, Z, V, C, and X flags are all affected in the same way as by the SUB instruction.

SUBX — Subtract with Extend Register to Register

This instruction subtracts both the contents of the source data register and the value of the Extend (X) flag from the contents of the destination data register. The result is stored in the destination data register. The operation size can be byte, word, or long word.

The object code for this instruction is:

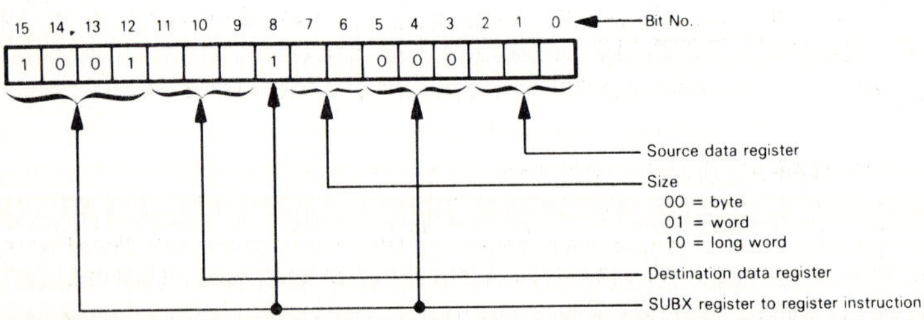

Operation of the SUBX instruction is essentially the same as that illustrated for the ADDX instruction. You should refer to that instruction's description and Figure 22-7 for an illustration of its execution.

The Carry (C) and Extend (X) flags are set if a borrow is generated as a result of the operation and are cleared otherwise. The Zero (Z) flag is cleared if the result is nonzero and is unchanged if the result is zero. The Negative (N) flag is set if the result is zero and cleared otherwise. The Overflow (V) flag is set if there is an overflow and cleared otherwise.

Note that the Zero flag is not changed if the result is zero. To perform multiple precision arithmetic, first set the Zero flag (using MOVE to CCR), then perform the operation. If any part of the result is nonzero, the Zero flag will be cleared; otherwise, the result is zero and the Zero flag remains set.

SUBX — Subtract with Extend Memory to Memory

This instruction binarily subtracts both the contents of the source memory location and the value of the Extend (X) flag from the contents of the destination memory location. The result is stored in the destination memory location. The memory address for the source operand is held in one address register and the memory address of the destination operand is held in the second address register. The contents of both address registers are decremented before the operation.

The object code for this form of the SUBX instruction is:

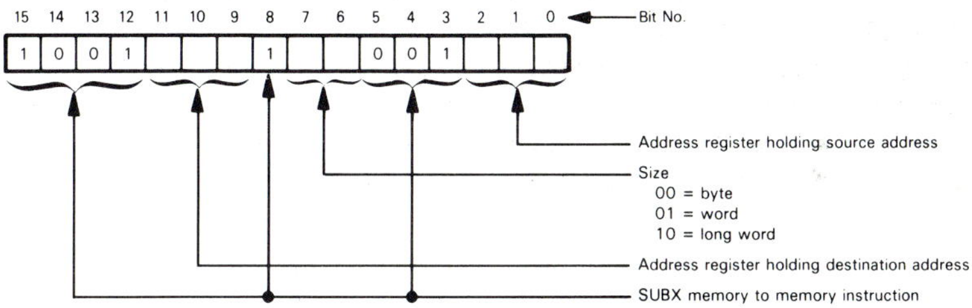

The data size for this version of the SUBX instruction can be byte, word, or long word.

Operation of this instruction is essentially the same as that illustrated for the ADDX memory to memory instruction and you should refer to the description of that instruction and Figure 22-8 for an illustration of its execution.

The register indirect with predecrement mode of operation used with the SUBX instruction facilitates multiple-precision binary arithmetic since the address registers are automatically modified to access the next byte, word, or long word to be used. Refer to Chapter 8 for discussion of multiple-precision arithmetic.

The SUBX instruction modifies the X, N, Z, V, and C status flags.

SWAP — Swap Register Halves

This instruction exchanges the contents of the least significant word of a data register with the contents of the most significant word of that data register.

The object code for the SWAP instruction is:

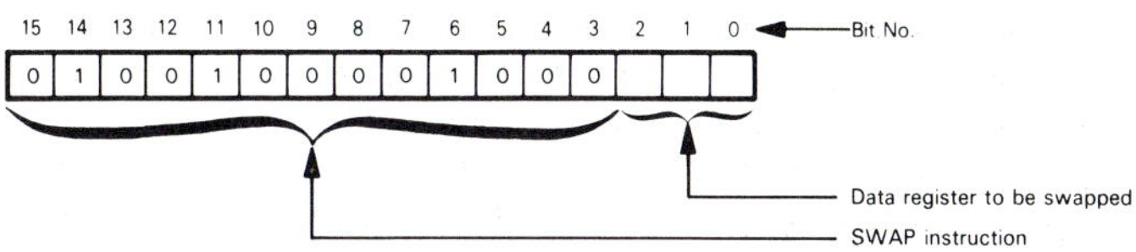

Figure 22-52 illustrates execution of the SWAP instruction with the contents of register D3 being swapped. After the instruction shown in this figure is executed, the least significant 16 bits of D3 will contain xxxx and the most significant 16 bits will contain yyyy.

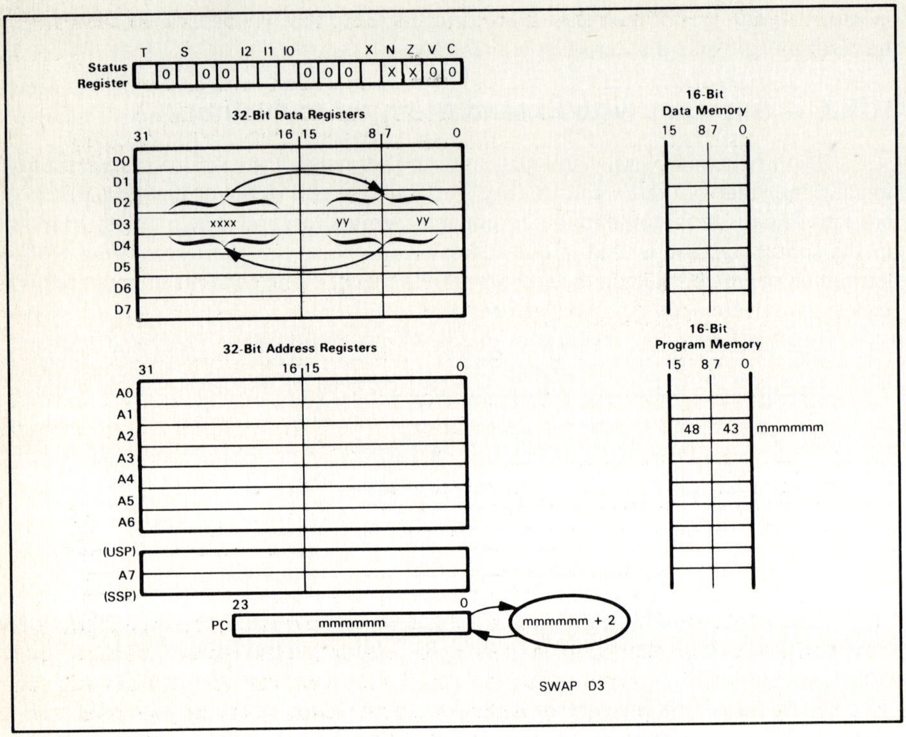

Figure 22-52. Execution of the SWAP Instruction

The Negative (N) flag will be set if the new value of bit 31 is 1 and will be cleared otherwise. The Zero (Z) status flag will be set if the 32-bit result after the swap equals zero, and will be cleared otherwise.

The Overflow (V) and Carry (C) status flags will always be cleared. The Extend (X) status flag is not affected.

TAS — Indivisible Test and Set

This instruction tests a byte of data in the destination operand, sets the N and Z status flags according to the results of the test, and then sets the high-order bit of the destination to one. The instruction is performed by the processor using a read-modify-write memory cycle and thus the operation is indivisible; it cannot be interrupted, and no other processor or external device in the system can access the operand during the operation.

The addressing modes that can be used to specify the byte operand to be tested are as follows:

Addressing Modes Allowed	Operand		Destination ea Field	
		Destination	Mode	Register No.
Data register direct		X	000	rrr
Address register direct				
Address register indirect		X	010	rrr
Postincrement register indirect		X	011	rrr
Predecrement register indirect		X	100	rrr
Register indirect with displacement		X	101	rrr
Register indirect with index		X	110	rrr
Absolute short		X	111	000
Absolute long		X	111	001
Program counter relative with displacement				
Program counter relative with index				
Immediate				

The object code for the TAS instruction is:

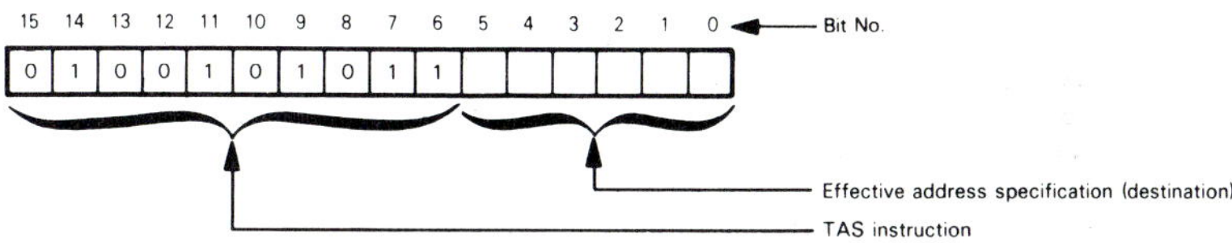

The TAS instruction provides a method for programs that are executing independently to synchronize their activities, for example, to synchronize references to shared data. With TAS, you can test a data flag to see if another program has set it, and also set the flag at the same time. Without this instruction, your program might test a flag and find it to be zero, then get interrupted before setting it. The interrupting program might also test a flag, find it to be zero and set it. After the interrupt your program would proceed as if the flag were still zero. With the TAS instruction, interrupt requests or bus requests from external devices are not honored while a TAS instruction is being executed, since the read-modify-write memory cycle is utilized. This guarantees that the entire instruction will execute without the possibility of the destination operand being changed during execution of the instruction.

The Negative (N) status flag is set if the most significant bit of the operand is set and is cleared otherwise. Note that this test is made at the beginning of the instruction (after the read portion of the memory access cycle): the most significant bit will then always be set during the write portion of the read-modify-write memory cycle.

The Zero (Z) status flag will be set if the contents of the operand equal zero and will be cleared otherwise. The Overflow (V) and Carry (C) status flags are always cleared. The Extend (X) status flag is not affected.

TRAP — Trap

This instruction initiates exception processing. The current program counter value, incremented to address the next sequential instruction, is pushed onto the system stack; then the current status register word is pushed onto the stack. Two words are then read from the appropriate location in the exception vector table and loaded into the program counter. Instruction execution will then continue at the location indicated by the new program counter value.

The TRAP instruction always pushes data onto the supervisor stack; that is to say, the supervisor stack pointer (SSP) is used, irrespective of whether the TRAP instruction is executed out of supervisor mode or user mode.

The object code for the TRAP instruction is:

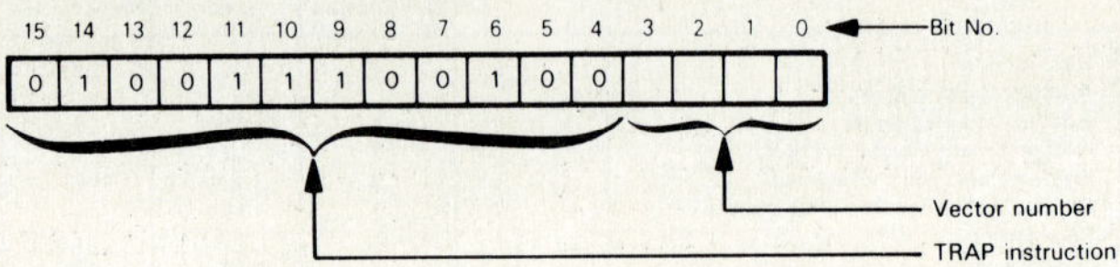

Sixteen different TRAP instruction vectors numbers can be specified. Table 22-4 shows the entire exception vector table. In this table, the TRAP instruction vector

Table 22-4. Exception Vector Table

Vector Number(s)	Address		Assignment
	Dec	Hex	
0	0	000	Reset: Initial SSP
	4	004	Reset: Initial PC
2	8	008	Bus Error
3	12	00C	Address Error
4	16	010	Illegal Instruction
5	20	014	Zero Divide
6	24	018	CHK Instruction
7	28	01C	TRAPV Instruction
8	32	020	Privilege Violation
9	36	024	Trace
10	40	028	Line 1010 Emulator
11	44	02C	Line 1111 Emulator
12*	48	030	(Unassigned, reserved)
13*	52	034	(Unassigned, reserved)
14*	56	038	(Unassigned, reserved)
15*	60	03C	(Unassigned, reserved)
16-23*	64	040	(Unassigned, reserved)
	95	05F	—
24	96	060	Spurious Interrupt
25	100	064	Level 1 Interrupt Autovector
26	104	068	Level 2 Interrupt Autovector
27	108	06C	Level 3 Interrupt Autovector
28	112	070	Level 4 Interrupt Autovector
29	116	074	Level 5 Interrupt Autovector
30	120	078	Level 6 Interrupt Autovector
31	124	07C	Level 7 Interrupt Autovector
32	128	080	TRAP Instruction #0
33	132	084	TRAP Instruction Vector #1
34	136	088	TRAP Instruction Vector #2
45	18C	0B4	TRAP Instruction Vector #13
46	184	0B8	TRAP Instruction Vector #14
47	188	0BC	TRAP Instruction Vector #15
48-63*	192	0C0	(Unassigned, reserved)
	255	0FF	—
64-255	256	100	User Interrupt Vectors
	1023	3FF	—

* Reserved for use by Motorola. To ensure compatibility with Motorola systems, avoid using these locations.

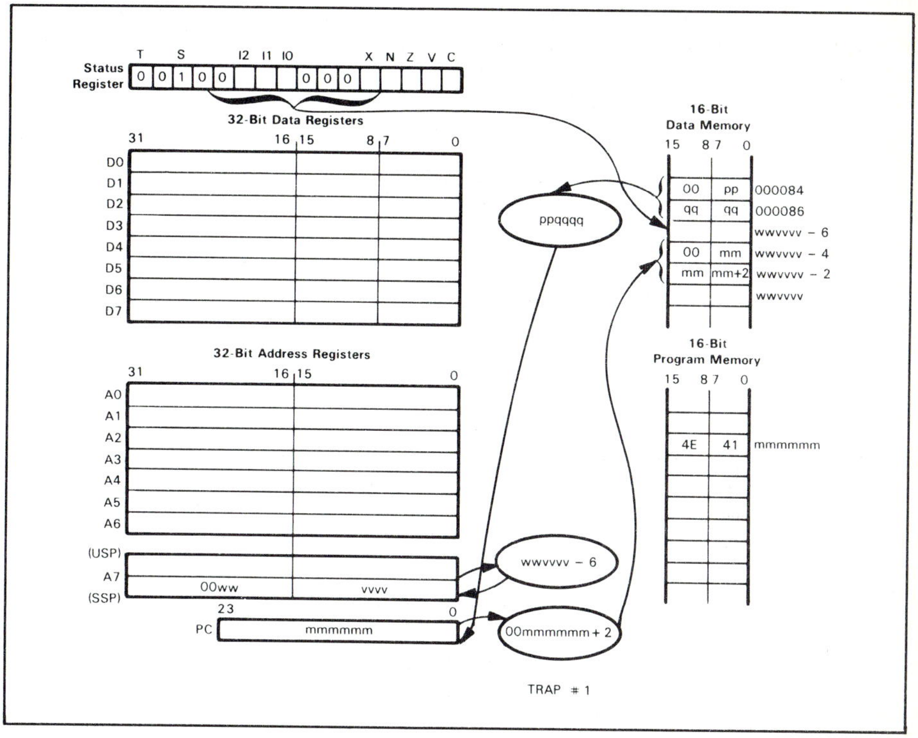

Figure 22-53. Execution of the TRAP Instruction

addresses occupy vector numbers 32 through 47. Each vector address consists of two words (four bytes) of data which will be loaded into the program counter. Thus the address for TRAP #0 occupies memory locations $080\text{-}083_{16}$; the address for TRAP #15 occupies memory locations $0BC\text{-}0BF_{16}$.

Figure 22-53 illustrates execution of the TRAP instruction. The instruction shown in this figure is TRAP #1 which accesses a four-byte vector address beginning at memory location 084_{16}. The contents of those two words (00ppqqqq) are loaded into the program counter after the previous contents of the program counter and the status register have been saved on the system stack.

Note that, after saving the contents of the status register, the Trace (T) flag is set to zero and the Supervisor (S) flag is set to one as the TRAP instruction is executed. No other bits in the status register are affected.

The sequence illustrated in Figure 22-53 is also executed when traps are automatically initiated by the processor as the result of such operations as an attempt to divide by zero or an attempt to execute an illegal or unimplemented opcode. These other types of exception processing simply access different vector numbers in the exception vector table as shown in Table 22-4.

For a thorough discussion of traps, and other types of exception processing, refer to Chapter 15.

TRAPV — Trap on Overflow

This instruction will initiate exception processing if the Overflow (V) bit in the status register is set when the instruction is executed. The sequence that is performed is identical to that illustrated in Figure 22-53 except that the vector that will be accessed from the vector table is the TRAPV instruction vector number 7 located beginning at memory location $01C_{16}$ as shown in Table 22-4.

The object code for the TRAPV instruction is:

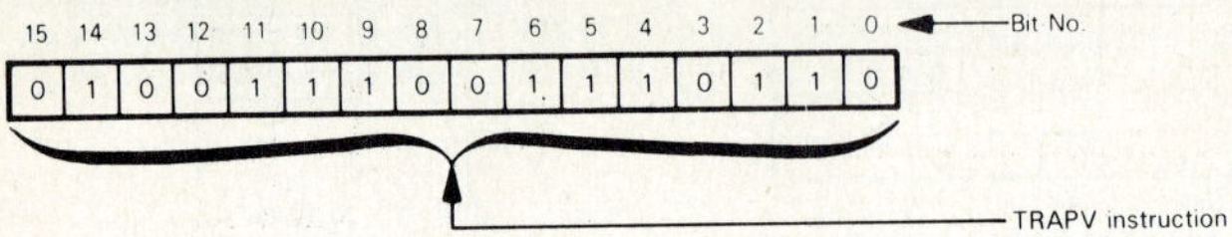

TST — Test an Operand

This instruction sets the Negative (N) and Zero (Z) status flags according to the contents of the destination operand. The addressing modes that can be used to specify the operand to be tested are:

Addressing Modes Allowed	Operand		Destination ea Field	
	Source	Destination	Mode	Register No.
Data register direct		X	000	rrr
Address register direct				
Address register indirect		X	010	rrr
Postincrement register indirect		X	011	rrr
Predecrement register indirect		X	100	rrr
Register indirect with displacement		X	101	rrr
Register indirect with index		X	110	rrr
Absolute short		X	111	000
Absolute long		X	111	001
Program counter relative with displacement				
Program counter relative with index				
Immediate				

The object code for the TST instruction is:

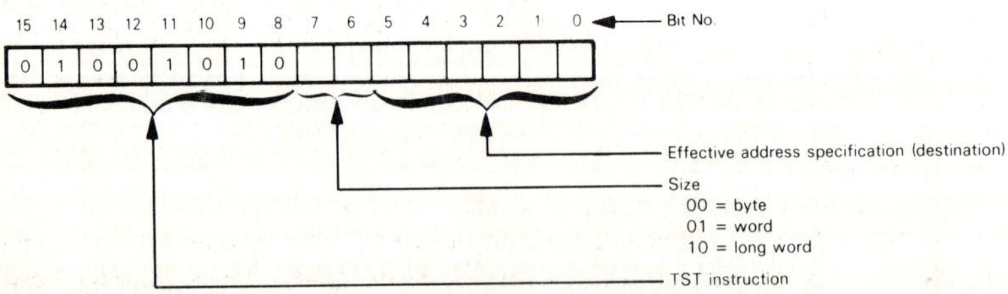

The operand to be tested can be either a byte, a word, or a long word.

Figure 22-54 illustrates execution of the TST instruction using address register indirect addressing. Register A4 is used to specify the word in memory whose contents are to be tested. Suppose that $xxxx=0000_{16}$. After the processor executes the instruction TST (A3), the Carry (C) and Overflow (V) flags will contain zero, the Negative (N) flag will contain zero, and the Zero (Z) flag will contain 1. No registers or memory location contents will be changed by the TST instruction.

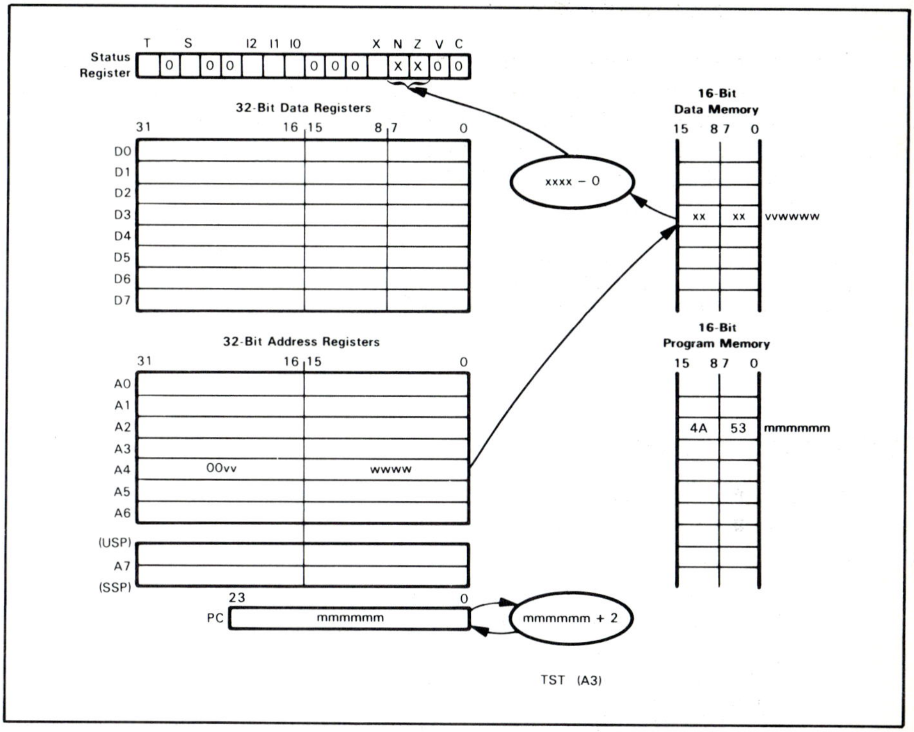

Figure 22-54. Execution of the TST Instruction Using Address Register Indirect Addressing

The TST instruction allows the programmer to set the flags according to the contents of a memory location or register without performing any operations or changing the contents of any register or memory location.

The Negative (N) flag will be set if the operand tested is negative and will be cleared otherwise. The Zero (Z) flag is set if the operand tested is zero and will be cleared otherwise. The Overflow (V) and Carry (C) flags are always cleared. The Extend (X) flag is not affected.

UNLK — Unlink

This instruction loads the system stack pointer with the contents of a specified address register (a "frame pointer"). This frame pointer is then loaded with a long word pulled from the top of the stack. Thus, both the frame pointer and system stack pointer will be restored to values they held before a link instruction was executed.

The object code for the UNLK instruction is:

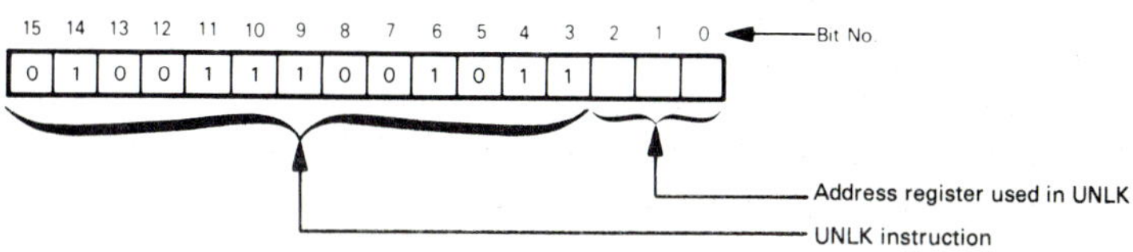

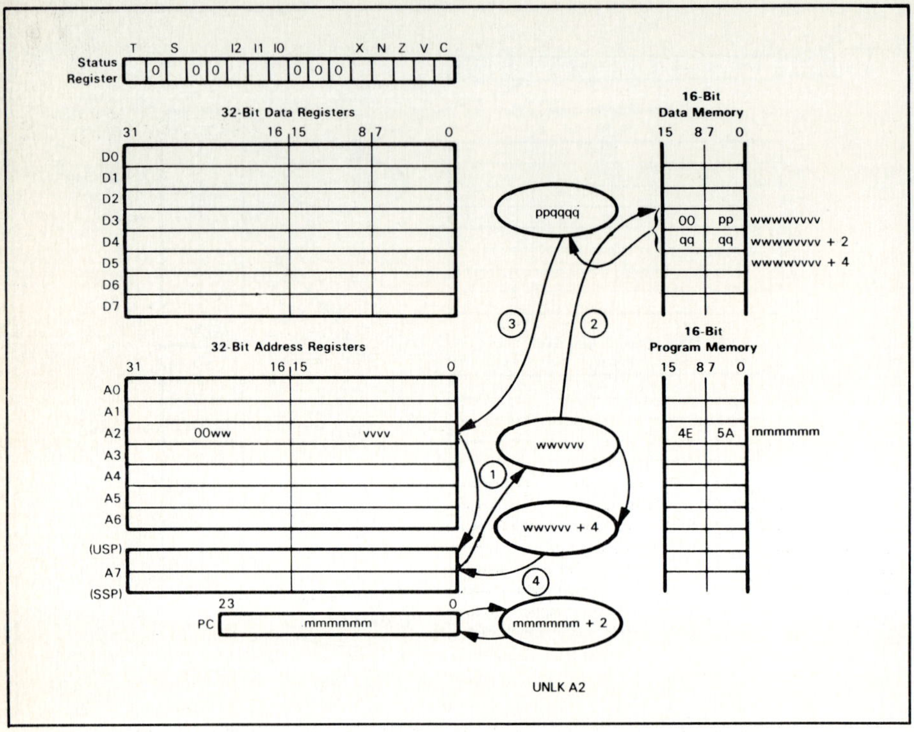

Figure 22-55. Execution of the UNLK Instruction

Figure 22-55 illustrates execution of the UNLK instruction with register A2 being used as the frame pointer. The UNLK instruction will be used to clean up the stack at the end of subroutine which started with a LINK instruction. Refer to the description of the LINK instruction for further discussion of the use of LINK and UNLINK.

None of the flags in the status register is affected by the UNLK instruction.

VI
Appendices

The following section presents a complete set of reference tables for the MC68000 instruction set.

Appendix A summarizes MC68000 instruction operations and effects, and is organized by function to display the capabilities of the MC68000 processor. Appendix B shows the object code for each MC68000 instruction (listed alphabetically by instruction mnemonic) and its execution time in clock cycles. Appendix B can serve as an aid to hand assembly of MC68000 instructions. Appendix C lists all valid object codes and their instruction mnemonics in numerical order and can be used for hand-checking and disassembly of object code — tasks sometimes required in the debugging of an assembly language progam.

A
The Instruction Set Summary

Table A-2 summarizes the MC68000 instruction set. The MNEMONIC column lists the instruction mnemonic (e.g., MOVE, ADD, JMP). The OPERAND(S) column lists the operands used with the instruction mnemonic.

The fixed part of an assembly language instruction is shown in UPPER CASE. The variable part (register number, address, immediate data, etc.) is shown in lower case.

The BYTES and CLOCK CYCLES are repeated in this table for reader convenience. Refer to Appendix B for a description of these entries.

ALTERNATE MNEMONICS

The MC68000 instruction set allows a choice of mnemonics for many operations. An "I" can be appended to the instruction mnemonic for an immediate operation. An "A" can be appended to the instruction mnemonic for an Address register operation. An ".S" can be appended to force a short-form conditional branch instruction.

Mnemonic choices are summarized in Table A-1 under these headings:

Primary Mnemonic	Lists the nominal mnemonic form.
Alternate Mnemonic	Lists the alternate choices that can be used in place of the primary mnemonic.

Operand — Shows the operand category to which the primary and alternate mnemonics apply. xx is any allowed operand selection.

Description — Identifies the operation.

For simplicity, only the primary mnemonics are shown in the instruction set tables that follow.

Note that there are no mnemonic alternates for the instruction variations X (Extend), M (Multiple), and P (Peripheral Data). These suffixes cannot be omitted from their respective instruction mnemonics.

Bear in mind that the assembler will select the "Quick" version of an instruction (e.g., MOVEQ, ADDQ, SUBQ) whenever possible. Thus you can use the alternates for these mnemonics — the more general MOVE, ADD and SUB — without sacrificing any opportunities for code shortening.

For example: MOVE.L #40,D2
is coded as: MOVEQ #40,D2

Another example: ADD #1, D0
is coded as: ADDQ.W #1,D0

STATUS

The effect of instruction execution on the status bits is listed in Table A-2. The status bits are:

T — Trace mode
S — Supervisor state
X — Extend bit
N — Negative (or Sign) bit
Z — Zero bit
V — Overflow bit
C — Carry bit

The following symbols are used in the STATUS columns:

X — flag is affected by operation
(blank) — flag is not affected by operation
1 — flag is set by operation
0 — flag is cleared by operation

OPERATION PERFORMED

This column shows the sequence of operations that occurs when the instruction is executed. (Instruction fetches are not shown, nor is the incrementing of the Program Counter for the purpose of instruction fetches.) Each operation is generally shown in the following form:

destination ← source

indicating that the source contents move to the destination, replacing the destination contents. For example, the LEA instruction operation is:

[An] ← jadr

The effective address, which may be any of the jadr forms, is loaded into the specified Address register.

Following the arrow sequence is a description of the operation in words.

ABBREVIATIONS

Following are the abbreviations used for instruction formats and operation descriptions.

addr Direct address (16 or 32 bits)

An Address registers, n = 0-7 (8, 16, or 32 bits, depending on the instruction size)

bitb Bit number of byte 0-7

bitl Bit number of long word 0-31

cc Condition code:

CC	Carry clear	0100
CS	Carry set	0101
EQ	Equal	0111
F	False	0001
GE	Greater than or equal	1100
GT	Greater than	1110
HI	High	0010
LE	Less than or equal	1111
LS	Low or same	0011
LT	Less than	1101
MI	Minus	1011
NE	Not equal	0110
PL	Plus	1010
T	True	0000
VC	No overflow	1000
VS	Overflow	1001

CCR Condition Code register — the low-order byte of the Status register

count Shift count (1-8)

dadr Destination address, which may be any of the following addressing modes:

(An)	Register indirect
(An)+	Register indirect with postincrement
−(An)	Register indirect with predecrement
d16(An)	Register indirect with displacement
d8(An,i)	Register indirect, indexed
addr	Direct address

dAn Destination Address register. This form is used only when there are two An operands.

aDn Destination Data register. This form is used only when there are two Dn operands.

data3 3 bits of immediate data
data8 8 bits of immediate data
data16 16 bits of immediate data
data32 32 bits of immediate data

Dn Data register, n = 0-7 (8, 16, or 32 bits, depending on instruction size)
d8 8-bit address displacement. Required, even if zero on indexed instructions.
d16 16-bit address displacement
i Index register (An or Dn)
jadr Jump address — same as sadr except no (An)+ or −(An)
label Address label
madr Multiple-instruction address — same as dadr except no (An)+ or −(An)
reg-list Register list naming one or more registers, each item in the list separated by a comma. Items may have the form:

Dn	Single data register
An	Single address register
rn_1-rn	Range of registers

rd Destination registers (dDn or dAn)
rs Source register (sDn or sAn)
sadr Source address, which may be any of the following address modes:

(An)	Register indirect
(An)+	Register indirect with postincrement
−(An)	Register indirect with predecrement
d16(An)	Register indirect with displacement
d8(An,i)	Register indirect, indexed
addr	Direct address
label	Program relative
label (i)	Program relative, indexed

sAn Source Address register. This form is used only when there are two An operands.
sDn Source Data register. This form is used only when there are two Dn operands.
SR Status register (16 bits)
USP User Stack Pointer. Note that this is Register A7.
vector Trap address vector. the memory location containing the address of the Trap routine.
[[ ]] The contents of the memory location whose address is contained in the designated register (indirect memory addressing, or implied addressing).
[ ] The contents of a register or memory location (register addressing or direct memory addressing).

For example:

[Dn] ← [[An]]

indicates that the contents of the memory location addressed by Register An are loaded into Dn, whereas:

[Dn] ← [An]

indicates that the contents of Register An itself are loaded into Dn.

$\overline{x}$	Complement the value of x.
x<y-z>	Bits y through z of x. For example, Dn<0-7> means the low-order byte of Dn. If the z term is omitted, then only the bit selected by y is being referenced. Thus Dn<0> means the least significant bit of Dn.
+	Add
−	Subtract
x	Multiply
÷	Divide
∧	Logical AND
∨	Logical OR
⊻	Logical Exclusive-OR
=	Equals
←	Data move in the direction of the arrow
←→	Data are exchanged between two locations

Table A-1. Alternate Instruction Mnemonics

Primary Mnemonic	Alternate Mnemonic	Operand	Description
ADD. B	ADDI. B	data8,xx	Add Immediate Byte
ADD. W	ADD	xx,xx	Add Word
	ADDA.W	xx,An	Add Address Register Word
	ADDI. W	data16,xx	Add Immediate Word
ADD. L	ADDA.L	xx,An	Add Address Register Long
	ADDI.L	data32,xx	Add Immediate Long
ADDQ.B	ADD.B	data3,xx	Add Quick Byte
ADDQ.W	ADD	data3,xx	Add Quick Word
	ADD. W		
ADDQ.L	ADD. L	data3,xx	Add Quick Long
AND.B	ANDI.B	data8,xx	AND Immediate Byte
AND.W	AND	xx,xx	AND Word
	ANDI.W	data16,xx	AND Immediate Word
AND. L	ANDI.L	data32,xx	AND Immediate Long
Bcc	Bcc.S	xx	Conditional Branch Short
CLR.W	CLR	xx	Clear Word
CMP.B	CMPI.B	data8,xx	Compare Immediate Byte
CMP.W	CMP	xx,xx	Compare Word
	CMPA.W	xx,An	Compare Address Register Word
	CMPI.W	data16,xx	Compare Immediate Word
CMP. L	CMPA.L	xx,An	Compare Address Register Long
	CMPI.L	data32,xx	Compare Immediate Long
EOR.B	EORI. B	data8,xx	Exclusive OR Immediate Byte
EOR. W	EOR	xx,xx	Exclusive OR Word
	EORI. W	data16,xx	Exclusive OR Immediate Word
EOR. L	EORI. L	data32,xx	Exclusive OR Immediate Long
MOVE. W	MOVE	xx,xx	Move Word
	MOVEA. W	xx,An	Move Address Register Word
MOVE. L	MOVEA.L	xx,An	Move Address Register Long
MOVEQ	MOVE. L	data8,xx	Move Quick (always Long)
OR. B	ORI. B	data8,xx	OR Immediate Byte
OR. W	OR	xx,xx	OR Word
	ORI. W	data16,xx	OR Immediate Word
OR. L	ORI. L	data32,xx	OR Immediate Long
SUB. B	SUBI. B	data8,xx	Subtract Immediate Byte
SUB.W	SUB	xx,xx	Subtract Word
	SUBA. W	xx,An	Subtract Address Register Word
	SUBI.W	data16,xx	Subtract Immediate Word
SUB. L	SUBA. L	xx,An	Subtract Address Register Long
	SUBI. L	data32,xx	Subtract Immediate Long
SUBQ. B	SUB. B	data3,xx	Subtract Quick Byte
SUBQ. W	SUB	data3,xx	Subtract Quick Word
	SUB.W		
SUBQ.L	SUB. L	data3,xx	Subtract Quick Long

Table A-2. MC68000 Instruction Set Summary

	Mnemonic	Operand(s)	Bytes	Clock Cycles	Status T	S	X	N	Z	V	C	Operation Performed
I/O and Primary Memory Reference	LEA	jadr,An	2,4, or 6	2(0/0)+								[An] ← jadr Load effective address into specified address register. The addressing size is long, although the address loaded may be byte, word, or long, depending on how it is subsequently used.[2]
	MOVE.B	(An),Dn	2	8(2/0)				X	X	0	0	[Dn<0-7>] ← [[An]] Register indirect
		(An) +,Dn	2	8(2/0)				X	X	0	0	[Dn<0-7>] ← [[An]], [An] ← [An] + 1 Register indirect with postincrement[1]
		−(An),Dn	2	10(2/0)				X	X	0	0	[An] ← [An] − 1, [Dn<0-7>] ← [[An]] Register indirect with predecrement[1]
		d16(An),Dn } sadr	4	12(3/0)				X	X	0	0	[Dn<0-7>] ← [[An] + d16] Register indirect with displacement
		d8(An,i),Dn	4	14(3/0)				X	X	0	0	[Dn<0-7>] ← [[An] + d8 + [i]] Register indirect, indexed
		addr,Dn	4 or 6	4(1/0)+				X	X	0	0	[Dn<0-7>] ← [addr] Direct address
		label,Dn	4	12(3/0)				X	X	0	0	[Dn<0-7>] ← [[PC] + d16] Program relative
		label(i),Dn	4	14(3/0)								[Dn<0-7>] ← [[PC] + d8 + [i]] Program relative, indexed Load byte to data register from memory location specified by any of the addressing modes above. Bits 8-31 of the data register are not affected.
	MOVE.B	Dn(An)	2	9(1/1)				X	X	0	0	[[An]] ← [Dn<0-7>] Register indirect
		Dn,(An)+	2	9(1/1)				X	X	0	0	[[An]] ← [Dn<0-7>], [An] ← [An] + 1 Register indirect with postincrement[1]
		Dn,−(An)	2	9(1/1)				X	X	0	0	[An] ← [An] − 1, [[An]] ← [Dn<0-7>] Register indirect with predecrement[1]
		Dn,d16(An) } dadr	4	13(2/1)				X	X	0	0	[[An] + d16] ← [Dn<0-7>] Register indirect with displacement
		Dn,d8(An, i)	4	15(2/1)				X	X	0	0	[[An] + d8 + [i]] ← [Dn<0-7>] Register indirect, indexed
		Dn,addr	4 or 6	5(0/1)+				X	X	0	0	[addr] ← [Dn<0-7>] Direct address Store byte from data register to memory location specified by any of the addressing modes above.
	MOVE.B	sadr,dadr	2, 4 6, 8 or 10	5(1/1)+				X	X	0	0	[dadr] ← [sadr] Store byte from specified source memory location to specified destination memory location.[1]

Notes:

1. Postincrement and predecrement change by 1, unless the address register specified is the Stack Pointer (A7), where the address is changed by 2 rather than 1 to keep the Stack Pointer on a word boundary.
2. The effective address must be on an even word boundary (0000, 0002, 0004, etc.).
3. Postincrement and predecrement change by 2.
4. Postincrement and predecrement change by 4.

Table A-2. MC68000 Instruction Set Summary (Continued)

	Mnemonic	Operand(s)	Bytes	Clock Cycles	Status T	S	X	N	Z	V	C	Operation Performed
I/O and Primary Memory Reference (Continued)	MOVE.W	sadr, Dn	2, 4 or 6	4(1/0)+				X	X	0	0	[Dn<0-15>] ← [sadr] Load word to data register from memory location. Bits 16-31 of the data register are not affected.[2, 3]
	MOVE.W	sadr,An	2, 4 or 6	4(1/0)+								[An]<0-15>] [An <16-31>] ← [An<15>] Load word to address register from memory location. The sign is extended to all upper bits of the register.[2, 3]
	MOVE.W	rs,dadr	2, 4 or 6	5(0/1)+				X	X	0	0	[dadr] ← [rs<0-15>] Store word to memory location from data or address register.[2, 3]
	MOVE.W	sadr,dadr	2, 4 6, 8 or 10	5(0/1)+				X	X	0	0	[dadr] ← [sadr] Store word from source memory location to destination memory location.[2, 3]
	MOVE.L	sadr,Dn	2, 4 or 6	4(1/0)+				X	X	0	0	[Dn<0-31>] ← [sadr] Load long word to data register from memory location.[2, 3]
	MOVE.L	sadr,An	2, 4 or 6	8(2/0)+								[An<0-31>] ← [sadr] Load long word to address register from memory location.[2, 4]
	MOVE.L	rs,dadr	2, 4 or 6	10(0/2)+				X	X	0	0	[dadr] ← [rs<0-31>] Store long word from data or address register to memory location.[2, 4]
	MOVE.L	sadr,dadr	2, 4 6, 8 or 10	14(1/2)+				X	X	0	0	[dadr] ← [sadr] Store long word from source memory location to destination memory location.[2, 4]
	MOVEM.W	jadr,reg-list	4, 6 or 8	8 + 4n(2 + n/0)+								[reg_1<0-15>] ← [[An]], [reg_1<16-31>] ← [reg_1<15>] [reg_2<0-15>] ← [[An + 2]],[reg_2<16-31>] ← [reg_2<15>] [reg_3<0-15>] ← [[An + 4]],[reg_3<16-31>] ← [reg_3<15>] . . . [reg_n<0-15>] ← [[An + 2n-2)]],[reg_n<16-31>] ← [reg_n<15>] Load multiple words from sequential memory locations to specified registers, in order D0-D7, A0-A7. The sign is extended to all upper bits of the register.[2]
	MOVEM.W	(An)+,reg-list	4	8 + 4n(2 + n/0)								[reg_1<0-15>] ← [[An]],[reg_1<16-31>] ← [reg_1<15>],[An] ← [An + 2] [reg_2<0-15>] ← [[An]],[reg_2<16-31>] ← [reg_2<15>],[An] ← [An + 2] [reg_3<0-15>] ← [[An]],[reg_3<16-31>] ← [reg_3<15>], [An] ← [An + 2] . . . [reg_n<0-15>] ← [[An]], [reg_n<16-31>] ← [reg_n<15>],[An] ← [An + 2] Same as above except with postincrement.[3]

Table A-2. MC68000 Instruction Set Summary (Continued)

	Mnemonic	Operand(s)	Bytes	Clock Cycles	Status T	S	X	N	Z	V	C	Operation Performed
I/O and Primary Memory Reference (Continued)	MOVEM.W	reg-list,madr	4, 6 or 8	4 + 5n(1/n)+								[[An]] ← [reg_1<0-15>] [[An + 2]] ← [reg_2<0-15>] [[An + 4]] ← [reg_3<0-15>] . . . [[An + (2n-2)] ← [reg_n<0-15>] Store multiple words to sequential memory locations from specified registers, in order D0-D7, A0-A7.[2]
	MOVEM.W	reg-list,−(An)	4	4 + 5n(1/n)+								[An] ← [An-2],[[An]] ← [reg_n<0-15>] . . . [An] ← [An-2],[[An]] ← [reg_3<0-15>] [An] ← [An-2],[[An]] ← [reg_2<0-15>] [An] ← [An-2],[[An]] ← [reg_1<0-15>] Store multiple words to sequential memory locations with predecrement to specified registers, in order A7-A0, D7-D0.[2, 3]
	MOVEM.L	jadr,reg-list (An)+,reg-list reg-list,madr reg-list,−(An)	4, 6 or 8 4 4, 6 or 8 4	8 + 8n(2 + 2n/0) 8 + 8n(2 + 2n/0) 4 + 10n(1/n)+ 4 + 10n(1/n)								Same as MOVEM.W except that all 32 bits of the registers are moved.[2, 4]
	MOVEP. W	d16(An),Dn	4	16(4/0)								[Dn<8-15>] ← [[An] + d16],[An] ← [An] + 2 [Dn<0-7>] ← [[An] + d16] Load peripheral data bytes from alternate memory locations to data register word. The address is a byte address.[3]
	MOVEP.W	Dn,d16(An)	4	18(2/2)								[[An] + d16] ← [Dn<8-15>],[An] ← [An] + 2 [[An] + d16] ← [Dn<0-7>] Store peripheral data bytes from data register long to alternate memory locations. The address is a byte address.[3]
	MOVEP.L	dos(An),Dn	4	24(6/0)								[Dn<24-31>] ← [[An] + d16],[An] ← [An] + 2 [Dn<16-23>] ← [[An] + d16],[An] ← [An] + 2 [Dn<8-15>] ← [[An] + d16],[An] ← [An] + 2 [Dn<0-7>] ← [[An] + d16] Load peripheral data bytes from alternate memory locations to data register long. The address is a byte address.[3]
	MOVEP.L	Dn,d16(An)	4	28(2/4)								[[An] + d16] ← [Dn<24-31>],[An] ← [An] + 2 [[An] + d16] ← [Dn<16-23>],[An] ← [An] + 2 [[An] + d16] ← [Dn<8-15>],[An] ← [An] + 2 [[An] + d16] ← [Dn<0-7>] Store peripheral data bytes from data register long to alternate memory locations. The address is a byte address.[3]

Table A-2. MC68000 Instruction Set Summary (Continued)

	Mnemonic	Operand(s)	Bytes	Clock Cycles	Status T	Status S	Status X	Status N	Status Z	Status V	Status C	Operation Performed
Secondary Memory Reference (Memory Operate)	ABCD	−(sAn),−(dAn)	2	19(3/1)			X	U	X	U	X	[sAn] ← [sAn] − 1 [dAn] ← [dAn]−1 [[dAn]] ← [[dAn]] + [[sAn]] + X Add decimal memory byte to memory byte with carry (Extend bit). Both addresses are byte[1].
	ADD.B	sadr,Dn	2, 4 or 6	4(1/0)+			X	X	X	X	X	[Dn<0-7>] ← [Dn<0-7>] + [sadr] Add byte to data register from memory location. Bits 8-31 of the data register are not affected.[1]
	ADD.B	Dn,dadr	2, 4 or 6	9(1/1)+			X	X	X	X	X	[dadr] ← [dadr] + [Dn<0-7>] Add byte to memory location from data register.[1]
	ADD.W	sadr,Dn	2, 4 or 6	4(1/0)+			X	X	X	X	X	[Dn<0-15>] ← [Dn<0-15>] + [sadr] Add word to data register from memory location. Bits 16-31 of the data register are not affected.[2, 3]
	ADD.W	sadr,An	2, 4 or 6	8(1/0)+								[An<0-31>] ← [An<0-31>] + [sadr] (sign extended) Add word to address register from memory location. The sign of the memory word is extended to a full 32 bits for the operation.[2, 3]
	ADD. W	Dn,Dadr	2, 4 or 6	9(1/1)+			X	X	X	X	X	[dadr] ← [dadr] + [Dn<0-15>] Add word to memory location from data register.[2, 3]
	ADD.L	sadr,Dn	2, 4 or 6	6(1/0)+			X	X	X	X	X	[Dn<0-31>] ← [Dn<0-31>] + [sadr] Add long word to data registers from memory location.[2, 4]
	ADD.L	sadr,An	2, 4 or 6	6(1/0)+								[An<0-31>] ← [An<0-31>] + [sadr] Add long word to address register from memory location.[2, 4]
	ADD.L	Dn,dadr	2, 4 or 6	14(1/2)+			X	X	X	X	X	[dadr] ← [dadr] + [Dn<0-31>] Add long word to memory locations from data register.[2, 4]
	ADDX.B	−(sAn),−dAn)	2	19(3/1)			X	X	X	X	X	[sAn] ← [sAn] − 1 [dAn] ← [dAn] − 1 [[dAn]] ← [[dAn]] + [[sAn]] + X Add memory byte to memory byte with carry (Extend bit). Both addresses are byte.[1]
	ADDX.W	−(sAn),−(dAn)	2	19(3/1)			X	X	X	X	X	[sAn] ← [sAn] − 2 [dAn] ← [dAn] − 2 [[dAn]] ← [[dAn]] + [[sAn]] + X Add memory word to memory word with carry (Extend bit). Both address are word.[2, 3]
	ADDX.L	−(sAn),−(dAn)	2	32(5/2)			X	X	X	X	X	[sAn] ← [sAn] − 4 [dAn] ← [dAn] − 4 [[dAn]] ← [[dAn]] + [[sAn]] + X Add memory long word to memory long word with carry (Extend bit). Both addresses are long word.[2, 4]
	AND.B	sadr,Dn	2, 4 or 6	4(1/0)+				X	X	0	0	[Dn<0-7>] ← [Dn<0-7>] ∧ [sadr] AND byte to data register from memory location. Bits 8-31 of the data register are not affected.[1]
	AND.B	Dn,dadr	2, 4 or 6	9(1/1)+				X	X	0	0	[dadr] ← [dadr] ∧ [Dn<0-7>] AND byte to memory location from data register.[1]

Table A-2. MC68000 Instruction Set Summary (Continued)

	Mnemonic	Operand(s)	Bytes	Clock Cycles	Status T	S	X	N	Z	V	C	Operation Performed
Secondary Memory Reference (Memory Operate) (Continued)	AND.W	sadr,Dn	2, 4 or 6	4(1/0)+				X	X	0	0	[Dn<0-15>] ← [Dn<0-15>] ∧ [sadr] AND word to data register from memory location. Bits 16-31 of the data register are not affected.[2, 3]
	AND.W	Dn,dadr	2, 4 or 6	9(1/1)+				X	X	0	0	[dadr] ← [dadr] ∧ [Dn<0-15>] AND word to memory location from data register.[2, 3]
	AND.L	sadr,Dn	2, 4 or 6	6(1/0)+				X	X	0	0	[Dn<0-31>] ← [Dn<0-31>] ∧ [sadr] AND long word to data register from memory location.[2, 4]
	AND.L	Dn,dadr	2, 4 or 6	14(1/2)+				X	X	0	0	[dadr] ← [dadr] ∧ [Dn<0-31>] AND long word to memory location from data register.[2, 4]
	CLR.B	dadr	2, 4 or 6	9(1/1)+				0	1	0	0	[dadr] ← 0 Clear memory byte to zeroes.[1]
	CLR.W	dadr	2, 4 or 6	9(1/1)+				0	1	0	0	[dadr] ← 0 Clear memory word to zeroes.[2, 3]
	CLR.L	dadr	2, 4 or 6	14(1/2)+				0	1	0	0	[dadr] ← 0 Clear memory long word to zeroes.[2, 4]
	CMP.B	sadr,Dn	2, 4 or 6	4(1/0)+				X	X	X	X	[Dn<0-7>] − [sadr] Compare data register byte with memory byte and set condition codes accordingly. Register/memory data are not changed on any compares.[1]
	CMP.W	sadr,Dn	2, 4 or 6	4(1/0)+				X	X	X	X	[Dn<0-15>] − [sadr] Compare data register word with memory word and set condition codes accordingly.[2, 3]
	CMP.W	sadr,An	2, 4 or 6	6(1/0)+				X	X	X	X	[An<0-15>] − [sadr] Compare address register word with memory word and set condition codes accordingly.[2, 3]
	CMP.L	sadr,Dn	2, 4 or 6	6(1/0)+				X	X	X	X	[Dn<0-31>] − [sadr] Compare data register with memory long word and set condition codes accordingly.[2, 4]
	CMP.L	sadr,An	2, 4 or 6	6(1/0)+				X	X	X	X	[An<0-31>] − [sadr] Compare address register with memory long word and set condition codes accordingly.[2, 4]
	CMPM.B	(sAn)+,(dAn)+	2	12(3/0)				X	X	X	X	[[dAn]] − [[sAn]] [dAn] ← [dAn] + 1 [sAn] ← [sAn] + 1 Compare memory bytes and set condition codes accordingly. The memory data are not changed on any compares.[1]
	CMPM.W	(sAn)+,(dAn)+	2	12(3/0)				X	X	X	X	[[dAn]] − [[sAn]] [dAn] ← [dAn] + 2 [sAn] ← [sAn] + 2 Compare memory words and set condition codes accordingly.[2, 3]
	CMPM.L	(sAn)+,(dAn)+	2	20(5/0)				X	X	X	X	[[dAn]] − [[sAn]] [dAn] ← [dAn] + 4 [sAn] ← [sAn] + 4 Compare memory long words and set condition codes accordingly.[2, 4]

Table A-2. MC68000 Instruction Set Summary (Continued)

	Mnemonic	Operand(s)	Bytes	Clock Cycles	Status							Operation Performed
					T	S	X	N	Z	V	C	
Secondary Memory Reference (Memory Operate) (Continued)	DIVS	sadr,Dn	2, 4 or 6	< 158(1/0)+				X	X	X	0	[Dn<0-15>] ← [Dn<0-31>] ÷ [sadr] [Dn<16-31>] ← remainder Divide signed numbers. Division by zero causes a TRAP. The source address is a word address.[2, 3]
	DIVU	sadr,Dn	2, 4 or 6	≤140(1/0)+				X	X	X	0	[Dn<0-15>] ← [Dn<0-31>] ÷ [sadr] [Dn<16-31>] ← remainder Divide unsigned numbers. Division by zero causes a TRAP. The source address is a word address.[2, 3]
	EOR.B	Dn,dadr	2, 4 or 6	9(1/1)+				X	X	0	0	[dadr] ← [dadr] ⊻ [Dn<0-7>] Exclusive-OR byte to memory location from data register.[1]
	EOR.W	Dn,dadr	2, 4 or 6	9(1/1)+				X	X	0	0	[dadr] ← [dadr] ⊻ [Dn<0-15>] Exclusive-OR word to memory location from data registers.[2, 3]
	EOR.L	Dn,dadr	2, 4 or 6	14(1/2)+				X	X	0	0	[dadr] ← [dadr] ⊻ [Dn<0-31>] Exclusive-OR long word to memory location from data register.[2, 4]
	MULS	sadr,Dn	2, 4 or 6	< 70(1/0)+				X	X	0	0	[Dn<0-31>] ← [Dn<0-15>] × [sadr] Multiply two 16-bit signed numbers, yielding a 32-bit signed product. The source address is a word address.[2, 3]
	MULU	sadr,Dn	2, 4 or 6	< 74(2/0)+				X	X	0	0	[Dn<0-31>] ← [Dn<0-15>] × [sadr] Multiply two 16-bit unsigned numbers, yielding a 32-bit unsigned product. The source address is a word address.[2, 3]
	NBCD	dadr	2, 4 or 6	9(1/1)+			X	U	X	U	X	[dadr] ← 0 − [dadr] − X Negate decimal memory byte. This operation produces the tens complement if X = 0 or the nines complement if X = 1.
	NEG.B	dadr	2, 4 or 6	9(1/1)+			X	X	X	X	X	[dadr] ← 0 − [dadr] Negate memory byte.[1]
	NEG.W	dadr	2, 4 or 6	9(1/1)+			X	X	X	X	X	[dadr] ← 0 − [dadr] Negate memory word.[2, 3]
	NEG.L	dadr	2, 4 or 6	14(1/2)+			X	X	X	X	X	[dadr] ← 0 − [dadr] Negate memory long word.[2, 4]
	NEGX.B	dadr	2, 4 or 6	9(1/1)+			X	X	X	X	X	[dadr] ← 0 − [dadr] − X Negate memory byte with Extend bit.[1]
	NEGX.W	dadr	2, 4 or 6	9(1/1)+			X	X	X	X	X	[dadr] ← 0 − [dadr] − X Negate memory word with Extend bit.[2, 3]
	NEGX.L	dadr	2, 4 or 6	14(1/2)+			X	X	X	X	X	[dadr] ← 0 − [dadr] − X Negate memory long word with Extend bit.[2, 4]
	NOT.B	dadr	2, 4 or 6	9(1/1)+				X	X	0	0	[dadr] ← [$\overline{\text{dadr}}$] Ones complement memory byte.[1]
	NOT.W	dadr	2, 4 or 6	9(1/1)+				X	X	0	0	[dadr] ← [$\overline{\text{dadr}}$] Ones complement memory word.[2, 3]
	NOT.L	dadr	2, 4 or 6	14(1/2)+				X	X	0	0	[dadr] ← [$\overline{\text{dadr}}$] Ones complement memory long word.[2, 4]
	OR.B	sadr,Dn	2, 4 or 6	4(1/0)+				X	X	0	0	[Dn<0-7>] ← [Dn<0-7>] ∨ [sadr] OR byte to data register from memory location. Bits 8-31 of the data register are not affected.[1]
	OR.B	Dn,dadr	2, 4 or 6	9(1/1)+				X	X	0	0	[dadr] ← [dadr] ∨ [Dn<0-7>] OR byte to memory location from data register.[1]

Table A-2. MC68000 Instruction Set Summary (Continued)

	Mnemonic	Operand(s)	Bytes	Clock Cycles	Status T	Status S	Status X	Status N	Status Z	Status V	Status C	Operation Performed
Secondary Memory Reference (Memory Operate) (Continued)	OR.W	sadr,Dn	2, 4 or 6	4(1/0)+				X	X	0	0	[Dn<0-15>] ← [Dn<0-15>] ∨ [sadr] OR word to data register from memory location. Bits 16-31 of the data register are not affected.[2, 3]
	OR.W	Dn,dadr	2, 4 or 6	9(1/1)+				X	X	0	0	[dadr] ← [dadr] ∧ [Dn<0-15>] OR word to memory location from data register.[2, 3]
	OR.L	sadr,Dn	2, 4 or 6	6(1/0)+				X	X	0	0	[Dn<0-31>] ← [Dn<0-31>] ∨ [sadr] OR long word to data register from memory location.[2, 4]
	OR.L	Dn,dadr	2, 4 or 6	14(1/2)+				X	X	0	0	[dadr] ← [dadr] ∧ [Dn<0-31>] OR long word to memory location from data register.[2, 4]
	SBCD	−(sAn),−(dAn)	2	19(3/1)			X	U	X	U	X	[sAn] ← [sAn] − 1 [dAn] ← [dAn] − 1 [[dAn]] ← [[dAn]] − [[sAn]] − X Subtract decimal memory byte from memory byte with carry (Extend bit). Both addresses are byte.[1]
	SCC	dadr	2, 4 or 6	9(1/1)+								[dadr] ← [all 1's if cc = TRUE [dadr] ← all 0's if cc = FALSE Set status in memory byte.[1]
	SUB.B	sadr,Dn	2, 4 or 6	4(1/0)+			X	X	X	X	X	[Dn<0-7>] ← [Dn<0-7>] − [sadr] Subtract memory byte from byte in data register. Bits 8-31 of the data register are not affected.[1]
	SUB.B	Dn,dadr	2, 4 or 6	9(1/1)+			X	X	X	X	X	[dadr] ← [dadr] − [Dn<0-7>] Subtract byte in data register from memory byte.[1]
	SUB.W	sadr,Dn	2, 4 or 6	4(1/0)+			X	X	X	X	X	[Dn<0-15>] ← [Dn<0-15>] − [sadr] Subtract memory word from word in data register. Bits 16-31 of the data register are not affected.[2, 3]
	SUB.W	sadr,An	2, 4 or 6	8(1/0)+			X	X	X	X	X	[An<0-31>] ← [An<0-31>] − [sadr] (sign extended) Subtract memory word from address register contents. The sign of the memory word is extended to a full 32 bits for the operation.[2, 3]
	SUB.W	Dn,dadr	2, 4 or 6	9(1/1)+			X	X	X	X	X	[dadr] ← [dadr] − [Dn<015>] Subtract data register word from memory location word.[2, 3]
	SUB.L	sadr,Dn	2, 4 or 6	6(1/0)+			X	X	X	X	X	[Dn<0-31>] ← [Dn<0-31>] − [sadr] Subtract memory long word from data register contents.[2, 4]
	SUB.L	sadr,An	2, 4 or 6	6(1/0)+			X	X	X	X	X	[An<0-31>] ← [An<0-31>] − [sadr] Subtract memory long word from address register contents.[2, 4]
	SUB.L	Dn,dadr	2, 4 or 6	14(1/2)+			X	X	X	X	X	[dadr] ← [dadr] − [Dn<0-31>] Subtract contents of data register from memory long word.[2, 4]
	SUBX.B	−(sAn),−(dAn)	2	19(3/1)			X	X	X	X	X	[sAn] ← [sAn] − 1 [dAn] ← [dAn] − 1 [[dAn]] ← [[dAn]] − [[sAn]] − X Subtract memory byte from memory byte with borrow (Extend bit). Both addresses are byte.[1]
	SUBX.W	−(sAn),−(dAn)	2	19(3/1)			X	X	X	X	X	[sAn] ← [sAn] − 2 [dAn] ← [dAn] − 2 [[dAn]] ← [[dAn]] − [[sAn]] − X Subtract memory word from memory word with borrow (Extend bit). Both addresses are word.[2, 3]

Table A-2. MC68000 Instruction Set Summary (Continued)

	Mnemonic	Operand(s)	Bytes	Clock Cycles	Status T	Status S	Status X	Status N	Status Z	Status V	Status C	Operation Performed
I/O and Primary Memory Reference (Continued)	SUBX.L	−(sAn),−(dAn)	2	32(5/2)			X	X	X	X	X	[sAn] ← [sAn] − 4 [dAn] ← [dAn] − 4 [[dAn]] ← [[dAn]] − [[sAn]] − X Subtract memory long word from memory long word with borrow (Extend bit). Both addresses are long word.[2, 4]
	TAS	dadr	2, 4 or 6	11(1/1)+				X	X	0	0	[dadr < 7 >] ← 1 Test status of memory byte and set high-order bit to 1.
	TST.B	dadr	2, 4 or 6	4(1/0)+				X	X	0	0	[dadr] − 0 Test status of memory byte. The byte value is not changed.
	TST.W	dadr	2, 4 or 6	4(1/0)+				X	X	0	0	[dadr] − 0 Test status of memory word. The word value is not changed.
	TST.L	dadr	2, 4 or 6	4(1/0)+				X	X	0	0	[dadr] − 0 Test status of memory long word. The long word value is not changed.
Immediate	MOVEQ	data8,Dn	2	4(1/0)				X	X	0	0	[Dn < 0-7 >] ← data8 [Dn < 8-32 >] ← [Dn < 7 >] Load immediate data byte to data register. The sign is extended to all upper bits of the data register.
	MOVE.B	data8,Dn	4	8(2/0)				X	X	0	0	[Dn < 0-7 >] ← data8 Load immediate data byte to data register. Bits 8-31 of the data register are not affected.
	MOVE.B	data8,dadr	4, 6 or 8	9(1/1)+				X	X	0	0	[dadr] ← [data8] Load immediate data byte into memory location.[1]
	MOVE.W	data16,Dn	4	8(2/0)				X	X	0	0	[Dn < 0-15 >] ← data16 Load immediate data word to data register. Bits 16-31 of the data register are not affected.
	MOVE.W	data16,An	4	8(2/0)								[An < 0-15 >] ← data16 [An < 16-31 >] ← [An < 15 >] Load immediate data word to address register. The sign is extended to all upper bits of the register.
	MOVE.W	data16,dadr	4, 6 or 8	9(1/1)+				X	X	0	0	[dadr] ← data16 Load immediate data word into memory location.[2, 3]
	MOVE.L	data32,Dn	6	12(3/0)				X	X	0	0	[Dn < 0-31 >] ← data32 Load immediate data long word into data register.
	MOVE.L	data32,An	6	12(3/0)								[An < 0-31 >] ← data32 Load immediate data long word into address register.
	MOVE.L	data32,dadr	6, 8 or 10	18(2/2)+				X	X	0	0	[dadr] ← data32 Load immediate data long word into memory location.[2, 4]
Immediate Operate	ADD.B	data8,Dn	4	8(2/0)			X	X	X	X	X	[Dn < 0-7 >] ← [Dn < 0-7 >] + data8 Add immediate data byte to data register. Bits 8-31 of the data register are not affected.
	ADD.B	data8,dadr	4, 6 or 8	13(2/1)+			X	X	X	X	X	[dadr] ← [dadr] + data8 Add immediate data byte to memory location.[1]
	ADD.W	data16,Dn	4	8(2/0)			X	X	X	X	X	[Dn < 0-15 >] ← [Dn < 0-15 >] + data16 Add immediate data word to data register. Bits 16-31 of the data register are not affected.

Table A-2. MC68000 Instruction Set Summary (Continued)

	Mnemonic	Operand(s)	Bytes	Clock Cycles	Status T	Status S	Status X	Status N	Status Z	Status V	Status C	Operation Performed
Immediate Operate (Continued)	ADD.W	data16,An	4	8(2/0)								[An < 0-31 >] ← [An < 0-31 >] + data 16 (sign extended) Add immediate data word to address register. The sign of the data word is extended to a full 32 bits for the operation.
	ADD.W	data16,dadr	4, 6 or 8	13(2/1)+			X	X	X	X	X	[dadr] ← [dadr] + data16 Add immediate data word to memory location.[2, 3]
	ADD.L	data32,Dn	6	16(3/0)			X	X	X	X	X	[Dn < 0-31 >] ← [Dn < 0-31 >] + data32 Add immediate data long word to data register.
	ADD.L	data32,An	6	16(3/0)								[An < 0-31 >] ← [An < 0-31 >] + data32 Add immediate data long word to address register.
	ADD.L	data32,dadr	6, 8 or 10	22(3/2)+			X	X	X	X	X	[dadr] ← [dadr] + data32 Add immediate data long word to memory location.[2, 4]
	ADDQ.B	data3,Dn	2	4(1/0)			X	X	X	X	X	[Dn < 0-7 >] ← [Dn < 0-7 >] + data3 Add immediate three bits to data register byte. Bits 8-31 of the data register are not affected.
	ADDQ.B	data3,dadr	2, 4 or 6	9(1/0)+			X	X	X	X	X	[dadr] ← [dadr] + data3 Add immediate three bits to memory byte.[1]
	ADDQ.W	data3,Dn	2	4(1/0)			X	X	X	X	X	[Dn < 0-15 >] ← [Dn < 0-15 >] + data3 Add immediate three bits to data register word. Bits 16-31 of the data register are not affected.
	ADDQ.W	data3,An	2	4(1/0)								[An < 0-15 >] ← [An < 0-15 >] + data3 Add immediate three bits to address register word. Bits 16-31 of the address register are not affected.
	ADDQ.W	data3,dadr	2, 4 or 6	9(1/1)+			X	X	X	X	X	[dadr] ← [dadr] + data3 Add immediate three bits to memory word.[2, 3]
	ADDQ.L	data3,Dn	2	8(1/0)			X	X	X	X	X	[Dn < 0-31 >] ← [Dn < 0-31 >] + data3 Add immediate three bits to data register long word.
	ADDQ.L	data3,An	2	8(1/0)								[An < 0-31 >] ← [An < 0-31 >] + data3 Add immediate three bits to address register long word.
	ADDQ.L	data3,dadr	2, 4 or 6	14(1/2)			X	X	X	X	X	[dadr] ← [dadr] + data3 Add immediate three bits to memory long word.[2, 4]
	AND.B	data8,Dn	4	8(2/0)				X	X	0	0	[Dn < 0-7 >] ← [Dn < 0-7 >] ∧ data8 AND immediate data byte to data register. Bits 8-31 of the data register are not affected.
	AND.B	data8,dadr	4, 6 or 8	13(2/1)+				X	X	0	0	[dadr] ← [dadr] ∧ data8 AND immediate data byte to memory byte.[1]
	AND.W	data16,Dn	4	8(2/0)				X	X	0	0	[Dn < 0-15 >] ← [Dn < 0-15 >] ∧ data16 AND immediate data word to data register. Bits 16-31 of the data register are not affected.
	AND.W	data16,dadr	4, 6 or 8	13(2/1)				X	X	0	0	[dadr] ← [dadr] ∧ data16 AND immediate data word to memory word.[2, 3]
	AND.L	data32,Dn	6	16(3/0)				X	X	0	0	[Dn < 0-31 >] ← [Dn < 0-31 >] ∧ data32 AND immediate data long word to data register.
	AND.L	data32,dadr	6, 8 or 10	22(3/2)+				X	X	0	0	[dadr] ← [dadr] ∧ data32 AND immediate data long word to memory.[2, 4]

Table A-2. MC68000 Instruction Set Summary (Continued)

	Mnemonic	Operand(s)	Bytes	Clock Cycles	Status							Operation Performed
					T	S	X	N	Z	V	C	
Immediate Operate (Continued)	CMP.B	data8,Dn	4	8(2/0)				X	X	X	X	[Dn<0-7>] – data8 Compare data register byte with immediate data byte and set condition codes accordingly. Register data are not changed on any compares.
	CMP.B	data8,dadr	4, 6 or 8	8(2/0)+				X	X	X	X	[dadr] – data8 Compare memory byte with immediate data byte and set condition codes accordingly.[1]
	CMP.W	data16,Dn	4	8(2/0)				X	X	X	X	[Dn<0-15>] – data16 Compare data register word with immediate data word and set condition codes accordingly.
	CMP.W	data16,An	4	8(2/0)				X	X	X	X	[An<0-15>] – data 16 Compare address register word with immediate data word and set condition codes accordingly.
	CMP.W	data16,dadr	4, 6 or 8	8(2/0)+				X	X	X	X	[dadr] – data16 Compare memory word with immediate data word and set condition codes accordingly.[2, 3]
	CMP.L	data32,Dn	6	14(3/0)				X	X	X	X	[Dn<0-31>] – data32 Compare data register with immediate data long word and set condition codes accordingly.
	CMP.L	data32,An	6	14(3/0)				X	X	X	X	[An<0-31>] – data32 Compare address register with immediate data long word and set condition codes accordingly.
	CMP.L	data32,dadr	6, 8 or 10	12(3/0)–				X	X	X	X	[dadr] – data32 Compare memory long word with immediate data long word and set condition codes accordingly.[2, 4]
	DIVS	data16,Dn	4	≤162(2/0)				X	X	X	0	[Dn<0-15>] ← [Dn<0-31>] ÷ data16 [Dn<16-31>] ← remainder Divide signed numbers. Division by zero causes a TRAP.
	DIVU	data16,Dn	4	≤148(2/0)				X	X	X	0	[Dn<0-15>] ← [Dn<0-31>] ÷ data16 [Dn<16-31>] ← remainder Divide unsigned numbers. Division by zero causes a TRAP.
	EOR.B	data8,Dn	4	8(2/0)				X	X	0	0	[Dn<0-7>] ← [Dn<0-7>] ⊻ data8 Exclusive-OR data byte to data register. Bits 8-31 of the data register are not affected.
	EOR.B	data8,dadr	4, 6 or 8	13(2/1)+				X	X	0	0	[dadr] ← [dadr] ⊻ data8 Exclusive-OR data byte to memory byte.[1]
	EOR.W	data16,Dn	4	8(2/0)				X	X	0	0	[Dn<0-15>] ← [Dn<0-15>] ⊻ data16 Exclusive-OR data word to data register. Bits 16-31 of the data register are not affected.
	EOR.W	data16,dadr	4, 6 or 8	13(2/1)+				X	X	0	0	[dadr] ← [dadr] ⊻ data16 Exclusive-OR immediate data word to memory word.[2, 3]
	EOR.L	data32,Dn	6	16(3/0)				X	X	0	0	[Dn<0-31>] ← [Dn>0-31>] ⊻ data32 Exclusive-OR immediate data long word to data register.
	EOR.L	data32,dadr	6, 8 or 10	22(3/2)+				X	X	0	0	[dadr] ← [dadr] ⊻ data32 Exclusive-OR immediate data long word to memory.[2, 4]

Table A-2. MC68000 Instruction Set Summary (Continued)

	Mnemonic	Operand(s)	Bytes	Clock Cycles	Status T	Status S	Status X	Status N	Status Z	Status V	Status C	Operation Performed
Immediate Operate (Continued)	MULS	data16,Dn	4	≤74(2/0)				X	X	0	0	[Dn<0-311>] ← [Dn<0-15>] × data16 Multiply two 16-bit signed numbers, yielding a 32-bit signed product.
	MULU	data16,Dn	4	≤74(2/0)				X	X	0	0	[Dn<0-31>] ← [Dn<0-15>] × data16 Multiply two 16-bit unsigned numbers, yielding a 32-bit unsigned product.
	OR.B	data8,Dn	4	8(2/0)				X	X	0	0	[Dn<0-7>] ← [Dn<0-7>] ∨ data8 OR immediate data byte to data register. Bits 8-31 of the data register are not affected.
	OR.B	data8,dadr	4, 6 or 8	13(2/1)+				X	X	0	0	[dadr] ← [dadr] ∨ data8 OR immediate data byte to memory byte.[1]
	OR.W	data16,Dn	4	8(2/0)				X	X	0	0	[Dn<0-15>] ← [Dn<0-15>] ∨ data16 OR immediate data word to data register. Bits 16-31 of the data register are not affected.
	OR.W	data16,dadr	4, 6 or 8	13(2/1)+				X	X	0	0	[dadr] ← [dadr] ∨ data16 OR immediate data word to memory word.[2, 3]
	OR.L	data32,Dn	6	16(3/0)				X	X	0	0	[Dn<0-31>] ← [Dn<0-31>] ∨ data32 OR immediate data long word to data register.
	OR.L	data32,dadr	6, 8 or 10	22(3/2)+				X	X	0	0	[dadr] ← [dadr] ∨ data32 OR immediate data long word to memory.[2, 4]
	SUB.B	data8,Dn	4	8(2/0)			X	X	X	X	X	[Dn<0-7>] ← [Dn<0-7>] − data8 Subtract immediate data byte from data register. Bits 8-31 of the data register are not affected.
	SUB.B	data8,dadr	4, 6 or 8	13(2/1)+			X	X	X	X	X	[dadr] ← [dadr] − data8 Subtract immediate data byte from memory byte.[1]
	SUB.W	data16,Dn	4	8(2/0)			X	X	X	X	X	[Dn<0-15>] ← [Dn<0-15>] − data16 Subtract immediate data word from data register. Bits 16-31 of the data register are not affected.
	SUB.W	data16,An	4	8(2/0)								[An <0-31>] ← [An<0-31>] − data16 (sign extended) Subtract immediate data word from address register. The sign of the data word is extended to a full 32 bits for the operation.
	SUB.W	data16,dadr	4, 6 or 8	13(2/1)+			X	X	X	X	X	[dadr] ← [dadr] − data16 Subtract immediate data word from memory word.[2, 3]
	SUB.L	data32,Dn	6	16(3/0)			X	X	X	X	X	[Dn<0-31>] ← [Dn<0-31>] − data32 Subtract immediate long word from data register contents.
	SUB.L	data32,An	6	16(3/0)								[An<0-31>] ← [An<0-31>] − data32 Subtract immediate data long word from address register.
	SUB.L	data32,dadr	6, 8 or 10	22(3/2)+			X	X	X	X	X	[dadr] ← [dadr] − data32 Subtract immediate data long word from memory word.[2, 4]
	SUBQ.B	data3,Dn	2	4(1/0)			X	X	X	X	X	[Dn<0-7>] ← [Dn<0-7>] − data3 Subtract immediate three bits from data register byte. Bits 8-31 of the data register are not affected.
	SUBQ.B	data3,dadr	2, 4 or 6	9(1/1)+			X	X	X	X	X	[dadr] ← [dadr] − data3 Subtract immediate three bits from memory byte.[1]

Table A-2. MC68000 Instruction Set Summary (Continued)

	Mnemonic	Operand(s)	Bytes	Clock Cycles	Status T	S	X	N	Z	V	C	Operation Performed
Immediate Operate (Continued)	SUBQ.W	data3,Dn	2	4(1/0)			X	X	X	X	X	[Dn < 0-15 >] ← [Dn < 0 >] − data3 Subtract immediate three bits from data register word. Bits 16-31 of the data register are not affected.
	SUBQ.W	data3,An	2	4(1/0)								[An < 0-15 >] ← [An < 0-15 >] − data3 Subtract immediate three bits from address register word. Bits 16-31 of the address register are not affected.
	SUBQ.W	data3,dadr	2, 4 or 6	9(1/1)+			X	X	X	X	X	[dadr] ← [dadr] − data3 Subtract immediate three bits from memory word.[2, 3]
	SUBQ.L	data3,Dn	2	8(1/0)			X	X	X	X	X	[Dn < 0-31 >] ← [Dn < 0-31 >] − data3 Subtract immediate three bits from data register contents.
	SUBQ.L	data3,An	2	8(1/0)								[An < 0-31 >] ← [An < 0-31 >] − data3 Subtract immediate three bits from address register contents.
	SUBQ.L	data3,dadr	2, 4 or 6	14(1/2)+			X	X	X	X	X	[dadr] ← [dadr] − data3 Subtract immediate three bits from memory long word.[2, 4]
JUMP, BRANCH	BRA	label	2 or 4	10(2/0)								[PC] ← label Branch unconditionally (short).
	JMP	jadr	2, 4 or 6	4(1/0)+								[PC] ← jadr Jump unconditionally.
Subroutine CALL and RETURN	BSR	label	2 or 4	10, 8(1/0) 10, 12(2/0)								[A7] ← [A7] − 2 [[A7]] ← [PC] [PC] ← label Branch to subroutine (short).
	JSR	jadr	2, 4 or 6	14(1/2)+								[A7] ← [A7] − 2 [[A7]] ← [PC] [PC] ← jadr Jump to subroutine.
	RTS		2	16(4/0)								[PC] ← [[A7]] [A7] ← [A7] + 2 Return from subroutine
	RTR		2	20(5/0)								[SR < 0-4 >] ← [[A7 < 0-4 >]] [A7] ← [A7] + 2 [PC] ← [[A7]] [A7] ← [A7] + 2 Restore condition codes and return from subroutine.
Branch on Condition	Bcc	label	2 or 4	10, 8(1/0) 10, 12(2/0)								[PC] ← label Branch if condition met.
	DBcc	Dn,label	4	12(2/0) 10(2/0), 14(3/0)								If cc then no further action. [Dn < 0-15 >] ← [Dn < 0-15 >] − 1 If [Dn < 0-15 >] = −1 then no further action. [PC] ← label Test condition, decrement and branch. Loop until the specified condition is true or until the loop count is exhausted.

Table A-2. MC68000 Instruction Set Summary (Continued)

	Mnemonic	Operand(s)	Bytes	Clock Cycles	Status T	Status S	Status X	Status N	Status Z	Status V	Status C	Operation Performed
Register-Register Move	MOVE.B	sDn,dDn	2	4(1/0)				X	X	0	0	[dDn < 07 >] ← [sDn < 0-7 >] Move one byte of any data register to any data register. Bits 8-31 of the destination register are not affected.
	MOVE.W	rs,Dn	2	4(1/0)				X	X	0	0	[Dn < 0-15 >] ← [rs < 0-15 >] Move one word of any data or address register to any data register. Bits 16-31 of the destination register are not affected.
	MOVE.W	rs,An	2	4(1/0)								[An < 015 >] ← [rs < 0-15 >] [An < 16-31 >] ← [An < 15 >] Move one word of any data or address register to any address register. The sign is extended to all upper bits of the address register.
	MOVE.L	rs,Dn	2	4(1/0)				X	X	0	0	[Dn < 0-31 >] ← [rs < 0-31 >] Move the contents of any data or address register to any data register.
	MOVE.L	rs,An	2	4(1/0)								[An < 0-31 >] ← [rs < 0-31 >] Move the contents of any data or address register to any address register.
Register-Register Operate	ABCD	sDn,dDn	2	6(1/0)			X	U	X	U	X	[dDn < 0-7 >] ← [dDn < 0-7 >] + [sDn < 0-7 >] + X Add decimal source data register byte to destination data register byte with carry (Extend bit). Bits 8-31 of the destination data register are not affected.
	ADD.B	sDn,dDn	2	4(1/0)			X	X	X	X	X	[dDn < 0-7 >] ← [dDn < 0-7 >] + [sDn < 0-7 >] Add byte from data registers to data register. Bits 8-31 of the destination data register are not affected.
	ADD.W	rs,Dn	2	4(1/0)			X	X	X	X	X	[Dn < 0-15 >] ← [Dn < 0-15 >] + [rs < 0-15 >] Add word from source register to data register. Bits 16-31 of the destination data register are not affected.
	ADD.W	rs,An	2	8(1/0)								[An < 0-15 >] ← [An < 0-15 >] + [rs < 0-15 >] (sign extended) Add word from source register to address register. The sign of the source word is extended to a full 32 bits for the operation.
	ADD.L	rs,Dn	2	8(1/0)			X	X	X	X	X	[Dn < 0-31 >] ← [Dn < 0-31 >] + [rs < 0-31 >] Add long word from source register to data register.
	ADD.L	rs,An	2	8(1/0)								[An < 0-31 >] ← [An < 0-31 >] + rs < 0-31 >] Add long word from source register to address register.
	ADDX.B	sDn,dDn	2	4(1/0)			X	X	X	X	X	[dDn < 0-7 >] ← [dDn < 0-7] + [sDn < 0-7 >] + X Add source data register byte to destination data register byte with carry (Extend bit). Bits 8-31 of the destination data register are not affected.
	ADDX.W	sDn, dDn	2	4(1/0)			X	X	X	X	X	[dDn < 0-15 >] ← [dDn < 0-15 >] + [sDn < 0-15 >] + X Add source data register word to destination data register word with carry (Extend bit). Bits 16-31 of the destination data register are not affected.
	ADDX.L	sDn,dDn	2	8(1/0)			X	X	X	X	X	[dDn < 0-31 >] ← [dDn < 0-31 >] + [sDn < 0-31 >] + X Add source data register long word to destination data register long word with carry (Extend bit).
	AND.B	sDn,dDn	2	4(1/0)				X	X	0	0	[dDn < 0-7 >] ← [dDn < 0-7 >] ∧ [sDn < 0-7 >] AND byte from data register to data register. Bits 8-31 of the destination data register are not affected.

Table A-2. MC68000 Instruction Set Summary (Continued)

	Mnemonic	Operand(s)	Bytes	Clock Cycles	Status T	Status S	Status X	Status N	Status Z	Status V	Status C	Operation Performed
Register-Register Operate (Continued)	AND.W	sDn,dDn	2	4(1/0)				X	X	0	0	[dDn < 0-15 >] ← [dDn < 0-15 >] ∧ [sDn < 0-15 >] AND word from data register to data register. Bits 16-31 of the destination data register are not affected.
	AND.L	sDn,dDn	2	8(1/0)				X	X	0	0	[dDn < 0-31 >] ← [dDn < 0-31 >] ∧ [sDn < 0-31 >] AND long word from data register to data register.
	CMP.B	sDn,dDn	2	4(1/0)				X	X	X	X	[dDn < 0-7 >] − [sDn < 0-7 >] Compare data register bytes and set condition codes accordingly. Register data are not changed on any compares.
	CMP.W	rs,Dn	2	4(1/0)				X	X	X	X	[Dn < 0-15 >] − [rs < 0-15 >] Compare data register word with register word and set condition codes accordingly.
	CMP.W	rs,An	2	6(1/0)				X	X	X	X	[An < 0-15 >] − [rs < 0-15 >] Compare address register word with register word and set condition codes accordingly.
	CMP.L	rs,Dn	2	6(1/0)				X	X	X	X	[Dn < 0-31 >] − [rs < 0-31 >] Compare data register with register and set condition codes accordingly.
	CMP.L	rs,An	2	6(1/0)				X	X	X	X	[An < 0-31 >] − [rs < 0-31 >] Compare address register with register and set condition codes accordingly.
	DIVS	sDn,dDn	2	≤158(1/0)				X	X	X	0	[dDn < 0-15 >] ← [dDn < 0-31 >] ÷ [sDn < 0-15 >] [dDn < 016-31 >] ← remainder Divide signed numbers. Division by zero causes a TRAP.
	DIVU	sDn,dDn	2	≤140(1/0)				X	X	X	0	[dDn < 0-15 >] ← [dDn < 0-31 >] ÷ [sDn < 0-15 >] [dDn < 16-31 >] ← remainder Divide unsigned numbers. Division by zero causes a TRAP.
	EOR.B	sDn,dDn	2	4(1/0)				X	X	0	0	[dDn < 0-7 >] ← [dDn < 0-7 >] ⊻ [sDn < 0-7 >] Exclusive-OR byte from data register to data register. Bits 8-31 of the destination data register are not affected.
	EOR.W	sDn,dDn	2	4(1/0)				X	X	0	0	[dDn < 0-15 >] ← [dDn < 0-15 >] ⊻ [sDn < 0-15 >] Exclusive-OR word from data register to data register. Bits 16-31 of the destination data register are not affected.
	EOR.L	sDn,dDn	2	8(1/0)				X	X	0	0	[dDn < 0-31 >] ← [dDn < 0-31 >] ⊻ [sDn < 0-31 >] Exclusive-OR long word from data register to data register.
	EXG	rs,rd	2	6(1/0)								[rd] ←→ [rs] Exchange the contents of two registers. This is always a long word operation.
	MULS	sDn,dDn	2	≤70(1/0)				X	X	0	0	[dDn < 0-31 >] ← [dDn < 0-15 >] × [sDn < 0-15 >] Multiply two 16-bit signed numbers, yielding a 32-bit signed product.
	MULU	sDn,dDn	2	≤70(1/0)				X	X	0	0	[dDn < 0-31 >] ← [dDn < 0-15 >] × [sDn < 0-15 >] Multiply two 16-bit unsigned numbers, yielding a 32-bit unsigned product.
	OR.B	sDn,dDn	2	4(1/0)				X	X	0	0	[dDn < 0-7 >] ← [dDn < 0-7 >] ∨ [sDn < 0-7 >] OR byte from data register to data register. Bits 8-31 of the destination dat register are not affected.

Table A-2. MC68000 Instruction Set Summary (Continued)

	Mnemonic	Operand(s)	Bytes	Clock Cycles	Status T	S	X	N	Z	V	C	Operation Performed
Register-Register Operate (Continued)	OR.W	sDn,dDn	2	4(1/0)				X	X	0	0	[dDn<0-15>] ← [dDn<0-15>] ∨ [sDn<0-15>] OR word from data register to data register. Bits 16-31 of the destination data register are not affected.
	OR.L	sDn,dDn	2	8(1/0)				X	X	0	0	[dDn<0-31>] ← [dDn<0-31>] ∨ [sDn<0-31>] OR long word from data register to data register.
	SBCD	sDn,dDn	2	6(1/0)			X	U	X	U	X	[dDn<0-7>] ← [dDn<0-7>] − [sDn<0-7>] − X Subtract decimal source data register byte from destination data register byte with carry (Extend bit). Bits 8-31 of the destination data register are not affected.
	SUB.B	sDn,dDn	2	4(1/0)			X	X	X	X	X	[dDn<0-7>] ← [dDn<0-7>] − [sDn<0-7>] Subtract data register bytes. Bits 8-31 of the destination data register are not affected.
	SUB.W	rs,Dn	2	4(1/0)			X	X	X	X	X	[Dn<0-15>] ← [Dn<0-15>] − [rs<0-15>] Subtract register words. Bits 16-31 of the destination data register are not affected.
	SUB.W	rs,An	2	8(1/0)								[An<0-15>] ← [An<0-15>] − [rs<0-15>] (sign extended) Subtract source register word from address register. The sign of the source word is extended to a full 32 bits for the operation.
	SUB.L	rs,Dn	2	8(1/0)			X	X	X	X	X	[Dn<0-31>] ← [Dn<0-31>] − [rs<0-31>] Subtract source register long word from data register.
	SUB.L	rs,An	2	8(1/0)								[An<0-31>] ← [An<0-31>] − [rs<0-31>] Subtract source register long word from address register.
	SUBX.B	sDn,dDn	2	4(1/0)			X	X	X	X	X	[dDn<0-7>] ← [dDn<0-7>] − [sDn<0-7>] − X Subtract source data register byte from destination data register byte with borrow (Extend bit). Bits 8-31 of the destination data register are not affected.
	SUBX.W	sDn,dDn	2	4(1/0)			X	X	X	X	X	[dDn<0-15>] ← [dDn<0-15>] − [sDn<0-15>] − X Subtract source data register word from destination data register word with borrow (Extend bit). Bits 16-31 of the destination data registers are not affected.
	SUBX.L	sDn,dDn	2	8(1/0)			X	X	X	X	X	[dDn<0-31>] ← [dDn<0-31>] − [sDn<0-31>] − X Subtract source data register long word from destination data register long word with borrow (Extend bit).
Register Operate	CLR.B	Dn	2	4(1/0)				0	1	0	0	[Dn<0-7>] ← 0 Clear data register byte to zeroes. Bits 8-31 of the data register are not affected.
	CLR.W	Dn	2	4(1/0)				0	1	0	0	[Dn<0-15> ← 0 Clear data register word to zeroes. Bits 16-31 of the data register are not affected.
	CLR.L	Dn	2	6(1/0)				0	1	0	0	[Dn<0-31>] ← 0 Clear data register to zeroes
	EXT.W	Dn	2	4(1/0)				X	X	0	0	[Dn<8-15>] ← [Dn<7>] Extend sign bit of data byte to data word size. Bits 16-31 of the data register are not affected.
	EXT.L	Dn	2	4(1/0)				X	X	0	0	[Dn<16-31>] ← [Dn<15>] Extend sign bit of data word to long data word size.

Table A-2. MC68000 Instruction Set Summary (Continued)

	Mnemonic	Operand(s)	Bytes	Clock Cycles	Status T	S	X	N	Z	V	C	Operation Performed
Register Operate (Continued)	NBCD	Dn	2	6(1/0)			X	U	X	U	X	[Dn<0-7>] ← [Dn<0-7>] − X Negate decimal register byte. Bits 8-31 of the data register are not affected.
	NEG.B	Dn	2	4(1/0)			X	X	X	X	X	[Dn<0>] ← 0 − [Dn<0-7>] Negate register byte. Bits 8-31 of the data register are not affected.
	NEG.W	Dn	2	4(1/0)			X	X	X	X	X	[Dn<0-15>] ← 0 − [Dn<0-15>] Negate register word. Bits 16-31 of the data register are not affected.
	NEG.L	Dn	2	6(1/0)			X	X	X	X	X	[Dn<0-31>] ← 0 − [Dn<0-31>] Negate register long word.
	NEG.B	Dn	2	4(1/0)			X	X	X	X	X	[Dn<0-7>] ← 0 − [Dn<0-7] − X Negate register byte with Extend. Bits 8-31 of the data register are not affected.
	NEG.W	Dn	2	4(1/0)			X	X	X	X	X	[Dn<0-15>] ← 0 − [Dn<0-15>] − X Negate register word with Extend. Bits 16-31 of the data register are not affected.
	NEG.L	Dn	2	6(1/0)			X	X	X	X	X	[Dn<0-31>] ← 0 − [Dn<0-31>] − X Negate register long word with Extend.
	NOT.B	Dn	2	4(1/0)				X	X	0	0	[Dn<0-7>] ← $\overline{[Dn<0-7>]}$ Ones complement data register byte. Bits 8-31 of the data register are not affected.
	NOT.W	Dn	2	6(1/0)				X	X	0	0	[Dn<0-15>] ← $\overline{[Dn<0-15>]}$ Ones complement data register word. Bits 16-31 of the data register are not affected.
	NOT.L	Dn	2	6(1/0)				X	X	0	0	[Dn<0-3>] ← $\overline{[Dn<0-31>]}$ Ones complement data register contents.
	Scc	Dn	2	9(1/1)								[Dn<0-7>] ← all 1's if cc = TRUE [Dn<0-1>] ← all 0's if cc = FALSE Set status in data register byte.
	SWAP	Dn	2	4(1/0)				X	X	0	0	[Dn<0-15>] ←→ [Dn<16-31>] Exchange the two 16-bit halves of a data register.
	TAS	Dn	2	4(1/0)				X	X	0	0	[Dn<7>] ← 1 Test status of data register byte and set bit 7 to 1.
	TST.B	Dn	2	4(1/0)				X	X	0	0	[Dn<0-7>] − 0 Test status of data register byte. The data register contents are not changed.
	TST.W	Dn	2	4(1/0)				X	X	0	0	[Dn<0-15>] − 0 Test status of data register word. The data register contents are not changed.
	TST.L	Dn	2	4(1/0)				X	X	0	0	[Dn<0-31>] − 0 Test status of data register long word. The data register contents are not changed.

Table A-2. MC68000 Instruction Set Summary (Continued)

	Mnemonic	Operand(s)	Bytes	Clock Cycles	Status T	S	X	N	Z	V	C	Operation Performed
Shift	ASL	dadr	2, 4 or 6	9(1/1)+			X	X	X	X	X	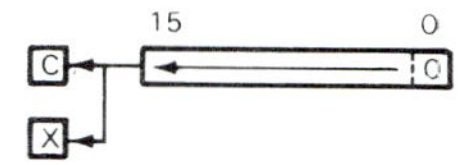 Arithmetic shift left one bit of memory word. A zero is shifted into bit 0. Bit 15 is shifted into both Carry and Extend bits.[2, 3]
	ASL.B	count,Dn Dn,dDn	2 2	6 + 2N(1/0) 6 + 2N(1/0)			X X	X X	X X	X X	X X	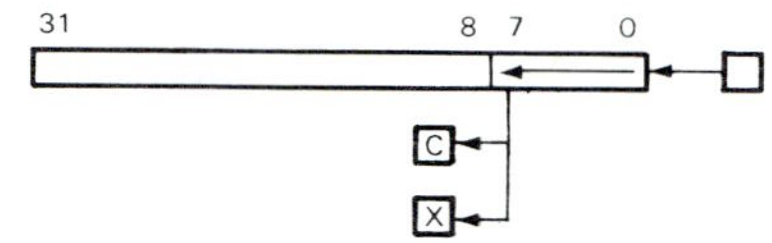 Arithmetic shift left of data register byte. The number of shifts is specified as a direct count (1-8) or in a data register (1-63). Zeroes are shifted into bit 0. Bit 7 is shifted into both Carry and Extend bits.
	ASL.W	count,Dn Dn,dDn	2 2	6 + 2N(1/0) 6 + 2N(1/0)			X X	X X	X X	X X	X X	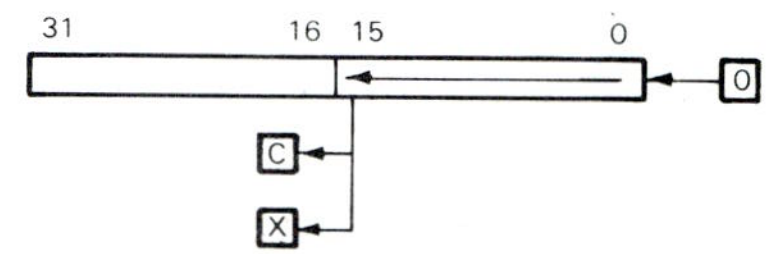 As ASL.B except shifts are for one word.
	ASL.L	count,Dn Dn,dDn	2 2	8 + 2N(1/0) 8 + 2N(1/0)			X X	X X	X X	X X	X X	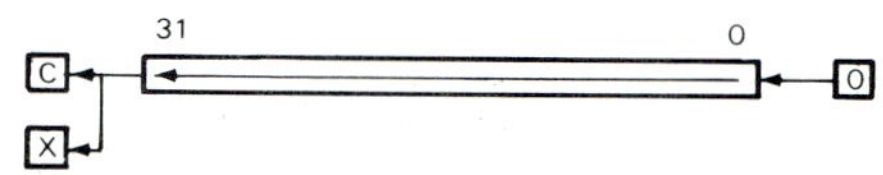 As ASL.B except shifts are for entire register.
	ASR	dadr	2, 4 or 6	9(1/1)+			X	X	X	X	X	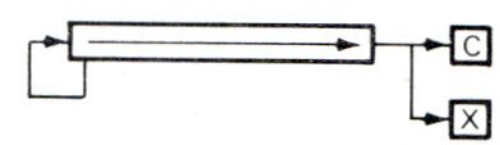 Arithemtic shift right one bit of memory word. Bit 15 is propagated to bit 14. Bit 0 is shifted into both Carry and Extend bits.
	ASR.B	count,Dn Dn,dDn	2 2	6 + 2N(1/0) 6 + 2N(1/0)			X X	X X	X X	X X	X X	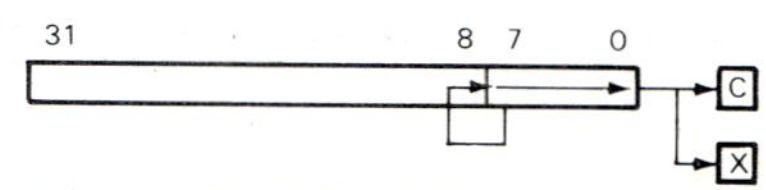 Arithmetic shift right of data register byte. The number of shifts is specified as a direct count (1-8) or in a data register (1-63). Bit 7 is propagated to the right. Bit 0 is shifted into both Carry and Extend bits.

Table A-2. MC68000 Instruction Set Summary (Continued)

	Mnemonic	Operand(s)	Bytes	Clock Cycles	Status T	Status S	Status X	Status N	Status Z	Status V	Status C	Operation Performed
Shift (Continued)	ASR.W	count,Dn Dn,dDn	2 2	6 + 2N(1/0) 6 + 2N(1/0)			X X	X X	X X	X X	X X	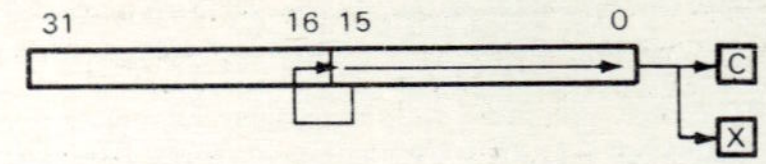 As ASR.B except shifts are for one word.
	ASR.L	count,Dn Dn,dDn	2 2	8 + 2N(1/0) 8 + 2N(1/0)			X X	X X	X X	X X	X X	 As ASR.B except shifts are for entire register.
	LSL	dadr	2, 4 or 6	9(1/1)+			X	X	X	0	X	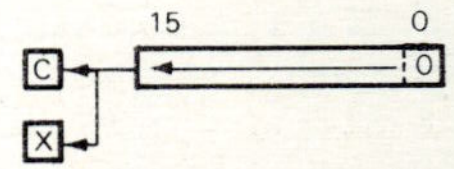 Logical shift left one bit of memory word. A zero is shifted into bit 0. Bit 15 is shifted into both Carry and Extend bits. (Note that LSL is identical to ASL except for the Overflow condition.)[2, 3]
	LSL.B	count,Dn Dn,dDn	2 2	6 + 2N(1/0) 6 + 2N(1/0)			X X	X X	X X	0 0	X X	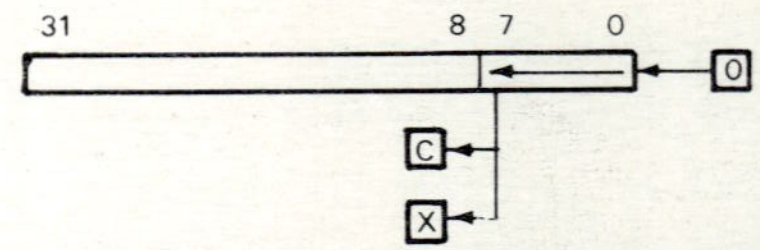 Logical shift left of data register byte. The number of shifts is specified as a direct count (1-8) or in a data register (1-63). Zeroes are shifted into bit 0. Bit 7 is shifted into both Carry and Extend bits.
	LSL.W	count,Dn Dn,dDn	2 2	6 + 2N(1/0) 6 + 2N(1/0)			X X	X X	X X	0 0	X X	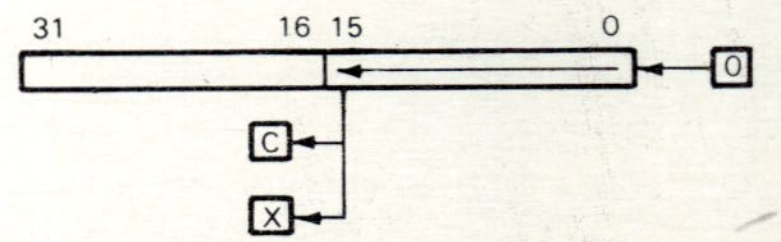 As LSL.B except shifts are for one word.
	LSL.L	count,Dn Dn,dDn	2	8 + 2N(1/0) 8 + 2N(1/0)			X X	X X	X X	0 0	X X	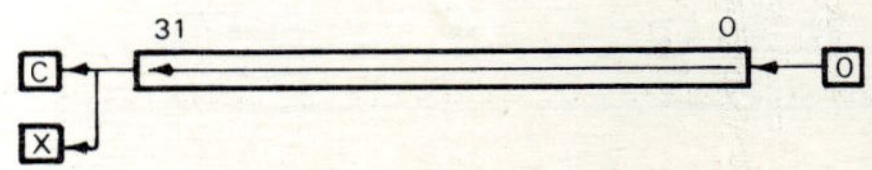 As LSL.B except shifts are for entire register.

Table A-2. MC68000 Instruction Set Summary (Continued)

	Mnemonic	Operand(s)	Bytes	Clock Cycles	Status							Operation Performed
					T	S	X	N	Z	V	C	
Shift (Continued)	LSR	dadr	2, 4 or 6	9(1/1)+			X	X	X	0	X	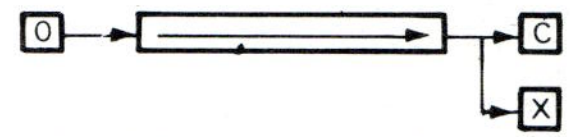 Logical shift right one bit of memory word. A zero is shifted into bit 15. Bit 0 is shifted into both Carry and Extend bits.
	LSR.B	count,Dn Dn,dDn	2 2	6 + 2N(1/0) 6 + 2N(1/0)			X X	X X	X X	0 0	X X	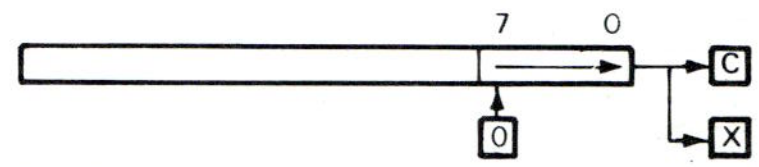 Logical shift right of data register byte. The number of shifts is specified as a direct count (1-8) or in a data register (1-63). Zeroes are shifted into bit 7. Bit 0 is shifted into both Carry and Extend bits.
	LSR.W	count,Dn Dn,dDn	2 2	6 + 2N(1/0) 6 + 2N(1/0)			X X	X X	X X	0 0	X X	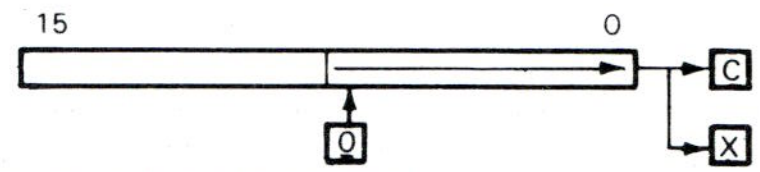 As LSR.B except shifts are for one word.
	LSR.L	count,Dn Dn,dDn	2 2	8 + 2N(1/0) 8 + 2N(1/0)			X X	X X	X X	0 0	X X	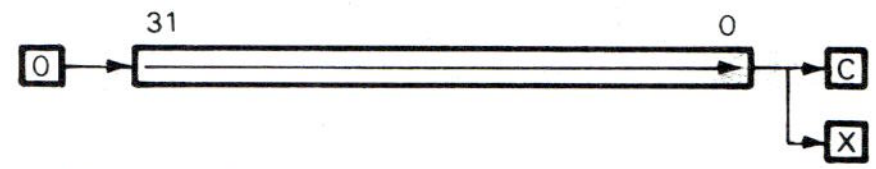 As LSR.B except shifts are for entire register.
	ROL	dadr	2, 4 or 6	9(1/1)+				X	X	0	X	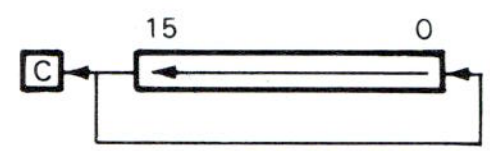 Rotate left one bit of memory word. Bit 15 is shifted into bit 0 and into the Carry.
	ROL.B	count,Dn Dn,dDn	2 2	6 + 2N(1/0) 6 + 2N(1/0)				X X	X X	0 0	X X	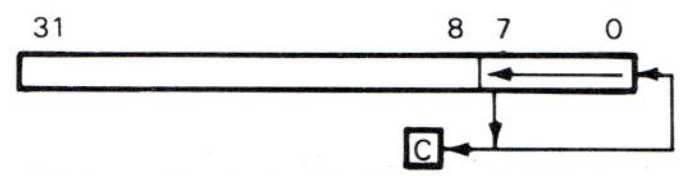 Rotate left of data register byte. The number of shifts is specified as a direct count (1-8) or in a data register (1-63). Bit 7 is shifted into bit 0 and into the Carry.

Table A-2. MC68000 Instruction Set Summary (Continued)

	Mnemonic	Operand(s)	Bytes	Clock Cycles	Status T	S	X	N	Z	V	C	Operation Performed
Shift (Continued)	ROL.W	count,Dn Dn,dDn	2 2	6 + 2N(1/0) 6 + 2N(1/0)				X X	X X	0 0	X X	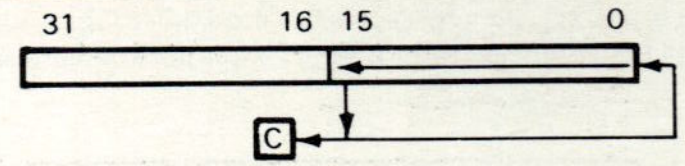 As ROL. B except shifts are for one word.
	ROL.L	count,Dn Dn,dDn	2 2	8 + 2N(1/0) 8 + 2N(1/0)				X X	X X	0 0	X X	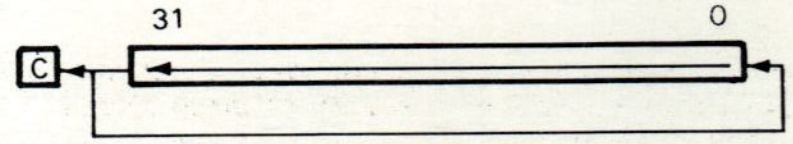 As ROL.B except shifts are for entire register.
	ROR	dadr	2, 4 or 6	9(1/1)+				X	X	0	X	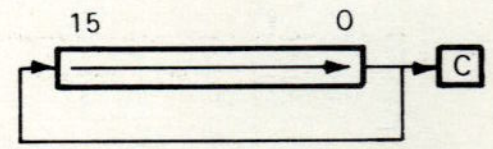 Rotate right one bit of memory word. Bit 0 is shifted into bit 15 and into the Carry.
	ROR.B	count,Dn Dn,dDn	2 2	6 + 2N(1/0) 6 + 2N(1/0)				X X	X X	0 0	X X	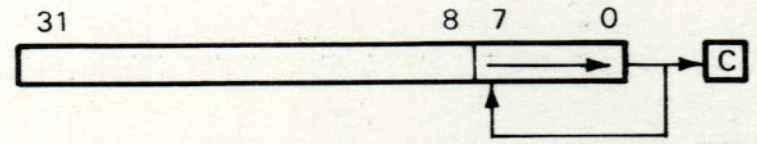 Rotate right of data register byte. The number of shifts is specified as a direct count (1-8) or in a data register (1-63). Bit 0 is shifted into bit 7 and into the Carry.
	ROR.W	count,Dn Dn,dDn	2 2	6 + 2N(1/0) 6 + 2N(1/0)				X X	X X	0 0	X X	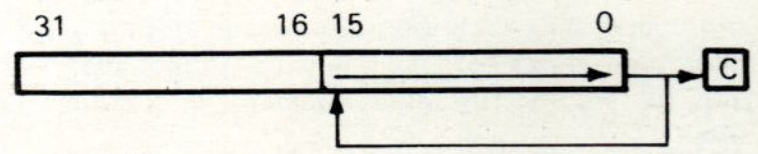 As ROR.B except shifts are for one word.
	ROR.L	count,Dn Dn,dDn	2 2	8 + 2N(1/0) 8 + 2N(1/0)				X X	X X	0 0	X X	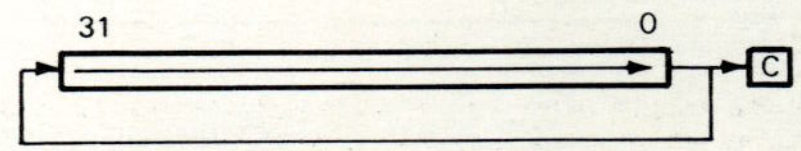 As ROR.B except shifts are for entire register.
	ROXL	dadr	2, 4 or 6	9(1/1)+				X	X	0	X	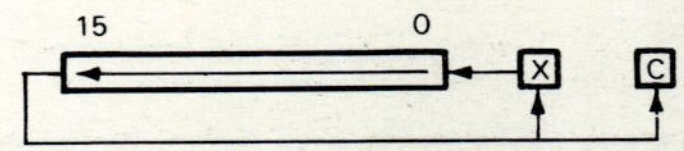 Rotate left one bit of memory word and Extend one bit. Bit 15 is shifted into both Extend and Carry bits. The Extend bit is shifted into bit 0.

Table A-2. MC68000 Instruction Set Summary (Continued)

	Mnemonic	Operand(s)	Bytes	Clock Cycles	Status T	S	X	N	Z	V	C	Operation Performed
Shift (Continued)	ROXL.B	count,Dn Dn,dDn	2 2	6 + 2N(1/0) 6 + 2N(1/0)				X X	X X	0 0	X X	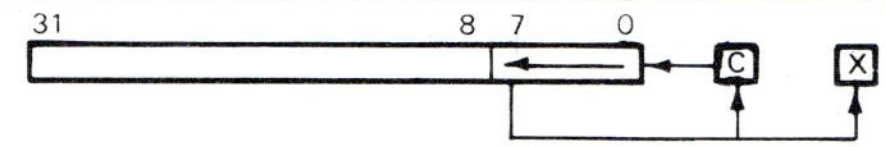 Rotate left of data register byte with Extend. The number of shifts is specified as a direct count (1-8) or in a data register (1-63). Bit 15 is shifted into both Extend and Carry bits. The Extend bit is shifted into bit 0.
	ROXL. W	count,Dn Dn,dDn	2 2	6 + 2N(1/0) 6 + 2N(1/0)				X X	X X	0 0	X X	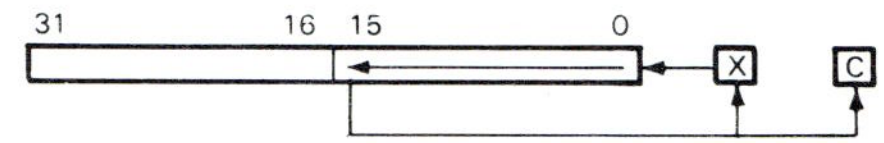 As ROXL.B except shifts are for one word.
	ROXL.L	count,Dn Dn,dDn	2 2	8 + 2N(1/0) 8 + 2N(1/0)				X X	X X	0 0	X X	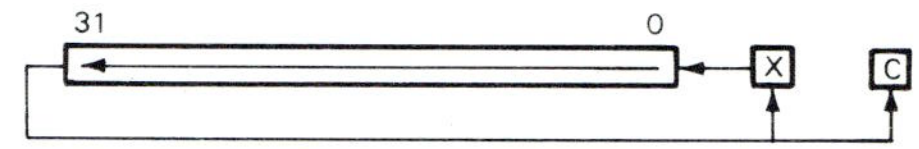 As ROXL.B except shifts are for entire register.
	ROXR	dadr	2, 4 or 6	9(1/1)+				X	X	0	X	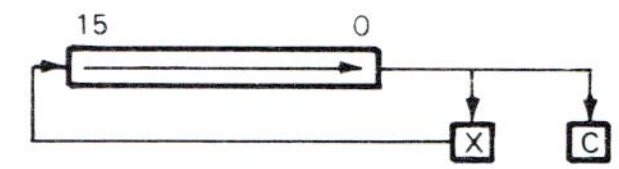 Rotate right one bit of memory word and Extend. Bit 0 is shifted into both Extend and Carry bits. The Extend bit is shifted into bit 15.
	ROXR.B	count,Dn Dn,dDn	2 2	6 + 2N(1/0) 6 + 2N(1/0)				X X	X X	0 0	X X	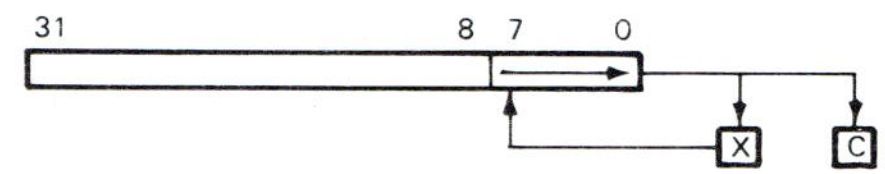 Rotate right of data register byte with Extend. The number of shifts is specified as a direct count (1-8) or in a data register (1-63). Bit 0 is shifted into both Extend and Carry bits. The Extend bit is shifted into bit 7.
	ROXR.W	count,Dn Dn,dDn	2 2	6 + 2N(1/0) 6 + 2N(1/0)				X X	X X	0 0	X X	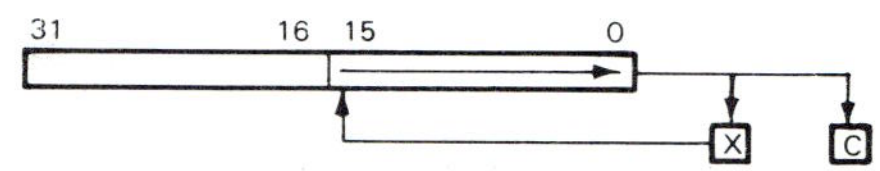 As ROXR.B except shfits are for one word.
	ROXR.L	count,Dn Dn,dDn	2 2	8 + 2N(1/0) 8 + 2N(1/0)				X X	X X	0 0	X X	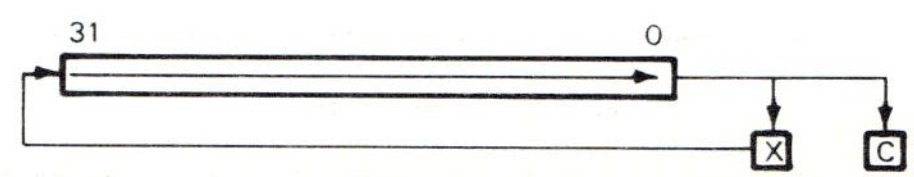 As ROXR.B except shifts are for entire register.

Table A-2. MC68000 Instruction Set Summary (Continued)

	Mnemonic	Operand(s)	Bytes	Clock Cycles	Status T	S	X	N	Z	V	C	Operation Performed
Bit Manipulation	BTST	bitl,Dn	4	10(2/0)					X			[Z] ← $\overline{\text{Dn<bitl>}}$
		Dn,dDn	2	6(1/0)					X			[Z] ← $\overline{\text{dDn<[Dn]>}}$ Test a bit of a data register and reflect status in Zero bit. The bit to be tested may be specified directly or in a data register (bit 0-31 in either case).
	BTST	bitb,dadr	4, 6 or 8	8(2/0)+					X			[Z] ← $\overline{\text{dadr<bitb>}}$
		Dn,dadr	2, 4 or 6	4(1/0)+					X			[Z] ← $\overline{\text{dadr<[Dn]>}}$ Test a bit of a memory byte and reflect status in Zero bit. The bit to be tested may be specified directly or in a data register (bit 0-7 in either case).[1]
	BSET	bitl,Dn	4	12(2/0)					X			[Z] ← $\overline{\text{Dn<bitl>}}$, [Dn<bitl>] ← 1
		Dn,dDn	2	8(1/0)					X			[Z] ← $\overline{\text{dDn<[Dn]>}}$, [dDn<[Dn]> ← 1
		bitb,dadr	4, 6 or 8	13(2/1)+					X			[Z] ← $\overline{\text{dadr<bitb>}}$, [dadr<bitb>] ← 1
		Dn,dadr	2, 4 or 6	9(1/1)+					X			[Z] ← $\overline{\text{dadr<[Dn]>}}$, [dadr<[Dn]>] ← 1 Test a bit as (BTST) and then set the specified bit.
	BCLR	bitl,Dn	4	14(2/0)					X			[Z] ← $\overline{\text{Dn<bitl>}}$, [Dn<bitl>] ← 0
		Dn,dDn	2	8(1/0)					X			[Z] ← $\overline{\text{dDn<[Dn]>}}$, [dDn<[Dn]>] ← 0
		bitb,dadr	4, 6 or 8	13(2/1)+					X			**[Z]** ← **$\overline{\text{dadr<bit b>}}$, [dadr<bit b>] ← 0**
		Dn,dadr	2, 4 or 6	9(1/1)+					X			[Z] ← $\overline{\text{dadr<[Dn]>}}$, [dadr<[Dn]>] ← 0 Test a bit (as BTST) and then clear the specified bit.
	BCHG	bitl,Dn	4	12(2/0)					X			[Z] ← $\overline{\text{Dn<bitl>}}$, [Dn<bitl>] ← [Dn $\overline{\text{<bitl>}}$]
		Dn,dDn	2	8(1/0)					X			[Z] ← $\overline{\text{dDn ← [Dn]>}}$, [dDn<[Dn]>], $\overline{\text{dDn<[dDn]>}}$
		bitb,dadr	4, 6 or 8	13(2/1)					X			[Z] ← $\overline{\text{dadr<bitb>}}$, [dadr<bitb>] ← $\overline{\text{[dadr<bitb>}}$
		Dn,dadr	2, 4 or 6	9(1/1)					X			[Z] ← $\overline{\text{dadr<[Dn]>}}$, [dadr<[Dn]>] ← $\overline{\text{dadr<[Dn]>}}$ Test a bit (as BTST) and then complement the specified bit.
Stack	MOVE	An,USP	2	4(1/0)								[USP] ← [An] Move contents of address register to User Stack Pointer. **This is a privileged instruction.**
	MOVE	USP,An	2	4(1/0)								[An] ← [USP] Move contents of User Stack Pointer to address register. **This is a privileged instruction.**
	LINK	An,d16	4	18(2/2)								[A7] ← [A7] − 2 [[A7]] ← [An] [An] ← [A7] [A7] ← [A7] + d16 Save the contents of the specified address register on the Stack, load the current Stack Pointer to the specified address register, and set the Stack Pointer to point beyond the temporary stack storage area.
	PEA	jadr	2, 4 or 6	10(1/2)+								[A7] ← [A7] − 2 [[A7]] ← jadr Compute long word address and push address onto the Stack.[3]

Table A-2. MC68000 Instruction Set Summary (Continued)

	Mnemonic	Operand(s)	Bytes	Clock Cycles	Status T	Status S	Status X	Status N	Status Z	Status V	Status C	Operation Performed
Stack (Cont')	UNLIK	An	2	12(3/0)								[A7] ← [An] [An] ← [[A7]] [A7] ← [A7] + 2 Store the contents of the specified address register to the Stack Pointer (A7) and load the specified address register from the stack.
Interrupt and Trap	CHK	data16,Dn	4	49(6/3), 12(2/0)				X	U	U	U	If [Dn < 0-15 >] < 0 or [Dn < 0-15 >] > data16 then [PC] ← CHK interrupt vector
		Dn,dDn	2	45(5/3), 8(1/0)				X	U	U	U	If [dDn < 0-15 >] < 0 or [dDn < 0-15 >] > [Dn < 0-15 >] then [PC] ← CHK interrupt vector
		sadr,Dn	2, 4 or 6	45(5/3), 8(1/0)				X	U	U	U	If [Dn < 0-15 >] < 0 or [Dn < 0-15 >] > [sadr] then [PC] ← CHK interrupt vector Check register against bounds and initiate Check interrupt processing if register word is out of bounds. The upper bound is a twos complement integer specified as immediate data, in a data register, or in a memory word.[2, 3]
	TRAP	vector	2	37(4/3)								[A7] ← [A7] − 2 [[A7]] ← [PC] [A7] ← [A7] − 2 [[A7]] ← [SR] [PC] ← vector Initiate exception processing through specified vector.
	TRAPV		2	37(5/3), 4(1/0)								If Overflow = 1 then TRAP Initiate exception processing through Overflow vector if the Overflow bit is on.
	RTE		2	20(5/0)			X	X	X	X	X	[SR] ← [[A7]], [A7] ← [A7] + 2 [PC] ← [[A7]], [A7] ← [A7] + 2 Return from exception.
Status	MOVE	Dn,CCr	2	12(2/0)			X	X	X	X	X	[SR < 0-4 >] ← [Dn < 0-4] Move status data from data register to condition codes.
	MOVE	sadr,CCR	2, 4 or 6	12(2/0)+			X	X	X	X	X	[SR < 0-4 >] [sadr < 0-4 >] Move status data from memory location to condition codes. The source address is a word address.[2, 3]
	MOVE	data8,CCR	4	16(3/0)			X	X	X	X	X	[SR < 0-4 >] ← data8 < 0-4 > Move immediate status data to condition codes.
	MOVE	Dn,SR	2	12(2/0)	X	X	X	X	X	X	X	[SR] ← [Dn < 0-15 >] Moves status word from data register to Status register. This is a privileged instruction.
	MOVE	sadr,SR	2, 4 or 6	12(2/0)+	X	X	X	X	X	X	X	[SR] ← [sadr] Move status word from memory location to Status register. This is a privileged instruction. The source address is a word address.[2, 3]
	MOVE	data16,SR	4	16(3/0)	X	X	X	X	X	X	X	[SR] ← data16 Move immediate status word to Status register. This is a privileged instruction.
	MOVE	SR,Dn	2	6(1/0)								[Dn < 0-15 >] ← [SR] Move contents of Status register to data register. Bits 16-31 of the data register are not affected.

Table A-2. MC68000 Instruction Set Summary (Continued)

	Mnemonic	Operand(s)	Bytes	Clock Cycles	Status							Operation Performed
					T	S	X	N	Z	V	C	
Status (Continued)	MOVE	SR,dadr	2, 4 or 6	9(1/1)+								[dadr] ← [SR] Move contents of Status register to memory location. The destination address is a word address. 2, 3
	AND.B	data8,SR	4	20(3/0)			X	X	X	X	X	[SR<0-7>] ← [SR<0-7>] ∧ data8 AND immediate data byte to low-order Status register byte.
	AND.W	data16,SR	4	20(3/0)	X	X	X	X	X	X	X	[SR] ← [SR] ∧ data16 AND immediate data with Status register. **This is a privileged instruction.**
	EOR.B	data8,SR	4	20(3/0)			X	X	X	X	X	[SR<0-7>] ← [SR<0-7>] ⊻ data8 Exclusive-OR immediate data byte to low-order Status register byte.
	EOR.W	data16,SR	4	20(3/0)	X	X	X	X	X	X	X	[SR] ← [SR] ⊻ data16 Exclusive-OR immediate data with Status register. **This is a privileged instruction.**
	OR.B	data8,SR	4	20(3/0)			X	X	X	X	X	[SR<0-7>] ← [SR<0-7>] ∧ data8 OR immediate data byte to low-order Status register byte.
	OR.W	data16,SR	4	20(3/0)	X	X	X	X	X	X	X	[SR] ← [SR] V data16 OR immediate data with Status register. **This is a privileged instruction.**
Miscellaneous Control	NOP		2	4(1/0)								No operation.
	RESET		2	132(1/0)								Reset. **This is a privileged instruction.**
	STOP	data16	4	8(2/0)			X	X	X	X	X	[SR] ← data16 Stop processor. **This is a privileged instruction.**

B
Instruction Object Code Tables

The object code for each MC68000 instruction is shown alphabetically by instruction mnemonic in this appendix.

For instruction words which have no variations, object codes are represented as four hexadecimal digits; for example, 4E71.

For instruction words with variation in one of the two bytes, the object code is shown as a combination of lower-case variables, hex digits, and binary digits. Each byte of an instruction word is subdivided into two "nibble" fields (1 nibble = 4 bits). If a single digit appears in a nibble field, it is a hexadecimal digit. If four digits, or a combination of digits and lower-case variables (for example, 1rrr), appear in a nibble field, each digit represents a single bit.

Note that some lower-case variables are used to represent hexadecimal digits rather than binary digits. When four of these hexadecimal variable characters (for example xxxx or yyyy) are used to represent a 16-bit word, they will appear grouped together in the center of the 2-byte column comprising that word.

INSTRUCTION EXECUTION TIMES

This appendix lists the instruction execution time in clock cycles. Each cycle = 125 nanoseconds (when $f_{CLK} = 8.0$ MHz).

The abbreviations and notations used in the "clock cycles" column are defined as follows:

+ea Effective address overhead. This is the additional time required to execute the instruction for addressing modes that take longer to execute than the nominal register indirect address. The following are the additional clock cycles required:

Addressing Mode	Additional Clock Cycles
(An)	0
(An)+	0
−(An)	2
d16(An)	5
d8(An,i)	7
addr-16-bit	5
addr-32-bit	10
label	5
label(i)	7

N For shift instructions, the number of shifts. For move multiple instructions, the number of registers being moved.

***** The first value is for branch or trap taken, the second is for branch or trap not taken. In the case of Bcc, the first of the latter numbers is for a two-byte instruction (8-bit displacement), and the second is for a four-byte instruction (16-bit displacement). In the case of DBcc, the first of the latter numbers is for branch not taken due to condition true, and the second is for branch not taken due to counter timeout.

****** Indicates maximum value.

******* The lower value is for condition false (byte set to all ones); the higher value is for condition true (byte cleared to all zeroes).

The following abbreviations are used in this appendix:

a Operand addressing mode (1 bit)
0 = data register to data register
1 = memory to memory

bbb 3 bits of immediate data. In bit operations the bit numbers 0 - 7.

bbbbb Bit numbers 0 - 31.

ccc Shift count 000 = 8 shifts
001 = 1 shift
010 = 2 shifts
011 = 3 shifts
100 = 4 shifts
101 = 5 shifts
110 = 6 shifts
111 = 7 shifts

ddd Destination register — same coding as rrr.

eeeee Source effective address (6 bits)

Address Mode	Mode/Register	[EXT]
(An)	010rrr	---
(An)+	011rrr	---
-(An)	100rrr	---
d16(An)	101rrr	xxxx
d8(An,i)	110rrr	a iii w 000 xx
addr-16-bit	111000	pppp
addr-32-bit	111001	pppp qqqq
label	111010	xxxx
label(i)	111011	a iii w ooo xx

[EXT] One or two optional words of extension addressing that may or may not appear, depending on the addressing mode (see the Addressing Modes description).

ffffff Destination effective address — same as eeeeee except no label or label(i).

gggggg Destination effective address but in a format with the MODE and REGISTER fields switched (e.g., (An)=rrr010).

hhhhhh Multiple-destination effective address — same as ffffff except no (An)+ or −(An).?

iii Index register — same coding as rrr.

jjjjjj Jump effective address — same as eeeeee except no (An)+ or −(An).

kkkk Register mask list for predecrement mode, in the following format (a "1" selects the register):

15	14	13	12	11	10	9	8	7	6	5	4	3	2	1	0
D0	D1	D2	D3	D4	D5	D6	D7	A0	A1	A2	A3	A4	A5	A6	A7

mmmm Register mask list for non-predecrement modes, in the format (a "1" selects the register):

15	14	13	12	11	10	9	8	7	6	5	4	3	2	1	0
A7	A6	A5	A4	A3	A2	A1	A0	D7	D6	D5	D4	D3	D2	D1	D0

pppp 16-bit address word or most significant word of 32-bit address

qqqq Least significant word of 32-bit address

rrr Register 000 = D0 or A0
001 = D1 or A1
010 = D2 or A2
011 = D3 or A3
100 = D4 or A4
101 = D5 or A5
110 = D6 or A6
111 = D7 or A7

sss Source register — same coding as rrr

t Type of register 0 = Dn
1 = An

vvvv 4-bit vector

w Index size. 0 = sign-extended, low-order integer in index register
1 = long word value in index register

xx 8-bit address displacement

xxxx 16-bit address displacement

yy 8-bit immediate data

yyyy 16-bit immediate data or most significant word of 32-bit data

zzzz Least significant word of 32-bit data

Table B-1. MC68000 Instruction Object Codes

Instruction		Byte 1	Byte 2	Byte 3	Byte 4	Byte 5	Byte 6	Byte 7	Byte 8	Byte 9	Byte 10	Bytes	Clock Cycles
ABCD	−(SAn),−(dAn)	C dddd1	0 1sss									2	19(3/1)
	sDn,dDn	C dddd1	0 0sss									2	6(1/0)
ADD.B	data8,dadr	0 6	00ff ffff	00	yy	[EXT]		[EXT]				4, 6, or 8	13(2/1)+
	data8,Dn	0 6	0 0ddd	00	yy							4	8(2/0)
	Dn,dadr	D sss1	00ff ffff	[EXT]		[EXT]						2, 4, or 6	9(1/1)+
	sadr,Dn	D ddd0	00ee eeee	[EXT]		[EXT]						2, 4, or 6	4(1/0)+
	sDn,dDn	D ddd0	0 0sss									2	4(1/0)
ADD.L	data32,An	D ddd1	F C	yyyy		zzzz						6	16(3/0)
	data32,dadr	0 6	10ff ffff	yyyy		zzzz		[EXT]		[EXT]		6, 8, or 10	22(3/2)+
	data32,Dn	0 6	8 0ddd	yyyy		zzzz						6	16(3/0)
	Dn,dadr	D sss1	10ff ffff	[EXT]		[EXT]						2, 4, or 6	14(1/2)+
	rs,An	D ddd1	C tsss									2	8(1/0)
	rs,Dn	D ddd0	8 tsss									2	8(1/0)
	sadr,An	D ddd1	11ee eeee	[EXT]		[EXT]						2, 4, or 6	6(1/0)+
	sadr,Dn	D ddd0	10ee eeee	[EXT]		[EXT]						2, 4, or 6	6(1/0)+
ADD.W	data16,An	D ddd0	F C	yyyy								4	8(2/0)
	data16,dadr	0 6	01ff ffff	yyyy		[EXT]		[EXT]				4, 6, or 8	13(2/1)
	data16,Dn	0 6	4 0ddd	yyyy								4	8(2/0)
	Dn,dadr	D ssss1	01ff ffff	[EXT]		[EXT]						2, 4, or 6	9(11)+
	rs,An	D ddd0	C tsss									2	8(1/0)
	rs,Dn	D ddd0	4 tsss									2	4(1/0)
	sadr,An	D ddd0	11ee eeee	[EXT]		[EXT]						2, 4, or 6	8(1/0)+
	sadr,Dn	D ddd0	01ee eeee	[EXT]		[EXT]						2, 4, or 6	4(1/0)+
ADDQ.B	data3,dadr	5 bbb0	00ff ffff	[EXT]		[EXT]						2, 4, or 6	9(1/0)+
	data3,Dn	5 bbb0	0 0ddd									2	4(1/0)
ADDQ.L	data3,An	5 bbb0	8 1ddd									2	8(1/0)
	data3,dadr	5 bbb0	10ff ffff	[EXT]		[EXT]						2, 4, or 6	14(1/2)+
	data3,Dn	5 bbb0	8 0ddd									2	8(1/0)
ADDQ.W	data3,An	5 bbb0	4 1ddd									2	4(1/0)
	data3,dadr	5 bbb0	01ff ffff	[EXT]		[EXT]						2, 4, or 6	9(1/1)+
	data3,Dn	5 bbb0	4 0ddd									2	4(1/0)
ADDX.B	−(sAn),−(dAn)	D ddd1	0 1sss									2	19(3/1)
	sDn,dDn	D ddd1	0 0sss									2	4(1/0)
ADDX.L	−(sAn),−(dAn)	D ddd1	8 1sss									2	32(5/2)
	SDn,dDn	D ddd1	8 0sss									2	8(1/0)
ADDX.W	−(sAn),−(dAn)	D ddd1	4 1sss									2	19(3/1)
	sDn,dDn	D ddd1	4 0sss									2	4(1/0)
AND.B	data8,dadr	0 2	00ff ffff	00	yy	[EXT]		[EXT]				4, 6, or 8	13(2/1)+
	data8,Dn	0 2	0 0ddd	00	yy							4	8(2/0)
	data8,SR	0 2	3 C	00	yy							4	20(3/0)
	Dn,dadr	C sss1	00ff ffff	[EXT]		[EXT]						2, 4, or 6	9(1/1)+
	sadr,Dn	C ddd0	00ee eeee	[EXT]		[EXT]						2, 4, or 6	4(1/0)+
	sDn,dDn	C ddd0	0 0sss									2	4(1/0)
AND.L	data32,dadr	0 2	10ff ffff	yyyy		zzzz		[EXT]		[EXT]		6, 8, or 10	22(3/2)+
	data32,Dn	0 2	8 0ddd	yyyy		zzzz						6	16(3/0)
	Dn,dadr	C sss1	10ff ffff	[EXT]		[EXT]						2, 4, or 6	14(1/2)+
	sadr,Dn	C ddd0	10ee eeee	[EXT]		[EXT]						2, 4, or 6	6(1/0)+
	sDn,dDn	C ddd0	8 0sss									2	8(1/0)
AND.W	data16,dadr	0 2	01ff ffff	yyyy		[EXT]		[EXT]				4, 6, or 8	13(2/1)+
	data16,Dn	0 2	4 0ddd	yyyy								4	8(2/0)
	data16,SR	0 2	7 C	yyyy								4	20(3/0)
	Dn,dadr	C sss1	01ff ffff	[EXT]		[EXT]						2, 4, or 6	9(1/1)
	sadr,Dn	C ddd0	01ee eeee	[EXT]		[EXT]						2, 4, or 6	4(1/0)

Table B-1. MC68000 Instruction Object Codes (Continued)

Instruction		Byte 1	Byte 2	Byte 3	Byte 4	Byte 5	Byte 6	Byte 7	Byte 8	Byte 9	Byte 10	Bytes	Clock Cycles
	sDn,dDn	C ddd0	4 0sss									2	4(1/0)
ASL	dadr	E 1	11ff ffff	[EXT]		[EXT]						2, 4, or 6	9(1/1)+
ASL.B	count,Dn	E ccc1	0 0ddd									2	6 + 2N(1/0)
	Dn,dDn	E rrr1	2 0ddd									2	6 + 2N(1/0)
ASL.L	count,Dn	E ccc1	8 0ddd									2	8 + 2N(1/0)
	Dn,dDn	E rrr1	A 0ddd									2	8 + 2N(1/0)
ASL.W	count,Dn	E ccc1	4 0ddd									2	6 + 2N(1/0)
	Dn,dDn	E rrr1	6 0ddd									2	6 + 2N(1/0)
ASR	dadr	E 0	11ff ffff	[EXT]		[EXT]						2, 4, or 6	9(1/1)+
ASR.B	count,Dn	E ccc0	0 0ddd									2	6 + 2N(1/0)
	Dn,dDn	E rrr0	2 0ddd									2	6 + 2N(1/0)
ASR.L	count,Dn	E ccc0	8 0ddd									2	8 + 2N(1/0)
	Dn,dDn	E rrr0	A 0ddd									2	8 + 2N(1/0)
ASR.W	count,Dn	E ccc0	4 0ddd									2	6 + 2N(1/0)
	Dn,dDn	E rrr0	6 0ddd									2	6 + 2N(1/0)
BCC	label	6 4	0 0	xxxx								4	10, 12(2/0)
	label	6 4	x x									2	10, 18(1/0)
BCHG	bitb,dadr	0 8	01ff ffff	00	0 0bbb	[EXT]		[EXT]				4, 6, or 8	13(2/1)+
	bitl,Dn	0 8	4 0ddd	00	000b bbbb							4	12(2/0)
	Dn,dadr	0 rrr1	01ff ffff	[EXT]		[EXT]						2, 4, or 6	9(1/1)+
	Dn,dDn	0 rrr1	4 0ddd									2	8(1/0)
BCLR	bitb,dadr	0 8	10ff ffff	00	0 0bbb	[EXT]		[EXT]				4, 6, or 8	13(2/1)+
	bitl,Dn	0 8	8 0ddd	00	000b bbbb							4	14(2/0)
	Dn,dadr	0 rrr1	10ff ffff	[EXT]		[EXT]						2, 4, or 6	9(1/1)+
	Dn,dDn	0 rrr1	8 0ddd									2	8(1/0)
BCS	label	6 5	0 0	xxxx								4	10, 12(2/0)
	label	6 5	x x									2	10, 18(1/0)
BEQ	label	6 7	0 0	xxxx								4	10, 12(2/0)
	label	6 7	x x									2	10, 8(1/0)
BGE	label	6 C	0 0	xxxx								4	10, 12(2/0)
	label	6 C	x x									2	10, 8(1/0)
BGT	label	6 E	0 0	xxxx								4	10, 12(2/0)
	label	6 E	x x									2	10, 8(1/0)
BHI	label	6 2	0 0	xxxx								4	10, 12(2/0)
	label	6 2	0 0									2	10, 8(1/0)
BLE	label	6 F	0 0	xxxx								4	10, 12(2/0)
	label	6 F	x x									2	10, 8(1/0)
BLS	label	6 3	0 0	xxxx								4	10, 12(2/0)
	label	6 3	x x									2	10, 8(1/0)
BLT	label	6 D	0 0	xxxx								4	10, 12(2/0)
		6 D	x x									2	10, 8(1/0)
BMI	label	6 B	0 0	xxxx								4	10, 12(2/0)
	label	6 B	x x									2	10, 8(1/0)
BNE	label	6 6	0 0	xxxx								4	10, 12(2/0)
	label	6 6	x x									2	10, 8(1/0)
BPL	label	6 A	0 0	xxxx								4	10, 12(2/0)
	label	6 A	x x									2	10, 8(1/0)
BRA	label	6 0	0 0	xxxx								4	10(2/0)
	label	6 0	x x									2	10(1/0)
BSET	bitb,dadr	0 8	11ff ffff	00	0 0bbb	[EXT]		[EXT]				4, 6, or 8	13(2/1)+
	bitl,Dn	0 8	C 0ddd	00	000b bbbb							4	12(2/0)
	Dn,dadr	0 rrr1	11ff ffff	[EXT]		[EXT]						2, 4, or 6	9(1/1)+
	Dn,dDn	0 rrr1	C 0ddd									2	8(1/0)

Table B-1. MC68000 Instruction Object Codes (Continued)

Instruction		Byte 1	Byte 2	Byte 3	Byte 4	Byte 5	Byte 6	Byte 7	Byte 8	Byte 9	Byte 10	Bytes	Clock Cycles
BSR	label	6 1	0 0	xxxx								4	10, 12(2/0)
	label	6 1	x x									2	10, 8(1/0)
BTST	bitb,dadr	0 8	00ff ffff	00	0 0bbb	[EXT]		[EXT]				4, 6, or 8	8(2/0)+
	bitl,Dn	0 8	0 0ddd	00	000bbbbb							4	10(2/0)
	Dn,dadr	0 rrr1	00ff ffff	[EXT]		[EXT]						2, 4, or 6	4(1/0)
	Dn,dDn	0 rrr1	0 0ddd									2	6(1/0)
BVC	label	6 8	0 0	xxxx								4	10, 12(2/0)
	label	6 8	x x									2	10, 8(1/0)
BVS	label	6 9	0 0	xxxx								4	10, 12(2/0)
		6 9	x x									2	10, 8(1/0)
CHK	data16,Dn	4 ddd1	B C	yyyy								4	49(6/3),12(2/0)
	Dn,dDn	4 ddd1	8 0rrr									2	45(5/3),8(1/0)
	sadr,Dn	4 ddd1	10ee eeee	[EXT]		[EXT]						2, 4, or 6	45(5/3)+,81/0)
CLR.B	dadr	4 2	00ff ffff	[EXT]		[EXT]						2, 4, or 6	9(1/1)+
	Dn	4 2	0 0ddd									2	4(1/0)
CLR.L	dadr	4 2	10ff ffff	[EXT]		[EXT]						2, 4, or 6	14(1/2)+
	Dn	4 2	8 0ddd									2	6(1/0)
CLR.W	dadr	4 2	01ff ffff	[EXT]		[EXT]						2, 4, or 6	9(1/1)
	Dn	4 2	4 0ddd									2	4(1/0)
CMP. B	data8,dadr	0 C	00ff ffff	00	yy	[EXT]		[EXT]				4, 6, or 8	8(2/0)
	data8,Dn	0 C	0 0ddd	00	yy							4	8(2/0)
	sadr,Dn	B ddd0	00ee eeee	[EXT]		[EXT]						2, 4, or 6	4(1/0)+
	sDn,dDn	B ddd0	0 0sss									2	4(1/0)
CMP. L	data32,An	B ddd1	F C	yyyy		zzzz						6	14(3/0)
	data32,dadr	0 C	10ff ffff	yyyy		zzzz		[EXT]		[EXT]		6, 8, or 10	12(3/0)+
	data32,Dn	0 C	8 0ddd	yyyy		zzzz						6	14(3/0)
	rs,An	B ddd1	C tsss									2	6(1/0)
	rs,Dn	B ddd0	8 tsss									2	6(1/0)
	sadr,An	B ddd1	11ee eeee	[EXT]		[EXT]						2, 4, or 6	6(1/0)+
	sadr,Dn	B ddd0	10ee eeee	[EXT]		[EXT]						2, 4, or 6	6(1/0)+
CMP. W	data16,An	B ddd0	F C	yyyy								4	8(2/0)
	data16,dadr	0 C	01ff ffff	yyyy		[EXT]		[EXT]				4, 6, or 8	8(2/0)+
	data16,Dn	0 C	4 0ddd	yyyy								4	8(2/0)
	rs,An	B ddd0	C tsss									2	6(1/0)
	rs,Dn	B ddd0	4 tsss									2	4(1/0)
	sadr,An	B ddd0	11ee eeee	[EXT]		[EXT]						2, 4, or 6	6(1/0)+
	sadr,Dn	B ddd0	01ee eeee	[EXT]		[EXT]						2, 4, or 6	4(1/0)+
CMPM. B	(sAn)+,(dAn)+	B ddd1	0 1sss									2	12(3/0)
CMPM. L	(sAn)+,(dAn)+	B ddd1	8 1sss									2	20(5/0)
CMPM. W	(sAn)+,(dAn)+	B ddd1	4 1sss									2	12(3/0)
DBCC	Dn,label	5 4	C 1rrr	xxxx								4	12(2/0),10(2/0),14(3/0)
DBCS	Dn,label	5 5	C 1rrr	xxxx								4	12(2/0),10(2/0),14(3/0)
DBEQ	Dn,label	5 7	C 1rrr	xxxx								4	12(2/0),10(2/0),14(3/0)
DBF	Dn,label	5 1	C 1rrr	xxxx								4	12(2/0),10(2/0),14(3/0)
DBGE	Dn,label	5 C	C 1rrr	xxxx								4	12(2/0),10(2/0),14(3/0)
DBGT	Dn,label	5 E	C 1rrr	xxxx								4	12(2/0),10(2/0),14(3/0)
DBHI	Dn,label	5 2	C 1rrr	xxxx								4	12(2/0),10(2/0),14(3/0)
DBLE	Dn,label	5 F	C 1rrr	xxxx								4	12(2/0),10(2/0),14(3/0)
DBLS	Dn,label	5 3	C 1rrr	xxxx								4	12(2/0),10(2/0),14(3/0)
DBLT	Dn,label	5 D	C 1rrr	xxxx								4	12(2/0),10(2/0),14(3/0)
DBMI	Dn,label	5 B	C 1rrr	xxxx								4	12(2/0),10(2/0),14(3/0)
DBNE	Dn,label	5 6	C 1rrr	xxxx								4	12(2/0),10(2/0),14(3/0)
DBPL	Dn,label	5 A	C 1rrr	xxxx								4	12(2/0),10(2/0),14(3/0)

Table B-1. MC68000 Instruction Object Codes (Continued)

Instruction		Byte 1	Byte 2	Byte 3	Byte 4	Byte 5	Byte 6	Byte 7	Byte 8	Byte 9	Byte 10	Bytes	Clock Cycles
DBRA	Dn,label	(same as DBF)											
DBT	Dn,label	5 0	C 1rrr	xxxx								4	12(2/0),10(2/0),14(3/0)
DVC	Dn,label	5 8	C 1rrr	xxxx								4	12(2/0),10(2/0),14(3/0)
DVS	Dn,label	5 9	C 1rrr	xxxx								4	12(2/0),10(2/0),14(3/0)
DIVS	data16,Dn	8 ddd1	F C	yyyy								4	< 162(2/0)
	sadr,Dn	8 ddd1	11ee eeee	[EXT]		[EXT]						2, 4, or 6	< 158(1/0)+
	sDn,dDn	8 ddd1	C 0sss									2	< 158(1/0)
DIVU	data16,Dn	8 ddd0	F C	yyyy								4	< 148(2/0)
	sadr,Dn	8 ddd0	11ee eeee	[EXT]		[EXT]						2, 4, or 6	< 140(1/0)+
	sDn,dDn	8 ddd0	C 0sss									2	< 140(1/0)
EOR.B	data8,dadr	0 A	00ff ffff	00	yy	[EXT]		[EXT]				4, 6, or 8	13(2/1)+
	data8,Dn	0 A	0 0ddd	00	yy							4	8(2/0)
	data8,SR	0 A	3 C	00	yy							4	20(3/0)
	Dn,dadr	B sss1	00ff ffff	[EXT]		[EXT]						2, 4, or 6	9(1/1)+
	sDn,dDn	B sss1	0 0ddd									2	4(1/0)
EOR.L	data32,dadr	0 A	10ff ffff	yyyy		zzzz		[EXT]		[EXT]		6, 8, or 10	22(3/2)+
	data32,Dn	0 A	8 0ddd	yyyy		zzzz						6	16(3/0)
	Dn,dadr	B sss1	10ff ffff	[EXT]		[EXT]						2, 4, or 6	14(1/2)+
	sDn,dDn	B sss1	8 0ddd									2	8(1/0)
EOR.W	data16,dadr	0 A	01ff ffff	yyyy		[EXT]		[EXT]				4, 6, or 8	13(2/1)+
	data16,Dn	0 A	4 0ddd	yyyy								4	8(2/0)
	data16,Sr	0 A	7 C	yyyy								4	20(3/0)
	Dn,dadr	B sss1	01ff ffff	[EXT]		[EXT]						2, 4, or 6	9(1/1)+
	sDn,dDn	B sss1	4 0ddd									2	4(1/0)
EXG	An,An	C sss1	4 1ddd									2	6(1/0)
	An,Dn	C sss1	8 1ddd									2	6(1/0)
	Dn,An	(same as An,Dn)											
	Dn,Dn	C sss1	4 0ddd									2	6(1/0)
EXT.L	Dn	4 8	C 0ddd									2	4(1/0)
EXT.W	Dn	4 8	8 0ddd									2	4(1/0)
JMP	jadr	4 E	11jj jjjj	[EXT]		[EXT]						2, 4, or 6	4(1/0)+
JSR	jadr	4 E	10jj jjjj	[EXT]		[EXT]						2, 4, or 6	14(1/2)+
LEA	jadr,An	4 ddd1	11jj jjjj	[EXT]		[EXT]						2, 4, or 6	2(0/0)+
LINK	An,d16	4 E	5 0rrr			xxxx						4	18(2/2)
LSL	dadr	E 3	11ff ffff	[EXT]		[EXT]						2, 4, or 6	9(1/1)+
LSL.B	count,Dn	E ccc1	0 1ddd									2	6 + 2N(1/0)
	Dn,dDn	E rrr1	2 1ddd									2	6 + 2N(1/0)
LSL.L	count,Dn	E ccc1	8 1ddd									2	8 + 2N(1/0)
	Dn,dDn	E rrr1	A 1ddd									2	8 + 2N(1/0)
LSL.W	count,Dn	E ccc1	4 1ddd									2	6 + 2N(1/0)
	Dn,dDn	E rrr1	6 1ddd									2	6 + 2N(1/0)
LSR	dadr	E 2	11ff ffff	[EXT]		[EXT]						2, 4, or 6	9(1/1)+
LSR.B	count,Dn	E ccc0	0 1ddd									2	6 + 2N(1/0)
	Dn,dDn	E rrr0	2 1ddd									2	6 + 2N(1/0)
LSR.L	count,Dn	E ccc0	8 1ddd									2	8 + 2N(1/0)
	Dn,dDn	E rrr0	A 1ddd									2	8 + 2N(1/0)
LSR.W	count,Dn	E ccc0	4 1ddd									2	6 + 2N(1/0)
	Dn,dDn	E rrr0	6 1ddd									2	6 + 2N(1/0)
MOVE	An,USP	4 E	6 0sss									2	4(1/0)
	data8,CCR	4 4	F C	00	yy							4	16(3/0)
	data16,SR	4 6	F C	yyyy								4	16(3/0)
	Dn,CCR	4 4	C 0sss									2	12(2/0)
	Dn,SR	4 6	C 0sss									2	12(2/0)

Table B-1. MC68000 Instruction Object Codes (Continued)

Instruction		Byte 1	Byte 2	Byte 3	Byte 4	Byte 5	Byte 6	Byte 7	Byte 8	Byte 9	Byte 10	Bytes	Clock Cycles
	sadr,CCR	4 4	11ee eeee	[EXT]		[EXT]						2, 4, or 6	12(2/0)+
	sadr,SR	4 6	11ee eeee	[EXT]		[EXT]						2, 4, or 6	12(2/0)+
	SR,dadr	4 0	11ff ffff	[EXT]		[EXT]						2, 4, or 6	9(1/1)+
	SR,Dn	4 0	C 0ddd									2	6(1/0)
	USP,An	4 E	6 1sss									2	4(1/0)
MOVE.B	data8,Dn	1 ddd0	3 C	00	yy							4	8(2/0)
	data8,dadr	1 gggg	gg11 C	00	yy	[EXT]		[EXT]				4, 6, or 8	9(1/1)+
	Dn,dadr	1 gggg	gg00 0sss	[EXT]		[EXT]						2, 4, or 6	5(0/1)+
	sDn,dDn	1 ddd0	0 0sss									2	4(1/0)
	sadr,dadr	1 gggg	ggee eeee	[EXT$_s$]		[EXT$_s$]		[EXT$_d$]		[EXT$_d$]		2, 4, 6, 8 or 10	5(1/1)+
	sadr,Dn	1 ddd0	00ee eeee	[EXT]		[EXT]						2, 4, or 6	4(1/0)+
MOVE.L	An,dadr	2 gggg	gg00 1sss	[EXT]		[EXT]						2, 4, or 6	10(0/2)+
	data32,An	2 ddd0	7 C	yyyy		zzzz						6	12(3/0)
	data32,dadr	2 gggg	gg11 C	yyyy		zzzz		[EXT]		[EXT]		6, 8, or 10	18(2/2)+
	data32,Dn	2 ddd0	3 C	yyyy		zzzz						6	12(3/0)
	Dn,dadr	2 gggg	gg00 0sss	[EXT]		[EXT]						2, 4, or 6	10(0/2)+
	rs,An	2 ddd0	4 tsss									2	4(1/0)
	rs,Dn	2 ddd0	0 tsss									2	4(1/0)
	sadr,An	2 ddd0	01ee eeee	[EXT]		[EXT]						2, 4, or 6	8(2/0)+
	sadr,dadr	2 gggg	ggee eeee	[EXT$_s$]		[EXT$_s$]		[EXT$_d$]		[EXT$_d$]		2, 4, 6, 8, or, 10	14(1/2)+
	sadr,Dn	2 ddd0	00ee eeee	[EXT]		[EXT]						2, 4, or 6	4(1/0)+
MOVE.W	An,dadr	3 gggg	gg00 1sss	[EXT]		[EXT]						2, 4, or 6	5(0/1)+
	data16,An	3 ddd0	7 C	yyyy								4	8(2/0)
	data16,dadr	3 gggg	gg11 C	yyyy		[EXT]		[EXT]				4, 6, or 8	9(1/1)+
	data16,Dn	3 ddd0	3 C	yyyy								4	8(2/0)
	Dn,dadr	3 gggg	gg00 0sss	[EXT]		[EXT]						2, 4, or 6	5(0/1)+
	rs,An	3 ddd0	4 tsss									2	4(1/0)
	rs,Dn	3 ddd0	0 tsss									2	4(1/0)
	sadr,An	3 ddd0	01ee eeee	[EXT]		[EXT]						2, 4, or 6	4(1/0)+
	sadr,dadr	3 gggg	ggee eeee	[EXT$_s$]		[EXT$_s$]		[EXT$_d$]		[EXT$_d$]		2, 4, 6, 8, or 10	5(0/1)+
	sadr,Dn	3 ddd0	00ee eeee	[EXT]		[EXT]						2, 4, or 6	4(1/0)+
MOVEM.L	(An)+,reg-list	4 C	E 0sss	mmmm								4	8 + 8n(2 + 2n/0)
	jadr,reg-list	4 C	11jj jjjj	mmmm		[EXT]		[EXT]				4, 6, or 8	8 + 8n(2 + 2n/0)+
	reg-list,−(An)	4 8	E 0ddd	kkkk								4	4 + 10n(1/n)
	reg-list,madr	4 8	11hh hhhh	mmmm		[EXT]		[EXT]				4, 6, or 8	4 + 10n(1/n)+
MOVEM.W	(An)+,reg-list	4 C	A 0sss	mmmm								4	8 + 4n(2 + n/0)
	jadr,reg-list	4 C	10jj jjjj	mmmm		[EXT]		[EXT]				4, 6, or 8	8 + 4n(2 + n/0)+
	reg-list,−(An)	4 8	A 0ddd	kkkk								4	4 + 5n(1/n)
	reg-list,madr	4 8	10hh hhhh	mmmm		[EXT]		[EXT]				4, 6, or 8	4 + 5n(1/n)+
MOVEP.L	d16(An),Dn	0 ddd1	4 1sss	xxxx								4	24(6/0)
	Dn,d16(An)	0 sss1	C 1ddd	xxxx								4	28(2/4)
MOVEP.W	d16(An),Dn	0 ddd1	0 1sss	xxxx								4	16(4/0)
	Dn,d16(An)	0 sss1	8 1ddd	xxxx								4	18(2/2)
MOVEQ	data8,Dn	7 ddd0	y y									2	4(1/0)
MULS	data16,Dn	C ddd1	F C	yyyy								4	< 74(2/0)
	sadr,Dn	C ddd1	11ee eeee	[EXT]		[EXT]						2, 4, or 6	< 70(1/0)+
	sDn,dDn	C ddd1	C 0sss									2	< 70(1/0)
MULU	data16,Dn	C ddd0	F C	yyyy								4	< 74(2/0)
	sadr,Dn	C ddd0	11ee eeee	[EXT]		[EXT]						2, 4, or 6	< 70(1/0)+
	sDn,dDn	C ddd0	C 0sss									2	< 70(1/0)
NBCD	dadr	4 8	00ff ffff	[EXT]		[EXT]						2, 4, or 6	9(1/1)+
	Dn	4 8	0 0ddd									2	6(1/0)
NEG.B	dadr	4 4	00ff ffff	[EXT]		[EXT]						2, 4, or 6	9(1/1)+

Table B-1. MC68000 Instruction Object Codes (Continued)

Instruction		Byte 1	Byte 2	Byte 3	Byte 4	Byte 5	Byte 6	Byte 7	Byte 8	Byte 9	Byte 10	Bytes	Clock Cycles
	Dn	4 4	0 0ddd									2	4(1/0)
NEG.L	dadr	4 4	10ff ffff	[EXT]		[EXT]						2, 4, or 6	14(1/2)+
	Dn	4 4	8 0ddd									2	6(1/0)
NEG.W	dadr	4 4	01ff ffff	[EXT]		[EXT]						2, 4, or 6	9(1/1)
	Dn	4 4	4 0ddd									2	4(1/0)
NEGX.B	dadr	4 0	00ff ffff	[EXT]		[EXT]						2, 4, or 6	9(1/1)+
	Dn	4 0	0 0ddd									2	4(1/0)
NEGX.L	dadr	4 0	10ff ffff	[EXT]		[EXT]						2, 4, or 6	14(1/2)+
	Dn	4 0	8 0ddd									2	6(1/0)
NEGX.W	dadr	4 0	01ff ffff	[EXT]		[EXT]						2, 4, or 6	9(1/1)+
	Dn	4 0	4 0ddd									2	4(1/0)
NOP		4 E	7 1									2	4(1/0)
NOT.B	dadr	4 6	00ff ffff	[EXT]		[EXT]						2, 4, or 6	9(1/1)+
	Dn	4 6	0 0ddd									2	4(1/0)
NOT.L	dadr	4 6	10ff ffff	[EXT]		[EXT]						2, 4, or 6	14(1/2)+
	Dn	4 6	8 0ddd									2	6(1/0)
NOT.W	dadr	4 6	01ff ffff	[EXT]		[EXT]						2, 4, or 6	9(1/1)+
	Dn	4 6	4 0ddd									2	6(1/0)
OR.B	data8,dadr	0 0	00ff ffff	00	yy	[EXT]		[EXT]				4, 6, or 8	13(2/1)+
	data8,Dn	0 0	0 0ddd	00	yy							4	8(2/0)
	data8,SR	0 0	3 C	00	yy							4	20(3/0)
	Dn,dadr	8 sss1	00ff ffff	[EXT]		[EXT]						2, 4, or 6	9(1/1)+
	sadr,Dn	8 ddd0	00ee eeee	[EXT]		[EXT]						2, 4, or 6	4(1/0)+
	sDn,dDn	8 ddd0	0 0sss									2	4(1/0)
OR.L	data32,dadr	0 0	10ff ffff	yyyy		zzzz		[EXT]		[EXT]		6, 8, or 10	22(3/2)+
	data32,Dn	0 0	8 0ddd	yyyy		zzzz						6	16(3/0)
	Dn,dadr	8 sss1	10ff ffff	[EXT]		[EXT]						2, 4, or 6	14(1/2)+
	sadr,Dn	8 ddd0	10ee eeee	[EXT]		[EXT]						2, 4, or 6	6(1/0)+
	sDn,dDn	8 ddd0	8 0sss									2	8(1/0)
OR.W	data16,dadr	0 0	01ff ffff	yyyy		[EXT]		[EXT]				4, 6, or 8	13(2/1)+
	data16,Dn	0 0	4 0ddd	yyyy								4	8(2/0)
	data16,SR	0 0	7 C	yyyy								4	20(3/0)
	Dn,dadr	8 ss1	10ff ffff			[EXT]		[EXT]				2, 4, or 6	9(1/1)+
	sadr,Dn	8 ddd0	01ee eeee	[EXT]		[EXT]						2, 4, or 6	4(1/0)+
	sDn,dDn	8 ddd0	4 0sss									2	4(1/0)
PEA	jadr	4 8	01jj jjjj	[EXT]		[EXT]						2, 4, or 6	10(1/2)+
RESET		4 E	7 0									2	132(1/0)
ROL	dadr	E 7	11ff ffff	[EXT]		[EXT]						2, 4, or 6	9(1/1)+
ROL.B	count,Dn	E ccc1	1 1ddd									2	6 + 2N(1/0)
	Dn,dDn	E rrr1	3 1ddd									2	6 + 2N(1/0)
ROL.L	count,Dn	E ccc1	9 1ddd									2	8 + 2N(1/0)
	Dn,dDn	E rrr1	B 1ddd									2	8 + 2N(1/0)
ROL.W	count,Dn	E ccc1	5 1ddd									2	6 + 2N(1/0)
	Dn,dDn	E rrr1	7 1ddd									2	6 + 2N(1/0)
ROR	dadr	E 6	11ff ffff	[EXT]		[EXT]						2, 4 or 6	9(1/1)+
ROR.B	count,Dn	E ccc0	1 1ddd									2	6 + 2N(1/0)
	Dn,dDn	E rrr0	3 1ddd									2	6 + 2N(1/0)
ROR.L	count,Dn	E ccc0	9 1ddd									2	8 + 2N(1/0)
	Dn,dDn	E rrr0	B 1ddd									2	8 + 2N(1/0)
ROR.W	count,Dn	E ccc0	5 1ddd									2	6 + 2N(1/0)
	Dn,dDn	E rrr0	7 1ddd									2	6 + 2N(1/0)
ROXL	dadr	E 5	11ff ffff	[EXT]		[EXT]						2, 4, or 6	9(1/1)+
ROXL.B	count,Dn	E ccc1	1 0ddd									2	6 + 2N(1/0)

Table B-1. MC68000 Instruction Object Codes (Continued)

Instruction		Byte 1	Byte 2	Byte 3	Byte 4	Byte 5	Byte 6	Byte 7	Byte 8	Byte 9	Byte 10	Bytes	Clock Cycles
	Dn,dDn	E rrr1	3 0ddd									2	6 + 2N(1/0)
ROXL.L	count,Dn	E ccc1	9 0ddd									2	8 + 2N(1/0)
	Dn,dDn	E rrr1	B 0ddd									2	8 + 2N(1/0)
ROXL.W	count,Dn	E ccc1	5 0ddd									2	6 + 2N(1/0)
	Dn,dDn	E rrr1	7 0ddd									2	6 + 2N(1/0)
ROXR	dadr	E 4	11ff ffff	[EXT]		[EXT]						2, 4, or 6	9(1/1)+
ROXR.B	count,Dn	E ccc0	1 0ddd									2	6 + 2N(1/0)
	Dn,dDn	E rrr0	3 0ddd									2	6 + 2N(1/0)
ROXR.L	count,Dn	E ccc0	4 0ddd									2	8 + 2N(1/0)
	Dn,dDn	E rrr0	B 0ddd									2	8 + 2N(1/0)
ROXR.W	count,Dn	E ccc0	5 0ddd									2	6 + 2N(1/0)
	Dn,dDn	E rrr0	7 0ddd									2	6 + 2N(1/0)
RTE		4 E	7 3									2	20(5/0)
RTR		4 E	7 7									2	20(5/0)
RTS		4 E	7 5									2	16(4/0)
SBCD	−(sAn),−(dAn)	8 ddd1	0 1sss									2	19(3/1)
	sDn,dDn	8 ddd1	0 0sss									2	6(1/0)
SCC	dadr	5 4	11ff ffff	[EXT]		[EXT]						2, 4, or 6	9(1/1)+
	Dn	5 4	C 0ddd									2	6, 4(1/0)
SCS	dadr	5 5	11ff ffff	[EXT]		[EXT]						2, 4, or 6	9(1/1)+
	Dn	5 5	C 0ddd									2	6, 4(1/0)
SEQ	dadr	5 7	11ff ffff	[EXT]		[EXT]						2, 4, or 6	9(1/1)+
	Dn	5 7	C 0ddd									2	6, 4, (1/0)
SF	dadr	5 1	1fff ffff	[EXT]		[EXT]						2, 4, or 6	9(1/1)+
	Dn	5 1	C 0ddd									2	6, 4(1/0)
SGE	dadr	5 C	11ff ffff	[EXT]		[EXT]						2, 4, or 6	9(1/1)+
	Dn	5 C	C 0ddd									2	6, 4(1/0)
SGT	dadr	5 E	11ff ffff	[EXT]		[EXT]						2, 4, or 6	9(1/1)
	Dn	5 E	C 0ddd									2	6, 4(1/0)
SHI	dadr	5 2	11ff ffff	[EXT]		[EXT]						2, 4, or 6	9(1/1)+
	Dn	5 2	C 0ddd									2	6, 4,(1/0)
SLE	dadr	5 F	11ff ffff	[EXT]		[EXT]						2, 4, or 6	9(1/1)+
	Dn	5 F	C 0ddd									2	6, 4(1/0)
SLS	dadr	5 3	11ff ffff	[EXT]		[EXT]						2, 4, or 6	9(1/1)+
	Dn	5 3	C 0ddd									2	6, 4(1/0)
SLT	dadr	5 D	11ff ffff	[EXT]		[EXT]						2, 4, or 6	9(1/1)+
	Dn	5 D	C 0ddd									2	6, 4(1/0)
SMI	dadr	5 B	11ff ffff	[EXT]		[EXT]						2, 4, or 6	9(1/1)+
	Dn	5 B	C 0ddd									2	6, 4(1/0)
SNE	dadr	5 6	11ff ffff	[EXT]		[EXT]						2, 4, or 6	9(1/1)+
	Dn	5 6	C 0ddd									2	6, 4(1/0)
SPL	dadr	5 A	11ff ffff	[EXT]		[EXT]						2, 4, or 6	9(1/1)+
	Dn	5 A	C 0ddd									2	6, 4(1/0)
ST	dadr	5 0	11ff ffff	[EXT]		[EXT]						2, 4, or 6	9(1/1)+
	Dn	5 0	C 0ddd									2	6, 4(1/0)
STOP	data16	4 E	7 2	yyyy								4	8(2/0)
SUB.B	data8,dadr	0 4	00ff ffff	00	yy	[EXT]		[EXT]				4, 6, or 8	13(2/1)+
	data8,Dn	0 4	0 0ddd	00	yy							4	8(2/0)
	Dn,dadr	9 sss1	00ff ffff	[EXT]		[EXT]						2, 4, or 6	9(1/1)+
	sadr,Dn	9 ddd0	00ee eeee	[EXT]		[EXT]						2, 4, or 6	4(1/0)+
	sDn,dDn	9 ddd0	0 0sss									2	4(1/0)
SUB.L	data32,An	9 ddd1	F C	yyyy		zzzz						6	16(3/0)
	data32,dadr	0 4	10ff ffff	yyyy		zzzz		[EXT]		[EXT]		6, 8, or 10	22(3/2)+

Table B-1. MC68000 Instruction Object Codes (Continued)

Instruction		Byte 1	Byte 2	Byte 3	Byte 4	Byte 5	Byte 6	Byte 7	Byte 8	Byte 9	Byte 10	Bytes	Clock Cycles
	data32,Dn	0 4	8 0ddd	yyyy		zzzz						6	16(3/0)
	Dn,dadr	9 sss1	10ff ffff	[EXT]		[EXT]						2, 4, or 6	14(1/2)+
	rs,An	9 ddd1	C tsss									2	8(1/0)
	rs,Dn	9 ddd0	8 tsss									2	8(1/0)
	sadr,An	9 ddd1	11eeeeee	[EXT]		[EXT]						2, 4, or 6	6(1/0)+
	sadr,Dn	9 ddd0	10eeeeee	[EXT]		[EXT]						2, 4, or 6	6(1/0)+
SUB.W	data16,An	9 ddd0	F C	yyyy								4	8(2/0)
	data16,dadr	0 4	01ff ffff	yyyy		[EXT]		[EXT]				4, 6, or 8	13(2/1)+
	data16,Dn	0 4	4 0ddd	yyyy								4	8(2/0)
	Dn,dadr	9 sss1	01ff ffff	[EXT]		[EXT]						2, 4, or 6	9(1/1)+
	rs,An	9 ddd0	C tsss									2	8(1/0)
	rs,Dn	9 ddd0	4 tsss									2	4(1/0)
	sadr,An	9 ddd0	11eeeeee	[EXT]		[EXT]						2, 4, or 6	8(1/0)+
	sadr,Dn	9 ddd0	01eeeeee	[EXT]		[EXT]						2, 4, or 6	4(1/0)+
SUBQ.B	data3,dadr	5 bbb1	00ff ffff	[EXT]		[EXT]						2, 4, or 6	9(1/1)+
	data3,Dn	5 bbb1	0 0ddd									2	4(1/0)
SUBQ.L	data3,An	5 bbb1	8 1ddd									2	8(1/0)
	data3,dadr	5 bbb1	10ff ffff	[EXT]		[EXT]						2, 4, or 6	14(1/2)+
	data3,Dn	5 bbb1	8 0ddd									2	8(1/0)
SUBQ.W	data3,An	5 bbb1	4 1ddd									2	4(1/0)
	data3,dadr	5 bbb1	01ff ffff	[EXT]		[EXT]						2, 4, or 6	9(1/1)+
	data3,Dn	5 bbb1	4 0ddd									2	4(1/0)
SUBX.B	−(sAn), −(dAn)	9 ddd1	0 1sss									2	19(3/1)
	sDn, dDn	9 ddd1	0 0sss									2	4(1/0)
SUBX.L	−(sAn),−(dAn)	9 ddd1	8 1sss									2	32(5/2)
	sDn,dDn	9 ddd1	8 0sss									2	8(1/0)
SUBX.W	−(sAn),−(dAn)	9 ddd1	4 1sss									2	19(3/1)
	sDn,dDn	9 ddd1	4 0sss									2	4(1/0)
SVC	dadr	5 8	11ff ffff	[EXT]		[EXT]						2, 4, or 6	9(1/1)+
	Dn	5 8	C 0ddd									2	6, 4(1/0)
SVS	dadr	5 9	11ff ffff	[EXT]		[EXT]						2, 4, or 6	9(1/1)+
	Dn	5 9	C 0ddd									2	6, 4(1/0)
SWAP	Dn	4 8	4 0rrr									2	4(1/0)
TAS	dadr	4 A	11ff fffff	[EXT]		[EXT]						2, 4, or 6	11(1/1)+
	Dn	4 A	C 0rrr									2	4(1/0)
TRAP	vector	4 E	4 0vvv									2	36(4/3)
TRAPV		4 E	7 6									2	37(5/3),4(1/0)
TST.B	dadr	4 A	00ff ffff	[EXT]		[EXT]						2, 4, or 6	4(1/0)+
	Dn	4 A	0 0rrr									2	4(1/0)
TST.L	dadr	4 A	10ff ffff	[EXT]		[EXT]						2, 4, or 6	4(1/0)+
	Dn	4 A	8 0rrr									2	4(1/0)
TST.W	dadr	4 A	01ff ffff	[EXT]		[EXT]						2, 4, or 6	4(1/0)+
	Dn	4 A	4 0rrr									2	4(1/0)
UNLK	An	4 E	5 1rrr									2	12(3/0)

C
Numerically-Ordered List of Instruction Object Codes

This appendix lists valid instruction object codes in numerically ascending order. For a discussion of format, abbreviations and notations used in this appendix, refer to the first three pages of Appendix B.

Table C-1. MC68000 Object Codes in Numerical Order

Instruction		Byte 1	Byte 2	Byte 3	Byte 4	Byte 5	Byte 6	Byte 7	Byte 8	Byte 9	Byte 10
OR.B	data8,Dn	00	0 0ddd	00	yy						
OR.B	data8,dadr	00	00ff ffff	00	yy	[EXT]		[EXT]			
OR.B	data8,SR	00	3 C	00	yy						
OR.W	data16,Dn	00	4 0ddd	yyyy							
OR.W	data16,dadr	00	01ff ffff	yyyy		[EXT]		[EXT]			
OR.W	data16,SR	00	7 C	yyyy							
OR.L	data32,Dn	00	8 0ddd	yyyy		zzzz					
OR.L	data32,dadr	00	10ff ffff	yyyy		zzzz		[EXT]		[EXT]	
BTST	Dn,dDn	0 rrr1	0 0ddd								
MOVEP.W	d16(An),Dn	0 ddd1	0 1sss								
BTST	Dn,dadr	0 rrr1	00ff ffff	[EXT]		[EXT]					
BCHG	Dn,dDn	0 rrr1	A 0ddd								
MOVEP.L	d16(An),Dn	0 ddd1	A 1sss	xxxx							
BCHG	Dn,dadr	0 rrr1	01ff ffff	[EXT]		[EXT]					
BCLR	Dn,dDn	0 rrr1	8 0ddd								
MOVEP.W	Dn,d16(An)	0 sss1	8 1ddd	xxxx							
BCLR	Dn,dadr	0 rrr1	10ff ffff	[EXT]		[EXT]					
BSET	Dn,dDn	0 rrr1	C 0ddd								
MOVEP.L	Dn,d16(An)	0 sss1	C 1ddd	xxxx							
BSET	Dn,dadr	0 rrr1	11ff ffff	[EXT]		[EXT]					
AND.B	data8,Dn	02	0 0ddd	00	yy						
AND.B	data8,dadr	02	00ff ffff	00	yy	[EXT]		[EXT]			
AND.B	data8,SR	02	3 C	00	yy						
AND.W	data16,Dn	02	4 0ddd	yyyy							
AND.W	data16,dadr	02	01ff ffff	yyyy		[EXT]		[EXT]			
AND.W	data16,SR	02	7 C	yyyy							
AND.L	data32,Dn	02	8 0ddd	yyyy		zzzz					
AND.L	data32,dadr	02	10ff ffff	yyyy		zzzz		[EXT]		[EXT]	
SUB.B	data8,Dn	04	0 0ddd	00	yy						
SUB.B	data8,dadr	04	00ff ffff	00	yy	[EXT]		[EXT]			
SUB.W	data16,Dn	04	4 0ddd	yyyy							
SUB.W	data16,dadr	04	01ff ffff	yyyy		[EXT]		[EXT]			
SUB.L	data32,Dn	04	8 0ddd	yyyy		zzzz					
SUB.L	data32,dadr	04	10ff ffff	yyyy		zzzz		[EXT]		[EXT]	
ADD.B	data8,Dn	06	0 0ddd	00	yy						
ADD.B	data8,dadr	06	00ff ffff	00	yy	[EXT]		[EXT]			
ADD.W	data16,Dn	06	4 0ddd	yyyy							
ADD.W	data16,dadr	06	01ff ffff	yyyy		[EXT]		[EXT]			
ADD.L	data32,Dn	06	8 0ddd	yyyy		zzzz					
ADD.L	data32,dadr	06	10ff ffff	yyyy		zzzz		[EXT]		[EXT]	
BTST	bitl,Dn	08	0 0ddd	00	000b bbbb						
BTST	bitb,dadr	08	00ff ffff	00	0 0bbb	[EXT]		[EXT]			
BCHG	bitl,Dn	08	4 0ddd	00	000b bbbb						
BCHG	bitb,dadr	08	01ff ffff	00	0 0bbb	[EXT]		[EXT]			
BCLR	bitl,Dn	08	8 0ddd	00	000b bbbb						
BCLR	bitb,dadr	08	10ff ffff	00	0 0bbb	[EXT]		[EXT]			
BSET	bitl,Dn	08	C 0ddd	00	000b bbbb						
BSET	bitb,dadr	08	11ff ffff	00	0 0bbb	[EXT]		[EXT]			
EOR.B	data8,Dn	0A	0 0ddd	00	yy						
EOR.B	data8,dadr	0A	00ff ffff	00	yy	[EXT]		[EXT]			
EOR.B	data8,SR	0A	3 C		yy						
EOR.W	data16,Dn	0A	4 0ddd	yyyy							
EOR.W	data16,dadr	0A	01ff ffff	yyyy		[EXT]		[EXT]			
EOR.W	data16,SR	0A	7 C	yyyy							
EOR.L	data32,Dn	0A	8 0ddd	yyyy		zzzz					
EOR.L	data32,dadr	0A	10ff ffff	yyyy		zzzz		[EXT]		[EXT]	
CMP.B	data8,Dn	0C	0 0ddd	00	yy						
CMP.B	data8,dadr	0C	00ff ffff	00	yy	[EXT]		[EXT]			
CMP.W	data16,Dn	0C	4 0ddd	yyyy							
CMP.W	data16,dadr	0C	01ff ffff	yyyy		[EXT]		[EXT]			
CMP.L	data32,Dn	0C	8 0ddd	yyyy		zzzz					
CMP.L	data32,dadr	0C	10ff ffff	yyyy		zzzz		[EXT]		[EXT]	
MOVE.B	sDn,dDn	1 ddd0	0 0sss								
MOVE.B	sadr,dDn	1 ddd0	00ee eeee	[EXT]		[EXT]					
MOVE.B	data8,Dn	1 ddd0	3 C	00	yy						
MOVE.B	Dn,dadr	1 gggg	gg00 0sss	[EXT]		[EXT]					
MOVE.B	sadr,dadr	1 gggg	ggee eeee	[EXT$_s$]		[EXT$_s$]		[EXT$_d$]		[EXT$_d$]	
MOVE.B	data8,dadr	1 gggg	gg11 C	00	yy	[EXT]		[EXT]			
MOVE.L	rs,Dn	2 ddd0	0000 tsss								
MOVE.L	sadr,Dn	2 ddd0	00ee eeee	[EXT]		[EXT]					
MOVE.L	data32,Dn	2 ddd0	3 C	yyyy		zzzz					
MOVE.L	rs,An	2 ddd0	0100 tsss								
MOVE.L	sadr,An	2 ddd0	01ee eeee	[EXT]		[EXT]					

Table C-1. MC68000 Object Codes in Numerical Order (Continued)

Instruction		Byte 1	Byte 2	Byte 3	Byte 4	Byte 5	Byte 6	Byte 7	Byte 8	Byte 9	Byte 10
MOVE.L	data32,An	2ddd0	7 C	yyyy		zzzz					
MOVE.L	rs,dadr	2gggg	gg00 tss	[EXT]		[EXT]					
MOVE.L	sadr,dadr	2gggg	ggee eeee	[EXT$_s$]		[EXT$_s$]		[EXT$_d$]		[EXT$_d$]	
MOVE.L	data32,dadr	2gggg	gg11 C	yyyy		zzzz		[EXT]		[EXT]	
MOVE.W	rs,Dn	3ddd0	0 tsss								
MOVE.W	sadr,Dn	3ddd0	00ee eeee	[EXT]		[EXT]					
MOVE.W	data16,Dn	3ddd0	3 C	yyyy							
MOVE.W	rs,An	3ddd0	4 tsss								
MOVE.W	sadr,An	3ddd0	01ee eeee	[EXT]		[EXT]					
MOVE.W	data16,An	3ddd0	7 C	yyyy							
MOVE.W	rs,dadr	3gggg	gg00 tsss	[EXT]		[EXT]					
MOVE.W	sadr,dadr	3gggg	ggee eeee	[EXT$_s$]		[EXT$_s$]		[EXT$_d$]		[EXT$_d$]	
MOVE.W	data16,dadr	3gggg	gg11 C	yyyy		[EXT]		[EXT]			
NEGX.B	Dn	40	0 0ddd								
NEGX.B	dadr	40	00ff ffff	[EXT]		[EXT]					
NEGX.W	Dn	40	4 0ddd								
NEGX.W	dadr	40	01ff ffff	[EXT]		[EXT]					
NEGX.L	Dn	40	8 0ddd								
NEGX.L	dadr	40	10ff ffff	[EXT]		[EXT]					
MOVE	SR,Dn	40	C 0ddd								
MOVE	SR,dadr	40	11ff ffff	[EXT]		[EXT]					
CHK	Dn,dDn	4ddd1	8 0rrr								
CHK	sadr,Dn	4ddd1	10ee eeee	[EXT]		[EXT]					
CHK	data16,Dn	4ddd1	B C	yyyy							
LEA	jadr,An	4ddd1	11jj jjjj	[EXT]		[EXT]					
CLR.B	Dn	42	0 0ddd								
CLR.B	dadr	42	00ff ffff	[EXT]		[EXT]					
CLR.W	Dn	42	4 0ddd								
CLR.W	dadr	42	01ff ffff	[EXT]		[EXT]					
CLR.L	Dn	42	8 0ddd								
CLR.L	dadr	42	10ff ffff	[EXT]		[EXT]					
NEG.B	Dn	44	0 0ddd								
NEG.B	dadr	44	00ff ffff	[EXT]		[EXT]					
NEG.W	Dn	44	4 0ddd								
NEG.W	dadr	44	01ff ffff	[EXT]		[EXT]					
NEG.L	Dn	44	8 0ddd								
NEG.L	dadr	44	10ff ffff	[EXT]		[EXT]					
MOVE	Dn,CCR	44	C 0sss								
MOVE	sadr,CCR	44	11ee eeee	[EXT]		[EXT]					
MOVE	data8,CCR	44	F C	00	yy						
NOT.B	Dn	46	0 0ddd								
NOT.B	dadr	46	00ff ffff	[EXT]		[EXT]					
NOT.W	Dn	46	4 0ddd								
NOT.W	dadr	46	01ff ffff	[EXT]		[EXT]					
NOT.L	Dn	46	8 0ddd								
NOT.L	dadr	46	10ff ffff	[EXT]		[EXT]					
MOVE	Dn,SR	46	C 0sss								
MOVE	sadr,SR	46	11ee eeee	[EXT]		[EXT]					
MOVE	data16,SR	46	F C	yyyy							
NBCD	Dn	48	0 0ddd								
NBCD	dadr	48	00ff ffff	[EXT]		[EXT]					
SWAP	Dn	48	4 0rrr								
PEA	jadr	48	01jj jjjj	[EXT]		[EXT]					
EXT.W	Dn	48	8 0ddd								
MOVEM.W	reg−list,madr	48	10hh hhhh	mmmm		[EXT]		[EXT]			
MOVEM.W	reg−list,−(An)	48	A 0ddd	kkkk							
EXT.L	Dn	48	C 0ddd								
MOVEM.L	reg−list,madr	48	11hh hhhh	mmmm		[EXT]		[EXT]			
MOVE.L	reg−list,−(An)	48	E 0ddd	kkkk							
TST.B	Dn	4A	0 0rrr								
TST.B	dadr	4A	00ff ffff	[EXT]		[EXT]					
TST.W	Dn	4A	4 0rrr								
TST.W	dadr	4A	01ff ffff	[EXT]		[EXT]					
TST.L	Dn	4A	8 0rrr								
TST.L	dadr	4A	10ff ffff	[EXT]		[EXT]					
TAS	Dn	4A	C 0rrr								
TAS	dadr	4A	11ff ffff	[EXT]		[EXT]					
MOVEM.W	jadr,reg−list	4C	10jj jjjj	mmmm		[EXT]		[EXT]			
MOVEM.W	(An)+,reg−list	4C	A 0sss	mmmm							
MOVEM.L	(An)+,reg−list	4C	E 0sss	mmmm							
MOVEM.L	jadr,reg−list	4C	11jj jjjj	mmmm		[EXT]		[EXT]			
MOVEM.L	(An)+,reg−list	4C	E 0sss	mmmm							
TRAP	vector	4E	4 vvvv								

Table C-1. MC68000 Object Codes in Numerical Order (Continued)

Instruction		Byte 1	Byte 2	Byte 3	Byte 4	Byte 5	Byte 6	Byte 7	Byte 8	Byte 9	Byte 10
LINK	An,d16	4E	5 0rrr	xxxx							
UNLK	An	4E	5 1rrr								
MOVE	An,USP	4E	6 0sss								
MOVE	USP,An	4E	6 1sss								
RESET		4E	7 0								
NOP		4E	7 1								
STOP	data16	4E	7 2	yyyy							
RTE		4E	7 3								
RTS		4E	7 5								
TRAPV		4E	7 6								
RTR		4E	7 7								
JSR	jadr	4E	10jj jjjj	[EXT]		[EXT]					
JMP	jadr	4E	11jj jjjj	[EXT]		[EXT]					
ADDQ.B	data3,Dn	5 bbb0	0 0ddd								
ADDQ.B	data3,dadr	5 bbb0	00ff ffff	[EXT]		[EXT]					
ADDQ.W	data3,Dn	5 bbb0	4 0ddd								
ADDQ.W	data3,An	5 bbb0	4 1ddd								
ADDQ.W	data3,dadr	5 bbb0	01ff ffff	[EXT]		[EXT]					
ADDQ.L	data3,Dn	5 bbb0	8 0ddd								
ADDQ.L	data3,An	5 bbb0	8 1ddd								
ADDQ.L	data3,dadr	5 bbb0	01ff ffff	[EXT]		[EXT]					
ST	Dn	50	C 0ddd								
DBT	Dn,label	50	C 1rrr	xxxx							
ST	dadr	50	11ff ffff	[EXT]		[EXT]					
SUBQ.B	data3,Dn	5 bbb1	0 0ddd								
SUBQ.B	data3,dadr	5 bbb1	00ff ffff	[EXT]		[EXT]					
SUBQ.W	data3,Dn	5 bbb1	4 0ddd								
SUBQ.W	data3,An	5 bbb1	4 1ddd								
SUBQ.W	data3,dadr	5 bbb1	01ff ffff	[EXT]		[EXT]					
SUBQ.L	data3,Dn	5 bbb1	8 0ddd								
SUBQ.L	data3,An	5 bbb1	8 1ddd								
SUBQ.L	data3,dadr	5 bbb1	01ff ffff	[EXT]		[EXT]					
SF	Dn	51	C 0ddd								
DBF	Dn,label	51	C 1rrrr	xxxx							
SF	dadr	51	11ff ffff	[EXT]		[EXT]					
SHI	Dn	52	C 0ddd								
DBHI	Dn,label	52	C 1rrrr	xxxx							
SHI	dadr	52	11ff ffff	[EXT]		[EXT]					
SLS	Dn	53	C 0ddd								
DBLS	Dn,label	53	C 1rrr	xxxx							
SLS	dadr	53	11ff ffff	[EXT]		[EXT]					
SCC	Dn	54	C 0ddd								
DBCC	Dn,label	54	D 1rrr	xxxx							
SCC	dadr	54	11ff ffff	[EXT]		[EXT]					
SCS	Dn	55	C 0ddd								
DBCS	Dn,label	55	C 1rrr	xxxx							
SCS	dadr	55	11ff ffff	[EXT]		[EXT]					
SNE	Dn	56	C 0ddd								
DBNE	Dn,label	56	C 1rrr	xxxx							
SNE	dadr	56	11ff ffff	[EXT]		[EXT]					
SEQ	Dn	57	C 0ddd								
DBEQ	Dn,label	57	C 1rrrr	xxxx							
SEQ	dadr	57	11ff ffff	[EXT]		[EXT]					
SVC	Dn	58	C 0ddd								
DVC	Dn,label	58	C 1rrr	xxxx							
SVC	dadr	58	11ff ffff	[EXT]		[EXT]					
SVS	Dn	59	C 0ddd								
DVS	Dn,label	59	C 1rrr	xxxx							
SVS	dadr	59	11ff ffff	[EXT]		[EXT]					
SPL	Dn	5A	C 0ddd								
DBPL	Dn,label	5A	C 1rrr	xxxx							
SPL	dadr	5A	11ff ffff	[EXT]		[EXT]					
SMI	Dn	5B	C 0ddd								
DBMI	Dn,label	5B	C 1rrr	xxxx							
SMI	dadr	5B	11ff ffff	[EXT]		[EXT]					
SGE	Dn	5C	C 0ddd								
DBGE	Dn,label	5C	C 1rrr	xxxx							
SGE	dadr	5C	11ff ffff	[EXT]		[EXT]					
SLT	Dn	5D	C 0ddd								
DBLT	Dn,label	5D	C 1rrr	xxxx							
SLT	dadr	5D	11ff ffff	[EXT]		[EXT]					
SGT	Dn	5E	C 0ddd								
DBGT	Dn,label	5E	C 1rrr	xxxx							

Table C-1. MC68000 Object Codes in Numerical Order (Continued)

Instruction		Byte 1	Byte 2	Byte 3	Byte 4	Byte 5	Byte 6	Byte 7	Byte 8	Byte 9	Byte 10
SGT	dadr	5E	11ff ffff	[EXT]		[EXT]					
SLE	Dn	5F	C 0ddd								
DBLE	Dn,label	5F	C 1rrr	xxxx							
SLE	dadr	5F	11ff ffff	[EXT]		[EXT]					
BRA	label	60	0 0	xxxx							
BRA	label	60	xx								
BSR	label	61	00	xxxx							
BSR	label	61	xx								
BHI	label	62	00	xxxx							
BHI	label	62	xx								
BLS	label	63	00	xxxx							
BLS	label	63	xx								
BCC	label	64	00	xxxx							
BCC	label	64	xx								
BCS	label	65	00	xxxx							
BCS	label	65	xx								
BNE	label	66	00	xxxx							
BNE	label	66	xx								
BEQ	label	67	00	xxxx							
BEQ	label	67	xx								
BVC	label	68	00	xxxx							
BVC	label	68	xx								
BVS	label	69	00	xxxx							
BVS	label	69	xx								
BPL	label	6A	00	xxxx							
BPL	label	6A	xx								
BMI	label	6B	00	xxxx							
BMI	label	6B	xx								
BGE	label	6C	00	xxxx							
BGE	label	6C	xx								
BLT	label	6D	00	xxxx							
BLT	label	6D	xx								
BGT	label	6E	00	xxxx							
BGT	label	6E	xx								
BLE	label	6F	00	xxxx							
BLE	label	6F	xx								
MOVEQ	data8,Dn	7ddd0	yy								
OR.B	sDn,dDn	8ddd0	0 0sss								
OR.B	sadr,Dn	8ddd0	00eeeeee	[EXT]		[EXT]					
OR.W	sDn,dDn	8ddd0	4 0sss								
OR.W	sadr,Dn	8ddd0	01eeeeee	[EXT]		[EXT]					
OR.L	sDn,dDn	8ddd0	8 0sss								
OR.L	sadr,Dn	8ddd0	10eeeeee	[EXT]		[EXT]					
DIVU	sDn,dDn	8ddd0	C 0sss								
DIVU	sadr,Dn	8ddd0	11eeeeee	[EXT]		[EXT]					
DIVU	data16,Dn	8ddd0	F C	yyyy							
SBC	sDn,dDn	8ddd1	0 0sss								
SBCD	−(sAn),−(dAn)	8ddd1	0 1sss								
OR.B	Dn,dadr	8sss1	00ff ffff	[EXT]		[EXT]					
OR.W	Dn,dadr	8sss1	01ff ffff	[EXT]		[EXT]					
OR.L	Dn,dadr	8sss1	10ff ffff	[EXT]		[EXT]					
DIVS	sDn,dDn	8ddd1	C 0sss								
DIVS	sadr,Dn	8ddd1	11ee eeee	[EXT]		[EXT]					
DIVS	data16,Dn	8ddd1	F C	yyyy							
SUB.B	sDn,dDn	9ddd0	0 0sss								
SUB.B	sadr,Dn	9ddd0	00ee eeee	[EXT]		[EXT]					
SUB.W	rs,Dn	9ddd0	4 tsss								
SUB.W	sadr,Dn	9ddd0	01ee eeee	[EXT]		[EXT]					
SUB.L	rs,Dn	9ddd0	8 tsss								
SUB.L	sadr,Dn	9ddd0	10eeeeee	[EXT]		[EXT]					
SUB.W	rs,An	9ddd0	C tsss								
SUB.W	sadr,An	9ddd0	11eeeeee	[EXT]		[EXT]					
SUB.W	data16,An	9ddd0	F C	yyyy							
SUBX.B	sDn,dDn	9ddd1	0 0sss								
SUBX.B	−(sAn),−(dAn)	9ddd1	0 1sss								
SUB.B	Dn,dadr	9sss1	00ffffff	[EXT]		[EXT]					
SUBX.W	sDn,dDn	9ddd1	4 0sss								
SUBX.W	−(sAn),−(dAn)	9ddd1	4 1sss								
SUB.W	Dn,dadr	9sss1	01ff ffff	[EXT]		[EXT]					
SUBX.L	sDn,dDn	9ddd1	8 0sss								
SUBX.L	−(sAn),−(dAn)	9ddd1	8 1sss								
SUB.L	Dn,dadr	9sss1	10ffffff	[EXT]		[EXT]					
SUB.L	rs,An	9ddd1	C tsss								

Table C-1. MC68000 Object Codes in Numerical Order (Continued)

Instruction		Byte 1	Byte 2	Byte 3	Byte 4	Byte 5	Byte 6	Byte 7	Byte 8	Byte 9	Byte 10
SUB.L	sadr,An	9 ddd1	11eeeeee	[EXT]		[EXT]					
SUB.L	data32,An	9 ddd1	F C	yyyy		zzzz					
CMP.B	sDn,dDn	B ddd0	0 0sss								
CMP.B	sadr,Dn	B ddd0	00eeeeee	[EXT]		[EXT]					
CMP.W	rs,Dn	B ddd0	4 tsss								
CMP.W	sadr,Dn	B ddd0	01eeeeee	[EXT]		[EXT]					
CMP.L	rs,Dn	B ddd0	8 tsss								
CMP.L	sadr,Dn	B ddd0	10eeeeee	[EXT]		[EXT]					
CMP.W	rs,An	B ddd0	C tsss								
CMP.W	sadr,An	B ddd0	11eeeeee	[EXT]		[EXT]					
CMP.W	data 16,An	B ddd0	F C	yyyy							
EOR.B	sDn,dDn	B sss1	0 0ddd								
CMPM.B	(sAn)+,(dAn)+	B ddd1	0 1sss								
EOR.B	Dn,dadr	B sss1	00ffffff	[EXT]		[EXT]					
EOR.W	sDn,dDn	B sss1	4 0ddd								
CMPM.W	(sAn)+,(dAn)+	B ddd1	4 1sss								
EOR.W	Dn,dadr	B sss1	01ffffff	[EXT]		[EXT]					
EOR.L	sDn,dDn	B sss1	8 0ddd								
CMPM.L	(sAn)+,(dAn)+	B ddd1	8 1sss								
EOR.L	Dn,dadr	B sss1	10ffffff	[EXT]		[EXT]					
CMP.L	rs,An	B ddd1	C tsss								
CMP.L	sadr,An	B ddd1	11eeeeee	[EXT]		[EXT]					
CMP.L	data32,An	B ddd1	F C	yyyy		zzzz					
AND.B	sDn,dDn	C ddd0	0 0sss								
AND.B	sadr,Dn	C ddd0	00eeeeee	[EXT]		[EXT]					
AND.W	sDn,dDn	C ddd0	4 0sss								
AND.W	sadr,Dn	C ddd0	01eeeeee	[EXT]		[EXT]					
AND.L	sDn,dDn	C ddd0	8 0sss								
AND.L	sadr,Dn	C ddd0	10eeeeee	[EXT]		[EXT]					
MULU	sDn,dDn	C ddd0	C 0sss								
MULU	sadr,Dn	C ddd0	11eeeeee	[EXT]		[EXT]					
MULU	data16,Dn	C ddd0	F C	yyyy							
ABCD	sDn,dDn	C ddd1	0 0sss								
ABCD	−(sAn),−(dAn)	C ddd1	0 1sss								
AND.B	Dn,dadr	C sss1	00ffffff	[EXT]		[EXT]					
EXG	Dn,Dn	C sss1	4 0ddd								
EXG	An,An	C sss1	4 1ddd								
AND.W	Dn,dadr	C sss1	01ffffff	[EXT]		[EXT]					
EXG	Dn,An or An,Dn	C sss1	8 1ddd								
AND.L	Dn,dadr	C sss1	10ffffff	[EXT]		[EXT]					
MULS	sDn,dDn	C ddd1	C 0sss								
MULS	sadr,Dn	C ddd1	11eeeeee	[EXT]		[EXT]					
MULS	data16,Dn	C ddd1	F C	yyyy							
ADD.B	sDn,dDn	D ddd0	0 0sss								
ADD.B	sadr,Dn	D dddC	00eeeeee	[EXT]		[EXT]					
ADD.W	rs,Dn	D ddd0	4 tsss								
ADD.W	sadr,Dn	D ddd0	01eeeeee	[EXT]		[EXT]					
ADD.L	rs,Dn	D ddd0	8 tsss								
ADD.L	sadr,Dn	D ddd0	10eeeeee	[EXT]		[EXT]					
ADD.W	rs,An	D ddd0	C tsss								
ADD.W	sadr,An	D ddd0	11eeeeee	[EXT]		[EXT]					
ADD.W	data16,An	D ddd0	F C	yyyy							
ADDX.B	sDn,dDn	D ddd1	0 0sss								
ADDX.B	−(sAn),−(dAn)	D ddd1	0 1sss								
ADD.B	Dn,dadr	D sss1	00ffffff	[EXT]		[EXT]					
ADDX.W	sDn,dDn	D ddd1	4 0sss								
ADDX.W	−(sAn),−(dAn)	D ddd1	4 1sss								
ADD.W	Dn,dadr	D sss1	01ffffff	[EXT]		[EXT]					
ADDX.L	sDn,dDn	D ddd1	8 0sss								
ADDX.L	−(sAn),−(dAn)	D ddd1	8 1sss								
ADD.L	Dn,dadr	D sss1	10ffffff	[EXT]		[EXT]					
ADD.L	rs,An	D ddd1	C tsss								
ADD.L	sadr,An	D ddd1	11eeeeee	[EXT]		[EXT]					
ADD.L	data32,An	D ddd1	F C	yyyy		zzzz					
ASR.B	count,Dn	E ccc0	0 0ddd								
LSR.B	count,Dn	E ccc0	0 1ddd								
ROXR.B	count,Dn	E ccc0	1 0ddd								
ROR.B	count,Dn	E ccc0	1 1ddd								
ASR.B	Dn,dDn	E rrr0	2 0ddd								
LSR.B	Dn,dDn	E rrr0	2 1ddd								
ROXR.B	Dn,dDn	E rrr0	3 0ddd								
ROR.B	Dn,dDn	E rrr0	3 1ddd								

Table C-1. MC68000 Object Codes in Numerical Order (Continued)

Instruction		Byte 1	Byte 2	Byte 3	Byte 4	Byte 5	Byte 6	Byte 7	Byte 8	Byte 9	Byte 10
ASR.W	count,Dn	E ccc0	4 0ddd								
LSR.W	count,Dn	E ccc0	4 1ddd								
ROXR.W	count,Dn	E ccc0	5 0ddd								
ROR.W	count,Dn	E ccc0	5 1ddd								
ASR.W	Dn,dDn	E rrr0	6 0ddd								
LSR.W	Dn,dDn	E rrr0	6 1ddd								
ROXR.W	Dn,dDn	E rrr0	7 0ddd								
ROR.W	Dn,dDn	E rrr0	7 1ddd								
ASR.L	count,Dn	E ccc0	8 0ddd								
LSR.L	count,Dn	E ccc0	8 1ddd								
ROXR.L	count,Dn	E ccc0	9 0ddd								
ROR.L	count, Dn	E ccc0	9 1ddd								
ASR.L	Dn,dDn	E rrr0	A 0ddd								
LSR.L	Dn,dDn	E rrr0	A 1ddd								
ROXR.L	Dn,dDn	E rrr0	B 0ddd								
ROR.L	Dn,dDn	E rrr0	B 1ddd								
ASR	dadr	E 0	11ffffff	[EXT]		[EXT]					
ASL.B	count,Dn	E ccc1	0 0ddd								
LSL.B	count,Dn	E ccc1	0 1ddd								
ROXL.B	count,Dn	E ccc1	1 0ddd								
ROL.B	count,Dn	E ccc1	1 1ddd								
ASL.B	Dn,dDn	E rrr1	2 0ddd								
LSL.B	Dn,dDn	E rrr1	2 1ddd								
ROXL.B	Dn,dDn	E rrr1	3 0ddd								
ROL.B	Dn,dDn	E rrr1	3 1ddd								
ASL.W	count,Dn	E ccc1	4 0ddd								
LSL.W	count,Dn	E ccc1	4 1ddd								
ROXL.W	count,Dn	E ccc1	5 0ddd								
ROL.W	count,Dn	E ccc1	5 1ddd								
ASL.W	Dn,dDn	E rrr1	6 0ddd								
LSL.W	Dn,dDn	E rrr1	6 1ddd								
ROXL.W	Dn,dDn	E rrr1	7 0ddd								
ROL.W	Dn,dDn	E rrr1	7 1ddd								
ASL.L	count,Dn	E ccc1	8 0ddd								
LSL.L	count,Dn	E ccc1	8 1ddd								
ROXL.L	count,Dn	E ccc1	9 0ddd								
ROL.L	count,Dn	E ccc1	9 1ddd								
ASL.L	Dn,dDn	E rrr1	A 0ddd								
LSL.L	Dn,dDn	E rrr1	A 1ddd								
ROXL.L	Dn,dDn	E rrr1	B 0ddd								
ROL.L	Dn,dDn	E rrr1	B 1ddd								
ASL	dadr	E 1	11ffffff	[EXT]		[EXT]					
LSR	dadr	E 2	11ffffff	[EXT]		[EXT]					
LSL	dadr	E 3	11ffffff	[EXT]		[EXT]					
ROXR	dadr	E 4	11ffffff	[EXT]		[EXT]					
ROXL	dadr	E 5	11ffffff	[EXT]		[EXT]					
ROR	dadr	E 6	11ffffff	[EXT]		[EXT]					
ROL	dadr	E 7	11ffffff	[EXT]		[EXT]					

A

B

C

T

U

V

X

Z